WORKING IN Restructured Workplaces

WORKING IN Restructured Workplaces

Challenges and New Directions for the Sociology of Work

Edited by
Daniel B. Cornfield · Karen E. Campbell
Holly J. McCammon

Sage Publications
International Educational and Professional Publisher
Thousand Oaks ▪ London ▪ New Delhi

For information:

Sage Publications, Inc.
2455 Teller Road
Thousand Oaks, California 91320
E-mail: order@sagepub.com

Sage Publications Ltd.
6 Bonhill Street
London EC2A 4PU
United Kingdom

Sage Publications India Pvt. Ltd.
M-32 Market
Greater Kailash I
New Delhi 110 048 India

Printed in the United States of America

Library of Congress Cataloging-in-Publication Data

Working in reconstructured workplaces: Challenges and new directions for the sociology of work / Daniel Cornfield, Karen Campbell, and Holly McCammon [editors].
p. cm.
Includes bibliographical references and index.
ISBN 0-7619-0782-3 (p)
1. Industrial sociology. I. Cornfield, Daniel. II. Campbell, Karen.
III. McCammon, Holly.
HD6955 .W675 2001
306.3′6—dc21
2001003572

This book is printed on acid-free paper.

01 02 03 04 05 06 7 6 5 4 3 2 1

Acquisition Editor: Stephen D. Rutter
Editorial Assistant: Kirsten Stoller
Production Editor: Sanford Robinson
Copy Editor: Joyce Kuhn
Editorial Assistant: Candice Crosetti
Typesetter: Marion Warren
Indexer: Teri Greenberg
Cover Designer: Michelle Lee

Contents

Preface

The death of William H. Whyte, Jr. in 1999 seemed to signify the end of one era of employment relations and the advent of another. In his 1956 classic, *The Organization Man*, Whyte announced the demise of the individualistic entrepreneur and the entry of the "organization man" who sought belongingness in the large corporation through a lifetime career of mutual commitment with his employer. The emergence of the organization man in the 1950s symbolized the dawning of the bureaucratic employment relationship. As Whyte's *New York Times* obituary put it,

> Mr. Whyte's book challenged and refuted claims of entrepreneurial vigor and daring in business by describing an ongoing bureaucratization of white-collar environments—board rooms, offices, laboratories. . . . Mr. Whyte wrote that corporate norms based on the pursuit of safety and security and characterized by conformity had spread to academic and scientific institutions and prevailed in the white-collar suburbs then proliferating across America.[1]

What is more, the arrival of the organization man, and of the organization woman (with women's increasing employment in the corporate environment), deeply influenced the image of employment relations that has pervaded social scientific research on social relations and career mobility in the workplace. It is inside the bureaucratic workplace, among the organization women and men who work in a single "internal labor market," where social scientists have typically researched the formation of work attitudes and work group cohesion, the sources of worker productivity, and inequality in pay, job security, and prospects for career mobility.

Whyte's death then, it seems, marks the passage of an era of bureaucratic, corporate employment relations. Increasingly, the workplace is populated by a contingent workforce of part-time and temporary workers, independent contractors, and other workers employed in transient relations with their employers. As managers respond to mounting global economic competitive pressures and collective bargaining and the decline in labor union membership as a percentage of the national labor force, more and more employment relations emerge as casual, low-paying arrangements that marginalize contingent workers from their higher paid full-time coworkers. In many workplaces, we are witnessing the emergence of a dual or two-tiered workforce that may further indicate an erosion of the workplace community and internal labor market that have shaped social relations and the career mobility chances of organization men and women. Indeed, these changes in the workplace have been accompanied by increasing income polarization in the United States over the past 30 years.

Yet contemporary workplace restructuring consists of contradictory tendencies. The recent diffusion of self-supervised work groups and production teams in many workplaces is consistent with Whyte's imagery of bureaucratic, corporate employment relations. Already by the 1930s, Elton Mayo had uncovered—in his legendary Hawthorne experiments—the powerful community- and productivity-enhancing benefits of semiautonomous, cohesive work groups. Following Mayo's communitarian lead, Whyte observed that the organization man sought to belong not only to the organization but to small work groups and project teams within the organization. The contemporary spreading of worker self-management, production teams, quality circles, total quality management, and the like continues to shape the workplace community of organization women and men in a manner consistent with that identified earlier by Mayo and Whyte.

Thus the question arises, will the workplace continue to constitute a community for organization men and women, or will it come to consist of increasingly individualistic employment relations? We, the editorial team of the sociological quarterly *Work and Occupations*, have assembled this volume, *Working in Restructured Workplaces*, to address the contradictory nature of contemporary workplace restructuring, its impact on worker livelihoods, and the prospects for future changes in the workplace. This volume consists of works previously published in *Work and Occupations* and several others commissioned specifically for the book.

So as to paint a broad portrait of workplace restructuring and to assess its multiple implications for worker livelihoods and actions, we develop a new conceptualization of "workplace restructuring" in our introductory chapter and have organized the chapters of *Working in Restructured Workplaces* into four major themes, which also are the titles of the four parts of the book:

1. Reconfiguring workplace status hierarchies
2. Casualization of employment relationships
3. Restructuring and worker marginalization
4. Comparative labor responses to global restructuring

The two concluding chapters present important implications for the agendas of future scholarly, social scientific research on the workplace. These chapters suggest that social scientists should now assume the existence of multiple models of employment relations. Future research ought to be directed at documenting the prevalence and diffusion of employment relations models across industries, occupations, workplaces, and groups of workers of different demographic backgrounds and the impact of these models on worker livelihoods.

Regardless of its changing, contradictory character, the workplace continues to be an important social arena for the formation of social relations and the determination of career mobility chances. Workplace restructuring has altered the web of employment relations in which people work, compelling social scientists to reexamine their images of the workplace and modify their research agendas accordingly. It is our hope that this volume will both stimulate new scholarly research on workplace restructuring and illuminate how working in restructured workplaces influences worker livelihoods.

DANIEL B. CORNFIELD
KAREN E. CAMPBELL
HOLLY J. MCCAMMON

NOTE

1. Michael T. Kaufman, "William H. Whyte, 'Organization Man' Author and Urbanologist, Is Dead at 81," *New York Times on the Web*, January 13, 1999, Wednesday, The Arts/Cultural Desk, http://archives.nytimes.com/archives/search/fastweb?getdoc+allyears2+db365+269384+1+wAAA+whyte

Working in Restructured Workplaces: An Introduction

DANIEL B. CORNFIELD
KAREN E. CAMPBELL
HOLLY J. McCAMMON

What is workplace restructuring, and what is its impact on workers' livelihoods inside and outside the workplace? The sociology of work addresses the relationships among worker life chances and worldviews, work processes, and the social organization of workplaces and markets. Restructuring of workplaces challenges sociologists of work to examine the many sociological implications of restructuring for the development of social inequality and the nature of the workplace. The purpose of this volume, *Working in Restructured Workplaces,* is to examine the impact of restructuring on workers and to explore the implications of restructuring for the sociology of work. We hope to encourage new directions for research in the sociology of work that extend and adapt the enduring mission of the sociology of work to workplace restructuring.

Workplace restructuring coincides with growing income polarization in the United States. Downsizing and displacement of workers, the advent of the contingent, just-in-time workforce, the effacement of middle management, the virtual disappearance of labor unions and collective bargaining, as well as increasing employee involvement in team-based decision making, have accompanied a 30-year trend of income polarization. According to the U.S. Bureau of the Census (1999b), the Gini coefficient, a leading statistical indicator of income inequality in the nation, increased by 15% between 1967 and 1997. Over the same period of time, the percentage of people in poverty changed little, fluctuating between 11% and 15%, but the share of aggregate income received by the 20% of families with the highest incomes rose from 41% to 47% (U.S. Bureau of the Census, 1999a, 1999c).

Moreover, workplace restructuring suggests, somewhat ironically, a growing disarticulation between worker and workplace at the same time as the employer devolves more job responsibilities onto a "self-supervised" nonsupervisory workforce (Smith, 1998). In its special report titled *The Downsizing of America,* the *New York Times* notes from its 1995 opinion survey of U.S. workers that approximately two thirds of survey respondents felt that employers and employees had become less loyal toward one another over the past 10 years and that coworkers were more competitive than cooperative with one another. Over half of the respondents felt that an "angrier mood" had developed in many workplaces (*New York Times,* 1996, p. 55). According to the U.S. Bureau of Labor Statistics' 1997 national survey of "contingent workers"—that is, "workers who do not perceive themselves as having an explicit or implicit contract with their employers for ongoing employment"—some two thirds of men and women contingent workers preferred a "noncontingent" employment arrangement to a contingent one (Hipple, 1998, p. 28; also see Smith, 1998).

Social scientific research has documented some consequences of workplace restructuring for workers (Smith, 1998). Organizational downsizing and company closures have displaced workers in a wide range of ailing "smokestack" industries and growing white-collar service industries (Gardner, 1995; Hipple, 1997). Many communities have been devastated by these large-scale displacements (Dudley, 1994; Illes, 1996; *New York Times*, 1996). U.S. Bureau of Labor Statistics (BLS) surveys of displaced workers suggest that ethnic-racial minorities and men tend to be more likely than other workers to be displaced by company closures and other types of involuntary job loss and that displaced women workers are more likely than displaced men to become reemployed with earnings lower than those of their previous jobs (Gardner, 1995; Hipple, 1997). For workers who survive a restructuring and downsizing, organizational paths to success may become chaotic and unclear or disappear altogether, and workers may become demoralized, emotionally stressed and burned out, and disaffected from their employers (Arthur & Rousseau, 1996, pp. 3-13; Cappelli et al., 1997, pp. 195-203; Hirsch, 1993; Osterman, 1996, pp. 1-20; Schellenberg, 1996; Smith, 1998).

While economic inequality has increased as with workplace restructuring, the ways in which restructuring may be producing inequality are not entirely clear, for four reasons. First, as a set of new and variegated employment relations, restructuring itself is unclear. The U.S. Commission on the Future of Worker-Management Relations (a.k.a. the "Dunlop Commission") was appointed recently by the U.S. Secretaries of Labor and Commerce to encourage the development of productive, cooperative and participatory employment relations. In its final report, the Commission (1994) argued that changes in work organization have clouded the meaning of the employment relationship and blurred the lines of authority in the workplace:

> New forms of organizing work, new workplaces (including work at home), new work relations (including with customers), new work hours, and new legal forms have emerged and become more common in which there is ambiguity and often no clear responsibility for training, health and safety, benefits, legal obligations, and the other societal demands of the workplace. These new and more diverse relations raise questions about the definitions of employee and employer, supervisor and professional used in labor relations and employment law. (pp. 1-2)

Second, the socioeconomic status of workers in "nonstandard or alternative employment arrangements" is complex and not straightforward (Barker & Christensen, 1998; Ferber & Waldfogel, 1998; Hipple & Stewart, 1996). On one hand, those who work in alternative employment arrangements (e.g., contingent work, independent contracting) are much less likely than those employed in "standard" or "traditional" full-time steady situations with one employer to be covered by employer-provided fringe benefits. In 1997, according to the BLS, 53.9% of "noncontingent workers" but only 20.7% of contingent workers and 7.0% of temporary help agency workers were covered by employer-provided health insurance; 44.2% of noncontingent workers but only 14.8% of contingent workers, 10.4% of temporary help agency workers, and 3.6% of independent contractors were included in an employer-provided pension plan. Furthermore, the 1997 median weekly earnings of full-time contingent workers were 12% to 23% lower than those of full-time noncontingent workers within all gender and major ethnic-racial groups (U.S. Bureau of Labor Statistics, 1998b, 1998c).

Yet, on the other hand, the earnings of workers employed in different types of nonstandard employment arrangements and of diverse demographic backgrounds vary widely in relation to those of workers employed in standard or traditional employment situations (Cohany, 1996, 1998). Among full-time workers in 1997, for example, the median weekly earnings of male "workers provided by contract firms" were 19%

greater than those of men employed in "traditional arrangements"; for female workers, however, the earnings of those who were provided by contract firms were 2.4% less than those of women in traditional arrangements. Considering the ethnicity-race of full-time workers, the median weekly earnings of White and Hispanic "independent contractors" exceeded those of White and Hispanic workers in traditional arrangements by 10% to 19% in 1997; the median weekly earnings of Black independent contractors, however, were 11% lower than those of Blacks employed in traditional arrangements (U.S. Bureau of Labor Statistics, 1998c).

Third, the magnitude of the socioeconomic impact of displacement on workers varies over time but does not appear to be moving either upward or downward. The BLS calculates changes in the median weekly earnings of workers who were displaced from their full-time wage and salary jobs due to plant and company closures and relocations, abolition of positions, and other causes and who were reemployed one to three years after their displacement. Over the period of its 1994, 1996, and 1998 surveys of reemployed displaced workers, the BLS found that the percentage of reemployed displaced workers whose earnings at least equaled those of their lost jobs shifted from 52.9% to 46.6% to 55.2%, respectively; the percentage of displaced workers whose earnings at reemployment were at least 20% lower than those of their lost jobs changed from 31.2% to 33.9% to 24.9%, respectively (Gardner, 1995; Hipple, 1997; U.S. Bureau of Labor Statistics, 1998d).

Fourth, the impact of workplace restructuring on economic inequality is unclear because of the absence of longitudinal data on the prevalence and diffusion of workplace restructuring in the national economy. We lack long-term time series data on changes in the employment relationship and in the organization of production and managerial decision making in workplaces. Consequently, it is difficult to monitor and assess the degree of association over time between workplace restructuring, on one hand, and indicators of economic inequality, on the other hand, much less compare the magnitude of the effects of restructuring and other causes of economic inequality (on methodological issues in researching restructuring, see Ichniowski, Kochan, Levine, Olson, & Strauss, 1996).

In order, therefore, to examine the nature of workplace restructuring and its impact on economic inequality, it is important to reexamine the meaning of fulfilling work and productive employment relationships as the workplace is restructured. Sociologists have begun to clarify the nature and impact of workplace restructuring (Castillo, 1997; Gamst, 1995; Leicht, 1998; Smith, 1997, 1998; Vallas, 1999). We, the editorial team of the sociological quarterly *Work and Occupations*,[1] have witnessed a growing number of manuscript submissions and books about workplace restructuring. This line of research has pertained to a wide range of topics about restructuring—its nature, variations, determinants, and consequences for worker livelihoods and employment relations. It signaled to us the import of restructuring for the sociology of work.

Indeed, restructuring compels sociologists of work to revisit basic assumptions of workplace bureaucracy and employment relations that underlie much of the sociology of work. Revisiting these assumptions, furthermore, compels sociologists of work not only to examine understandings of the structure of workplaces but also to examine the nature and impact of workplace restructuring on worker livelihoods.

"Workplace restructuring" is a term with multiple meanings. If sociologists of work are to analyze effectively this transformation of workplaces, we must first define the changes and examine their implications for the mission and practice of the sociology of work.

WHAT IS "WORKPLACE RESTRUCTURING"?

We conceive of "workplace restructuring" as a *three-dimensional transformation of workplace social structure.* As we discuss shortly, the three dimensions are devolution of decision making, casualization of the employment relationship, and a shift from collective bargaining to individual bargaining. To develop this three-dimensional perspective of workplace restructuring, we first elaborate on the concept of workplace social structure, describe recent concrete instances of restructuring, and then critically review the image of bureaucracy that underlies much of contemporary sociology of work.

Kalleberg and Berg's (1987) definition of "work structures" captures the meaning of workplace social structure that many sociologists of work use implicitly:

> These are the *rules* on which many people have agreed and thus legitimated, for longer or shorter periods, as effective means of solving the economic and political problems of production and distribution. Work structures also represent the *hierarchical orderings* of persons and clusters of interests, configurations of norms, and the rights and obligations that characterize the relations among different types of actors in the economy. (p. 2, emphasis added)

Kalleberg and Berg (1987) emphasize six concrete work structures: nation-states, industries, business organizations, occupations, classes, and unions. In light of the recent institutionalization of transnational arrangements for global economic integration, such as the European Union, MERCOSUR among the Southern cone nations of South America, and NAFTA, we add "transnational economic institutions" to Kalleberg and Berg's list of work structures that influence the functioning and outcomes of labor markets and labor-management relations and are associated with "restructuring" (Cornfield, 1997a).

Contemporary workplace restructuring constitutes a reconfiguration of the sociological image of "bureaucracy" that developed in the 1950-1980 era and that inheres in much contemporary scholarship in the sociology of work. The image of bureaucracy that is embedded in contemporary research in the sociology of work derived from Max Weber's classic essay on bureaucracy and responded to the advent of the large-corporate, oligopolistic economy in which mass production occurred in bureaucratic, Fordist-Taylorist organizations. Several writers during the 1950s developed bureaucracy as an image of economic institutions and labor processes in industrial nations in which an individual employee, unlike the disappearing individualistic entrepreneur, would become immersed in an organizational community. Referring to his fabled "organization man" in 1956, William H. Whyte, Jr., wrote,

> It is the organization man . . . who most urgently wants to belong. . . . The group that he is trying to immerse himself in is not merely the larger one—The Organization, or society itself—but the immediate, physical group as well: the people at the conference table, the workshop, the seminar, . . . the project team. . . . Where the immersion of the individual used to be cause for grumbling and a feeling of independence lost, the organization man of today is now welcoming it. (pp. 46-47)

In this image, bureaucracy was a formal organization that consisted of a pyramidal authority structure; a complex occupational division labor with highly specialized jobs arrayed in a maze of career lines; potent informal work groups that influenced worker attitudes and productivity; mass production technology; and unionization. The stability and structural stasis of this bureaucracy rested on U.S. manufacturing and financial dominance in the world market and a strong industrial labor union in the workplace and industry. In this bureaucracy, a worker, independent of collar color, typically expected job security with long-term prospects of upward career mobility at the same employer. The bureaucracy of the 1950s became the emerging arena for upward social mobility and for claiming prestige. As C. Wright Mills put it in 1951,

> The fetishism of the enterprise, and identification with the firm, are often as relevant for white-collar hirelings as for managers. This identification may be implemented by the fact that the work itself . . . offers little chance for external pres-

tige claims and internal self-esteem. . . . In identifying with a firm, the young executive can sometimes line up his career expectations with it, and so identify his own future with that of the firm's. (pp. 243-244)

It is this image of worker, work, and workplace that pervaded Miller and Form's (1951) *Industrial Sociology*, a text that pioneered and guided the sociology of work for the next quarter-century (also see Smith, 1998).

Beginning in the early 1970s, this image of bureaucracy was modified in four ways in response to growing sociological interest in organizational career and social mobility processes, the demographic diversification of the labor force, and the globalization and transnationalization of economic production. First, with the publication of Doeringer and Piore's (1971) *Internal Labor Markets and Manpower Analysis*, sociologists borrowed the concept of internal labor market from institutional economics in order to explain more precisely how the structure and functioning of bureaucracy shaped individual careers, especially long-term careers at the same employer. Second, with the publication of *Men and Women of the Corporation*, Kanter (1977a) elaborated on the image of bureaucracy as an institutional arena culturally imbued with societal norms about group relations and roles, such as gender roles. These norms effectively created minority and token employees whose work attitudes and career prospects were constrained by a bureaucracy managed by White men. Third, in *Work and Family in the United States*, Kanter (1977b) argued that organizational careers and work attitudes were shaped not only by workplace factors but also by important mutually causal relations between the workplace and the family. Fourth, with the publication of Cole's (1979) *Work, Mobility, and Participation* on U.S.-Japan differences in organizational careers and work attitude formation, bureaucracy came to be seen as a work institution whose organization and organizational impact on workers derived partly from societal values about work and self-society relationships and from state regulation of labor and economic processes.

Notwithstanding this evolution of the image of bureaucracy since the 1950s, the current dominant image forged by the 1970s among sociologists continues to assume that bureaucracy is a stable and structurally static institution that houses and shapes important processes of social mobility and work attitude formation. Yet by the 1980s, proclaimed Leinberger and Tucker (1991), the stable economic basis of the organization man *qua* model had eroded, leading to "his" retirement from the corporate bureaucracy. In their study of the children of the same organization men whom Whyte had interviewed for his 1956 book *The Organization Man*, Leinberger and Tucker (1991) argued that

> under the pressure of global competition and advances in communication technology, there have appeared almost overnight new organizational forms that are the antithesis of the centered, functional hierarchies elaborated during the era of the organization man. . . . Many organizations now more closely resemble the decentered networks of which the organizations are a part. . . . Increasingly, the model of organization is coming to be that of the network, with constantly shifting nodes of power and influence, often geographically distant from each other, but tightly linked by communications. (pp. 332, 334)

As for the contemporary social mobility prospects and career paths of the children of the organization men, Leinberger and Tucker (1991) wrote that

> many of the organization offspring certainly appear to take bold risks; they change jobs and even careers with startling frequency, choose where they want to live and only then look for work, desert orthodox career paths in favor of fashioning their own situations, and prize personal freedom over job security and creativity over productivity. . . . The children, utterly lacking their fathers' loyalty to a specific organization but under no illusions about how the world's work gets done, will be antiorganization but not antiorganizational, more inclined to join many

ever-shifting networks than to seek a niche in one immortal hierarchy. (pp. 18, 21)

"Workplace restructuring" has assumed a specific historical meaning about contemporary changes in the organization of workplaces (Smith, 1998). In his review of recent scholarship on restructuring, Leicht (1998, p. 37) highlights six concrete forms of restructuring:

1. Flattening of organizational hierarchies
2. Growing use of temporary workers
3. Extensive use of subcontracting and outsourcing
4. Massive downsizing of the permanent workforce
5. A postunionized bargaining environment
6. Virtual organizations that exist as webs of technologically driven interaction

Sociologically, we argue, contemporary workplace restructuring is a three-dimensional change in the structure of the bureaucratic workplace. The three dimensions of change may or may not occur together in a particular workplace and do not necessarily cohere logically as a unified strategy of organizational change (Drago, 1998). These changes are typically implemented by a corporate management attempting to reduce production costs and increase decision-making flexibility in an increasingly volatile and uncertain product market (Osterman, 1996; Rubin, 1996; Smith, 1997; Vallas, 1999; Vallas & Beck, 1996).

The first dimension of workplace restructuring—the *devolution of decision making*—pertains to the shape of the authority structure and occupational division labor of the bureaucratic workplace. As Leicht (1998) suggests, the flattening of organizational hierarchies in "post-Taylorist/Fordist" directions entails the shift in production decision making, and to a lesser extent personnel decision making, away from middle management and first-line supervision toward self-supervised shop- and office-floor teams of nonsupervisory workers.

The extent and degree to which devolution of decision making has occurred, as well as its impact on occupational skill levels, are subject to scholarly estimation and speculation (Appelbaum & Batt, 1994; Cappelli et al., 1997; Crompton, Gallie, & Purcell, 1996; Nissen, 1997; Osterman, 1996; Smith, 1997; Vallas, 1999). Estimates of the progress and prevalence of devolution depend on its empirical operationalization and the characteristics of the sample used to observe devolution (Ichniowski et al., 1996). The 1993 BLS Survey of Employer Provided Training in some 6,000 private, nonagricultural U.S. business establishments is one of the most comprehensive national surveys of work organization. According to this survey, 42% of establishments practiced at least one of the following types of decentralized decision making: worker teams, total quality management, quality circles, peer review of employee performance, worker involvement in purchase decisions, and job rotation (Gittleman, Horrigan, & Joyce, 1998, p. 104). Decentralized decision making is most likely to be instituted in large organizations (Gittleman et al., 1998; Marsden, Cook, & Kalleberg, 1996; Osterman, 1994). Presently, it is difficult to track the depth and diffusion of the devolution of decision making partly because insufficient scholarly attention has been given to several important features of decision-making decentralization *within the firm.* These features of decentralization include the frequency with which it is practiced, the range of policy domains to which it is applied, the organizational level of authority that makes final, binding decisions, and the proportion of the firm workforce that makes decisions.

To the extent it has occurred, devolution constitutes a decentralization of the authority structure and a "craftist" simplification of the occupational division of labor of bureaucracy. It is decentralization in that more formal decision-making authority is lodged at lower levels of the authority structure than in the Taylorist bureaucracy. Devolution simplifies the occupational division of labor by effectively enlarging the range of production tasks and responsibilities of production and frontline service jobs, reminiscent of pre-Taylorist craft organization.

The second dimension of workplace restructuring is the *casualization of the employment relationship* inside the bureaucratic workplace. The internal labor market was predicated on the mutual expectations of employer and employee that the employee would remain employed for much of his or her career in a single employer. What is more, the internal labor market assumes implicitly that coworkers work with one another on the same physical premises rather than being dispersed widely in telecommuting and other "virtual" relationships via electronic media (e.g., e-mail and beepers). With fringe benefit generosity, promotion chances, and job security accruing with employment seniority, the successful full-time employee could expect upward career mobility and a retirement pension; the employer could expect employment stabilization, few interruptions in production that resulted from employee turnover, and the development of an on-the-job trained workforce.

The advent of the contingent "just-in-time" workforce, outsourcing to parts and business-service suppliers, knowledge- and productivity-based compensation systems, and other "nonstandard or alternative work arrangements" constitute a declining commitment to the seniority-based internal labor market and a growing casualization of the employment relationship (Arthur & Rousseau, 1996; Barker & Christensen, 1998; Barry & Crant, 1994; Cappelli et al., 1997; Cornfield, 1997b; Herzenberg, Alic, & Wial, 1998, chap. 7; O'Reilly & Fagan, 1998; Osterman, 1996; Rubin, 1996; Tilly, 1996). Much like the workers in the prebureaucratic, casual employment relationship that preceded the internal labor market at the beginning of the 20th century (Cornfield, 1997b; Jacoby, 1985), the growing numbers of part-time and temporary workers, self-employed homeworkers, and independent contractors lack long-term mutual commitments and relationships with their multiple, short-term, and often "virtual" employers. In this casual employment relationship, employer and employee have a limited engagement with one another, and the employer typically provides no fringe benefits to the contingent worker. What is more, the full-time worker no longer expects to ascend a single corporate career ladder. In the casual employment relationship, the full-time worker achieves upward career mobility through a series of interfirm job shifts during his or her career. More scholarly research needs to be directed at discerning (a) the extent to which workers opt for the schedule flexibility associated with casual employment relations or default into these casual employment relations and (b) the role of management in instituting casual employment relations (Barker & Christensen, 1998; Gonos, 1998; Hipple, 1998; Jurik, 1998; O'Reilly & Fagan, 1998; Smith, 1998).

The multiplicity of casual employment relationships complicates the calculation of the prevalence of casualization. Four BLS concepts—multiple jobholding, part-time work, contingent work, and alternative employment arrangements—can be used to operationalize casual employment relationships and track their diffusion. The percentage of the employed who worked multiple jobs declined from 5.5% in 1956 to 4.5% in 1974 and then rose to 6.0% by 1998 (Jacobs, 1997, pp. 68-69; U.S. Bureau of Labor Statistics, 1983, p. 114; 1999a, p. 211). Part-time employment as a percentage of employment increased from 14.0% to 17.7% between 1968 and 1998 (Jacobs, 1997, p. 45; U.S. Bureau of Labor Statistics, 1999a, p. 184). Using the BLS's three definitions of contingent workers,[2] contingent workers composed 1.9% to 4.4% of employment in 1997 (Hipple, 1998, p. 23). The BLS's alternative employment arrangements, as opposed to its "traditional arrangements," are workers paid by temporary help agencies or contract companies, on-call workers, and independent contractors (Hipple, 1998, p. 35; for definitions of alternative employment arrangements, see Cohany, 1998, p. 4.; Cohany, Hipple, Nardone, Polivka, & Stewart, 1998). According to the BLS, workers in alternative employment arrangements accounted for 9.9% of employment in 1997 (Cohany, 1998, p. 4).

The future direction of casualization is uncertain for two reasons. First, little or no scholarly research has addressed the ambiguous interpretation of the youthfulness of contingent workers. Workers 16 to 24 years old are much more likely than older workers to prefer contingent work over noncontingent work and to be employed as contingent workers (Hipple, 1998). It is unclear whether this reflects a growing age-generational shift in preferences for contingent work or an enduring conception of this age group in each cohort that contingent work constitutes a temporary way station in the life cycle. Second, BLS occupational employment forecasts suggest that on-the-job training is likely to decline, implying a weakening of the rationale for firm-specific internal labor markets. The BLS projects that employment in jobs that require short-, moderate-, and long-term on-the-job training will grow by only 8.7% to 13.3% between 1996 and 2006 and that jobs requiring a bachelor's degree or more formal education will increase by 18.0% to 25.4% (U.S. Bureau of Labor Statistics, 1998a). This suggests that casualization will continue if employers externalize job training and the occupational division of labor shifts in favor of occupations whose incumbents have historically been trained and licensed by government, educational, professional, and occupational institutions rather than by employers. More scholarly research, therefore, should be addressed to the evolution of labor-supply processes and institutions (Gonos, 1998).

The third dimension of workplace restructuring is the *shift from collective bargaining to individual bargaining* over the terms of employment (Edwards, 1993; Freeman, 1994). This shift is signified by the decline in the percentage of the national labor force that belongs to unions. From its all-time high of 35.5% in 1945, the percentage unionized declined to 13.9% in 1998 (U.S. Bureau of Labor Statistics, 1979, p. 507; 1999b). Union decline has resulted from several forces, including employer resistance to unionization and limited demand for unionization among workers (Stern & Cornfield, 1996).

In the absence of a union and labor agreement, workers bargain individually with their employers. Formal individual bargaining tactics and strategies include quitting voluntarily, litigation and acquiescence (U.S. Commission on the Future of Worker-Management Relations, 1994). Moreover, collective bargaining and litigation may be deployed in tandem (McCann, 1994). Informal individual bargaining may take a variety of legal and extralegal forms. Informal types of individual bargaining tactics include noncollegial behavior and deviant behavior such as sabotage and workplace violence (see, for example, the February 1999 special issue of *Work and Occupations* on "Crime and the Workplace"). Little scholarly attention has been given to the prevalence of formal and informal individual bargaining and the extent to which deviant behavior in the workplace may have arisen with the decline of collective bargaining (for an exception, see Hodson, 1995).

We close this introduction to our volume on working in restructured workplaces with the observation that this three-dimensional contemporary workplace restructuring challenges sociologists who study the workplace to reexamine the image of bureaucracy developed before the present wave of workplace restructuring. Restructuring also challenges researchers to widen their mission to encompass the rate, extent, and variations in workplace restructuring and the impact of workplace restructuring on worker life chances and the quality of employment relations.

WORKPLACE RESTRUCTURING: ITS IMPLICATIONS FOR RESEARCH IN THE SOCIOLOGY OF WORK

In assembling *Working in Restructured Workplaces*, we have reprinted *Work and Occupations* articles and commissioned several new ones that address the nature, causes, and consequences of workplace restructuring.[3] We organized the chapters according to four broad themes that suggest new directions for research in the sociology of work. These themes, identified as Parts I through IV in the table of contents, address the transformations in workplace status hierarchies and employment relations that are associated with workplace restructuring. The conclusion consists of two chapters that chart new research agendas on the extent and durability of workplace restructuring.

Part I, "Reconfiguring Workplace Status Hierarchies," treats the implications of workplace restructuring for the reproduction of existing status hierarchies and the development of new hierarchies in the workplace. Among the varied research issues addressed by these chapters are the ways in which managers cope with contradictory employment systems that emerge when permanent and temporary workers labor side by side; the impact of reorganization and new technology on worker skill levels, unequal employment relations, and upward career mobility; the circumstances shaping worker assessments of status hierarchies during restructuring; the implications of legal policies for earnings differentials; and the outcome of transferring one set of workplace hierarchies into an alternative cultural environment.

Part II, "Casualization of Employment Relationships," assesses the factors that promote and erode long-term employment relations. Two chapters focus on the experiences of self-employed workers, particularly women; two others explore the history of and recent changes in the Japanese system of permanent employment. All four may be read through a lens of gender: In the United States, women and men follow different routes into self-employment, and self-employed women are—like other groups of women— disproportionately responsible for child care, whereas in Japan, no matter the current state of the practice, permanent employment has not been available to women nor even to all men. Thus, trends in the longevity and formality of employment relations cannot be understood adequately without attention to the ways in which these trends reinforce existing privilege and disadvantage.

Part III, "Restructuring and Worker Marginalization," considers the impact of workplace restructuring on interpersonal relations in the workplace, worker emotional states, and individual coping strategies. Its seven chapters, while varied, draw our attention to the negative consequences for individual workers (and for coworkers and management) of alienating workplace structures and practices, which affect a broad range of workers and threaten even self-employed physicians. Marginalization of workers is often signaled by their exclusion from decision making, limited interaction with others on the job, and lack of understanding about the purpose of their daily activities. More positively, some of the research in Part III demonstrates the good that can come from structures and practices that afford workers the resources with which to do their jobs well, voices in decision making, and opportunities to interact constructively with coworkers.

Part IV, "Comparative Labor Responses to Global Restructuring," discusses labor's responses to the dramatic changes in the global economy. Its five chapters represent diverse approaches to understanding labor's actions in an era of international competition and corporate flexibility, yet all have some common themes running through them. A key concern of this section is with the implications of broad political and economic contexts for labor's responses. Many of the chapters consider the consequences for workers and labor movements of national or transnational policies. Some of the work presented here views, for instance, new global trade policies as providing opportunities for labor to turn its focus to more international concerns. Another theme developed in these chapters highlights the role of the economic context for labor's willingness and ability to respond to corporate strategies designed to respond to increasingly competitive international markets.

Finally, the volume's two concluding chapters present complementary agendas for research on the trajectory of, and variations in, workplace restructuring. In Chapter 23, Paul Hirsch and Charles Naquin address the implications of restructuring for the system of career mobility. Their research agenda rests on the assertion that the restructured workplace has not fully supplanted the bureaucratic, "organization man" system of careers in the firm-specific internal labor market. Hirsch and Naquin suggest that the variations in institutionalized career patterns that have resulted from workplace restructuring necessitate a reformulation of theories of careers.

In Chapter 24, Arne Kalleberg concludes that restructured workplaces themselves are sufficiently diverse and pervasive to indicate a variety of new avenues of research on their consequences for work organization, employment relations, and interorganizational relations. He details three types of firm "flexibility," each of which raises research questions:

- The institution of functional flexibility has implications for the direction of worker control.
- The establishment of numerical flexibility implies that nonstandard employment arrangements may influence worker life chances and socioeconomic status.
- The advent of flexible network organizations raises questions about interorganizational trust relations and relationship durability.

The new sociological research on workplace restructuring will illuminate the nature and durability of workplace restructuring. Moving the sociology of work in this direction will generate theoretical insights about institutional change in the workplace and its consequences for worker livelihoods and life chances, as well as policies for tackling problems associated with working in restructured workplaces.

NOTES

1. Daniel Cornfield, Karen Campbell, and Holly McCammon have been Editor, Book Review Editor, and Deputy Editor, respectively, of the journal *Work and Occupations* since 1995.

2. The three BLS definitions of contingent workers range from narrow to broad. The narrowest excludes the self-employed and independent contractors and consists of wage and salary workers who expect to work in their current job for one year or less and who had worked for their current employer for one year or less. The next broader definition includes self-employed workers, independent contractors, temporary help, and contract company workers. The broadest definition removes the one-year duration and tenure requirements. For further elaboration, see Hipple (1998, pp. 34-35).

3. The commissioned chapters in order of appearance in this volume are authored by Vicki Smith (Chapter 1), Beth Rubin and Brian Smith (Chapter 17), Paul Hirsch and Charles Naquin (Chapter 23), and Arne Kalleberg (Chapter 24).

REFERENCES

Appelbaum, E., & Batt, R. (1994). *The new American workplace.* Ithaca, NY: ILR Press.

Arthur, M., & Rousseau, D. (Eds.). (1996). *The boundaryless career: A new employment principle for a new organizational era.* New York: Oxford University Press.

Barker, K., & Christensen, K. (Eds.). (1998). *Contingent work: American employment relations in transition.* Ithaca, NY: Cornell University Press.

Barry, B., & Crant, J. (1994). Labor force externalization in growing firms. *International Journal of Organizational Analysis, 2,* 361-383.

Cappelli, P., Bassi, L., Katz, H., Knoke, D., Osterman, P., & Useem, M. (1997). *Change at work.* New York: Oxford University Press.

Castillo, J. J. (1997). Looking for the meaning of work. *Work and Occupations, 24,* 413-425.

Cohany, S. (1996, October). Workers in alternative employment arrangements. *Monthly Labor Review,* pp. 31-45.

Cohany, S. (1998, November). Workers in alternative employment arrangements: A second look. *Monthly Labor Review,* pp. 3-21.

Cohany, S., Hipple, S., Nardone, T., Polivka, A., & Stewart, J. (1998). Counting the workers: Results of a first survey. In K. Barker & K. Christensen (Eds.), *Contingent work: American employment relations in transition* (pp. 41-68). Ithaca, NY: Cornell University Press.

Cole, R. (1979). *Work, mobility, and participation: A comparative study of American and Japanese industry.* Berkeley: University of California Press.

Cornfield, D. (1997a). Labor transnationalism? An editorial introduction to "Labor in the Americas." *Work and Occupations, 24,* 278-287.

Cornfield, D. (1997b). Labor union responses to technological change: Past, present, and future. *Perspectives on Work, 1,* 35-38.

Crompton, R., Gallie, D., & Purcell, K. (Eds.). (1996). *Changing forms of employment: Organisations, skills and gender.* New York: Routledge.

Doeringer, P. B., & Piore, M. J. (1971). *Internal labor markets and manpower analysis.* Lexington, MA: D. C. Heath.

Drago, R. (1998). New systems of work and new workers. In K. Barker & K. Christensen (Eds.), *Contingent work: American employment relations in transition* (pp. 144-169). Ithaca, NY: Cornell University Press.

Dudley, K. (1994). *The end of the line: Lost jobs, new lives in postindustrial America.* Chicago: University of Chicago Press.

Edwards, R. (1993). *Rights at work: Employment relations in the post-union era.* Washington, DC: Brookings Institution.

Ferber, M., & Waldfogel, J. (1998, May). The long term consequences of nontraditional employment. *Monthly Labor Review,* pp. 3-12.

Freeman, R. (Ed.). (1994). *Working under different rules.* New York: Russell Sage.

Gamst, F. (Ed.). (1995). *Meanings of work: Considerations for the twenty-first century.* Albany: State University of New York Press.

Gardner, J. (1995, April). Worker displacement: A decade of change. *Monthly Labor Review,* pp. 45-57.

Gittleman, M., Horrigan, M., & Joyce, M. (1998). "Flexible" workplace practices: Evidence from a nationally representative survey. *Industrial and Labor Relations Review, 52,* 99-115.

Gonos, G. (1998). The interaction between market incentives and government actions. In K. Barker & K. Christensen (Eds.), *Contingent work: American employment relations in transition* (pp. 170-191). Ithaca, NY: Cornell University Press.

Herzenberg, S., Alic, J., & Wial, H. (1998). *New rules for a new economy: Employment and opportunity in post-industrial America.* Ithaca, NY: Cornell University Press.

Hipple, S. (1997, December). Worker displacement in an expanding economy. *Monthly Labor Review,* pp. 26-39.

Hipple, S. (1998, November). Contingent work: Results from the second survey. *Monthly Labor Review,* pp. 22-35.

Hipple, S., & Stewart, J. (1996, October). Earnings and benefits of workers in alternative work arrangements. *Monthly Labor Review,* pp. 46-54.

Hirsch, P. (1993). Undoing the managerial revolution? Needed research on the decline of middle management and internal labor markets. In R. Swedberg (Ed.), *Explorations in economic sociology* (pp. 145-157). New York: Russell Sage.

Hodson, R. (1995). The worker as active subject: Enlivening the "new sociology of work." In D. Bills (Ed.), *The new modern times: Factors reshaping the world of work* (pp. 253-280). Albany: State University of New York Press.

Ichniowski, C., Kochan, T., Levine, D., Olson, C., & Strauss, G. (1996). What works at work: Overview and assessment. *Industrial Relations, 35,* 299-333.

Illes, L. (1996). *Sizing down.* Ithaca, NY: Cornell University Press.

Jacobs, E. (Ed.). (1997). *Handbook of U.S. labor statistics.* Lanham, MD: Bernan Press.

Jacoby, S. (1985). *Employing bureaucracy: Managers, unions, and the transformation of work in American industry, 1900-1945.* New York: Columbia University Press.

Jurik, N. (1998). Getting away and getting by: The experiences of self-employed homeworkers. *Work and Occupations, 25,* 7-35.

Kalleberg, A., & Berg, I. (1987). *Work and industry: Structures, markets, and processes.* New York: Plenum.

Kanter, R. (1977a). *Men and women of the corporation.* New York: Basic Books.

Kanter, R. (1977b). *Work and family in the United States: A critical review and agenda for research and policy.* New York: Russell Sage.

Leicht, K. (1998). Work (if you can get it) and occupations (if there are any)? What social scientists can learn from predictions of the end of work and radical workplace change. *Work and Occupations, 25,* 36-48.

Leinberger, P., & Tucker, B. (1991). *The new individualists: The generation after the organization man.* New York: HarperCollins.

Marsden, P., Cook, C., & Kalleberg, A. (1996). Bureaucratic structures for coordination and control. In A. Kalleberg, D. Knoke, P. Marsden, & J. Spaeth (Eds.), *Organizations in America* (pp. 69-86). Thousand Oaks, CA: Sage.

McCann, M. (1994). *Rights at work: Pay equity reform and the politics of legal mobilization.* Chicago: University of Chicago Press.

Miller, D., & Form, W. (1951). *Industrial sociology: An introduction to the sociology of work relations.* New York: Harper & Brothers.

Mills, C. W. (1951). *White collar.* New York: Oxford University Press.

New York Times. (1996). *The downsizing of America.* New York: Times Books.

Nissen, B. (Ed.). (1997). *Unions and workplace reorganization.* Detroit: Wayne State University Press.

O'Reilly, J., & Fagan, C. (Eds.). (1998). *Part-time prospects: An international comparison of part-time work in Europe, North America and the Pacific Rim.* New York: Routledge.

Osterman, P. (1994). How common is workplace transformation and who adopts it? *Industrial and Labor Relations Review, 47,* 173-188.

Osterman, P. (Ed.). (1996). *Broken ladders: Managerial careers in the new economy.* New York: Oxford University Press.

Rubin, B. (1996). *Shifts in the social contract.* Thousand Oaks, CA: Pine Forge Press.

Schellenberg, K. (1996). Taking it or leaving it: Instability and turnover in a high-tech firm. *Work and Occupations, 23,* 190-213.

Smith, V. (1997). New forms of work organization. *Annual Review of Sociology, 23,* 315-339.

Smith, V. (1998). The fractured worlds of the temporary worker: Power, participation, and fragmentation in the contemporary workplace. *Social Problems, 45,* 411-430.

Stern, R., & Cornfield, D. (1996). *The U.S. labor movement: References and resources.* New York: G. K. Hall.

Tilly, C. (1996). *Half a job: Bad and good jobs in a changing labor market.* Philadelphia: Temple University Press.

U.S. Bureau of Labor Statistics. (1979). *Handbook of labor statistics, 1978* (Bulletin No. 2000). Washington, DC: Government Printing Office.

U.S. Bureau of Labor Statistics. (1983). *Handbook of labor statistics* (Bulletin No. 2175). Washington, DC: Government Printing Office.

U.S. Bureau of Labor Statistics. (1998a). *Table 5. Employment and total job openings, 1996-2006, and 1996 median weekly earnings by education and training category,* published September 9, 1998 [Online]. Available at: http://www.bls.gov/news.release/ecopro.table5.htm

U.S. Bureau of Labor Statistics. (1998b). *Table 9. Employed contingent and noncontingent workers and those with alternative and traditional work arrangements by health insurance coverage and eligibility for employer-provided pension plans, February 1997,* published February 3, 1998 [Online]. Available at: http://www.bls.gov/news.release/conemp.t09.htm

U.S. Bureau of Labor Statistics. (1998c). *Table 13. Median usual weekly earnings of full- and part-time contingent and noncontingent wage and salary workers and those with alternative and traditional work arrangements by sex, age, race, and Hispanic origin, February 1997,* published February 3, 1998 [Online]. Available at: http://www.bls.gov/news.release/conemp.t13.htm

U.S. Bureau of Labor Statistics. (1998d). *Table 7. Displaced worker(1) who lost full-time wage and salary jobs and were reemployed in February 1998 by industry of lost job and characteristics of new job,* published August 19, 1998 [Online]. Available at: http://www.bls.gov/news.release/disp.t07.htm

U.S. Bureau of Labor Statistics. (1999a, January). *Employment and Earnings,* No. 46.

U.S. Bureau of Labor Statistics. (1999b). *Table 1. Union affiliation of employed wage and salary workers by selected characteristics,* published January 25, 1999 [Online]. Available at: http://www.bls.gov/news.release/union2.t01.htm

U.S. Bureau of the Census. (1999a). *Table F-2. Share of aggregate income received by each fifth and top 5 percent of families (all races): 1947 to 1997,* published March 22, 1999 [Online]. Available at: http://www.census.gov/hhes/income/histinc/f02.html

U.S. Bureau of the Census. (1999b). *Table H-4. Gini ratios for households, by race and Hispanic origin of householder: 1967 to 1997,* published February 3, 1999 [Online]. Available at: http://www.census.gov/hhes/income/histinc/h04.html

U.S. Bureau of the Census. (1999c). *Table 2. Poverty status of people, by family relationship, race, and Hispanic origin: 1959 to 1997,* published February 3, 1999 [Online]. Available at: http://www.census.gov/hhes/poverty/histpov/hstpov2.html

U.S. Commission on the Future of Worker-Management Relations. (1994). *Report and recommendations.* Washington, DC: Author.

Vallas, S. (1999). Re-thinking post-Fordism: The meaning of workplace flexibility. *Sociological Theory, 17,* 68-101.

Vallas, S., & Beck, J. (1996). The transformation of work revisited: The limits of flexibility in American manufacturing. *Social Problems, 43,* 339-361.

Whyte, W., Jr. (1956). *The organization man.* New York: Simon & Schuster.

PART I

Reconfiguring Workplace Status Hierarchies

A key question that any student of workplace restructuring must ask is what is the impact of workplace reorganization on the equalities and inequalities of the workplace? The six chapters in this opening section consider a variety of ways in which workplace reconfiguration alters dimensions of workplace hierarchy, including differences in worker power, status, compensation, skill, and career trajectories and even differences in organizational status within firms. The perspectives and conclusions of the authors are quite varied and provide for a theoretically and empirically rich overview of a topic that is critical to understanding the implications of workplace restructuring. Each of the following chapters also reveals important new avenues for research.

Chapter 1 by Vicki Smith, "Teamwork vs. Tempwork: Managers and the Dualisms of Workplace Restructuring," provides one of the first investigations of how managers, particularly lower-level managers, cope with the everyday workplace dynamics that result from corporate reorganization. Smith begins with a discussion of the increasingly common coexistence of, on one hand, permanent workers who are asked to participate in self-managed teams, quality circles, or other progressive employee arrangements and, on the other hand, temporary workers hired for impermanent, sometimes even part-time work. Smith finds that in her study of a corporation these two very different types of workers are supervised and coordinated by the same manager. She reveals how managers simultaneously manage workers who labor within very different employment systems, and she uncovers some surprising findings. Where one might expect managers to reinforce status distinctions among the permanent and temporary workers, Smith finds that the managers instead attempt by various means to bridge some of the inherent inequities in the temporary hiring relationship.

Smith concludes by pointing out that we know little about the extent to which these contradictory employment relations exist side by side in today's workplace. She calls for more study in this area, not only to gauge how frequently this arrangement occurs but also to explore further how managers—and we might add to this, workers as well—cope with such contradictory logic in restructured workplaces.

Ian Taplin, in Chapter 2, "Flexible Production, Rigid Jobs: Lessons From the Clothing Industry," discusses the implications of moves by firms in the textile industry to make production more efficient, flexible, and profitable in an increasingly competitive marketplace. Taplin finds that the men's and boys' apparel firms he studies have undergone significant reorganizations involving the introduction of microprocessor technologies and often the formation of work teams. Taplin's particular concern as he studies these reorganizations is with the consequences of change for the production workers. Taplin asks whether the workplace changes have also meant a move away from the traditional Fordist work environment with labor-intensive mass production and low-skilled workers having little power in the workplace. But what emerges quite clearly from his analysis is that, at least in the textile industry, there is no "post-Fordism" emerging but, rather, "neo-Fordism." The new computer technology brought about not only a reorganization of work but a reliance on fewer and even less skilled workers, and these workers, even though they frequently participate in work groups, have no greater authority in their work than previously.

A key question that remains, as Taplin himself points out, is just how generalizable the finding is. Does the introduction of new technology and more flexible production in other industries produce the same results for workers, that is, reduced skill requirements, greater job insecurity, and no greater workplace power? Is the pattern unique to textile production, or is it the case as well in other labor-intensive, competitive industries? Further research is needed to map more systematically these patterns of change across work settings.

In Chapter 3, "The Technological Foundations of Task-Coordinating Structures in New Work Organizations: Theoretical Notes From the Case of Abdominal Surgery," James Zetka echoes many of these same concerns in presenting a fascinating look at the consequences of a new technology in surgical work. He finds that in various medical subspecialties when surgeons use video laparoscopy, the task coordination between the primary and assistant surgeons alters. Zetka relies on contingency theory to examine the effects of the video technology and illustrates with his analysis that in conventional surgery (without the new technology) neo-Fordist conditions prevail where the lead surgeon routinely unilaterally controls the surgery process. But the introduction of the technology produces post-Fordist working relations. With the technology, lead surgeons pair themselves with able assistant surgeons, and because of the demands of the technology, the two work as partners in a more equal work relationship. The technology reduces the unequal power relations.

But, as with Taplin's work, Zetka's case study raises these questions: How generalizable is this finding? In which working environments can we expect a reduction in status hierarchies with the introduction of new technology? Taplin's study of the textile industry demonstrates little change in unequal workplace relations, whereas Zetka's reveal significant changes. What accounts for this difference? What are the circumstances in which each occurs? What role does the nature of the technology play? Clearly, broader research spanning multiple cases can help answer these questions.

In Chapter 4, "A Tale of Two Career Paths: The Process of Status Acquisition by a New Organizational Unit," Elizabeth Briody, Marietta Baba, and Lindsay Cooper explore the ramifications of organizational restructuring in General Motors' Sales and Service Division. In the study, GM had recently established a new telemarketing unit within its service and sales division. The new unit allowed GM to service its lower volume sales dealerships indirectly through telecommunication facilities. Briody, Baba, and Cooper trace the development of a unit hierarchy within the reorganized division in which the new unit ranked below the traditional zone unit that provided direct contact with the higher volume dealerships. The authors examine a number of factors that GM employees use as indicators of unit status, but particularly important to their investigation is career mobility. Units providing greater chances of upward mobility for employees (which the zone unit did) were perceived to have higher organizational status.

The authors point out that little is known about the impact of corporate restructuring on the possibilities for career trajectories (although see Chapter 23 by Hirsch and Naquin, this volume). But their work also reveals how employees socially construct perceptions of organizational status (in this case unit status), and this, too, is understudied in the literature on workplace organization; particularly unexamined are changes in perceptions during periods of rapid restructuring. We know little about how workplace cultures may influence workers' perceptions of changing organizational status in firms and how employees' perceptions may then influence their work commitment during periods of organizational change.

Chapter 5 is by Martin Kenney, W. Richard Goe, Oscar Contreras, Jairo Romero, and Mauricio Bustos, whose work titled "Learning Factories or Reproduction Factories? Labor-Management Relations in the Japanese Consumer Electronics Maquiladoras in Mexico" offers an unusual but important look at the consequences of altered workplace relations. Rather than examining changing workplace arrangements within a particular firm, Kenney and his collaborators compare labor-management practices in Japanese electronics firms to those in Japanese-owned electronics maquiladoras in Mexico. Through interviews with production workers concerning hiring, training, job mobility, and the labor process in the maquiladoras, the authors find that although the Japanese firm owners have transferred operations to Mexico they have not fully transferred Japanese management practices to the maquiladoras. Kenney and his colleagues conclude that a "hybrid labor-management system" exists in the Japanese-owned firms which, unlike the firms in Japan, devolve little power to workers but also, unlike in Japan, rely on regular employees (rather than contingent or contract workers) to do routine tasks. But in the end, the findings show that in many respects a worker hierarchy is more pronounced in the Japanese maquiladoras than in the plants in Japan.

The larger question that Kenney and his coauthors pose is a fascinating one. What sorts of workplace relations and hierarchies result when, in the global economy, a firm from one culture with its distinct work practices is transported to another culture with its unique workplace forms? Which form prevails, if either? Does an initial hybrid model exist and then gradually transform into the locally dominant model, as Kenney and the others speculate might be the case in Mexico?

In a unique chapter, Deborah Figart and June Lapidus examine the potential impact of a hypothetical piece of national comparable worth legislation on earnings inequality. In Chapter 6, "The Impact of Comparable Worth on Earnings Inequality," these authors provide a quantitative model to demonstrate the effects of wage legislation imposed externally by the government on workplace gender inequality, and their dramatic results suggest the possibility of greater equality through legal means. Figart and Lapidus's findings reveal that not only would such policy reduce overall earnings inequality in the economy, but comparable worth legislation would also decrease inequality between women and men and among women of different class locations.

Researchers studying workplace restructuring often do not consider the organizational and hierarchical consequences of changes due to government policy. But in an age when the workplace is highly regulated by legal policies, perhaps this emphasis should change. Legal developments can have profound impacts on the workplace, including their impacts on workplace inequalities. Moreover, the government has and will play a role in regulating the pace of corporate change to accommodate changing global markets. This, too, offers important avenues for researchers.

The chapters presented in Part I offer a wide array of empirical research concerning the impact of workplace reconfigurations on workplace hierarchies. These studies offer a broad look at this crucial outcome of workplace restructuring, and students of restructuring should find them highly useful.

1

Teamwork vs. Tempwork

Managers and the Dualisms of Workplace Restructuring

VICKI SMITH

Recent overviews of corporate restructuring have pointed to the simultaneous and oftentimes contradictory growth of workplace decentralization, employee participation, and empowerment, on the one hand, and contingent employment, on the other (Cappelli et al., 1997; Kalleberg, Knoke, Marsden, & Spaeth, 1996; Smith, 1997; Smith, 2001; Vallas, 1999). Whereas the first set of changes (often grouped under the rubric *functional* flexibility) maximizes business adaptability at the level of organizational arrangements—by redesigning production and decision-making processes—the second set (*numerical* flexibility) maximizes business adaptability at the level of employment contracts—by hiring workers on a temporary basis in order to adjust staffing levels. Most empirical studies about the two sets of changes have focused on shopfloor workers, neglecting the central role of supervisors and middle-level managers in shaping these new forms of work and employment relations. Given the dramatic transformation of the American workplace in recent years, the absence of inquiry about managers' work process is puzzling.

To be sure, managers have not been altogether ignored as corporations have restructured, downsized, and flattened. Numerous studies have documented macrolevel transformations in management: Cuts in middle management across corporate America have been deep and wide; job and career instability and downward mobility have become normative for middle managers and professionals (Baker & Aldrich, 1996; DiTomaso, 1996; Doeringer et al., 1991; Heckscher, 1995; Hirsch, 1993; Hirsch & Shanley, 1996; Newman, 1988; Osterman, 1996; Smith, 1997). Yet, to date, managers don't appear in studies of the micropolitics of shopfloor change. Researchers studying flexible production, employee involvement, contingent work, and other new forms of work organization depict (if they depict them at all) managerial strategies in shops and offices in a one-dimensional, untextured way or assume that their interests converge with those of executives who dictate corporate policy. Supervisors and middle managers are assumed to be the coercive executors of new restrictive corporate policies, defenders of more traditional hierarchical and centralized organizational arrangements (e.g., Shaiken, Herzenberg, & Kuhn, 1986), or resistors to any change that challenges their authority and their organizational privilege (see Smith, 1990, for criticisms of these assumptions).

Such one-dimensional and simplistic conceptualizations are inadequate for explaining workplace change, however. Historically, lower-level managers have been designated the agents for shaping antithetical, destabilizing currents of change (Smith, 1988, 1990). Their resistance to and endorsement of contemporary currents are important to study in depth because they may explain the possible limits to which corporate employers can continue to turn stable, permanent jobs into transient or bad ones (Kalleberg, Hudson, & Reskin, 2000) in the American economy.

This chapter strives to advance our understanding of workplace restructuring by examining and explaining supervisors' and middle managers' organizational interests in new production arrangements, especially when new sets of employment relations are superimposed on them. Specifically, I focus on an emergent workplace arrangement, in which functional flexibility and numerical flexibility overlap. Such workplaces represent in microcosm what Appelbaum and Batt (1994, p. 157) have noted about the American employment relations model more generally: a hybrid or piecemeal model of workplace change resulting from employer-initiated innovations to build progressive new workplaces in their pursuit of competitiveness, and their simultaneous reluctance to let go of long-standing cost-minimizing approaches. The convergence of these two trends, previously believed to exist autonomously, is important, for it both challenges conventional expectations about patterns of the implementation of flexibility on the shopfloor and calls for refinement of social science theory about the managerial labor process.

THE CONVERGENCE OF FUNCTIONAL AND NUMERICAL FLEXIBILITY: IMPLICATIONS FOR THEORIES OF LABOR PROCESS AND WORKFORCE MANAGEMENT

As we begin the 21st century, our understanding of workplace reform has become extensive. As American businesses modified their production and employment practices in order to remain competitive, many sociologists, industrial relations researchers, and organizational specialists have vigorously pursued the task of documenting the forms and the frequency of such modifications and have identified two general trends.

The first, *functional flexibility,* encompasses organizational mechanisms and work flow innovations that "build in" employee participation: new technologies, inventory methods, job enlargement schemes, self-managed teams, and quality circles (Smith, 1997). This set of innovations is premised on securing the deeper engagement and commitment of core workers, on continually training them, and on exploiting their accumulated knowledge and experience (Osterman, 1994; Wood, 1989). The second, *numerical flexibility,* refers to contingent jobs, which Polivka (1996) defines as "any job in which an individual does not have an explicit or implicit contract for long-term employment" (p. 4). The contingent labor force includes temporary, subcontracted, and occasionally part-time positions that are organized on an impermanent externalized (Pfeffer & Baron, 1988) or nonstandard (Reskin, 1996) basis.[1]

Whereas functional flexibility theoretically enables workers to adjust their production methods, to respond quickly to changes in inventory, supplies, or demand for product, and to specialize in making a broader range, but smaller batches, of goods and services, numerical flexibility theoretically enables firms to adjust their staffing levels, to bring workers in when needed, and to discard them when they are no longer needed.

A large and growing body of literature has emerged to analyze these two trends (Appelbaum & Batt, 1994; Arthur, 1992; Callaghan & Hartmann, 1991; Cappelli et al., 1997; Colclough & Tolbert, 1992; Harrison, 1994; O'Reilly, 1994; Osterman, 1999; Rubin, 1996; Smith, 1997; Smith, 2001; Vallas, 1999; Wood, 1989). Many studies have assumed that functional and numerical flexibility are two separate systems with their own internal logics and that the numerically flexible approach marginalizes temporary workers. Functional flexibility, it has been argued, is targeted at privileged ranks of workers, such as skilled core workers whom employers wish to nurture as a permanent, loyal labor force. In this line of reasoning, these workers' and companies' interests converge: Companies invest in a smaller core workforce that would be trained and retrained, would develop technical and organizational expertise, and in the process become a loyal partner, enthusiastically throwing its efforts behind the goals of corporate-level management. From the point of view of the company, the costs of continually training and developing core employees are far outweighed by the benefits reaped from workers' increased knowledge about how to do things right and from their heightened commitment to the firm.

Numerical flexibility is expected to target a different set of workers and production settings and to be governed by a different set of cost-benefit calculations. To avoid excessive training costs and organizational disruption, to make it easier to quickly adjust the levels of this variable labor, and to maximize quality control and security, managers will place temporary workers in low-level positions that are least skilled and responsible, most peripheral and routinized, tightly controlled, and least integrated with the firm's core workers. Even when they work in the same space with permanent employees, temporaries' tasks are seen as set apart by their deskilled and devalued character (Rogers, 1999). In this framework, employers wishing to promote numerical flexibility strive to marginalize their temporary workers, both organizationally and culturally, by depriving them of opportunities for involvement, learning, and teamwork. By deliberately marginalizing temporary workers and treating them as "disposable" labor (Thomas, 1994), companies minimize rather than invest in the costs of their human resources. The possible costs of disaffection and alienation on the part of temporaries who resent being used in this manner are far outweighed by the benefits, to the firm, of having a lean permanent workforce.

Two claims about temporary workers follow from the core/margins hypothesis. First, the expectation that temporary workers will be marginalized leads to the claim of "convenience." In this view, using temporary workers is seamless, entailing minimal transaction or organizational costs; managers view temporary workers as disposable and cheap, as little more than mechanical factors of production that they can acquire and discard, depending on business fluctuations. This, indeed, is assumed to be the raison d'être for American employers' heightened interest in using temporary workers (Pfeffer & Baron, 1988).

Second, the hypothesis that managers and employers marginalize temporary workers leads to an expectation that the former will rule the latter with an iron hand. Implicit in the "iron hand" hypothesis is the long-standing assumption that strategies of control and coordination together with managers' needs for consent correspond neatly to the tenure and attachments of workers. Theorists have argued that in firms where employers have an interest in keeping workers on a long-term basis, in maximizing their investments in workers' training and developing their organization-specific skills, managers will adopt noncoercive, bureaucratic, hegemonic, or paternalistic control mechanisms designed to build the consent, participation, and commitments of workers over time (Burawoy, 1985; Edwards, 1979; Hodson, 1996). In this framework, employers wishing to promote functional flexibility would most likely encourage worker self-reliance, autonomous teams, continual learning, and workers' stakeholding in the policies and goals of the company.

Conversely, theorists have argued that in firms where employers lack the incentive to keep and train workers—firms that employ significant numbers of people in temporary, part-time and seasonal low-skill jobs—managers do not view consent as problematic (Doeringer & Piore, 1970; Gordon, Edwards, & Reich, 1982). Indeed, it is believed that they actively discourage commitment and participation and accordingly design control strategies that are antagonistic, coercive (Edwards, 1979), despotic (Burawoy, 1985), or objectifying (Rogers & Henson, 1997) since their interest in keeping workers long term is minimal. In other words, the prevailing typology, to date, suggests two dissimilar, if not antithetical, approaches to managerial strategies: one set designed to deepen the attachment and commitment of workers needed for the long haul, and one set designed to strategically discourage the attachment of workers whom employers need on a short-term basis only.

In this chapter, I explore these expectations and present a more fine-grained understanding of workplace transformation as it is currently playing out in the American workplace. Emerging evidence suggests that more firms are bringing temporary workers into their core activities (Thompson, 1967) and that numerical flexibility is spreading into functionally flexible work settings rather than being siphoned off into distinct settings and distinct groups of workers. In carrying out what Callaghan and Hartmann (1991) have called "business as usual," firms are having temporary workers work side by side with permanent workers, converting permanent employment contracts into temporary contracts, and using temporary workers to perform job tasks formerly done exclusively by permanent workers. A new variant of temporary employment is growing, in which temporary positions are being incorporated into core workplaces, jobs are ongoing but workers are not, and the boundaries between permanent and temporary workers are blurred (for evidence, see Geary, 1992; Graham, 1995; Kunda, 1992; Thomas, 1994). Very often, they are used in settings that can be characterized as highly participative (Hodson, 1996), which utilize the techniques and practices grouped under functional flexibility.

The introduction of temporary workers into work settings where they are integrated into the ranks of permanent workers raises many areas for sociological research. In this chapter, I focus on the microlevel dynamics resulting from the intersection of functional and numerical flexibility, of a commitment-maximizing and a cost-reduction approach, and of a logic of teamwork and a logic of tempwork. Specifically, I analyze the group of corporate employees positioned at the intersection of and responsible for merging functional and numerical flexibility: supervisors and mid-level managers. I first explore the "marginalization" hypothesis, the expectation that to maximize cost-effectiveness and minimize disruption, supervisors and their managers will position temporary workers in jobs that require minimal discretionary power, few opportunities for involvement and mutual collaboration, the least training, and the lowest degree of integration with permanent workers in the firm.

Second, I explore the "convenience" hypothesis, the expectation that managers welcome the use of temporary workers because they feel that it entails a straightforward and seamless business transaction (hire when needed, terminate when not) that gives them greater flexibility. Third, I explore the "iron hand" hypothesis that suggests that because temporary workers lack the legal/temporal attachment to the firm that is assumed to be a foundation for eliciting work effort, discipline, and commitment, managers will use coercive or discouraging tactics.

I explore these claims using data from inductive case study research, in which I formally and informally interviewed managers and temporary workers and observed different work sites in a high-technology firm. These data indicate that the success of or barriers to the spread of new transient, nonstandard work arrangements—arrangements of increasing concern to social scientists and policy researchers—can be explained in large part by looking in depth at the managers responsible for introducing them. How temporary jobs and employment relations are socially organized, including the degree of alienation and degradation experienced, and the opportunity or lack thereof that inheres in such work, directly stems from managerial interventions, which are in turn shaped by organizational constraints and cultural frameworks. Data derived from an inductive approach to the dynamics between managers and their temporary workers allow us to generalize about some of the causes and consequences of this labor market arrangement.

METHODS AND CASE STUDY: THE BACKGROUND

The data are from an in-depth case study of "CompTech," a pseudonym for a leading high-technology firm. This large firm designs and manufactures a range of hardware and software products that are sold around the world. For reasons I discuss shortly, CompTech exemplifies a case in which temporary employment has been institutionalized, fully incorporated into management policy to allow for flexibility, cost reduction, and fine-tuning of staffing levels. CompTech's utilization of a temporary workforce reflects a broader trend in which more jobs are being permanently organized on a nonstandard basis (Reskin, 1996).

In one of the company's divisions in Northern California, I conducted 45 semistructured interviews between August 1996 and January 1997. I interviewed 13 managers, supervisors, and staffing specialists from five production settings. Seven of the 13 managers and staffing specialists were located in business units where they were directly responsible for overseeing factory and office workers. Throughout this chapter I refer to them as the supervisors and their managers, or middle managers. Other interviewees included 22 entry-level assembly line, warehouse, and distribution workers (of whom 13 were temps and 9 were "converts," my term for former temporary workers who had been hired on as permanent workers and had viewed the temporary work relationship from both sides of the divide), 3 high-level, high-paid contract workers, 3 white-collar administrative assistants (entry-level, 1 of whom was a temp and 2 of whom were converts), and 3 representatives of a temporary help service agency that recruited temporary workers for the company. I also interviewed the director of personnel over a period of several months.

The average length of time that the 25 assembly, warehouse, and clerical workers were in temporary positions was 27 noncontinuous months. (Current temps had worked an average of 27.6 months; converts had worked as temps for an average of 26.5 months. As I'll discuss shortly, managers were required to release temps after 18 months but could rehire them after 3 months off.)[2] All workers and work settings were nonunionized. Of the formal interviews with 25 entry-level workers, 12 were with women and 13 were with men. Three of the entry-level workers were Hispanic and the rest were White, although I talked with 5 additional workers of color (2 African Americans and 3 Hispanics) informally. On only one line—the deskilled line—did I observe a significant number of people of color; in other areas, their numbers were small. The *Whiteness,* and especially the *male Whiteness,* of the temporary labor force seemed to me to be a significant finding, as it suggests that temporary work here is not simply a ghetto for the most marginalized members of the labor force. (I'll discuss the implications of this demographic finding shortly.) About two thirds of the workers I interviewed and observed appeared to be in their late 20s or early 30s, whereas the other third appeared to be in their 40s and 50s. Tape-recorded interviews with managers and supervisors averaged 90 minutes in length, whereas interviews with entry-level workers averaged 30 minutes.

I observed 21 additional workers, both temporary and permanent, while they were working, and I informally interviewed 10 of that group who were temporary employees. (In these informal interviews, conducted while "hanging out," I asked workers detailed questions about their jobs and, when it felt appropriate, about their past work histories and their feelings about temporary employment.) The division had several thousand employees dispersed across nearly 30 functions and businesses, ranging from research and development to order fulfillment, production, distribution, and shipping. I studied a small percentage of the total number of employees, but I studied close to 100% of employees in a handful of work settings. For example, I observed all of the workers working three separate assembly lines (two assembling servers and one assembling PCs), and I interviewed and observed about 60% of the workers on one other line. Observations allowed me to assess the skill levels and interactions entailed in different jobs and to cross-check information about production processes that interviewees, managerial and nonmanagerial, described to me. This chapter draws its conclusions from observations in work areas and from integrating and cross-checking interview data from multiple occupational groups.

The findings are generalizable to a specific subset of workplaces. First, as I note shortly,

CompTech has some of the most progressive employment policies in American industry. It is well known for its generous treatment of company workers. Thus, the analysis that follows would be generalizable to companies with similar progressive employment frameworks. Other companies that have more coercive management policies across the board might perceive fewer risks in marginalizing and alienating their temporary employees.

Second, the desirability of permanent employment at CompTech strengthened temporary workers' willingness to work as reliable, dedicated employees. In companies where permanent employment is not a long-term goal for temporary workers, managers would be unable to exploit this desire in their efforts to sustain worker commitment.

Third, the high proportion of White men that I observed indicates that CompTech is distinct. This demographic finding is at odds with what we know to be true about the temporary labor force in the aggregate: that it is disproportionately filled with White women and with men and women of color (Callaghan & Hartman, 1991; Polivka, 1996). The fact that I collected most of my interview and observational data from factorylike settings most likely explains the higher numbers of White men. Such individuals may have been more likely to seek temporary employment in a setting that held out two things that were compatible with their gendered expectations about work: a blue-collar job and permanent employment. I speculate that we would find this configuration of demographics and temporary work in manufacturing and assembly work sites in other core firms, where men have traditionally been located. It is possible that this gender composition affected managers' efforts to treat temps equitably, but the more compelling explanation rests, I will argue, in CompTech's paternalistic culture.

CompTech Management Systems

CompTech managers historically have managed their workforce using an incentive-based, hegemonic system of control (Burawoy, 1985) governed by rewards, generous benefits, and promises of advancement. The company is a prime example of a firm characterized by a participative culture (Hodson, 1996). Many amenities and benefits were available to permanent workers across the board, production arrangements afforded even the lowest-level assembly workers some degree of autonomy, multiple opportunities existed for employees to make decisions and give their input to company managers, there were opportunities for employees to maneuver through mobility paths from the ground up, and last, but not least, the company had a policy of redeploying rather than laying off workers in sluggish economic times. Employees strongly felt that CompTech manifested and rewarded a culture of respect and equality, a value system in part generated by this participative organizational context. According to secondary sources, the high-commitment, inclusive approach to organizing work in CompTech is a long-standing one reinforced over the years by various CEOs who publicly and repeatedly stressed this aspect of the company organization and culture.

Managers have provided symbolic rewards to their permanent workforce, such as social functions, employee of the month certificates, and balloons and banners for outstanding achievers but also cash and benefit rewards, such as paid days off and gift, travel, and restaurant certificates. Moreover, the company expected managers to continually develop their employees professionally, to point workers to training opportunities, mentor them for promotions and nurture them to take on more responsibilities for eventual lateral or upward mobility. For these reasons, it is easy to appreciate why employees I interviewed held the view that CompTech is a good employer, particularly given their less favorable employment options in our current era, in which downsizing and restructuring have created enormous instability, distrust, inequality, and, some would say, degradation for U.S. workers. Indeed, virtually all the temporary workers I interviewed desired permanent employment with CompTech, a desire that was an active ingredient in their compliance with the temporary work regime (I analyze the experiences of temporary workers themselves in Smith, 1998).

In recent years, the company has employed a significant number of temporary workers, following larger trends in American industry. The decision to significantly increase the ratio of temporary to permanent workers was made in the early 1990s by top-level management in corporate headquarters. They made the decision at a point in company history where they needed new "tools" to survive in a increasingly fluctuating economy. Short of laying off permanent workers, top managers first imposed a hiring freeze; when business prospects improved, additional labor was brought in by hiring temporary workers. The personnel director, company staffing personnel, and department managers and supervisors routinely recited to me that top management had decided to implement a temporary employment system for two reasons. In their understanding, the use of temps was both a flexibility strategy—the company gained new capacities for immediately accommodating increases in demand cycles—and a cost-saving strategy—the company could avoid having unnecessary workers on the payroll during periods of slack demand. They also insisted that these strategies were adopted in order to protect core workers. At the time I did my fieldwork, approximately 25% of the company's several-thousand-member workforce were employed on a temporary basis.

The decisions of department managers (those who managed distinct business units or divisions within the company) to hire temporary or permanent labor thus were constrained by corporate-level managers. And while department managers faced a limit on the number of people they could hire into permanent positions and had to go through arduous, bureaucratic, often futile processes to acquire approval for a permanent position, they were able to hire temps with relative ease.[3] Corporate approval of contract rather than fixed labor had led to many instances in which the workers were temporary but the jobs were not; in other words, managers filled temporally open-ended positions with temporary labor. The majority of temporary entry-level white- and blue-collar workers were paid slightly above minimum wage, received no benefits from the firm, and were formally employees of temporary help agencies. (Toward the end of my research there was some evidence that wages for temps were increasing because of tighter labor market conditions in the region.)

By using temps, department managers and supervisors were able to meet their production quotas and to accommodate unexpected work loads. Managers were able to identify why, theoretically, temps were supposed to facilitate these goals—they could hire temps when needed and let them go when the need disappeared or for reasons of poor performance—but, as we shall see, the deeper reality of the temporary employment system is that it is less seamless or static than current discussions about its benefits, among both management practitioners and consultants, would suggest.

Policies for Managing Temporary Employees

Along with the increased use of temporary workers came a new policy framework for managing temporary workers, a framework that disrupted CompTech's historically incentive-based work system. To stay within the boundaries of employment law regarding the use of temporary workers (such as continually emphasizing that temps were not legally employees of CompTech but of temp agencies) and to ease liability concerns (such as eliminating the possibility that a temp would be injured while attending a CompTech social function), the company had elaborated a set of policies that production supervisors and managers were to follow, by which they could draw a clear line between temporary and permanent employees. There was to be no confusion over who the temporaries worked for: Experientially they were employees of CompTech, but formally/legally they were employees of temporary agencies.

Temporary workers wore badges (purple) that were a different color from the badges of the regular workers (orange), highlighting a two-tiered employment system in a context where historically all workers were to be treated equally and respectfully. The company imposed an 18-month cap on the employment of temporaries, although they could be, and often were, hired back ("recalled") after a 3-month break. Temps were officially excluded from specific brainstorming and work-related meetings on the grounds that information was confidential or that they simply didn't need to know what was being discussed. Supervisors and managers were not supposed to lavish the same kinds of rewards for achievement on the temps (such as having on-site dessert parties or giving gifts) nor were the temps invited to dinners and other parties which were held for regular workers. Formally, supervisors and managers were to refrain from developing, counseling, and evaluating the temporary worker. This task rested in the hands of the representatives of the agency that employed the temporary worker. And, of course, supervisors and managers ultimately could simply call the agency and tell them to inform the temporary worker that she or he was to be reassigned.

In other words, managers were supposed to manage using a set of policies found to be difficult to reconcile with incentive-based treatment of employees. The very principles of trust and inclusion, which had formed a basis for commitment to CompTech, and are typical of many "high-trust" workplaces (Appelbaum & Batt, 1994) were identified by top management as inappropriate principles to apply to temporary workers, potentially costly, and disruptive to the shop and office floor.

MERGING TEMPORARY WORKERS WITH A PARTICIPATIVE WORK SYSTEM: ORANIZATIONAL OUTCOMES OF THE CORPORATE MANDATE TO USE TEMPS

Marginalization?

As suggested earlier, the literature on temporary work has often assumed a polarized division of labor, in which temps are typically found marginalized into the least skilled, least responsible, dirtiest, and generally most undesirable positions. In CompTech, a temporary employment system had become institutionalized, and top management of the company had mandated a limit on the size of CompTech's permanent workforce but augmented budgets for a contracted labor force. Where department managers thus had been given no choice but to hire temporary workers to meet their production and organizational goals, and where temporary workers labored in positions that were ongoing, managers' and supervisors' ability to keep distinct boundaries between permanent and temporary workers, to keep the two groups segregated, was limited.

I found temporary workers employed in a range of jobs, differing by skill, responsibility, autonomy, and degree of integration into the ranks of permanent workers. Temporary workers were employed, in one setting, at skilled "parallel" production processes, in which each worker assembled-to-order large, expensive, and complex units that differed from piece to piece. They were responsible for putting together each unit from beginning to end. These individuals often had extensive experience, worked independently, and in some cases had trained other temporary as well as permanent workers. Their team was a work group composed of other assembly workers, about half temporary and half permanent, producing units in parallel. This autonomous, self-paced work unit was exemplary of functional flexibility, with temporaries and permanents working side by side in comparably skilled and self-paced work and without company managers hovering over them.

In distinct contrast, other temporary workers worked on a "deskilled" model, a fast-moving serial production process in which small PCs were pushed down a traditional assembly line, ready to have cables, boards, modems and memory inserted into a chassis by the next individual, under pressured, repetitive, chaotic, and loud work conditions. Yet even in this deskilled work environment, the configuration of authority and autonomy was unanticipated. The deskilled group I observed was coordinated by a team leader, also a temporary. The entire team (14 members) was composed of temporary workers. Temporary workers were trained to work at every work station, thus allowing for interchangeability and variety in work routines.

Another line I observed was midway between the skilled team and the deskilled team. Nine of its 10 members were temps who again were led by a temporary worker. This team worked on an assembly line (serial rather than parallel production) that had very few stations, where they worked interchangeably at a moderate pace, and where the units they were producing were customized, although not significantly complex. Even in these predominantly temporary work groups, workers had substantial levels of interaction with permanent workers in surrounding production areas and ancillary positions. Yet a fourth production area also fell on the mid-point of the spectrum; this group employed about 50% temps and 50% permanents.

Thus, the day-to-day experiences of many temporary workers were indistinguishable from those of permanent workers. Temporaries had accumulated much organization-specific knowledge in the course of their employment. All temps I interviewed had been cross-trained for different positions. Although many positions required simple skill levels, temporaries had had the opportunity to develop a cross-organizational perspective, gaining knowledge of many different functions in their production area. I found temporary workers in a variety of work situations, often working side by side with permanent workers, occasionally located at the top of group hierarchies monitoring and supervising their temporary coworkers (I found no instances of temps managing permanents), demonstrating varied skill levels, and, in some cases, working in semiautonomous groups composed exclusively of other temps. These examples illustrate the complexity of power relations among temps and their diverse organizational statuses but also their high degree of integration into, not marginalization from, the company's permanent workers.

Convenience?

The discovery of the integration of temporary workers into everyday organizational and labor processes provides a backdrop for interpreting supervisors' and managers' views of the convenience or the awkwardness of using temporary workers. Expectations for convenience assume that when managers manage temporary workers, it is a seamless effort, a straightforward and cost-effective substitute for permanent workers. Supervisors and managers mechanistically exploit temps' labor while they're on the job and can, in an instant, let them go when their labor is no longer needed, when their work performance is shoddy, or when their attitude is poor or antagonistic. In this simplified depiction, neither the social organization of the workplace nor managers' work practices substantively change or become more complicated with the introduction of temps. In this section, I show the organizational implications, from managers' and supervisors' point of view, of being forced to officially treat temporary workers as low-status organizational members in an otherwise inclusive workplace. In contrast to the assumption of convenience, supervisors and managers viewed this new arrangement as anything but convenient, finding instead that it expanded and complicated their jobs.

Supervisors' and managers' organizational interests were divided. On one hand, they were required to carry out corporate-level management's mandate to hire some portion of the workforce on a temporary basis and manage temps differently from their permanents. On the other hand, they were constrained by their local circumstances: Their need to achieve production goals led them to alternative efforts to maintain the consent of temporaries and to defuse the more demoralizing effects of the temporary employment system. In this context, managers developed attachments to valued temporary workers but had to act on those attachments within an employment framework based on detachment. In this section, I lay out supervisors' and managers' understandings of the difficulties of merging teamwork with tempwork, and their frustrations about bringing together a long-enduring framework emphasizing inclusiveness with a new framework emphasizing exclusion and unequal distinction.

MANAGERS' NARRATIVE OF TEMPWORK VS. TEAMWORK

The manager's dilemma can be summarized in the following way. Managers in companies that historically have encouraged and sustained progressive, or incentive-based, management practices have had significant positive resources at their disposal to solicit participation and consent to work goals. In hegemonic (Burawoy, 1985), bureaucratically controlled (Edwards, 1979), paternalistic (Smith, 1990) or participative (Hodson, 1996) work settings, managers use salaries, raises, bonuses, and opportunities for training and upward mobility to gain employee consent to work hard and productively. CompTech's incentive system likewise had historically hooked the firm's permanent workers with monetary rewards, social rewards, and the reward of security: the explicit promise that workers would be afforded career development, mobility, and tenure within the company if they worked hard, worked smart, and demonstrated that they were CompTech "material." If workers gave their best to CompTech, CompTech would take care of them. Thus, granting more or less permanent attachment to the firm was the linchpin holding together the incentive-based management system.

The introduction of the new regime of temporary employment in theory reversed these principles. As I described earlier, managers were given a new set of exclusionary rules applying to temporaries only, rules that potentially undermined the premises of participation, community and cohesion that managers manipulated as a powerful ingredient in reaching their own production objectives. Lacking the ability to offer social functions, meaningful gifts, access to brainstorming meetings, and, above all, permanent jobs, managers' authority and their ability to control shopfloor activities were potentially eroded.

Because temporaries were integrated into and throughout a regular workforce (which managers had been forced to do in order to reach their own work goals), they had numerous opportunities to learn about the culture of the firm. Applying coercive management to them would have stood in stark contrast to incentive-based management applied to permanent workers: Highlighting such inequality in a culture that was allegedly grounded in equality could have led to ongoing contestation of management's goals.

The following accounts indicate shopfloor managers' awareness of this constraint and their concern about reconciling the contrasting logics of work organization. An interview I conducted with a production supervisor early in the research first alerted me to the teamwork versus tempwork problem and I quote him extensively because his point of view was clear and well elaborated. Moreover, as I will show shortly, his perspective is forcefully echoed in the comments of other supervisors. When I asked him about the advantages and disadvantages of using temporary workers, he responded,

> Um, see, my thinking on this is, it's true they're [temps] coming from the outside; but the only differences between the CompTech employees and themselves is they are employed through a different organization. The meaning of *why* they come to work is the same. They need the job, they need the cash flow. And they want some options. My commitment to them is, to build them into a team. . . . If a contract employee feels this product . . . needs some involvement, then they have the same input and I will support that. . . . That's the way I am. Um, I also provide development opportunities equally for those individuals, as part of the team if they are not evolving technically, or if they don't understand how to run UNIX, or they need some in-depth things, uh, such as, more unstructured type of environments to be exposed to. I expose them to that. The net [*sic*] is, they grow, the team grows, and our overall success, uh, is better postured.[4] The things I do not

like about contracts are, one is we are not recognizing them . . . , to a large degree, in the same framework as we do for CompTech employees, *for what they [temps] do for the programs and the teams and the project and of course, for the dollars.*

This particular supervisor, who was responsible for 43 workers, put his finger precisely on the potentially counterproductive outcome of combining a work system based on participation and commitment with an employment system based on transience. He was critical of policies handed down from top management excluding temporary workers from events such as training and brainstorming sessions that are the formal hallmark of an involved work system, saying that

they're [high-level management] forgetting that the people are the glue that makes this thing work. And if for some reason everyone decided to turn their switch off, nothing's going out this door. . . . What I think is, we tend to invest in the wrong areas. We think, we gotta make the process better, we gotta do this better.

He went on to distinguish between the infrastructure of people in his division, which refers to all the people working day to day, and the "gang," those who are integrated into CompTech's participative and inclusive work culture. He said, "Well, if you don't have your immediate infrastructure of people in the gang with you, understanding the plans and the directions and the whys, I don't care what you do to the process, I don't care what you do with the infrastructure." He elaborated,

The minute you start talking like that [about temps vs. teams] and start setting boundaries up, you start dividing a team. You also start dividing, you also start seeing that these people are on this level of plateau, like "Yeah, you guys are here and you show up and you make things happen. But, by the way, you're these contract-type employees." And the minute you put a label on something like that, you are already dividing the team. You've already said "You're a different class of folk." And so I totally disagree with it. . . . It's a team environment, not one individual running the show here.

Another interviewee, a department manager responsible for 350 people, including 12 supervisors and a workforce that was about 60% temporary workers, identified the disjuncture between tempwork as corporate-level management envisioned it and tempwork as he experienced it in CompTech's traditional work system. Expressing frustration about top management's prohibition on hiring permanent workers, he said,

[Top management] doesn't deal with it. They don't deal with frustrating (*sic*), they don't deal with the morale issues. They don't deal with the frustration of supervisors who can't reward or recognize people that are contributing to the success of the company the same way they can for a different class of citizens. High-level managers just don't, they don't get to deal with that kind of day-to-day, week-to-week, month-to-month frustration.

He claimed that the widespread use of temps was creating a "morale problem, morale inhibitor or morale drag."

It is difficult to promulgate a shared culture of teamwork, democratic participation and involvement if some individuals perceive that the payoff for involvement is significant for only a fraction of the team. A woman who managed a production line of 18 workers, about 50% of whom were temps and the other 50% permanents, claimed that the formal mandate to actively distinguish between the two groups was not feasible since it directly conflicted with CompTech's philosophy:

You know, if you go to any meetings around here it's team—you're on a team, part of team, team, team, team team, it's just boom, boom in your head. And then you get out here, and you have ta (*sic*) manage this mix of people, and you need to be able to treat 'em all equally so they feel that way.

She went on to succinctly voice the dilemma:

> It's hard, because you know, you try to, you try to discipline when necessary out there and motivate, and it's two different trees we have to go up when we do this stuff, you know. And, it's hard as managers because I wanna do it all the same way. You know, the philosophy has been, ah, "Well, if they're contracted, Norma, don't spend so much time in developing them. If the behavior's not there and they're not up to performance, get rid of 'em. Call the agency, get somebody else." Let me tell you something, when you're down there on the front line, you can't do that, because, again, you're not just about specific performance. You've got a team dynamic that you're creating, that you're tryin' to develop, you're tryin' to encourage.

Another woman who managed a production line lamented that

> CompTech has gotten more strict on the kind of activities that contract workers can participate in. So when we have an off-site [author's note: a function for employees], if there's information that is important for the temp to do their job, they can participate. But if it's a reward—like this Friday I'm taking everybody out for lunch—well, I can't do that for my temps. I used to do that. I used to just do it and not tell anybody and just do it because I thought it was important, because it's a team. And we worked really hard to make sure that the temps feel like they're part of the team, but they're not always part of the team. And then you get resentments that build up, both on the *permanents'* side. . . . I mean we've had some of my regular employees get *very* upset about the fact that the temps can't participate in certain things, more so than from the temps.

She went on to note that the permanent workers' dismay was spurred by their knowledge that many of the temporary jobs were in fact "permanent in nature."

These narratives reveal how, in supervisors' and managers' minds, the foundations of temporary employment—in theory built on transience, detachment, and disposability—threatened the building blocks of CompTech's participative work culture: its stated commitment to employee involvement, teamwork, and self-governance and an ideology about egalitarian work relations that has been very productive for managers. Managing temporary workers in a context where temps enable managers to fulfill production goals has added a new layer of work tasks to managers' jobs. In coordinating assembly lines and offices where temps and permanent workers work side by side, supervisors and managers have had to develop new sensitivities to the differing conditions and constraints surrounding each workforce. They have to daily put out fires, that resulted from using temps, that were never envisioned or at least never acknowledged by executive-level top management. In other words, an entirely new social relations system has emerged. But these are spoken accounts, not descriptions of managers' actions. How do managers act on their interpretation of the teamwork versus tempwork dualism?

Ruling With an Iron Hand?

I noted earlier in the chapter that an expectation has emerged, following from many studies of temporary work, that managers will rule with an iron hand and will discourage temporary workers' goodwill toward the company that might eventuate in raised expectations for permanent employment. Contrasting with the picture of such coercive management, in CompTech I found three sets of comparatively paternalistic strategies that managers and supervisors used to merge and contain the different organizational logics of teamwork and tempwork. The strategies were consistent with the dominant control framework used for the firm's permanent workers, but managers crafted them in ways that were consistent with the firm's official line—which could indeed be labeled coercive—on exclusion for temporary workers. Specifically, managers and supervisors created a positive shopfloor culture for temporaries; they found ways to keep a pool of available temporary workers; and they manipulated the temporary help agencies, new agents in the equation of shopfloor control. This paternalistic treatment, while productive, entailed additional inconveniences and costs for managers and supervisors.

PARALLEL PATERNALISM

First, supervisors and managers built a positive work and cultural environment for their temporary employees. While they were careful not to mislead temps about their prospects for permanent employment, in the everyday workings of shopfloor life they muted the divisions between the two groups of workers. The possible costs of not doing so—resentment, alienation, and even illegal behavior—simply threatened to undermine their own production goals. If I had heard this from managers only I would have suspected that I was merely hearing the CompTech party line on management philosophy, a narrative about their *theory* of management that wouldn't match the lived experience of the workers under them. But the majority of temporary workers I interviewed corroborated managers' accounts of their refusal to bifurcate their workforce through differential treatment.

Managers used various measures, consistent with the traditional, incentive-based regime of governance, to preempt feelings of hostility or antagonism on the part of temps. For example, temps from different settings (including white-collar) recited many instances in which their managers, quietly and casually, had included them in on-the-job minor social functions, given them occasional paid days off, given them modest cash awards, counseled them, developed them, sent them for training classes, and helped them polish resumés and prepare for interviews for permanent employment. In one case, a manager coordinated the work efforts of temporaries and permanents so as to minimize distinction and inequality. This factory supervisor felt that if demand for the product accelerated enough to require adding extra shifts or asking people to work overtime, asking temporaries only to put in overtime hours would undermine an ethos of teamwork by highlighting the essentially exploitive nature of temp employment: "There's only a few areas where we can *try to bring equality to the work team.* Overtime is one of them." He elaborated,

> We try not to have the regular employees work only 40 hours and this contract labor base just workin' all the extra hours and so forth. They're, we try to keep 'em equal, because they work so closely together. . . . If you expect your team to work overtime, there's no difference in whether you're a regular full-time employee or a contract laborer. The team is expected to work overtime, everyone's gonna participate in that type of situation. So that helps so you don't have the "us versus them" type scenarios out there.

Other managers cited instances in which they had maneuvered to bring greater equity into the wage process, a point I describe in a moment.

MAINTAINING A NETWORK OF "ON CALL" QUALIFIED TEMPORARY WORKERS

Managers stayed in contact with workers to whom they had become attached because they did their job well. Managers' desire to find ways around the formal dictates of the temporary employment regime was deepened by what they viewed as the multilayered and excessive costs of having to let temporary workers go when temps reached the limits of their contract. Some of their temporary workers had been on the job longer than permanent workers, had been cross-trained in a number of functional areas, and had accumulated valuable levels of expertise, skill, and experience. Adding to the evidence about inconvenience and complexity, managers reported significant frustration with the disruption to production processes and production goals. They had to train new individuals over and over for ongoing positions that had been staffed by often highly competent temporary labor; they had to find replacements for outstanding temporaries who were lured away by better, permanent job offers from other companies; and they had to let go of temporary workers and use permanent workers who were not as skilled or as qualified.

Managers cited various strategies for getting around this disruptive potential and for maintaining an "on call" qualified temporary workforce. These included rehiring an individual for a temporary position multiple times after the person took the mandatory 3 months off, finding loopholes in the policy on an 18-month cap so as to avoid letting valued temps go, reassigning temps to other tasks in their unit rather than letting them go when the workload ebbed,[5] and, in one fascinating instance, having two temporary workers on different contract schedules share a job so that at any given time across the year there was always at least one knowledgeable and qualified individual on the job. I also encountered two cases in which managers had exploited top-level managers' concern about security and quality to justify their plea to hire workers, in sensitive areas or jobs, permanently rather than temporarily.

MANIPULATING AGENCIES

Sociologists who study work and the labor process have noted the variety of ways in which the management process has been made more complex by the addition of other individuals and groups (including consultants, engineers, human resources personnel, and customers) into the monitoring, disciplinary, and control process (Kunda, 1992; Noble, 1977). As has been typical with the increased use of temporary workers (Gottfried, 1991; Rogers & Barrett, 1998), the new regime of temporary employment in CompTech has brought an additional actor into the shopfloor: the temporary help agency. Although typically the agency had little to do with the day-to-day work lives of its temps, the agency representatives did occasionally get entangled enough that managers reported spending significant amounts of time negotiating and planning with them.

Under some circumstances, agencies fractured and complicated the authority of managers. The disruption and frustration that can result from the involvement of temp agencies emerge in the following story. An individual who supervised warehouse workers recounted how he had had to "do battle with an agency." The agency responsible for placing the bulk of the temporary warehouse workers had, unbeknown to him, created a two-tier wage policy. They started offering higher wages to new temps in order to attract a higher quality workforce, a startling reversal of the more typical punitive two-tier wage strategies where employers bring in new workers at *lower* rates than their senior workers. This set off a tempest among his more experienced temporary workers, who protested what they viewed as unacceptable inequality within their own ranks. The agency, for all intents and purposes, was pitting temps against one another, and this manager recalled how a "politics of equality" (my term) exploded:

> Soon as that was found out on the floor, which was within a very short period of time, everybody was coming knocking, saying "I've been here 6 months, I've been here 9 months, I've been here a year, and I'm making less money than this person who just started yesterday." Those kinds of things sweep through the warehouse very quickly—then I have to go back and talk to the agency again.

Managers tried to counteract the effects of the agencies and to manipulate the agencies to facilitate parallel paternalism. First, as noted earlier, for legal reasons CompTech's official policy insisted that managers clearly draw the lines between its regular workforce and temporary workers; thus the managers were expressly forbidden from including temps in a number of social functions and amenities that represented a resource available to managers for gaining consent and for creating cohesion and goodwill among CompTech workers. In interviews, however, managers repeatedly told me of otherwise having established inclusionary rituals for the temporary workers by mobilizing the agency itself. By pressing agencies to offer social events or recreational outings to temporaries—events that managers felt were important to minimize temporaries' feelings of exclusion and maximizing morale—managers further shaped a positive temporary culture, leaving the official policy of unattachment intact.

Typically, a manager would approach the representatives of the agency and tell them that he or she wanted the agency to organize an event. The events that were held were much like the events for permanent workers—smaller in scale but generally held off-site, with food, awards to outstanding temporaries, and occasionally the distribution of small gifts, such as modest certificates for restaurants or retail establishments or movie tickets. In this way, managers reinforced the paternalistic culture for temporary workers that mirrored the culture of the permanent workers. At the same time, managers remained within the legal mandate, honoring the formal contract specifying that the temp was an employee of the agency not CompTech.[6] Nearly all the temporary workers I interviewed had attended one or more of these segregated events. Even though such events did little to dispel the fact that temporaries were on the margins with respect to their employment status, they reinforced temps' view that CompTech was a good employer and promoted a work culture of which they wished to become permanent members.

Second, managers similarly reported mobilizing the agencies to bring greater equity into temporary employees' wages. Agencies set the wages for their employees, removing control over one important inducement for effort and hard work traditionally held by managers. To offset the agencies' power, supervisors and middle managers reported that periodically they spoke with agency representatives about readjusting wages for temporary workers, even though this was discouraged in official corporate policy.[7] Occasions arose in which managers felt that to secure their own production objectives it was necessary to motivate or reward particular individuals and thus to shape the determination of wages. One supervisor explained her need for such intervention. She had recently hired onto her line temporary workers who were employed by one of the agencies. She claimed that these new hires earned substantially lower wages than other temporaries on her line who were employed by another agency:

> [Agency A] was payin' their people a *whole* lot less than [Agency B] does. And I have given those folks gradual raises over time to get them up to the same level. So I'm managing all those people, too, at their technical skills, their time on the job, as to where their pay is in relationship to other people on the team. So I'm kinda doin' my own, like, mental ranking of people for wage administration to make it fair and equitable out there.

In her words, "people need to be paid equitably for what they're adding to the team." To do otherwise would introduce tensions and politics around fairness and equity within the ranks of her temps.

Significantly, managers were forced to work with a new partner, and more of their time was spent devoted to managing, via this additional institutional actor, the unique dynamics of temporary workers. Thus, as noted by Pfeffer and Baron (1988), Gottfried (1991), Smith (1994), and Uzzi and Barsness (1998), the increased externalization of employment, sometimes used to justify the use of temporary employees because it is hypothesized to reduce the time and costs entailed in administration, in fact has added organizational and temporal complexity to management's work. As one manager put it, the unquantifiable, unofficial time spent on administering and coordinating temporary workers, was a "sink hole," bottomless and indefinable. Having to continually negotiate with the agencies, while allowing managers to create a culture for temporary workers that was not at odds with CompTech's broader culture, deepened the inconvenience and disruptions in managers' work.

DISCUSSION

I have investigated three claims or hypotheses in the burgeoning literature on contingent work by taking an in-depth and up-close look at the social organization of a temporary employment system within one firm. I first considered the claim for marginalization, which suggests that temporary workers will be segregated into the lowest organizational levels and into separate sites of work away from core permanent workers. Contrary to expectations of marginalization, I found an unexpected degree of integration of temporary workers into the ranks of permanent workers and into the organization itself. Supervisors and managers, in responding to new policies on the part of top management to cut the company's fixed labor costs, had no choice but to use temporary workers in work positions that were not temporary.

Second, I considered the claim that employing temporary workers is convenient, that managers will view using temporary workers as a straightforward business or organizational transaction—bring them in when needed, let them go when not needed. Analyzing interview and observational data, I found instead that supervisors and managers objected to the destabilizing possibilities of the temporary employment system and that they wove these objections into the way they handled and coordinated their temporary workers and in the way they merged their temps with their permanent workers.

Finally, I explored the claim that low-level managers will rule temporaries with an iron hand and found instead that supervisors and shop managers went to extensive lengths to build a parallel positive culture for temps, to maintain an on-call, available pool of qualified temporary workers, and to manipulate temporary help service agencies to mute the overt exploitation of temporary workers.

This case study material presents compelling evidence for rethinking current typologies about managers' strategies of coordination and control at work. As I noted earlier, labor process and work studies have categorized managers' actions into one-dimensional boxes. Managers of long-term, even permanent workforces, it is argued, use a set of strategies that differs from the strategies used by managers of impermanent workforces. This one-dimensional categorization holds for the way managers are hypothesized to treat work groups of different skills and different organizational positions as well. Managers who direct professionals and other managers have used bureaucratic procedures, relying on the organization of internal labor markets and the guarantee of mobility and autonomy to maintain commitment and effort. Managers who oversee manufacturing or assembly workers have used technology and/or direct supervision to guarantee pacing and quantity of output. Managers in charge of frontline service workers or manual laborers have overbearingly watched their workers, observing their job performance and warning them or otherwise punishing them on the spot when they violate organizational rules. In other words, the current sociological paradigm for explaining management control strategies typically asserts a "one workforce/one labor process/one control strategy" correspondence.

The study of CompTech, and additional evidence about ongoing workplace change, which I discuss in a moment, suggests the need to deepen this typology and to contextualize it in dynamic historical circumstances. CompTech managers, as a result of top management's quest to make labor more variable and impermanent in the face of unpredictable market fluctuations, had received a new mandate to manage two very different workforces and, moreover, two different employment systems. This created a complicated space and contradictory organizational logic within which managers managed. On one hand, they were instructed to continually bifurcate workers into two groups, with respect to formal treatment, evaluation, inclusion, and so forth. On the other hand, managers believed, and acted on this belief, that they should not overtly bifurcate the workforce in their day-to-day work relations and experiences and that they would pay severe costs if they did so. Ironically, managers did bifurcate their strategies but in a fashion unanticipated and unauthorized by top-level management. They were required, in complex and numerous ways, to continually work on both labor forces but differentially and subtly in such a way as to merge their efforts and solicit the loyalty of both. On the stage, managers were to present a unified strategy, but behind the scenes, managers spent significant time pondering and planning how to manage two workforces with differential status. Managers in this case, then, were maintaining dual and parallel control systems: one developed in a historical context of growth, stability, and prosperity and one imposed in an era of constraint, unpredictability of markets, and a global culture of postbureaucratic organizational structure.

When analyzing the role of managers in transforming the workplace, it is crucial to identify different levels of management and to identify the intraorganizational conflicts in perceptions of what is best for the company, of what best maximizes the corporate interest (Smith, 1990). In the case of CompTech, it was top- or executive-level managers, far removed from everyday work practices and from knowledge of organizational dynamics, who decided to increase the size of their temporary or contract workforce to maximize the firm's ability to fine-tune staff, cut costs, and achieve production goals. When such policies were implemented, however, *lower levels* of management—supervisors directly overseeing production and office workers, and middle managers responsible for the outcomes of particular units, departments, or divisions—had little choice but to contend with the contradictory logics characterizing, on one hand, the upgraded work environments enjoyed by permanent workers, and, on the other hand, the downgraded expectations for weak commitment of temporary workers. The corporate-level mandate to increase the utilization of temporary workers forced supervisors and managers to craft new strategies for control and coordination. The analysis presented here suggests that managers devised multilayered strategies to reconcile the attached/involved model of work for permanent workers with the presumably unattached/uninvolved model of work for temporary workers.

Not inconsequentially, the dualistic control system served to blunt some of the blatant inequities in the temporary hiring relationship. Integrating temporary workers into participative work processes, creating an alternative positive culture, and stressing that many temps were of great value to their managers were ongoing sources of attachment for temps: of commitment to their jobs in the face of no real security and of desire to become full-fledged members of this company's workforce (see Smith, 1998, for an analysis of the "fractured world" of temporary workers). In making this claim I do not mean to suggest that managers always succeeded in these efforts. I do mean to highlight, however, what the overlapping systems of work and employment looked like from managers' perspective, organizationally situated as they were. I also intend to highlight the concrete and varied ways that managers established the temporary employment system in the context of their organizationally constructed interests.

CONCLUSION

What do these findings have to tell us about broad changes for managers and workers in American society? The CompTech data allow us to make some larger generalizations about workplace transformation. First, it is clear that the way in which temporary employment plays out significantly depends on the managers who execute these new systems of work. In CompTech, supervisors and managers softened the overtly exploitive aspects of temporary work. Whereas top management envisioned the utilization of temps in mechanistic terms—use them when necessary, stave off their expectations for permanent work, suppress commitment, let them go—they had not counted on the supervisors' and middle managers' need for quality participation and worker consent. Supervisors and their managers in effect redesigned the temporary employment system, making it plausibly consistent with the larger corporate culture, and even developed some temps for future permanent employment.

Shortly before I left the field, there were indications that top management was recognizing the dilemmas and costs built into the system. A highly respected corporate-level planner had circulated a paper calling for a moratorium on hiring temporary workers and outlining many of the same weaknesses and costs of using temps that I have outlined here. Although no immediate changes in policy had followed from this report, the existence of the document suggests that lower-level managers may have partially succeeded in putting the brakes on temporary employment and perhaps limited its spread to an even greater proportion of the workforce. A number of managers I interviewed claimed that they had complained about the new system of contract labor to *their* managers. We could anticipate that managers in other work settings and other companies, faced with similar legitimacy and credibility problems, would exert a similar braking influence (although this clearly would vary depending on the firm's culture and employment relations framework). But will this alone stop the growth of temporary and other forms of contingent employment in the United States?

The answer to this is indeterminate. When companies do segregate their temporary workers from their permanent workforce or when the permanents are treated to coercive management that is automatically extended to temporary workers, conditions are ripe, although not perfect, for this secondary employment arrangement to thrive. But in a significant number of American workplaces, the shopfloor dynamics are rarely so single-tiered or one-dimensional, and as employers become cognizant of the extensive administrative, financial, and morale costs of using temporary workers, they may seek other ways to resolve the problem of labor flexibility.

A company dedicated to maintaining progressive work conditions for its employees could, for example, establish an in-house temporary pool filled with truly flexible but permanent workers. Such workers could be trained to circulate continually throughout the firm to fill in where needed on either a short-term or a long-term basis. This model already exists in some large retail and service establishments where permanently employed "floaters" constitute the company's flexible labor force. And, of course, if labor organizing efforts directed at unionizing temporary workers succeed (Carre, duRivage, & Tilly, 1995), temporary workers may no longer look like an easily manipulable and exploitable labor source to company executives.

Some will argue that CompTech is extremely atypical in the quality of and the degree to which it has developed its temporary employment system. This we will only know from continued research. As I noted in the beginning of the chapter, there is emergent evidence that suggests that CompTech is not alone in these practices, and one purpose of this chapter is to open up a line of pursuit directed at filling in the gap in our knowledge about this. But beyond this case study, it is increasingly clear that the complex dynamics resulting from mixing new production arrangements and new staffing arrangements have become widespread as diverse production settings, occupations, and industries move toward flexibility. Cappelli et al. (1997), Gordon (1996), Kalleberg et al. (1996), Osterman (1996), and numerous other sociologists and labor relations researchers point out that the "high performance" functionally flexible approach and the "low cost" numerically flexible approach to achieving economic competitiveness are widely accepted by corporate managements; as global trends they are growing at one and the same time and are continuing to place wedges between different groups of American workers. We might predict that these two global trends will, as they have in CompTech, merge more and more in the microlevel organization of different workplaces and that, subsequently, managers at the lower levels of corporations will be pressured to implement dualistic control strategies across the board.

Also in this vein, DiTomaso (1996) problematizes permanent employment, suggesting that commitment and effort increasingly are expected from workers but will not necessarily be rewarded with permanent attachment. As she has found, even high-level permanent employees are having to develop a mind-set that they too are subcontracted; that they must do everything they can for the company but that they should be prepared always for change, to do the best they can until they have done all they can and then move on. With the growing emphasis on career resiliency (Waterman, Waterman, & Collard, 1994) and employability rather than employment security (Kanter, 1995), managers across the board face the uneasy task of maintaining worker commitment in the face of lack of commitment from employing organizations.

What remains to be investigated is the extent to which such contradictory dynamics are emerging in other workplaces, with special emphasis on cataloguing the types of work sites and industries where the coupling of the two trends occurs, enumerating the categories of workers who will be affected by the coupling process, explaining situations where coupling is not likely to be found, and explaining outcomes as the trends are combined at work.

Finally, the findings presented here may be significant for thinking about other aspects of corporate restructuring. One of the outcomes of downsizing and restructuring is that managerial positions have been cut and the span of control for remaining managers subsequently increases. Thus, the "survivors" of cutbacks must manage greater numbers of workers, and presumably workgroups that are, to a greater degree, differentiated by function. Additionally, such cutbacks are often undertaken in companies that stress quality and commitment from its employees, another antithetical merging of trends (Cameron, 1995). These twists and turns in organizational structure and policy imply that the administrative complexities and costs that Pfeffer and Baron (1988) predicted would accompany the growing externalization of workers will also grow with internally employed workers whose jobs, mobility paths, and cultures are differentially changing in the context of flexibility. In this context, supervisors and managers may have to develop dualistic control strategies just to do "business as usual," which increasingly will be defined as business that is unusual and unpredictable (Smith, 2001). However, the data presented here imply that corporate America faces substantial obstacles to seamlessly merging the commitment-maximizing practices associated with a privileged permanent workforce, with the cost-reduction practices used to manage disadvantaged insecure workers. The hidden costs are high, and key actors such as managers, in many ways the linchpin of the system, will continue to deploy workers at all levels in ways that are consistent with their own situated organizational interests rather than with the several-times-removed interests and profit-maximizing agenda of top-level corporate managers. I hope that this inductive study has shed new light on such issues and has succeeded in identifying important organizational dynamics that shape the way that temporary employment works for a growing number of Americans.

NOTES

1. This chapter focuses on entry-level temporary workers, the strategic pillar of the contingent workforce. On part-time employment, see Tilly (1996); on high-level contract workers, see Meiksins and Whalley (1995) and Reskin (1996). For studies addressing the importance of the growth of the temporary labor force, as well as measurements of the contingent workforce as a whole, see Barker and Christensen (1998), Belous (1989), Callaghan and Hartmann (1991), Cohen and Haberfeld (1993), Davis-Blake and Broschak (1997), Henson (1996), *Monthly Labor Review* (1996), Nardone, Veum, and Yates (1997), Parker (1994), and Rogers and Barrett (1998).

2. These tenure figures are also indicative of how deeply institutionalized the temporary employment system is. Current Population Survey figures collected on the contingent workforce for the Bureau of Labor Statistics in 1995 suggest shorter tenure rates for most temporary workers. The CPS found that only 24% of those surveyed had worked more than 1 year as a temp; 42% had been at their current assignment for 3 months or less; 17% had been at their current assignment for 9 months or less; but 16% had been at their current work assignment for 1 year or more (Cohany, 1996). Rogers and Witkowski (1997) found that 16.5 months was the mean time that individuals worked in temporary employment.

3. On this finding, an interesting yet sobering observation: The procedures for hiring temps were consistent with a flatter "postbureaucratic" organizational structure because managers had only to get one signature from the manager directly above them to hire temps; they were thus able to expedite the hiring process. Procedures for hiring permanent workers, however, were comparatively anachronistic, a relic of a hierarchical, time-absorbing

large bureaucracy, in that managers had to obtain multiple signatures from several layers above. In other words, it is not merely that temporary *labor* is a source of flexibility for the firm; it is the temporary *hiring practice* itself that yields flexibility for managers. I found this discouraging because corporate-level managers can exploit the rhetoric of the virtues of the flexible organization, so powerful in the 1990s, to promote a temporary employment system, arguing that the latter is an essential ingredient for achieving the former, indeed, that such flexible hiring practices are necessary for the very survival of the corporation.

4. The term "posturing" is not clear to me. This was a particularly long and at times tedious interview, and I only picked this term up when reading the transcript.

5. This individual noted that "[corporate-level] rationale behind it [hiring temps] is because of the way our marketplace is, it's so volatile, we're up, we're down, we're up, we're down, and what that does is it allows us to transition people in and out. . . . That's the philosophy behind it. Um, I don't manage that way. What I do is, um, if I have an opportunity, where our work load is light out there, I will find them something to do elsewhere."

6. The finding that temporary agencies adopted practices that reflected the culture of CompTech casts new light on social science researchers' understanding of the temporary help service industry more generally. In contrast to the suggestion that companies purchase a fixed commodity when they contract for the services of temporary workers, temp agency practices can be shaped by—indeed, they customize their services to—the organizational and cultural context in which they operate. More generally, recent findings about the autonomous dynamics of the temporary help service industry are provocative. The points mentioned above and other findings about the ways in which this industry, state by state, shaped labor law to facilitate and protect its own growth strategies (Gonos, 1997), the ways in which the industry has actively worked to create demand for its services and customize them to the needs of the companies they serve (Ofstead, 1999), and the different trajectories of growth cross-nationally (Gottfried, 2000) open an enormous spectrum of possibilities for future research. It is clear that the conventional explanation that the temporary help service industry has grown so astronomically but passively in response to changing supply-and-demand factors (Koster, 1997) is in serious need of revision.

7. The situation described earlier, in which a supervisor had to contend with the fallout from the two-tiered wage policy for temps, exemplifies the dilemma of wage inequity.

REFERENCES

Appelbaum, E., & Batt, R. (1994). *The new American workplace.* Ithaca, NY: ILR Press.

Arthur, J. (1992). The link between business strategy and industrial relations systems in American steel minimills. *Industrial and Labor Relations Review, 45,* 488-506.

Baker, T., & Aldrich, H. (1996). Prometheus stretches: Building identity and cumulative knowledge in multiemployer careers. In M. Arthur & D. Rousseau (Eds.), *Boundaryless careers: Employment in the new organizational era* (pp. 132-149). New York: Oxford University Press.

Barker, K. & Christensen, K. (1998). *Contingent work: American Employment Relations in Transition.* Ithaca: Cornell University/ILR Press.

Belous, R. (1989). *The contingent economy: The growth of the temporary, part-time, and subcontracted workforce.* Washington, DC: National Planning Association.

Burawoy, M. (1985). *The politics of production.* London: Verso.

Callaghan, P., & Hartmann, H. (1991). *Contingent work: A chart book on part-time and temporary employment.* Washington, DC: Institute for Women's Policy Research/Economic Policy Institute.

Cameron, K. (1995). Downsizing, quality and performance. In R. Cole (Ed.), *The death and life of the American quality movement* (pp. 93-114). New York: Oxford University Press.

Cappelli, P., Bassi, L., Katz, H., Knoke, D., Osterman, P., & Useem, M. (1997). *Change at work.* New York: Oxford University Press.

Carre, F., duRivage, V., & Tilly, C. (1995). Piecing together the fragmented workplace: Unions and public policy on flexible employment. In L. Flood (Ed.), *Unions and public policy* (pp. 11-35). Westport, CT: Greenwood.

Cohaney, S. (1996). Workers in alternative employment arrangements. *Monthly Labor Review, 119*(10), 31-45.

Cohen, Y., & Haberfeld, Y. (1993). Temporary help service workers: Employment characteristics and wage determination. *Industrial Relations, 32*(2), 272-287.

Colclough, G., & Tolbert, C. (1992). *Work in the fast lane.* Albany: State University of New York Press.

Davis-Blake, A., & Broschak, J. (1997, August). *The consequences of temporary worker use: How temporary staffing affects attitudes and productivity of permanent and temporary employees.* Paper presented at the annual meeting of the American Sociological Association, Toronto.

DiTomaso, N. (1996, August). *The loose coupling of jobs: The subcontracting of everyone?* Paper presented at the annual meeting of the American Sociological Association, New York.

Doeringer, P., Christensen, K., Flynn, P., Hall, D., Katz, H., et al. (1991). *Turbulence in the American workplace.* New York: Oxford University Press.

Doeringer, P., & Piore, M. (1970). *Internal labor markets and manpower analysis.* Washington, DC: Office of Manpower Research, U.S. Department of Labor.

Edwards, R. (1979). *Contested terrain.* New York: Basic Books.

Geary, J. (1992). Employment flexibility and human resource management. *Work, Employment and Society, 6*(2), 251-270.

Gonos, G. (1997). The contest over "employer" status in the post-war U.S.: The case of temporary help firms. *Law and Society Review, 31*(1), 81-110.

Gordon, D., Edwards, R., & Reich, M. (1982). *Segmented work, divided workers: The historical transformation of labor in the United States.* New York: Cambridge University Press.

Gottfried, H. (1991). Mechanisms of control in the temporary help service industry. *Sociological Forum, 6*(4), 699-713.

Gottfried, H. (2000). Compromising positions: Emergent neo-Fordisms and embedded gender contracts. *British Journal of Sociology, 52*(2), 235-259.

Harrison, B. (1994). *Lean and mean: The changing landscape of corporate power in the age of flexibility.* New York: Basic Books.

Heckscher, C. (1995). *White collar blues.* New York: Basic Books.

Henson, K. (1996). *Just a temp.* Philadelphia: Temple University Press.

Hirsch, P. (1993). Undoing the managerial revolution? Needed research on the decline of middle management and internal labor markets. In R. Swedberg (Ed.), *Explorations in economic sociology* (pp. 145-157). New York: Russell Sage.

Hirsch, P., & Shanley, M. (1996). The rhetoric of "boundaryless": How the newly empowered and fully networked managerial class of professional bought into and self-managed its own marginalization. In M. Arthur & D. Rousseau (Eds.), *Boundaryless careers: Employment in the new organizational era* (pp. 218-233). New York: Oxford University Press.

Hodson, R. (1996). Dignity in the workplace under participative management: Alienation and freedom revisited. *American Sociological Review, 61*(5), 719-738.

Kalleberg, A., Hudson, K., & Reskin, B. (2000). Bad jobs in America: Standard and nonstandard employment relations and job quality in the United States. *American Sociological Review, 65*(2), 256-278.

Kalleberg, A., Knoke, D., Marsden, P., & and Spaeth, J. (1996). *Organizations in America: Analyzing their structures and human resource practices.* Thousand Oaks, CA: Sage.

Kanter, R. (1995). Nice work if you can get it. *The American Prospect, 23,* 52-58.

Koster, M. (1997). New employment relationships and the labor market. *Journal of Labor Research, 18*(4), 551-559.

Kunda, G. (1992). *Engineering culture.* Philadelphia: Temple University Press.

Meiksins, P., & Whalley, P. (1995, August). *Technical workers and reduced work: Limits and possibilities.* Paper presented at the annual meeting of the American Sociological Association, Washington, DC.

Monthly Labor Review. (1996). Special issue on contingent employment and alternative work arrangements. Vol. 119(10).

Nardone, T., Veum, J., & J. Yates, J. (1997). Measuring job security. *Monthly Labor Review, 120*(6), 26-33.

Newman, K. (1988). *Falling from grace.* New York: Vintage.

Noble, D. (1977). *America by design.* Oxford, UK: Oxford University Press.

Ofstead, C. (1999). Temporary help firms as entrepreneurial actors. *Sociological Forum, 14*(2), 273-294.

O'Reilly, J. (1994). *Banking on flexibility.* Aldershot, UK: Avebury.

Osterman, P. (1994). How common is workplace transformation and who adopts it? *Industrial Relations Review, 47*(2), 173-188.

Osterman. P. (Ed.). (1996). *Broken ladders: Managerial careers in the new economy.* New York: Oxford University Press.

Osterman, P. (2000). *Securing Prosperity.* Princeton: Princeton University Press.

Parker, R. (1994). *Flesh peddlers and warm bodies.* New Brunswick, NJ: Rutgers University Press.

Pfeffer, J., & Baron, J. (1988). Taking the workers back out: Recent trends in the structuring of employment. *Research in Organizational Behavior, 10,* 257-303.

Polivka, A. (1996). A profile of contingent workers. *Monthly Labor Review, 119*(10), 10-21.

Reskin, B. (1996, August). *A queuing perspective on nonstandard employee/employer relationship.* Paper presented at the annual meeting of the American Sociological Association, New York.

Rogers, J. (1999). Deskilled and devalued: Changes in the labor process in temporary clerical work. In M. Wardell, P. Meiksins, & T. Steiger (Eds.), *Rethinking the labor process* (pp. 53-78). Albany: State University of New York Press.

Rogers, J., & Barrett, M. (1998). *Barriers and building blocks: Organizing temporary workers in a contingent economy.* Unpublished paper, Department of Labor Studies and Industrial Relations, Pennsylvania State University, University Park.

Rogers, J., & Henson, K. (1997). Hey, why don't you wear a shorter skirt? Structural vulnerability and the organization of sexual harassment in temporary clerical employment. *Gender & Society, 11*(2), 215-237.

Rogers, J., & Witkowski, K. (1997, August). *Determinants and outcomes of voluntary vs. involuntary temporary employment.* Paper presented at the annual meeting of the American Sociological Association, Toronto.

Rubin, B. (1996). *Shifts in the social contract.* Thousand Oaks, CA: Pine Forge Press.

Shaiken, H., Herzenberg, S., & Kuhn, S. (1986). The work process under more flexible production. *Industrial Relations, 25*(2), 167-183.

Smith, V. (1988). Restructuring management and managing restructuring: The role of managers in corporate change. *Research in Politics and Society, 3,* 221-239.

Smith, V. (1990). *Managing in the corporate interest.* Berkeley: University of California Press.

Smith, V. (1994). Institutionalizing flexibility in a service firm: Multiple contingencies and hidden hierarchies. *Work and Occupations, 21*(3), 284-307.

Smith, V. (1997). New forms of work organization. *Annual Review of Sociology, 23,* 315-339.

Smith, V. (1998). The fractured world of the temporary worker: Power, participation, and fragmentation in the postindustrial workplace. *Social Problems, 45*(4), 411-430.

Smith, V. (2001). *Crossing the great divide: Worker risk and opportunity in the new economy.* Ithaca: Cornell/ILR Press.

Thomas, R. (1994). *What machines can't do.* Berkeley: University of California Press.

Thompson, J. (1967). *Organizations in action.* New York: McGraw-Hill.

Tilly, C. (1996). *Half a job: Bad and good part-time jobs in a changing labor market.* Philadelphia: Temple University Press.

Uzzi, B., & Barsness, Z. (1998). Contingent employment in British establishments: Organizational determinants of the use of fixed-term hires and part-time workers. *Social Forces, 76*(3), 967-1005.

Vallas, S. (1999). Re-thinking post-Fordism: The meaning of workplace flexibility. *Sociological Theory, 17*(1), 68-101.

Waterman, R., Waterman, J., & Collard, B. (1994). Toward a career-resilient workforce. *Harvard Business Review, 72*(4), 87-95.

Wood, S. (1989). *The transformation of work?* Boston: Unwin Hyman.

2

Flexible Production, Rigid Jobs

Lessons From the Clothing Industry

IAN M. TAPLIN

Macroeconomic crises and declining rates of corporate profit during the 1970s prompted critical interest in the organizational principles of mass production and their continued effectiveness in a more integrated and interdependent world economy (Best, 1990; Piore & Sabel, 1984; Reich, 1983). Firms that face the most difficulties in the new globalized marketplace are often those with labor intensive, standardized manufacturing processes. These firms, and their production systems, have proved vulnerable to increased competition from low-wage producers in countries that have predicated economic growth strategies on export-led industrialization (Deyo, 1987; Dicken, 1992). Because Fordism, as a labor intensive, low-skilled system of standardized mass production, was easily replicated, it is perhaps not surprising that it should emerge in virtual paradigmatic form in regions of the world where abundant unskilled labor occurs.

The response to this challenge in the high-wage economies of the West, and particularly the United States, has been a mixture of defensive tactics (trade quotas and tariffs immediately come to mind) and, at the firm level, proactive organizational changes designed to take advantage of microelectronic innovations and labor market changes. The latter falls under the general rubric of restructuring, where many firms have attempted to reconfigure work places and production systems (flatter hierarchies and lean production systems are two such examples). The presumption is that such changes will enable a firm to attain the much vaunted "flexibility," seen by many as crucial to maintaining competitive advantage in the next century. Flexible production systems, made possible by these organizational changes and new technologies, permit shortened product development time and allow small batch production that enhances firm responsiveness to more segmented markets. In other words, they permit firms to substitute economies of scope for economies of scale, to lessen their reliance on large numbers of unskilled or semiskilled workers, and to better coordinate production so that supply matches demand variability. As such, what is being suggested is a new way of organizing production and a departure from Fordist principles and all that they entail.

What is the reality of the transformed workplace if such production changes associated with new technology have occurred? Can firms lower costs and find production flexibility without necessarily developing a self-regulated labor force of skilled, highly trained workers? In this study, based on an analysis of technological innovation and organizational change in a segment of the U.S. apparel industry, I examine the contradictory tendencies that exist in many apparent post-Fordist arrangements. By examin-

From *Work and Occupations*, Vol. 22, No. 4, November 1995, pp. 412-438. Reprinted by permission.

ing managerial implementation of changes dictated by heightened competition within the industry, I show how flexible production technologies and labor process organization coexist with "rigid" low-skill, low-paid workers. The "new" workplace, involving heightened pressure on workers and managers alike, raises interesting questions about the routinization of work for all groups within organizations as well as the meaning and character of post-Fordist arrangements.

FORDISM AND BEYOND

The growth of standardized mass production in the United States is generally associated with the emergence of managerial hierarchies (Chandler, 1977) and the search for ways to coordinate and control a diverse workforce (Best, 1990). The logic of Taylorism was derived from general managerial needs to reduce the independence of skilled workers and accelerate the pace of work (Waring, 1991) in the emergent mass production sector. Fordism meanwhile, as Lazonick (1990) argues, was part of new ideologies that "enabled value creation to depend upon greater effort by shop floor workers *and* the planned coordination of effort saving technology by managers" (p. 182, emphasis added).

Under Fordism it was assumed that managers would seek ways to integrate workers into the production process without meaningfully involving them in the design of that process. Because planning the organization of work was removed from the factory floor, and hence from the purview of skilled workers, managerial structures were able to relieve workers of authority and responsibility for the flow of work (Lazonick, 1990, p. 183). The actual system of production was designed to decompose worker skills through an elaborate division of labor within firms. Although it furthered the rationalization of production inherent in the separation of thinking and doing under Taylorism, it also legitimized managerial hierarchies and helped solidify managerial power within firms. Furthermore, it enabled managers to "regulate" production and safeguard their own position within firms as well as meeting the efficiency criteria set by the organization's owners.

Not surprisingly, Fordism acquired normative status in oligopolistic firms where wage-based competitive pressures were subsequently reduced and production stabilized. It benefitted organizations because workers were consigned the status of a variable cost faced equitably by competitors, and managers could be reasonably expected to further the firm's success because their own fortunes were intricately linked with it.

Fordism proved particularly suitable to durable goods manufacture in a mass consumption economy. It required only periodic innovation of products; it had product specific capital equipment; the commodities produced were most likely to be of a low-quality, low-value, high-volume nature; and competition was price based.

The above characteristics admittedly represent an ideal type of Fordism, one that seems rigid and inflexible. The reality of workplace production often produced a combination of rigidity and flexibility with many firms predicating their success, as Wood (1993) argues, by modifying stereotypical Fordism into a more flexible system. With limited training times, workers could be easily hired and fired, therefore providing firms with numerical flexibility (Streeck, 1987). Furthermore, internal labor markets provided firms with core workers who were given stable employment in return for displaying functional flexibility (Procter, Rowlinson, McArdle, Hassard, & Forrester, 1994).

Notwithstanding the obvious efficiencies of Fordism, some of the very features that were responsible for the economic successes of this system also proved problematic. Low quality could easily become poor quality; workers were poorly motivated with resulting high labor turnover and absenteeism; and coordinating the flow of materials through production processes was difficult (Wood, 1993). Labor-management demarcations and responsibilities were rigidly defined and separated, the result being that workers were often as unwilling to provide input into solving production problems as were managers in soliciting that input (Williams, Cutler, Williams, & Haslam, 1991).

The Technological Basis

Technology's role in Fordism has been crucially important for managers because it afforded them opportunities to coordinate and control production in ways that enhanced their own supervision of the workforce. It also increased the speed of the production process, permitting the economies of scale associated with low unit costs. Machines, products, and processes were standardized, and rationality and efficiency became the hallmark of managerial justification for their power in the bureaucratic organization (Kanter, 1977).

Despite technology's centrality under Fordism, one cannot unambiguously assume a distinctive technological logic that shaped the organization of work (Kelley, 1986; Spenner, 1988), even though the context and the content of jobs were often changed (Attewell, 1987; Taplin, 1992; Wallace, 1989). Furthermore, technology's role is often muddled to an outsider because it appears to serve multiple, sometimes conflicting purposes even when ostensibly introduced as part of firm efficiency mandates. For example, technical changes can make a firm more responsive to the market, increase both the volume and the rate of production, or reduce unit costs while maintaining established levels of production.

Because various constituencies within an organization might view the function of new technology in dramatically different terms (Smith, 1990), the deployment of similar technology in different firms can result in dramatically different organizational outcomes (Kelley, 1990). For example, McLoughlin and Clark (1988) argue that senior managers often envisage changes in strategic terms while line managers seek an expansion of their control over labor. As implementation is often the responsibility of midlevel managers, the latters' situational uncertainty in the face of technological innovation can be a powerful contingent force constraining change. Recent research shows how incentive structures by top management encourage line managers to pursue their own self-interests (Prechel, 1991). A similar pattern is discernible when competitive pressures force firms to innovate technologically, but when actual workplace agendas are set by line managers. This is central to Thomas's (1994) "power-process" perspective that he developed to understand the role of power brokering strategies by managers in determining the form and content of new technology in firms.

Because it is difficult to make universal assertions about the impact of technology on workers under Fordism, especially given its multiple aims, it is not surprising that its role in promoting flexibility in the workplace is similarly ambiguous (Schoenberger, 1989). Once again, organizational intent, actual deployment, and the consequences innovations have for workers can vary considerably from setting to setting and in some instances appear contradictory.

Flexible Production

Pressures from increased market segmentation, the need for shortened product development cycles and greater operating flexibility, plus intense competition in standardized product lines from low-wage newly industrialized countries (NICs), have forced many firms with standardized products to experiment with new microprocessor technologies. In particular, computer-aided-design (CAD) and computer-aided-manufacturing (CAM) systems have been used to provide firms with flexibility and cost-effective shortened production runs.

In its prescriptive form, the shift from large batch, standardized production to small volume, demand-driven, and higher value-added manufacturing suggests a new, possibly post-Fordist manufacturing policy. Referred to as *flexible specialization* (Piore & Sabel, 1984) or *flexible accumulation* (Harvey, 1989), the process implies alterations in both labor market structure and industrial organization. Under such systems, managerial hierarchies are flattened, firms become smaller and leaner, and responsibility for monitoring production devolves to a higher skilled shop floor workforce.

Such flexible production methods appear most appropriate for the manufacture of durable goods where a relatively high-wage work force uses capital-intensive technologies to mass produce or customize goods of a lasting nature. However, because many of the above changes have become subsumed under the panoply of post-Fordism, they have come to represent a set of policy recommendations more than an empirical trend, with their appeal extending beyond the durable goods sector.

Because technological changes (primarily microelectronic innovations) are driving the apparent transformation, the ensuing flexibility provisions inexorably assume the need for a skilled workforce that enjoys task discretion and decision-making autonomy, and a managerial attitude that views labor as a resource to be developed rather than a cost to be contained (Barlow & Winterton, 1995). In other words, flexible technologies and innovative organizational forms that are central to post-Fordism presuppose a dramatically different managerial orientation to workers (and the use of technology) to that found under Fordism. Furthermore, the objective conditions of labor undergo changes that are both qualitative and quantitative. Such changes distinguish post-Fordism from the minor production modifications that are part of the general processes of long-run capitalist restructuring (neo-Fordism).

Post-Fordist Evidence and Counterclaims

As evidence of these tendencies, flexible specialization proponents point to multiskilling and teamworking in Japanese factories and the growth of "lean production" (Womack, Jones, & Roos, 1990); job enrichment through upskilling and autonomy in German automobile production (Lane, 1989); and the ubiquitous "artisanal production" supposedly characteristic of the Third Italy (Piore & Sabel, 1984). More recently, Hirst and Zeitlin (1991) have defended flexible specialization against its critics by arguing that the existence of hybrid forms of production (a combination of mass production and flexible specialization) that is frequently apparent in all of the above cited cases in no way detracts from the general assertion. Because they view flexible specialization and mass production as dichotomous, hybridization is merely seen as a stage on the process toward a purer form of flexible specialization.

Critics of the flexible specialization thesis have been trenchant in their opposition on a number of theoretical and empirical grounds. First, they claim that it is too simplistic to argue that mass production and flexible specialization are opposite paradigms because there is ample evidence of the two coexisting under capitalism (Hyman, 1988; Sayer, 1989). Second, it is not clear that Fordism was ever as pervasive a generic production system as many claim, because much durable and nondurable goods manufacture involves small-batch production (Williams et al., 1987). Third, sufficient evidence exists to show that what flexible specialization often entails is a more sophisticated use of labor that masks intensification of effort (Pollert, 1988), therefore making it indistinguishable from neo-Fordism. Relatedly, even in regions where its successes have been proclaimed, such as Japan and Italy, intensification of effort rather than job enrichment are often the norm for production workers (Taplin, 1989; Wood, 1993). In a similar vein, studies suggest Japanese worker acquiescence is often manufactured through fear, normative subcultural pressures, and dual labor markets (a secondary labor market of workers without extensive benefit packages working under virtual Taylorist conditions) rather than a meaningful incorporation into the work process (Tomaney, 1990). Finally, too much emphasis on demand driven (market saturation and subsequent segmentation) technological innovation puts too much emphasis on an inferential approach without questioning why alternative responses might have occurred.

Key to many of these critical concerns is the role of technology. Flexible specialization assumes ceteris paribus that technological innovation both entails and necessitates a dramatic rethinking of existing production methods. But sometimes new technology is used to attain flexibility in ways that are consistent with past organizational practices rather than part of new systems. For example, Cohen and Zysman (1987) argue that many U.S. firms prefer a form of "static" flexibility because it entails incremental adjustments rather than the dramatic transformations of production policies that would be necessitated under "dynamic" flexibility. Even high-tech firms in unstable market environments display a propensity for static flexibility (Colclough & Tolbert, 1992).

Whither Fordism?

The central issue in the discussion thus far is whether flexible production systems made possible by new technologies are sufficiently distinct from past practices to warrant use of the term post-Fordist? Or, has the increased information potential inherent in microprocessor technologies provided firms with requisite flexibility while enabling them to retain existing production relations (neo-Fordism)? If the latter is the case, under what conditions does this exist? Might microprocessor technologies function efficiently as part of Fordist structures, rationalizing production in certain functional areas while allowing managers to devise ways of intensifying work effort in others?

It is apparent that we need clarification of what conditions promote the use of new technology to buttress Fordist work organization and which ones are conducive to flexible specialization. This means examining external influences on firms as well as understanding the intrafirm forces that shape managerial behavior and their rationale for the deployment of new technology. For example, do labor market conditions inhibit the use of flexible production arrangements, and if so, are there related institutional forces that further discourage managerial adoption of "dynamic" flexibility? Is managerial preference for the production modifications found in "static" flexibility indicative of systemic obduracy because to do otherwise may result in "uncertainties of management" (Streeck, 1987, p. 286)? Or does it suggest managerial attempts at compromise, seeking to balance the beneficial aspects of technological innovation with any adverse effects it might have on their own status and job performance (Smith, 1990)?

These questions concern the meaning and character of post-Fordist arrangements and the conditions under which they are likely to emerge. It seems appropriate therefore that one examine a specific industry where Fordist production has been the manufacturing norm and yet where organizational changes associated with new technologies are currently under way. This is done not as a basis for a putative countergeneralization but to illustrate the broad framework that shapes the innovation process, how managers interpret and implement these changes, and what the resulting production system looks like.

The case selected is apparel manufacturing, a labor-intensive industry undergoing change following innovations in microprocessor technologies (American Apparel Manufacturers Association [AAMA], 1988; Hoffman & Rush, 1988; Office of Technology Assessment [OTA], 1987) and one that currently faces intense competitive pressure from low-cost NIC producers.

It has been argued that mass market apparel firms in high-wage economies will logically subcontract labor-intensive assembly tasks to firms in low-wage economies (Frobel, Heinrichs, & Kreye, 1981). Although this has happened in many cases, other firms have innovated technologically and reconfigured production systems to remain competitive and attain requisite levels of flexibility. Several firms that have restructured in this fashion are the subject of this study. I suggest that the direction and shape of production change in these firms are partly determined by historical decisions regarding the use of low-wage, unskilled workers in this industry as well as new technology that promotes efficiency while further routinizing work.

DATA AND RESEARCH DESCRIPTION

Data for this research were derived from interviews with 13 managerial personnel of 5 plants in North Carolina conducted during 1990 and 1991.[1] I followed up these interviews in 1993 and 1994 with more specific questions designed to amplify key points that were crucial to the focus of this study. All of the plants produced men's and boys' shirts (SIC 2321): 2 were plants (employing 700 and 900 workers, respectively) of multiestablishment, diversified conglomerates; the other 3 were single-establishment firms. They were selected in consultation with informed sources in the industry because each had implemented production changes as part of cost reduction and enhanced market share strategies. Although they are not necessarily representative of the industry as a whole, they do illustrate how firms with proactive competitive strategies have tackled the technology-organization fit issues in increasingly unstable product market environments.

In each case, I was permitted to tour the plant, talk with key supervisory personnel, and be provided with summary details of recent technological changes, current operating procedures, and production goals. Background information from published reports (of the two larger firms) complemented these interview data, as did aggregate industry sector data published by the Census of Manufactures. I supplemented this information with published data from the AAMA together with technical details provided in interviews with key personnel of the AAMA.

APPAREL INDUSTRY STRUCTURE

Apparel is a highly competitive, fragmented, and frequently labor-intensive industry. For classification purposes, one can divide the industry into two sectors. In the more fashion-oriented women's and girls' clothing sector, short production runs and small batches are associated with a disaggregated production system of vertically linked small firms. In this sector, 56% of establishments employed fewer than 20 workers in 1987.

The other sector includes hosiery, knit products, and men's and boys' wear. Long production runs and standardized batches are possible in this sector because of infrequent style changes. Consequently, firms are more likely to be larger than in women's and girls' products because size becomes a critical factor in attaining economies of scale. In men's and boys' shirts (SIC 2321), the subject of this study, there were 585 establishments employing 77,600 workers in 1987. The leading state in terms of employment (13,600 workers) and number of establishments (74) was North Carolina.

Since the 1970s, the apparel industry has faced intense competitive pressures from imports of clothing manufactured in low-wage NICs. In 1993, imports exceeded domestic production in most segments, including that of men's and boys' shirts. Despite annual productivity growth of 2.4% since the late 1970s, a rate nevertheless slower than the 3.1% for manufacturing as a whole, domestic labor costs have increased, the value of the dollar has risen against foreign currencies, domestic market growth has been sluggish, and high interest rates have stifled further capital spending (Avery & Sullivan, 1985).

In men's and boys' clothing, competitive strategies have often centered on yield improvements and cost reduction through technological innovation, reorganization of work, and the use of a smaller and less skilled labor force. This contrasts with the labor-intensive women's and girls' clothing sector where subcontracting is widely used and wage depressing tactics are intricately linked with the availability and employment of immigrant populations.

Because the focus of this study is the impact of technological change on the organization of production, the remainder of the discussion is devoted to an analysis of firm behavior in the men's and boys' sector.

Product and Labor Market Factors

As raw materials (fabric) can represent up to 60% of garment manufacturing costs, it is not surprising that companies (a) seek ways to reduce wastage and (b) rationalize materials flow through inventory reduction and increased production turnaround. These were paramount concerns in each of the firms studied. Moreover, each faced pressure from major retailers to expedite the supply of restocked items, thereby adding to their own need for improved materials management.

After raw materials, labor remains the next significant cost factor, constituting approximately 25% of total costs. Earlier industry relocation to the largely nonunion and low-tax South gave firms access to a workforce that could be paid low wages, made to work longer hours, and accept heightened levels of work intensity (Leiter, Schulman, & Zingraff, 1991; Wright, 1986). The malleability of this labor force, and its parallel among immigrant workers in New York and California,[2] was precisely what companies sought in their efforts to depress labor costs.[3] But increasingly even these tactics have been insufficient for companies producing goods for the lower end of the market and for whom competition from low-wage NICs has intensified. Furthermore, tight labor markets in some growth areas of the South have shrunk this traditional labor pool (Falk & Lyson, 1988).

Attempts by firms to address the materials handling and labor use issues have centered around three interrelated changes. First, microprocessor technologies have been introduced into the preparation functions (design, grading, and marking and fabric cutting) (Kazis, 1989; OTA, 1987). Such technologies reduce material wastage, lessen the need for skilled operatives, and dramatically increase the speed with which design information can be transmitted. Second, firms have introduced computerized monitoring systems to track the flow of material and better coordinate the output of sewing machine operators. Third, attempts to improve productivity in garment assembly functions have centered on technological and organizational changes in the batch system of transporting goods through the production process (AAMA, 1988). Each involves changes to traditional mass manufacturing techniques, but do they entail mere modifications to extant practices, or the adoption of a new organizational paradigm?

TECHNOLOGICAL AND ORGANIZATIONAL INNOVATIONS

Garment Preparation

Because much of fabric wastage occurs in the preparation stages, computer-aided-design (CAD) and numerically controlled (NC) cutting systems have been introduced (Hoffman & Rush, 1988). CAD systems permit designs to be easily transferred to visual display terminal (VDT) screens for markers to arrange jigsaw-like for pattern cutting. Such systems reduce fabric wastage and cut product development time. NC cutting systems permit large quantities of fabric to be cut accurately and quickly and/or allow smaller and more varied production lots to be cut by firms adopting flexible manufacturing. One semiskilled worker, positioning the reciprocating knife that performs the actual cutting, can do the work of three or four skilled cutters in about 1/10 of the time. Such a worker requires two days of training as opposed to the 6 to 12 months needed before manual cutters become proficient (Cedrone, 1994). Here then, flexibility is squarely predicated on a system that uses a smaller and less skilled workforce engaged in the performance of simple, repetitive tasks. Such a system is a far cry from the use of multiskilled, autonomous workers of flexible specialization lore.

Garment Assembly

Although preparation functions have been rationalized around increased production speed and deskilling criteria, assembly functions remain labor intensive with little change in the requisite skill level of operators.

It is difficult to automate garment assembly because fabric is limp. Some peripheral operations such as pleating, hemming, needle positioning, and thread cutting have been automated, but nothing has yet replaced the sewing machine as the primary assembly tool. Here, operators pass material through sewing machines—repetitive tasks that nevertheless defy automation because the fabric has to be individually positioned.

Some productivity gains together with quality improvements have nevertheless been possible in standardized batch production through the use of dedicated machines such as buttonholers (Riley, 1987). However, because sewing machines are worker-paced rather than automated, efforts to further rationalize work have focused on improved coordination of production.

As part of electronic data interchange (EDI) systems that have often been mandated by retailers,[4] manufacturers have introduced computerized tracking systems to monitor production. Digitized information on task performance by sewing machine operators permits sophisticated monitoring of worker productivity and easier identification of quality problems. Such impersonal supervision obviates the need for direct oversight yet provides improved managerial coordination of, and control over, production workers. Again, no suggestion of upgraded skills, greater worker autonomy, or decreased routinization of work is apparent.

Because technological innovation in the apparel industry has moved away from mechanical engineering systems to microelectronic processing, many of the above changes necessitate organizational restructuring to take into account the "total systems" basis of such technology (OTA, 1987). In other words, the benefits of microelectronic application in one area of the production process can often only be fully realized by complementary applications in related areas. This is best seen in attempts to rethink the "bundle" system of materials handling.

Technological Innovation and Work Reorganization

The traditional "bundle" system hinders attempts to speed product flow in the factory. Under such a system, garment components are cut and packed in bundles of 25 to 30 parts and then sent to the sewing floor for assembly. Here individual sewing machine operators untie the bundle, perform a particular sewing operation on each part, and then retie the bundle and deposit it in a bin where it awaits the next requisite operation. Such a system results in the slow movement of goods through production, with an item taking up to a month before it is finally assembled.

Efforts to improve product throughput and reduce time spent in inventory have led recently to experiments with alternative production systems. These include unit production systems (UPS), where computers balance the work flow as individual components are shipped to operators working alongside a transporter, and modular and related forms of team-based sewing (AAMA, 1988). Although UPS remains in the experimental stage, team systems have become more widespread, in part because they easily blend with existing managerial orientations to workers.

Modular manufacturing borrows heavily from the production organization found in Japanese auto manufacturing. Teams of cross-trained workers, organized into small groups (modules), together assemble an entire garment (Mazziotti, 1993). Small bundles are shipped to these work stations where each worker performs a particular assembly task. Not only does such a system speed the flow of the product and reduce work-in-process inventory, it invokes group effort to maximize both productivity and enhanced product quality (Shepherd, 1987).

Variations on modules, such as a progressive bundle system or teams with workers cross-trained in only two functional tasks, are also popular. The virtues of such team-based work systems lie in their ability to induce improved worker performance while reducing supervision and without compromising quality. However, Celia Cody's (1993) study of alternative manufacturing systems at Levi Strauss and Tom Bailey's (1993) sample of standardized product manufacturers both illustrate how firms have used team systems to improve quality and timeliness while retaining a treatment of labor characteristic of mass production.

DETAILED MANAGEMENT STRATEGY

The aforementioned general industry trends indicate ways in which flexibility and cost containment have been accomplished and age-old quality problems have been addressed. When work systems have been reconfigured to make these changes, there is nevertheless little evidence of firms departing from basic Fordist principles.

Why have firms in this industry apparently chosen to seek the benefits associated with flexibility without necessarily changing production relations? The proponents of flexible specialization argue that its benefits are maximized when skill upgrading occurs to complement the new technology. Are firms in this industry failing to realize the full potential of these changes, prisoners as they might be of outmoded system paradigms? Or might such partial change represent an alternative way of attaining certain attributes of flexibility?

To answer such questions, we examine specific firms, looking closely at the rationale of managerial behavior because managers are responsible for system implementation in specific settings.

In each firm where interviews were conducted, cost savings were sought through improved flexibility and shorter product turnaround time. Changes also included efforts to rationalize inventory control and achieve productivity gains without compromising quality levels. This is certainly consistent with industrywide priorities, of which "ability to respond faster" and "managing inventory" are, respectively, first and second according to the latest Kurt Salmon Associates' survey (KSA, 1995). Of the five firms in our sample, Plants A, B, and D have introduced modular or team manufacturing, Plant C has a bundle system that is computer monitored, and Plant E had introduced UPS. Labor shortages and equipment breakdown problems have since forced Plant E to abandon UPS and adopt a team system.[5] All the plants had CAD systems, but only Plants A, B, and D had NC cutters. Each of the plants has introduced dedicated purpose sewing machines, and Plant C was currently examining new "quick change" attachments to these machines.

Fewer Workers, Lower Skills

Whenever I asked about the purpose and benefits of CAD and NC systems, the reply was virtually always the same, as summarized in the following comments of the Plant B production manager:

> This equipment allows us to be flexible, responsive to rapid style shifts, improve our productivity and allows us to use fewer and less skilled workers. The savings on wages and inventory easily offset the initial capitalization. We have less problems hiring and retaining skilled cutters and graders because we don't really need them anymore. And when we get big orders, we can fill them more quickly than in the past.

The engineering director of Plant D did say that equipment malfunctions proved problematic and he was forced to hire an additional mechanic/ technician. But this cost was offset by savings associated with improved product turnaround. Other firms reported no specific problems in this area.

Use of the term "deskilled" to refer to the benefits of such systems was redolent among each of the managers. Clearly, automation for them meant less dependence on skilled workers plus reduced labor costs and productivity improvements. Because labor markets in this region were tight, managers were enthusiastic about finding ways to simultaneously reduce labor needs and increase production. Each said the innovation period was fraught with coordination problems, largely because production was speeded up. But once established, such systems dramatically increased managerial ability to systematize and standardize many of these traditionally skilled preparation function tasks.

When asked about automation in garment assembly, each of the managers interviewed said they make every effort to reduce the human element of discretion and find ways of further standardizing procedures. The engineering manager of Plant A said,

> The beauty of machines is not that they don't make mistakes: they do. But when they do, it's the same mistake, repeated over and over again. Once you identify it, you know what to look for in the batch and it's easily rectified. Even the most skilled workers here can make mistakes. We all do, especially at this speed. But they're not consistent and it's damn hard to find them. As a result the less human contact there is in the assembly process, the more reliable the finished product quality is.

Two managers, in different plants, did say that constant monitoring and team pressures have resulted in a marked reduction in defective products. Because poor quality is often cited as a problem associated with overseas manufacturing, such gains without adding to costs are a significant competitive strength.

Reconfigured Work Organizations

Central to the efficiency aims of firms has been the introduction of team manufacturing systems. These are seen as a way of structuring work to improve productivity while reducing supervision and of making workers pay closer attention to quality issues.

The two largest firms (Plant A with 700 workers and Plant B with 900 workers) reconfigured production in the mid-1980s, one with modular and the other with a team manufacturing system. They each developed strategies to increase their market share; improved profits would then come from an increase in the volume of unit sales if associated with a simultaneous lowering of unit production costs. In each of the plants, the plant manager said he was given a work organization framework to implement and allowed to modify it only if local labor markets dictated changes. If the latter occurred, it was clear that each manager would be accountable for any problems that might subsequently arise.

In both plants it was initially difficult to make workers accept a modified piece rate system that was team instead of individual based. Workers found it particularly difficult to adapt to team production norms because it took away much of the individual initiative and control over the pace of work. Managers also reported difficulty in motivating workers in teams where discrete tasks might require extreme functional skill variations. Workers in more complex tasks did not like cooperating in team-based remuneration with those whose tasks were simple. There were also some initial problems in costing quotas to reflect various tasks, ability to perform interconnected functions, and how much time should be allotted to such efforts. A manager in each plant commented on the difficulty in calculating ways to measure performance in a team-based system. "Everything is so interdependent now," said one, "it's hard to determine where one job ends and the other one begins." Of modular manufacturing, a Plant A supervisor said it required more active supervision of cross-trained workers, ensuring that they slot into the required tasks. He went on to comment that

> getting someone who is both good and reliable can be difficult. Just when I think I've found someone who can move easily, understanding the difficulties of integrating people into different teams, they quit to get married, get pregnant, or go and work at IBM as a secretary (where they can earn 5 to 10 cents an hour more). I guess the problem is ours because for years we've wanted them to come to work, do their job, not ask any questions, and then go home. Now we're saying they have to think a bit; try and figure out what their contribution to this new system might be.

This statement is typical of managerial ambivalence towards workers. On one hand, they lament the absence of workers' ability and willingness to work with greater responsibility; on the other hand, few systematic attempts have been made to encourage the growth of such a work culture.

When asked to describe current team operating procedures, managers of each of the firms provided similar comments. The assistant plant manager's description of Plant A operations is typical of the replies I received. The team system, with 10 workers to a team, allowed work-in-process to be cut by 90% with products turned around in 2 to 3 hours. Production quotas are established for the teams, and workers in the team are paid a base rate of $7.00 per hour. Any production in excess of the predetermined quota is rewarded as a proportion of the base rate. A typical team in Plant A, for instance, will produce 20% more than the predetermined quota; hence their earnings will be $8.40 per hour ($7.00 plus $1.40—20% of $7.00).

In every case, managers determined the quotas, the optimum number of teams, and the payment scales. They also provided short training programs for all workers, designed to introduce variations on the modular concept of self-directed teams. This was seen as important if workers were to be weaned away from the old status quo of traditional piece rate systems. But it also meant that workers were denied opportunities to provide input into the design of work teams, thereby restricting their discretionary behavior. However, every team in each of the plants regularly exceeded the production quota; in exceptional cases, it could be by as much as 21%, but more likely it is in the region of 8% to 11%.

Managerial enthusiasm for teams was obvious when productivity increases and lessened supervision were the focus of conversation. As the team becomes accountable for meeting standard quotas together with agreed-on group production in excess of these quotas, pressure on individual workers is displaced from managers to a more abstract group norm. In each of the firms with teams, the plant manager said fewer supervisors were needed and consequently cost savings were made.

Workers in each of the teams are cross-trained to perform a series of different tasks within the team. But the cycle of tasks (hemming, collar attachment, and so forth) remains standardized and repetitive with little if any opportunity for individual workers to have input into variations on the design of the job task. Managers at Plants A and B said that few workers were trained to do all the tasks because such workers would be so skilled they would deem their pay inadequate. Yet those same managers said that one of their major problems with team sewing is absenteeism and labor turnover. Workers use allotted sick days for holidays so that on some days as much as 3% of the workforce would be absent. When this occurs, "floaters" (workers who are not assigned a permanent team) work temporarily with the team but lack the social integration necessary to be committed to the group incentives of a permanent member. Consequently, production suffers. A manager in Plant A was quite straightforward about this problem:

> At $7 to $8 an hour let's face it, we're paying close to what the welfare levels most of these people could get. The work is boring, repetitive, and pretty low skilled. Most of our workers (in actuality 87%) are female, in their late 20s and 30s and married. Anybody who is smart and going anywhere is not going to work in a mill. Even if they're not smart but still want to go somewhere, they're not going to be wanting to come here. If we trained them for multiple tasks they wouldn't work for this low wage. If we're going to stay competitive, we have to keep our labor costs down at this wage level. So we do the best we can, trying to make the atmosphere as nice as possible, going easy on them when it comes to absences but also not being too lenient.

Such comments illustrate the managerial dilemma. How do you keep wages low and skill levels about the same while simultaneously demanding greater effort from your workforce? It appears that teams provided the answer for these firms through an appeal to basic acquisitive interests. At the surface, workers are "sold" on the new production systems with a combination of financial incentives and production changes that promise better work arrangements, even though the latter are largely cosmetic. Work tasks meanwhile have been fragmented and further routinized, with individual effort "rationalized" through the mediation of group norms.

Plant D has used team manufacturing systems since 1985. The director of engineering, discussing the rationale for the system, said,

> Workers internalize this work effort that is team induced. We encouraged the election of team leaders but made sure each team had several workers who were both popular and productive. That way we stacked the productivity cards in our favor. Since then, it's been a great success; labor turnover is down to less than 2%, productivity is up, as is quality. The latter is especially important because we have been able to cut the number of people in inspection and put them into production and coordination tasks. This means more productive work for more of the work force.

Here again, with little training and no new technology, skills have been merely reconfigured and productivity increases related to labor intensification.

Plant C (with 250 employees) does not use team or modular systems but attempted to modify the bundle system with extensive computer monitoring of production. Here, senior management strategies have focused on moving into niche markets where product quality standards are more demanding. Consequently, there has been pressure to design systems to monitor the location of a product in the production process, provide detailed information about work performance, and build in ways of implementing better quality control. Now, according to the data processing manager, "one can both better track people and products; productivity has increased but most importantly so has product quality." Defects have fallen by 80%, which is important to this company because of its strategies for going up-market with its product line. If it is to compete in a higher priced market, its product must reflect the better quality that such a market demands. In the words of Plant C's data processing manager, this means

> making improvements in moving the garment around the factory and making sure that the work done was performed in accordance with the new standards we established. Computer monitoring is great because the workers feel they are being held to objective standards. There's nothing arbitrary about this system. After some initial problems, they all accepted it and work accordingly. They know if they screw up, they end up paying for it by having to work on the problem without pay.

Here, new technology enables managers to more subtly control their workforce in ways that mask discipline under the cloak of microelectronic rationality. The plant manager of Plant C said that such monitoring systems have reduced his need to actively supervise and improved the flow of goods through production. This matches the reduction in supervision that accompanied team manufacturing in Plants A, B, and D.

The manager of Plant E said that these were his intentions when a modified UPS system was introduced, but he abandoned it when his workforce could not cope with the requisite productivity imperatives and work backed up when machines malfunctioned. Following this impasse, the firm reduced its labor force and switched all but the high-quality product manufacturing offshore. I asked what pressures have been imposed by the firm's owners, and his reply was a judicious mixture of optimism and concern:

> They told me to try UPS; I did and it didn't work. I didn't think it would given what I know about the workers here. Some have been here for years and are really good. The others come and go and I don't think they have the aptitude for sustained effort. They're just doing this until something better comes up. I figured it was best to stick with the good ones, let them learn a progressive bundle system, and give them the chance to earn more money if they could work even faster and

do quality work. I got rid of the other workers and now use contractors to pick up the slack or when we have a really big rush order.[6]

Flexibility vs. Skill

Although all the managers were committed to flexible production, they defined it as a way of lowering costs and becoming more responsive to the market without making significant investments in worker training and job enrichment. In other words, flexibility was possible without departing from existing "command and control" managerial orientations. Not only had none of the firms provided anything but rudimentary training programs for workers, invariably new technology and production systems were chosen to match the capability of the existing workforce. In most cases, work tasks had become simplified with workers performing repetitive discrete tasks in a team setting. Work teams were organized around specific product lines with flexibility and yield improvements coming from improved coordination of functional assembly tasks. This enabled firms to avoid any of the costs for worker training that are associated with multiskilled teams. All but Plant E nonetheless experienced productivity growth of between 3% and 6% annually, each had seen incremental improvements in quality, and all reported increased profitability of their respective organizational unit.[7]

From what I could discern, management successfully cultivated an atmosphere of instrumental paternalism in each of the firms. Relative to depressed wages and sweatshop work conditions among a largely immigrant labor force in areas such as California and New York, the wages paid workers in my North Carolina sample were quite good.[8] All the plants were nonunion in a state where unions are an institutional anathema and where work opportunities for unskilled workers traditionally have been plentiful in textiles and apparel (Leiter, 1982, p. 1986). Health care and generous sick day provisions, plus a workplace subculture that attempts to distill the beneficial aspects of a "company town" (softball leagues, company picnics, and so on), all combine to generate worker compliance within the restructured work environment.

It was apparent that worker-management adversarialism of the type found in some manufacturing industries was conspicuously absent here. Management capitalized on this acquiescence, using work reorganization (and the benign "worker empowerment" implicit in it) as the means to improve the efficiency of workers without increasing overt supervision. As one assistant manager told me, "The new systems better utilize existing workers making task performance more standardized without me having to constantly check up on them." And the shift supervisor of Plant B added,

With most of our workers not graduating from high school, it's been difficult to devise new systems that would match their skill levels. Some are great workers, and we should pay them more. Others don't give a damn, are lazy, and we should pay them less. Team systems' been good because it evens them all out. Essentially the good now monitor the bad.

How much gender is a factor in these events is difficult to assess.[9] All of the managerial and supervisory staff interviewed were male; depending on the plant, between 72% and 87% of workers were female. Male workers occupied some of the skilled positions (grading, marking, and cutting for example) but were overrepresented in the most unskilled (finishing and shipment) positions.

It could be argued that considerations about training and skill, integral to new productive arrangements, are significantly shaped by (biased) managerial beliefs about women's weaker attachment to work. In other words, managers might be reluctant to upgrade female workers' skills because high turnover renders such investments too costly. However, several plants with low turnover rates were also the ones that had routinized work the most. Also, the jobs that were targeted for deskilling were more likely to be the ones where a tight labor market made it difficult for firms to hire and retain skilled workers, no matter what their gender. Finally, some of the most routinized jobs were occupied by males.

This suggests that gender is less of an issue than might be the case in other settings. Managers still view apparel workers in general as typical of "traditional" workers with average attachment to jobs, low educational levels, and limited aspirations. The fact that a majority of them are women might have initially contributed to such a predisposition. Current managerial thinking is more circumspect, because workers who are skilled or have the potential to become skilled (regardless of gender) are often the ones whose labor turnover is highest. Perhaps because of this, managers have favored the adoption of new techniques designed to match the skill levels of their existing workforce. This enables them to avoid having to deal with costly skill upgrading, minimizes their dependence on the exigencies of the labor market, and allows continued reliance on an instrumental-based motivation that remains central to apparel workplace cultures in this region (Leiter, 1986).

Despite managerial obduracy concerning change, the pattern of reorganization in each of the plants appears similar. New technology and organizational changes have been introduced to meet the efficiency requirements mandated by firm owners. This follows exogenous pressures from an uncertain external environment that includes vendor and supplier problems, increased regulatory pressure from federal and state agencies, and heightened competitive pressures from overseas manufacturers.

Because apparel manufacturing is not especially capital intensive, it is not surprising that options for changing the organization of the labor process fall short of post-Fordist worker empowerment. Although all the managers interviewed shared the need to improve the speed and flexibility of the production process, they each sought ways of doing so that might lessen their dependence on the vagaries of the workforce, thereby reducing one aspect of the "management of uncertainty."

There are, however, important systemic and institutional constraints on managerial behavior that should be noted. In making the decision at the outset to use a low-wage labor force, firms imposed a wage-depressing logic for managers to follow. Managers recognize that resulting low investments in human capital preclude post-Fordist agendas predicated on skill upgrading. In fact, once the apparel industry decided to move south and employ low-wage labor, ostensibly the decision about post-Fordist production methods was made for them. When the potential for flexibility in microprocessor technologies was realized, not surprisingly managers sought to blend such innovations with the existing characteristics of a low-wage work force in ways that precluded any dramatic skill changes.

Intensifying their use of resources (personnel and products), but within frameworks that preserved as many of their prerogatives as possible, has allowed managers to attempt a reconciliation of the contradiction between the mass production imperative for cheaper labor costs and the post-Fordist belief that only extensive investment in human capital will improve production methods and make producers competitive. Such changes have rendered oversight of workers less problematic while achieving productivity gains.

FLEXIBLE REGIMES AND ROUTINIZED WORK

Although I do not presume to generalize from this clothing case, trends in one sector of the apparel industry can tell us something about what flexibility in practice can entail. In this case, firms have been able to achieve productivity gains (shortening start-up and production time), rationalize batch production to meet exogenous demands by retailers (flexibility), and yield quality improvements. This has been accomplished without upgrading worker skills or adding worker training and by decreases in supervision and reductions in the number of skilled workers. Each of the firms attained greater operating flexibility, but none of the managers or engineers acknowledged that this flexibility had involved them rethinking the way they treat their workforce.

Contrary to what proponents of "flexible specialization" argue, technological innovation here has actually deskilled high-skilled functional tasks and has led to job losses in these areas. Work reorganization meanwhile has embedded the control of semiskilled workers into group-based norms of self-exploitation, further routinizing such work tasks. Together both changes have enabled firms to speed the flow of goods through the manufacturing process. Managers have successfully incorporated workers into the mandates of flexible production, neither improving nor decreasing the dimensions of their work nor altering base pay scales. Because microprocessor technology permits companies to monitor performance rates and the quality of that performance without recourse to more confrontational forms of personal supervision, it has reduced some of the anxiety and pressure experienced by line managers. This is consistent with other findings on the preservation of managerial self-interest in the face of externally mandated changes (Attewell, 1992; Prechel, 1991). It is also similar to Prechel's (1994) recent findings in his study of the capital-intensive steel industry, in which he describes an emerging neo-Fordist mode of control as simply another stage in scientific management.

For each apparel firm, work reorganization occurred during a period of labor market changes, notably a shrinking pool of low-wage labor caused in part by the growth of alternative opportunities in the burgeoning service sector of the South. Companies in my sample continue to recruit mainly females from rural or small town backgrounds. Presumably, this group remains open to quasi-paternalist appeals of the type that traditionally characterized production relations in mill communities (Simon, 1991) and remain commonplace today. But the changes cited above allow managers more subtle control over the work effort of individual workers and conceivably provide productivity gains from a smaller workforce.

Historically, the technological impediments to the automation of work organization limited managerial options for labor force control to quasi-paternalistic methods of supervision (Leiter et al., 1991). Partial technological transformations, however, now permit an increased regulation of workers and more extensive coordination of production without increasing the managerial reliance on such forms of consent. Where technology has permitted automation and deskilling of tasks, it has been introduced; in functional areas that limit its substitutability, reconfigured work practices have produced requisite results. In each case, the goal of flexibility has been attained.

CONCLUSION

Firms in a highly competitive industry such as apparel, increasingly segmented along firm and product market lines, will presumably be more subject to the vicissitudes of the market than an oligopolistic firm. Although clothing firms are engaged in the active generation of new "demands" (new fashion items, for example), from the standpoint of one firm, fashion changes are more or less exogenous. As price takers therefore, most firms seek ways of containing production costs and becoming more flexible in their response to market volatility.

Yield and quality improvements, although strategically conceived as part of flexibility drives, often result in a managerial focus on improving productivity because this is the area in which managerial accountability is highest and more easily measured. Not surprisingly perhaps, managers rely on extant practices when deploying new technology because systemic and institutional forces often constrain them from doing otherwise. They also seek to protect their own positions and invariably use technological changes and work reconfiguration as a way of safeguarding such a position. Evidence from our study on this point is certainly consistent with the findings of others (Smith, 1990; Thomas, 1994). Also, despite being labor-intensive, the organization of apparel production uses the same strategies and technologies as the capital-intensive steel industry in Prechel's (1994) study. This further strengthens the generalizability of the conceptual argument about the absence of post-Fordist modes of control in flexible production systems.

The resulting organizational form of such changes suggests a type of "flexible Fordism" but more than what Howard (1985) terms "technocratic control." Labor-intensive firms in competitive markets can, it seems, attain flexible production through reconfigured work and without the addition of highly skilled artisanal workers suggested in the Piore and Sabel (1984) agenda. Under this system, managers can still preserve a hierarchical work organization that retains a sharp distinction between themselves and shop floor workers. In fact, comments by managers suggest that they are as ambivalent about technological change as workers are and do their utmost to avoid it unless it can be used to consolidate their own position.

Finally, what this study shows is that managers can mold new techniques and work practices to suit the capabilities of an existing workforce. In other words, restructuring is resulting in a neo-Fordist mode of control, not a post-Fordist one as many argue. Furthermore, within such a system, managers can balance competing exigencies to safeguard their own position in the organization while attaining flexible production without compromising their traditional control prerogatives.

NOTES

1. In Plant A (700 workers), I interviewed the regional engineering manager, the plant and assistant plant managers, and a senior production supervisor; in Plant B (900 workers), I interviewed the vice president for human resources, the plant manager, and a shift manager; in Plant C (250 workers), I interviewed the vice president for data processing and the assistant plant manager; in Plant D (350 workers), I interviewed the director of engineering and the plant manager; and in Plant E (80 workers), I interviewed the operations manager and the assistant plant manager. In each case, my questions were designed to determine what technology had been introduced, the rationale for its introduction, and what its effects were on workers and managers alike. Managers were asked to articulate the concerns, if any, they had, how their jobs had been altered, and the extent to which production changes necessitated a rethinking of the way in which worker consent (the legitimacy dimension) is manufactured.

2. For discussions of the role that immigrants have played and continue to play in the garment industry, see Waldinger (1986), Light and Bonacich (1987), and Bonacich (1989).

3. Relative to manufacturing in general, apparel industry wages have always been low; since the 1950s, that gap has widened: from 77% of manufacturing wages in 1950 to 54% in 1988.

4. Under such a system, retailers electronically transmit daily or weekly restocking orders to manufacturers. The latter are forced to manufacture smaller batches on demand or maintain a large goods inventory themselves. Because such inventory is too costly, manufacturers have been forced to become more flexible, introduce shorter start-up times, and improve product monitoring. For a full description of such microelectronic mediated efficiency pressures on manufacturers, see Hammond (1993).

5. In fact, this firm now contracts 40% of the garment assembly and finishing stages to four contractors (two of whom are Dominican Republic-based subsidiaries) while retaining the design, marking, grading, and sometimes even cutting in-house.

6. During my interview with the operations manager, he received a telephone order for 15,000 dozen boys' shirts from Sears. He immediately called a contractor in the Dominican Republic to arrange production, then turned to me and said, "That's flexible production for a small firm without the headaches and cost of UPS! If we were bigger, however, we could produce in-house and get a bigger margin from the markup. In order to grow, we need guaranteed orders on a regular basis, but unless you're big, you don't get them. It's a vicious circle and we're completely at the mercy of the market."

7. In marked contrast to the women's and girls' sector, men's and boys' clothing has witnessed productivity increases since the early 1970s that reflect the consolidation of the industry into larger sized establishments, mechanization of some sewing tasks, and better materials handling. Although industry output has declined, largely because of increased import penetration, the number of employees has shrunk even further. For a useful discussion of the important variables explaining these trends in men's and boys' suits and coats, see Sieling and Curtin (1988).

8. Plant C paid the highest wages (approximately $9 an hour), had the most stable workforce (an average employment period of 8 years for the workforce as a whole), and had the lowest annual labor turnover rate (less than 1%).

9. I am indebted to one of the anonymous reviewers whose comments on this issue forced me to go back and

ask more questions about gender. Unfortunately, I did not find evidence that could unambiguously support gender as an organizing principle, but it did enable me to probe more into managerial stereotypes of apparel workers. Ellen Rosen's (1994) recent article on women workers in men's tailoring discusses many of these gender issues in greater detail.

REFERENCES

American Apparel Manufacturers Association. (1988). *Flexible apparel manufacturing* [Report of the Technical Advisory Committee]. Washington, DC: Author.

Attewell, P. (1987). The deskilling controversy. *Work and Occupations, 4,* 323-346.

Attewell, P. (1992). Skill and occupational change in U.S. manufacturing. In P. Adler (Ed.), *Technology and the future of work* (pp. 46-88). New York: Oxford University Press.

Avery, D., & Sullivan, G. D. (1985, November). Changing patterns: Reshaping the southeastern textile-apparel complex. *Economic Review of the Federal Reserve Bank of Atlanta,* pp. 34-44.

Bailey, T. (1993). Organizational innovation in the apparel industry: Strategy or technique. *Industrial Relations, 32,* 30-48.

Barlow, A., & Winterton, J. (1995). Restructuring production and work organization: U.K. clothing industry. In I. M. Taplin & J. Winterton (Eds.), *Restructuring within a labour intensive industry,* Aldershot, UK: Avebury.

Best, M. (1990). *The new competition.* Cambridge, MA: Harvard University Press.

Bonacich, E. (1989). *Asian immigrants in the Los Angeles garment industry.* Unpublished manuscript.

Cedrone, J. (1994, April). New issues drive cutting technology. *Bobbin,* pp. 42-55.

Chandler, A. (1977). *The visible hand.* Cambridge, MA: Harvard University Press.

Cody, C. (1993). *Team work, piece work, or both: Work reform at Levi Strauss.* Unpublished master's thesis, Massachussetts Institute of Technology.

Cohen, S., & Zysman, J. (1987). *Manufacturing matters: The myth of the post-industrial economy.* New York: Basic Books.

Colclough, G., & Tolbert, C., II. (1992). *Work in the fast lane.* Albany: State University of New York Press.

Deyo, F. (1987). *The political economy of the new Asian industrialism.* Ithaca, NY: Cornell University Press.

Dicken, P. (1992). *Global shift.* New York: Guilford.

Falk, W., & Lyson, T. (1988). *High tech, low tech, no tech.* Albany: State University of New York Press.

Frobel, F., Heinrichs, J., & Kreye, O. (1981). *The new international division of labor.* Cambridge, UK: Cambridge University Press.

Hammond, J. (1993). Quick response in retail/manufacturing channels. In S. Bradley, J. Hausman, & P. Nolan (Eds.), *Technology and competition* (pp. 185-214). Cambridge, MA: Harvard Business School Press.

Harvey, D. (1989). *The condition of Postmodernity.* Oxford, UK: Basil Blackwell.

Hirst, P., & Zeitlin, J. (1991). Flexible specialization versus post-Fordism: Theory, evidence, and policy implications. *Economy and Society, 20*(1), 1-52.

Hoffman, K., & Rush, H. (1988). *Micro-electronics and clothing.* New York: Praeger.

Howard, R. (1985). *Brave new workplace.* New York: Penguin.

Hyman, R. (1988). Flexible specialization: Miracle or myth? In R. Hyman & W. Streeck (Eds.), *New technology and industrial relations.* Oxford, UK: Basil Blackwell.

Kanter, R. (1977). *Men and women of the corporation.* New York: Basic Books.

Kazis, R. (1989, August/September). Rags to riches? One industry's strategy for improving productivity. *Technology Review,* pp. 42-53.

Kelley, M. (1986). Programmable automation and the skill question: A reinterpretation of the cross-national evidence. *Human Systems Management, 6,* 223-241.

Kelley, M. (1990). New process technology, job design, and work organization: A contingency model. *American Sociological Review, 55,* 191-208.

Kurt Salmon Associates. (1995, January). Optimism high for '95. *Bobbin,* pp. 42-53.

Lane, C. (1989). *Management and labour in Europe.* Aldershot, UK: Edward Elgar.

Lazonick, W. (1990). *Competitive advantage on the shop floor.* Cambridge, MA: Harvard University Press.

Leiter, J. (1982). Continuity and change in the legitimation of authority in Southern mill towns. *Social Problems, 29,* 540-550.

Leiter, J. (1986). Reactions to subordination: Attitudes of Southern textile workers. *Social Forces, 64,* 948-974.

Leiter, J., Schulman, M. D., & Zingraff, R. (1991). *Hanging by a thread.* Ithaca, NY: ILR Press.

Light, I., & Bonacich, E. (1987). *Immigrant entrepreneurs.* Berkeley: University of California Press.

Mazziotti, B. (1993, April). Modular manufacturing's new breed. *Bobbin,* pp. 36-42.

McLoughlin, I., & Clark, J. (1988). *Technological change at work.* Milton Keynes, UK: Open University Press.

Office of Technology Assessment. (1987). *The U.S. textile and apparel industry: A revolution in progress.* Washington, DC: Author.

Piore, M., & Sabel, C. (1984). *The second industrial divide.* New York: Basic Books.

Pollert, A. (1991). *Farewell to flexibility?* Oxford, UK: Basil Blackwell.

Prechel, H. (1991). Irrationality and contradiction in organizational change: Transformation in the corporate form of a U.S. steel corporation. *Sociological Quarterly, 32,* 423-455.

Prechel, H. (1994). Economic crisis and the centralization of control. *American Sociological Review, 59*(5), 723-745.

Procter, S. J., Rowlinson, M., McArdle, L., Hassard, J., & Forrester, P. (1994). Flexibility, politics, and strategy: In defence of the model of the flexible firm work. *Employment and Society, 8*(2), 221-242.

Reich, R. (1983). *The next American frontier.* Harmondsworth, UK: Penguin.

Riley, S. (1987, April). The industrial revolution: Our time has arrived. *Bobbin,* pp. 67-88.

Rosen, E. (1994). Women workers in a restructured domestic apparel industry. *Economic Development Quarterly, 8*(2), 197-210.

Sayer, A. (1989). Post-Fordism in question. *International Journal of Urban and Regional Research, 13,* 666-695.

Schoenberger, E. (1989). Thinking about flexibility: A response to Gertler. *Transaction of the Institute of British Geographers, 14,* 98-108.

Shepherd, J. N. (1987, May). Mechanizing the sewing room. *Bobbin* pp. 92-96.

Sieling, M., & Curtin, D. (1988, November). Patterns of productivity change in men's and boys' suits and coats. *Monthly Labor Review,* pp. 25-31.

Smith, V. (1990). *Managing in the corporate interest.* Berkeley: University of California Press.

Spenner, K. (1988). Technological change, skill requirements, and education: The case for uncertainty. In R. Cyert & D. Mowery (Eds.), *The impact of technological change on employment and economic growth* (pp. 131-184). Cambridge, MA: Ballinger.

Streeck, W. (1987). The uncertainties of management in the management of uncertainty: Employers, labor relations and industrial adjustment in the 1980s. *Work, Employment, and Society, 1,* 281-308.

Taplin, I. M. (1989). Segmentation and the organisation of work in the Italian apparel industry. *Social Science Quarterly, 70,* 408-424.

Taplin, I. M. (1992). Rising from the ashes: The deskilling debate and tobacco manufacturing. *Social Science Journal, 29,* 87-106.

Thomas, R. (1994). *What machines can't do.* Berkeley: University of California Press.

Tomaney, J. (1990). The reality of workplace flexibility. *Capital and Class, 40,* 29-60.

Waldinger, R. (1986). *Through the eye of the needle.* New York: New York University Press.

Wallace, M. (1989). Brave new workplace. *Work and Occupations, 16,* 363-392.

Waring, T. (1991). *Taylorism transformed.* Chapel Hill: University of North Carolina Press.

Williams, K., Cutler, T., Williams, J., & Haslam, C. (1987). The end of mass production. *Economy and Society, 16,* 405-439.

Womack, J. P., Jones, D. T., & Roos, D. (1990). *The machine that changed the world.* New York: HarperCollins.

Wood, S. (1993). The Japanization of Fordism. *Economic and Industrial Democracy, 14,* 535-555.

Wright, G. (1986). *Old South, new South.* New York: Basic Books.

The Technological Foundations of Task-Coordinating Structures in New Work Organizations

Theoretical Notes From the Case of Abdominal Surgery

JAMES R. ZETKA, JR.

By many accounts, we are witnessing a transition to a new work organization (Appelbaum & Batt, 1994; Capelli et al., 1997; Heydebrand, 1989; Kenney & Florida, 1993). The demands of variegated markets and flexible technologies have challenged the efficacy of Taylorist and bureaucratic production organization (Piore & Sabel, 1984; Streeck, 1987). These demands include more complex intraorganizational coordination, more effective patterns of communication across occupational boundaries within work units, and a capacity to respond quickly to contingencies (Galegher & Kraut, 1990; Weick & Roberts, 1993). The new environment demands workplace flexibility and team-based competencies (see Capelli et al., 1997; Ozaki, 1992). Organizations are passing decision-making authority to the work unit in response.

Many post-Fordists see this transformation as signifying progress toward workplace empowerment and democracy because such a transformation demands more skills, grants workers more autonomy and responsibility, and involves teamwork (Florida & Kenney, 1991; Walton, 1985; Womack, Jones, & Roos, 1991; see also Capelli et al., 1997, chap. 3). Many neo-Fordists, however, see the newly decentralized work unit as a despotic extension of hierarchical control (see Dohse, Jürgens, Malsch, & Dohse, 1993; Graham, 1995; Jürgens, Malsch, & Dohse, 1993; Turnbull, 1988; Turnbull & Graham, 1988). They argue that such units, especially when monitored through new information technologies (see Prechel, 1994; Vallas, 1993, chap. 4), grant upper-level management more knowledge and resources to control and intensify work processes.

The evidence is mixed. Some studies support the post-Fordist imagery (see Florida & Kenney, 1991; Hodson, 1996; Kelley, 1990), some support the neo-Fordist position (see Dawson & Webb, 1989; Graham, 1995; Prechel, 1994; Shaiken, Herzenberg, & Kuhn, 1986; Taplin, 1995; Vallas & Beck, 1996), and some report significant variation within organizations (see Geary, 1993; Smith, 1994, 1996; Vallas, 1993). The only conclusion we can draw is that a good deal of diversity exists in the population.

The response of contingency theory to such a predicament involves embracing such diversity as inevitable and developing the nuanced theo-

From *Work and Occupations*, Vol. 25, No. 3, August 1998, pp. 356-379. Reprinted by permission.

retical constructs required to explain it. Here, I extend contingency arguments to the work unit level. Rather than focus on the impact of work reorganization on individual skills—a typical focus of work transformation studies—I examine changes in task coordination practices and the structures regulating them. I argue that there are distinctive technological foundations for post-Fordist and neo-Fordist coordination structures.

The hypotheses developed to support this contention are generalized from an analysis of task coordination in abdominal surgery, an admittedly atypical work setting. Video laparoscopy—a procedure involving miniaturized cameras, television monitors, long instruments, and small puncture wounds—has changed the nature of task coordination in the operating room. Understanding the impact of this technology on surgical work has general relevance to our understanding of contemporary workplace transformations. Task coordination in major conventional and video surgeries involves reciprocal and team-flow interdependencies (for definitions, see Van de Ven, Delbecq, & Koenig, 1976), interdependencies associated with new work organizations (see Adler & Borys, 1989, pp. 393-395). Yet, with these interdependencies held constant, the coordination structures used in each type of surgery are quite distinct. Comparative analysis of these types of surgery will provide general insight into the different coordination structures that are technically feasible for decentralized work units.

The chapter develops as follows. First, I review the return of contingency arguments to the work organization literature and refine the classical specification of the relationship between task interdependence and coordination structures. I then link two coordination structures found in complex abdominal surgeries to their technological demands. Finally, I generalize the theoretical linkages made in the analysis of abdominal surgery, arguing that there are distinctive technological foundations for either a neo-Fordist or post-Fordist coordination structure.

CONTINGENCY THEORY AND NEW WORK ORGANIZATION

Classical contingency theory links variation on organizational structures to efficiency demands emanating from the work process. In this perspective, the requirement of rational production, coupled with variation in factors like task predictability (Perrow, 1967; Van de Ven & Delbecq, 1974) and the structure of information flows (Stinchcombe, 1990), influences how work is organized and partially determines work outcomes. Although external forces are critical in determining the choice of a technology (see Noble, 1984; Thomas, 1994; Walsh, 1991), contingency theorists view problems inherent in making the technology work efficiently as largely shaping practices associated with it.

Recent Findings

Although popular in the 1960s, contingency theory took a back seat to the "new structuralist" and "social choice" paradigms of the 1970s and 1980s, as the explanatory locus shifted from the workplace to societal forces (see Adler & Borys, 1989; Hodson, 1995; Simpson, 1989). However, research concerning the impact of new machining technology on work skills has stimulated a revival of contingency arguments. Programmable automation was originally designed to wrest from workers control over machining processes (see Noble, 1984). Managers in the United States and Great Britain initially implemented this technology with deskilling strategies (see Buchanan & Boddy, 1983; Kelley, 1986; Noble, 1984). Such strategies, however, often failed as management proved unable to shake machining processes free from dependency on an experiential, worker-controlled knowledge base (see Fadem, 1984; Noble, 1984, chap. 11). In response, the technology has been redesigned for operator input. Kelley (1990), for example, found that U.S. managers acquiring the newer versions of this technology in the 1980s were more likely to pass control over programming to workers, as were those who had instituted reforms that promoted cooperation and flexibility in labor relations. Others have documented similar adjustments in response to difficulties in implementing new technologies with a Taylorist agenda (Clark, McLoughlin, Rose, & King, 1988; McLoughlin & Clark, 1988; Noble, 1984, chap. 11; Orr, 1996, pp. 150-151; Vallas, 1993, chap. 4; Zetka, 1991, 1995, chap. 9).

Such studies show the obstinacy of technical-efficiency demands even when managerial strategies run contrary to them. Making work systems run effectively with new technology is problematic and often forces unanticipated change. Studies that pinpoint the strategic choices that managements make as the key variable determining practice often restrict their focus to early phases of implementation. Contingency theorists argue that, over longer stretches of time, managers in competitive markets are forced to adjust their practices so that they are consistent with efficiency demands (see Adler, 1992; Adler & Borys, 1989; McLoughlin & Clark, 1988).

As recent research demonstrates, contingency arguments are still useful (see Gutek, 1990). As societal-level concepts prove incapable of accounting for the diversity found in industries and firms, labor process scholars have turned increasingly to contingency arguments (e.g., see Leidner, 1993; Vallas, 1993; Walsh & Bayema, 1996; Zetka, 1992, 1995). Such arguments are being grafted onto other theoretical frameworks as well (e.g., see Barley, 1986, 1990; Burawoy, 1985; Piore & Sabel, 1984). And, or course, the transition to post-Taylorist organization was predicted by the early contingency theorists (see Blauner, 1964; Trist, 1981; Woodward, 1970).

Interdependence Levels and Coordination Structures

Nonetheless, the impact of new technology on task interdependence and coordination—a key focus of early contingency research—has been neglected in the recent literature. The best specification of this relationship is found in classical sources. Thompson (1967, pp. 54-56) developed a hierarchical scale for operationalizing interdependence and its relationship to authority structures. Interdependence refers to "the extent to which personnel are dependent upon one another to perform their individual jobs" (Van de Ven et al., 1976, p. 324).

At the lowest level of the scale is pooled interdependence, in which task performances are segmented from one another. The next levels are sequential interdependence, in which the output of a given unit becomes the input of another's work process, and reciprocal interdependence, in which outputs and inputs are shared by coordinating workers. Van de Ven et al. (1976, p. 323) add team work flow as the highest level of interdependence. In team work flow, all components of the task are mutually performed by each team member (Van de Ven, 1977, pp. 239-240).

Each level of interdependence demands a different coordination structure. In pooled and sequential interdependence, workers do not interact with one another while performing tasks. Because of this, coordination and control can be centralized. Standardized programming is sufficient to coordinate work flow with pooled interdependence; standardized programming with a scheduling plan is sufficient with sequential interdependence. With reciprocal interdependence, feedback flows among workers, and mutual adjustments must take place when they perform tasks. With team-flow interdependence, worker interactions intensify during the task. Such interaction adds levels of complexity and uncertainty. Because of this, these latter interdependence levels require a coordination structure that is increasingly decentralized (i.e., one that passes decision making to the task level) and unstandardized (i.e., one that allows for flexible responses) (Van de Ven et al., 1976, p. 325). Such a structure allows the work unit to make adjustments quickly during task performances.

Although this conceptualization has proved useful, more fine-grained distinctions are needed to explain variation within newly reorganized work units, many of which are experiencing reciprocal or team-flow interdependencies as a result of either new technology or related transformations. This chapter suggests that two structures are technically efficient under different sets of conditions for managing reciprocal and team-flow interdependencies within decentralized work units. The first employs unilateral decision making by those in the dominant work role. This structure does not require situationally specific and dedicated groups.

The case study suggests that such a coordination structure is effective when (1) critical tasks within the coordinating team are segmented, (2) the tasks performed by subordinates are relatively simple, and (3) task coordination occurs in a natural, face-to-face interaction context. These conditions allow the dominant actor in the team to control the actions of his of her subordinates directly and effectively through simple commands. This structure is compatible to those anticipated in neo-Fordist arguments and is referred to here as *neo-Fordist.* If adopted on a large scale, such a structure may mark a reversion from bureaucratic to simple, personal control (see Edwards, 1979).

The second structure requires the development of mature groups. Here, partners synchronize the speech and nonverbal cues necessary for performing tasks effectively to one another over time so that such tasks can be performed consensually without much explicit direction or command. Partners process information quickly and develop idiosyncratic action repertoires that allow them to react instantly as a team to contingencies. Such interaction repertoires are emergent and relationally specific. They develop only with repeated experience in stable, dedicated groups. Levels of in-group familiarity are very high, as are levels of trust in each team member's competencies (see Gabarro, 1990, pp. 82-87; on familiarity, see Goodman & Shah, 1992; on trust, see Lorenz, 1993). When such groups break up or are reformulated, vital collectively generated skills die and must be re-created. This type of structure is similar to that anticipated in the synergistic team conceptualization lauded in some post-Fordist arguments and is referred to here as *post-Fordist.*

As will be suggested in the case analysis below, a coordination structure involving this type of mature team is required when two conditions are present conjointly. The first occurs when the critical tasks being coordinated are performed on the same work object on a moment-by-moment basis. This tightens the couplings of the interactions occurring in time and increases complexity. Mature cohesive groups, working under these conditions, can react to contingencies more effectively than work units composed of a dominant actor coordinating the actions of relative strangers through unilateral control. In some work contexts, the speed facilitated by this type of well-developed team is vital.

The second condition occurs when tasks are coordinated collectively through a surreal or virtual context (i.e., through an exclusively symbolic medium, like a computer monitor or video screen) that is divorced from the spatial and/or tactile sensory feedback that facilitates understanding and effective action in face-to-face settings (on such environments, see Barley & Orr, 1997b, p. 10; Zuboff, 1988). To compensate for communication restrictions in such environments, workers in tightly coupled and interactively complex settings must develop and then routinize patterns of collective action through idiosyncratic experience together so that such actions can be performed as a conditioned reflex. Routinization spares workers from having to rely on detailed verbal commands for communicating their intentions and for coordinating actions. Relying on such formal commands can be quite cumbersome when interrelating in virtual environments and can slow down and confuse collective performances in work systems with little slack.

METHODOLOGY

Interview Design

The perspective guiding this study holds that only those who do the work are in a position to know how new technology affects task organization. Given this assumption, the appropriate method for eliciting workplace information is a grounded theoretical approach that primarily employs qualitative interviewing (Glaser & Strauss, 1967; see also Zetka & Walsh, 1994). This type of interviewing takes the form of a flexible, guided conversation that allows informants to bring up information relevant to the topic that cannot be anticipated a priori. It elicits from informants detailed accounts of their personal experiences (see Weiss, 1994).[1]

Interviews of this sort were conducted with 37 physicians using video or laser procedures in six communities from upstate New York. From January to October 1994, 22 informants were interviewed; from March to August 1994, 15 were interviewed. The interviews typically lasted from 40 to 60 minutes and focused on comparisons of the skills demanded in conventional and video procedures. Direct observations, used primarily to visualize what was being discussed and to develop probing skills, were made of two procedures.

A methodological problem that can plague such a study is the validity of retrospective accounts. For a number of reasons, I do not feel that this threat is severe. First, the video technology was introduced during 1990 and 1991, and its impact was dramatic. My informants had given considerable thought to the issues, and their accounts were quite rich. Second, unlike the case with skill-displacing technology, video surgeons continued to perform conventional, open-incision surgeries as well. Their understanding of both technologies and their critical differences were being constantly refreshed and tested in practice. Third, all but one informant[2] using advanced video procedures performed in both primary and assistant surgeon positions. As such, these informants knew firsthand the task demands of each position.[3]

Sampling Design

The adequacy of the sample must be assessed in terms of the theoretical purposes for which it is used. Theoretical sampling, as defined by Glazer and Strauss (1967, chap. 3), was employed in selecting informants. Informants were sought who had direct experience with minimally invasive surgical technology. In reviewing the early transcripts (approximately $n = 5$), a decision was made to focus primarily on the video component of the technology rather than the laser because the video camera and television monitor were reported to have had the greatest impact on work skills and interactions. After the first wave of interviewing ($n = 22$), all information was coded and analyzed. This crystallized data patterns, underscored where the study was thin empirically, and led to refined approaches to collect additional information. Informants for the second wave of interviewing ($n = 15$) were selected both to minimize the differences thought to be most relevant to the study (e.g., advanced video laparoscopists were sought who worked in hospitals with a partner) and to maximize differences thought to be less relevant (e.g., informants were sought from the specialties of general surgery, gynecology, and urology in communities outside the influence of a local medical center).

The informants interviewed were primarily those who listed a new procedure in the classified pages of their local phone book.[4] The response rate from the potential informants selected was 49%. The new technology generated negative media reports ("Surgical Injuries," 1992; "When Patient's Life Is Price of Learning," 1992). Those suspicious of the motives for a study coming after such reports, or those experiencing catastrophes like those reported, would likely refuse the interview request. No informant mentioned experiencing such a catastrophic case. Informants were aware of the technology's potential hazards, however, and their work routines were structured to avoid them.

The informant sample is skewed by medical specialty. Those from specialties doing advanced video surgeries are overrepresented. The sample includes 16 gynecologists, 12 surgeons (10 general surgeons and 2 specialty surgeons), 6 urologists, 2 gastroenterologists, and 1 dermatologist. The sample is diverse demographically, although none of these variations had systematic effects on informants' accounts of the coordination demands in question. A range of experiences is also represented. Twenty-nine informants had experience with video laparoscopy and open surgery, and their accounts are primarily used in drawing the findings reported here. However, information from the 8 informants not using laparoscopic techniques was vital for comparing and contrasting the work demands of the technology's components (e.g., the video monitor versus the energy source used) and for distinguishing each component's specific effects.[5]

Informants are listed in Table 3.1 by respondent number in the order interviewed. The respondent number is used to identify each quotation below. However, these quotations illustrate general patterns and were selected from several text units. Information from informants that might challenge the pattern reported is addressed in footnotes.

TASK COORDINATION IN CONVENTIONAL SURGERY

The coordination of retraction and dissection in conventional surgery involves team-flow interdependencies, as both the primary and assistant surgeons are working close together and mutually adjusting their actions on a moment-by-moment basis.[6] These interdependencies are determined by the tight timing of the actions performed. However, the anatomical structures upon which each surgeon works are separate, and this allows for segmentation. Typically, the primary surgeon alone manipulates the structure being dissected; the assistant secures the primary's work space by holding back adjacent structures. As stated by a general surgeon,

> The assistant is sort of holding . . . structures not being operated on out of the way—the bowels, the stomach. So he or she is not really involved in the procedure per se. He or she is just kind of keeping an open field. You [the primary surgeon] are the one controlling the whole operative field. (31)

The assistant's function is not particularly complex.[7] It consists of placing one's grasping instruments in the open wound space and holding back structures on cue or command. As stated by a general surgeon,

> The assistant has really a smaller role in an open procedure. I can take someone who has no surgical training and get him to assist me. Just say, "O.K. Put your hand here and pull. Hold this retractor here." I don't think that the assistant needs to be as knowledgeable with the technique as in the laparoscopic procedure. (32)

Deciding what to hold back and when to do it are the basic decisions made and communicated. The low level of task complexity involved allows the retraction task of the assistant to be coordinated quickly with the dissection task of the primary surgeon with simple commands (see Katz, 1981, p. 343), thereby allowing the primary surgeon to dominate the coordination process in a unilateral manner (see Coser, 1958; Freidson, 1970, pp. 128-130; Katz, 1981, 1985). Because actions unfold under immediate view, primaries have spatial control over what their assistants do. They can compensate for their assistants' shortcomings by manually directing them. As stated by a general surgeon,

> When you are directing somebody to do something [in an open procedure], you can point: "Do this. Do that." And you have a little bit of control. You can always stick your hand in there and you can sort of move them. (14)

Thus, although the task performances of retracting and dissecting in conventional surgery involve reciprocal and team-flow interdependencies, task segmentation, coupled with a low level of task complexity in the assistant's function, lends itself to a particular type of coordination. Flexibility is achieved through unilat-

TABLE 3.1 Informant Profiles

Interview Number	*Informant Specialty*	*Hospital Type*[a]	*Practice Location*[b]	*Years in Practice*[c]	*Resident Training*
Video laparoscopy informants					
3	Gynecology	Teaching	Metro	2.0	Local
4	Gynecology	Teaching	Metro	15.5	Local
5	Gynecology	Teaching	Metro	17.0	Local
6	General surgery	Teaching	Metro	23.0	Local
7	Gynecology	Teaching	Metro	1.0	Local
8	Gynecology	Teaching	Metro	6.0	Local
9	Gynecology	Community	Metro	22.0	Outside
11	Gynecology	Community	Metro	18.0	Outside
12	Surgical specialty	Teaching	Metro	4.0	Local
14	General surgery	Teaching	Metro	3.0	Local
15	General surgery	Teaching	Metro	35.0	Local
16	Gynecology	Community	City	36.0	Outside
17	General surgery	Community	City	20.0	Local
18	Urologist	Teaching	Metro	6.0	Local
19	Gynecology	Community	City	35.0	Outside
22	Gynecology	Teaching	Metro	0.5	Local
23	Gynecology	Community	Outer	3.5	Local
25	Gynecology	Community	Outer	4.0	Local
26	General surgery	Community	Outer	27.0	Local
28	General surgery	Community	Outer	23.0	Outside
29	Gynecology	Community	Outer	26.0	Outside
30	General surgery	Community	Outer	23.0	Local
31	General surgery	Community	Outer	4.0	Outside
32	General surgery	Community	Outer	9.0	Local
33	Gynecology	Community	City	21.0	Outside
34	Gynecology	Community	Outer	25.0	Outside
35	Urologist	Community	Outer	16.0	Outside
36	Gynecology	Community	Outer	26.0	Outside
37	General surgery	Community	Outer	35.0	Local
Video endoscopy informants					
10	Gastroenterology	Community	City	12.0	Outside
13	Gastroenterology	Community	City	19.0	Outside
20	Urologist	Community	Metro	9.0	Outside
21	Urologist	Community	City	10.0	Outside
24	Urologist	Teaching	Metro	5.0	Local
27	Urologist	Community	City	12.0	Outside
Laser surgery informants					
1	Surgical specialty	Community	Metro	1.5	Outside
2	Surgical specialty	Teaching	Metro	13.0	Local

a. The teaching hospitals include hospitals with a residency program or affiliation.
b. "Metro" is used to designate that an informant's primary hospital affiliation is in the largest city in the SMSA studied. "City" is used to designate that an informant's primary hospital affiliation is in a smaller city bordering the largest city in the SMSA. "Outer" is used to designate that an informant's primary hospital affiliation is in a small city in a different county over 30 miles from the largest city in the SMSA.
c. "Years in Practice" does not include the residency period, which typically involves 4 to 5 years, or the years involved in earning specialty or subspecialty fellowships (usually an additional 1 to 2 years).

eral decision making by the primary surgeon and through the on-the-spot subordination of the assistant to the primary's commands.

TASK COORDINATION IN VIDEO SURGERY

By the mid-1980s, it became technically feasible for surgeons to insert cameras through a small incision and project images of the inner abdomen onto television screens. Working from these images, surgeons could then perform complex operations without major incisions by manipulating long instruments through trocar ports inserted through small puncture wounds in the abdomen. This change significantly affected task coordination. Whereas in open surgery assistants hold back adjacent structures and provide work space while the primary surgeon unilaterally manipulates and dissects the target structure, in video surgery the task of manipulating the target structure while it is being dissected is a collective action, involving a division of labor and much closer effort coordination.[8] Here, the primary works the operating instrument—that is, the laser, electrocautery wand, or scissors—through one port. The assistant, controlling graspers through two auxiliary ports, manipulates the targeted structure, coordinating his or her actions with the directing surgeon dissecting the structure.

Take, for example, the critical task of identifying, clamping, and dissecting the cystic duct in a laparoscopic gallbladder removal. The cystic duct transports wastes from the gallbladder to the point at which the cystic and common bile ducts join together. In an open procedure, the primary alone identifies, manipulates, clamps, and dissects this structure. In the laparoscopic procedure, the assistant exposes the cystic duct and allows the surgeon to distinguish it from the common bile duct by pulling on the gallbladder at its base with grasping instruments and stretching the point on the "Y" where the cystic and common bile ducts converge. Once adequately exposed, the primary clamps and then dissects the duct with a blade tool in concert with the assistant moving the gallbladder. As stated by a general surgeon (when showing pictures of the procedure),

> The more closed that Y is, the more risk you have in getting the wrong structure. For safety's sake, the best thing you can do is stretch that and open up that Y as much as possible. . . . [The assistant] sort of uses the abdominal wall as a fulcrum. . . . He takes [his grasper] against the abdominal wall and pushes it to open up that Y, and then sort of pushes the gallbladder up towards the head of the patient. He is stretching it that way, and I am stretching it this way [while dissecting].

Here, the type of complex coordination taking place between the surgeon's eyes and hands in the open case must be produced as a collective, communicative act. Four hands must be coordinated in tight sequence. Each actor must transmit information to the other and react to it instantly.

This coordination demand makes the performance and skill of the assistant more vital to the video operation's success. As stated by a urological surgeon,

> I think that probably in laparoscopy . . . the role of the assistant is more important than any other procedure. You can't really do it without somebody else doing it with you. (35)

Unlike in open procedures, primary surgeons cannot compensate well for the shortcomings of their assistants. Primary surgeons cannot see their assistants' hand motions because they take place above the closed abdomen, outside the view projected to the video screen. Primaries cannot reach over the table and take control over their assistants' tool as in conventional surgery. An ob/gyn surgeon stated,

> With laparoscopic surgery you are limited with space and you cannot tell somebody to hold this, because it is coordination and you are looking at TV. And if the guy doesn't know to move left or

right, looking at the TV, you can't teach them instantly. That's experience. It is a reflex. (5)

Some informants reported difficulty in directing residents in teaching hospitals because of spatial limitations inherent in the video laparoscopic technology. A general surgeon stated,

> You have to always be turning around in front of the TV screen. The TV screen is behind you, and the person on the other side of the table looks up at the screen over your shoulder. So, I've got to turn around and point to the screen and show him to do this and do that. I think [working with residents] puts a little more stress on the surgeon than in the open because you can't exactly show them what to do. (14)

An ob/gyn surgeon also stated,

> For this particular laparoscopic surgery to go really well you need a good assistant, or somebody who is already working with you. . . . And I think that that is a real problem. . . . It's a team. That's the thing. You start getting the real process in an institution where they just do that [create dedicated teams] and there are no residents. (5)

Thus, as in conventional surgery, the performance of the primary and assistant surgeons' tasks during dissection involves reciprocal and team-flow interdependencies. The video modality greatly intensifies such interdependencies, however. First, unlike the case of open surgery, the primary and assistant share an identical work object. Each manipulates the same structure in the same moment. There is no segmentation. Second, the time spans within which the primary and assistant mutually adjust their actions are shortened. In conventional surgery, the assistant acts to move and hold back nonessential structures as the surgeon dissects. While the surgeon manipulates the target structure, the assistant simply holds others out of the way. In video surgery, the assistant makes many more intricate adjustments during the same time span because he or she is responsible for pulling and turning the target structure as the surgeon dissects. Third, in video surgery as in open surgery, speed is an important and vital element to success. Seconds gained or lost during a procedure can seriously affect the outcome achieved. Reducing complexity by stretching out greatly the time it takes to perform the operation is simply not a serious option.

The type of work system created by the video technology shares many of the characteristics that Perrow (1984; 1986, chap. 4) associates with "normal accidents" in larger complex organizations—interactive complexity, interdependence, and the tight coupling of performances. And, as Perrow's model predicts, catastrophes did occur in the early stages of the video technology's diffusion ("Surgical Injuries," 1992; "When Patient's Life Is Price of Learning," 1992). Fortunately, such catastrophes have become uncommon. These catastrophes are routinely avoided with the use of a different type of coordination structure.

To use the new technology effectively, informants suggested that primary and assistant surgeons develop working relationships within which effective patterns of coordination and communication develop. The typical approach involves working with a dedicated partner, one with whom surgeons have worked repeatedly and have built up considerable trust and tacit understanding.[9] Interactions, even of a very complex nature, become routinized. Communication becomes attenuated and largely nonverbal to facilitate quickness. As expressed by a general surgeon,

> [My partner] has been assisting me on almost every case that I have done. So, it's just like a dancing partner. You start to understand each other immediately with a little touch or something. . . . He knows exactly what I am talking about, sometimes without going in detail. (6)

The comfortable interactive rhythms emerging from such "dancing partner" relationships are essential for reacting effectively to the many contingencies jointly managed in the surreal video environment. As stated by an ob/gyn surgeon,

> Eventually there becomes a silent communication among the partners. If you scrub together all the time, you know what the person is going to do next, and you can do things to make that task easier for the person. . . . You need someone [like that], because [then] as soon as you start to run into a little bit of a problem, you can nip it in the bud and it remains a small problem. If you can't nip it in the bud—an inexperienced person would not allow you to do that—all of a sudden you wind up with a bigger problem, a complication where you might have to open the belly. (23)

In experienced teams, the authority relationship between the primary and assistant changes. Unlike in open procedures, assistants have the same view of structures on the screen as the primary. Consequently, they can be called upon to interpret difficult anatomy and to reassure judgments. This is done when levels of trust are quite high. As expressed by a general surgeon,

> We work together a lot and we go back and forth. If my assistant doesn't think that I am in the right plane, or if he doesn't think that I got the right structure, I don't cut it or clip it until we come to an agreement. (37)

An ob/gyn surgeon stated,

> The extra pair of eyes, the extra brain that can tell you if you are too deep or too shallow, position—you have another fellow on the other side of the table who can get a better angle at it than you do. Umh. In my own personal experience . . . it is always good to have another fellow who knows what the procedure is—is trained as well as you, if not better. You stay out of trouble and you want that. . . . So, it is a give-and-take relationship that is very beneficial. (36)

Thus, to manage the coordination demands of advanced video procedures, surgeons typically attach themselves to competent partners and develop the high level of trust that comes only with repeated, idiosyncratic experience. These experienced dyads routinize complex interactions so that surgeons can swing their coordinated efforts quickly into motion in response to the screen images they interpret. Such relationships allow surgeons to coordinate their actions collectively without relying on much conscious, verbal direction. They enable surgeons to focus on what to do in surgery rather than on how to do it with an unfamiliar partner or on how to communicate prescriptions. Whereas the ability to both emit and take cues effectively can be taken for granted when coordinating activities in the face-to-face setting in conventional surgery (a setting managed effectively with unilateral control), shifting to the screen image appears to make such basic communicative competence problematic in work units that are complex and tightly coupled in time. Forming dedicated and experienced teams frees surgeons from having to build such basic communicative competence anew with different partners.

This team-based response is dictated, for the most part, by the technical demands of the technology; specifically, its increased complexity, its demand for moment-by-moment coordination, and the shift from a natural face-to-face context to a two-dimensional screen environment. The latter environment is surreal, accessed from a distance, and, for the most part, detached from easily interpretable spatial and tactile input.

NEO-FORDIST VS. POST-FORDIST TASK-COORDINATING STRUCTURES

Drawing from the case study, I hypothesize that specific technological variables influence generally whether a given organization adopts either a post-Fordist or a neo-Fordist coordination structure. These variables have a long track record in contingency theory. They include the extent to which interconnected task performances are tightly coupled in time, the complexity of tasks being coordinated, and the type and complexity of the communicative competence required for mutually adjusting courses of action during tasks. Whereas classical contingency theory employs these variables to explain variation in complex organizations (see Perrow, 1986, chap. 4), this chapter employs them at a more micro level to explain variation within decentralized work units. The general pressures encouraging organizations to decentralize task units—that is, high levels of complexity and uncertainty—are not fine-grained enough to dictate specific workplace patterns. Such pressures signal the need to make decisions on the spot. However, specifically how such decisions are made and how efforts are coordinated in response can vary significantly. In the empirical analysis above, two very different structures were found to work efficiently under different conditions. I have labeled them neo-Fordist and post-Fordist. Here, I specify their technical determinants and discuss where they are likely to be found in the population.

The Technical Determinants of Neo-Fordist Coordination

The dominant response to the demand for decentralized task units may well take a unilateral form—a course consistent with neo-Fordist predictions. Here, teams manage complex contingencies with a single knowledgeable actor commanding performance in the work group. As in conventional surgery, this type of coordination can be effective when simple and complex interconnected tasks are segmented from one another and when subordinates are assigned the simpler tasks. Such conditions grant flexibility without forcing the development of costly new communicative competencies among coordinating teammates. Such conditions also allow teams to function without extraordinary levels of familiarity or trust. New personnel, as long as they have basic task skills and general interaction competencies, do not threaten the team's ability to function.

This may explain why corporations recently have promoted teamwork structures in the workplace while subjecting their workforces to severe labor market fluctuation and uncertainty. Capelli et al. (1997) view these strategies as contradictory. However, they may not be in neo-Fordist structures. Here, the only shop floor personnel that need to be stable over time to operate effectively are lead workers. As long as a given organization maintains a stable cadre of such workers, the rest of the workforce can be employed on a contingent basis. Although brutal, the lesson from abdominal surgery is that such practices may not sacrifice efficiency when the technical conditions specified above hold.

The team leader position used to coordinate work in Japanese auto transplants represents a nonsurgical example of this type of unilateral coordination structure. Those holding this position are empowered to make critical staffing and production decisions for the work team on the spot (see Florida & Kenney, 1991; Graham, 1995; Kenney & Florida, 1993; Shaiken, Lopez, & Mankita, 1997). In most cases, the tasks coordinated through such a position are segmented from one another with rather low levels of complexity. This technical foundation, I argue, enables such a structures to work well without developing new group-based coordination skills.

In intraoccupationally coordinated units, the actor with the higher occupational status, or those whose skills are most central to the production outcome sought, will likely take the lead position. In the case of the German auto body plant studied by Dankbaar (1988, pp. 169-172), for example, this position went to the line controller. In the case of the paper-processing plants studied by Vallas and Beck (1996), this position went to process engineers who were integrated into work teams with new technology. In the case of the photoduplicating firm studied by Smith (1994), the dominant position went to permanent over temporary employees.

A neo-Fordist coordination structure is likely to be prevalent when organizations, without adopting new information-mediating and skill-disruptive technologies, implement reorganization schemes in routinized task structures. A prime example is the implementation of just-in-time inventory systems in assembly processes (see Dawson & Webb, 1989; Turnbull, 1988). Although task variation and reciprocal coordination increase among workers, such developments do not make the task unit so complex that it cannot be coordinated with simple, unilateral control. Although true team-based coordination may have some advantages in such settings, such capacities are costly. The general role-taking and communicative skills that most workers possess will usually suffice.

The Technical Determinants of Post-Fordist Coordination

I hypothesize that post-Fordist task coordination structures are demanded only in work settings that (a) produce outputs collectively in delimited units of time and space in tightly coupled work units and (b) employ complex information-mediating technology in doing so. The second condition forces tightly coupled work units to abandon unilateral control. The use of such technologies shifts interactions from a face-to-face to a surreal or a virtual context, as represented in the case of surgery by the shift to the video screen. Effective coordination in this virtual context appears to require new collectively based interactive skills, at least when the task performed demands that workers use information from the surreal medium to guide collective action in the actual spatial medium where the work transformation is performed. General interaction scripts do not suffice here because subordinates must have a much fuller intuitive understanding of their lead actors' particularistic intentions, proclivities, and moves. Functioning requires the work team to think and move as one. This demands groups with collective capacities that cannot be reproduced individually.

Many manufacturing organizations have adopted new technologies that force workers to coordinate their activities from a symbolic or virtual medium. However, I suspect that the first technical condition making post-Fordist structures necessary rarely holds for them because the tasks directed by such technology are not usually tightly coupled to one another. Automated machining processes, for instance, often can be monitored individually in segmented units (see Faunce, 1958a, 1958b). Ozaki (1992, p. 25), however, does link advanced microelectronic machining technology, such as flexible manufacturing systems, to the type of team coordination that I have labeled post-Fordist. The extent to which such technology demands true group coordination is still an open question. More fine-grained analysis of what is done in the actual tasks performed in such contexts is needed. Most studies of such settings have not focused explicitly on task coordination patterns.

I suspect that most technical service work contexts also lack the first technological condition that makes a post-Fordist coordination structure necessary. Much technical service work involving a staff, maintenance, or repair function is uncoupled from the core tasks of organizations. This uncoupling frees technicians from the moment-by-moment constraints experienced by abdominal surgeons. When work teams are needed in this type of setting, they typically have adequate resources at hand (i.e., time) to work out their coordination problems before any outcomes are affected. If nothing else, they can stop for lengthy "bull sessions" until they stumble on the level of understanding and agreement required to accomplish the task. As such, dedicated, long-tenured teams are not technically necessary.

Hence, post-Fordist coordination structures may be technically necessary for only those production workers experiencing what Barley and Orr (1997a) refer to as "technization"—those manipulating things in delimited units of time and space with complex information-mediating technologies. As such, true post-Fordist coordination structures may have the potential to reach only a minority of the technical labor force and a very small fragment of the total labor force. For the rest of the workforce experiencing workplace decentralization, little more than unilateral, personal control may be necessary to coordinate work flow.

Finally, the technological determinism suggested in these preliminary hypotheses is soft. The hypotheses assume that technically efficient structures will be chosen over alternatives. This assumption has been challenged (see Noble, 1984). Institutional, class, and political forces, some of which may be at times more pressing than those emanating from the workplace, also affect how technological outcomes are managed (see Zetka, 1991). However, the cost of a workplace failure may have a causal influence on determining which set of forces predominates. When this failure is very high to catastrophic, as it is in surgery, I argue that the workplace demands specified here will likely predominate (on such high-reliability organization, see Roberts, 1993).

CONCLUSION

To conclude, this chapter's contribution to the new work organization debate is twofold. First, it shifts the focus of the debate from individual to team-based coordination skills and defines the demand for a qualitatively different type of task coordination as marking the significant break with past practice that should be labeled post-Fordist. Because the team is defined as a critical component of new work organizations, we should develop distinctive team-level conceptualizations for categorizing organizations and explaining their differences. This chapter makes a contribution to this end by extending contingency arguments regarding interdependence and coordination to decentralized work units. Second, this chapter links distinct coordination structures to distinct sets of technological conditions, arguing that both neo-Fordist and post-Fordist coordination structures have technological foundations similar to those found in surgical work. I contend that the case of abdominal surgery is useful as a critical case for developing such general theoretical linkages because the professional dominance that surgeons enjoy over their operating rooms effectively holds the effects of external forces constant. Nonetheless, surgical work is atypical, and the generalizations drawn are speculative. Much conceptual and empirical work is needed to develop a fuller understanding of contemporary workplace transformations and their outcomes.

NOTES

1. There is disagreement in qualitative sociology regarding the proper method for generating theory. Some argue primarily for direct participant observation in the setting, assuming that folks operating there lack the cognitive and communication skills required to account sufficiently for what is going on (e.g., see Barley, 1986, p. 83). Although this position is appropriate for some topics (i.e., those that do not require the actor's conscious reflection and accounting, such as the nuanced use of conversational strategies), this approach has shortcomings. In addition to real spatial and temporal restrictions on what can be observed, the definitional frame employed in participant observation is typically that of a neophyte ("new hire") to the work setting. Although this frame is as important as any other, the frame of the "old timer" is often the most vital one for understanding how a workplace change affects existing practices, skills, and interactions. Intensive, empathetic interviewing is the only practical way of achieving access to this perspective.

2. This informant, although trained in another specialty, routinely assisted general surgeons conducting gallbladder procedures. He did not perform as the primary surgeon for this procedure.

3. The surgeon in charge of the case takes responsibility for it and performs the primary surgeon's role in the operating room. In community hospitals, other surgeons serve as assistants. Most commonly, partners reciprocate for one another. This gives the typical surgeon multiple experiences in both primary and assistant roles. In teaching hospitals, attending surgeons are nominally in charge of the cases but routinely pass them to advanced residents. When this is done, the attending often performs the assisting role. Some community hospitals hire permanent assistants.

4. I began making lists of surgeons from the 1993 and 1994 phone books. Surgeons who had reputations for performing video surgeries tended to advertise or list the specific procedure they performed in the Physicians and Surgeons sections of the classified pages in 1993 and 1994. Fewer surgeons did this in subsequent years. This sampling procedure, although convenient, leaves out those surgeons choosing not to advertise, especially those holding staff positions and not seeking to expand their caseloads. With the increasing competition for surgical markets, surgeons who refuse to advertise are becoming rare. Surgeons identified by informants as the major laparoscopists in their communities listed their procedures in the phone books.

5. Six informants had little to no experience with video laparoscopy but considerable experience with video endoscopy, a sister technology involving an endoscope inserted into a natural orifice, television monitors, and instruments snaked through the scope. Three informants had no experience in open abdominal surgery (2 gastroenterologists [who were endoscopists] and the dermatologist), and 2 informants only had experience with laser instruments in a freehand modality (the dermatologist and a specialty surgeon).

6. This chapter focuses exclusively on the relationship between the primary and first assistant. This is the most critical relationship in abdominal surgery. The surgical team in open surgery also includes a scrub nurse, a circulating nurse, and other assistants, depending on the operation. In video surgery, a second assistant or scrub nurse may operate the video camera. Although this is an important job, it is not as critical to the success of the operation as that of the first assistant.

7. One surgeon's response did not concur with the general pattern. This informant stated that the assistant's job was actually more important for conventional procedures than for video laparoscopic ones. This informant's point of reference was the nature of the open gallbladder procedures since the the advent of video laparoscopy. Experience in open procedures had changed significantly with the new technology's diffusion. The gallbladder cases done openly now are the very complicated ones that cannot be done safely with the video procedure—ones with high risks of bleeding, difficult anatomy, and so on. This informant also claimed to favor a retraction technique in doing video laparoscopy that would minimize dependence on group-based coordination skills (see Note 9).

8. The point of reference here are those complex video cases that require the removal of a major structure from the abdomen, such as the gallbladder, uterus, or kidney. More minor procedures, such as ligating a fallopian tube, or taking a specimen, do not require the same level of coordination as do the complicated procedures. These procedures were performed with the surgeon looking directly through the lens of the scope long before the introduction of the video equipment.

9. Three informants mentioned an alternative technique that allowed the primary to minimize the procedure's dependence on team-based skills. Two felt that, with this technique, they could perform the procedure alone. Here, the surgeon uses two hands in the dissection/retraction task: one hand to retract by holding and pulling the structure of interest with a grasping instrument protruding through one port; the other to dissect with a cutting instrument protruding through another part. The advantage is that both critical tasks—retraction and dissection—stay mostly under the primary surgeon's unilateral control. The assistant simply holds the organ through one port in a stationary position. This two-handed approach is not dominant, however, because it requires considerable—perhaps extraordinary—individual dexterity in using both hands. One informant claimed that the two-handed approach was much too awkward to be practical, and most informants made no reference to it. It is interesting that none of the three talking up the alternative approach was actually using it routinely at the time of the interviews. One suggested that the two-handed approach was used primarily in rural communities where help was difficult to find.

REFERENCES

Adler, P. S. (Ed.). (1992). *Technology and the future of work.* New York: Oxford University Press.

Adler, P. S., & Borys, B. (1989). Automation and skill. *Politics and Society, 17,* 377-402.

Appelbaum, E., & Batt, R. (1994). *The new American workplace.* Ithaca, NY: ILR Press.

Barley, S. R. (1986). Technology as an occasion for structuring. *Administrative Science Quarterly, 31,* 78-108.

Barley, S. R. (1990). The alignment of technology and structure through roles and networks. *Administrative Science Quarterly, 35,* 61-103.

Barley, S. R., & Orr, J. E. (Eds.). (1997a). *Between craft and science.* Ithaca, NY: Cornell University Press.

Barley, S. R., & Orr, J. E. (1997b). Introduction: The neglected workforce. In S. R. Barley & J. E. Orr (Eds.), *Between craft and science* (pp. 1-9). Ithaca, NY: Cornell University Press.

Blauner, R. (1964). *Alienation and freedom.* Chicago: University of Chicago Press.

Buchanan, D. A., & Boddy, D. (1983). *Organizations in the computer age.* Aldershot, UK: Gower.

Burawoy, M. (1985). *The politics of production.* London: Verso.

Capelli, P., Bassi, L., Katz, H., Knoke, D., Osterman, P., & Useem, M. (1997). *Change at work.* New York: Oxford University Press.

Clark, J., McLoughlin, I., Rose, H., & King, R. (1988). *The process of technological change.* Cambridge, UK: Cambridge University Press.

Coser, R. L. (1958). Authority and decision-making in a hospital. *American Sociological Review, 23,* 56-63.

Dankbaar, B. (1988). Teamwork in the West-German car industry and the quality of work. In W. Buitelaar (Ed.), *Technology and work* (pp. 165-181). Aldershot, UK: Avebury.

Dawson, P., & Webb, J. (1989). New production arrangements. *Work, Employment & Society, 3,* 221-238.

Dohse, K., Jürgens, U., & Malsch, T. (1985). From "Fordism" to "Toyotism"? *Politics and Society, 14,* 115-146.

Edwards, R. (1979). *Contested terrain.* New York: Basic Books.

Fadem, J. A. (1984). Automation and work design in the U.S. In M. Warner (Ed.), *Microprocessors, manpower and society.* Aldershot, UK: Gower.

Fantasia, R., Clawson, D., & Graham, G. (1988). A critical view of worker participation in American industry. *Work and Occupations, 15,* 468-488.

Faunce, W. A. (1958a). Automation and the automobile worker. *Social Problems, 6,* 68-78.

Faunce, W. A. (1958b). Automation in the automobile industry. *American Sociological Review, 23,* 401-407.

Florida, R., & Kenney, M. (1991). Transplanted organizations. *American Sociological Review, 56,* 381-398.

Freidson, E. (1970). *Profession of medicine.* New York: Dodd, Mead.

Gabarro, J. J. (1990). The development of working relationships. In J. Galegher, R. E. Kraut, & C. Egido (Eds.), *Intellectual teamwork* (pp. 79-110). Hillsdale, NJ: Lawrence Erlbaum.

Galegher, J., & Kraut, R. E. (1990). Technology for intellectual teamwork. In J. Galegher, R. E. Kraut, & C. Egido (Eds.), *Intellectual teamwork* (pp. 1-20). Hillsdale, NJ: Lawrence Erlbaum.

Geary, J. F. (1993). New forms of work organization and employee involvement in two case study sites. *Economic and Industrial Democracy, 14,* 511-534.

Glaser, B. G., & Strauss, A. L. (1967). *The discovery of grounded theory.* New York: Aldine.

Goodman, P. S., & Shah, S. (1992). Familiarity and work group outcomes. In S. Worchel, W. Wood, & J. A. Simpson (Eds.), *Group process and productivity* (pp. 276-298). Newbury Park, CA: Sage.

Graham, L. (1995). *On the line at Subaru-Isuzu.* Ithaca, NY: Cornell University Press.

Gutek, B. A. (1990). Work group structure and information technology. In J. Galegher, R. E. Kraut, & C. Egido (Eds.), *Intellectual teamwork* (pp. 63-78). Hillsdale, NJ: Lawrence Erlbaum.

Heydebrand, W. V. (1989). New organizational forms. *Work and Occupations, 16,* 323-357.

Hodson, R. (1995). The worker as active subject. In D. B. Bills (Ed.), *The new modern times* (pp. 253-280). Albany: State University of New York Press.

Hodson, R. (1996). Dignity in the workplace under participative management. *American Sociological Review, 61,* 719-738.

Jürgens, U., Malsch, T., & Dohse, K. (1993). *Breaking from Taylorism.* London: Cambridge University Press.

Katz, P. (1981). Ritual in the operating room. *Ethnology, 20,* 335-350.

Katz, P. (1985). How surgeons make decisions. In R. A. Hahn & A. D. Gaines (Eds.), *Physicians of Western medicine* (pp. 155-175). Hingham, MA: Kluwer Academic.

Kelley, M. R. (1986). Programmable automation and the skill question. *Human Systems Management, 6,* 223-241.

Kelley, M. R. (1990). New process technology, job design, and work organization. *American Sociological Review, 55,* 191-208.

Kenney, M., & Florida, R. (1993). *Beyond mass production.* New York: Oxford University Press.

Leidner, R. (1993). *Fast food; fast talk.* Berkeley: University of California Press.

Lorenz, E. H. (1993). Flexible production systems and the social construction of trust. *Politics and Society, 21,* 307-324.

McLoughlin, I., & Clark, J. (1988). *Technological change at work.* Milton Keynes, UK: Open University Press.

Noble, D. (1984). *Forces of production.* New York: Knopf.

Orr, J. E. (1996). *Talking about machines.* Ithaca, NY: Cornell University Press.

Ozaki, M. (1992). Technological change and labour relations. In M. Ozaki et al. (Eds.), *Technological change and labour relations* (pp. 1-46). Geneva: International Labour Office.

Perrow, C. (1967). A framework for the comparative analysis of organizations. *American Sociological Review, 32,* 194-208.

Perrow, C. (1984). *Normal accidents.* New York: Basic Books.

Perrow, C. (1986). *Complex organizations.* New York: McGraw-Hill.

Piore, M., & Sabel, C. (1984). *The second industrial divide.* New York: Basic Books.

Prechel, H. (1994). Economic crisis and the centralization of control over the managerial process. *American Sociological Review, 59,* 723-745.

Roberts, K. H. (1993). *New challenges to understanding organizations.* New York: Macmillan.

Shaiken, H., Herzenberg, S., & Kuhn, S. (1986). The work process under more flexible production. *Industrial Relations, 25,* 167-183.

Shaiken, H., Lopez, S., & Mankita, I. (1997). Two routes to team production. *Industrial Relations, 36,* 17-45.

Simpson, I. H. (1989). The sociology of work. *Social Forces, 67,* 563-581.

Smith, V. (1994). Institutionalizing flexibility in a service firm. *Work and Occupations, 21,* 284-307.

Smith, V. (1996). Employee involvement, involved employees. *Social Problems, 43,* 166-179.

Stinchcombe, A. L. (1990). *Information and organizations.* Berkeley: University of California Press.

Streeck, W. (1987). The uncertainties of management in the management of uncertainty. *Work, Employment & Society, 1,* 281-308.

Surgical injuries lead to new rule. (1992, June 14). *New York Times,* p. A1.

Taplin, I. M. (1995). Flexible production, rigid jobs. *Work and Occupations, 22,* 412-438.

Thomas, R. J. (1994). *What machines can't do.* Berkeley: University of California Press.

Thompson, J. D. (1967). *Organizations in action.* New York: McGraw-Hill.

Trist, E. L. (1981). The evolution of sociotechnical systems as a conceptual framework and as an action research program. In A. H. Van de Ven & W. F. Joyce (Eds.), *Perspectives on organization design and behavior* (pp. 19-76). New York: John Wiley.

Turnbull, P. J. (1988). The limits to "Japanisation"—Just-in-time, labour relations and the UK automotive industry. *New Technology, Work and Employment, 3,* 7-20.

Vallas, S. P. (1993). *Power in the workplace.* Albany: State University of New York Press.

Vallas, S. P., & Beck, J. P. (1996). The transformation of work revisited. *Social Problems, 43,* 339-361.

Van de Ven, A. H. (1977). A panel study on the effects of task uncertainty, interdependence, and size on unit decision making. *Organization and Administrative Sciences, 8,* 237-253.

Van de Ven, A. H., & Delbecq, A. L. (1974). A task contingent model of work unit structure. *Administrative Science Quarterly, 19,* 183-197.

Van de Ven, A. H., Delbecq, A. L., & Koenig, R., Jr. (1976). Determinants of coordination modes within organizations. *American Sociological Review, 41,* 322-338.

Walsh, J. P. (1991). The social context of technological change. *Sociological Quarterly, 32,* 447-468.

Walsh, J. P., & Bayema, T. (1996). Computer networks and scientific work. *Social Studies of Science, 26,* 663-703.

Walton, R. E. (1985). From control to commitment in the workplace. *Harvard Business Review, 63*(2), 76-84.

Weick, K. E., & Roberts, K. H. (1993). Collective mind in organizations. *Administrative Science Quarterly, 38,* 357-381.

Weiss, R. S. (1994). *Learning from strangers.* New York: Free Press.

When patient's life is price of learning new kind of surgery. (1992, June 23). *New York Times,* p. C3.

Womack, J. P., Jones, D. T., & Roos, D. (1991). *The machine that changed the world.* New York: HarperCollins.

Woodward, J. (1970). *Industrial organization.* Oxford, UK: Oxford University Press.

Zetka, J. R., Jr. (1991). Automated technologies, institutional environments, and skilled labor processes. *Sociological Quarterly, 32,* 557-574.

Zetka, J. R., Jr. (1992). Work organization and wildcat strikes in the U.S. automobile industry, 1946 to 1963. *American Sociological Review, 57,* 214-226.

Zetka, J. R., Jr. (1995). *Militancy, market dynamics, and workplace authority.* Albany: State University of New York Press.

Zetka, J. R., Jr., & Walsh, J. P. (1994). A qualitative protocol for studying technological change in the labor process. *Bulletin de Methodologie Sociologique, 45,* 37-73.

Zuboff, S. (1988). *In the age of the smart machine.* New York: Basic Books.

4

A Tale of Two Career Paths

The Process of Status Acquisition by a New Organizational Unit

ELIZABETH K. BRIODY
MARIETTA L. BABA
LINDSAY COOPER

Career path selection and planning have been central issues for individual employees and organizations. The stakes are high for both: The individual seeks more challenging work opportunities and their associated rewards, and the organization's effectiveness, morale, and productivity are likely to suffer if a good match is not found between employee characteristics and job requirements.

Career development matters become more complex during periods of organizational change. When company reorganizations and downsizings occur, turmoil tends to reverberate throughout the firm's operations, including its policies and procedures related to personnel management. Implementing personnel processes to ensure stability is critical to the firm's long-term outlook. However, in the course of restructuring, organizational members may find that their roles and statuses have undergone considerable change. Some may encounter upward job mobility, whereas others experience constraints in opportunities or a change which they interpret as significantly worse for their careers.

In this chapter, we explore organizational change using an anthropological approach. This approach consists of a focus on "native" perspectives in which we compare various employee groups and describe and explain our results and conclusions in a holistic manner. Through our inductive investigation, we hope to shed light on two aspects of organizational change that have not received much attention in the literature. First, we examine the changing structure of the firm as seen in the creation of a new organizational unit, the developing career structure associated with the new unit, and participant evaluations of that career structure. Second, we focus on the topic of organizational inequality by introducing the concept of organizational status. As such, we present a case study of how a new organizational unit acquired status over time, and the way in which this process influenced career paths. Interestingly, this case is an example of unplanned career and status consequences resulting from a largely involuntary corporate reorganization designed to accomplish tasks more efficiently and at a lower cost. This type of restructuring is frequently found in U.S. firms as they attempt to respond to global competitive pressures.

The topic of socioeconomic inequality, both in society at large and in organizational settings, has long interested social scientists. We review this literature briefly because status is associ-

From *Work and Occupations*, Vol. 22, No. 3, August 1995, pp. 301-327. Reprinted by permission.

ated with socioeconomic inequality. Two paradigms have been discussed at length in the literature—one focused on "individual" variables and the other on "structural" variables (Jencks, 1980; Rosenbaum, 1986; Rosenfeld, 1992; Sorensen, 1986). Whereas the former views individuals as the causal forces in charting their own career opportunities, the latter emphasizes a predetermined organizational structure that either fosters or constrains an individual's career mobility. Potential structural explanations, particularly those identified with internal labor markets,[1] have been directed at employment practices found in firms. Factors such as firm size, growth, vacancy chains, demography, managerial selection preferences, career ladders, technology, and unionization have been investigated with respect to employment practices (Baron, 1984; Gaertner, 1980; Kanter, 1977; Stewman & Konda, 1983).

Attempts have been made to integrate the individual and structural explanations. For example, Granovetter (1981) suggested that there are three main factors contributing to earned income: the characteristics of the job and the employer, the characteristics of the job holder, and processes that match both factors. Althauser and Kalleberg (1990) argued that mobility is a function of the skill and knowledge acquired by an employee. In Rosenbaum's (1986, 1990) "tournament model," the career selection system is viewed as a "series of implicit meritocratic competitions which progressively differentiate a cohort of individuals" (Rosenbaum, 1986, p. 154). The career system not only fills vacancies on an as-needed basis but also defines patterns for career advancement.

Structural theories, as well as frameworks that attempt to integrate both individual and structural explanations of inequality, may be critiqued from at least three standpoints. First, organizational structure is viewed as a given, as fixed in time. Such a static view does not lend itself to analyses of organizational change when organizations are redesigned, reorganized, or downsized (Keller, 1989; Tomasko, 1987, 1993). Second, structural conceptualizations do not address or emphasize how change is interpreted by organizational members, Thomas (1994) being one notable exception. Individual or group perceptions of the changing work environment are not viewed as relevant or important to understanding the context in which organizational restructuring occurs, or to outcomes of restructuring (Rosenbaum, 1989; White, 1970). Third, the unit of analysis is restricted to the individual. All focus is directed toward the effect of employment practices on individual employees rather than some larger collectivity that might be uniformly affected by company policies.

Recent work in internal labor market research appears to have taken a somewhat broader orientation toward differences in organizational forms and changes and their impact on career path issues. Kanter (1984) compared structural differences between the "classic functional-line ladder" career and the "high-tech" career. Rather than placing primary emphasis on the internal workings of the firm, some researchers have underscored the key role of the external environment in shaping organizational outcomes (Jacoby, 1985; Rosenfeld, 1992). Others have emphasized the examination of "process" as it applies to organizational change (Jacoby, 1985; Sorensen, 1986). Thomas (1994), in particular, argued that structure should be viewed as a "constructive activity" rather than a "static set of offices or rules" (p. 226).

We build on Thomas's (1994) work on process by analyzing the changing internal labor market as seen through employee[2] career paths in a particular General Motors (GM) sales and marketing division. In so doing, we attempt to move away from the overly static analyses of career mobility toward a more dynamic description and interpretation of organizational change. Our study describes the creation of a new organizational unit that set in motion a reexamination of the system of organizational ranking for sales-and-service units. As in many restructuring cases (Davenport, 1993; Hammer, 1990), this restructuring involved the introduction of a new technology—telemarketing techniques such as computers and telephones—for selected sales-and-service employees. Our research focuses attention on the evaluations made by these employees about their work and career paths.

Our research also is aligned with selected literature on the topic of status. Of course, much work has been conducted on the status of an individual, status attainment, and intergenerational mobility in which variables such as education and father's occupation are viewed as key status determinants (Blau & Duncan, 1967; Goldthorpe, 1980; Sewell & Hauser, 1975; Weber, 1946). Other literature has directed attention to the status of groups, namely ethnic and occupational groups (Feagin, 1978; Slocum, 1974; Trice, 1993; Van Maanen & Barley, 1984; Warner & Srole, 1945). Less well-developed is the literature on "organizational status" in which an organizational unit's ranking is a by-product of certain material, environmental, and perceptual conditions. A few exceptions come to mind: Talbert and Bose's (1977) study of department store clerks, referred to as an occupational group although status differences across store departments are later identified, and Thomas's (1994) description of the status of manufacturing and product engineers.

In this chapter, we define *organizational status* as the position or rank of one organization relative to another. Our definition assumes that organizations and their units constitute a status hierarchy (Stinchcombe, 1965) in which various objective and subjective criteria are used to rank groups relative to one another. This definition expands on one proposed by Linton (1936, p. 113) wherein a status is both "a position in a particular pattern" (e.g., based on gender, age, income, education) and "a collection of rights and duties."

Thus we propose to examine career path development through a focus on both organizational process and organizational status. Based on our case, we outline a four-step model in which a newly created organizational unit acquires status under conditions of organizational upheaval. We also assess the generalizability of this model to other organizational restructurings. As such, our research is aligned with an internal labor market emphasis, albeit in a changing external and internal environment, and directed at organizational status inequality as evident in career path structures. We believe that an emphasis on status considerations not only may provide insights into the outcomes of organizational redesign processes but also may enable better understanding of the organizational culture[3] of GM and American work organizations generally.

DATA AND METHODS

Our data collection efforts were targeted largely at employees of the newly created organizational unit known as the Telemarketing Assistance Group (TAG). In the TAG we conducted semistructured and structured interviews with 39 sales-and-service employees (55% of TAG employees). Between February and July 1988, we spent many hours observing their work environment and, on average, 45 to 60 minutes each in discussions with individual employees. Our discussions were focused on the history and culture of sales-and-service work, individual work histories, current job tasks and working conditions, and future career expectations. We were able to secure such divisional archival documents as newsletters, training materials, employee survey results, and mission statements, and to interview members of the personnel staff. Our findings were validated with information gathered during three presentations of results and recommendations to study participants.

Our TAG respondents were not selected randomly but, rather, through a network-based approach. Our initial introduction to the TAG was facilitated by a personnel staff manager who not only asked us to assess the TAG's culture but whose contacts served as a starting point for our sample; we then sought other TAG respondents on our own. Because our interest was focused on the change in sales-and-service work due to the reorganization, our TAG sample was purposely overrepresented by 33 sixth-level employees (85%)—referred to as district sales managers (DMs) and district service managers

TABLE 4.1 Sample Distribution, by Previous Employment and Phase

	Previous Employment			
Phase	*Former Zone*	*Former Non-Zone*	*Total*	*Percentage TAG Employees*
Phase I	16	4	20	28
Phase II	24	9	33	46
Totala	30	9	39	55

a. Note that many of those interviewed in Phase I were interviewed again in Phase II. All 39 employees were with the TAG in Phase II, representing 55% of the 71 employees at that time.

(DSMs)—compared with the proportion of these employees in the TAG population (68%). Sixth-level employees filled entry-level sales-and-service positions, responding to dealership matters; their day-to-day work was impacted most directly by the technological and organizational changes that took place in this unit. It was these employees who previously had the greatest face-to-face contact with dealerships and, following the reorganization, interacted with their dealerships via telemarketing technology. Other TAG employees in our sample included 5 higher ranking branch and area managers and 1 clerical support employee.

The analysis consisted of separating the data into two periods: Phase I (Winter 1988) and Phase II (Summer 1988). Table 4.1 shows the distribution of our sample by phase and previous employment. The variable—previous employment—refers to employee work experience in a sales-and-service "zone" (administrative unit) somewhere in the United States. We will see that previous employment emerges as a variable critical to our identification of organizational status; the proportions in our sample on this variable were approximately equivalent for the TAG population during both Phase I and Phase II. We used both content and statistical analysis techniques with our data. Content categories and their subcategories associated with the interviews from Phase I and Phase II were developed by one of us using an inductive approach.[4] We then compared and contrasted the data from these content categories across the two periods.

BACKGROUND PERIOD

During the mid-1980s, in an effort to increase competitiveness in the American automobile industry, this GM division began to review the effectiveness and efficiency of its sales-and-service operations. To compete more effectively, the division had two goals: to increase the sales volume in its low volume dealerships—those that sold fewer than 200 vehicles per year—and to reduce employee-incurred costs, including the use of company-owned vehicles and expense accounts associated with coordinating sales and service. It was anticipated that the newly available telemarketing technology[5] would achieve both aims. No downsizing in the form of a headcount reduction was planned.

Faced with these motivators, the division restructured its operations through the consolidation of a number of U.S. sales-and-service zones. It was decided that larger volume dealerships would continue to be serviced through direct contact with zone employees, whereas smaller, low-volume, and geographically dispersed dealerships would be serviced through telemarketing techniques of the newly created TAG unit located at divisional headquarters. The vast majority of new TAG employees were transferred involuntarily from the zones, although some were selected from other divisional units—predominantly from the Purchaser Service Group (PSG), whose responsibilities included addressing specific customer complaints about vehicles via telephone. Consequently, the TAG was staffed by two diverse groups of employees whose prior work assignments, methods, and status were substantially different.

Another dimension of TAG operations was the introduction of a new work organization based on teamwork and participative management, in accordance with the sociotechnical systems approach (Trist, 1981). TAG working relationships were designed to be based on information sharing and consensus decision making, in contrast with the individualistic and hierarchical nature of work relations in the zones. Prior to the start of TAG operations in 1987, TAG employees received both a "cultural" orientation to their work and computer training. During these training sessions, it was already evident that employee reactions to a TAG assignment were either very positive, among the PSG transferees, or quite negative, among zone transferees. Whereas divisional management provided information on selected aspects of a TAG assignment (e.g., eventual rotation of all sales-and-service employees through the TAG, assignments limited to 2 years, and the promise of a raise at the start of the assignment), other concerns related to the TAG's place in the division's career path progression, the eventual usefulness of computer skills for an individual's career, and the loss of material benefits such as a company-owned vehicle were not addressed. These mixed signals made it difficult to interpret the relative benefit of a TAG assignment, creating ambiguity that would be continually subject to discussion, examination, and negotiation both by individuals and organizational units within the division.

PRELIMINARY INDICATORS OF ORGANIZATIONAL STATUS

As the TAG operations began, several managerial decisions pertaining to divisional sales and service were crystallized. These decisions focused on both tangible, material aspects of sales and service that would enable the division to implement its TAG objectives, and selected aspects of the newly designed TAG work culture. Decisions were made regarding the relative monetary value of work output in the TAG, the work process, and the TAG reward system; all of these decisions were used by employees in evaluating and assigning status to the TAG. We discuss these decisions now because chronologically in the process of status acquisition these decisions and their impacts preceded employee interpretation.

One important traditional status indicator was created by the formal division of labor that separated employees on the basis of function and market, and correspondingly, *unit profitability.* Whereas zone employees were responsible for the high-volume dealers who produced the greatest profits for the division, TAG employees were associated with the low-volume dealers who reaped far less profit. Complaints of individual customers, representing the smallest unit of profit (or indeed, loss of profit) were handled by PSG employees.

This division of labor also had implications for other aspects of the job, as traditionally defined, including *classification level.* Prior to the reorganization, the majority of zone employees were sixth-level employees. These employees enjoyed certain *perquisites,* including the use of company-owned vehicles and access to expense accounts for travel. The majority of non-zone employees were fifth-level employees with no such perquisites. With the advent of the TAG, the majority of the TAG positions were classified as sixth-level with no such perquisites.

Another tangible, material factor that differentiated organizational units, but was not part of GM's traditional pattern of status markers, was the availability of computerized *job tools.* Whereas both TAG and PSG employees routinely used computers in their work, TAG employees' access to computerized information was more extensive. Although initial employee evaluations of computer training were overwhelmingly positive, it was not yet clear that this factor would ultimately play a role in the status of the TAG.

A second set of indicators relates to factors in the work environments of the three sales-and-service units. The TAG had been predicated on the innovative concepts of *teamwork and participative management,* whereas decision making in the zones and the PSG usually was relegated to higher-ranking employees. During the training sessions, TAG employees indicated strong support for the introduction of these two attributes into their work environment. However, as with the job tools, it was unclear whether teamwork and participative management skills might become valued by the division, adopted in other divisional units such as the zone or PSG, or serve as important future indicators of a unit's status.

Other more traditional facets of the work environment also distinguished the three units. For example, divisional personnel generally placed a high value on an employee's *interpersonal skills,* that is, the ability to interact well on a face-to-face basis with clients. This method of conducting business provided the opportunity for an in-depth exchange of information and ideas that could serve as the foundation for a long-standing professional relationship. Zone employees were positioned to develop and use such skills; TAG and PSG employees were not. Finally, despite the lack of consensus decision making in the zone, the structure of work there enabled zone employees to act autonomously by making quick, local-level decisions with respect to their dealerships. They also had the freedom to structure their work activities in an independent fashion. This characteristic of *autonomy* was far less evident in the TAG and the PSG, despite its high value within the division.

On balance, it appeared that the zone was ranked highest overall on five of the seven preliminary indicators of organizational status, the PSG ranked lowest, and the TAG situated somewhere in between. However, two of the indicators—job tools and teamwork/participative management—were such innovative features, and limited to the TAG, that their significance had not yet been established. Nevertheless, TAG employees believed that knowledge of computerized tools and the ability to work as a member of a team in a participative management environment represented the "wave of the future" in business methods and would provide them with a distinct career advantage over other divisional employees. We now turn to a discussion of employee evaluations of the TAG during the TAG's first phase of operations.

PHASE I

The Content and Distribution of Employee Perceptions

We begin with a discussion of employee perceptions of the TAG during February and March 1988. Employee evaluations of job attributes provided us with further clues about the relationship between individual and organizational status and were assigned either a positive or a negative value. Such statements were identified by the use of value-laden words such as "good," "beneficial," "desirable," or "not good," "not effective," "not conducive." To be included in our analysis, each evaluative statement had to fulfill the following conditions: reference the TAG directly, focus on the respondent's own experience, and provide some explanation for the opinion if the explanation was not implicit. Our content analysis of the field notes yielded 112 evaluative statements.

Next, we identified three major content categories into which these statements could be categorized: job task, work environment, and rewards and incentives. Although these categories were developed inductively based on the field data, they are consistent with categories used in the organizational literature (Gresov, Drazin, & Van de Ven, 1989; Herzberg, Mausner, & Snyderman, 1959; Tushman & Nadler, 1978). The following are our definitions of these major categories:

- *Job task* includes any statement pertaining to the nature or substance of work duties and tasks that were assigned to an employee.

TABLE 4.2 Net Difference in TAG Employee Evaluative Statements During Phase I, by Content, Value, and Previous Job Assignment

	Previous Job Assignment					
	Zone			*Non-Zone*		
Content Categories	+	–	*Net*	+	–	*Net*
Job task						
Computers	4	1	3	1	2	–1
Sales and service	1	5	–4	1	0	1
Perform well/efficient	0	4	–4	0	1	–1
Dealer interface	1	1	0	0	1	–1
Hours of work	2	0	2	0	0	0
Other	0	3	–3	1	0	1
Work environment						
Teamwork/share information	11	0	11	2	0	2
Competition	2	9	–7	0	2	–2
Participative management/access to management	5	4	1	2	0	2
Autonomy/freedom	1	0	1	1	0	1
Work load	1	2	–1	0	2	–2
Costs/sales	3	0	3	0	0	0
TAGers' personal qualities	1	0	1	1	0	1
Access to sales/service	1	0	1	0	0	0
Adjustment to TAG	0	1	–1	0	0	0
Management visibility	1	0	1	0	0	0
Other	0	1	–1	0	0	0
Rewards and incentives						
Company-owned vehicle	2	9	–7	0	0	0
Raise/promotion at outset	0	6	–6	1	0	1
Amount of travel on the job	3	2	1	1	0	1
Monetary situation at outset	0	1	–1	0	0	0
Other	0	5	–5	0	0	0
Grand total	39	54	–15	11	8	3

- *Work environment* includes any statement pertaining to work activity excluding the task itself (e.g., day-to-day operational constraints, social relationships, rules pertaining to decision making).
- *Rewards and incentives* includes any statement pertaining to monetary and nonmonetary compensation and other benefits (or lack thereof) associated with a job assignment (e.g., raises, change in classification level).

Many of the statements implicitly or explicitly compared previous job assignments with current assignments in the TAG, or compared TAG assignments with anticipated future assignments. Although employees typically did not use the term "status" in discussing these job attributes, their comments point to distinctions that implied differences in ranking within the division. All evaluative statements were assigned to one of the three categories using the three definitions outlined above. Table 4.2

shows the distribution of these statements by the number of positive and negative evaluations, previous employment, and type of content categories and subcategories.

Most notable about Table 4.2 is that former zone and former non-zone employees differed in their evaluations of the rewards and incentives category. Former zone employees described losing their company-owned vehicles as "a big chunk out of our pockets" because they had to pay for their own cars, car insurance, and maintenance costs previously covered by the division. There were also complaints that the "promised raise had never materialized." On the other hand, former PSG employees spoke very positively about their move to the TAG. One former PSG employee stated, "I had been trying for a long time to get out of the PSG; this (move) was an actual promotion for me to a level six."

Interestingly, the evaluations of all of the respondents, regardless of former employment, seemed to be aligned on many other aspects of the TAG assignment. For example, they all seemed to support the teamwork and participative management concepts, associated with the work environment category, and most indicated that these new practices appeared to be working relatively well. One individual remarked,

> The team effort at the TAG is good. When anyone is absent, there are other people to fill in for them. This is something that did not happen in the zones at all. There were no teams (nor was there) a team concept in the zones. There was a lot more competition in the zones which is something that is not good for the TAG.

Both the emphasis on a "team" working together rather than individuals competing against one another (as in the zone) and the opportunity to participate in decisions related to the management of the unit were aspects of the TAG work culture that not only differentiated the TAG from other divisional units such as the zone and PSG but also appeared to be viewed as superior by TAG employees.

Employees also commented favorably on the computer experience, associated with the job task category, that they acquired in the TAG. One individual stated, "I like it here (in the TAG). I feel this is an opportunity to learn new things and that the computers are very good and very helpful to me in reducing my workload. I am really happy here." Another indicated that it was an opportunity to gain new skills in "state-of-the-art business procedures."

Former zone and former non-zone employees also agreed on the increasingly competitive nature of sales-and-service work in the TAG. One employee commented,

> The original idea of helping each other goes out the window when things get really competitive during the first days of every week (a time when TAG employees must allocate their weekly allotment of vehicles to their dealers). Very often (TAG employees) seem to be moving away from the initial concept which was to help each other.

Employees clearly were reacting to the apparent growth of competition in the TAG, which, in their view, conflicted with teamwork. Indeed, employees indicated to us that their "culture was slipping" to highlight the development of this unwanted competition. If this emerging aspect of their work culture were to persist, the TAG would stray further from its ideal "cultural" design and, as such, be less distinctive in comparison with other divisional units.

Based on the compilation of the Phase I evaluative statements, it is clear that working in the TAG is associated with both benefits and disadvantages such that the overall evaluation of the TAG assignment remained ambiguous. It was uncertain how the computer and teamwork/participative management features ranked relative to other divisional organizations, in part because the long-term effects of a TAG assignment on an individual's career and the overall unit's success were not well known. Nevertheless, there were clear indications of the negative reaction by former zone employees to the loss of certain material or financial benefits or both, concerns that surfaced initially during the cultural training. Whereas the relationship between previous job assignment and the positive or negative value associated with employee statements was not statistically significant, it was in the expected direction; 58% of the former zone employee statements were negative, whereas 58% of the non-zone employee statements were positive.

Distinctive Career Path Models

This bifurcation phenomenon based on previous employment provided us with two distinct views of the TAG, suggesting an implicit status hierarchy. As we will demonstrate in this section, former non-zone employees viewed the TAG as "up," whereas former zone employees perceived it to be "down." Especially important to this conceptualization was the modeling of ideal employee career paths. We asked TAG employees questions focused on their perceptions of their own career paths. Our content analysis of their responses revealed two distinctive career path models—one for the zone and one for the non-zone—both with important implications for TAG status.

THE CAREER PATH MODEL OF FORMER NON-ZONE EMPLOYEES

Former non-zone employees indicated that they had a "sense of having been chosen" for new and exciting job responsibilities in the TAG. Most, if not all, former non-zone employees experienced a promotion to a sixth level and its associated raise upon arrival in the TAG. They indicated that they were treated "more professionally" than they had been in their previous assignments where they performed clerical/administrative duties and were subject to a constant stream of customer complaints. Accordingly, they positively evaluated their move to the TAG as an upward career progression.

All 9 former non-zone employees expected future upward career moves as they became ready to move on to other job responsibilities. These individuals anticipated transfers to the zone as either a DM or DSM. For example, one

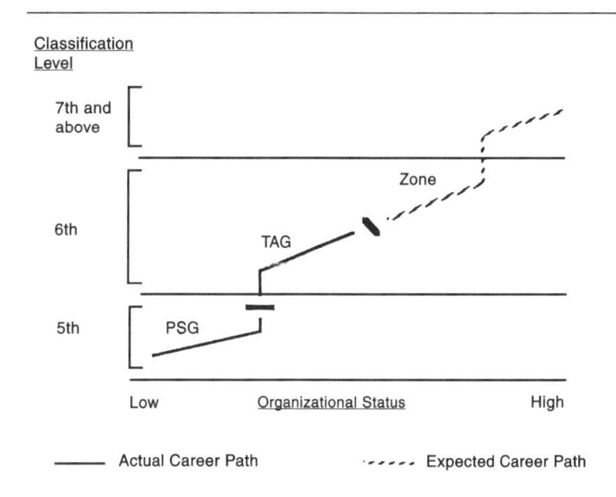

Figure 4.1. The Career Path Model of Former Non-Zone Employees

individual stated, "I would hope to go out into the field (zone).... Right now I am enjoying the home office atmosphere, but would like to move up eventually." Several indicated no desire to be transferred until they had acquired sufficient experience and confidence in their TAG jobs. These statements, together with level change and acquisition of knowledge and skills useful for career development, reflect important intervals in an upwardly mobile career path. Figure 4.1 illustrates these intervals as a "step-up" progression within the sales-and-service career path.

THE CAREER PATH MODEL OF FORMER ZONE EMPLOYEES

By contrast, former zone employees' reactions to the TAG frequently dealt with two distinct types of "losses." First, as indicated previously, former zone employees experienced a financial loss related to the company-owned vehicle and no upward-level change or its accompanying raise when they were transferred to the TAG. Second, they also experienced a loss in autonomy and "professionalism" in performing their assignments. Whereas telemarketing techniques require some degree of professionalism and technical skill, the fact that the job was performed over the telephone meant that certain traditional aspects of doing business were sharply reduced or curtailed. Specifically, TAG employees did not have the same types of ongoing opportunities to establish and maintain personal relationships with dealership personnel simply because they did not routinely have the occasion to interact directly with them. Furthermore, TAG employees did not travel outside the TAG on a regular basis or have as much flexibility with respect to their hours of work as zone employees. As a result of these losses, employees from the zone viewed the TAG as a "holding tank" or a "delay" in their career path. A transfer to the TAG involved a lateral move, but employees perceived it as a "demotion" because its practices and procedures did not compare favorably with those of the zone.

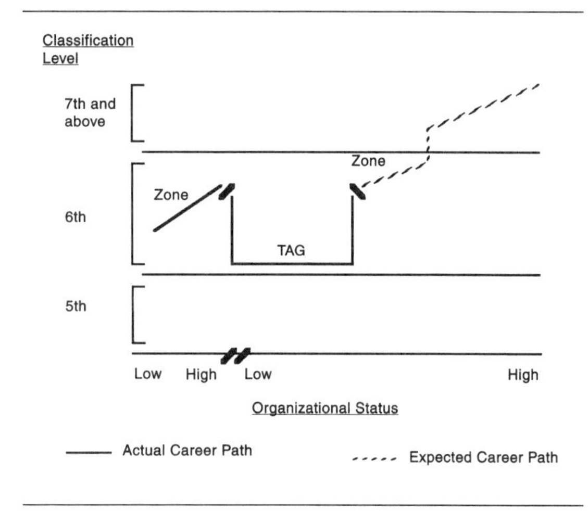

Figure 4.2. The Career Path Model of Former Zone Employees

When asked specifically about their next job assignments, 15 of the 23 former zone employees anticipated being transferred back to the zone; use of the phrase "being promoted out to the zone" was common. One individual commented, "I expect that in 6 to 8 more months, I will be moved to a metro district (the highest volume and most prestigious zone assignment)." The 8 remaining employees either wanted to leave sales for some other functional area, remain in the TAG as a seventh-level employee, or had no hopes for either leaving the TAG for the zone or moving up to a seventh-level position in the TAG. We illustrated the intervals in their career path graphically by depicting the "holding tank" model (see Figure 4.2). This conceptualization suggests that the TAG is perceived as a (possibly temporary) step downward in the career path, but a step from which most hope to recover. In the next section of the chapter, we examine the development of employee viewpoints regarding the status of the TAG during Phase II.

PHASE II

The Content and Distribution of Employee Perceptions

Between May and July 1988, we engaged in the second period of TAG fieldwork and followed the same analytic procedures used in Phase I. First, we isolated evaluative statements from the responses to our interview questions. There were 339 evaluative statements—111 positive statements and 228 negative statements. We applied the same three content categories to the Phase II data because the content analysis was conducted simultaneously; nine additional subcategories were created based on the Phase II data and assigned to each of the three content categories.

Employee differences based on previous job assignment became more pronounced during Phase II. Table 4.3 shows the distribution of employee evaluations of the TAG and their previous job assignment. In addition to the predominance of negative statements from former zone employees associated with the rewards and incentives category, both former zone and former non-zone employees emphasized the TAG's increasing workload. Statements such as "the workload is too much; there's no relief in sight . . . " reflected the increase in the number of dealerships from 55 to 70 assigned to each TAG employee. By contrast, current zone employees were assigned between one quarter and one third the number of dealers. In general, former zone employees were significantly less favorable to the TAG then were non-zone employees both in Phase II and overall when Phases I and II data were combined ($p \leq .01$).[6]

TABLE 4.3 Net Difference in TAG Employee Evaluative Statements During Phase II, by Content, Value, and Previous Job Assignment

	Previous Job Assignment					
	Zone			*Non-Zone*		
Content Categories	+	–	*Net*	+	–	*Net*
Job task						
Computers	15	5	10	0	0	0
Sales and service	6	8	–2	6	1	5
Perform well/efficient	4	3	1	0	0	0
Dealer interface	4	7	–3	4	0	4
How the division works	4	0	4	2	0	2
Hours of work	2	0	2	0	0	0
Other	4	3	1	1	0	1
Work environment						
Teamwork/share information	8	15	–7	2	1	1
Competition	2	5	–3	0	2	–2
Participative management/access to management	5	14	–9	1	0	1
Autonomy/freedom	3	7	–4	3	0	3
Workload	3	19	–16	1	7	–6
Costs/sales	3	0	3	0	0	0
TAGers' personal qualities	6	0	6	4	0	4
Zone rotation into TAG	0	9	–9	0	1	–1
Access to sales/service data	9	0	9	0	0	0
Adjustment to TAG	0	4	–4	0	0	0
Management action	0	4	–4	0	0	0
Management visibility	3	0	3	0	0	0
TAG career path	0	2	–2	0	1	–1
Selection of TAGers at outset	0	3	–3	0	0	0
Other	0	8	–8	0	1	–1
Rewards and incentives						
Company-owned vehicle	0	7	–17	0	0	0
Raise/promotion at outset	1	8	–17	1	1	0
Amount of travel on the job	4	9	–5	0	0	0
Monetary situation at outset	0	17	–17	0	0	0
Incentives/raises/promotions	0	11	–11	0	2	–2
Geographic location	0	10	–10	0	0	0
Anticipated future promotions	0	5	–5	0	3	–3
TAG office design	0	2	–2	0	3	–3
Other	0	10	–10	0	0	0
Grand total	86	205	–119	25	23	2

Perceived Trends Beyond the Tag

Although we did not have the opportunity to interview non-TAG personnel as part of this study, we did collect TAG employees' perceptions of dealer and current zone employees' attitudes toward the TAG. We examined these perceptions to gauge the extent to which they corroborated or refuted TAG employee evaluations of a TAG assignment and to identify possible effects of these perceptions on TAG employees. Of the 38 statements made concerning perceived dealer reactions to the TAG, 12 were associated with Phase I and 26 with Phase II. Over that time period, the proportion of positive responses increased from 58% to 73% and focused on the benefits related to service, attention, and assistance that TAG dealers received from the new telemarketing system. Clearly, dealership personnel increasingly indicated their application of the quick response time via telephone and computer to dealership queries. There was no relationship between a TAG employee's previous job assignment and their interpretation of the dealers' attitudes.

During Phase II, TAG employees also commented on the views about the TAG held by current zone employees.[7] According to TAG employees, 17 of the 18 statements made by current zone employees about the TAG were negative. The largest category of negative responses focused on the perceived status of the TAG relative to the zone. For example, one TAG employee stated, "Zone people really don't like the TAG. They feel people working in the TAG are beneath them (while) working in the zone is a heavier weighted job even though it's on the same level as people in the TAG." Another indicated, "Most of them (current zone employees) feel that they are too good for the TAG." Former zone employees made all but one of the 17 negative comments.

Dealer and current zone employees' attitudes about a TAG assignment diverge. According to TAG employees, the dealership community is favorably impressed with the TAG's telemarketing capabilities and service. Because dealerships are directly connected with TAG employees in the organization and structure of work, their views have the potential to send an important message to divisional management about the value of the telemarketing method. On the other hand, current zone employees are reported to confine their remarks to the personal and organizational drawbacks of a TAG assignment; dealer satisfaction or other external factors such as cost savings are not relevant to their assessment of the TAG's work or status.

THE ACQUISITION OF ORGANIZATIONAL STATUS

Based on the analysis of our case study, we now propose a four-part process model focused on the acquisition of organizational status. We use the phrase "acquisition of status" rather than "determination of status" because of the as-yet-unknown effects that computer skills or the ability to work with colleagues in a team/participative management environment might have on the assignment of status to the TAG. We recognize that this model may not be generalizable to all corporate restructurings since it is based on a particular case. For example, there were specific conditions associated with this reorganization (e.g., there were relatively favorable economic conditions in the United States at the time of the reorganization, many TAG transfers were involuntary, many TAG employees perceived their transfers as a demotion) that would not be present in all reorganizations. Nevertheless, in this era of corporate reorganizations and downsizing, we suspect that the staffing conditions and assignment interpretations described in this case study are fairly common in today's business environment—from the standpoint of employee reaction to the change. Future case study research would be useful in testing the applicability of our model to other reorganized work groups under different environmental circumstances.

Environmental Shift/Reorganization

As a first step in our model, we hypothesize that the attribution of status to a new organizational unit often occurs within the context of an environment shift followed by a reorganization. In this case, the competitive economic climate within the United States was exerting significant pressure on GM generally and on the sales-and-service division specifically. The organizational response to this pressure was to assess sales revenues relative to costs: Vehicle sales associated with lower-volume dealerships were viewed as too low, whereas divisional costs to coordinate sales and service in those dealerships were perceived as too high. Within the cultural environment of GM such an assessment often leads to a cost-cutting program. In this case, cost cutting was achieved through a reorganization and the creation of a new, low-cost organizational unit.

Managerial Decision Making

A second step in the process of status acquisition concerns the impact of managerial decision making on organizational units. Managers make choices about actions that they hope will be most effective; their choices give affected organizational members important clues about status. With these choices, the acquisition of status actively begins. Managerial decisions were made related to the selection of the cost-saving telemarketing techniques, staffing the new telemarketing office, identifying other cost savings, and the training of employees. As indicated, some overt attempts were made to make it appear as though TAG and zone employees were roughly equivalent in status. However, in fact, most indicators suggested that they were not. Based on both the preliminary indicators of organizational status present at the outset of the study and our interview and observational data, we propose four cultural principles manifest in the decisions made by divisional leadership that contributed to employee interpretations of the TAG's status.

First, *size* matters at GM (Keller, 1989); big, profitable units are more highly valued than small, less profitable ones—regardless of efficiency. Managers targeted small, geographically dispersed zones for the TAG. Thus the TAG was associated with smallness. Second, *cars* are symbolic at GM; employees who have regular use of a company-owned vehicle are regarded more highly than those who must purchase their own cars. TAG employees lost their cars, reflecting a lost of status at GM. Third, *autonomy and individualism* matter at GM (Keller, 1989; Metcalf & Briody, 1995); those who appear to be independent operators concerning how and when their work gets done are considered more prestigious than those whose work procedures and schedules are more tightly controlled. Former zone employees lost much of the autonomy to control their own work schedules and now were confined to an office in divisional headquarters instead of being able to ride about freely in the zone. Fourth, being an active participant in the *career mainstream* matters at GM; those who remain associated with the traditional work and methods of the organization often are held in higher regard than those associated with or transferred to an experimental or nonmainstream unit (perhaps with some exceptions such as GM Europe). Employees transferred out of the mainstream often are believed to be those who have "plateaued" or reached a "dead end" in their careers (Briody & Baba, 1991; Metcalf & Briody, 1995). Taken together, managerial choices about the TAG and its employees suggest that this new unit was not of primary importance to the division, was not highly favored, and was not part of the mainstream.

Employee Interpretations

The third step in our model of status acquisition consists of reactions to and interpretations of events by nonmanagerial employees. In this case, TAG employees made note of managerial decisions concerning the TAG and interpreted the status implications of these decisions within the context of GM culture; indeed, these managerial decisions served as important organizational symbols for the employees. Whereas telemarketing technology, for example, may have been viewed as cost-effective for TAG operations, the bias toward traditional face-to-face contact within the hierarchical zone structure persisted. The strong preference for face-to-face contact continued to flourish despite advances in technology and a movement toward a more team-based, participative management work environment in the larger national culture. Although there was some discussion of introducing computers into the zone offices, there were no immediate implementation plans. In addition, most higher-ranking managerial employees did not use computers in their work, whereas lower-ranking, nonmanagerial employees (e.g., clerical) did. Furthermore, there were serious doubts, even by TAG employees, that they would be able to sustain their own organizational culture. As conditions in the external environment became even more competitive with further losses in sales and profits, the mandates for work performance in the division increased and the teamwork/participative management elements of the TAG's culture waned. Although former non-zone employees were somewhat more favorably disposed to their TAG assignments in comparison with former zone employees, by Phase II, all TAG employees were able to articulate the ideal sales-and-service work environment in terms of tasks, work methods, work culture, and perquisites.

Similarly, the divisional management group had sent mixed messages to TAG employees about their TAG positions and their relationship with the zone. Prior to the start of TAG operations, promises apparently were made in an effort to address some of the career-path concerns voiced by TAG recruits. However, promises such as zone rotation or a 2-year TAG tenure could not be ascertained immediately. During the first year of TAG operations, the initial uncertainty surrounding these concerns was transformed into disbelief when the promises were not kept. Thus managerial actions that could have balanced these negative status indicators and placed the TAG on a level playing field with the zone were not taken.

Community Consensus on Organizational Status

The final step in our status acquisition process model is the emergence of a general consensus regarding the relative status ranking of the new organizational unit. TAG employees, as a group, ultimately recognized the status superiority of the zone. Even though the low-volume dealership community appears to have been satisfied with the TAG's output, this satisfaction had only limited influence initially in the reckoning of the TAG's status. The differential distribution of material factors to the zone and TAG, corroborated by work environment factors and an overall negative evaluation from current zone employees, contributed to and later confirmed TAG employees' perceptions of their lower status.

Those most heavily affected by this conclusion—former zone employees—came to terms with their TAG assignment in two important ways. First, they appeared to compensate for their loss of organizational status by continuing to emphasize the importance of their telemarketing and work culture skills—skills that could not be obtained anywhere else in the division. Second, they looked forward to their future assignments in the zone. We know that as early as Summer 1988, TAG employees were being transferred or notified of their pending transfer to the zone—rather than to any other unit.[8]

A new career progression began to emerge spontaneously within sales and service (see Figure 4.3). This new career path began with employment in an entry-level position in the PSG, followed by a change in classification level to the TAG, and culminated most often with a lateral transfer to the prestigious zone (although some employees may remain in the TAG, other opt for positions outside of sales and service). Even though the organizational literature has identified alternative patterns of career move-

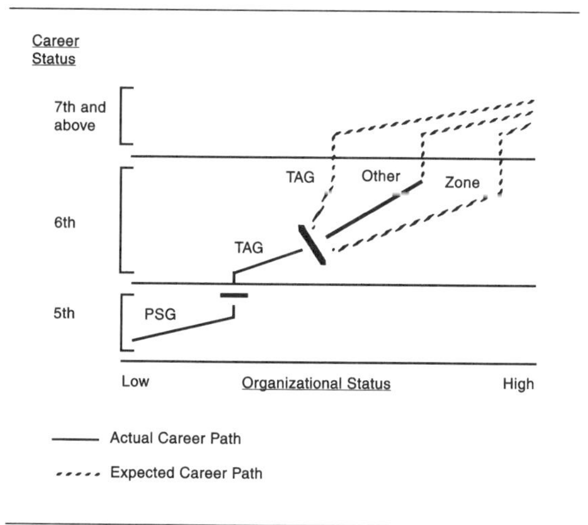

Figure 4.3. The Emergent Career Path Model

ment, including lateral movement across functional or technical boundaries, or movement toward centrality or inclusion within the "inner circle or the core" of an organization or occupation (Schein, 1971; Van Maanen & Barley, 1984), our data suggest that advancement up the division's hierarchy is preferred by employees. This new career path reflects both the modal pattern, that is, the actual sequence of promotions observed, and the ideal career progression desired by sales-and-service employees.

It is important to note that consensus regarding a new unit's status may be relevant for only a given period of time until other factors intervene, stimulating a new interpretation and resolution.[9] The entire process of status acquisition and change thus reflects an evolutionary process. Furthermore, although organizational participants may not agree on whether or not the conclusions drawn are justified, this process copes with members' uncertainty regarding the way in which the new organizational unit will be ranked relative to other units.

CONCLUSIONS

In this study, we examined a corporate restructuring that had a profound effect on both organizational status and organizational career structures. Evident at the outset of the study was the changing nature of the corporate environment and associated work settings as the sales-and-service division began to accommodate the new telemarketing unit. Our status acquisition model proposed four steps (i.e., environmental shift followed by a reorganization, managerial decision making, employee interpretations, and community consensus on organizational status) in which organizational units came to be associated with a particular status relative to other units. Once the status was acquired, the ambiguity and uncertainty surrounding organizational change dissipated. In our case study, the direction and expectations of career-path movement was one of several indicators of organizational status. Career structures were subject to change, particularly when the telemarketing segment of the sales-and-service career path was introduced; its position in the broader sales-and-service career structure was interpreted and reinterpreted over a period of many months. Eventually, a new sales-and-service career path structure was established, incorporating the experience from a TAG assignment.

We believe that our analysis has underscored the importance of three aspects of organizational change, filling gaps in the literature on internal labor markets and organizational status. First, during periods of organizational restructuring, organizational structures are in flux. The dynamic nature of the changes have important implications for business goals, day-to-day operations, a variety of social processes including employee reactions, and future restructurings. Indeed, we found that despite attention to planning and training, and the achievement of the TAG's initial objectives to increase sales and reduce costs, the restructured sales-and-service activities were short-lived. Within 3 years of the restructuring, divisional management already was planning to integrate the TAG's operations with those of the zone. We argue that the continuing importance of traditional sales-and-service culture patterns in the zone—namely face-to-face relationships and individual autonomy—along with selected material factors (such as the symbolic significance of a company-owned vehicle) played a central role in restructuring sales and service back to its more traditional form. As others have discovered (Martin & Siehl, 1983; Trist, 1981), when the larger divisional culture is not aligned with its subcultures, it becomes very difficult for the subculture to sustain its own defining characteristics in the long run.

Second, we focused on the process of organizational change, independent of any restructuring attempts. Althauser and Kalleberg (1990, p. 323) asked what processes "govern movement through sequences of ILM (internal labor market) jobs?" We suggest a broader question: What effects will restructurings have on individual jobs and careers paths, and the ways in which they are evaluated? Interpretations or "sense making" (Louis, 1980) are based both on past experiences and on anticipated projections. We found that employees relied on four sources of information to formulate their opinions about the TAG's status: material considerations, conditions in the work environment, other employee and dealer perceptions of the TAG, and the direction and expectations of future career moves. Their initial clues were derived from the material indicators, made somewhat uncertain by aspects of the work environment, then corroborated by non-TAG perceptions, and finally confirmed by the direction of career-path transfer from the TAG. Thus interpretations of organizational change may be quite protracted and, in this case, fluctuate over a period of time until employees' attention is diverted to new concerns.

Finally, as part of our investigation of organizational change, we introduced and discussed the concept of organizational status. Although our sample was composed of individuals, some of whom might have considered themselves part of an occupational "sales" and "service" culture, both American and GM culture appeared to have had an overriding effect on employee interpretations of their careers. Career paths, rather than some aspect of occupational life or the particular tasks or job status an individual held, turned out to be a defining attribute of employment. Not only was an individual's status based on his or her job mobility, and perceived movements "up" or "down" between units of differential status, but the status of individual units appeared tied to the sequence of job moves as well. Job moves following an upward progression were preferred and consistent with the strong preference for career advancement within American culture generally (Hall & Hall, 1989; Metcalf & Briody, 1995). The status associated with an organizational unit mirrored its place in the sales-and-service career path.

NOTES

1. An internal labor market has been defined as "firmwide organizational structures—including administrative or bureaucratic personnel rules, job classification systems with job and salary grades, or simply all the jobs within a firm" (Althauser & Kalleberg, 1990, p. 322).

2. We use the term *employee* to include both managers and nonmanagers.

3. We define *organizational culture* as an enduring system of ideas and related behavior distinctive to particular organizational setting or settings.

4. To check the reliability of our content categories, one of the authors independently categorized a 5% sample (N = 23) of the 451 employee evaluative statements into these content categories. The reliability was 91%. This same individual also reviewed the subcategory labels in conjunction with the statements associated with them; she recommended relabeling 3 of the 28 subcategories. In addition, the authors decided to move one of the subcategories, hours of work, from the rewards and incentives category to the job task category.

5. The telemarketing approach consists of the use of computer databases containing information on dealership automobile inventory, financing, and other quantitative information. An employee has the ability to access information quickly via computer while simultaneously discussing the information with dealership personnel over the telephone. Use of the databases enabled employees to have accurate, up-to-date information on the exact number and type of automobiles that each dealer had in stock, thus facilitating sales-and-service exchange negotiations.

6. During Phase II, zone employees had 70% negative statements, whereas overall they had 67% negative statements. Former non-zone employees had 48% negative statements during Phase II and 46% negative statements overall.

7. Because only a few TAG employees commented about other divisional employees during Phase I, we were not able to compare them with our Phase II results. For additional analyses of other divisional employees' reactions to a TAG assignment, see Briody, Baba, and Cooper (1991).

8. Indeed, the flow of transferees was unidirectional (e.g., TAG to zone but not zone to TAG), in which "you could count on one hand" the number of zone transfers to the TAG. By the late 1980s, most new TAG employees either transferred in from the PSG and selected manufacturing facilities or were newly hired college graduate employees.

9. Since the competition of this study in 1990, some significant changes have occurred at the division. In large part due to the strong positive dealership assessment of the TAG's telemarketing methods, sales-and-service work was restructured once again. High-volume dealers reportedly heard about the telemarketing system's capabilities and efficiency and wanted to benefit from it. At the same time, the division reevaluated the role of face-to-face contact in conducting divisional/dealership business. A decision was made to employ the face-to-face method with both high- and low-volume dealerships while simultaneously making available laptop computers to all sales-and-service employees. At the time of this writing, the TAG was in the process of being dissolved, with all personnel circulating to zone positions. Although further study would be required to determine whether either computers or teamwork/participative management became an integral part of the zone's status system, we speculate that computer knowledge and use was folded into the traditional set of status markers for zone personnel.

REFERENCES

Althauser, R. P., & Kalleberg, A. L. (1990). Identifying career lines and internal labor markets within firms: A study in the interrelationships of theory and methods. In R. L. Breiger (Ed.), *Social mobility and social structure* (pp. 308-356). Cambridge, UK: Cambridge University Press.

Baron, J. N. (1984). Organizational perspectives on stratification. *Annual Review of Sociology, 10*, 37-69.

Blau, P., & Duncan, O. D. (1967). *The American occupational structure.* New York: John Wiley.

Briody, E. K., & Baba, M. L. (1991). Explaining differences in repatriation experiences: The discovery of coupled and decoupled systems. *American Anthropologist, 93*(2), 322-344.

Briody, E. K., Baba, M. L., & Cooper, L. (1991). *A tale of two career paths: The impact of reorganization on employee career development.* Warren, MI: GMR Publication No. 7506.

Davenport, T. H. (1993). *Process innovation: Reengineering work through information technology.* Boston: Harvard Business School Press.

Feagin, J. R. (1978). *Racial and ethnic relations.* Englewood Cliffs, NJ: Prentice Hall.

Gaertner, K. N. (1980). The structure of organizational careers. *Sociology of Education, 53*, 7-20.

Goldthorpe, J. H. (1980). *Social mobility and class structure in modern Britain.* Oxford, UK: Clarendon.

Granovetter, M. (1981). Toward a sociological theory of income differences. In I. Berg (Ed.), *Sociological perspectives on labor markets* (pp. 11-47). New York: Academic Press.

Gresov, C., Drazin, R., & Van de Ven, A. H. (1989). Work-unit task uncertainty, design and morale. *Organization Studies, 10*(1), 45-62.

Hall, E. T., & Hall, M. R. (1989). *Understanding cultural differences: Keys to success in West Germany, France, and the United States.* Yarmouth, ME: Intercultural Press.

Hammer, M. (1990). Reengineering work: Don't automate, obliterate. *Harvard Business Review, 68*(4), 104-112.

Hayes, R. H., & Jaikumar, R. (1988). Manufacturing's crisis: New technologies, obsolete organizations. *Harvard Business Review, 66*(5), 77-85.

Herzberg, F., Mausner, B., & Snyderman, B. (1959). *The motivation to work.* New York: John Wiley.

Jacoby, S. M. (1985). *Employing bureaucracy: Managers, unions, and the transformation of work in American industry, 1900-1945.* New York: Columbia University Press.

Jencks, C. (1980). Structural versus individual explanations of inequality: Where do we go from here? *Contemporary Sociology, 9*, 762-767.

Kanter, R. M. (1977). *Men and women of the corporation.* New York: Basic Books.

Kanter, R. M. (1984). Variations in managerial careers structures in high-technology firms: The impact of organizational characteristics on internal labor market patterns. In P. Osterman (Ed.), *Internal labor markets* (pp. 109-131). Cambridge: MIT Press.

Keller, M. A. (1989). *Rude awakening: The rise, fall and struggle for recovery of General Motors.* New York: William Morrow.

Linton, R. (1936). *The study of man.* New York: Appleton-Century-Crofts.

Louis, M. R. (1980). Surprise and sense making: What newcomers experience in entering unfamiliar organizational settings. *Administrative Science Quarterly, 25*, 226-251.

Martin, J., & Rosenbaum, K. (1983, Autumn). Organizational culture and counterculture: An uneasy symbiosis. *Organizational Dynamics*, pp. 52-63.

Metcalf, C., & Briody, E. K. (1995). Reconciling perceptions of career advancement with organizational change: A case from General Motors. *Human Organization, 54*, 417-428.

Rosenbaum, J. E. (1986). Institutional career structures and the social construction of ability. In J. G. Richardson (Ed.), *Handbook of theory and research for the sociology of education* (pp. 139-171). New York: Greenwood.

Rosenbaum, J. E. (1989). Organizational career systems and employee misperceptions. In M. B. Arthur, D. T. Hall, & B. S. Lawrence (Eds.), *Handbook of career theory* (pp. 329-353). Cambridge, UK: Cambridge University Press.

Rosenbaum, J. E. (1990). Structural models of organizational careers: A critical review and new directions. In R. L. Breiger (Ed.), *Social mobility and social structure* (pp. 272-307). Cambridge, UK: Cambridge University Press.

Rosenfeld, R. A. (1992). Job mobility and career processes. *Annual Review of Sociology, 18,* 39-61.

Schein, E. H. (1971). The individual, the organization, and the career: A conceptual scheme. *Journal of Applied Behavioral Science, 7,* 401-426.

Sewell, W., & Hauser, R. (1975). *Education, occupation, and earnings.* New York: Academic Press.

Slocum, W. L. (1974). *Occupational careers: A sociological perspective.* Chicago: Aldine.

Sorensen, A. B. (1986). Theory and methodology in social stratification. In U. Himmelstrand (Ed.), *Sociology from crisis to science? The sociology of structure and action* (Vol. 1, pp. 69-95). Beverly Hills, CA: Sage.

Stewman, S., & Konda, S. L. (1983). Careers and organizational labor markets: Demographic models of organizational behavior. *American Journal of Sociology, 88*(4), 637-685.

Stinchcombe, A. L. (1965). Social structure and organizations. In J. G. March (Ed.), *Handbook of organizations* (pp. 142-193). Chicago: Rand McNally.

Talbert, J., & Bose, C. E. (1977). Wage-attainment processes: The retail clerk case. *American Journal of Sociology, 83*(2), 403-424.

Thomas, R. J. (1994). *What machines can't do: Politics and technology in the industrial enterprise.* Berkeley: University of California Press.

Tomasko, R. M. (1987). *Downsizing: Reshaping the corporation for the future.* New York: American Management Association.

Tomasko, R. M. (1993). *Rethinking the corporation: The architecture of change.* New York: American Management Association.

Trice, H. (1993). *Occupational subcultures in the workplace.* Ithaca, NY: ILR Press.

Trist, E. (1981). *The evolution of socio-technical systems: A conceptual framework and an action research program* (Occasional Paper No. 2). Toronto: Ontario Quality of Working Life Center.

Tushman, M. L., & Nadler, D. A. (1978). Information processing as an integrating concept in organizational design. *Academy of Management Review, 3,* 613-624.

Van Maanen, J., & Barley, S. R. (1984). Occupational communities: Culture and control in organizations. *Research in Organizational Behavior, 6,* 287-365.

Warner, W. L., & Srole, L. (1945). *The social systems of American ethnic groups.* New Haven, CT: Yale University Press.

Weber, M. (1946). *From Max Weber: Essays in sociology.* New York: Oxford University Press.

White, H. C. (1970). *Chains of opportunity: System models of mobility in organizations.* Cambridge, MA: Harvard University Press.

Learning Factories or Reproduction Factories?

Labor-Management Relations in the Japanese Consumer Electronics Maquiladoras in Mexico

MARTIN KENNEY
W. RICHARD GOE
OSCAR CONTRERAS
JAIRO ROMERO
MAURICIO BUSTOS

In recent years, Japanese firms have dramatically increased their direct investment in *maquiladora* operations in Mexico.[1] In 1996, Japanese firms employed approximately 40,000 Mexican workers in more than 100 factories.[2] Large Japanese firms such as Sony and Matsushita now employ more than 5,000 workers each in their various Mexican operations. The investment in Japanese maquiladoras has involved not only assembly but manufacturing; numerous Japanese suppliers are making parts and components in Mexico (Curry & Kenney, 1996). As part of a movement to establish offshore production, the Japanese maquiladoras serve as production platforms for North American markets.

Japanese factories are considered by many observers to set the global standard for production management (Dertouzos, Lester, & Solow, 1989). A key facet of Japanese production management is its work organization and labor-management system. Japanese factories are managed as learning environments in which shop floor workers not only produce items but continuously gain new knowledge that is employed to improve the production process and enhance product quality (Adler & Cole, 1993; Cole, 1989; Fruin, 1997; Kenney & Florida, 1993). The possibility of learning while producing has led to great interest in the transfer of Japanese production practices to developing countries (Humphrey, 1993, 1995; Kaplinsky, 1994, 1995).

The operation of the Japanese maquiladoras appears to offer Mexican workers the opportunity to work in and become familiar with global-class production facilities. It is uncertain, however, that these facilities represent the "learning factories" described by Fruin (1997) and Kenney and Florida (1993). For example, research conducted during the 1980s found little evidence that the maquiladoras were using advanced Japanese labor-management practices (Carrillo & Hernandez, 1985; Fernandez-Kelly, 1983). More recent research has yielded mixed

From *Work and Occupations,* Vol. 25, No. 3, August 1998, pp. 269-304. Reprinted by permission.

findings. Several studies have found that such practices are being used more extensively in some maquiladoras (Gonzalez-Arechiga & Ramirez, 1992; Pelayo-Martinez, 1992; P. Wilson, 1992). Other studies have found that the use of Japanese labor-management practices in the maquiladoras continues to be minimal at best (Kamiyama, 1994; Kenney & Florida, 1994). The primary objective of this research is to compare and contrast the labor-management practices of Japanese consumer electronics maquiladoras in the 1990s to those of consumer electronics factories in Japan and assess the extent to which the labor-management practices used in Japanese factories have been transferred to maquiladoras in Mexico.

This study is based on in-depth interviews with 75 Mexican production workers in Japanese consumer electronics maquiladoras. Most previous research on Japanese (or any other) maquiladoras has relied on the reports of managers to measure the transfer of either Japanese or advanced labor-management methods (Coronado, 1992; Echeverri-Carroll, 1988; Kenney & Florida, 1994; Rodriguez, 1990; Shaiken & Browne, 1991). Our research provides a shop floor worker's perspective. This permits an examination of the characteristics of shop floor workers in Japanese consumer electronics maquiladoras, the training they receive, and the work practices they use. In turn, this allows an assessment of the ways in which the labor-management practices employed in consumer electronics factories in Japan are being transferred and implemented in the maquiladoras.

This chapter is organized as follows. The first section delineates a stylized model of the labor-management practices of Japanese consumer electronics factories. The second section examines previous research on the transfer of Japanese labor-management methods to overseas consumer electronics factories in general, and the maquiladoras in particular. The third section describes the research methods used in the study. The fourth section describes the findings from the interviews with the production workers. Finally, the implications of the findings are discussed. We suggest that the consumer electronics maquiladoras are using a hybrid labor-management system that is similar to but differs in important ways from the system used in consumer electronics factories in Japan.[3]

THE JAPANESE LABOR MANAGEMENT SYSTEM IN CONSUMER ELECTRONICS

Western understanding of the Japanese labor-management system has been heavily influenced by descriptions of the Toyota production system that in immortalized in Womack, Jones, and Roos's (1990) characterization of lean production. More recently, there have been some doubts as to whether this model is a universal description of the organization of Japanese industry. There can be little doubt that there must be some variation across industries according to the technical complexity of the production process and set of labor skills required, among other factors. Thus, it is reasonable that the labor-management system used in automobile assembly factories might differ from that used in television assembly plants. In comparison to automobile factories, there has been limited previous research concerning the labor-management system used by Japanese television and consumer electronics factories.[4] Nonetheless, the context within which the Japanese consumer electronics industry developed was the same as that of the auto industry and included long-term employment for regular employees; a complicated pay system based on seniority, skills, and job grade; enterprise unions; a blurred white collar–blue collar role division; the use of temporary (contract) workers; and the use of relational contracting with supplier firms for requisite parts and supplies (Aoki, 1988; Dore, 1973, 1986; Koike, 1988).

The available literature and interviews by one of the authors suggest that an important dimension of the labor-management system of the typical Japanese consumer electronics factory is the stratification of production workers on the basis of the type of contract held with the firm.[5]

The lowest stratum of production workers consists of a group of fixed-term, contract (i.e., temporary) workers. Above the contract workers is a stratum of regular shop floor workers who are hired on a long-term basis (Kenney, 1995; Nakamura, Demes, & Nagano, 1994). This distinction influences the type of testing administered to prospective workers during the hiring process.

In Japan's long-term employment system, hiring is a very important function. Manufacturing employees are hired once annually through the recruitment of regular and industrial high school graduates. All regular employees receive written, oral, and medical examinations. The written examination includes surprisingly difficult algebra, contemporary economics, and English-language questions. The oral examination is meant to establish the worker's personality and motivation and lasts between 30 and 60 minutes. There is also at least one medical examination.

The distinction between contract workers and regular workers influences the type of work performed, as well as wage levels. Contract workers tend to perform simple, routinized assembly tasks requiring minimal skills and are paid relatively low wages, whereas regular workers are paid higher wages and perform higher level work tasks (Kenney, 1995; Nakamura et al., 1994). In a study of a VCR factory, Nakamura et al. (1994) found that the assembly of VCRs was done almost entirely by contract workers and involved very routinized work tasks. Even though they were officially defined as contract workers, these employees were relatively permanent workers in practice because their contracts were almost invariably renewed. Although assembly work was organized on the basis of teams, regular workers did not typically perform any assembly tasks. Instead, regular workers primarily engaged in supervisory and control duties. Moreover, there were few or no contract workers engaged in jobs requiring greater skill and/or a broader range of knowledge such as those in the adjustment and inspection, engineering, materials supply, and parts subsections.

Trends in the broader Japanese economy indicate that the use of contract workers is increasing in manufacturing (Ministry of Labor, 1996, p. 416). Recent interviews conducted by Kenney (1995, 1996a, 1996b) suggest, however, that the use of contract workers in Japanese television assembly factories has declined.[6] For example, at one television assembly facility, nearly all workers were found to be regular employees, although many were employed as contract assembly workers at an earlier point in time. Recently, due to the continuing transfer of television assembly offshore, increasing automation, and the unwillingness of Japanese workers to accept such jobs, the television assembly factories have begun to eliminate contract workers.[7] This indicates that some regular employees are now performing assembly tasks.

The distinction between contract workers and regular workers influences opportunities for training and learning available to production workers. All regular employees receive a period of orientation of from 1 to 5 days of training after being hired, depending on the particular company. After beginning their jobs in a factory, production workers receive on-the-job training. An important aspect of Japanese on-the-job training mentioned in the literature is job rotation, whereby workers are trained to perform a broad range of work tasks. Different types of job rotation are used. Toyota, for example, employs short-term task rotation, in which each member of a work team (see discussion below) receives training in and performs all or most of the work tasks undertaken by the team, and longer-term rotation (or transfer), in which workers are transferred between positions in entirely different work groups or units and receive training in and perform tasks within these different groups (Cole, 1989).

In Japanese consumer electronics factories, regular workers are exposed to longer-term rotation, or transfer, whereas contract workers are not. Upon entry into the factory, regular workers are transferred through various jobs during their first 3 months on the job. After this, they are assigned to a particular section in which the group leader is responsible for their further on-the-job training, although the actual training is largely provided by senior workers (Kenney, 1996a, 1996b). Thus, the scope of tasks undertaken by regular workers over time tends to be relatively broad, and cross training is used (Kenney, 1995; Nakamura et al., 1994).

Short-term task rotation is not typically used in Japanese consumer electronics factories. For example, at a Japanese television factory studied by Kenney (1995), assembly line contract workers perform the same work task each day. The lack of use of short-term task rotation in Japanese consumer electronics factories is not due to Western-style job control rights. Rather, Japanese managers believed it was better that personnel learn to do a particular job well (Kenney, 1995).

The use of longer-term rotation, or transfer, is also part of an internal job ladder. Japanese consumer electronics firms fill all higher level shop-floor positions through internal promotion. Nakamura et al. (1994) describe an elaborate system by which regular employees enter the firm and gradually are promoted and transferred to different functions. Most begin in adjustment and inspection and transfer through different posts in the sections as they receive steadily higher grades. After sufficient experience, some move into the first supervisory positions as team leaders; others move into the senior ranks of the maintenance, inspection, and quality control sections. During this entire process, regular workers are receiving on-the-job training across a broad scope of work activities. When organized and exploited, such learning can become a powerful mechanism for increasing a factory's capabilities.

During this process, regular workers also tend to receive opportunities for off-the-job training, whereas contract workers do not. Off-the-job training represents a more substantial investment compared to on-the-job training because workers are not producing for the factory while they are training. There are various levels of off-the-job training. First, there are plant-level training courses in robotics, integrated circuitry, and various other technical topics taught by senior factory personnel (Kenney, 1996b). There are also companywide training courses. Finally, there are courses offered by outside organizations. Overall, the training component for regular production workers plays a central role in preparing these employees for the internal job ladder and represents a significant investment in these workers by the Japanese firm. However, the actual acquisition of a new skill (i.e., completing a course or receiving a national license) does not automatically guarantee a promotion, although such accomplishments are necessary to be considered for one (Kenney, 1996b).

In Japanese television assembly, just as in automobile factories (Cole, 1989), production workers are organized into work teams or groups (*han*). There are, however, qualitative differences in the role of groups in each industry. Due to the physical layout of the assembly line and the actual work activities, nearly all the individual jobs on a television assembly line can be done by a single worker. As a result, there is less need for tight within-group coordination and/or work sharing. Therefore, in contrast to the Toyota model, the work group in television assembly has less of a production management role and is more a supervisory institution. Other small-group activities, however, such as quality control circles and safety improvement groups, are also central to television assembly and include each factory worker. Small-group activities have a process improvement aspect and, perhaps more important, a social aspect. These activities are geared not only to technical improvement but to developing a social solidarity (Adler, 1999).

Japanese manufacturing success centers on the ability of Japanese factories to manufacture efficiently and to continually increase productivity and product quality (see Adler & Cole, 1993; Fruin, 1992, 1997; Kenney & Florida, 1993). A factory has the potential not only to produce goods but to generate knowledge about production. As an organization, the factory learns and innovates, thereby increasing productivity as part of its normal operation. This is exemplified in the role Nakamura et al. (1994, pp. 42-44) describe for production workers in the process of developing and introducing new consumer electronics products. In the early stages, their role is auxiliary and is confined to supplying data. However, in the pilot run and pre-production phases, they are actively involved in working "with production engineers on video assembly, adjustment and inspection, and they actively put forward their own ideas on how to improve work steps."

The ongoing training and education promoted in the Japanese system provides the context for the production worker's direct role in spearheading continuous improvement and quality control activities. An indirect factory output can be the development of new skills and capabilities. As Koike (1988) pointed out, many of these skills are partly firm specific and often tacit. As a result, such skills are not easily transportable (on the importance of tacit skills for Japanese firms, see Nonaka & Takeuchi, 1995). The factory evolves to higher levels of efficiency because it is populated by workers who continuously develop new capabilities.

THE ROLE OF GENDER IN THE JAPANESE LABOR-MANAGEMENT SYSTEM

An additional dimension of Japanese labor-management in consumer electronics is a system of gender stratification. First, the stratum of contract workers performing low-skilled work on the assembly line and receiving lower wages consists mostly of females, whereas the stratum of regular production workers tends to consist predominantly of males. Although there are no legal or formal distinctions, within the stratum of regular shop floor workers, opportunities for promotion and training tend to be stratified on the basis of gender. Regular employees who are male typically have greater seniority and substantially better opportunities for training. Moreover, they also tend to have higher skills and their "duties are mainly maintenance-related" (Abo, 1994a, p. 157). Regular employees who are male are also more apt to be promoted to first-line supervisors and higher level positions. In these supervisory positions, they are responsible for managing employees, setting standard processing times, spearheading operational improvements, and evaluating performance (Abo, 1994a, p. 158).[8]

In contrast, opportunities are typically more circumscribed for regular employees who are female. For example, at most companies, promotions for women usually progress no higher than the group leader, although all Japanese consumer electronics firms have some females in supervisor positions. There are inconsistent findings concerning whether the opportunity for transfer through a broad variety of jobs is stratified by gender. For example, Nakamura et al. (1994) found that all regular employees received this type of transfer, whereas Abo (1994a) found that this type of transfer was restricted to males. In either case, mobility and opportunities for participating in more skilled work activities tend to be limited for female workers.

Although female workers are treated differently than male workers, labor turnover for both sexes is low in Japanese factories. Hiramoto (1995, p. 246) found that annual turnover at a Hitachi television assembly facility in Japan was 1% for male workers and 4.2% for female workers. At one Japanese television assembly facility, male turnover was "almost zero except for retirement" and women's turnover was 1% a year. Female turnover was usually due to marriage and pregnancy (but usually these women plan on returning). The inclusion of secretaries (office personnel) raises turnover to approximately 5% per year (Nakamura et al., 1994). In other words, even female workers on the assembly line do not tend to leave.

TRANSFER OF THE JAPANESE LABOR-MANAGEMENT SYSTEM

Research concerning the overseas transfer of Japanese labor-management methods has multiplied over the last decade. Most research has concentrated on the operations of Japanese firms in developed countries. These studies have concluded that the most comprehensive transfer of Japanese labor-management methods has taken place within the automobile and auto parts sectors (Abo, 1994a; Adler, 1993; Kenney & Florida, 1993). Although some studies have disputed this conclusion (Fucini & Fucini, 1990; Graham, 1995; Parker & Slaughter, 1988), there can be little doubt that Japanese firms in the automobile and auto parts sectors have implemented some Japanese-style labor-management practices in their offshore factories. At issue for most critics is the range of practices that have been transferred and the degree to which these practices have been accepted or viewed as desirable by workers.

The transfer of Japanese labor-management methods to transplants in consumer electronics has received less attention. Most studies of Japanese consumer electronics factories in the United States have found a more limited transfer compared to the automobile and auto parts sectors (Abo, 1994a; Hiramoto, 1995; Kenney & Florida, 1993; Milkman, 1991; Sato, 1991). This finding has been confirmed in studies of Japanese consumer electronics firms in the United Kingdom (Delbridge, 1995; Oliver & Wilkinson, 1988; Taylor, Elger, & Fairbrother, 1994).

There have been only two multinational (as opposed to binational) studies on the transfer of Japanese labor-management techniques in consumer electronics. Abo (1994a, p. 13) found that there was greater transfer of the Japanese system to Asian factories as compared to U.S. factories. Nomura (1992) compared Japanese consumer electronics plants with their transplants in Europe and other parts of Asia and concluded that they exhibited a high degree of similarity in terms of the use of internal promotion, employment of peripheral workers, and overtime. They also exhibited some similarity in the use of in-house union organizations, qualification systems, and personal evaluation but exhibited little similarity with regard to turnover, wage systems, the use of subcontracting, and the degree of flexibility of the work system.

Koike and Inoki (1990) studied the skill formation systems of Japanese subsidiaries in Southeast Asia and found limited evidence of the transfer of Japanese skill formation practices. On the other hand, Kawabe (1991) found the development of a hybrid of local and Japanese management styles in offshore factories in Malaysia. Beechler and Taylor (1995) found a mixed record concerning the transfer of Japanese human resource management practices to the offshore factories of Japanese consumer electronics firms operating in Malaysia. Hiramoto (1995) compared two Japanese television assembly factories in Taiwan and Malaysia to those in Japan and found that the Malaysian factory was similar with regard to the use of internal promotion, performance evaluation, education and training, regular bonuses, and small-group activities.

It is difficult to summarize this broad range of studies adequately given the differing firms, nations, methodologies, and perspectives involved. However, the one conclusion that can be drawn with regard to consumer electronics assembly is that Japanese labor-management practices are transferred more to factories in Asian countries, especially transports meant to be export platforms, than to factories in other countries. It is interesting to study Mexico, since Mexico is a non-Asian country that receives large-scale Japanese investment and has established export platforms.

RESEARCH ON THE MAQUILADORAS

Research on the use of Japanese labor-management methods in Mexican maquiladoras has produced contradictory findings. Much of the research carried out in the 1980s concluded that the maquiladoras were only low-skill sweatshops that exhibited little if any evidence of using advanced manufacturing techniques (Carrillo & Hernandez, 1985; Fernandez-Kelly, 1983). Several recent studies of Japanese-operated maquiladoras also found the extent of transfer of Japanese labor-management methods to be minimal at best. Using the framework developed by Abo (1994a), Kamiyama (1994) found that Japanese-operated maquiladoras are characterized by certain features of the Japanese system such as the lack of unions and the use of

Japanese machinery. However, there was little evidence of job rotation, worker involvement in quality control circles, internal training, and other Japanese work organization characteristics. Consistent with this study, Kenney and Florida (1994) found little evidence of Japanese management techniques in the consumer electronics maquiladoras based on interviews with managers. They did find, however, that managers were trying to develop and retain a stable core of production workers that could be considered as analogous to the regular employees in Japanese factories.

In contrast to these studies, other recent research has found evidence that advanced manufacturing techniques are now being used more extensively in some maquiladoras (Gonzalez-Arechiga & Ramirez, 1992; Pelayo-Martinez, 1992; P. Wilson, 1992). Using samples not differentiated by the nationality of the firm, a number of researchers found that there are a significant number of maquiladoras using "flexible" organizational practices (Carrillo, 1993; Carrillo & Santibanez, 1993; P. Wilson, 1992). For example, Carrillo (1993) found in a sample of electronics maquiladoras that 33% use quality control circles, 39% have multiskilled workers, and 40% use some form of job rotation among operators on the production line. On the basis of this evidence, one would conclude that Japanese (or what many, such as Osterman, 1994, now call "advanced") management techniques have been transferred to Mexico.

Based on managerial interviews, Shaiken (1990) found that advanced manufacturing techniques such as "just-in-time" delivery, continuous process improvement, and job rotation were already in use at three Japanese-operated electronics maquiladoras, although overall transfer remained limited.[9] These findings were replicated in studies by Echeverri-Carroll (1988) and, to a lesser degree, Beechler and Taylor (1995). In response to these apparent differences, Gereffi (1994) theorized that there is a difference between the "old" and "new" maquiladoras regarding levels of training and skill upgrading. In this case, the old maquiladoras were those in the low-technology garment, footwear, and furniture industries. The new maquiladoras were in relatively higher technology fields such as consumer electronics assembly. It was expected that the newer maquiladoras would invest more in workers because of their more sophisticated production process. Thus, by Gereffi's definition, the firms studied would be included among the new maquiladoras.

In a recent study of factories of a major Japanese multinational television assembler in Japan, Mexico, and the United Kingdom (most probably Matsushita), Lowe, Morris, and Wilkinson (1996) found that the roles of supervisory-level personnel at the Japanese and Mexican plants were similar. At the Mexican plant, the supervisors and group leaders were able to "evaluate the industrial engineering implications" of a new product (Lowe et al., 1996, p. 16). Moreover, they found that in the maquiladoras, there was a seniority form of payment in an effort to reduce turnover. They theorize that in the nonunion environment, the Japanese found it much easier to transfer their supervisory system to Mexico. There was, however, one important difference. They found that in the Mexican factory its operators would only rarely be promoted to group leader and supervisor.

As indicated by this brief review of the literature, previous research has yielded inconsistent findings regarding the use of Japanese labor-management practices in the Japanese maquiladoras. From a methodological standpoint, the use of mail surveys as means of collecting data from firms can provide misleading results. For example, S. Wilson (1992, pp. 82-84) found that although many companies responded to his mail questionnaire asking whether they encouraged employee suggestions his follow-up interviews revealed that the use of these techniques was actually quite minimal. Additionally, studies that have employed interviews with managers as a sole or primary means of collecting data may yield misleading findings if managers believe that their responses could be scrutinized by higher level personnel and/or used for purposes that could be construed as being against the interests of the firm.

Previous research suggests that the maquiladoras in general, and Japanese maquiladoras in particular, may be in the process of beginning to use Japanese-style labor-management practices. If so, it is not surprising that inconsistent findings have been uncovered with regard to the transfer and implementation of these practices, simply as a result of the particular firms that were selected for examination. Thus, further research is needed to monitor this process as it unfolds over time and diffuses across a greater number of Japanese maquiladoras. There are several environmental conditions faced by Japanese factories operating in Mexico that could serve as obstacles to the full-scale implementation of Japanese labor-management practices.

First, labor turnover rates in the maquiladoras are high compared to the minimal turnover rates experienced by consumer electronics factories in Japan. In a 1994 study, turnover rates in Japanese maquiladoras were estimated to range between 5% and 10% per month (Kenney & Florida, 1994). In 1991, Abo (1994b, p. 185) found that Sanyo's Tijuana factory had the highest turnover (180% per year) of five Sanyo overseas television factories. The next highest turnover rate (25%) occurred in the factory in the United Kingdom. In comparing labor turnover rates in border cities, Alonso, Carillo, and Contreras (1996, p. 16) found that Tijuana had the highest turnover rates, with an average of 12.7% per month.

One reason that has been given for the high turnover rates is the oppressiveness of work conditions in the maquiladoras (Paik & Teagarden, 1995). However, some studies have found that high labor turnover has resulted in cases where employees report being satisfied with and committed to their jobs. For example, Beechler and Taylor (1995, pp. 177-180) report that the firm they found to have the highest level of employee satisfaction and commitment (probably Sony) had a relatively high turnover rate (9% per month).

Contreras and Fouquet (1995) contend that the high labor turnover can be attributed to the following: First, there are few opportunities for workers to develop a "job career" in the maquiladoras; second, there is a permanent labor shortage in local industrial labor markets, which provides ample opportunities to secure jobs (thus, there is little need to be concerned about finding employment); third, jobs are not very important for workers' fulfillment or self-expression, since their main goals are related to family and home. A more structural explanation rooted in Thompson's (1966) discussion of the creation of the English working class has been proposed by Kenney and Florida (1994): That is, Tijuana does not yet have a settled working class habituated to factory work.

These factors pose obstacles to the implementation of Japanese labor-management practices in the consumer electronics maquiladoras in that the Japanese system requires a stable core of production workers (e.g., the regular employees in the Japanese factories). As discussed above, such workers receive substantial training aimed at providing new skills and upgrading the quality of their job performance. The justification for investment in worker training is that the skills learned will lead to greater productivity.[10] It is here that longer-term employment becomes important. If employees resign, the firm cannot recoup its training costs. Thus, there is little incentive to invest beyond minimal training if the firm does not expect to retain employees. The growth of Japanese maquiladoras suggests that this obstacle is not viewed as severe enough to prevent investment altogether.

Another factor to be considered, beyond labor turnover and the development of the Mexican working class, is the role played by maquiladoras in the technical division of labor of Japanese firms producing consumer electronics on an international scale. For example, Ohgai (personal communication, 1996) reports that consumer electronics factories in Japan are now oriented toward introducing new products into a firm's product line. This orientation has become more pronounced as firms have shifted production offshore, downsized their workforce, and eliminated contract workers. If offshore factories are used primarily for the routine assembly of mature products, then it is reasonable to assume that a different set of labor-management practices will be used in the offshore factories in Mexico compared to the factories in Japan, particularly given the high labor turnover rates and comparatively lower level of working-class development.

The following analysis will explore the ways in which the stylized model of Japanese labor-management practices employed in the consumer electronics sector is, or is not, being replicated in Japanese consumer electronics maquiladoras. This study differs from previous studies of Japanese consumer electronics maquiladoras in that data are collected from personal interviews with samples of production workers drawn from eight consumer electronics maquiladoras. Informal interviews were conducted with production workers in their homes in an effort to encourage openness about their work experiences and minimize any perceived fear of managerial retribution as a result of their responses.

TABLE 5.1 Maquiladoras Sample Firms, Number of Employees, and Date of First Operation

Company Name	*Number of Employees*	*Product*	*Date of Establishment*
Matsushita	2,100	Televisions	1982
Sony	3,000	Televisions	1980
Mutsutech	100	Plastic parts	1989
Sanyo TV	2,000	Televisions	1982
Sanmex	270	Electric fans	1982
SMK	500	Remote controls	1988
Arcosa	300	Wire harnesses	1986
KSC	360	Remote controls	1987

DATA AND RESEARCH METHODS

Data were collected in personal interviews with 75 production workers employed at 8 Japanese maquiladoras located in Tijuana. Interviewees included 4 consumer electronics assemblers and 4 electronic parts suppliers. The interviews were conducted from October through December 1993. Tijuana has the largest concentration of Japanese consumer electronics assemblers and electronics parts suppliers in Mexico. At the time of the study, there were 8 Japanese assemblers and more than 30 Japanese parts suppliers operating in Tijuana. The 8 maquiladoras were selected for participation on the basis of their size and importance to the regional economy. As Table 5.1 indicates, at the time of the study, all the firms were relatively well established. The newest factory, a supplier, was 4 years old in 1993. The oldest factory was 13 years old, and all of the others were at least 5 years old. We believe all the plants were sufficiently mature to have developed a stable management system.

Management was not involved in selecting interviewers or administering the interviews. Rather, trained interviewers were dispatched to stand outside each factory at the time the day shift was ending. Workers were contacted by these interviewers as they walked out of the target factory at the end of the day shift and were asked to participate in the study. If they agreed to participate, arrangements were made to conduct the interview in the worker's home the following weekend.

This method of selecting workers for participation ensured that different types of shop floor workers would be represented in the sample and that management or any other party would not influence the composition of the sample or the responses. This sampling design also ensured that shop floor workers from the largest, most important Japanese maquiladoras in Tijuana would be represented, and it also allowed the names of the firms employing these workers to be identified. This provides a benchmark for other researchers to compare their results. Firms examined in many studies are anonymous. As a result, researchers have no way of ensuring strict comparability.

The advantages of this strategy for selecting workers for participation were obtained at the cost of an inability to draw valid statistical inferences from the resulting data, since the strategy represents a nonprobability sampling design. The sample is, in essence, a convenience sample. As such, any conclusions drawn from this data can only be viewed as suggestive because probabilities cannot be validly estimated concerning the accuracy of generalizations drawn from the sample data to the population of all production workers employed in Japanese consumer electronics maquiladoras in Tijuana. The data are adequate for the purposes of "analytical generalizability" (Yin, 1989), that is, for determining whether there is empirical support for the stylized model described above and whether further testing and development of the model is warranted.

All interviews were conducted in Spanish in workers' homes and were approximately 1 hour in duration. Workers were administered a structured questionnaire that contained both open-ended and close-ended questions. The questionnaire was designed to collect information on the extent to which a worker's employment experience within a maquiladora involved elements of the Japanese system as identified in the research literature. This included questions designed to elicit information about a worker's previous work experience, current job characteristics, the nature of the training received, and involvement in work teams and quality control activities, among other dimensions of employment. Usable interviews with 75 shop floor workers from the 8 maquiladoras were completed.[11]

THE SAMPLE: CHARACTERISTICS OF FIRMS AND WORKERS

The Japanese firms from which the sample of production workers was selected are listed in Table 5.1. As previously stated, the firms in the sample consist of both consumer electronics assemblers and suppliers. In Japan, the use of the Japanese labor-management system is more limited at supplier firms, particularly small supplier firms. The supplier maquiladoras included in the sample are subsidiaries of medium-sized companies and, as such, can be expected to use most features of the stylized Japanese system (Chalmers, 1989). In Japan, the factories of the assembly firms represented in the sample employ the labor-management practices described above.

Assuming that the term refers to the badly lit, dirty, dangerous, and crowded factories that characterize such industries as apparel and shoes, the maquiladoras operated by the consumer electronics firms in the sample could not be termed sweatshops. Rather, the Mexican factories appeared to be modern, well lit, and clean like their Japanese counterparts. However, some interesting differences were identified between the maquiladoras operated by these firms and the factories they operate in Japan. First, the maquiladoras did not produce the newest products developed by their parent firms. Second, the maquiladoras that were television assemblers were found to manufacture some routine components such as printed circuit boards in-house rather than being supplied by external vendors.[12] Third, factories were not unionized, and none of the workers belonged to any union. Finally, maquiladoras did not hire contract workers on a temporary basis.

The sample of 75 production workers contained 48 workers who classified their work position as a direct operator responsible for work tasks such as assembly, welding, or painting (see Table 5.2). This represented approximately 64.9% of the sample. The sample also contained 26 production (i.e., nonmanagerial) workers who reported their jobs as higher level non-operator work positions. In descending order of ranking, this included 3 supervisors or assistant supervisors, 2 line chiefs (*jefe de linea*), 2 technicians, 5 production assistants (assistants to the line chief, warehouse assistants), and 14 quality inspectors.[13] Of the sample of 75 shop floor workers, 1 could not be assigned a work position due to a refusal to answer the question (see Table 5.2).

TABLE 5.2 Characteristics of Workers in the Sample (n = 75)

Variable	n	%
Work position (n = 74)		
Operator	48	64.9
Nonoperator		
Supervisor	3	4.0
Quality inspector	13	17.6
Chief of the line	3	4.0
Production assistant	5	6.8
Technician	2	2.7
Gender (n = 75)		
Males	33	44.0
Females	42	56.0
Education (n = 74)		
1-6 years	18	24.3
7-12 years	55	74.3
+12 years	1	1.4
Age (n = 75)		
15-20 years	42	56.0
21-25 years	17	22.7
26-30 years	9	12.0
+31 years	7	9.3
Marital status (n = 75)		
Single	58	77.3
Married	17	22.7
Divorced/separated/ widowed	0	0.0
Emigrated to Tijuana from other Mexican states (n = 75)	54	72.0

NOTE: Weekly salary in new pesos for all workers = 213.8.

Although none of the production workers were hired on temporary contracts, many of the work tasks performed by the operators are similar to the tasks performed by contract workers in Japan. Moreover, the tasks performed by those in higher level nonoperator positions more closely resemble those performed by the regular workers and lower level supervisors in Japanese factories. If a labor-management system is being implemented in the maquiladoras that is modeled after that used in the Japanese factories, then it would be expected that these two groups of workers should exhibit differences in labor practices that correspond to the stylized model of the Japanese system in consumer electronics detailed above. More specifically, workers in nonoperator positions should engage in higher skilled work activities, be paid higher wages, and receive more extensive training both on the job and off the job compared to workers in operator positions.

The gender composition of workers in the sample was 56% females and 44% males. Additionally, production workers in the sample predominantly (a) had between 7 to 12 years of formal education, (b) were less than 25 years old (56% were between 15 and 20 years of age), (c) were single, and (d) had immigrated to Tijuana from other states in Mexico. The average weekly wage for the entire sample was approximately $213 per week in new pesos (NP) (US$60).[14] Also, none of the workers belonged to any union.

Substantial differences were found in the gender composition of the operator and nonoperator groups in the sample. Following the system of gender stratification in Japanese factories, the operator group consisted of 67% females and 33% males, whereas the nonoperator group comprised 61.5% males and 38.5% females. Also, wages were found to differ substantially on the basis of gender. Production workers in the operator group averaged NP$186.9 per week (US$53.40), whereas the nonoperator group averaged NP$264.5 (US$75.57) per week.[15] This difference became more distinct when further divided by gender. Female operators were found to average NP$180.2 per week (US$51.49) compared to NP$200.3 per week (US$57.23) for male operators. Females in nonoperator work positions were found to average NP$216.6 per week (US$61.89) compared to NP$294.5 per week (US$84.14) for males in the nonoperator group.

Nonwage benefits were not differentiated on the basis of work position or gender with several exceptions. The majority of workers in the sample among both operators and nonoperators received paid vacations, medical insurance, on-site dispensary medical treatment, punctuality bonuses for arriving at work on time, and company-sponsored parties for Christmas and other holidays. Although not received by the majority of workers in the sample, a substantially greater percentage of workers in the operator group received subsidized cafeteria meals and food coupons and participated in a company-sponsored savings plan compared to workers in the nonoperator group.

FINDINGS

Hiring

In contrast to Japanese consumer electronics factories, the maquiladoras in the sample were found to continuously hire new production workers rather than hire workers once annually. This was the result of high labor turnover. A 1993 study found that maquiladoras in Tijuana experience turnover rates of between 5% and 15% per month (Kenney & Florida, 1993). Assuming this rate, companies such as Sony or Matsushita with 2,000 employees would be hiring 100 to 300 persons per month—a significant task. Hiring was found to be an ongoing activity for the firms in the sample, which contrasts sharply with the Japanese factories in which all hiring is undertaken once annually.

Additionally, unlike the Japanese factories, the consumer electronics maquiladoras did not extensively use screening and testing in hiring production workers. With the varied educational backgrounds of Mexican workers, it might be assumed that rigorous screening would be used in the hiring process. However, only 50% of the workers in the sample took a written examination prior to their employment and even fewer (36%) had oral interviews. The only examination that the majority of workers (72%) were required to take was a medical examination. Apparently, the existing capabilities of the operators was of limited interest in the hiring process. However, with turnover rates of 5% to 15% per month, it might be more efficient to allow new employees' performances to undergo the winnowing function that an exam normally performs.

The policy regarding written examinations seemed to vary, even at the same company. For example, at Arcosa (the Onamba and Sumitomo Electric wire harness supplier joint venture), one respondent applying for an assembly job said she received a written examination asking her to do "some addition and logical thinking problems." Another Arcosa assembler said she just had to complete an application. For the assembler position, it may not be worthwhile to use written and/or oral interviews in all cases. Even the larger companies had a similarly sporadic testing policy. This differs significantly from factories in Japan, where all regular workers received written, oral, and medical examinations.

Training

Unlike workers in the Japanese consumer electronics factories, a substantial component of production workers in the maquiladoras did not receive any initial training. Approximately 68.6% of the production workers in the sample received some form of initial training, whereas 31.4% did not. When asked about her training experience, one worker said,

> When I entered I also asked the [other] girls if they received any training, because they had never done this kind of work. But, they said no, they had only received a paper, which they also gave me. It had all the component names, the polarity and everything.

Whether a production worker received initial training, or whether a production worker was hired for a nonoperator work position versus an operator position, did not vary substantially by gender.

Of the workers in the maquiladoras who did receive initial training, the length of the training received was comparable to that in Japanese factories. On average, workers hired as operators received approximately 4.3 days of training compared to 7 days for those hired for nonoperator positions. The most predominant form of initial training for workers in the sample was related to the tasks and skills specific to their work positions. Approximately 65.7% of the workers in the sample reported receiving initial training of this type. In comparison, 41.4% of the workers received some initial training in safety procedures, 37.1% received initial training in quality control, and less than 15% received initial training in teamwork techniques and statistical process control. Most typically, initial training was administered by the workers' immediate supervisor or fellow workers in the same work position.

Like the stratified system of training found in Japanese consumer electronics factories, workers in higher level nonoperator positions in the maquiladoras were found to receive a broader and more extensive scope of on-the-job training through the use of longer-term rotation or job transfers. Nonoperators were found to have changed their work position an average of 1.7 times since being employed by their current firm compared to an average of 0.5 times for workers in the operator group. In total, 83.3% of the nonoperators had changed their work position at least one time compared to 30.4% of the operators. Furthermore, 33.3% of the nonoperators had changed their work position 2 or more times compared to 10.9% of the operators. Thus, nonoperators were transferred more extensively and thereby experienced broader on-the-job training.

In contrast to Japanese consumer electronics factories, few production workers in the maquiladoras were found to receive off-the-job training. However, corresponding to the Japanese model, workers in higher level nonoperator positions were more likely to receive off-the-job training. Among all production workers in the sample, only 13.5% received any off-the-job training since being employed by their current firm. When broken down by type of work position, 34.6% of the nonoperators received off-the-job training compared to only 2% of the operators.

The allocation of off-the-job training was not stratified on the basis of gender in the maquiladoras, since equal numbers of males and females in both operator and nonoperator work groups were found to have received this type of training. Interestingly, those who received off-the-job training had changed their work position a greater number of times compared to those who did not receive this form of training. Also, a greater proportion of the workers who received off-the-job training also had received initial training compared to the workers who were not given off-the-job training.[16]

Of those nonoperators who received off-the-job training, only two received further training outside the plant in which they were working. One of these nonoperators, Mr. A, had a junior high school education and had been working at Matsushita for 10 years. He received training in-house and twice attended quality control courses in Tijuana-area hotels. Mr. A said that his immediate supervisors had been sent to Japan to learn about the "company's policies and quality control mainly, and about [the worker's] work and to reinforce their knowledge about machines and robotics. The main reason they send them to Japan is to specialize in robotics." The duration of these trips was as long as 3 months.

Interestingly, when asked whether these workers who received off-the-job investments in training stayed with Matsushita, Mr. A answered,

> Usually, they [these trained workers] wait awhile and then go to work at other companies where they get paid better. . . . Because they are more specialized, they have other opportunities. . . . The company gets mad because they had [invested in the training of] the person, but it's also the company's fault. . . . The company, instead of saying "do not go, we are going to pay you [the] same as the new firm will pay" [lets them go].

This suggests that, at least within Matsushita's Tijuana factory, turnover remains a problem among those who receive significant corporate investment in off-the-job training.[17]

In sum, the evidence suggests that, unlike the Japanese consumer electronics factories, substantially less investment is made in training production workers in the maquiladoras. Moreover, training is allocated on a more selective basis. Corresponding to the Japanese model, workers in nonoperator positions receive broader on-the-job training through job transfers and are more likely to receive off-the-job training, particularly if they received initial training and were transferred more extensively.

TABLE 5.3 Job Mobility of Production Workers in Sample

	Initial Position	
Current Position	*Operator*	*Nonoperator*
Operator	44	2
	(95.6%)	(2.4%)
Nonoperator	19	5
	(79.2%)	(20.8%)

Internal Job Mobility

In contrast to the Japanese model, a substantial component of the workers in higher level nonoperator positions was found to have been hired into these positions rather than being promoted via an internal job ladder. Still, more of workers in these higher level positions were internally promoted. Of those workers in nonoperator positions, 79.2% (19/24) began their jobs with their present firm as operators, whereas 20.8% (5/24) were initially hired in nonoperator positions (see Table 5.3). This suggests that the sample firms predominantly tend to fill higher level shop floor positions by promoting from within rather than recruiting from the outside. As previously reported, the nonoperator group comprised 54.6% males and 45.4% females. Thus, like the system of gender stratification in the Japanese factories, males were more likely (but emphatically not exclusively) to receive promotions.

Promotion is one of the most important motivations for workers and forms the basis of an internal job ladder necessary to retain workers and establish expertise in the factory. One of the most successful workers interviewed was a junior high school graduate working for Matsushita. He began as an operator and moved up to technician assistant and then to technician; he was promoted to junior supervisor and transferred to quality control. This pattern is almost exactly the same as the one Nakamura et al. (1994) describe in the Japanese VCR plant. There were other examples. At Videotec (Sony), a 17-year-old woman was promoted to inspector and given off-the-job training concerning inspection techniques. A female inspector at SMK (a parts supplier) said vacancies are advertised internally. She said that those who wish to apply are given a course and then tested; if they pass, they are considered for the job. These findings suggest that there is a career ladder available to the maquiladora operators.

The reasons given by nonoperators for their promotions were remarkably similar. Of the nonoperators, 75% believed promotion was due to good performance in their previous position and 12.5% believed promotion was due to seniority. This differs from the findings of Carrillo (1993, pp. 166-167), which indicate that the most important factor affecting workers' promotions in the electronics industry is their level of work discipline, followed by seniority, knowledge of operations, and attendance. There are two possible explanations for this: The Japanese electronics firms have different criteria, or the workers misunderstand the reasons for their promotions. The findings of Carrillo (1993) also differ from those of Kenney and Florida (1994), who report that Japanese managers in the maquiladoras stated that seniority was not important for deciding promotions. Of course, in one sense, seniority is a precondition for promotion because of the use of the internal job market for recruitment to higher level positions (i.e., if you do not stay you cannot be promoted).

The supervisors were responsible for deciding on the lower level promotions (e.g., operator to quality inspector). This is interesting because these supervisors often are former shop floor workers who have been promoted. Promotions to line chief or supervisor were made by the managers. In the Japanese factories, the group leader has the most important voice with regard to the promotion of subordinates, but the final decision rests with the factory manager and personnel office.

In sum, the evidence suggests that the maquiladoras both deviate from and conform to the idealized model with respect to the use of internal promotions. The maquiladoras deviate in that a substantial component of workers in higher level nonoperator positions are hired from the outside, although the majority are promoted internally. Also, workers reported that seniority is not used in promotions. The maquiladoras conform to the pattern of gender stratification in that women are less likely to get hired and/or promoted to a nonoperator position. Additionally, promotions are handled in a somewhat similar manner as they are in Japan. We were not able to assess the possibility that workers could be promoted to the managerial ranks. If this were true, the blurred blue collar–white collar role division would be indicated.

The Labor Process

Unlike the idealized model, a small component of workers in operator positions in the maquiladoras did not engage strictly in assembly work, although the vast majority of operators did. A small component was found to perform maintenance on tools and machines in addition to assembly work, and a smaller component engaged strictly in the inspection of parts and supplies or assembled components. In total, 89.6% of the operators engaged in assembly work; 28.6% performed maintenance on tools and machines; and 10.4% were responsible for formally inspecting parts, supplies, or assembled components (see Table 5.4). Corresponding to the idealized model, the performance of maintenance work by operators was stratified on the basis of gender because male operators were more than twice as likely to perform such work.

Conforming to the Japanese model, the majority of nonoperators engaged in the formal inspection of parts, supplies, or assembled components (i.e., control activities). In total, 65.4% of the nonoperators were engaged in these types of inspection (see Table 5.4). Also consistent with the idealized model, a much higher percentage of the nonoperators in the maquiladoras engaged in technical work, such as testing parts, supplies, and assembled components or performing maintenance on tools and machines, compared to the operators. Furthermore, a much higher percentage of the nonoperators engaged in control activities such as administrative work and supplying materials and inputs to the production line. Very few nonoperators performed any assembly tasks (see Table 5.4).

Also conforming to the Japanese model was the pattern of gender stratification observed among the nonoperators in the maquiladoras with regard to the performance of higher level work activities. Female nonoperators were relatively more likely to be engaged in the inspection or testing of parts, supplies, or assembled components, whereas male operators were relatively more likely to be engaged in supplying materials and inputs to the production line, administrative work, or performing maintenance on tools and machines (see Table 5.4).

Japanese firms are noted for delegating quality control responsibilities to individual line workers. However, they have also developed inspection systems to ensure quality. Quality control processes in the maquiladoras were found to differ from the idealized Japanese model in several respects. First, a substantial percentage of the operators (23.4%) reported that they were not authorized to reject parts that were not correctly assembled, although the majority did have such authorization (see Table 5.4). Moreover, a small percentage of the nonoperators reported not having this authorization (see Table 5.4). Second, a small percent-

TABLE 5.4 Characteristics of Work Activity, by Type of Work Position and Gender (in percentages)

Variable	*Total Operators*	*Female Operators*	*Male Operators*	*Total Nonoperators*	*Female Nonoperators*	*Male Nonoperators*
Does the worker's current position involve:						
Assembly work?						
Yes	89.6	90.6	87.5	7.7	10.0	6.2
No	10.4	9.4	12.5	92.3	90.0	93.8
Formal inspection of parts, supplies, or assembled components?						
Yes	10.4	9.4	12.5	65.4	90.0	50.0
No	89.6	90.6	87.5	34.6	10.0	50.0
Testing of parts, supplies, or assembled components?						
Yes	0.0	0.0	0.0	26.9	40.0	18.7
No	100.0	100.0	100.0	73.1	60.0	81.3
Supplying materials and inputs to the production line?						
Yes	0.0	0.0	0.0	30.8	10.0	43.8
No	100.0	100.0	100.0	69.2	90.0	56.2
Maintenance on tools and machines?						
Yes	28.6	19.4	44.4	45.0	33.3	54.6
No	71.4	80.6	54.6	55.0	66.7	45.4
Administrative work?						
Yes	0.0	0.0	0.0	34.6	20.0	43.8
No	100.0	100.0	100.0	65.4	80.0	56.2
Is the worker authorized to reject parts that were not correctly assembled?						
Yes	76.6	75.9	77.8	86.7	100.0	75.0
No	23.4	24.1	22.2	13.3	0.0	25.0
Does the worker's duties include checking his or her own work?						
Yes	86.0	84.4	88.9	95.5	90.0	100.0
No	14.0	15.6	11.1	4.5	10.0	0.0
Does the worker have his or her work inspected by a higher level employee?						
Yes	100.0	100.0	100.0	100.0	100.0	100.0
No	0.0	0.0	0.0	0.0	0.0	0.0

age of both operators and nonoperators reported that their duties did not include checking their own work, although the duties of the vast majority of workers in both groups did. This was more likely to be true of operators than nonoperators. Finally, all workers in both groups reported that their work was also inspected by a higher level employee (see Table 5.4).

As reported earlier, most of the workers in the nonoperator group engaged in the inspection of parts, supplies, or assembled components. This position is often the first promotion from an operator and represents a second line of quality control. In the maquiladoras, the checking and quality control activities of the operators are reinforced with the liberal use of inspectors, as in the work of those in nonoperator positions. In-line inspection is also used in Japanese television factories. But we have no information on the density of inspection and the number of inspectors, although we believe that such inspection is used more extensively than in the Japanese factories.

The data suggest that the operators are not fully entrusted with the responsibility for quality control. However, the operators and nonoperators believed that the quality of the goods they produced was an important factor in their performance evaluations. Approximately 87% of the operators and 76% of the workers in the nonoperator group listed quality in their job performance as the most important criterion affecting their work evaluation; this is compared to other criteria such as speed, level of cooperation, and the provision of suggestions. Similarly, most of the respondents in both groups said that they were asked to provide quality improvement suggestions. Approximately 70% of the operators and 57% of the workers in nonoperator positions stated that they were asked to provide such suggestions. But suggestions were not mandatory as they are in every Japanese television assembly factory. Also, 69.2% of the workers in nonoperator positions and 60.4% of the operators stated that their immediate supervisor discussed work-related quality control problems directly with them.

Some workers described their experiences as quality control inspectors. A female quality control inspector with 4.5 years at Sanyo described her responsibilities. She said she was responsible for three lines and her responsibilities included checking the entire production process, inspecting the final process, and inspecting all soldering. Upon being hired at Sanyo as a quality control inspector, she received training in statistical quality control. Every year she attends further quality control training, and her supervisor has given her training in using and maintaining the equipment she uses. This was clearly an exception in the amount of training but did not seem atypical of the quality control inspectors in our sample. Another inspector, at SMK, received off-the-job quality control training and described it as being conducted in a classroom (2 hours a day for 2 days) where instructors explained "theory and practice on a blackboard."

These findings suggest that Japanese maquiladoras place a strong emphasis on quality and this emphasis is perceived by shop floor workers. For operators, the emphasis on quality does not appear to be supported by formal training in quality control techniques. Thus, for the majority of shop floor workers, any quality control techniques the operators know must have been learned on the job. Clearly, in Japan, a far higher percentage of the operators would have had training in formal quality control techniques or have learned them through various activities such as quality control circle activities. Here, there seems to be a fundamental division between our operator and nonoperator groups.

Work Groups and Small-Group Activities

The maquiladoras were also found to differ from the idealized Japanese model in that a substantial percentage of workers reported that they did not work as part of a work group or team, although the majority did. Of the workers, 65.7% reported that they worked as part of a work group whereas 34.3% did not. This was not found to vary substantially on the basis of the type of work position or gender. The majority of those working in groups reported that their groups met regularly to discuss production issues. Moreover, the majority of these groups had a designated leader, and group leaders were either supervisors (in the case of workers) or the chiefs of the line (in the case of operators). The responses regarding work groups suggest that they were used more as a channel for one-way communication to the workers than as a means of eliciting dialogue with workers. This is illustrated in the description of a daily group meeting provided by an operator at the Matsushita facility:

Question: You have a meeting everyday?
Response: Yes. In those everyday meeting they tell us if the work is fine, or to hurry

a little bit more, or that we need more production or that we are getting behind.

Q: And does he ask you for an opinion, or does he just tell you?

R: No, he sort of demands from us, because we do not make all the production we have to.

This type of response was quite typical of the operator's perspectives on work group meetings.

Labor Stability and Turnover

Like the Japanese consumer electronics factories, the maquiladoras were attempting to build a stable core of production workers via internal promotion, although they encountered constant turnover among both operators and nonoperators. Approximately 77% of the operators and 88% of the nonoperators had previously been employed by another firm. This is a reflection of the high-labor-turnover environment in the maquiladoras.

There were major differences between operators and nonoperators with regard to the average employment tenure at their present firm. The average employment tenure for operators was approximately 10 months, whereas the average employment tenure for nonoperators was 34 months. Thus, nonoperators (most of whom had been promoted via internal job ladders) tended to have relatively stable tenures at their current jobs compared to their jobs with their previous employer.

Given the longer job tenure, higher wages, greater training, and increased responsibility, it is expected that nonoperators will exhibit a higher level of work satisfaction than the operators. This pattern was observed: 65.4% of the nonoperators rated their job as "interesting and pleasant" compared to 35.4% of the operators. Level of work satisfaction also was stratified on the basis of gender. Among the operators, 56.3% of the male operators rated their job as interesting and pleasant compared to only 25% of the female operators. Moreover, among the nonoperators, 70% of the females rated their jobs as interesting and pleasant compared to 62.5% of the males. Thus, most of the females in nonoperator positions tended to evaluate their job positively or neutral.

Another indicator of work satisfaction is the desire of workers to continue working in the factory. This directly addresses the turnover issue that is central to the ability to build a knowledgeable labor force. Respondents were asked to specify how much longer they would likely work at the factory. Approximately 25% ($n = 23$) of the sample stated that they did not know how long they would continue working at the factory. Thus, there was no clear expected length of tenure for these workers. Of these respondents, 12 rated their jobs as interesting and agreeable, which indicates that they might be relatively stable. Another 10 rated their jobs as fine but not interesting. Of these 10, 2 said they would stay "as long as they could stand it" and 2 said they would stay "until they fire me." One worker stated that the job was "easy, but sometimes boring." These responses suggest that these workers might be unstable.

For workers who did provide a valid response to their expected length of tenure, important differences were observed in the expected tenure of workers on the basis of type of work position and gender. Operators expected to stay in their jobs an average of 6.4 additional months compared to an average of 11.1 additional months for workers in nonoperator positions. However, female operators expected to stay in their jobs an average of 5.3 additional months versus 8.8 additional months for male operators, 8.4 additional months for female nonoperators, and 12.5 additional months for male nonoperators. These findings suggest that the female operators are the most fluid component of the shop floor workforce in the Japanese maquiladoras and are most likely to resign from their jobs. However, the average expected tenure for male operators, female nonoperators, and male nonoperators was not long either.[18] These data must be treated with some caution because of the large number of workers who liked their jobs but gave no estimate of how long they would stay.

These findings suggest that there is likely to be immanent turnover among the workers, particularly the female operators. There were important exceptions. Mr. A at Matsushita was a junior supervisor with 10 years' experience and intended to stay with the firm until retirement. Few other workers expressed an interest in staying so long with a single firm. However, some other senior workers also had either long-term plans or no clear intention to leave. Generally, the operators, especially the women, had a short tenure and were intending to leave soon. In Japan, the tenures of the vast majority of both regular workers and contract workers tend to be stable for long periods of time.

DISCUSSION

The findings from this research suggest that a hybrid labor-management system is being employed in the Japanese consumer electronics maquiladoras that is similar to but yet differs from the labor-management system of consumer electronics factories in Japan. The maquiladoras are different from the home plants in that they tend not to produce new products and produce some routine components in-house that often would be contracted out in Japan. This means that much of the work that would be done by contract workers in Japan is done by regular workers in Mexico. Furthermore, the maquiladoras do not employ any contract workers on a temporary basis. At the same time, however, the labor-management system employed among production workers in the maquiladoras exhibits similarities to that used in Japanese factories.

First, a similar pattern of stratifying shop floor work positions on the basis of gender was observed in the Japanese maquiladoras. Workers who performed assembly and production tasks similar to those of the contract workers in Japanese factories (i.e., the operators) were predominantly female, and workers who performed higher level production tasks similar to the regular workers in the Japanese factory (i.e., the nonoperators) were predominantly male. This pattern of shop floor stratification appears to be less distinct in the maquiladoras in that males were also operators. Second, although wages are substantially lower and nonwage benefits less extensive, the pattern of wage stratification on the basis of gender in the Japanese maquiladoras was similar to that in Japanese consumer electronics factories. Males in nonoperator positions were paid substantially higher wages and had more seniority than females in nonoperator positions.

Additionally, similar patterns of stratification were observed in the Japanese maquiladoras in terms of work activities, training, and promotion. Like the regular workers in the Japanese factory, workers in higher level nonoperator positions typically did not engage in assembly work and were much more likely to perform higher level control and technical tasks (i.e., inspection, administrative tasks, machine maintenance, and testing of parts, supplies, and assembled components) compared to workers in operator positions. Furthermore, specific types of control and technical work tasks in the nonoperator group did tend to be stratified by gender in that male nonoperators were more likely to be involved in administrative work, machine maintenance, and the supply of materials and inputs to the production line. There was also evidence of an internal job ladder as the majority of workers in higher level nonoperator positions were recruited internally and experienced transfer through a variety of work positions. There were also cases of off-the-job training for workers in higher level nonoperator positions. Finally, the majority of workers at all levels work as part of a team, and a strong emphasis is placed on quality control as part of the labor process.

The evidence from this study suggests that the hybrid labor-management system of Japanese maquiladoras exhibits a number of additional characteristics that make it different from the hybrid labor-management system of Japanese consumer electronics factories. First, the maquiladoras do not use the extensive screening and testing in hiring that is used in Japan. Second, the initial training provided to workers is much less extensive, and a significant proportion of production workers do not receive any formal, initial training for their jobs. Furthermore, with the exception of the nonoperator group, little off-the-job training is given to production workers. This differs dramatically from the situation of regular workers in Japan but conforms quite closely to the situation of contract workers.

As previously mentioned, the findings suggest that gender stratification in the maquiladoras is somewhat less distinct than in Japan. This difference can be summarized along the following dimensions. First, many males are hired as operators to directly perform assembly tasks in the maquiladoras, whereas these tasks are performed by female workers in factories in Japan. Second, among the workers in nonoperator positions, the allocation of off-the-job training was not highly stratified on the basis of gender.

Differences were also found in the Japanese maquiladoras in relation to the quality control process. Like Japanese consumer electronics factories, a strong emphasis was placed on quality control in the maquiladoras as part of the labor process. However, a sizable number of operators and some nonoperators were not authorized to reject parts that were not assembled correctly, some workers were not mandated to check their own work, and all workers in both operator and nonoperator groups reported that their work was inspected by higher level employees. This suggests that production workers in the maquiladoras are not highly entrusted with the responsibility of quality control. Additionally, the majority of production workers received no formal training in quality control. One possible explanation for this is that the routinization of production is so advanced that the necessary quality control techniques can be learned on the job or are embedded in the design of the production process. Another difference was that a sizable component of workers in the maquiladoras did not work in teams. One possible explanation for this is that certain parts of the labor process may be routinized to the point that teams are not necessary or that some parts are organized more in the American style (where workers report to a foreman).

The findings suggest that, at best, the Japanese consumer electronics maquiladoras are only in the process of implementing the labor-management system used in Japanese factories. Central to this process seems to be the establishment of a stable core of production workers who are selectively identified and developed. The vast majority of higher level production workers began as operators. Some workers received formal, initial training concerning the specific tasks involved in their jobs, although it is difficult to be sure whether this was critical for their future employment trajectories.[19] A subset of workers receives extensive training in such areas as plant safety, quality control, teamwork, and statistical control processes. Among these operators, a select group is promoted to higher level positions and receives more extensive on-the-job training. Among this core group, a select few are provided with additional off-the-job training. This core group of production workers is paid higher wages and is engaged in higher level, supervisory, and maintenance tasks including the provision of initial training to new operators. The findings suggest that some workers may begin engaging in tasks of these types while still at the operator level.

Through this process, the Japanese maquiladoras seem to be trying to establish a stable, core group of production workers with longer employment tenure at the factory. As a result, the firm-specific knowledge and skills acquired by these workers can be retained (at least for longer periods of time). And yet, as one interviewee suggested, these trained employees also are often lost after receiving significant training. This is reasonable because at the moment there is a shortage of higher level production workers and supervisors.[20] This is in contrast to the bottom of the shop floor hierarchy that consists of the lowest paid workers (likely to be females), who receive no formal initial training and engage in routine assembly tasks. This component of the shop floor workforce is the most fluid and experiences the highest turnover rates. The findings concerning job satisfaction can be viewed as being supportive of this conclusion in that female operators tended to have the shortest expected job tenure and very few female operators viewed their jobs as interesting and pleasant.

In conclusion, the findings of this study indicate that the labor-management system of Japanese consumer electronics factories has been only partially transferred to the maquiladoras examined in this study at the time of data collection. It remains to be seen whether the hybrid labor-management system employed by these maquiladoras will be transformed over time to correspond more closely to the system used in the Japanese factories. It would seem that the perpetuation of the high-labor-turnover problem and the role of the maquiladoras in producing mature, routinized products and components would work against this occurrence. More extensive investments in transferring the Japanese system would appear to be risky under conditions in which a stable workforce cannot be maintained. Moreover, a more extensive transfer of the Japanese system may not be necessary in the production of routinized products.

However, the findings suggest that even in the manufacture of routinized products, certain elements have been transferred. This is understandable, since even routine production requires equipment that must be maintained, line-based decisions on product quality, and operator supervision. These tasks require higher level skills that can only be learned through practice. A more extensive transfer of the Japanese system to a larger number of workers may be based on decisions by Japanese firms to transfer higher order activities (e.g., product design and development, systems engineering) to the maquiladoras that are currently undertaken in Japan. This would require the development of the capacity to introduce and stabilize production of these new products in Mexico. It would be facilitated by the development of a stable working class in the maquiladora region that is habituated to factory work. The evidence uncovered in this study suggests that at the present time the consumer electronics maquiladoras do not primarily represent "learning" factories as described by Fruin (1992). Rather, they may be more appropriately viewed as "reproduction" factories, in which most workers have simple standardized tasks to fulfill in assembling routinized products.

NOTES

1. The term *maquiladora* refers to factories established under a special Mexican government program. These factories are licensed to import parts and components for assembly on the proviso that the finished goods be exported. In other words, the factories are treated as free trade zones. For further discussion, see Sklair (1989).

2. In 1995, there were approximately 3,000 maquiladoras employing nearly 600,000 Mexicans (Alonso, Carrillo, & Contreras, 1996). It is difficult to be absolutely sure how many Japanese maquiladoras are operating in Mexico, but Szekely (1991) estimates the number of maquiladoras to be 70. There are clearly more factories currently in operation, although no definitive roster exists.

3. For a discussion of Japanese hybrids overseas, see Abo (1994a).

4. To supplement our limited access to Japanese-language materials, we asked a Japanese-speaking graduate student, Shoko Tanaka, to search the literature, but few useful references were found. Inquiries about Japanese-language references were made of Professor Michio Nitta, labor relations expert at the Institute of Social Science, University of Tokyo; Atsushi Hiramoto, a professor of economics and expert on the Japanese television industry; and Professor Shuichi Hashimoto, a labor relations expert at Kokugakuin University—who provided us with some of the most important references. Curiously, most of the Japanese literature on television assembly studies transplants in great detail but provides little discussion of the factories in Japan.

5. The Nakamura, Demes, and Nagano (1994) study and the interviews conducted by Kenney (1995, 1996a, 1996b) concentrate on the same Japanese consumer electronics firm. The authors recognize that each Japanese firm is different, so generalizations should be drawn carefully. However, there are also many similarities between companies.

6. At the firm studied by Kenney (1995, 1996a, 1996b), these contract workers are represented by the company union.

7. According to an informant, there were previously three strata of workers: male permanent employees, female permanent employees, and female contract workers. Because of the recession and restructuring of the company's global television production, now only 25 of the 450 female workers are contract workers. This pattern has

been repeated at nearly every firm's television assembly facility in Japan.

8. Until recently, these tasks were normally reserved for industrial engineers and managers in the typical U.S. firm.

9. "Just-in-time" refers to the industrial practice of having components arrive at the point of production when needed. This technique eliminates buffers, shrinks inventories, and assists in locating problems that would affect quality.

10. Koike (1988) discusses, in great detail, the role and importance of firm-specific knowledge.

11. Interviewers were instructed to secure participation from 15 workers at each of the 8 Japanese maquiladoras. The initial goal was to complete interviews with 10 of the workers at each factory for a total of 80 interviews. However, due to inability to find the domiciles of subjects because of lack of street signs, faulty addresses, or a lack of time before nightfall, only 75 interviews could be completed.

12. This is significant because in Japan printed circuit board production, though highly automated, still requires some laborious hand insertion, a task often relegated to lower paid suppliers.

13. Supervisors are included as nonoperators because in Japan and in Mexico they are not considered managers. In Japanese television factories, the managerial ranks begin at the *kacho* (section manager). When employees are promoted to kacho, they then leave the union and are considered managers. Therefore, although a supervisor is no longer a direct worker, he or she is not a manager.

14. In dollar terms, wages in Tijuana increased at a rate of approximately 10% per annum from 1990 to 1994 (Alonso et al., 1996). Ten percent per annum is a relatively high rate of increase, particularly when compared to wage increases in most advanced industrial nations. In interviews conducted with Japanese managers in Mexican maquiladoras, Kenney and Florida (1992) found that they were trying to hold down wages but recognized and accepted wage increases of 10% per annum in dollar terms. Of course, with the Mexican devaluation in 1994, these gains were eliminated as wages decreased nearly 40% in real terms.

15. All conversions are made at the prevailing November 1993 exchange rate of NP$3.5 = US$1.

16. In total, 80% of the workers who received off-the-job training also received initial training compared to 69.2% of the workers who did not receive off-the-job training. Furthermore, workers who received off-the-job training had changed their work position an average of 2.6 times since they were employed with their current firm compared to an average of 0.6 times for workers who did not receive off-the-job training.

17. Labor turnover rates are lower for the nonoperators than for the operators. This is not surprising, since generally the highest turnover for maquiladora workers occurs in the first month after hire.

18. Our interviews were conducted in October and November. This was immediately before the December Christmas holidays when large numbers of workers return to their homes in central Mexico. Many return, but others do not. Thus, the length of service may be underestimated because many workers already planned to leave in December. If the interviews had been conducted in January, many workers might have responded that they intended to stay until December. For example, of the 10 respondents (all operators) at the Sony plant, 5 said they would be leaving in December. Often, if and when these workers return to Tijuana they find another employer. To help mitigate these losses, Sony now dispatches buses to various cities in southern Mexico to collect its workers and return them to Tijuana.

19. This was found to vary according to the firm involved. For example, Arcosa provides initial training to the majority of its workers, whereas Matsushita seems to be less uniform in its initial training regimen.

20. A number of Korean firms have recently established large production facilities in Tijuana and are actively hiring trained personnel. This provides an excellent environment for job hopping.

REFERENCES

Abo, T. (1994a). *Hybrid factories.* New York: Oxford University Press.

Abo, T. (1994b). Sanyo's overseas production activities: Seven large plants in U.S., Mexico, U.K., Germany, Spain and China. In H. Schutte (Ed.), *The global competitiveness of the Asian firm* (pp. 179-202). New York: St. Martin's.

Adler, P. (1993). Time-and-motion regained. *Harvard Business Review, 71*(1), 97-108.

Adler, P. (1999). Teams at NUMMI. In J.-P. Durand, P. Stewart, & J. J. Castillo (Eds.), *Teamwork in the automotive industry* (pp. 126-150). Oxford, UK: Oxford University Press.

Adler, P., & Cole, R. (1993). Designed for learning: A tale of two auto plants. *Sloan Management Review, 34,* 85-94.

Alonso, J., Carrillo, J., & Contreras, O. (1996). *Working in the Mexican maquiladoras: Challenges of the contemporary industrial transition and its interpretation.* Unpublished mimeo, El Colegio de la Sonora.

Aoki, M. (1988). *Information, incentives and bargaining in the Japanese economy.* Cambridge, UK: Cambridge University Press.

Beechler, S., & Taylor, S. (1995). The transfer of human resource management systems overseas. In N. Campbell & F. Burton (Eds.), *Japanese multinationals: Strategies and management in the global kaisha* (pp. 157-185). London: Routledge.

Carrillo, J. (1993). *Mercados de trabajo en la industria maquiladora de exportación.* Tijuana: El Colegio de la Frontera Norte.

Carrillo, J., & Hernández, A. (1985). *Mujeres fronterizas en la industria maquiladora, Mexico.* Mexico City: SEP-CEFNOMEX.

Carrillo, J., & Santibánez, J. (1993). Empleo y capacitación en las plantas maquiladoras. In J. Carrillo (Ed.), *Condiciones de empleo y capacitación en las maquiladoras de exportación en Mexico* (pp. 135-172). Tijuana: El Colegio de la Frontera Norte.

Chalmers, N. (1989). *Industrial relations in Japan: The peripheral workforce.* London: Routledge.

Cole, R. (1989). *Strategies for learning.* Berkeley: University of California Press.

Contreras, O., & Fouquet, A. (1995, June). *Trajectoires professionnelles et perception du travail a la Frontiere Mexique/Etats-Unis.* Paper presented at the Deuxieme Journess D'Etude CEREQ-LASMAS-IDL, Caen, France.

Coronado, B. (1992). *La localización como estrategia de competitividad de las firmas Japonesas: El caso de la industria electronica.* Unpublished master's thesis, Colegio de la Frontera Norte, Tijuana.

Curry, J., & Kenney, M. (1996, September). *The Japanization of Baja California: Japanese-owned maquiladoras and the rise of integrated production complexes in Tijuana and Mexicali.* Paper presented at the International Conference on Technological Learning, Innovation and Industrial Policy: National and International Experiences, Mexico City.

Delbridge, R. (1995). Surviving JIT: Control and resistance in a Japanese transplant. *Journal of Management Studies, 32*(6), 803-817.

Dertouzos, M., Lester, R., & Solow, R. (1989). *Made in America.* Cambridge: MIT Press.

Dore, R. (1973). *British factory, Japanese factory.* Berkeley: University of California Press.

Dore, R. (1986). *Flexible rigidities: Industrial policy and structural adjustment in the Japanese economy, 1970-80.* Stanford, CA: Stanford University Press.

Echeverri-Carroll, E. (1988). *Maquiladoras: Economic impacts and foreign investment opportunities: Japanese maquiladoras—A special case.* Austin: University of Texas, Bureau of Business Research, Graduate School of Business.

Fernandez-Kelly, M. P. (1983). *For we are sold: I and my people: Women and industry in Mexico's frontier.* Albany: State University of New York Press.

Fruin, M. (1992). *The Japanese enterprise system.* Oxford, UK: Clarendon.

Fruin, M. (1997). *Knowledge works.* New York: Oxford University Press.

Fucini, S., & Fucini, J. (1990). *Working for the Japanese.* New York: Free Press.

Gereffi, G. (1994, May). *Mexico's maquiladoras in the context of economic globalization.* Paper presented at the Maquiladoras in Mexico: Present and Future Prospects of Industrial Development workshop, El Colegio de la Frontera Norte, Tijuana.

González-Aréchiga, B., & Ramírez, J. (1992). La silenciosa integración de la industria Baja California a la cuenca de Pacífico. In J. J. Palacios Lara (Ed.), *La apertura economica do México y la cuenca del pacífico: Perspectivas de intercambio y cooperación* (pp. 169-191). Guadalajara, Mexico: Universidad de Guadalajara.

Graham, L. (1995). *On the line at Subaru-Isuzu.* Ithaca, NY: ILR Press.

Hiramoto, A. (1995). Overseas Japanese plants under global strategies: TV transplants in Asia. In S. Frenkel & J. Harrod (Eds.), *Industrialization and labor relations: Contemporary research in seven countries* (pp. 236-280). Ithaca, NY: ILR Press.

Humphrey, J. (1993). Japanese production management and labour relations in Brazil. *Journal of Development Studies, 30*(1), 92-114.

Humphrey, J. (1995). The adoption of Japanese management techniques in Brazilian industry. *Journal of Management Studies, 32*(6), 767-787.

Kamiyama, K. (1994, May). *Comparative study of Japanese maquiladoras with the plants in the United States and Asian countries.* Paper presented at the "Maquiladoras in Mexico: Present and Future Prospects of Industrial Development" workshop, El Colegio de la Frontera Norte, Tijuana.

Kaplinsky, R. (1994). *Easternization: The spread of Japanese management techniques to LDCs.* London: Frank Cass.

Kaplinsky, R. (1995). Technique and system: The spread of Japanese management techniques to developing countries. *World Development, 23*(1), 57-72.

Kawabe, N. (1991). Problems of and perspectives on Japanese management in Malaysia. In S. Yamashita (Ed.), *Transfer of Japanese technology and management to the ASEAN [Association of Southeast Asian Nations] countries* (pp. 239-268). Tokyo: University of Tokyo Press.

Kenney, M. (1995, December 14). [Personal interview and site visit at a Japanese television assembly factory site visit in Western Japan.]

Kenney, M. (1996a, November 28). [Personal interview and site visit at a Japanese television assembly factory in Northern Japan.]

Kenney, M. (1996b, December 25). [Personal interview and site visit at a Japanese television assembly factory in Western Japan.]

Kenney, M., & Florida, R. (1992, April). *Japanese maquiladoras.* Report to the U.S. Congress, Office of Technology Assessment.

Kenney, M., & Florida, R. (1993). *Beyond mass production: The Japanese system and its transfer to the United States.* New York: Oxford University Press.

Kenney, M., & Florida, R. (1994). Japanese maquiladoras: Production organization and global commodity chains. *World Development, 22*(1), 27-44.

Koike, K. (1988). *Understanding industrial relations in modern Japan.* New York: St. Martin's.
Koike, K., & Inoki, T. (1990). *Skill formation in Japan and Southeast Asia.* Tokyo: University of Tokyo Press.
Lowe, J., Morris, J., & Wilkinson, B. (1996, December). *Hanchos, floats and group leaders: An international comparison of front line management and supervision.* Paper presented at the ANZAM Diversity and Change Conference, University of Wollongong, Australia.
Milkman, R. (1991). *How "Japanese" are California's Japanese-owned plants.* Los Angeles: University of California, Institute of Industrial Relations.
Ministry of Labor. (1996). *The white paper on labor, 1996.* Tokyo: Author.
Nakamura, K., Demes, H., & Nagano, H. (1994). *Work organization in Japan and Germany: A research report on VCR production (1). Miscellanea, (6).* Tokyo: Philipp-Franz-von-Siebold-Stiftung, Deutsches Institut fur Japanstudien.
Nomura, M. (1992). Japanese personnel management transferred. In S. Tokunaga, N. Altmann, & H. Demes (Eds.), *Internationalization and changing corporate strategies* (pp. 117-132). Munich: Iudicum Verlag.
Nonaka, I., & Takeuchi, H. (1995). *The knowledge-creating company.* New York: Oxford University Press.
Oliver, N., & Wilkinson, B. (1988). *The Japanization of British industry.* Oxford, UK: Basil Blackwell.
Osterman, P. (1994). How common is workplace transformation and how can we explain who adopts it? *Industrial and Labor Relations Review, 47,* 175-188.
Paik, Y., & Teagarden, M. (1995). Strategic international human resource management approaches in the maquiladora industry: A comparison of Japanese, Korean and U.S. firms. *International Journal of Human Resource Management, 6,* 568-587.
Parker, M., & Slaughter, J. (1988). *Choosing sides: Trade unions and the team concept.* Boston: South End Press.
Pelayo-Martínez, A. (1992). *Nuevas technologías en la industria maquiladora de autopartes en Ciudad Juárez: Materiales y observaciones de campo* (Quadernos de Trabajo 6). Unidos de Estudios Regionales, Universidad Autónoma de Ciudad Juárez.
Rodriguez, I. (1990). *Las plantas maquiladoras Japonesas de Tijuana: Posibilidades y limitaciones para la integración con la industria nacional local.* Unpublished master's thesis, Colegio de la Frontera Norte, Tijuana.
Sato, A. (1991). Business as usual: Management practices of Japanese consumer electronics companies in the United States (Harvard University Occasional Paper No. 91-10). Cambridge, MA: Harvard University, Program on U.S.-Japan Relations.
Shaiken, H. (1990). *Mexico in the global economy: High technology and work organization in export industries.* San Diego: University of California, Center for U.S. Mexican Studies.
Shaiken, H., & Browne, H. (1991). Japanese work organization in Mexico. In G. Szekely (Ed.), *Manufacturing across border and oceans* (pp. 25-50). San Diego: University of California, Center for U.S. Mexican Studies.
Sklair, L. (1989). *Assembling for development.* Boston: Unwin Hyman.
Szekely, G. (Ed.). (1991). *Manufacturing across border and oceans.* San Diego: University of California, Center for U.S. Mexican Studies.
Taylor, B., Elger, T., & Fairbrother, P. (1994). Transplants and emulators: The fate of the Japanese model in British electronics. In T. Elger & C. Smith (Eds.), *Global Japanization* (pp. 196-228). London: Routledge.
Thompson, E. P. (1966). *The making of the English working class.* New York: Vintage.
Wilson, P. A. (1992). *Exports and local development: Mexico's new maquiladoras.* Austin: University of Texas Press.
Wilson, S. (1992). *Continuous improvement and the new competition: The case of U.S., European, and Japanese firms in the Mexican maquiladora industry.* Unpublished doctoral dissertation, University of Tennessee.
Womack, J., Jones, D., & Roos, D. (1990). *The machine that changed the world.* New York: Macmillan.
Yin, R. K. (1989). *Case study research.* Newbury Park, CA: Sage.

The Impact of Comparable Worth on Earnings Inequality

DEBORAH M. FIGART
JUNE LAPIDUS

Extensive research by sociologists and economists has demonstrated that a significant portion of the gender-based wage gap can be attributed to occupational gender segregation. A wage penalty exists for male and female incumbents in traditionally female occupations, even after accounting for human capital and institutional variables (England, 1992; Reskin, 1993; Sorensen, 1989a, 1989b, 1994; Treiman & Hartmann, 1981). Sociologists and others have studied the processes that perpetuate and exacerbate this wage penalty, including biased job-evaluation systems (Steinberg, 1992; Wajcman, 1991), socially designated conceptions of skill (Steinberg, 1990), organizational characteristics (Acker, 1990; Anderson & Tomaskovic-Devey, 1995; Baron & Bielby, 1985; Buswell & Jenkins, 1994), and the influence of market forces (Bridges & Nelson, 1989).[1] The relationship between wage inequality by gender and occupational segregation has been used to document the need for comparable worth policies designed to reduce the portion of the gender-based wage gap due to the undervaluation of female-dominated occupations (England, 1992; Sorensen, 1994; Treiman & Hartmann, 1981). Comparable worth has thus been viewed primarily as a strategy to address gender-based wage differentials.

Evidence on recent trends in earnings inequality suggests that policies targeting female-dominated occupations for wage increases could also have an impact on overall wage dispersion. Since 1979, there has been an observed increase in both overall and within-gender-group earnings inequality (see Levy & Murnane, 1992, for a review of this literature).[2] Two studies indicate that about one fifth of the increase in overall earnings inequality appears to be explained by the shift from manufacturing to more female-intensive service sector employment (Harrison & Bluestone, 1988, p. 120; Karoly, 1992, p. 114).[3] Although the service sector has produced more professional and managerial jobs than existed in manufacturing, it has also expanded employment in low-wage occupations, especially for workers without college degrees (Harrison & Bluestone, 1988). Concerns have been raised that a "pattern of dualism" is emerging (Kuhn & Bluestone, 1987, p. 17). Furthermore, the expansion of traditionally female industries has been accompanied by the "feminization" of occupations within industries due to the restructuring of work to reduce labor costs (Jenson, Hagen, & Reddy, 1988; Reskin & Roos, 1990). Thus, policies that raise the wages of female-dominated sectors could mediate rising inequality.

Within-group inequality has also increased for both women and men. For example, Wagman and Folbre (1988) pointed out that while some women have moved into higher paid professional and managerial occupations, the simultaneous expansion of low-wage

From *Work and Occupations*, Vol. 25, No. 3, August 1998, pp. 269-304. Reprinted by permission.

women's jobs has yielded an increase in the percentage of women at both the upper and lower tails of the earnings distribution (see also Katz & Murphy, 1992). Among men, the middle of the earnings distribution also declined, whereas the upper and lower tails grew (Burtless, 1990; Harrison & Bluestone, 1988; Levy & Murnane, 1992). The increase in inequality among men can be largely explained by the loss of jobs paying a so-called family wage. In fact, the gender-based wage gap declined with a fall in men's real wages, as well as the relative increase in women's education and experience (Bernhardt, Morris, & Handcock, 1995; Grubb & Wilson, 1989; Karoly, 1992; Levy & Murnane, 1992).

Despite the influence of the social construction of gender on these earnings trends, the relationship between the gender pay gap and overall earnings inequality has been relatively unexplored. In their comparative work, Blau and Kahn (1992, 1994) found that women benefit from a lower wage gap in countries with less overall earnings inequality. This article examines whether the converse is also true. That is, would a comparable worth policy designed to decrease the gender-based wage differential reduce other measures of earnings inequality?

Although intuition would lead to the presumption of a positive finding, the issue is complex. Pay equity is sometimes perceived as a middle-class women's issue, primarily benefiting jobs requiring relatively higher levels of education. Although supporting the policy, Malveaux (1985) questioned whether it would assist the lowest paid workers. Brenner (1987, p. 457) argued that "comparable worth is a relatively conservative approach to women's low pay" because it accepts the existence of occupational wage hierarchies. Pay equity is frequently omitted from policy agendas intended to address rising inequality (see, for example, Schafer & Faux, 1996). Therefore, the question posed above must be refined to ask which forms of earnings inequality might be alleviated by comparable worth. Would the policy largely decrease inequality between women and men, or would it also narrow intragroup inequality? Are the improvements greater for the middle ranges of the earnings distribution or the lowest paid workers?

In this research, we estimate the potential effect of a national comparable worth policy on earnings inequality, both among and between women and men.[4] Thus we ask what would happen if the negative correlation between wages and the percentage female in occupations were eliminated economywide. Although eliminating this wage penalty represents a narrow interpretation of a national comparable worth policy, this estimate provides insight into comparable worth's potential impact. We found a decrease in overall earnings inequality, inequality between women and men, and inequality among women. These outcomes held across choice of inequality index. Although the finding that comparable worth would reduce between-gender-group inequality was expected (as noted by Jacobs & Lim, 1992), the estimated reduction in overall and within-group inequality demonstrates the potential of comparable worth to reverse the so-called declining middle by revaluing historically devalued women's occupations.

DATA AND RESEARCH DESIGN

Wages and Comparable Worth

Occupational segregation by gender has had a measurable effect on wages. To estimate the effect of percentage female in occupation on wages, we replicated the multiple regression methodology used in previous studies. However, we also employed a technique to hypothetically eliminate the negative effect of percentage female on earnings to estimate wages under a comparable worth scenario, *ex ante*. Studies that estimate the potential impact of comparable worth implemented at the establishment level across the United States are *ex ante* studies. *Ex post* studies measure wages and the wage gap after realization of comparable worth wage adjustments. Some *ex ante* studies estimate the potential impact of comparable worth on other aspects of the labor market, including labor supply and employment (see Aldrich & Buchele, 1986; Ehrenberg & Smith, 1987; Killingsworth, 1985, 1987; Smith, 1988). None of these studies examines the potential impact of comparable worth on earnings inequality.

Most prior empirical research estimates that the negative impact of percentage female on wages is in the 10% to 17% range, depending upon model specification (Aldrich & Buchele, 1986; England, 1992; Gerhart & El Cheikh, 1991; Johnson & Solon, 1986). Two longitudinal investigations employing regression models with fixed effects reported coefficients in the 3% to 10% range, although the negative effect of working in a female-dominated job was higher for African American women (Kilbourne, England, & Beron, 1994; Kilbourne, Farkas, Beron, Weir, & England, 1994). On the higher end of cross-sectional studies, Blau and Beller (1988) and Sorensen (1989a, 1989b, 1990, 1994) estimated the impact at 15% to 20% for women and 20% to 27% for men, *ceteris paribus.* Studies on the low end of the spectrum emphasize that most of the difference in men's and women's occupational earnings is accounted for by industry or compensating differentials associated with job traits or characteristics. The addition of numerous measures of jobs traits (strength, working conditions, etc.) from the *Dictionary of Occupational Titles* (DOT) reduces the explanatory power of the percentage female variable (see England, 1992; Filer, 1985, 1989).

However, there is considerable disagreement about including job traits in the analysis. The more job traits (strength, working conditions, etc.) included in the regression equation, the more likely they are to capture how the market remunerates such characteristics. In other words, characteristics of work are themselves historically associated with the gender composition of the job and will reduce the direct effect of gender composition on wages. Therefore, the inclusion of job characteristics maintains some of the bias comparable worth advocates seek to avoid. Because job characteristics also correlate with human capital variables, overuse can result in multicollinearity, according to Sorensen (1990, 1994). Furthermore, research by Jacobs and Steinberg (1991, 1994) found that little of the gender gap in earnings was accounted for by compensating differentials, especially undesirable working conditions.

Using the March 1992 *Current Population Survey* (U.S. Bureau of the Census, 1992), we estimated wage regressions based upon Sorensen's methodology (1989a, 1990). Our sample included individuals ages 16 to 64 with earnings in the survey week. Earnings are expressed hourly (HRSPAY). Because returns to independent variables have historically differed for men and women, it is customary to run separate earnings equations for men and women. The semilogarithmic earnings equations for women and men respectively are

$$\ln W_F = \alpha_F + \beta_F X_F + \gamma_F Z_F + \varepsilon_F \quad (1)$$

$$\ln W_M = \alpha_M + \beta_M X_M + \gamma_M Z_M + \varepsilon_M \quad (2)$$

where X is a vector of human capital, demographic, regional, industrial/firm, and occupational characteristics that influence earnings and γ is the coefficient for percentage female, Z, in three-digit occupations.[5] This coefficient is interpreted as the percentage change in earnings with a 1 point increase in percentage female in each occupation.

A significantly negative γ is indicative of wage discrimination. The potential impact of comparable worth is then estimated by setting the percentage female coefficient equal to zero. Specifically, new wages (NEWPAY) are calculated using the estimated coefficients from the women's and men's equations respectively (β_{Fs} and β_{Ms} to generate a new wage equation in which $\gamma = 0$. Thus, women and men would be compensated as if percentage female in the occupation were not depressing the wage. This process assumes that wage penalties in occupations that are 99% female are greater than in occupations that are 70% female and that this relationship is linear. A potential drawback of the approach is allowing the rates of returns to characteristics, the βs in equations (1) and (2), to differ between women and men; this underestimates the interaction between occupational segregation and returns to human capital and demographic variables.

The wage adjustment process we define, setting γ equal to zero, is not procedurally equivalent to a comparable worth compensation policy of raising wages in female-dominated occupations up to a male, nonfemale (male plus neutral), or neutral pay line. There are several ways in which this methodology of assessing and correcting for wage discrimination differs from conventional comparable worth implementation. First, individuals and not jobs are the unit of analysis. Separate equations for individual women and men are substituted for female-dominated and male-dominated jobs. (In studies of gender- and race-based wage discrimination, four equations for race-gender groups have been used. See Cotton, 1988, and Gyimah-Brempong & Fichtenbaum, 1993.) This methodology was chosen to allow for pre– and post–comparable worth comparisons of wage inequality. Earnings inequality indexes are calculated with individuals as the unit of analysis. Furthermore, this approach permits use of a national sample, rather than firm-level data.

To replicate Sorensen and again contrast estimated coefficients with previous research, we added those job traits from the *Dictionary of Occupational Titles* that are summarized as scale variables in addition to conventional explanatory variables capturing human capital, demographic, industrial, and regional differences. The added job characteristics are cognitive skills, specific vocational training, strength, environment, and working conditions.[6] In addition, the inclusion of both full-time and part-time workers in the sample and allowing for the effect of both voluntary and involuntary part-time work on earnings, as we do, yields a lower coefficient for percentage female. We discuss the effects of modeling full-time workers only and the potential impact of eliminating the depreciation of wages for part-time workers in the results section.

The net effect of these methodological qualifications is that from a comparable worth perspective, the regression model will understate the effect of percentage female for women and likely overestimate it for men. The model intentionally biases γ against a hypothesis of a significantly negative impact of female occupational composition on earnings. Such restrictions incorporated into the methodology may produce a lower-bound estimate of the effect of comparable worth on earnings and inequality.[7]

With those conditions stipulated, we estimated comparable worth wage adjustments under a scenario that mirrors pay equity implementation and the parameters of similar social policies in the United States as much as possible. For example, the benefits of comparable worth wage increases were restricted to women and men in female-dominated occupations, defined as 70% or more female. This threshold is the most commonly used, although some jurisdictions have used more inclusive definitions. However, occupations that are less than 70% female nationally may qualify for comparable worth wage adjustments at the firm level due to intraoccupational segregation. Examples include social workers, bill or account collectors, office supervisors, food counter clerks, electrical assemblers, educational or vocational counselors, and psychologists. Because public policies such as Title VII of the U.S. Civil Rights Act of 1964 and the Family and Medical Leave Act of 1993 have excluded small firms, NEWPAY results assume that firms with fewer than 25 employees (at all locations) are excluded from a comparable worth mandate.[8] Finally, no one individual's wage is allowed to drop, mirroring historical precedent in compliance with the Equal Pay Act. Based upon previous research, we assume that comparable worth wage adjustments would not have major disemployment effects (see, for example, Ehrenberg & Smith, 1987; Hartmann & Aaronson, 1994; Kahn, 1992; O'Neill, Brien, & Cunningham, 1989).

Inequality Measures

Most sociological studies of inequality have used the popular Gini coefficient (Bailey, 1985). To assess the robustness of our results, we employed a variety of indexes. We calculated the following measures of earnings inequality: the coefficient of variation (CV); the variance of the natural log of earnings (VLN); the Gini coefficient (Gini); the Theil-Entropy Index (Theil); and Atkinson's measure when $\varepsilon = 1.5$ and 2.0. For Atkinson, ε measures the relative sensitivity of an underlying social welfare function to transfers at different income levels. As ε increases, more weight is attached to transfers at the lower end of the distribution and less to transfers among top earnings recipients (Allison, 1978; Atkinson, 1970).[9] We chose $\varepsilon = 1.5$ and 2.0 to emphasize those reductions in inequality that would result from increased earnings at the lower end of the distribution. Although there is heterogeneity among measures, studies that use a variety of scalar indexes for longitudinal analysis show consistent trends across measures (Karoly, 1992; Levy & Murnane, 1992).

The CV is most sensitive to changes in the upper tail and is therefore least preferred if, a priori, we expect comparable worth to help women in the lower to middle ranges of the distribution. Deciles and the Gini coefficient were used to better examine distribution at the middle ranges, although no measure is ideal for distinguishing what happens in the middle from other kinds of inequality. The VLN and Theil measures, and Atkinson when $\varepsilon = 1.5$ and 2.0, are well-suited to analyzing changes in the lower tail of the earnings distribution. In studying family income inequality, Treas (1983) selected the Theil index due to this property. VLN, Theil, and Atkinson are also exemplary because they can be decomposed into inequality within group and inequality between groups. We applied the decomposition methodology to ask, *ex ante*: How would comparable worth alter inequality *among* women and men as well as *between* women and men?[10]

RESULTS

This section first describes the results of the regression models used to calculate new predicted wages. The effect of the comparable worth wage adjustments on pay and earnings inequality is then presented. A summary of the estimated effect on overall earnings inequality is followed by a comparison of the decomposition of intergroup and intragroup inequality. The impact of comparable worth on measures of wage dispersion for women and men separately is discussed last.

Wages and Percentage Female

The estimated coefficients for the semilogarithmic equations for women and men are summarized in Table 6.1. The results are categorized by job characteristic, human capital, demographic, regional, and industrial factors including union membership and size of firm. The estimated coefficients for the independent variables were consistent with previous researchers' estimates, with the exception that marital status did not have a significant impact on women's earnings.

For example, human capital acquisition had a highly positive and significant effect on earnings, and more for high school- and college-educated men than women. The wage penalty for voluntary part-time work was higher for men than for women, and significant for both. The effect of marital status on men's earnings was positive and higher for men who were currently married. The negative impact on earnings of being African American, Latino/a, or a member of another minority group was higher for men than women (see Albelda, 1986; Sorensen, 1989a, 1990). Finally, the relative wage advantage of union membership was also slightly higher for men than women, although the effect seemed to be converging across gender groups compared to earlier studies. Our estimates for the relative wage effect of unionization, 16%, were closer to Johnson and Solon (1986) than to Sorensen (1990). However, the magnitude of the estimates reflected those in the literature (see Leicht, Wallace, & Grant, 1993; Lewis, 1986).

To predict what women and men would earn with comparable worth, the impact of an occu-

TABLE 6.1 Estimated Coefficients From Earnings Equations: Women and Men

Variable	*Women*	*Standard Error*	*Men*	*Standard Error*
Intercept	.571**	.076	.934**	.094
Job characteristics				
Percentage female	–.118**	.027	–.193**	.030
GED	.135**	.018	.035	.019
SVP	.035**	.009	.067**	.009
Strength	–.011	.012	–.082**	.017
Environment	–.039*	.017	.016	.012
Physical demands	.008	.010	–.018	.010
Human capital				
High school graduate	.096**	.017	.119**	.017
College	.291**	.022	.306**	.023
Graduate degree	.446**	.028	.389**	.028
Age	.029**	.003	.033**	.003
Age squared	–3.1E-04**	3.9E-05	–3.1E-04**	4.2E-05
Part-time	–.092**	.012	–.140**	.016
Involuntary part-time	–.032	.024	–.014	.066
Demographic				
African American	–.049**	.016	–.152**	.018
Latino/a	–.049**	.020	–.115**	.019
Other minority	–.037	.029	–.084**	.029
Married	.022	.015	.098**	.016
Once married	.031	.018	.052*	.021
Child under 6	.046**	.015	.009	.016
Number of dependents	–.010	.005	.009	.006
Regional				
Small SMSA	.051	.046	.079	.048
Medium SMSA	.094**	.022	.139**	.025
Large SMSA	.098**	.012	.125**	.012
Midwest	–.111**	.015	–.055**	.016
Northeast	.020	.016	–.032	.017
South	–.088**	.015	–.081**	.015
Industrial/firm				
Union member	.162**	.016	.168**	.015
Local government	–.017	.023	.071**	.028
State government	–.022	.028	–.008	.032
Federal government	.138**	.035	.115**	.034
Small firm	.018	.017	.107**	.018
Medium firm	.042**	.017	.134**	.018
Large firm	.078**	.022	.145**	.025
Very large firm	.122**	.014	.215**	.015
Agriculture	.070	.063	.054	.040
Business services	.168**	.028	.119**	.026

(*continued*)

TABLE 6.1 Continued

Variable	*Women*	*Standard Error*	*Men*	*Standard Error*
Communications	.329**	.043	.224**	.041
Construction	.254**	.051	.237**	.026
Education services	.044	.026	–.097**	.031
Entertainment	.111**	.044	.067	.044
Fire	.211**	.021	.199**	.027
Forestry/fishing	.071	.259	.053	.185
Hospital	.351**	.024	.083*	.040
Household services	–.194**	.047	–.051	.126
Manufactured durables	.250**	.024	.182**	.020
Manufactured nondurables	.199**	.024	.151**	.023
Mining	.226*	.096	.391**	.063
Personal services	.097**	.030	–.071*	.037
Other medical	.238**	.024	.207**	.051
Other professional	.255**	.028	.093**	.032
Public administration	.260**	.034	.116**	.035
Social services	–.102**	.030	–.317**	.054
Transportation	.348**	.037	.236**	.027
Utilities/sanitary	.322**	.059	.201**	.041
Wholesale trade	.265**	.033	.229**	.027
Adjusted R^2	.488		.532	
Sample size	7,280		7,538	

NOTE: Data were taken from England and Kilbourne (1989); U.S. Bureau of the Census (1992); U.S. Department of Labor (1993). SMSA = Standard Metropolitan Statistical Area.
*p .05; **p .01 (two-tailed t tests).

pation's percentage female composition on wages was used. The estimated coefficients for percentage female were –.118 for women and –.193 for men and are significant at the 1% level. The higher the percentage female in the occupation in which the person was employed, the greater the wage depreciation and hence the higher the comparable worth wage increase in percentage terms. Using the customary practice of separate wage equations for women and men, the penalty of being employed in a female-dominated occupation was greater for men. Although this appears to support the reasonable explanation that the benefits to men employed in male-dominated and neutral occupations are relatively greater than the benefits to women, these findings are actually contingent upon model specification.

To demonstrate how the regression model understated the effect of percentage female for women and overestimated it for men, two additional wage regressions were estimated: (a) without the job characteristics variables; and (b) a sample of full-time workers only, without the negative effect of part-time and involuntary part-time work depressing hourly wages. Dropping job characteristics and using full-time workers neither altered the arithmetic sign of the remaining coefficients nor changed their values significantly. However, the absolute value of the percentage female coefficient increased.[11] Both job traits and work hours reflect how gender is incorporated into the definition of jobs. Pooling the men's and women's equations into one sample yielded several additional insights. First, when a dummy variable for gender was added to the pooled regression (= 1 if female), its significant coefficient was –.124, indicating the presence of other forms of gender-based wage discrimination in addition to the devaluation of traditionally female occupations. The effect of pooling men and women of similar sample sizes averages their coefficients and thus the value of γ changed to –.136, in between the results for separate men's and women's equations.[12] We have retained the methodology of specifying separate equations by gender in calculating wage adjustments to isolate, as much as possible, comparable worth wage discrimination from other forms.

When post–comparable worth wages were estimated by setting $\gamma = 0$, we found that comparable worth could have a significant impact on women's hourly earnings and on the gender-based wage differential. The descriptive statistics are reported in Table 6.2. Women's median earnings increased 13.2%, and the median female-to-male wage ratio increased 13.4% relatively, from 72.2% to 81.9%. At the mean, the female-to-male wage ratio increased from 76.5% to 80.4%. These estimates conform to earlier research by Sorensen (1987) on the effect of comparable worth policies on earnings in five states. Although the wage depreciation for men working in female-dominated occupations was relatively larger, the percentage increase in average and median pay for men was less, 1.1%, reflecting the smaller number of men in female-dominated occupations.

The estimated increase in hourly wage costs as a result of comparable worth wage adjustments was 3.67%. Our estimated expenditure on comparable worth corresponds with the average and median cost of implementation across 20 state governments found by Hartmann and Aaronson. This is lower than the cost as a percentage of payroll incurred by implementation of pay equity for civil service employees in Washington, Oregon, Iowa, Connecticut, Vermont, New Mexico, and Massachusetts (Hartmann & Aaronson, 1994).

TABLE 6.2 Descriptive Statistics: Wages

	HRSPAY	*NEWPAY*	*Change*
Women (n = 7,280)			
Median	$8.04	$9.10	+13.2%
Mean	$9.79	$10.41[a]	+6.3%
	(5.94)	(5.83)	
Men (n = 7,538)			
Median	$10.99	$11.11	+1.1%
Mean	$12.80	$12.94	+1.1%
	(7.96)	(7.96)	
Female-male wage ratio (n = 14,818)			
Median	72.2%	81.9%	+13.4%
Mean	76.5%	80.4%	+5.1%

NOTE: Numbers in parentheses are standard deviations. Authors' calculations are based on U.S. Bureau of the Census (1992).
a. Indicates the change from HRSPAY to NEWPAY is significant at the .01 level (one-tailed t tests).

Comparable Worth's Effect on Measures of Earnings Inequality

All five measures of earnings inequality registered a decline with comparable worth. These inequality indexes are summarized in Table 6.3, with the change from HRSPAY to NEWPAY.[13] The largest relative declines were in Theil and VLN, two of the indexes capturing transfers at the lower tail. To test the significance of the declines, jackknife standard errors were calculated for CV, VLN, Theil, and Atkinson, using formulas derived by Karoly (1989).[14] The declines in CV, VLN, and Theil are significant at the 5% level. Although standard errors are not available for the Gini coefficient (Karoly, 1992, indicates that computational costs are too high), the unambiguous improvement in the Lorenz Curve discussed below suggests that this de-

TABLE 6.3 Measures of Wage Dispersion and Inequality: Men and Women (n = 14,818)

	HRSPAY	*NEWPAY*	*Absolute Δ*	*Relative Δ*
CV	.638 (.009)	.608 (.009)	–.030[a]	–4.7%
VLN	.352 (.007)	.326 (.007)	–.026[a]	–7.4%
Gini	.322	.308	–.014	–4.4%
Theil	.175 (.003)	.157 (.003)	–.018[a]	–10.3%
Atkinson (ϵ = 1.5)	.231 (.053)	.219 (.013)	–.012	– 5.2%
Atkinson (ϵ = 2.0)	.340 (.020)	.330 (.021)	–.010	–2.9%

NOTE: Jackknife standard errors are in parentheses. Authors' calculations are based on U.S. Bureau of the Census (1992).
a. Indicates the change from HRSPAY to NEWPAY is significant at the .05 level (one-tailed t tests).

TABLE 6.4 Decomposition of Inequality Indexes

Measure	*Overall*[a]	*Intergroup*	*Intragroup*
VLN			
HRSPAY	.352	.0214	.3369
NEWPAY	.326	.0081	.3177
% Δ	–7.4%	–62.1%	–5.7%
Theil			
HRSPAY	.175	.0129	.1622
NEWPAY	.157	.0059	.1509
% Δ	–10.3%	–54.3%	–7.0%
Atkinson (ϵ = 1.5)			
HRSPAY	.231	.0100	.2230
NEWPAY	.219	.0050	.2148
% Δ	–5.2%	–50.0%	–3.7%
Atkinson (ϵ = 2.0)			
HRSPAY	.340	.0103	.3335
NEWPAY	.330	.0016	.3263
% Δ	–2.9%	–84.5%	–2.2%

NOTE: Authors' calculations based on U.S. Bureau of the Census (1992).
a. Sum may vary due to rounding; for Atkinson, ATK = IA + IR – IA*IR.

cline is also due to something other than sampling variability.

Comparison with results of longitudinal changes in the distribution of earnings in Karoly (1992) suggests that declines in the indexes in Table 6.3 are dramatic. For example, Karoly (1992, pp. 109, 111) reported that the increase in the Theil-Entropy index from .353 in 1976 to .359 in 1986, or 1.7%, cannot be attributed to sampling variability. As a comparison, the decrease in Theil we report in Table 6.3 is 10.3%. Similarly, the 5.2% decline in Atkinson for ε = 1.5 is greater than a 4.3% decline from 1976 to 1986 measured and reported significant by Karoly (1992, p. 109).

Whereas comparable worth appears to reduce overall inequality, it is a policy that targets gender-based occupational segregation. Therefore, we decomposed VLN, Theil, and Atkinson (for ε = 1.5 and 2.0) by gender group to assess the potential effect of comparable worth on earnings inequality between as well as among women and men. Results of our decomposition analysis for intergroup (IR) and intragroup (IA) inequality are reported in Table 6.4.

Previous researchers who decomposed changes in inequality found that inequality within gender (and race, age, or industry, etc.) group was greater than between group. For example, Grubb and Wilson (1989) demonstrated that inequality within gender group, measured by decomposing the Theil index, was higher than between groups. Using Atkinson's measure, Conrad (1993) also found inequality within racial groups was far greater than inequality between groups. Consider height as an analogy. The difference between the tallest woman and the shortest woman is greater than the difference between the average woman and the average man.

We also found that within-group inequality was greater than between-group inequality. Intragroup inequality accounts for over 90% of total inequality. In their survey of the literature

TABLE 6.5 Disaggregated Measures of Wage Dispersion and Inequality

	CV	*VLN*	*Gini*	*Theil*	*Atkinson* (ϵ = 1.5)	*Atkinson* (ϵ = 2.0)
Women (*n* = 7,280)						
HRSPAY	.607	.309	.300	.154	.210	.311
	(.012)	(.009)		(.012)	(.044)	(.030)
NEWPAY	.571[a]	.280[a]	.280	.134	.175	.283
	(.011)	(.009)		(.024)	(.010)	(.034)
Δ	–.036	–.029	–.020	–.020	–.035	–.028
% Δ	–5.9%	–9.4%	–6.7%	–13.0%	–16.7%	–9.0%
Men (*n* = 7,538)						
HRSPAY	.625	.364	.323	.168	.239	.354
	(.012)	(.010)		(.010)	(.006)	(.029)
NEWPAY	.615	.354	.326	.164	.233	.349
	(.012)	(.010)		(.010)	(.009)	(.029)
Δ	–.010	–.010	.003	–.004	–.006	–.005
% Δ	–1.6%	–2.7%	0.9%	–2.4%	–2.6%	–1.4%

NOTE: Jackknife standard errors in parentheses. Source is U.S. Bureau of the Census (1992) and authors' calculations.
a. Indicates the change from HRSPAY to NEWPAY is significant at the .10 level (one-tailed *t* tests).

on U.S. earnings levels and inequality, Levy and Murnane (1992) encouraged researchers to explore this aspect of inequality.[15] As shown in Table 6.4, intragroup inequality would decline with comparable worth, but by much less than intergroup inequality in percentage terms. Consistent with a decline in the male-female wage gap under a comparable worth policy, inequality between women and men naturally declines for each of the measures used. Yet the magnitude of the relative change is striking. Intergroup inequality declined by 62.1% for VLN, by 54.3% for Theil, 50.0% and 84.5% for Atkinson (when ε = 1.5 and 2.0, respectively).

However, it is not possible to discern the differential effects of comparable worth on women and men from the decomposition analysis. Intragroup declines capture the combined effect of reductions in inequality among men and among women. We therefore calculated each index for men and women separately and report the results in Table 6.5. For women, each index declined markedly in absolute and relative terms. The percentage decreases in inequality ranged from 5.9% for the CV to 16.7% for the Atkinson (when ε = 1.5). With the exception of the Gini, indexes for men declined, but by a more modest amount. The average decrease was 2%, as measured by CV, Theil, Atkinson, and VLN. Changes in the CV and VLN are significant at the 10% level for women; none of the index declines for men are statistically significant.[16] It is unlikely that the increase in the third decimal place of the Gini for men is significant (see Karoly, 1992).

The indexes that exhibit the largest percentage decreases for women and men are those that best capture changes in the lower tail of the earnings distribution. In fact, the share of hourly earnings received by each of the first four deciles increased under comparable worth. This indicates that comparable worth potentially reduces earnings inequality by increasing the income of the lowest wage workers. This is consistent with earlier findings that comparable worth wage adjustments could reduce the percentage of women and men earning poverty-level wages by approximately 40% and 10%, respectively (Lapidus & Figart, 1994). Based on a study of the relationship between occupational segregation and earnings among life-course groupings by Witkowski and Leicht (1995), married women with children could especially benefit from policies to eliminate wage depreciation in female-dominated occupations, contrary to opponents' contention that comparable worth will redistribute income to childless, single women (see Nelson, Opton, & Wilson, 1980).

The estimated decline in the value of the Gini coefficient among women indicates that comparable worth could also affect the proportion of women in the middle earnings quintiles. Wagman and Folbre (1988) noted that, for women, the relative share of middle-wage jobs declined between 1970 and 1986. Because the Gini is most sensitive to changes in the middle of the earnings distribution, the nonintersecting Lorenz Curves in Figure 6.1 suggest that a comparable worth policy has the potential to reverse this decline.

Let us put the changes in these indexes into some context. Although the magnitude of the changes varies according to the different measures, they are not moderate. In longitudinal studies, large and pivotal shifts in U.S. income distribution in the past three decades, including an increase in earnings inequality called the great U-turn, have been noted when the inequality indexes change 5% to 10%, or movement occurs in the second decimal place. The overall changes in wage dispersion estimated in Tables 6.3 and 6.4 are within this range. The reduction in inequality among women noted in Table 6.5 exceeds this range for the Theil and Atkinson indexes. Furthermore, in longitudinal and economic development research, an immense shift in income distribution is needed to alter the Lorenz Curve. It appears that comparable worth would have this profound effect.

The comparable worth policy that we have modeled addresses the component of inequality and earnings disparities attributed to the gender composition of occupations. However, the devaluation of women's work is related to other forms of discrimination. A more comprehensive approach to pay equity would eliminate both the negative wage penalty associated with the gender of the job (through the percentage female variable) and the gender of its incumbent (through a gender dummy variable). In fact, had we used our pooled regression, the declines in inequality for women would be even greater. Future research could build upon our relatively conservative scenario to model these broader definitions of pay equity as well as alternative public policies. In a related study, Figart and Lapidus (1995) found that both pay equity and an increase in the minimum wage would reduce poverty rates among women workers significantly. Thus, the impact on earnings inequality of potentially complementary policies, such as an increase in the minimum wage or another expansion of the Earned Income Tax Credit, are worth examination and consideration.

CONCLUSION

Under the comparable worth scenario presented here, eliminating the wage penalty associated with employment in female-dominated occupations increases women's mean and median earnings and the gender-based wage ratio. Beyond this, an economywide comparable worth policy would decrease overall earnings inequality, inequality between women and men, and inequality among women. For three of four indexes for which jackknife standard errors are calculable, the overall decline in inequality is statistically significant. In the case of the Gini coefficient, examination of the Lorenz Curves indicates a clear improvement under comparable worth. In comparison with previously reported research, the declines in all of the inequality indexes are notable.

Comparable worth is sensitive to class as well as gender inequality, addressing intragroup as well as intergroup inequality. By focusing on inequality within gender groups, this analysis disputes the contention that compar-

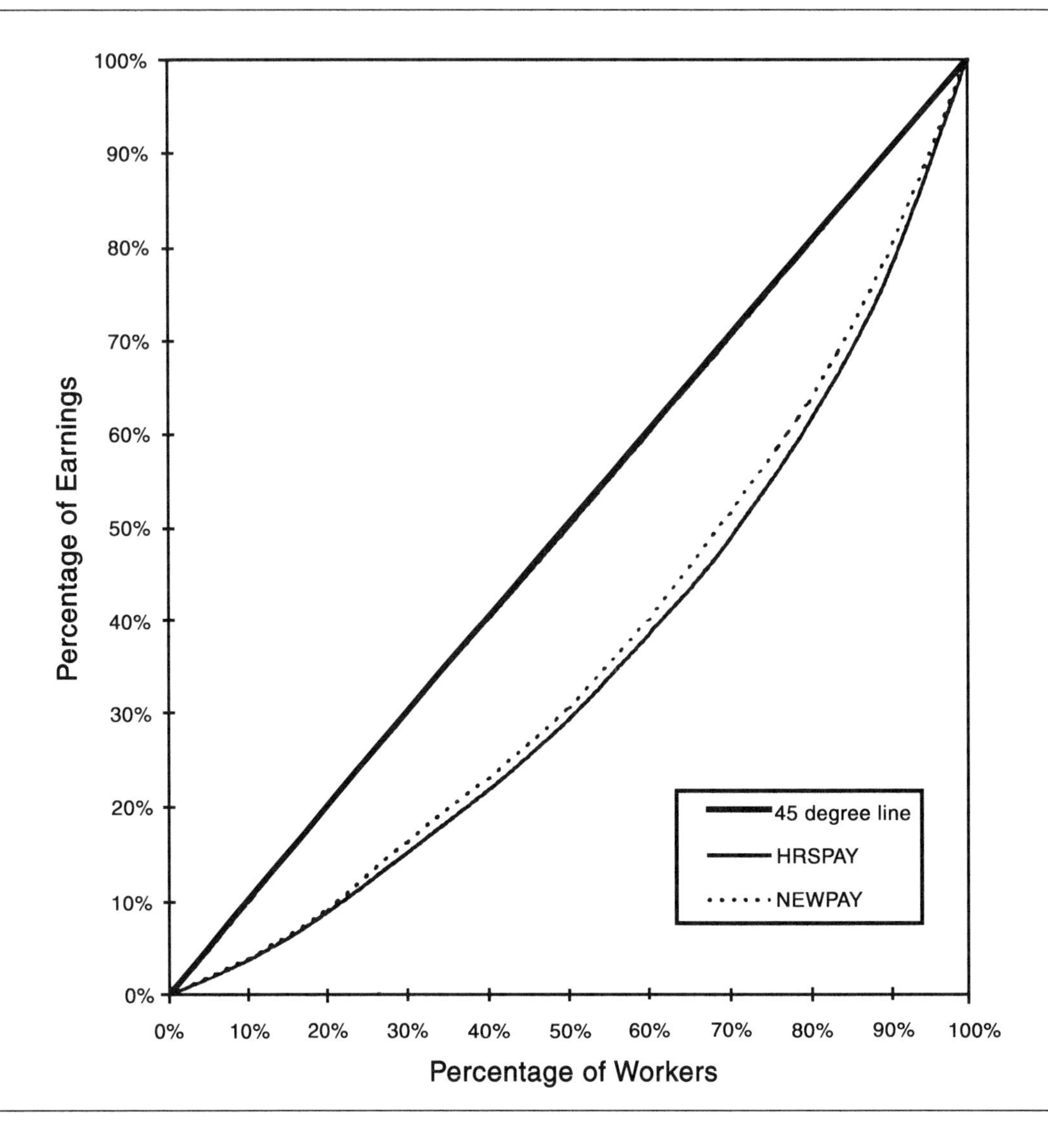

Figure 6.1. Lorenz Curves for Women

able worth primarily benefits middle-class women. In fact, a comparison of indexes indicates that reductions in inequality are concentrated in the lowest tails of the earnings distribution, raising wages of workers at the bottom of the ladder.

Our findings also indicate that a commitment to pay equity could serve to offset longitudinal trends of rising inequality brought about by industrial and occupational restructuring in the U.S. economy. Female-dominated occupations targeted by pay equity—in administrative support, sales, and service—are typical of the expanding, low-wage sectors frequently imputed to skew the earnings distribution downward. Comparable worth can be conceptualized as a means to minimize the disappearing middle in a feminizing labor force. It is a "low-pay campaign" in addition to an equity policy for the labor market.

NOTES

1. See Bielby (1991) for an overview of competing explanations of occupational segregation.

2. The focus is on wages rather than changes in the distribution of capital and labor's share of income.

3. However, growth of military spending and the expansion of male-dominated defense industries during the post–Vietnam War period, especially 1980 to 1986, have also been found to increase income inequality, especially between gender and race groups (Abell, 1994).

4. Our research is similar to Grubb and Wilson (1989), who calculated hypothetical changes in Theil measures of inequality under assumptions of change in, for example, the composition of the labor force, mean income ratios, or within group inequality, ceteris paribus.

5. Tenure was omitted from the model because it was not included in U.S. Bureau of the Census, 1992. Age and its square are proxies for experience. Marital status, presence of a younger child, and number of children were included in multiple regression analysis as proxies for supply-side variables that are not measured, such as time spent out of the labor force and other productivity-enhancing variables.

6. GED includes reasoning, mathematical, and language development; it measures the formal/informal education required to perform the job, which ranges from 1 to 6. SVP is specific vocational training required to perform the job and ranges from 1 to 9. SVP includes training in school, at work, and in the military, as well as institutional training and training in the vocational environment. STRENGTH ranges from 1 to 5 for work ranging from sedentary to very heavy, and includes standing, walking, sitting, lifting, carrying, pushing, and pulling. ENVIRONMENT is a measure of working conditions indicating the absence or presence of environmental factors; it includes extreme heat and cold, wet or humid conditions, noise, hazards, atmospheric conditions, and ranges from 1 to 6. PHYSICAL DEMANDS is a scale of four indicators gauging the absence or presence of physically demanding tasks; it includes climbing, stooping, reaching, and seeing.

7. According to Bryk and Raudenbush (1992), when the regression methodology combines individual and aggregate characteristics (e.g., firm size, industry, job traits, etc.), Hierarchical Linear Modeling (HLM) would be preferable to Ordinary Least Squares (OLS). OLS biases the results upward by lowering the size of the standard errors. However, HLM would require a substantial number of incumbents within each specific occupational group in the U.S. Bureau of the Census (1992) sample. We are indebted to a referee for this insight.

8. With the Current Population Survey, the possible choices for number of employees of the firm (at all locations) was under 10, 10 to 24, and 25 to 99. The Ontario, Canada, legislation is less restrictive; it covers private sector employers with 10 or more employees.

9. For discussion of the criteria or properties these indexes satisfy, such as independence of unit of measurement and the principle of transfers, see Slottje (1989), Karoly (1992), and Levy and Murnane (1992).

10. Equations used to compute these inequality measures and their decomposition are available from the authors, or alternatively: for the Gini, see Lerman and Yitzhaki, 1984, 1989; for decomposing the VLN, see Karoly, 1989; for decomposing the Theil, see Slottje, 1989; for the Atkinson and its decomposition, see Conrad, 1993.

11. Excluding the job trait variables raises the absolute value of the percentage female coefficients closer to the upper estimates for women found in previous research; γ was –.160 for women and –.125 for men without these controls. The wage equations for full-time workers reduce, in part, the effect of the gender-differentiated returns to human capital characteristics. The value of γ increases to –.210 for women and declines to –.156 for men.

12. Both variables are significant at the .01 level. The correlation coefficient between the percentage female variable and the gender dummy is .6220, less than the threshold necessary to drop one of the two variables.

13. Because a large part of the variation in annual wage and salary income is due to variation in hours worked, our index measures based on hourly earnings are consistently lower than estimates presented in studies focusing on wage and salary income (see, for example, Blackburn, 1990; Conrad, 1993; Grubb & Wilson, 1989; Karoly, 1992). By focusing on hourly wages, our estimates are net of differences in hours worked. The effect of being employed part-time is reflected indirectly in the value of γ.

14. The jackknife standard error procedure is based on sequentially omitting each observation in a data set and then calculating the desired statistic. In the case of inequality measures used, this would involve creating $N - 1$ new estimates of each index and using those new estimates to in turn calculate the standard error (by summing the squared difference between the omitted value and the mean of the distribution without the omitted value and using a degrees of freedom correction). This can be quite costly and time consuming in the case of very large data sets. Karoly (1989) has shown that jackknife estimates can be calculated with only a few passes through the data.

15. In Levy and Murnane's (1992) review of recent literature, inequality between gender groups was stable in the 1970s and grew in the 1980s, whereas inequality within groups has grown steadily since 1970. In fact, the increase in inequality within groups defined by gender was greater and dominated the decline in inequality between men and women (see Grubb & Wilson, 1989; Karoly, 1992).

16. Though the magnitude of our estimated changes is quite large, it is difficult to show statistical significance. Overall, the decision to use hourly earnings as the depen-

dent variable limited our sample to the outgoing rotation (one quarter of the U.S. Bureau of the Census, 1992, sample). Also, when indexes are calculated separately for women and men, the sample size is further reduced, increasing our jackknife estimates of standard errors.

REFERENCES

Abell, J. (1994). Military spending and income inequality. *Journal of Peace Research, 31,* 35-43.

Acker, J. (1990). Hierarchies, jobs, bodies: A theory of gendered organizations. *Gender & Society, 4,* 139-158.

Albelda, R. (1986). Occupational segregation by race and gender: 1958-1981. *Industrial and Labor Relations Review, 39,* 404-411.

Aldrich, M., & Buchele, R. (1986). *The economics of comparable worth.* Boston: Ballinger.

Allison, P. (1978). Measures of inequality. *American Sociological Review, 43,* 865-880.

Anderson, C., & Tomaskovic-Devey, D. (1995). Patriarchal pressures: An exploration of organizational processes that exacerbate and erode gender earnings inequality. *Work and Occupations, 22,* 328-356.

Atkinson, A. (1970). On the measurement of inequality. *Journal of Economic Theory, 2,* 244-263.

Bailey, K. (1985). Entropy measures of inequality. *Sociological Inquiry, 55,* 200-211.

Baron, J., & Bielby, W. (1985). Organization barriers to gender equality: Sex segregation of job opportunities. In A. Rossi (Ed.), *Gender and the life course* (pp. 233-251). New York: Aldine.

Bernhardt, A., Morris, M., & Handcock, M. (1995). Women's gains or men's losses? A closer look at the shrinking gender gap in earnings. *American Journal of Sociology, 101,* 302-328.

Bielby, W. (1991). The structure and process of sex segregation. In R. Cornwall & P. Wunnava (Eds.), *New approaches to economic and social analyses of discrimination* (pp. 97-112). New York: Praeger.

Blackburn, M. (1990). What can explain the increase in earnings inequality among males? *Industrial Relations, 29,* 441-456.

Blau, F., & Beller, A. (1988). Trends in earnings differentials by gender, 1971-1981. *Industrial and Labor Relations Review, 41,* 513-529.

Blau, F., & Kahn, L. (1992). The gender earnings gap: Learning from international comparisons. *American Economic Review, 82,* 533-538.

Blau, F., & Kahn, L. (1994). Rising inequality and the U.S. gender gap. *American Economic Review, 84,* 23-33.

Bound, J., & Freeman, R. (1989). Black economic progress: Erosion of the post-1965 gains in the 1980s? In S. Shulman & W. Darity (Eds.), *The question of discrimination: Racial inequality in the labor market* (pp. 32-49). Middletown, CT: Wesleyan University Press.

Brenner, J. (1987). Feminist political discourses: Radical versus liberal approaches to the feminization of poverty and comparable worth. *Gender & Society, 1,* 447-465.

Bridges, W., & Nelson, R. (1989). Markets in hierarchies: Organizational and market influences on gender inequality in a state pay system. *American Journal of Sociology, 95,* 616-658.

Bryk, A., & Raudenbush, S. (1992). *Hierarchical linear models: Applications and data analysis methods.* Newbury Park, CA: Sage.

Burtless, G. (1990). Earnings inequality over the business and demographic cycles. In G. Burtless (Ed.), *A future of lousy jobs* (pp. 77-122). Washington, DC: Brookings Institution.

Buswell, C., & Jenkins, S. (1994). Equal opportunities policies, employment, and patriarchy. *Gender, Work and Organization, 1,* 83-93.

Conrad, C. (1993). A different approach to the measurement of income inequality. *Review of Black Political Economy, 22,* 19-31.

Cotton, J. (1988). Discrimination and favoritism in the U.S. labor market: The cost to a wage earner of being female and black and the benefit of being male and white. *American Journal of Economics and Sociology, 47,* 15-28.

Ehrenberg, R., & Smith, R. (1987). Comparable worth wage adjustments and female employment in the state and local sector. *Journal of Labor Economics, 5,* 43-62.

England, P. (1992). *Comparable worth: Theories and evidence.* New York: Aldine de Gruyter.

England, P., & Kilbourne, B. S. (1989). Occupational measures from the Dictionary of Occupational Titles for 1980, Census Detailed Occupations. ICPSR.

Figart, D., & Lapidus, J. (1995). A gender analysis of U.S. labor market policies for the working poor. *Feminist Economics, 1*(3), 60-82.

Filer, R. (1985). Male-female wage differences: The importance of compensating differentials. *Industrial and Labor Relations Review, 38,* 426-437.

Filer, R. (1989). Occupational segregation, compensating differentials, and comparable worth. In R. Michael, H. Hartmann, & B. O'Farrell (Eds.), *Pay equity: Empirical inquiries* (pp. 153-170). Washington, DC: National Academy Press.

Flaherty, S., & Caniglia, A. (1992). The relative effects of unionism on the earnings distributions of women and men. *Industrial Relations, 31,* 382-393.

Gerhart, B., & El Cheikh, N. (1991). Earnings and percentage female: A longitudinal study. *Industrial Relations, 30,* 62-77.

Glass, J., Tienda, M., & Smith, S. (1988). The impact of changing employment opportunity on gender and ethnic earnings inequality. *Social Science Research, 17,* 252-276.

Grubb, W., & Wilson, R. (1989). Sources of increasing inequality in wages and salaries, 1960-1980. *Monthly Labor Review, 112,* 3-13.

Gyimah-Brempong, K., & Fichtenbaum, R. (1993). Black-White wage differential: The relative importance of human capital and labor market structure. *Review of Black Political Economy, 21,* 19-52.

Harrison, B., & Bluestone, B. (1988). *The great U-turn: Corporate restructuring and the polarizing of America.* New York: Basic Books.

Hartmann, H., & Aaronson, S. (1994). Pay equity and women's wage increases: Successes in the states, a model for the nation. *Duke Journal of Gender Law & Policy, 1,* 69-87.

Jacobs, J., & Lim, S. (1992). Trends in occupational and industrial sex segregation in 56 countries, 1960-1980. *Work and Occupations, 19,* 450-486.

Jacobs, J., & Steinberg, R. (1990). Compensating differentials and the male-female wage gap: Evidence from the New York State pay equity study. *Social Forces, 69,* 439-468.

Jacobs, J., & Steinberg, R. (1994). *Further evidence on compensating differentials.* Unpublished manuscript.

Jenson, J., Hagen, E., & Reddy, C. (1988). *Feminization of the labor force: Paradoxes and promises.* New York: Oxford University Press.

Johnson, G., & Solon, G. (1986). Estimates of the direct effects of comparable worth legislation. *American Economic Review, 76,* 1117-1125.

Kahn, S. (1992). Economic implications of public-sector comparable worth: The case of San Jose, California. *Industrial Relations, 31,* 270-291.

Karoly, L. (1989). *Computing standard errors for measures of inequality using the jackknife* [Photocopy, Department of Economics]. Santa Monica, CA: RAND.

Karoly, L. (1992). Changes in the distribution of individual earnings in the United States, 1967-1986. *Review of Economics and Statistics, 74,* 107-115.

Katz, L., & Murphy, K. (1992). Changes in relative wages, 1963-1987: Supply and demand factors. *Quarterly Journal of Economics, 107,* 34-78.

Kilbourne, B., England, P., & Beron, K. (1994). Effects of individual, occupational, and industrial characteristics on earnings: Intersections of race and gender. *Social Forces, 72,* 1149-1176.

Kilbourne, B., Farkas, G., Beron, K., Weir, D., & England, P. (1994). Returns to skill, compensating differentials, and gender bias: Effects of occupational characteristics on the wages of White women and men. *American Journal of Sociology, 100,* 689-719.

Killingsworth, M. (1985). The economics of comparable worth: Analytical, empirical, and policy questions. In H. Hartmann (Ed.), *Comparable worth: New directions for research.* Washington, DC: National Academy Press.

Killingsworth, M. (1987). Heterogeneous preferences, compensating wage differentials, and comparable worth. *Quarterly Journal of Economics, 102,* 727-741.

Kuhn, S., & Bluestone, B. (1987). Economic restructuring and the female labor market: The impact of industrial change on women. In L. Benera & C. Stimpson (Eds.), *Women, households, and the economy* (pp. 3-32). New Brunswick, NJ: Rutgers University Press.

Lapidus, J., & Figart, D. (1994). Comparable worth as an anti-poverty strategy: Evidence from the March 1992 CPS. *Review of Radical Political Economics, 26,* 1-10.

Leicht, K., Wallace, M., & Grant, D. (1993). Union presence, class, and individual earnings inequality. *Work and Occupations, 20,* 429-451.

Lerman, R., & Yitzhaki, S. (1984). A note on the calculation and interpretation of the Gini index. *Economics Letters, 15,* 363-368.

Lerman, R., & Yitzhaki, S. (1989). Improving the accuracy of estimates of Gini coefficients. *Journal of Econometrics, 42,* 43-47.

Levy, F., & Murnane, R. (1992). U.S. earnings levels and earnings inequality: A review of recent trends and proposed explanations. *Journal of Economic Literature, 30,* 1333-1381.

Lewis, H. G. (1986). *Union relative wage effects: A survey.* Chicago: University of Chicago Press.

Malveaux, J. (1985). Comparable worth and its impact on black women. *Review of Black Political Economy, 14,* 4-27.

McDermott, P. (1991). Pay equity in Canada: Assessing the commitment to reducing the wage gap. In J. Fudge & P. McDermott (Eds.), *Just wages: A feminist assessment of pay equity* (pp. 21-32). Toronto: University of Toronto Press.

Nelson, B., Opton, E., & Wilson, T. (1980). Wage discrimination and Title VII in the 1980s: The case against "comparable worth." *Employee Relations Law Journal, 6,* 380-405.

O'Neill, J., Brien, M., & Cunningham, J. (1989). Effects of comparable worth policy: Evidence from Washington State. *American Economic Review, 79,* 305-309.

Reskin, B. (1993). Sex segregation in the workplace. *Annual Review of Sociology, 19,* 241-270.

Reskin, B., & Roos, P. (1990). *Job queues, gender queues: Explaining women's inroads into male occupations.* Philadelphia: Temple University Press.

Schafer, T., & Faux, J. (Eds.). (1996). *Reclaiming prosperity: A blueprint for progressive economic reform.* Armonk, NY: M. E. Sharpe.

Slottje, D. (1989). *The structure of earnings and the measurement of income inequality in the U.S.* Amsterdam: North-Holland.

Smith, R. (1988). Comparable worth: Limited coverage and the exacerbation of inequality. *Industrial and Labor Relations Review, 41,* 227-239.

Sorensen, E. (1987). Effect of comparable worth policies on earnings. *Industrial Relations, 26,* 227-239.

Sorensen, E. (1989a). Measuring the effect of occupational sex and race composition on earnings. In R. Michael, H. Hartmann, & B. O'Farrell (Eds.), *Pay equity: Empirical inquiries* (pp. 49-60). Washington, DC: National Academy Press.

Sorensen, E. (1989b). The wage effects of occupational sex composition: A review and new findings. In M. A. Hill & M. Killingsworth (Eds.), *Comparable worth: Analyses and evidence* (pp. 57-79). Ithaca, NY: ILR Press.

Sorensen, E. (1990). The crowding hypothesis and comparable worth. *Journal of Human Resources, 25,* 55-89.

Sorensen, E. (1994). *Comparable worth: Is it a worthy policy?* Princeton, NJ: Princeton University Press.

Steinberg, R. (1990). Social construction of skill: Gender, power, and comparable worth. *Work and Occupations, 17,* 449-482.

Steinberg, R. (1992). Gendered instructions: Cultural lag and gender bias in the Hay system of job evaluation. *Work and Occupations, 19,* 387-423.

Treas, J. (1983). Postwar determinants of family income inequality. *American Sociological Review, 48,* 546-559.

Treiman, D., & Hartmann, H. (1981). *Women, work, and wages: Equal pay for jobs of equal value.* Washington, DC: National Academy Press.

U.S. Bureau of the Census. (1992, March). *Current Population Survey* [Computer tape]. Washington, DC: U.S. Department of Commerce.

U.S. Department of Labor, Bureau of Labor Statistics. (1993). *Employment and earnings, 40, January.* Washington, DC: Author.

Wagman, B., & Folbre, N. (1988, November-December). The feminization of inequality: Some new patterns. *Challenge,* pp. 56-59.

Wajcman, J. (1991). Patriarchy, technology, and conceptions of skill. *Work and Occupations, 18,* 29-45.

Witkowski, K., & Leicht, K. (1995). The effects of gender segregation, labor force participation, and family roles on the earnings of young adult workers. *Work and Occupations, 22,* 48-72.

PART II

Casualization of Employment Relationships

The chapters in this section are organized around two foci: the first two chapters explore the experiences of workers, particularly women, who are self-employed; the latter two describe recent changes in the Japanese employment system, the perquisites of which have been reserved primarily for men in white-collar occupations. Although quite different in their subjects, all four contributions highlight the consequences of change in work settings for continued patterns of inequality.

In Chapter 7, "Two Paths to Self-Employment? Women's and Men's Self-Employment in the United States, 1980," Deborah Carr notes that two prominent theories of self-employment do not account well for self-employment among women. Women neither pursue self-employment as a last resort when more traditional employment is closed to them (the default theory) nor pursue self-employment as a unique career for persons with high levels of distinctive human capital (the career theory).

Using data from the 1980 Census microdata sample, Carr demonstrates that self-employed women and men have quite different personal characteristics (e.g., human capital, parental and marital statuses). She finds that both the default and career theories are useful for explaining men's involvement in self-employment (that is, two fairly distinct types of men were self-employed in 1980). But the differences between women and men are intriguing: Married women were more likely than married men to be self-employed; the presence of young children had a substantial positive effect on the likelihood of women's self-employment, but fathers were only slightly more likely than childless men to be self-employed; and these gender differences hold across four occupational groups. Carr concludes that women and men enter self-employment for different reasons and with different types of resources. Her findings suggest that, for women, self-employment is a form of worker response to the fact that U.S. workplaces have *not restructured sufficiently* to meet the needs of the growing number of mothers who have entered the labor market since the 1960s.

Carr's findings pertain to self-employed persons no matter the physical setting of their businesses, whereas in Chapter 8, "Getting Away and

Getting By: The Experiences of Self-Employed Homeworkers," Nancy Jurik's focus is on the self-employed who work from their homes. Through qualitative interviews with 46 homeworkers (both women and men), Jurik tackles a central question: Is homeworking a form of liberation and flexibility, or is it a type of exploitation accepted in the face of limited choices for conventional employment? Many of the homeworkers she interviewed expressed desires for self-fulfillment and autonomy, for escape from workplace bureaucracies and office politics. In contrast with their expectations, Jurik finds that homeworkers often faced long hours of tedious work that failed to offer the flexibility they sought; out of economic necessity, self-employed homeworkers often imposed on themselves conditions similar to those they eschewed in "regular" employment. Further, women working from home were frequently interrupted by child care and household responsibilities, so self-employed homework did not challenge seriously the gendered division of household labor.

These two studies suggest that, on some dimensions, the more work changes, the more it remains the same: Workers who seek to escape the constraints of traditional employment or to organize work to complement family responsibilities often reproduce the gendered division of labor and even some of the oppressive features of wage work. Further research might tackle several questions: What are the continuing trends in which and how many workers "choose" self-employment? What are the consequences—for the self-employed and for wage workers—of trends toward self-employment? Will new services emerge to facilitate self-employment (such as integrated fax/e-mail/Web site technology or novel childcare arrangements)? Might more flexible worksite arrangements reduce the percentage of mothers who opt for homework as a way of meeting both wage-earning and domestic responsibilities?

The third and fourth chapters in Part II shift our focus to workplace restructuring in Japan. Long held up as a model of permanent employment (and therefore, the antithesis of "casual" employment), the Japanese system—and previous sociological research on it—has recently come under scrutiny. First, the system of "permanent employment" shows signs of wear; second, more writers are recognizing that permanent employment has been extended only to males, and primarily to those in white-collar occupations. These two chapters, then, are both particularly timely and contribute to the global flavor of this volume.

Mariah Mantsun Cheng and Arne Kalleberg, in Chapter 9, refine our understanding of Japanese employment in "How Permanent Was Permanent Employment? Patterns of Organizational Mobility in Japan, 1916-1975." Three cross-sectional national surveys conducted in 1955, 1965, and

1975 asked men for retrospective information about their careers; from these data, Cheng and Kalleberg estimate the age, period, and cohort effects on Japanese men's movement across organizations between 1916 and 1975. The results leave us better informed about the historical extent of permanent employment in Japan.

First, the permanency of employment clearly depended on macrostructural factors, particularly World War II. (Movement of workers across firms increased during the war.) Second, men employed in small firms reported significantly less stability over the life of their careers than did employees of large firms; those (particularly younger workers) in small firms were more likely to have had several employers. Third, blue-collar workers typically worked for more firms in their lifetimes than did white-collar men.

In Chapter 10, "The Transformation of the Japanese Employment System: Nature, Depth, and Origins," James Lincoln and Yoshifumi Nakata draw on a variety of sources to describe how a recent shift among Japanese firms toward greater emphasis on profits contributed to the restructuring of Japanese employment arrangements. The authors give careful attention to what they call "legitimacy constraints" on managerial decisions and actions; these constraints are grounded in postwar Japanese employment culture and are, they suggest, powerful forces for stability in the Japanese economy.

Lincoln and Nakata do identify numerous recent shifts in Japanese managerial practices, including greater emphasis on skills (rather than credentials) in hiring; flattening the organizational hierarchy by reducing the number of managerial slots (and, thus, line workers' expectations for rising into management); and moving away from seniority-based wages and salaries toward compensation linked more closely to productivity. But they also find evidence that some managerial practices are designed with the intent of protecting permanent employment for selected workers. Employers may, for example, protect permanent employees by using "buffer groups" when additional workers are needed. (This is similar to the situation at a U.S. computer firm described by Vicki Smith in Chapter 1, this volume.) Women and workers past typical retirement age are hired when demand for labor increases and let go when it slackens, protecting most male white-collar employees from market fluctuations. Japanese firms may also transfer workers to subsidiary firms, providing those workers with continued employment, albeit via often involuntary mobility.

Rather than viewing recent changes in Japanese managerial practices as evidence of the demise of permanent employment, Lincoln and Nakata conclude that such tactics are, in fact, culturally constrained efforts to *protect* permanent employment in an increasingly volatile global economy. The more detailed research that Lincoln and Nakata call for in their conclusion could illuminate whether these efforts will break down under the weight of the 1998-1999 Asian economic crisis. Taken together, Chapters 9 and 10 suggest interlocking observations: Permanent employment has historically been limited to male white-collar workers and/or those in large firms, and for that privileged sector of workers, permanent employment—under substantial economic pressure but strongly supported by cultural conventions—is still available. Questions remain: Are there additional factors (beyond the recent Asian economic crisis) that will force Japanese managers to retreat from permanent employment? Will typically disadvantaged groups (women, blue-collar, and employees of small firms) be able to claim more permanent employment contracts, and if so, how? Other questions link the opening two chapters of Part II to the latter two. For example, what role might unions in the United States and Japan play in narrowing the gap between privileged workers who enjoy relatively stable employment and those who rely on less-protected wage work or self-employment when other options fail?

Two Paths to Self-Employment?

Women's and Men's Self-Employment in the United States, 1980

DEBORAH CARR

Self-employment is a widely shared American ideal. A national survey of adults in the U.S. workforce in 1980 showed that 57% of all working class persons, two thirds of all men, and slightly less than one half of all women would like to be self-employed some day (Steinmetz & Wright, 1989). Opinion polls are not the only barometer of recent preferences for self-employment, however. Although the number of nonfarm self-employed workers steadily declined between 1920 and 1970, Current Population Survey data show that the number of self-employed workers in the United States rose by more than 1.1 million between 1972 and 1979 and increased by 23% between 1976 and 1983 (Becker, 1984; Fain, 1980).

An even more notable trend is the rise in female self-employment. Between 1972 and 1979, female self-employment increased by 43%—or five times faster than male self-employment—and 12% above the increase in the number of women employed as wage and salary workers. The Social Security Administration similarly reported an increase in the female share of self-employment, rising from 12% in 1955 to 17% in 1975 to 29% in 1986 (Aronson 1991, p. 4). This sharp rise in women's self-employment is difficult to explain, especially from a purely economic vantage point, given that self-employed women's earnings are well below those of both female wage and salary workers and self-employed men—even when adjusted for differences in industry, occupation, and hours worked. (Aronson, p. xi; Brown, 1976). This raises two important questions: Who are these self-employed women, and how do they differ from the male self-employed? I will argue that neither of the two prevailing theories of self-employment—the default theory (Schumpeter, 1934) nor the career theory (Knight, 1933)—offers an adequate theory of women's self-employment. Rather, I will argue that self-employment, like part-time or home-based work, is a flexible work strategy adopted by women to accommodate the competing demands of family and paid employment. Accordingly, a theory of self-employment that applies to women must incorporate family characteristics including marital status, parental status, and ages of children. These familial characteristics represent both enhancements and constraints to women's employment decisions.

Although several sociological studies have examined the characteristics of self-employed women, few have expanded their analyses to compare the characteristics of self-employed women and men, nor have they attempted to link their empirical research to extant theories of self-employment. Empirical studies limited to samples of women only have shown that having preschool-age children (Connelly, 1992) and that being married with school-age children

From *Work and Occupations,* Vol. 23, No. 1, February 1996, pp. 26-53. Reprinted by permission.

(MacPherson, 1988) increase the odds that a woman will work for herself. Neither study considered whether men's self-employment is affected by family characteristics, however. Although detailed bivariate analyses of self-employed women and men in 1975 and 1990 showed that a higher proportion of self-employed men than women are married, gender differences in the parental status of self-employed workers were not considered (Devine, 1994).

This chapter attempts to expand on past research by (a) identifying gender differences in the determinants of self-employment; (b) contrasting the determinants of both incorporated and unincorporated self-employment; and (c) developing a theory of self-employment that is applicable to women's work experiences. The theories of Schumpeter (1934) and Knight (1933) are modified to include family variables as sources of constraint and choice. Moreover, the gender model (Loscocco, 1990) is used as a theoretical starting point, so several hypotheses are based on the assumption that family characteristics will have different effects on the work outcomes of men and women (Loscocco & Leicht, 1993).

Using 1980 U.S. Census data, I first compare the demographic, human capital, and family characteristics of self-employed and salaried men and women.[1] Next, logistic regression analyses reveal the determinants of men's and women's self-employment versus wage/salary employment in a private company. The hypothesis that self-employment is a strategy whereby educated married women are able to combine work with family responsibilities is confirmed by the data; advanced education, being married, and having preschool children each have a large and positive effect on the odds of women's self-employment. For men, however, human capital characteristics rather than family characteristics are the strongest predictors of self-employment. These patterns generally persist even when analysis is limited to specific occupational groups (i.e., executive, professional, sales and service workers).

Finally, a multinomial logit model compares the determinants of two distinct classes of self-employment; self-employment in an incorporated business and self-employment in an unincorporated business versus wage and salary work. The latter analysis affords us a way to evaluate the two prevailing theories of entrepreneurship: self-employment as a default for marginal workers or self-employment as a career option for the most able and ambitious. Prior research on self-employment has treated the self-employed as a homogeneous category. By further dividing the self-employed into the incorporated and unincorporated, it might be possible to better evaluate whether the self-employed have unique capabilities or whether they are incapable of finding profitable employment in the wage and salary sector. Admittedly, incorporation status is not a perfect proxy for "skilled" versus "unskilled" self-employment. Incorporation status is, however, associated with higher earnings and professional occupations because personal incorporation carries both tax advantages and some protection against malpractice suits (Aronson 1991, pp. 88-89).

THEORETICAL BACKGROUND AND HYPOTHESES

Two classical theories of entrepreneurship provide a framework for examining characteristics of the self-employed. On one hand, the self-employed can be seen as persons with particular abilities and the self-knowledge of these abilities that motivates individuals to establish their own enterprises (Knight, 1933). Consistent with this theory, some authors have found that human capital variables including education, age, and past work experience have a positive effect on the odds of male self-employment. Borjas and Bronars (1989) found that college education and advanced chronological age increase the probability of a man's choosing self-employment over salaried work. Age is also a concomitant of past work experience, accumulation of sufficient amounts of start-up capital, and the establishment of an enduring professional reputation—attributes that may be crucial to the establishment of one's own business (Aronson, 1991, p. 23; Borjas, 1986). Devine's (1994) bivariate analysis of Current Population Survey data also showed that self-employed women, on average, are older and better educated than their salaried peers.

The contrasting perspective regards self-employment as a default option for those facing constraints to traditional wage and salary employment. The self-employed do not necessarily have unique abilities that differentiate them from individuals in wage and salary jobs but are merely responding to the structural constraints facing them (Schumpeter, 1934). In a pioneering study of self-employment, Phillips (1962) similarly concluded that self-employment would survive principally as a defense against unemployment or as a refuge for older workers, the disabled, and those with low personal productivity. This theory suggests that ethnic minorities, immigrants, the physically disabled, and those living in geographic areas with high unemployment may react to obstacles in the traditional wage and salary employment sector by forming their own businesses. Empirical support for this perspective is equivocal; analyses of national cross-sectional survey data in the United States and Great Britain estimated rates of self-employment to be highest among white immigrants (Borjas, 1986; Borjas & Bronars, 1989); the disabled and those with a work-limiting health condition (Fuchs, 1980; Quinn, 1980); those living in geographic areas or those formerly employed in industries with high unemployment rates (Johnson, 1981); and men whose past work histories included spells of unemployment, numerous job shifts, and low-paid wage work (Evans & Leighton, 1989). African Americans and other "visible minorities" are less likely than Whites to work for themselves, however; consumer discrimination and limited access to capital are obstacles to minority self-employment (Borjas; Maxim, 1992).

These two competing theories of self-employment share two important similarities, however; both are implicitly based on the standard model of labor market participation, wherein individuals behave rationally to maximize their financial rewards, and both were formulated to explain men's self-employment (Aronson, 1991, p. 21). I will argue that neither Schumpeter's (1934) constraint theory nor Knight's (1933) choice theory offers an adequate theory of women's self-employment. Rather, I will argue that self-employment offers women an adaptive alternative or "escape route" from less convenient or less flexible work arrangements in the wage and salary sector (Silver, 1989, p. 108). In other words, a new theory of women's self-employment can be developed, which draws both on the default and career theories. Although family characteristics—most notably, young children—place constraints on a woman's paid employment options, such human capital factors as education or the income of a spouse allow her to choose self-employment over less flexible salaried work. Women do not default to self-employment because they have no other options, as is suggested by Schumpeter's constraint theory. Rather, women—especially women with young children who have the resources to facilitate the starting of their own businesses (e.g., education and the second income of a spouse)—will opt for self-employment over wage and salary work because it allows more flexibility than traditional wage and salary employment and a greater degree of autonomy than other forms of contingent work, including part-time, shift, and temporary work.

One of the most consistent findings in the study of women's labor force participation is the constraining effect of young children on a woman's decision to work, hours worked per week, and occupation chosen (Presser & Baldwin, 1980). Occupations classified as more convenient, including employment close to home (Darian, 1975) and home-based work (Kraut & Grambsch, 1987), are filled at higher rates by women with young children. Similarly, "contingent" work, including part-time work or shift work (Presser & Baldwin) and temporary work is overwhelmingly done by married women with children (Christensen, 1987). Nearly 60% of all part-time workers in 1985 were married women living with their husbands. This is not surprising, given that part-time workers typically are not given discretionary company benefits, such as health insurance, paid sick leave, maternity leave, vacation time, or pension coverage. Likewise, temporary agencies, particularly those who hire clerical workers, more often fill their jobs with women than men. For many women, contingent work represents a work accommodation that serves their lifestyle and economic needs. Contingent work may fill a woman's desire for a flexible work schedule; may provide a supplemental income at times when one is necessary for married women; and may provide a more convenient option over full-time work (Christensen, 1987).

Self-employment is an occupational choice that is similar to shift work and home-based work in that it offers its incumbents schedule flexibility. Connelly and Rhoton's (1988, p. 225) qualitative analysis of female self-employed direct sales workers showed that the women's entry into self-employment is explained by "occupational drift"; women choose this occupation due to its flexible schedule.

The costs of self-employment are particularly high for women, however, and as a result, I expect to find that human capital variables and characteristics associated with greater choice, such as being White, married, and educated also increase the odds that a woman will work for herself. The U.S. Small Business Administration documents that the average business receipts of women's sole proprietorships were only 27% of the average for men's sole proprietorships in 1980 (Loscocco & Robinson, 1991). Even among full-time year-round self-employed female workers, the earnings disadvantage persists. In 1980, roughly half of all full-time year-round self-employed women workers were employed in 2 of the 13 major census occupational groups: sales and services. Their earnings in these occupational groups were just 45% and 50%, respectively, of self-employed men and 95% and 85%, respectively, of salaried women in like occupations (Carr, 1993, pp. 47-52).

Moreover, given the sporadic and/or seasonal earnings of all self-employed workers, the lack of pension and health insurance benefits afforded to self-employed workers, and the earnings disparity between self-employed women and female wage and salary workers (Brown, 1976), self-employment may be an option only to those women who have the financial cushion of a spouse's income.[2] A similar hypothesis was supported in Kraut and Grambsch's (1987) study of home-based workers; because the earnings of home-based workers are significantly less than those of on-site workers, White married women and other persons with household incomes over and above their own earnings are more likely to work at home.

Because the majority of self-employed women held occupations in which on-the-job training or extensive work experience was not vital to job entry in 1980 (e.g., child care workers, hairdressers/cosmetologists, door-to-door sales) (Aronson, 1991; Connelly, 1992), I expect that women with no work experience or part-time work experience in 1975 will have been more likely than those with full-time experience in 1975 to work for themselves in 1980.[3] The well-documented earnings disadvantage associated with women's self-employment would likely be least attractive to women with the most extensive work experience. Additionally, limited work experience may open few doors for women in the wage and salary sector.

I also expect to find several similarities between the male and female self-employed. Specifically, I expect to replicate the widespread finding that advanced age and higher education will increase the odds of both men's and women's self-employment. The association between age, education, and self-employment among men is widely documented (Borjas & Bronars, 1989; Fain, 1980; Fuchs, 1980; Quinn, 1980),[4] and preliminary bivariate analyses by Devine (1994) also show evidence that higher education and advanced age are associated with women's self-employment.

Finally, I expect that the self-employed in incorporated and unincorporated businesses will differ in terms of age, past work experience, and health status. Characteristics associated with greater choice and opportunity are expected to predict self-employment in an incorporated business, and traits that constrain one's labor force decisions are expected to predict self-employment in an unincorporated business only. Personal incorporation has become popular among many self-employed professionals because of the tax advantages, including the ability to shelter retirement income contributions in Keogh-type pension plans and the exemption of business expenses from taxation. Incorporation may also have provided some protection against malpractice suits (Aronson 1991, pp. 88-89). Therefore, because legislation makes it profitable for business owners to incorporate and become "employees" of their own corporations, the self-employed with the highest earnings—typically those in professional and managerial occupations—stand to benefit the most from incorporating their businesses. Thus I expect to find that the odds of having one's own incorporated business will be positively affected by higher education and full-time past work experience. I also expect that being of the most advanced age (age 55-64) and having a disability reduce the odds of incorporating one's business. Given historical shifts in occupational structure, it is probable that the oldest self-employed are clustered in crafts and sales occupations, jobs that are more common among the self-employed in unincorporated businesses.[5]

DATA AND METHODS

This study uses data from a 1:1,000 nationwide sample of the Census of Population and Housing, 1980, *Public Use Microdata Sample* (PUMS) (*A*), prepared by the Bureau of the Census (1983). The analysis is limited to a subsample of 55,502 (22,403 women and 33,099 men) noninstitutionalized civilian persons, aged 18 to 64, who worked for more than one hour for pay in both 1979 and 1980. Only nonfarm wage and salary workers for private companies and self-employed workers in both nonfarm incorporated and nonfarm unincorporated businesses are included in the sample.

The analysis has three parts. First, demographic and labor supply characteristics of male and female self-employed and salaried workers are presented in Tables 7.1 and 7.2. Second, two logistic regression models separately estimate the determinants of men's and women's self-employment. The dependent variable is the log-odds of a person's being a self-employed worker (incorporated or unincorporated) versus a wage/salary employee. It is based on the class of worker item in the PUMS and is operationalized as a dichotomous outcome (1 = *self-employed*, 0 = *employee*). This model replicates past studies by contrasting all self-employed workers with wage earners yet advances past research by considering the unique aspects of women's self-employment. To obtain a more detailed picture of the determinants of self-employment, separate logistic regression models are also run for each of four major occupational groups (executive, professional, sales and service).

Finally, to obtain an expanded description of the self-employed, a multinomial logit model with three outcome categories is estimated. The dependent variable is the log-odds that a self-employed person works for an unincorporated or an incorporated business versus being a wage and salary worker (2 = *incorporated business/employee of own corporation*, 1 = *unincorporated business*, 0 = *wage and salary work*). This approach is in contrast with past studies that did not differentiate between the two classes of self-employment (Borjas & Bronars, 1989; Brown, 1976) or studies that defined as self-employed only those persons who received no income from wages and salary (Moore, 1983). The latter operationalization excludes from study the self-employed whose businesses are incorporated. Since 1967, the U.S. Census and Current Population Survey began classifying the self-employed workers of incorporated businesses or "employees of own corporation" explicitly as wage earners.[6] Despite this differentiation, employees of their own corporation are conceptually similar to the self-employed whose businesses are unincorporated. They own all or most of the stock in a privately held corporation, and often consider themselves to be self-employed (Aronson, 1991).

TABLE 7.1 Demographic Characteristics of Private Wage and Salary Workers and Self-Employed Workers in the United States, by Sex (%): 1980 (N = 55,502)

Independent Variable	*Male Wage/Salary (n = 28,485)*	*Male Self-Employed (n = 4,614)*	*Female Wage/Salary (n = 21,115)*	*Female Self-Employed (n = 1,288)*
Age				
18-24	10.4	3.3	13.8	3.0
25-34	32.5	23.6	30.7	23.1
35-44	23.9	27.2	23.6	30.7
45-54	19.5	25.2	19.0	23.0
55-64	13.7	20.7	12.9	20.3
Education				
< 12 years	21.4	28.5	18.6	14.4
12 years	36.8	18.7	45.6	38.0
13-15 years	20.4	19.6	22.8	25.5
16 years	11.9	13.2	8.2	12.6
17+ years	9.4	20.0	4.8	9.4
Race				
White	88.6	94.3	86.2	92.9
Non-White	11.4	5.7	13.8	7.1
Ethnicity				
Hispanic	5.7	3.4	4.9	3.3
Non-Hispanic	94.3	96.6	95.1	96.7
Civil status				
Born in United States	93.0	92.8	92.7	91.8
Immigrant	7.0	7.2	7.3	8.2
Marital status				
Never married	8.3	9.0	10.2	4.4
Currently married	86.0	89.6	69.8	79.6
Divorced/separated/widowed	5.7	5.4	20.0	16.0
Kids at home				
None	46.4	47.4	53.1	50.6
< 6 years only	14.3	9.5	8.7	6.8
6-17 years only	28.3	32.1	31.2	33.9
0-17 years	11.0	11.0	7.0	8.7

SOURCE: *Public Use Microdata Samples (A)* (U.S. Bureau of the Census, 1983). Sample includes all civilian men and women aged 18-64 who worked as nonfarm wage and salary workers or nonfarm self-employed workers in 1979.

TABLE 7.2 Labor Supply and Contextual Characteristics of Wage and Salary Workers and Self-Employed Workers in the United States, by Sex (%): 1980 (N = 55,502)

Independent Variable	*Male Wage/Salary (n = 28,485)*	*Male Self-Employed (n = 4,614)*	*Female Wage/Salary (n – 21,115)*	*Female Self-Employed (n = 1,288)*
Hours worked per week				
< 15	1.4	2.3	4.3	11.5
15-34	2.8	6.3	19.5	27.7
35-40	60.2	35.2	66.4	32.8
41+	35.6	56.2	9.7	28.0
Mean hours worked, 1979	2,125.9	2,321.5	1,668.7	1,685.6
(SD)	(560.9)	(801.2)	(655.7)	(939.5)
Work in 1975				
Full-time	83.0	89.0	57.1	52.8
Part-time	6.5	5.2	16.7	24.1
Did not work	10.4	5.8	26.2	23.1
Location of work				
Home	0.6	5.9	1.0	20.3
On-site	99.4	94.1	99.0	79.7
Work disability				
Yes	4.5	6.3	3.1	5.0
No	95.5	93.7	96.9	95.0
Full-time year-round worker				
Yes	78.9	75.1	55.5	46.9
No	21.1	24.9	44.5	53.1
Metro residence				
In SMSA	82.5	79.0	83.5	79.8
Non-SMSA	17.5	21.0	16.5	20.2
Urban				
Central city	18.3	16.0	21.2	15.8
Non-central city	81.7	84.0	78.8	84.2
Area				
South	32.5	32.9	32.8	32.1
Non-South	67.5	67.1	67.2	67.9
SMSA unemployment rate	0.07	0.07	0.07	0.07
(SD)	(0.02)	(0.02)	(0.02)	(0.02)

SOURCE: *Public Use Microdata Samples (A)* (U.S. Bureau of the Census, 1983). Sample includes all civilian men and women aged 18-64 who worked as nonfarm wage and salary workers or nonfarm self-employed workers in 1979.
NOTE: SMSA = Standard Metropolitan Statistical Area.

The independent variables selected can be classified as those consistent with Knight's (1933) career theory of self-employment (i.e., age, education, and past work experience); and those considered to be indicators of Schumpeter's (1934) default path to self-employment (i.e., sex, race,[7] Hispanic ethnicity, immigrant status,[8] presence of a work-limiting health condition, residence in a Standardized Metropolitan Statistical Area [SMSA], and SMSA unemployment rate). As discussed earlier in this chapter, age, education, and work experience are indicators of human capital, or indicators of the skills and experiences that make one capable of forming a successful business (Aronson, 1991, p. 23; Borjas & Bronars, 1989; Fain, 1980). Becoming self-employed requires accumulated experience, skills, and material resources. Because time is required to garner these assets, self-employment is expected to be more common among older workers, although workers nearing retirement may be reluctant to leave secure wage and salary work for the uncertainties of entrepreneurship (Becker, 1984).

Conversely, the variables race, immigrant status, Hispanic ethnicity, and disability status are expected to increase the odds of self-employment if Schumpeter (1934) and Phillips (1962) are correct in arguing that self-employment is a refuge for those who are prevented from securing productive or profitable employment in the wage and salary sector. Similarly, unemployment rate is considered because the default theory of self-employment suggests that self-employment is a microlevel response by workers to economic duress (Steinmetz & Wright, 1989). Because SMSA-level unemployment rates are used in this analysis, an additional dummy variable indicating SMSA versus non-SMSA residents is necessary.[9]

A series of family characteristics are also included. As argued earlier, neither Schumpeter's (1934) nor Knight's (1933) model of self-employment offers an adequate explanation of women's self-employment. Given that women's work and family decisions are inextricably tied (Darian 1975; Loscocco & Leicht 1993; Sweet 1973), any theory of women's labor force participation must acknowledge that family characteristics differentially enhance and constrain men's and women's work decisions. Accordingly, marital status along with presence and ages of children (no children; ages 0-6 only; ages 6-17 only; ages 0-17) are considered as independent variables.

Finally, control variables are added for residence in a southern state and urban residence; these variables were included to account for regional differences in opportunity for small business growth. The "rural renaissance" of the 1970s was distinguished by a movement of Americans away from metropolitan areas and a mass migration to the South, which would likely create a demand for small business (Fuguitt, 1985).

Each of the variables is measured at the individual level, except unemployment rate, which is an area-level variable. The unemployment rate variable was created by matching the appropriate 1979 area unemployment rate to the person record. Although personal characteristics, tastes, whether one's parents were/are self-employed, whether one's spouse is self-employed, marketable job skills, and the availability of start-up capital may guide the decision to become self-employed (Carroll & Mosakowski, 1987; Fuchs, 1980), this chapter will be limited to examining only those characteristics obtained in the 1980 U.S. Census: the demographic and human capital determinants of self-employment.

FINDINGS AND DISCUSSION

Self-employed and wage and salary workers differ in several major respects, as shown by the descriptive statistics in Tables 7.1 and 7.2. The self-employed American is typically White and older and better educated than his or her salaried peers. On closer inspection, self-employed men have several characteristics that are associated with the marginality theory of entrepreneurship. Although 29% of self-employed men are high school dropouts, only 21% of male salaried workers have fewer than 12 years of schooling. This finding could reflect intercohort changes in levels of educational attainment. Given the fact that self-employment is more prevalent among older age cohorts who are also more likely to have completed fewer than 12 years of school, this pattern likely reflects the negative correlation between age and education. At the same time, however, nearly one third of self-employed men and 22% of self-employed women have at least a college education, and the figures for wage and salaried workers are 21% and 13%, respectively.

The hours and conditions under which the salaried and the self-employed work also differ in several respects. One of the most striking observations is that more than 20% of self-employed women work in their homes. This is in sharp contrast with the proportion of self-employed men (6%) and wage and salaried workers (< 1%) whose main place of employment is at home. Home-based work has been depicted as a way for women to work while caring for their families (Christensen, 1988; Kraut & Grambsch, 1987).

The work schedules of salaried and self-employed workers are also quite diverse. Roughly 40% of self-employed women work less than 35 hours per week, yet just 25% of the wage-earning women work part-time. The work schedules of self-employed men show great variety; although self-employed men are more likely than salaried men to work part-time (8.6% versus 4.2%), they are also more likely to work more than 40 hours per week (56% versus 36%).

The results suggest thus far that men's self-employment is a bimodal phenomenon, attracting the most educated and those investing the most hours per week in their careers, as well as those who turn to self-employment due to their limited education and/or poor health. For women, a different picture emerges; well-educated, married women who have limited past work experience appear to select self-employment as a flexible career option. Women's self-employment, therefore, cannot be succinctly described as a reaction to structural constraints or as a choice guided solely by the availability of skills and resources. Rather, women's self-employment decision reflects a combination of choice within structural constraints. The logistic regression results, shown in Table 7.3, offer support for these hypotheses.

The results in Table 7.3 display the marginal and adjusted odds of being self-employed (versus being a wage earner). The marginal odds show the proportion of persons in each sociodemographic category who are self-employed. The adjusted odds (exp β) are the odds of being self-employed relative to persons in the reference category, after controlling for a series of sociodemographic variables. Reference categories are bracketed in Tables 7.3 through 7.7, and the odds ratio for each equals 1.0. Because the variables of age, education, marital status, and presence and ages of children have significantly different effects ($p < .005$) on the odds of women's versus men's self-employment in a preliminary pooled model, separate logistic regression models are estimated for women and men.

Family Structure Variables

The odds of being self-employed are significantly affected by sex, age, ethnicity, marital status, age of children, and location of residence. As expected, family characteristics differentially constrain and enhance women's and men's employment choices: Being married and having preschool children each has a large and positive effect on the odds of women's—but not men's—self-employment. Table 7.3 shows that currently married women are 1.7 times as likely as never-married women to work for themselves, yet the difference between never-married and currently married men is much smaller, with married men just 1.14 times more likely than never-married men to be self-employed. Economists have reasoned that self-employment is a more rational choice for married men because, unlike the unmarried, they can ensure against the risk of unreliable employees by hiring their spouses (Borjas, 1986). Although this assumption has not been held to

TABLE 7.3 Logistic Regression Model of Self-Employment vs. Wage and Salary Employment in the United States, by Sex: 1980 (N = 55,502)

	Women			*Men*		
Independent Variable	*Marginal Odds*	*Adjusted Odds*	β/*SE*	*Marginal Odds*	*Adjusted Odds*	β/*SE*
Age						
[18-24**]	1.3	1.00		14.9	1.00	
25-34	4.4	3.13	6.52	10.5	1.79	6.19
35-44	7.3	6.48	10.40	15.6	2.78	10.19
45-54	6.9	6.98	10.77	17.3	3.37	12.03
55-64	8.8	9.9	12.62	19.7	4.07	13.67
Race						
[White]	6.2	1.00		14.7	1.00	
Non-White	3.0	0.52	–4.78	7.4	0.51	–8.25
Ethnicity						
Hispanic	3.9	0.79	–1.00	8.9	0.87	–1.13
[Non-Hispanic]	5.8	1.00		14.2	1.00	
Civil status						
[Born in United States]	5.7	1.00		13.9	1.00	
Immigrant	6.4	1.32	2.03	14.3	1.24	2.64
Education						
< 12 years**	4.5	0.8	–2.38	12.4	0.99	–0.26
[12 years]	4.8	1.00		11.1	1.00	
13-15 years	6.4	1.58	6.1	13.4	1.35	6.38
16 years	8.6	2.33	8.59	15.2	1.49	7.39
17+ years	10.6	2.81	9.26	25.6	2.83	20.78
Work disability						
Yes	9.0	1.51	2.95	18.3	1.32	3.99
[No]	5.6	1.00		13.7	1.00	

empirical test, Borjas argued that this type of labor allocation within the family is "optimal because both self-employed workers will have identical incentives—the maximization of family income or self-employment profits—and the shirking problem is solved." Given that marriage has a much larger effect on women's self-employment than on men's, it is also possible that having a husband with steady earnings and benefits affords women a financial cushion that increases the chances of her starting her own business. In 1990, roughly 15% of self-employed women received health insurance through their own job, versus 70% of salaried women and 40% of self-employed men (Devine, 1994). Additional research is needed to examine the role of spouse and family members in self-employed businesses. Moreover, the financial contributions of each spouse to the total family income must be considered.

The presence and ages of children also have a markedly different effect on the odds that

TABLE 7.3 Continued

Independent Variable	Women: Marginal Odds	Women: Adjusted Odds	Women: β/SE	Men: Marginal Odds	Men: Adjusted Odds	Men: β/SE
Marital status						
[Never married**]	2.6	1.00		9.0	1.00	
Currently married	6.5	1.69	3.59	13.2	1.14	1.28
Divorced/separated/widowed	4.7	1.18	1.03	14.4	1.18	2.09
Kids at home						
[None**]	6.1	1.00		15.7	1.00	
0-6 years only	4.5	1.45	2.81	9.7	0.94	–0.97
6-17 years only	6.2	1.04	0.48	15.5	1.03	0.58
0-17 years	7.1	1.66	4.10	13.9	1.18	2.60
Work in 1975**						
Full-time	5.3	0.89	–1.57	14.8	1.25	3.11
Part-time	8.1	1.34	3.39	11.3	1.37	3.25
[Did not work]	5.1	1.00		8.3	1.00	
South [vs. non-South]	5.6	1.09	1.41	14.1	1.08	2.27
Urban [vs. non-urban]	4.4	0.84	–2.11	12.4	0.96	–0.80
Metro [vs. non-SMSA]	5.3	0.76	–3.57	13.4	0.73	–7.43
Unemployment rate		0.99	–0.38		0.99	–1.63
Non-White immigrant*	4.0	0.72	–0.16	10.0	0.74	–1.00
Hispanic immigrant*	4.1	1.03	0.04	9.4	0.84	–1.35
Number of cases			22,403			33,099

SOURCE: *Public Use Microdata Sample (A)* (U.S. Bureau of the Census, 1983). Sample includes all civilian men and women aged 18-64 who worked as nonfarm wage and salary workers or nonfarm self-employed workers in 1979.
NOTE: SMSA = Standard Metropolitan Statistical Area. Brackets indicate a reference group.
* Indicates an interaction effect.
** Indicates that a sex = interaction term for this variable was significant at the .005 level in a pooled model.

women and men will be self-employed. The adjusted odds ratios in Table 7.3 show that men with both preschool children and school-age children (age 0-17 years) are 18% more likely than men with no children at home to be self-employed. A strikingly different pattern emerges for women. Relative to women with no children, women with only preschool children (i.e., age 0-6 only) are 1.5 times as likely to work for themselves, while women with both preschool and school-age children (i.e., ages 0-17) are nearly 1.7 times as likely to be self-employed. Having only school-age children (i.e., ages 6-17 only) does not have a significant effect on the odds of women's self-employment relative to salaried work. This is consistent with past findings that the constraint of children on women's participation in the traditional labor force decreases as children grow older; preschool age children require ongoing and close supervision, and school-age children do not require parental care during the school hours

(Stolzenberg & Waite, 1984; Sweet, 1973). The positive effect of preschool children on women's self-employment is also consistent with the assertion of Connelly (1992) that self-employment is often a strategy for working mothers to combine family and work responsibilities. Women with preschool children may find that being their own boss allows them to earn money yet still fulfill family responsibilities. This general pattern persists even when analysis is limited to specific occupational groups. Tables 7.4 and 7.5 show the results of logistic regression analyses conducted for each of four occupational groups: executives, professionals, sales workers, and those employed in service occupations. These four groups were selected for further analysis because roughly two thirds of self-employed women and more than one half of self-employed men work in these occupations (Carr, 1993, p. 48). Across each of the four occupational groups, the presence of preschool children increases the odds that a woman will be self-employed, ranging from log odds of 1.3 among sales workers and executives to 1.7 among professionals. Having preschool age children does not significantly affect the odds that a man—regardless of occupational group—will be self-employed.

Human Capital Variables

The monotonic effect of education supports the widely documented finding that both men and women with higher education are more likely to work for themselves. Even though men with less than a high school education are just about as likely as high school graduates to work for themselves, female high school dropouts are 20% less likely to work for themselves. Men and women with more than 4 years of college are almost three times as likely as high school graduates to be self-employed.

Age is also a powerful determinant of self-employment status, although analysis of cross-sectional data does not allow us to ascertain whether this effect is due to chronological age or unique attributes of the oldest age cohort in 1980. The odds of self-employment in 1980 increase monotonically with age, and the oldest male workers (ages 55-64) are more than four times as likely as 18- to 24-year-old males to work for themselves. Interestingly, this pattern is even more pronounced among women. Females in the oldest age group are 10 times as likely as 18- to 24-year-old women to be self-employed.

There are several possible explanations for this unexpected pattern. Labor force participation rates of older men dropped significantly between 1952 and 1982, and older wives may continue to work to supplement the family income. Current Population Survey data show that the labor force participation rate for husbands aged 65 and older dropped from 48% in 1952 to 19% in 1982. Corresponding rates for husbands aged 55 to 64 years of age were 89% and 71%, respectively (Waldman, 1983). Alternatively, it is possible that high rates of self-employment among older women reflect the same cohort changes in nonfarm self-employment that are evident among men. Older women may be self-employed in the same businesses as their husbands or may take over the businesses of their deceased or retired husbands. Herz (1988) reports that self-employed women may continue working later in life due to low earnings and lack of pension coverage.

Constraint Variables

My analysis thus far supports the career theory of self-employment and replicates the past finding that the accrual of human capital and life experience increases the odds of self-employment (Borjas, 1986; Fuchs, 1980). The data also offer limited support for the default hypothesis; part-time (versus full-time) work experience in 1975, having a disability, and being an immigrant increase the probability of individual self-employment. Having a disability also increases the odds of self-employment relative to wage work; both men and women with a work-limiting health condition are 1.4 times as likely as those without a disability to be self-employed.

Past work experience has very different effects on men's and women's chances of being self-employed. Men who worked part-time in

TABLE 7.4 Logistic Regression Model of Self-Employment vs. Wage and Salary Employment in the United States by Major Occupational Group: Women, 1980 (N = 22,403)

Independent Variable	*Total exp (β)*	*Executive exp (β)*	*Professional exp (β)*	*Sales exp (β)*	*Service exp (β)*
Age					
[18-24]	1.00	1.00	1.00	1.00	1.00
25-34	3.13	5.14	1.43	3.75	3.04
35-44	6.48	11.40	4.16	8.63	3.76
45-64	6.98	10.81	6.49	9.37	3.44
55-64	9.90	17.49	7.92	13.16	3.27
Race					
[White]	1.00	1.00	1.00	1.00	1.00
Non-White	0.52	0.59	1.07	0.70	0.42
Ethnicity					
Hispanic	0.79	1.41	2.03	1.29	0.71
Non-Hispanic	1.00	1.00	1.00	1.00	1.00
Civil status					
[Born in United States]	1.00	1.00	1.00	1.00	1.00
Immigrant	1.32	2.18	1.09	1.66	0.82
Education					
< 12 years	0.80	1.91	1.55	0.72	0.78
[12 years]	1.00	1.00	1.00	1.00	1.00
13-15 years	1.58	1.54	0.93	2.25	1.15
16 years	2.33	1.74	1.19	3.30	0.99
17+ years	2.81	2.74	0.98	2.89	0.86
Work disability					
Yes	1.51	1.99	1.37	1.87	0.87
[No]	1.00	1.00	1.00	1.00	1.00
Marital status					
[Never married]	1.00	1.00	1.00	1.00	1.00
Currently married	1.69	1.14	1.62	2.21	2.51
Divorced/separated/widowed	1.18	1.11	1.39	1.46	1.57
Kids at home					
[None]	1.00	1.00	1.00	1.00	1.00
0-6 years only	1.45	1.35	1.69	1.32	1.63
6-17 years only	1.04	0.81	1.32	1.03	0.93
0-17 years	1.66	0.97	2.49	1.23	1.76
Work in 1975					
Full-time	0.89	0.88	0.78	1.45	1.50
Part-time	1.34	1.80	1.26	1.13	1.71
[Did not work]	1.00	1.00	1.00	1.00	1.00
South [vs. non-South]	1.09	1.21	1.29	0.98	1.30
Urban [vs. non-urban]	0.84	1.41	0.69	0.56	0.63
Metro [vs. non-SMSA]	0.76	1.24	0.68	0.62	0.98
Unemployment rate	0.99	1.03	1.01	0.98	0.98
Non-White immigrant*	0.72	0.44	1.21	1.23	0.56
Hispanic immigrant*	1.03	4.26	1.10	2.74	0.75
Number of cases~	22,403	2,283	1,928	2,655	3,222

NOTE: SMSA = Standard Metropolitan Statistical Area. Bold-face indicates that β coefficient is significant at the .05 level. Results show log odds relative to reference group. Brackets indicate reference categories.
* Indicates an interaction effect.

TABLE 7.5 Logistic Regression Model of Self-Employment vs. Wage and Salary Employment in the United States by Major Occupational Group: Men, 1980 (N = 33,099)

Independent Variable	*Total exp (β)*	*Executive exp (β)*	*Professional exp (β)*	*Sales exp (β)*	*Service exp (β)*
Age					
[18-24]	1.00	1.00	1.00	1.00	1.00
25-34	1.79	1.34	1.62	1.35	1.63
35-44	2.78	1.91	2.46	2.45	3.25
45-64	3.37	2.75	2.84	3.20	2.47
55-64	4.07	4.54	3.22	4.43	2.49
Race					
[White]	1.00	1.00	1.00	1.00	1.00
Non-White	0.51	0.65	0.71	0.74	0.65
Ethnicity					
Hispanic	0.87	1.32	0.81	1.26	0.58
[Non-Hispanic]	1.00	1.00	1.00	1.00	1.00
Civil status					
[Born in United States]	1.00	1.00	1.00	1.00	1.00
Immigrant	1.24	0.93	1.81	1.68	1.31
Education					
< 12 years	0.99	1.53	1.54	1.46	0.90
[12 years]	1.00	1.00	1.00	1.00	1.00
13-15 years	1.35	0.95	0.85	1.31	1.44
16 years	1.49	1.02	0.89	1.04	0.47
17+ years	2.83	3.92	0.56	1.42	2.75
Work disability					
Yes	1.32	0.87	1.16	1.68	1.38
[No]	1.00	1.00	1.00	1.00	1.00
Marital status					
[Never married]	1.00	1.00	1.00	1.00	1.00
Currently married	1.14	1.08	1.18	1.33	1.59
Divorced/separated/widowed	1.18	1.35	1.23	1.13	1.24
Kids at home					
[None]	1.00	1.00	1.00	1.00	1.00
0-6 years only	0.94	1.09	0.93	1.18	1.11
6-17 years only	1.03	1.11	1.11	1.16	1.48
0-17 years	1.18	1.52	1.22	1.28	0.55
Work in 1975					
Full-time	1.25	1.48	1.21	1.19	1.25
Part-time	1.37	1.49	0.92	1.22	1.15
[Did not work]	1.00	1.00	1.00	1.00	1.00
South [vs. non-South]	1.08	1.15	0.90	0.96	1.07
Urban [vs. non-urban]	0.96	1.20	1.09	0.82	0.65
Metro [vs. non-SMSA]	0.73	0.72	0.69	0.66	0.70
Unemployment rate	0.99	1.04	0.95	1.01	1.11
Non-White immigrant*	0.74	0.60	1.74	2.47	0.31
Hispanic immigrant*	0.84	1.67	1.34	1.35	0.00
Number of cases	33,099	3,372	4,963	3,639	1,327

NOTE: SMSA = Standard Metropolitan Statistical Area. Bold-face indicates that β coefficient is significant at the .05 level. Results show log odds relative to reference group. Brackets indicate a reference group.
* Indicates an interaction effect.

1975 are slightly more likely than 1975 full-time workers to be self-employed in 1980, yet both are 25% to 40% more likely than those with no 1975 work experience to be self-employed in 1980. A different picture emerges for women, however; women who worked part-time in 1975 are 34% more likely, yet those who worked full-time in 1975 are 10% less likely, than non-workers in 1975 to be self-employed in 1980. This general pattern holds for women executives, professionals, and service workers, as revealed in Table 7.4. This is consistent with my hypothesis that extensive career experience may not be necessary for women's self-employment in 1980, given that the majority of these women were employed in retail sales and service occupations, including child care workers and hairdressers/cosmetologists—occupations where work experience may not be vital for job entry (Aronson, 1991; Connelly, 1992).

The data also offer mixed support for the argument that immigrants and ethnic minorities turn to self-employment as a mechanism to circumvent discriminatory practices in the wage labor force. For White immigrants, self-employment is a strategy for upward mobility; they are 30%-40% more likely than American-born Whites to have their own businesses. African Americans and Hispanics, both native born and immigrants, are significantly less likely than Whites to work for themselves, with similar effects for both men and women.

Comparing Classes of Self-Employment

The logistic regression analyses reveal that the odds of being self-employed are increased by both human capital characteristics (e.g., age and education) and characteristics that typically constrain one's labor force options (e.g., disability, immigrant status). In an effort to better evaluate the merits of the default and career theories of unemployment, the analysis will now move beyond the contrast of all self-employed versus wage and salary workers to a review of the results of a multinomial logit model in which self-employment in an incorporated business and self-employment in an unincorporated business are each contrasted with traditional wage and salary sector employment. The marginal odds show the proportion of persons in each sociodemographic category who work in either an incorporated or unincorporated self-employed business, relative to wage and salary work. The adjusted odds (exp β) are the odds of being self-employed (either incorporated or unincorporated) versus being a wage and salary worker, the reference category in both cases.

The multinomial regression results suggest that the determinants of self-employment are not as simplistic as early theories might have suggested. Results in Tables 7.6 and 7.7 offer only limited evidence for the possibility that self-employment in an incorporated business is a proxy for self-employment as a career or that self-employment in an unincorporated business is a proxy for self-employment as a default career choice. The results in Tables 7.6 and 7.7 show that higher education has a positive influence on the choice of either type of self-employment versus salaried work. The self-employed in unincorporated businesses are more likely than salaried workers to have part-time rather than full-time work experience and to have a disability. A male high school dropout is more likely than a male high school graduate to have his own unincorporated business. Moreover, although having a work-limiting health condition makes both men and women much more likely to be self-employed in an unincorporated business relative to salaried work, this is not true of self-employment in an incorporated business. The effect of past work experience also differs for the two classes of self-employment. Men who worked part-time in 1975 are more likely than those with no 1975 work experience to have their own unincorporated businesses in 1980, yet those with full-time work experience are no more likely than those with no 1975 work experience to be self-employed with an unincorporated business. Conversely, men who worked full-time in 1975 are 70% more likely than nonworkers in 1975 to have their own corporations in 1980. These results suggest that men with limited work experience and health problems may default to self-employment, but

TABLE 7.6 Multinomial Logit Model of Men's Self-Employment in an Unincorporated or Incorporated Business vs. Wage and Salary Employment in the United States: 1980 (N = 33,099)

	Self-Employment in an Unincorporated Business vs. Wage/Salary Work			*Self-Employment in an Incorporated Business vs. Wage/Salary Work*		
Independent Variable	*Marginal Odds*	*Adjusted Odds*	*β/SE*	*Marginal Odds*	*Adjusted Odds*	*β/SE*
Age						
[18-24]	3.67	1.00		1.29	1.00	
25-34	7.74	1.93	5.96	3.26	1.52	2.29
35-44	10.99	2.86	8.86	5.71	2.64	5.13
45-54	12.06	3.25	10.02	6.77	3.51	6.62
55-64	14.75	4.17	11.96	6.74	3.73	6.81
Race						
[White]	10.50	1.00		5.19	1.00	
Non-White	5.67	0.54	–6.64	1.99	0.42	–5.17
Ethnicity						
Hispanic	7.08	1.01	0.02	2.06	0.52	–2.33
[Non-Hispanic]	10.17	1.00		4.99	1.00	
Civil status						
[Born in United States]	10.02	1.00		4.78	1.00	
Immigrant	9.72	1.15	1.42	5.58	1.42	2.84
Education						
< 12 years	10.19	1.12	2.02	2.67	0.68	–4.12
[12 years]	8.15	1.00		3.53	1.00	
13-15 years	9.02	1.20	3.30	5.32	1.71	6.89
16 years	9.19	1.19	2.57	7.25	2.21	9.45
17+ years	18.78	2.69	10.88	10.17	3.15	13.93
Work disability						
Yes	15.09	1.49	5.21	4.45	0.91	–0.66
[No]	9.75	1.00		4.85	1.00	

they are defaulting to self-employment in an unincorporated business only. For men, then, characteristics associated with constraints to traditional wage and salary employment increase the likelihood of being self-employed in an unincorporated business. Both men and women who work for their own corporations are more highly educated than wage workers and are less likely to be disabled, Hispanic, or Black.

The traditional theories of entrepreneurship are not well suited to describe women's self-employment, however. Incorporation status does not provide an appropriate test for default versus choice as a theory of women's self-employment. Advanced education is positively associated with both classes of self-employment for women. Although part-time work experience in 1975 increases the odds that a woman will be self-employed in an unincorporated

TABLE 7.6 Continued

Independent Variable	*Self-Employment in an Unincorporated Business vs. Wage/Salary Work*			*Self-Employment in an Incorporated Business vs. Wage/Salary Work*		
	Marginal Odds	*Adjusted Odds*	*β/SE*	*Marginal Odds*	*Adjusted Odds*	*β/SE*
Marital status						
[Never married]	6.96	1.00		2.35	1.00	
Currently married	10.28	1.09	0.9	5.14	1.48	2.58
Divorced/separated/widowed	10.06	1.12	1.02	3.84	1.17	0.85
Kids at home						
[None]	10.38	1.00		4.72	1.00	
0-6 years only	6.83	0.91	–1.20	3.35	1.00	–0.02
6-17 years only	10.88	1.02	0.30	5.79	1.04	0.47
0-17 years	10.10	1.18	2.26	4.72	1.15	1.34
Work in 1975						
Full-time	10.48	1.12	1.40	5.35	1.67	3.69
Part-time	9.31	1.43	3.39	2.46	1.14	0.66
[Did not work]	6.48	1.00		2.07	1.00	
South [vs. non-South]	10.39	1.10	2.29	4.58	1.04	.70
Urban [vs. non-urban]	8.81	0.98	–0.56	4.48	0.96	–0.57
Metro [vs. non-SMSA]	9.37	0.66	–8.59	4.92	0.95	–0.68
Unemployment rate		0.99	–1.26		0.98	–1.10
Non-White immigrant*	7.32	0.71	–0.71	3.37	0.79	0.97
Hispanic immigrant*	8.96	.84	–1.50	4.33	0.84	0.36
Number of cases			3,166			1,448

SOURCE: *Public Use Microdata Sample (A)* (U.S. Bureau of the Census, 1983). Sample includes all civilian men and women aged 18-64 who worked as nonfarm wage and salary workers or nonfarm self-employed workers in 1979.
NOTE: SMSA = Standard Metropolitan Statistical Area. Brackets indicate a reference group.
* Indicates an interaction effect.

business, past work experience has no effect on the odds that a woman will work for her own corporation. Rather, family structure variables must be considered when examining women's self-employment; being married and having preschool children have large and significant effects on the odds that women will choose either variant of self-employment over wage and salary work. It appears that self-employment, either incorporated or unincorporated, is a strategy for women to circumvent the constraints that their child care needs may place on their traditional wage labor force participation. At the same time, self-employment is not an option readily available to all women. Personal resources, such as education and the financial security of having a spouse, appear to be prerequisites for a woman to select this flexible work strategy. Therefore, women's self-employment decisions do not comply neatly with either Schumpeter's (1934) or Knight's (1933) theory. Although women with preschool-age children may be constrained from securing wage and salary employment, only those with the advan-

TABLE 7.7 Multinomial Logit Model of Women's Self-Employment in an Unincorporated or Incorporated Business vs. Wage and Salary Employment in the United States: 1980 (N = 22,403)

	Self-Employment in an Incorporated Business vs. Wage/Salary Work			*Self-Employment in an Unincorporated Business vs. Wage/Salary Work*		
Independent variables	*Marginal Odds*	*Adjusted Odds*	*β/SE*	*Marginal Odds*	*Adjusted Odds*	*β/SE*
Age						
[18-24]	1.15	1.00		0.14	1.00	
25-34	3.79	3.22	6.12	0.67	3.54	2.38
35-44	5.44	5.71	8.82	2.12	12.55	4.77
45-54	5.47	6.35	9.43	1.57	12.10	4.69
55-64	6.73	8.33	10.62	2.34	23.10	5.89
Race						
[White]	4.87	1.00		1.62	1.00	
Non-White	2.40	0.52	–4.35	0.65	0.66	–1.5
Ethnicity						
Hispanic	2.94	1.00	0.02	0.76	0.37	–1.4
[Non-Hispanic]	4.61	1.00		1.36	1.00	
Civil status						
[Born in United States]	4.50	1.00		1.46	1.00	
Immigrant	4.94	1.35	1.97	1.59	1.38	1.22
Education						
< 12 years	3.96	0.96	–0.39	0.61	0.40	–4.05
[12 years]	3.63	1.00		1.30	1.00	
13-15 years	5.01	1.62	5.62	1.53	1.48	0.03
16 years	6.55	2.26	7.28	2.32	2.53	4.98
17+ years	9.17	3.08	9.25	1.73	1.80	2.27
Work disability						
Yes	8.22	1.76	3.93	0.91	0.67	–0.96
[No]	4.41	1.00		1.34	1.00	

tages of education and spousal income are afforded the choice of self-employment.

CONCLUSIONS

The main purpose of this chapter was to contrast the characteristics of the male and female self-employed and to consider whether either the default or career theory of self-employment is appropriate to explain the determinants of women's self-employment. Neither theory, as originally formulated, provides an adequate or complete theory of women's self-employment. Rather, family characteristics—especially having young children (which constrains women's workforce options) and marital status (which facilitates women's self-employment decision)—are the strongest predictors of women's self-employment. Human capital characteris-

TABLE 7.7 Continued

Independent variables	Self-Employment in an Incorporated Business vs. Wage/Salary Work			Self-Employment in an Unincorporated Business vs. Wage/Salary Work		
	Marginal Odds	*Adjusted Odds*	*β/SE*	*Marginal Odds*	*Adjusted Odds*	*β/SE*
Marital status						
[Never married]	2.31	1.00		0.28	1.00	
Currently married	5.05	1.53	2.71	1.61	3.23	2.76
Divorced/separated/widowed	3.83	1.16	0.88	0.89	1.64	1.10
Kids at home						
[None]	4.43	1.00		1.17	1.00	
0-6 years only	3.77	1.41	2.35	0.81	1.66	1.63
6-17 years only	4.64	0.96	–0.51	1.73	1.38	1.99
0-17 years	5.82	1.64	3.66	1.41	1.88	2.34
Work in 1975						
Full-time	4.01	0.84	–2.10	1.45	1.16	0.95
Part-time	7.01	1.49	4.19	1.26	0.89	–0.61
[Did not work]	4.05	1.00		1.13	1.00	
South [vs. non-South]	4.46	1.11	1.39	1.27	1.00	0.01
Urban [vs. non-urban]	3.54	0.86	–1.63	0.89	0.72	–1.84
Metro [vs. non-SMSA]	4.29	0.72	–3.95	1.33	0.99	–0.06
Unemployment rate		1.00	0.18		0.96	–1.19
Non-White immigrant*	3.29	0.80	0.44	1.02	0.48	–1.03
Hispanic immigrant*	4.44	0.85	–1.19	1.23	1.72	1.42
Number of cases			1,003			285

SOURCE: *Public Use Microdata Sample (A)* (U.S. Bureau of the Census, 1983). Sample includes all civilian men and women aged 18-64 who worked as nonfarm wage and salary workers or nonfarm self-employed workers in 1979.
NOTE: SMSA = Standard Metropolitan Statistical Area. Brackets indicate a reference group.
* Indicates an interaction effect.

tics, however, are the strongest predictors of men's self-employment. Although several characteristics associated with Schumpeter's (1934) default model predict self-employment, a closer inspection reveals that these characteristics (limited past work experience, disability, immigrant status) predict men's self-employment in unincorporated businesses only. We cannot conclude with certainty, however, that men "choose" to be self-employed in incorporated businesses and default to unincorporated self-employment. Incorporation status, as noted earlier, is a very weak proxy for skilled versus unskilled self-employment.

Overall, Knight's (1933) career theory emerges as the better explanation of men's and women's self-employment; advanced age and education, as hypothesized, are shown to be strong determinants of both women's and men's self-employment relative to wage and salaried work. These results do not necessarily confirm the findings of past researchers that advanced chronological age, and the work experience this age often carries, is a determinant of self-employment. Rather, future research must rely on longitudinal data to determine how men's and women's entrances to, and exits from, self-employment vary over the life course. It is crucial to examine whether past analyses of cross-sectional data have truly reflected age, rather than period or cohort effects.

Moreover, the relationship between age and probability of self-employment can be better understood by examining cohort differences in industry and occupation categories. It is expected that the most recent entrants to self-employment are white-collar professional workers, and older cohorts of nonfarm self-employed workers are clustered in crafts and manufacturing occupations. The large and significant effect of education on the odds of being self-employed is expected to persist in the future as more white-collar professionals—many the victims of corporate layoffs in the 1980s and 1990s—form their own businesses. Ironically, these well-educated workers may actually turn to self-employment as a default career choice; many of these newly self-employed "consultants" find their earnings to be significantly less than those earned at their former salaried occupations (Uchitelle, 1993). In the past decade, increasing numbers of corporations began to outsource work to "homeworkers," "independent contractors," and "freelancers": individuals who may be labeled self-employed by censuses and tax records but who actually have little autonomy or control over what they produce or how they produce it (Christensen, 1988; Dale, 1986).

Despite the numerous similarities between the male and female self-employed, two distinct differences exist: past work experience and family structure. Women who did not work or who worked only part-time in 1975 are shown to be more likely than 1975 full-time workers to be self-employed 5 years later. Men who worked part-time or full-time in 1975 are more likely than the 1975 nonworking to be self-employed after the same period of time. Given the recent rise in white-collar self-employment due to corporate layoffs and outsourcing, however, it seems likely that full-time work experience will be a prerequisite for both men's and women's self-employment in future years.

Finally, family characteristics must be considered when evaluating explanations of women's self-employment. The fact that women with preschool children are more likely than the childless or the mothers of school-age children to be self-employed provides empirical support for the hypothesis that self-employment resembles shift work and part-time work in that it is a strategy for working women to combine home and work responsibilities. To date, there has been only suggestive evidence that self-employment provides an avenue for women who want to or need to work yet must also balance the demands of family. Earlier research by Pleck, Staines, and Lang (1980) showed results from a national survey of workers, in which women more often than men reported schedule incompatibility between work and family, yet women's self-employment was unrelated to work-family conflicts. Self-employment does not appear to be an option available to all mothers who are prevented from taking full-time salaried work, however; the additional advantages of advanced education and the benefits of a spouse's income provide the necessary capital for a woman to form her own business.

The story of women's self-employment does not end here, however. Future research must consider spouses' joint employment decisions and the duration of women's self-employment. It is quite possible that husbands and wives working together in a family-owned business or that having a spouse who is employed at a stable, well-paying job offers greater latitude for one to take the risk of starting one's own business. The large and significant effect of age on women's self-employment also raises questions about the relationship between spousal retirement and a woman's work in her own business. Moreover, if a woman's entrance to self-employment is conditioned by family responsibilities, does she exit self-employment when her children are grown, or does she parlay her initial investment into a long-term career? Does experience obtained in the self-employed workforce carry over into the traditional salaried workforce, in terms of tenure and earnings for women?

By further examining such questions, the sociological study of women's labor force participation can be enhanced. Structured interviews with self-employed women could capture their motivations for forming their own businesses and their reasons for accepting low earnings for full-time work (Aronson, 1991). An examination of self-employed women's strategies for determining their fees and payment structures may also offer some insights into their earnings disadvantage. Although the present analysis of census data cannot answer such questions, it has provided some insights into the status of the self-employed, based on sex and incorporation status.

NOTES

1. This analysis used 1980 U.S. Census data because 1990 data were not yet available at the time the project began. Analysis of the 1980 data is crucial for two reasons: First, it represents the first census taken after the monotonic increase in self-employment rates began in the 1970s. Secondly, this analysis provides a baseline for the study of self-employment in the 1980s and offers a point of departure for examining the 1990 U.S. Census data.

2. Although data on total household income are available in the PUMS data, this is not used as an independent variable in the analysis. A woman's decision to be self-employed might be jointly determined with husband's income.

3. Past work experience is operationalized as whether the respondent worked part-time in 1975, worked full-time in 1975, or did not work in 1975. The more traditional approximation of one's labor force experience—age minus years of schooling minus six years—is not appropriate in a model attempts to measure men's and women's career experiences. Salvo and McNeil (1984) have concluded that women have much more disjointed career trajectories than men and that this disparity is exacerbated for married women and mothers. Therefore, a less precise, yet presumably less gender-biased, measure of workforce experience is included in the model.

4. The frequently documented finding that advanced chronological age has a positive effect on self-employment may reflect intercohort changes in the prevalence of self-employment. In other words, it is possible that older men are overrepresented among the self-employed simply because self-employment was more prevalent in the earlier decades when they began their careers. The bulk of research on the recent increase in self-employment rates has been conducted in the 1970s, and older chronological age in such studies may simply reflect older cohorts born prior to 1920. This assertion cannot be tested in the present cross-sectional data; future research should examine longitudinal data on the self-employment experience.

5. The following occupations are the most commonly held jobs by male and female nonfarm self-employed full-time year-round workers, based on incorporation status. The 1:100 1980 PUMS was used to calculate the following listings, and the occupations are defined by the three-digit census occupational codes (complete occupation and industry distributions available from author).

Males, unincorporated: Managers and administrators, not elsewhere classified (nec); carpenters; supervisors and proprietors, sales; lawyers; truck drivers; supervisors, electricians; automobile mechanics; painters, construction, and maintenance; real estate sales occupations; and physicians.

Males, incorporated: Managers and administrators, nec; supervisors and proprietors, sales; construction trades supervisors; physicians; sales reps, mining, manufacturing, wholesale; real estate sales occupations; supervisors, production occupations; lawyers; managers, marketing, advertising, public relations.

Females, unincorporated: Hairdressers and cosmetologists; managers and administrators, nec; child care workers; teachers, nec; real estate sales occupations; sales workers, other commodities; street and door-to-door vendors; bookkeepers and accounting clerks; designers; painters, sculptors.

Females, incorporated: Managers and administrators, nec; bookkeepers; secretaries; supervisors and proprietors, sales; real estate sales occupations; sales workers, other commodities; general office clerks; hairdressers and cosmetologists; cashiers.

6. This method of measuring self-employment is potentially inaccurate. Census respondents who report that they are self-employed are then asked whether their business is incorporated or not. Respondents who initially reported that they were wage and salary workers of private companies, however, were not subsequently asked whether they own the business. This asymmetry may lead to the misclassification of some self-employed workers in incorporated businesses as wage and salary workers.

The potential asymmetry in reporting class of worker status is not expected to be problematic in the present analysis. Haber, Lamas, and Lichtenstein (1987) compared estimates of the proportion reporting self-employment status in the *Current Population Survey* (CPS) and the *Survey of Income* and Program Participation (SIPP) and found few differences. In SIPP, all business owners are identified, whether or not they own incorporated businesses or "side" (unincorporated) businesses. The authors reported that 7.4% and 7.8%, respectively, of the employed report self-employment in unincorporated businesses in SIPP and CPS. From the SIPP data, they found that an additional 2.6% operate incorporated businesses, and the comparable CPS figure is 2.7%.

7. Race is coded into a dichotomous variable, wherein non-White equals 1, and White is the reference group. Of the 12% of sample respondents who are not White, roughly three quarters are Black. Although Asians and Blacks have been shown to have very different work histories and propensities towards self-employment (Boyd 1991; Zhou & Logan 1989), separate categories are not created for the two groups. Rather, the categories are grouped together for the purpose of sample size and parsimony, and interaction terms are added to represent non-white immigrants and Hispanic immigrants.

8. Hispanic ethnicity, regardless of race, is coded as 1. Immigrant status is also a dichotomous predictor variable and is derived from the census question regarding year of immigration. Individuals born in the United States or born abroad of American parents are the reference group. The year of immigration is not included in the analysis; rather, we are interested simply in whether or not the person immigrated to the United States.

9. The unemployment rates were obtained from the U.S. Department of Commerce (1982). For the New England states, however, New England County Metropolitan Area unemployment rates are matched to the corresponding Standard Metropolitan Statistical Area (SMSA) code. For the 32% of the sample who do not reside in SMSAs, the 1979 national unemployment rate of 7.1 is assigned as a proxy rate. The dummy variable for SMSA residence carries the effect of differences in self-employment between the actual rate and that expected from the national unemployment rate of 7.1%.

REFERENCES

Aronson, R. L. (1991). *Self employment: A labor market perspective.* Ithaca, NY: ILR Press.

Becker, E. H. (1984). Self-employed workers: An update to 1983. *Monthly Labor Review, 107,* 14-19.

Borjas, G. J. (1986). *The self-employment experience of immigrants* (NBER Working Paper No. 194). Cambridge, MA: National Bureau of Economic Research.

Borjas, G. J., & Bronars, S. G. (1989). Consumer discrimination and self-employment. *Journal of Political Economy, 97,* 581-605.

Boyd, R. L. (1991). A contextual analysis of black self-employment in large metropolitan areas, 1970-1980. *Social Forces, 70,* 409-429.

Brown, G. D. (1976). How type of employment affects earnings differences by sex. *Monthly Labor Review, 99,* 25-30.

Carr, D. (1993). *The determinants of women's and men's self-employment in the United States, 1980.* Unpublished master's thesis, University of Wisconsin, Madison.

Carroll, G. R., & Mosakowski, E. (1987). The career dynamics of self-employment. *Administrative Science Quarterly, 32,* 570-589.

Christensen, K. (1987). Women and contingent work. *Social Policy, 18,* 15-19.

Christensen, K. (1988). *Women and home-based work: The unspoken contract.* New York: Henry Holt.

Connelly, M., & Rhoton, P. (1988). Women in direct sales: A comparison of Mary Kay and Amway sales workers. In A. Stathan et al. (Eds.), *The worth of women's work: A qualitative synthesis.* Albany: State University of New York Press.

Connelly, R. (1992). Self-employment and providing child care. *Demography, 29,* 17-29.

Dale, A. (1986). Social class and the self-employed. *Sociology, 20,* 430-434.

Darian, J. C. (1975). Convenience of work and the job constraint of children. *Demography, 12,* 245-255.

Devine, T. (1994). Characteristics of self-employed women in the United States. *Monthly Labor Review, 117,* 20-34.

Evans, D. S., & Leighton, L. (1989). Some empirical aspects of entrepreneurship. *American Economic Review, 79,* 519-535.

Fain, T. S. (1980). Self-employed Americans: Their number has increased. *Monthly Labor Review, 103,* 3-8.

Fuchs, V. (1980). *Self-employment and labor force participation of older males* (NBER Working Paper No. 584). Cambridge, MA: National Bureau of Economic Research.

Fuguitt, G. (1985). The non-metropolitan turnaround. *Annual Review of Sociology, 11,* 259-280.

Haber, S. E., Lamas, L., & Lichtenstein, J. (1987). On their own: The self-employed and others in private business. *Monthly Labor Review, 111,* 17-23.

Herz, D. (1988). Job characteristics of older women, 1987. *Monthly Labor Review, 112,* 3-12.

Johnson, P. (1981). Unemployment and self-employment: A survey. *Industrial Relations Journal, 12,* 5-15.

Knight, F. H. (1933). *Risk, uncertainty and profit.* London: London School of Economics and Political Science.

Kraut, R. E., & Grambsch, P. (1987). Home-based white collar employment: Lessons from the 1980 Census. *Social Forces, 66,* 410-426.

Loscocco, K. A. (1990). Reactions to blue collar work: A comparison of women and men. *Work and Occupations, 17,* 152-177.

Loscocco, K. A., & Leicht, K. T. (1993). Gender, work-family linkages, and economic success among small business owners. *Journal of Marriage and the Family, 55,* 875-887.

Loscocco, K. A., & Robinson, J. (1991). Barriers to women's small-business success in the United States. *Gender & Society, 5,* 511-532.

MacPherson, D. (1988). Self-employment and married women. *Economic Letters, 28*(3), 281-284.

Maxim, P. S. (1992). Immigrants, visible minorities and self-employment. *Demography, 29,* 181-198.

Moore, R. (1983). Employer discrimination: Evidence from self-employed workers. *Review of Economics and Statistics, 65,* 496-501.

Phillips, J. D. (1962). *The self-employed in the United States.* Urbana: University of Illinois Press.

Pleck, J. H., Staines, G. L., & Lang, L. (1980). Conflicts between work and family life. *Monthly Labor Review, 103,* 29-32.

Presser, H. B., & Baldwin, W. (1980). Childcare as a constraint on employment: Prevalence, correlates, and bearing on the work and fertility nexus. *American Journal of Sociology, 85,* 1202-1213.

Quinn, J. F. (1980). Labor force participation patterns of older self-employed workers. *Social Security Bulletin, 43,* 17-28.

Salvo, J. J., & McNeil, J. M. (1984). *Lifetime work experience and its effect on earnings* (Current Population Reports P-23, p. 136).

Schumpeter, J. (1934). *The theory of economic development: An inquiry into profits, capital and credit.* Cambridge, MA: Harvard University Press.

Silver, H. (1989). The demand for housework: Evidence from the U.S. Census. In E. Boris & C. R. Daniels (Eds.), *Homework: Historical and contemporary perspectives on paid labor at home* (pp. 103-129). Chicago: University of Illinois Press.

Steinmetz, G., & Wright, E. O. (1989). The fall and rise of the petty bourgeoisie: Changing patterns of self-employment in the post-war United States. *American Journal of Sociology, 94,* 937-1018.

Stolzenberg, R., & Waite, L. (1984). Local labor markets, children and labor force participation of wives. *Demography, 21,* 157-170.

Sweet, J. (1973). *Women in the labor force.* New York: Academic Press.

Uchitelle, L. (1993, November 15). Newest corporate refugees: Self-employed but low-paid. *New York Times,* p. A1.

U.S. Bureau of the Census. (1983). *Public use microdata samples (A): Technical documentation.* Washington, DC: Author.

U.S. Bureau of the Census. (1984). *Survey of income and program participation (SIPP): Wave 1.* Washington, DC: Author / Ann Arbor, MI: InterUniversity Consortium for Political and Social Research.

U.S. Department of Labor. (1982). Labor force statistics derived from the *Current Population Survey* (Bulletin 2096). Washington, DC: Government Printing Office.

Waldman, E. (1983). Labor force statistics from a family perspective. *Monthly Labor Review, 106,* 16-20.

Zhou, M., & Logan, J. R. (1989). Returns on human capital in ethnic enclaves: New York City's Chinatown. *American Sociological Review, 54,* 809-820.

Getting Away and Getting By

The Experiences of Self-Employed Homeworkers

NANCY C. JURIK

The past two decades have witnessed a resurgence in the number of women and men in the United States who do paid work in their homes (Silver, 1989). Some scholars see this development as emancipatory—a fulfillment of worker demands for more flexibility and autonomy (Beach, 1989; Carter & Cannon, 1992; Toffler, 1980). But, critics warn of the exploitation associated with homework; they charge that homework reflects a trend toward worker insecurity and a decreased standard of living (Boris, 1994; Allan & Wolkowitz, 1987). Public debates are confused by the varied forms of homework and by differences in homework experiences along gender, class, and race lines.

Homework is a gendered phenomenon. It appeals to women who wish to combine paid work with domestic obligations. However, some women who work at home for piece rates in production or service-related industries are exploited (Allan & Wolkowitz, 1987; Christensen, 1989; Dangler, 1994; Phizacklea & Wolkowitz, 1995). Although defined as self-employed, these workers function as employees for one firm. Poor women, especially recent immigrants, tend to occupy the most exploitative homework positions. Thus, class and race relations also organize homework demands and experiences.

Some research suggests that the only liberated homeworkers are those who are truly self-employed (Allan & Wolkowitz, 1987; Dangler, 1994). Estimates suggest that anywhere from two thirds to 75% of homeworkers are self-employed (Heck, 1991; Walker & Heck, 1995). These individuals are more likely to be White, middle class, and highly educated than their disguised-employee counterparts; they may avoid the exploitations faced by employees working outside the home and by disguised employees working in the home.

Self-employment is a source of supplemental income and upward mobility for racial/ethnic minorities and immigrants (Castells & Portes, 1989; Light & Bonacich, 1988). Self-employed homework (SEH) also may be an avenue for women to enter masculine domains of business and to combine child care and earning activities (Brush, 1992; Else & Raheim, 1992).

Research has not sufficiently questioned this liberated image for self-employed homeworkers. Neither has it addressed variations in the SEH experience. This study examines the experiences of self-employed homeworkers. Through in-depth interviews with a sample of predominantly female, white-collar, professional SEH workers, it reveals how SEH challenges and reproduces conventional work arrangements. It considers the ways in which respondent social location in terms of gender, family status, race/ethnicity, resources, and market conditions frames SEH strategies.

From *Work and Occupations*, Vol. 25, No. 1, February 1998, pp. 7-35. Reprinted by permission.

THEORETICAL TREATMENTS OF SELF-EMPLOYMENT AND HOMEWORK

Research on small businesses, entrepreneurs, paid home labor, informalism, and gendered divisions of labor present two competing images of SEH (Carr, 1996). One view portrays self-employed homeworkers as liberated innovators "getting away" from many of the constraints of conventional employment (Beach, 1989; Carter & Cannon, 1992; Heck, Owen, & Roe, 1995). SEH is said to offer greater advancement, more satisfying work, and more flexibility (Beach, 1989; Edwards & Edwards, 1995). Self-employed homeworkers furnish their own work materials and set their own prices and work hours (Ellisburg, 1985).[1]

Small business, including home- and nonhome-based ventures, is portrayed as an avenue of empowerment for marginalized workers (Blackford, 1991; Else & Raheim, 1992). Members of racial/ethnic minority and newly immigrating groups pursue self-employment to achieve upward mobility (Light & Bonacich, 1988). Women choose self-employment as a means of overcoming "glass ceilings" (Goffee & Scase, 1985). The home offers a relatively inexpensive location for business start-up to marginalized workers with limited capital.

The home also offers the physical space to combine business and child care. Although both men and women entrepreneurs seek independence, achievement, and satisfaction, women are more likely to seek flexibility for combining paid work and family care (Hisrich & Brush, 1986; Smith, McCain & Warren, 1982). More than half of women-owned businesses are home-based (U.S. Department of Labor, Women's Bureau, 1992). Many women rely on SEH as a means to balance paid work and child care (Prugl & Boris, 1996).

In contrast to the liberated innovator image, structural theories of labor exploitation and socialist feminist analyses of homework see self-employed homeworkers as constrained, contingent workers, getting by amid limited options for secure, conventional employment. A structural orientation stresses the macroeconomic and cultural determinants of SEH options (Harvey, 1989; Schumpeter, 1934). The reemergence of self-employment is an outgrowth of global restructuring, technological advances, changing consumer demands, and corporate layoffs, as well as state fiscal crises that have led government to downsize its workforce (Aronson, 1991; Dantico & Jurik, 1986; Goss, 1991). Employers have expanded part-time and temporary staff, and subcontracted work to smaller firms (Bromley & Gerry, 1979). Advances in communication technology and consumer demand for crafts also have fueled the demand for small-scale services and production (Castells & Portes, 1989; Gerson, 1993).

Self-employment no longer embodies the autonomy and productive capacity of previous decades; it is vulnerable to market forces dominated by large corporations (Dale, 1986; Fernandez-Kelly & Garcia, 1985; Gerson, 1993; Scase & Goffee, 1982). Given that self-employed homeworkers are often the sole proprietors of very small businesses, they are especially susceptible to market cycles. Like temporary work, disguised-employee homework, and other contingent work, SEH is a strategy for getting by in an economy of diminishing job quality and security (Spalter-Roth, Soto, & Zandniapour, 1994).

Self-employed homeworkers who are members of financially and socially disadvantaged groups are the most marginalized. Socialist feminist analyses argue that for women, paid homework is an adaptation to life in capitalist, patriarchal society (Phizacklea & Wolkowitz, 1995). Historically and today, economic need converges with gender subordination to force women into exploitative homework arrangements (Allen & Wolkowitz, 1987; Boris, 1994). Women's disproportionate responsibilities for unpaid domestic labor and the inflexibility of nonhome employment make homework attractive to women. Women pay a price for this flexibility in the form of lower earnings and otherwise exploitative work arrangements (Dangler, 1994; Nelson, 1990; Prugl & Boris, 1996). Relative to work outside the home, homework is less visible to husbands who might otherwise help with domestic labor (Christensen, 1988).

Although they have more freedom than disguised-employee homeworkers, women doing SEH are more constrained than liberated. Because of the time and space demands of child care and limited access to investment capital, women's businesses are disproportionately small, home-based, and in low-growth industries (Brush, 1992; Carter & Cannon, 1992). Size and industrial location make women's home businesses especially precarious. If SEH is the best among limited options, structural models do not view it as a meaningful choice.

Some analyses combine individual agency with socialist feminist and structural exploitation models to explore the everyday struggles of homeworkers within a societal context of economic and gender oppression. Beneria and Roldan (1986) focus on both the empowering and constraining dimensions of paid homework for women subcontractors in Mexico City (see also Boris & Prugl, 1996; Nelson, 1990). Balkin (1989) has made a case for some limited empowering dimensions of self-employment among the U.S. poor. Goffee and Scase (1985) suggest that some British women use entrepreneurship to challenge patriarchal systems of doing business. Relations surrounding gender, family status, economic resources, and race/ethnicity influence the degree of liberation or oppression in SEH.

Lamphere, Zavella, Gonzales, and Evans (1993) use the term *social location* to specify the way in which political and economic conditions interact with class, ethnicity, culture, and sexual orientation to shape the meanings and strategies of working men and women (p. 4). This combined emphasis on structure, agency, and practice reveals points of convergence and divergence in workers' lives.

This study draws on the integrative work described above to examine both the empowering and constraining dimensions of SEH for women and a comparison group of men. Drawing on Lamphere et al. (1993), it examines both commonalities and variations in SEH workers' experiences by comparing respondents of differing social locations. It identifies both similarities and differences in workers' motivations for SEH, freedom to choose SEH, perceived success in SEH, and difficulties in balancing SEH with family and personal commitments. The findings reveal the importance of considering individual agency, structural economic forces, and gender, race, and class relations in the analysis of SEH.

METHODS

The analysis draws on interviews with 46 self-employed homeworkers living in New England and the Sun Belt states. Sampling self-employed homeworkers is difficult; some hide businesses to avoid tax and zoning regulations (Portes & Sassen-Koob, 1987; Pratt, 1987). It is also difficult to determine if an individual is truly self-employed.

Respondents were included in this study if during the preceding 6 months they: (a) had worked 40 or more hours a month at home, (b) had no outside office for their SEH, (c) considered themselves self-employed, and (d) had more than one client. These criteria helped screen disguised-employee homeworkers.

The sample was drawn from three organizations of self-employed homeworkers and through referrals. The sample was purposively varied along dimensions that the literature suggests shape the SEH experience (Babbie, 1992, pp. 230-231; Glaser & Strauss, 1967). These dimensions included gender, family status, race/ethnicity, age, family income, type of SEH, and SEH duration.

One organization was a subgroup of the Boston Computer Society, a voluntary association for amateur and professional computer users. This home enterprise subgroup included men and women planning or running home-based ventures in the Boston area. The second organization was a voluntary association for women who were self-employed in a variety of home- and non-home-based ventures; it was also located in the Boston area. Members of both groups were predominantly White and middle class. I attended meetings of both organizations, explained the research, and obtained membership lists with brief descriptions of group members. I selected respondents from the lists to vary them along the dimensions listed above. Although the membership of both organizations was largely White, I interviewed two members who were persons of color. The third organization was a nonprofit business training and loan program for low-income, self-employed men and women in the Phoenix area. All five clients in the program who were engaged in SEH agreed to be interviewed. Additional respondents in several states (Arizona, California, Maine, Massachusetts, Rhode Island, and Texas) were obtained through referrals from respondents and researcher acquaintances.

Respondents worked in a variety of fields. Table 8.1 lists the SEH types. Four respondents' concerns overlapped two SEH categories. The majority were white-collar and professional ventures. They ranged from 3 months to 11 years of operation. Three fourths of respondents were sole proprietors; seven were in partnerships. Of the respondents, 72% (n = 33) occasionally subcontracted work out or hired temporary help, 17% (n = 8) did not hire employees or subcontract work out, 11% (n = 5) maintained one or more employees; 35% (n = 16) were incorporated. With some exceptions, respondent earnings tended to be low as is the case for much SEH. Women's earnings tended to be lower than men's earnings. Of the sample, 15% (n = 7) also held full- or part-time jobs outside the home. Respondent background characteristics are summarized in Table 8.2.

Table 8.2 shows that the sample was predominantly White and middle-income. More than half were single or divorced. A large percentage (70%) had some college education. Most (95%) were between the ages of 26 and 60. Women comprised 76% (n = 35) of the sample; men comprised 24% (n = 11). Nevertheless, sample variation of gender, resource level, family status, and race/ethnicity was sufficient to permit exploratory comparisons.

National surveys of homeworkers are confusing and inaccurate because much homework is hidden and unrecorded, and definitions of homework vary from survey to survey (Pratt, 1987). The 1991 Supplement to the U.S. Census revealed homework occupational distributions similar to those in the present study. However, neither the Census (Deming, 1994) nor Small Business Administration surveys (U.S. Small Business Administration, 1989) provides a clear breakdown of self-employed and employee homeworkers along gender lines.

Walker and Heck's (1995) analysis of a nine-state survey of homeworkers offers the most detailed insight into the gender and occupational characteristics of the U.S. self-employed homeworker population (see also Owen, Heck, & Rowe, 1995). Respondents in Walker and Heck's (1995) study worked about the same number of SEH hours each week on average as did respondents in the present study. However, there also were significant differences between the two samples. This study oversampled women; women comprised only 42% of Walker and Heck's (1995) respondents. The present sample was younger (mean ages of 39 vs. 44), more highly educated, more likely to be single or divorced, and had lower mean SEH ($12,000 vs. $15,000) and family incomes ($38,000 vs. $41,000) than Walker and Heck's. The present sample also contains fewer women in clerical, sales, and artisan concerns, and more in professional fields. It contains fewer men in professions than did Walker and Heck (1995).[2] Nevertheless, the implications of these comparisons are limited because the Walker and Heck study excluded SEH concerns less than 1 year old and significantly oversampled rural areas.

Walker and Heck (1995) were silent on race, but rough national estimates suggest that home self-employment among Blacks and Hispanics is very low, around 5% for Blacks and 1% for Hispanics (Pratt, 1993). Thus, the present sample probably overrepresents Black and Hispanic self-employed homeworkers.

My intent was not to draw a representative sample of the population of self-employed homeworkers. I aimed to collect a detailed set of personal accounts of the motives and experi-

TABLE 8.1 Type of Self-Employed Homework (SEH), by Gender

Type of SEH and Abbreviation	*Women*	*Men*	*Total*
Professional services	16 (46%)	3 (27%)	19 (41%)
Accountant (Act)	1	1	2
Advertising (Adv)	2	—	2
Book indexing (Indx)	1	—	1
College counseling (Couns)	1	—	1
Computer programming (CP)	3	1	4
Legal research (LS)	1	—	1
Management and diversity training (MDT)	3	—	3
Marketing/evaluation research (Res)	1	1	2
Public relations (PR)	3	—	3
Clerical-related services	5 (14%)	—	5 (11%)
Wordprocessing (WP)	4	—	4
Wordprocessing training (WPT)	1	—	1
Other services	7 (20%)	2 (18%)	9 (19%)
Alterations/accessories (Alt)	1	—	1
Auto detailing (AD)	1	—	1
Child care (Child)	2	—	2
Furniture assembly (FA)	—	1	1
Housesitting service (HS)	1	—	1
Photography (Ph)	1	1	2
Travel agent (TA)	1	—	1
Sales-production	2 (6%)	3 (27%)	5 (11%)
Ad sales (AS)	—	1	1
Children's clothes (make & sell) (CC)	1	—	1
Computer sales/rentals (CSR)	1	1	2
Software marketing (SWM)	—	1	1
Crafts-artisans	3 (7%)	1 (9%)	4 (9%)
Painter (P)	—	1	1
Silk flower arrangements (SF)	1	—	1
Weavers (W)	2	—	2
Combination of types	2 (6%)	2 (18%)	4 (9%)
Computer programmer, hardware sales (CH)	—	1	1
Edit and sell ads for magazine (Mag)	—	1	1
Make purses, cartoonist, paint (PCP)	1	—	1
Weave, design, and manufacture drapes (WD)	1	—	1

ences from women and a small comparison group of men engaged in SEH who had varied background characteristics and who worked in different occupations and contexts. Most respondents were white-collar or professional SEH workers.

TABLE 8.2 SEH Sample Characteristics ($N = 46$)

Characteristics	*Women*	*Men*	*Total*
Gross yearly she income			
$50,000 +	11% (4)	36% (4)	17% (8)
$30,000–$49,000	23% (8)	27% (3)	24% (11)
$10,000–$29,000	31% (11)	27% (3)	30% (14)
Less than $10,000	34% (12)	9% (1)	28% (13)
Total	(35)	(11)	(46)
Annual family income			
$70,000 +	20% (7)	9% (1)	17% (8)
$23,301–$69,999	49% (17)	63% (7)	52% (24)
$23,300 or less	31% (11)	27% (3)	30% (14)
Total	(35)	(11)	(46)
Race/ethnicity			
African American	17% (6)	9% (1)	15% (7)
Hispanic	9% (3)	18% (2)	11% (5)
Caucasian	74% (26)	72% (8)	74% (34)
Total	(35)	(11)	(46)
Family status			
Married, child under 6	26% (9)	9% (1)	22% (10)
Married, child 6-17	9% (3)	(0)	7% (3)
Married, adult/no child	20% (7)	18% (2)	19% (9)
Divorced/single, child under 6	3% (1)	9% (1)	4% (2)
Divorced/single, child 6-17	9% (3)	0	7% (3)
Divorced/single, adult/no child	34% (12)	64% (7)	41% (19)
Total	(35)	(11)	(46)

NOTE: "Child" in this table means that the respondent was living with one or more children in that age category, unless "no child" is specified. "Adult/no child" means the respondent either had only children age 18 and older or had no children.

The interviews covered a range of topics: demographics, work history, reasons and goals for starting SEH, working conditions, time allocation, and perceived benefits, problems, and strategies to SEH. Each interview lasted about 1½ hours; all but 10 were taped. A subsample of 20 respondents was followed for periods of 6 to 24 months after the first interview. Five were interviewed after quitting SEH.

The analysis focuses on the liberating potential of SEH and the ways in which gender, race, resources, family status, and market conditions framed and were reproduced by such ventures. *Gender* refers to "patterned, socially produced distinctions between female and male, feminine and masculine" (Acker, 1992, p. 250; West & Zimmerman, 1987). *Race/ethnicity* refers to the socially constructed differences among individuals based on perceived skin color and group cultural practices (Nagel, 1994). *Resources* refer to respondents' access to education, skills, financial capital (e.g., income and assets of self or family), and the unpaid labor of family and friends. Individuals whose family income met HUD low-income guidelines were coded as low income.[3] Those with family incomes above that level were coded as middle-income. Family status addresses respondents' marital status, number and ages of children, and care needs of older relatives. Table 8.3 lists respondents' identification number, background, and SEH type.

GETTING AWAY: MOTIVATIONS AND IDEALS OF HOMEWORK

Respondent reasons for starting SEH ventures ranged from those who had "little choice" and few, if any, alternatives (20%) to those who emphasized that their SEH was "a choice," among other work alternatives (24%). The majority of respondents (56%) described some combination of constraints and agency in their decisions to begin SEH. However, most respondents, even those who felt forced into SEH, viewed it as an opportunity to get away from the constraints of traditional work. They assessed SEH in relation to paid and unpaid work options, and in relation to the constraints of resources, family status, gender, and race/ethnicity.

TABLE 8.3 Respondent ID No., Demographics, and SEH Type and Length

ID No.	*Gender*	*Race/ Ethnicity*	*Marital Status*	*Youngest Child's Age*	*SEH Type*	*Length*
1	Woman	White	Divorced	Grown	Book indexing	4 years
2	Man	Hispanic	Divorced	1.5 years	Editing/sales	3 years
3	Woman	White	Married	3 months	Wordprocessing trainer	8 months
4	Woman	White	Married	2 years	Computer programmer	2 years
5	Man	White	Single	None	Programmer/sales	2 years
6	Woman	White	Single	None	Tax accountant	2 years
7	Woman	White	Single	None	Wordprocessing	6 months
8	Woman	White	Married	Grown	Management training	5 years
9	Woman	White	Married	9 years	Travel agent	5 years
10	Woman	White	Married	2 years	Wordprocessing	1 year
11	Man	White	Married	Grown	Computer sales/rentals	11 years
12	Woman	Hispanic	Divorced	Grown	Legal research	3 years
13	Woman	White	Single	None	Wordprocessing	2 years
14	Man	White	Single	None	Accountant	3 years
15	Woman	White	Married	Grown	College counseling	2 years
16	Man	White	Single	None	Software marketing	1 year
17	Man	Black	Married	3 years	Furniture assembly	8 months
18	Woman	White	Married	5 years	Programmer	1.5 years
19	Woman	White	Married	Grown	Computer sales/rental	11 years
20	Man	White	Single/ cohabitating	None	Artist/painter	2 years
21	Man	White	Married	Grown	Ad sales	4 years
22	Woman	White	Divorced	Grown	House sitting	4 years
23	Man	Hispanic	Single	None	Programmer	1 month
24	Woman	White	Married	5 years	Child care	3 years
25	Woman	White	Divorced	Grown	Clothing alterations	2 years
26	Woman	White	Married	4 years	Programmer	4 years
27	Woman	White	Divorced	16 years	Market research	1 year
28	Woman	White	Single	None	Make purses, cartoonist, painter	8 years
29	Woman	White	Married	Grown	Wordprocessing	3 years
30	Woman	White	Married	Grown	Advertising	10 years
31	Woman	White	Married	Grown	Advertising	10 years
32	Woman	Hispanic	Divorced	Grown	Make/sell children's clothes	3 years
33	Woman	White	Married	5 years	Weaver	2 years
34	Woman	Black	Married	Grown	Management/diversity training	5 years
35	Woman	White	Married	10 years	Weave/make drapes	3 years
36	Woman	White	Married	10 years	Weave/quilt	3 years
37	Woman	Hispanic	Married	3 years	Auto detail	2 years
38	Woman	White	Single	None	Public relations	3.5 years
39	Woman	White	Single	5 years	Public relations	1 year
40	Man	White	Single	None	Photographer	3 years
41	Woman	Black	Single	None	Diversity training	2 years
42	Man	White	Divorced	None	Evaluation research	~2 years
43	Woman	Black	Married	3 years	Child care	1 year
44	Woman	Black	Divorced	8 years	Public relations	2.5 years
45	Woman	Black	Divorced	6 years	Silk flower arrangements	6 months
46	Woman	Black	Single	None	Photography	6 months

Forced Respondents

Women respondents who felt forced linked this pressure to their roles as wives and mothers. Two women (5%) were pressed into SEH to help their unemployed husbands:

> The business is his thing not mine. After he got laid off, he couldn't find anything. He was an unemployed Latino . . . his opportunities were not good. I had to help him get the business going, to keep him going, to keep our family going. (no. 37)

Prior research reports that women's unpaid labor is often essential to the survival of family businesses (Moallem, 1991).

Two women either had to quit their wage and salary sector jobs or return full-time after brief pregnancy leaves. They chose SEH instead:

> They said that I could work part-time . . . after I had my baby. Then they decided that it would set a bad precedent. I quit and looked for a part-time job, but I had to do something to make money in the meantime. (no. 26)

Inadequate pregnancy leaves and inflexible work options often limit women's paid employment choices (Reskin & Padavic, 1994).

Respondents who felt they did not have a choice also included individuals who were laid off, disabled, or fired and had difficulty obtaining a new job in their field ($n = 5$). This finding concurs with the view that core employment downsizing and increased subcontracting have increased homework (Harvey, 1989; Prugl & Boris, 1996):

> Working at home . . . was essentially a non-choice. We . . . got settled here and . . . the company decided to send us to New York. We were not interested in moving. I couldn't find a real job. . . . I started on contract . . . realized I could do it, and decided to go out on my own. (no. 11)

Respondents who felt they did not have a choice intended to work at home until they found regular jobs. However, their ability to get by doing SEH, and perhaps the human tendency to view one's own activities positively, later led them to more positive evaluations of the experience. Their views came to resemble those who chose SEH. "I really wanted a job at first . . . now I wouldn't go back to a conventional job ever" (no. 14).

Even for those who did not choose it, SEH often came to be seen as a viable alternative to conventional employment, as a chance to get away. These findings reveal the dynamic interplay between structural constraints and individual agency in the SEH decision.

Escape and Fulfillment

Respondents described a variety of motivations for SEH; there was rarely only one reason for making the transition. Most respondents (90%) named self-fulfillment as a motivation. They described self-fulfillment as autonomy, freedom from supervision, freedom to set their working conditions and hours, and the opportunity to perform varied, interesting, or challenging work. The desire for self-fulfillment characterized respondents of both genders, of all represented racial/ethnic groups, and those with varying resources, occupations, and family statuses.

For one fourth of respondents, SEH represented an escape from some unpleasant workplace condition. Women frequently referenced discrimination—against women, against women of color, or against women with small children. Research finds that women often begin businesses to escape gender discrimination in employment (Goffee & Scase, 1985).

Two women chose SEH to escape the tedium of child rearing. One said, "Working at home lets me keep my skills up . . . keeps me from going brain-dead while I raise my baby" (no. 4).

Men focused more on independence as a value in itself. Men respondents spoke about wanting to escape "office politics" ($n = 2$), and "constant supervision" ($n = 3$). "I . . . wasn't going to make a career . . . in corporate America. I was more interested in getting something done than going to bars with my coworkers and supervisors" (no. 16).

Respondent comments about self-fulfillment and escape offered a critique of conventional employment. Of the respondents, 20% (n = 9) described SEH as a challenge to conventional systems of work or business in the United States. "We are part of a workplace revolution, challenging office politics and the rigidity of the 9-to-5 workday" (no. 23).

Another 7% (n = 3) described how their religious values, gender, or racial/ethnic background motivated them to develop their business in a different way. "I want to make a space for women of all races to come together, to learn, and to challenge these male-dominated structures" (no. 41).

> My mother was from Mexico. . . . I saw her struggle to provide clothes for us . . . so we could look OK . . . and I mostly think of the Hispanic family. Their families are bigger and that's the market I reach. . . . I feel a lot of pride in it, being able to offer them . . . quality clothes . . . at low prices. (no. 32)

The childhood experiences of this woman shaped her desire to keep her prices low even if it meant lower profits for herself.

Escape was an important motivation for many respondents. White men respondents expressed a desire to escape what they saw as oppressive employment conditions. In line with previous research, interviews revealed that individuals from disadvantaged groups (e.g., White women, men and women of color) often viewed self-employment as a way to avoid or challenge discriminatory workplaces (Fernandez-Kelly & Garcia, 1985; Goffee & Scase, 1985; Light & Bonacich, 1988). These results are consistent with previous findings that women tend to emphasize personal relationships and concerns for others in entrepreneurial endeavors more so than do men (Brush, 1992). Such arguments draw on Carol Gilligan's (1982) studies of moral development, which argue that men are more likely to concentrate on abstract rights and duties, whereas women are more likely to focus on an ethic of care and concern for relationships with others.

Flexibility, Balance, and Care

Respondents across gender, race, and resource categories hoped that relative to conventional employment, SEH would offer them the flexibility to lead a balanced life. Despite common use of the terms, the specific meaning attached to flexibility and balance varied across gender and family status groups. For women who did not plan to have children or whose children were grown, and for men generally, flexibility meant a less stressful work life and more balance among work, leisure, and family.

Women with small children defined flexibility as time for child care. Married women respondents of all racial/ethnic groups were more likely than were men to mention care responsibilities (e.g., for children or older relatives) as a motivating factor for SEH. Women spoke in terms of "taking care of" children; the two men who mentioned children as a motivation for SEH described it as "having more time to spend with children." "I was not the primary caretaker for the kids . . . my wife was. But having the business at home meant that I could be around them more . . . could see them more" (no. 11). Like Christensen (1988), these findings suggest that SEH does little to alter traditional gender divisions of household labor.

These data also reveal that although child care was often a priority, it was seldom the only reason that mothers began SEH:

> I directed a large (child care) facility. . . our kids were getting bigger . . . [and my husband] works . . . one of us needs to be home . . . and I was breaking my neck for this woman employer and she didn't care. (no. 43)

For this respondent, SEH meant both better family care and career advancement.

Views about the appropriateness of SEH varied across gender, family status, and resource groups. Of 11 men, 9 described SEH as "irresponsible" for husbands and fathers unless they also held "outside" jobs. They viewed it as financially irresponsible given their family obligations. Two single men said they would get traditional jobs if they got married.

However, married women described homework as a "good alternative" for meeting their earning and family responsibilities. Single mothers with adult children (*n* = 3) expressed concern about homeworking mothers; they "waited until the kids left home to start" SEH.

Previous research (e.g., Simon, 1995) has found that women view employment as preventing them from fulfilling their primary responsibilities to nurture children and husbands. Husbands, in contrast, view employment to be the cornerstone of their contribution to the family, that of provider. These findings reflect culturally dominant notions of femininity, masculinity, and family responsibilities that prevail in U.S. society. Men, not women, are viewed as the primary wage earners in heterosexual couples. Regardless of skills and education, women are viewed as financially dependent on husbands (Connell, 1987; Reskin & Padavic, 1994).

One man's woman companion was financially supporting him. "She has given me a year to make this thing pay. She . . . got a job. She wanted to work at home in her business, but she made this sacrifice for me" (no. 20). He described his companion as making "a great sacrifice." Women described husbands' financial support positively, but not as an unusual sacrifice.

Monetary Goals

Although only two respondents expected to make more money in SEH than in outside employment, income was still a motivating factor for most. Resources, family status, and gender shaped respondent views about the need for SEH income. Respondents ranged from those who viewed SEH income as essential to those who said they did not need their SEH income. Of the respondents, 46% (*n* = 21) viewed SEH as essential to their family income.

Another 17% (*n* = 8) used SEH income as a supplement but hoped it would fully support them in the future. Four of them were living temporarily on savings or investments. "I have investment income that will support me while I try this business idea. I can live for a while, even if the business doesn't pay at first. . . . After the money is gone, I get a job" (no. 16). Four respondents with low family incomes held full- or part-time jobs and did SEH. They hoped to quit these jobs when their SEH income could support them.

Another group of respondents (22%; *n* = 10) wanted their SEH earnings as extra income for them or their families. Three of these were low-income respondents (two men and one woman) who wanted SEH to supplement nonhome wage earnings. Two others were divorced, middle-income women who relied on their SEH to supplement alimony income. Five middle-income women viewed their SEH income as a supplement to their husbands' wages.

The notion of men as primary wage earners in families is seen in respondents' discussions of the monetary goals for their SEH. Of the respondents, 15% (*n* = 7) said that they did not need the income from their SEH. Six of these seven respondents were White, married women, whose husbands earned what they perceived to be a "comfortable income." Their primary concern was self-fulfillment, not economic independence. "It probably sounds crazy, but the money just serves as an indicator of how I am doing. . . . It is a measure of my effectiveness at what I do" (no. 9). Only one man reported that he did not need the income from his SEH. He had a "good retirement income." His primary motivations were self-fulfillment and keeping busy.

For most respondents, SEH was more than just a means for getting by; it represented a chance to get away and carve out alternative work and/or family arrangements. SEH meant a chance to develop unique work lives: Respondents wanted independent, varied, interesting, and challenging work; an escape; and harmony between work and family/personal life. As suggested by Lamphere et al. (1993), respondents' social locations generated differences in the exact meanings of these motivational factors. Social location also affected the degree to which respondents were financially dependent on the SEH. However, regardless of economic need, they ultimately had to be concerned with the profitability of their venture. They had to worry about getting by.

GETTING BY: THE REALITY OF HOMEWORK

Because most respondents were engaged in SEH at the time of their interview, it is not surprising that most (80%) were generally satisfied with SEH and hoped to continue for the next 5 years. Satisfied respondents perceived that they had indeed gotten away from the limitations of conventional work. They had improved their work situation along one or more of the dimensions of flexibility, work quality, and achievement. They viewed themselves as distinct from disguised-employee homeworkers. "I don't think of myself as a homeworker. I'm an entrepreneur. I think of homeworkers as poor, immigrant women who do industrial work under awful conditions" (no. 3).

Despite their general satisfaction, respondents routinely confronted dilemmas that threatened the survival and benefits of SEH. To handle the dilemmas, they developed strategies to get by. Some strategies worked, but often they undermined respondents' other SEH goals. A major dilemma centered on reconciling profitability, other SEH goals, and the demands of family and friends. Strategies for coping with this dilemma were shaped by respondents' social location (i.e., by gender, family status, and resources) as well as by surrounding local and regional economic conditions.

Demands of SEH: Profitability

Business in a market economy requires profitability (Scase & Goffee, 1982). Even respondents who did not need their SEH income viewed profit as an indicator of success. However, maintaining profitability often interfered with SEH goals of self-fulfillment, escape, or caring for others. It often meant replicating the very problems with conventional work that respondents were trying to escape.

INSTABILITY AND BREAD-AND-BUTTER WORK

Profitability required clients, and obtaining clients was not always easy. It was easiest for respondents who possessed high-demand skills and business contacts. However, for most respondents, SEH was economically unstable:

> The worst thing about this [SEH] is the insecurity. I often don't know where my next work is coming from. When things get really bad, I pick up part-time work. . . . When things are bad I think . . . if a good [outside] job comes along, I would take it. (no. 7)

As a result, the employment statuses of my sample were fluid over time. Over the course of a year, some respondents shifted from SEH to outside employment. Of the respondents, 11% ($n = 5$) changed their status at least twice during a 12-month period. Their experiences reveal that SEH, like other small business, is highly vulnerable to local and regional market fluctuations (Goss, 1991). "Since I began my business, there has been a real glut of programmers who have been laid off. They all seem to have started their own businesses and are competing with me" (no. 4). The reputation of home enterprises as unstable led some clients to fear doing business with them. This further exacerbated SEH instability.

Many respondents developed stable work flows and eased marketing pressures by accepting subcontracting work, often from former employers. Such jobs provided income until more desirable work could be found. Respondents often referred to this as "bread-and-butter work." For an artist, it meant designing novelty purses; for a quilter, it meant sewing curtains for a large hotel chain. Often, however, the "bread-and-butter" jobs were the sort of mundane work that respondents wanted to escape:

> I want to do marketing research. Right now I am doing title searches for my former employer.... It keeps me going. I make the same hourly wage that I made as their employer.... Of course, now. ... I don't have any health insurance. (no. 27)

Bread-and-butter work also was problematic because it reduced the time available to search for more desirable jobs. Moreover, respondents who became dependent on a few large clients, were vulnerable to exploitations:

> I hate the way that client treats me ... making me wait forever to get paid. They often complain about the quality of what I do, when they really just changed their mind about what they wanted. As soon as I can get other clients, I want to stop doing so much work for them. Right now, I've got to have them to survive. (no. 7)

Bread-and-butter work for one or two large firms provided only temporary stability. More than half of my respondents had at least some large companies as major clients. The decisions of those firms could make or break SEH ventures. "The IRS has changed its guidelines for independent contractors again. That has caused some companies to stop using independent contractors altogether. I could be out of business" (no. 14). This quote illustrates the importance of both government regulations and corporate policies in framing the experiences of self-employed homeworkers and others in small businesses. As the small business literature suggests, the autonomy of such concerns is often illusory (Dale, 1986; Scase & Goffee, 1982).

Better resourced respondents were able to advertise for the type of work they wanted, or to refuse jobs while waiting for more desirable work. Still, even they were not completely immune from the pressures of bread-and-butter work.

MARKETING AND OTHER UNDESIRABLE WORK

Because most SEH ventures were small, sole proprietorships, respondents described problems of having to do every SEH chore themselves. Prior to doing SEH, most respondents had worked as employees in large firms. Thus, they were used to a division of labor wherein other staff shared the work. However, in their SEH, it was all up to them:

> I was used to handing my letters off to a secretary and saying type this, mail that, file that. Now, I have to do it.... I'm even my own janitor. It's easy to forget the little jobs we didn't have to do before. (no. 5)

Another homeworker agreed. "I hate bookkeeping.... As soon as I can afford it, I'm going to hire an accountant" (no. 10). All respondents identified some SEH tasks as boring or undesirable. Nonetheless, they noted that these tasks were vital to the survival of their business.

Marketing was the most disliked and feared SEH task. Marketing themselves to strangers was stressful for many respondents. Marketing also took time away from work that could be charged to clients. They described self-marketing as a distraction from the "real work" of their business. "I hate marketing myself. It is not the work I started this business to do" (no. 13).

Although both men and women expressed disdain for marketing, women did so with greater frequency. Even two women whose SEH was marketing expressed intense dislike for marketing themselves.

Respondents with more financial resources were able to hire someone to help with or do marketing for them. However, most respondents struggled with the problem alone.

SELF-EXPLOITATION

The more dependent respondents were on SEH income, the more profitability demands led to self-exploitation (i.e., long, hard hours for low pay). Unfortunately, long hours reduced flexibility. "Yes, I have flexibility. I have the flexibility to work all night, and weekends . . . if I want to keep eating" (no. 5). Women with small children found the long hours most problematic. "I work while the kids sleep . . . maybe 'til 2 a.m.!" (no. 36)

As suggested in the homework literature, those (most often women) also responsible for child or other family member care, experienced double workdays (Christensen, 1988; Phizacklea & Wolkowitz, 1995). The pressure toward self-exploitation often undermined other SEH goals, such as those of reducing work-related pressures, increasing personal time, and promoting greater balance between work and family commitments.

Low-income respondents combined SEH with full- or part-time jobs. This meant double and even triple workdays when unpaid domestic labor was also included.

BUSINESS GROWTH

Expanding the business and hiring employees increased profitability and facilitated a division of labor. But, growth created new management responsibilities that cut into autonomy (Scase & Goffee, 1982). "I subcontracted typing work and used an answering service. . . . That got expensive, so I hired a girl [*sic*] to work here with me. Then I had to manage her" (no. 5). Moreover, growth did not necessarily lead to fewer SEH hours:

> I thought that hiring people to help out might give me more free time. True, I worked less on some things, but my hours went up because of having to supervise the people and fill out the paperwork to hire them (no. 22)

Growth also jeopardized efforts to balance SEH earnings with the family care responsibilities of some women in the sample. Too much growth implied more SEH responsibilities and a move out of the home. Many mothers wanted to work at home:

> I need to expand the business if I . . . want to make money, but the house is too crowded now. If I get an office, I will have to be away from the kids more. . . . That defeats the purpose. . . . I might as well get a job. (no. 18)

For these reasons, several SEH mothers decided to limit their business growth. This pattern suggests some explanation for the low rates of business growth among women-owned businesses, and for the high percentages of women-owned home businesses (Carter & Cannon, 1992; U.S. Department of Labor, Women's Bureau, 1992).

RESOURCES TO MEDIATE PROFIT DILEMMAS

Access to credit or other financial resources mediated problems surrounding profitability. Most businesses were too small for conventional business loans so they relied on credit cards and personal loans from family to keep their businesses afloat in troubled times. In line with previous literature on small business, my data indicated that women were less likely to espouse hopes of future business loans than were men (Carter & Cannon, 1992). Only seven respondents had ever received such loans. Five of the seven received loans from the program developed for self-employed low-income persons (Cowgill, 1996).

Resources, gender, and family status often converged to heighten or mediate profitability concerns. For example, 15% said they were "only a little concerned" about profit. Only one male respondent was "not too concerned" about profit; he was living on retirement income. The rest were White, middle-class, married women supported by husbands' incomes.

> We don't really need the extra money. Bob's income is more than adequate for our family. I am doing this to keep my skills up and have something for my resume when I return to full-time work . . . when my son is old enough. (no. 4)[4]

These findings mirror research on self-employed men and women that suggests that married women's businesses are more likely to be smaller, informal, home-based, and low profit than those of married men (Carter & Cannon, 1992). The differences stem, in part, from married women's additional time allocations to unpaid domestic work and from reliance on husbands' earnings (Pratt, 1993). Still, most women need their paid work earnings (Reskin & Padavic, 1994). More than half of the married women (including low- and middle-income women) said that they needed their SEH income to help support their families. "We can't make it without my income. If this doesn't make money, I'll have to go back to work" (no. 43). Profitability pressures and resources to meet them shaped the SEH experience. These pressures often conflicted with family and friend relationships.

Social Demands and Support: Family and Friends

Family labor and support helped some respondents, but SEH demands also produced conflicts with family and friends. Gender, resources, and family status shaped the form and intensity of conflicts.

DEMANDS OF FAMILY AND FRIENDS

An earlier section noted the sense of stigma that accompanied the decision to begin SEH. Negative views of SEH held by family and friends framed the ongoing SEH experiences of men and women respondents. However, the ongoing experience of SEH stigma also continued to differ along gender and family status lines. Men, especially married men, were viewed as slackers. "A man working at home raises eyebrows, especially if people hear that his wife is out working" (no. 20).

These findings suggest that homework violated dominant cultural images of masculinity (Connell, 1987) and images of real work (Lozano, 1989). Men are expected to be breadwinners; real work is outside, not inside the home.

In contrast, paid labor is not an essential component of culturally dominant notions of femininity. The women in this study were more concerned that their husbands, friends, and family did not take them or their homework seriously. "My husband doesn't think I'm really going to make a go of it at home and he wants me to get a job" (no. 36). Another woman said, "I explained to a friend that I ran a home business; she responded with the equivalent of 'how cute' (no. 35). Thus, culturally dominant images of real work and gender-appropriate behavior often impeded respondents' dreams of achievement and recognition.

Negative views of family and friends also exacerbated respondents' sense of conflict between SEH and family/friend demands. "My friends call me in the middle of the day and want me to join them for a drink. They think because I work for myself, and work at home, that I can just take off anytime" (no. 5). "Because I worked at home, I was on every mother's emergency list at school. When their kids got sick, the school called me to come pick them up" (no. 31).

Family members, especially husbands, sometimes complained that SEH distracted their wives from family-related duties. For several married women, unsupportive family highlighted the invisibility of housework and child care labor (Christensen, 1988). The following woman described these conflicts as both gender and ethnic/cultural issues:

> My mother lives with us and helps me with my daughter. But my husband is a very traditional Latin man. He expects me to work with him in the business all day, and cook and clean and care for our daughter too. (no. 37)

Similar comments from Anglo-American women about their husbands' failure to help with child care indicate that this problem is common to women across racial/ethnic groups:

> When I quit my job to stay home with the kids, he said, "I'm not washing another dish." Even with the business, he refuses to help with housework

or child care. He says, "You're home all day. If you can't handle it, get a job" (no. 35).

Women with small children experienced the greatest demands from family responsibilities. This concurs with prior research; it is difficult for women with small children to simultaneously perform paid homework and child care (Christensen, 1988; Pratt, 1993). These women typically used some of the following strategies: hiring child care, quitting or slowing the business, working while children slept. One woman formed a child care exchange with another friend who was doing SEH. "You should see us each week trying to reconcile schedules. We both had to tone down what we were trying to do" (no. 18). Such solutions did not always work. Some respondents relied on financial assistance or unpaid labor from family members.

FAMILY AND FRIENDS AS RESOURCES FOR SEH

Strategies for confronting the SEH–child care dilemma were again shaped by the social location of respondents (i.e., gender, family status, resources, and race/ethnicity). Like other small business proprietors, self-employed homeworkers often used the unpaid labor of spouses, children, or other family and friends to boost profitability. A few married women respondents (n = 3) reported that they had help from husbands in their business. A few women (n = 6) and one man received assistance from mothers, sisters, or children. Two sisters became SEH partners. Two other women were partners in their husbands' businesses.

Both wives who became partners had to give up their preferred work plans. The literature on family-owned businesses suggests that women, more often than men, dedicate full-time unpaid labor to make such ventures viable (Moallem, 1991). My data presented no instances in which men gave up preferred work options to join their wives' businesses.

Single mothers often had the fewest financial resources to resolve family/paid work conflicts. They relied on unpaid family labor and tried to work despite interruptions. One respondent credited help from her parents and the strength of her experience as an African American woman in achieving balance:

> I think Black women are used to combining our [paid] work and child care. It is something we do and have seen each other do. The White women here . . . are in their mid 30s and just had babies. They talk about problems balancing work and kids. . . . I have had my daughter since I was 18. . . . I am used to balancing my life with hers. . . . I give her little things to do and she pretends that she is working like her mother. . . . My parents live with us. . . . They help a lot. (no. 44)

Although conclusions from such findings are limited by the small number of women of color in the sample, my findings concur with a large amount of literature that suggests that women of color are more adept at balancing work and family responsibilities because of a cultural history of such balancing and because their families and social networks are more supportive of such integration (Amott & Matthaei, 1991; Collins, 1990). Regular, unpaid labor from family members was more often reported by women of color than by White women or by men respondents. Five of eight respondents who had unpaid child care or SEH help from family members were women of color. In addition, one divorced Hispanic man had such help. "I drop [my] daughter off every morning and my mom watches her. That really helps me manage work and my daughter" (no. 2).

Satisfactory resolutions to SEH family conflicts required resources from one or more of the following: the unpaid labor of supportive family members, personal financial reserves, spousal financial assistance.

FINANCIAL RESOURCES TO MEDIATE FAMILY AND SEH

When available, financial resources helped to mediate conflicts between SEH and family responsibilities. If the SEH income was adequate, or if other financial assistance was available from family or savings, a respondent was able to hire help with the SEH or with household and child care work.

About half of the married women with small children relied on husbands' income to help pay for child care services. Even when women resolve these tensions through paid child care, another dilemma often arose. "I got child care . . . but that defeated the purpose of my being home with them. I had to slow the business back. . . . Now we are getting by on [my husband's] income" (no. 10).

When women decrease time allocations to their SEH, they may reaffirm stereotypes of self-employed homework as trivial. They also contribute to the slow rates of growth reported by women-owned businesses (U.S. Department of Labor, Women's Bureau, 1992).

In contrast, one respondent in a highly skilled occupation made enough money so that she could expand her business and hire full-time child care. "I have child care 8 hours a day, but I am still at home. . . . If there was an emergency, I'd be here" (no. 26).

Resources and family status also facilitated balance in other ways. Respondents with sufficient finances and older children worked in spaces separated from children's activities. They obtained separate business-only phone lines, and trained children not to interrupt them. These strategies reduced family intrusions into work hours. However, family and paid work conflicts were not easily managed for those who had limited resource reserves, had young children, or were financially dependent on their SEH.

SUMMARY

The dynamics surrounding the social location of respondents shaped SEH motivations and experiences. Gender, family status, resources, race/ethnicity, and market demands also shaped their strategies for confronting dilemmas of profitability and its conflicts with other personal and family goals.

Autonomy and flexibility were important SEH motivations for all respondents. The meaning of these concepts differed across respondents. Mothers were more likely to want SEH flexibility to care for children and family. Women without children were more likely to emphasize personal fulfillment. White men focused on independence and escape from office politics. A few men who were married or were anticipating marriage hoped that SEH would give them more time with families, but they did not describe it in terms of responsibility for caregiving. Men of color and women referenced SEH as a means for overcoming workplace racial barriers and discrimination. For some respondents, gender and race/ethnicity clearly shaped the goals and nature of SEH.

SEH entailed the negotiation of often competing personal goals, business demands, and family responsibilities. Trying to make a business profitable often reduced autonomy, work satisfaction, and flexibility. In other words, in trying to get by, respondents could not always get away. Their efforts to carve out alternative and more satisfying SEH arrangements were often co-opted, and replicated conventional employment problems of long hours, boring work, and limited mobility. Efforts to get by were often further exacerbated by local and regional economies of layoffs and high unemployment.

Women with young children have been identified as beneficiaries of SEH (Else & Raheim, 1992). In this study, they experienced the most problems reconciling SEH and family concerns. Like other working women, married women doing SEH bore a disproportionate share of household and child care responsibilities (Christensen, 1988).

Resources, financial support, or unpaid labor from family and friends helped to mediate problems of mundane work, self-exploitation, instability, and business growth. For women with young children, resources were important for balancing SEH with child care responsibilities. For women of color, the unpaid labor of family members often aided in balancing paid work and family demands. For some married women, husbands' incomes provided resources for mediating SEH-family tensions. However, that resolution reinforced economic dependence on husbands.

Respondents with substantial non-SEH income sources (e.g., women whose spouses earned an adequate family income; men and women respondents who had investment, interest, alimony, or retirement incomes) were less concerned about the profitability of SEH. They knew what the literature confirms; they would probably make less money in SEH than they would as employees (Walker & Heck, 1995). Nonetheless, given the guiding norms of business in a capitalist economy, all respondents, albeit to differing degrees, ultimately confronted concerns about SEH profitability.

Despite obstacles, most respondents continued their struggles to balance business and family demands; they achieved considerable work satisfaction. Most preferred their own venture to more conventional employment options. They developed creative solutions to their dilemmas. The most successful individuals had some combination of very marketable skills and supportive family and friendship networks. In all cases, satisfaction was the hard-won outcome of tension, innovation, and compromise.

CONCLUSION

To my respondents, SEH was an innovation; in a qualified sense, it was liberating and revolutionary. At the same time, self-employed homeworkers confronted the economic and cultural realities of balancing personal goals, earnings, and family responsibilities in a global economy. Thus, these findings offer support for theoretical models that combine individual agency and structural constraint in understanding worker experiences. The concept of social location defined by Lamphere et al. (1993) has proven useful in this study to elucidate the variations in opportunities, constraints, and practices that characterize the lives of workers across gender, race/ethnicity, family status, class, and economic markets (see Beneria & Roldan, 1986).

Only a few of my respondents viewed themselves as forced into SEH. Most viewed themselves as a category apart from disguised-employee homeworkers. They were predominantly in white-collar or professional SEH. Nevertheless, the dilemmas they faced locate SEH as one manifestation of a larger trend toward the casualization and decentralization of work (Harvey, 1989; Portes & Sassen-Koob, 1987). Although these self-employed homeworkers appear significantly better off than disguised-employee homeworkers (Allen & Wolkowitz, 1987), many still shared the growing insecurity that confronts informal workers and conventional employees worldwide. This insecurity is now a part of life in middle- as well low-income America (Goss, 1991; Lozano, 1989). Thus, although these workers did not fit the image of exploited home pieceworkers, neither did they conform to the image of self-employed homeworkers as liberated innovators.

The findings also reveal that SEH, like other forms of homework, is not a solution for gender divisions of labor. Married women doing SEH did a disproportionate share of housework and child care. Married men doing SEH did not radically redefine their share of domestic responsibilities. Success stories of women doing SEH often ignore the dependence on husbands' incomes that was apparent in this study. Accounts of men's business success often ignore the essential contribution of women's unpaid domestic and business labor (Moallem, 1991). These omissions fuel myths that even without social change and institutional support, women and men can have it all if they have it at home.

These findings suggest that policymakers' hopes for SEH and other small businesses as solutions to the economic devastation of corporate downsizing and family-work conflicts, are misplaced. SEH worked best for highly skilled individuals or for those with additional income sources (see Spalter-Roth et al., 1994).

Further research on larger and more representative samples of men and women performing SEH would strengthen the generalizability of the findings reported here. Such research should ensure sufficient variation along the lines of SEH type, income levels, race/ethnicity, and family status. In addition, such research should try to get information on both recorded and unrecorded ("under the table") SEH. More longitudinal studies of the trajectories of SEH endeavors would provide insights into SEH growth rates across gender, racial/ethnic, family status, and income groups. For example, future research could seek to distinguish, if possible, between long-term, career-type and more part-time, temporary, contingent SEH workers.

SEH is no panacea for workers' or women's liberation. Many people are saying no to restrictive work arrangements. Their activities are both adaptive and challenging to predominant institutional systems of work in our society (see Henry, 1978). They pay a cost for saying no to conventional employment, but they continue to struggle to forge work alternatives.

NOTES

1. These are the U.S. Department of Labor guidelines for distinguishing true employment from hidden employment. To avoid workers' compensation regulations and social security payments for employees, some firms often label individuals as "self-employed" when they actually function as employees (Ellisburg, 1985).

2. The present study contained a higher percentage of women in professional occupations (46% in the present study vs. 17% in Walker & Heck, 1995). It contained a much lower percentage of men in professional self-employed homework (SEH) than did Walker and Heck (27% vs. 55%, respectively). It also contained a lower percentage of women in clerical, sales, and artisan SEH than Walker and Heck's (1995) study. Finally, it had an equal percentage of men in sales SEH, a lower percentage of men in clerical SEH, and a higher percentage of men in artisan SEH.

3. HUD low-income guidelines label $23,300 for a family of one as low income. Any respondents whose family income was lower than this were treated as low income in my study. One third of respondents refused to give their gross business income. Their earnings were estimated by other information obtained in the interviews (e.g., their hourly rates by approximate hours worked or the percentage that their business earnings contributed to family income).

4. All respondent names are pseudonyms.

REFERENCES

Acker, J. (1992). Gendering organizational theory. In A. Mills & P. Tancred (Eds.), *Gendering organizational analysis* (pp. 248-260). Newbury Park, CA: Sage.

Allan, S., & Wolkowitz, C. (1987). *Homeworking*. London: Macmillan.

Amott, T., & Matthaei, J. (1996). *Race, gender, and work: A multicultural economic history of women in the United States*. Boston: South End Press.

Aronson, R. (1991). *Self-employment: A labor market perspective*. Ithaca, NY: ILR Press.

Babbie, E. (1992). *The practice of social research* (6th ed.). Belmont, CA: Wadsworth.

Balkin, S. (1989). *Self-employment for low income people*. New York: Praeger.

Beach, B. (1989). *Work and family life: The home working family*. Albany: State University of New York Press.

Beneria, L., & Roldan, M. (1986). *The crossroads of class and gender: Industrial homework, subcontracting, and household dynamics in Mexico City*. Chicago: University of Chicago Press.

Blackford, M. G. (1991). *A history of small business in America*. New York: Twayne.

Boris, E. (1994). *Home to work: Motherhood and the politics of industrial homework in the United States*. Cambridge, UK: Cambridge University Press.

Boris, E., & Prugl, E. (Eds.). (1996). *Homeworkers in global perspective: Invisible no more*. New York: Routledge.

Bromley, R., & Gerry, G. (1979). Who are the casual poor? In R. Bromley & C. Gerry (Eds.), *Casual work and poverty in Third World cities* (pp. 3-32). New York: John Wiley.

Brush, C. (1990). Women and enterprise creation: Barriers and opportunities. In S. Gould & J. Parzen (Eds.), *Enterprising women: Local initiatives for job creation* (pp. 37-58). Paris: Organization for Economic Cooperation and Development.

Brush, C. (1992, Summer). Research on women business owners: Past trends, a new perspective, and future directions. *Entrepreneurship Theory and Practice*, pp. 5-30.

Carr, D. (1996). Two paths to self-employment. *Work and Occupations, 23*, 26-53.

Carter, S., & Cannon, T. (1992). *Women as entrepreneurs: A study of female business owners, their motivations, experiences, and strategies for success*. New York: Academic Press.

Castells, M., & Portes, A. (1989). World underneath: The origins, dynamics, and effects of the informal economy. In A. Portes, M. Castells, & L. Benton (Eds.), *The informal economy: Studies in advanced and less developed countries* (pp. 11-40). Baltimore, MD: Johns Hopkins University Press.

Christensen, K. (1988). *Women and home-based work: The unspoken contract*. New York: Henry Holt.

Christensen, K. (1989). Home-based clerical work: No simple truth, no single reality. In E. Boris & C. Daniels

(Eds.), *Homework: Historical and contemporary perspectives* (pp. 183-197). Urbana: University of Illinois Press.

Collins, P. H. (1990). *Black feminist thought: Knowledge, consciousness, and the politics of empowerment.* Boston: Unwin Hyman.

Connell, R. W. (1987). *Gender and power: Society, the person, and sexual politics.* Cambridge, MA: Polity.

Cowgill, J. (1996). *Empowerment in a microenterprise loan program.* Unpublished master's thesis, Arizona State University.

Dale, A. (1986). Social class and the self-employed. *Sociology, 20,* 430-434.

Dangler, J. F. (1994). *Hidden in the home: The role of waged homework in the modern world economy.* Albany: State University of New York Press.

Dantico, M., & Jurik, N. (1986). Where have all the good jobs gone? The effect of government service privatization on women workers. *Contemporary Crises, 10,* 421-439.

Deming, W. (1994, February). Work at home: Data from the CPS. *Monthly Labor Review,* pp. 14-19.

Edwards, P., & Edwards, S. (1995). Foreword. In R. Heck, A. Owen, & B. Rowe (Eds.), *Home-based employment and family life* (pp. xiii-xv). Westport, CT: Auburn House.

Ellisburg, D. (1985). Legalities. In National Academy (Ed.), *Office workstations in the home* (pp. 59-65). Washington, DC: National Academy Press.

Else, J., & Raheim, S. (1992). AFDC clients as entrepreneurs. *Public Welfare, 50,* 36-41.

Fernandez-Kelly, M. P., & Garcia, A. M. (1985). The making of an underground economy: Hispanic women, homework, and the advanced capitalist state. *Urban Anthropology, 14,* 59-90.

Gerson, K. (1993). Reevaluating union policy toward white-collar home-based work. In D. Cobble (Ed.), *Women and unions: Forging a partnership* (pp. 246-259). Ithaca, NY: ILR Press.

Gilligan, C. (1982). *In a different voice: Psychological theory and women's development.* Cambridge, MA: Harvard University Press.

Glaser, D., & Strauss, A. (1967). *The discovery of grounded theory.* Chicago: Aldine.

Goffee, R., & Scase, R. (1985). *Women in charge: The experiences of female entrepreneurs.* London: Allen and Unwin.

Goss, D. (1991). *Small business and society.* London: Routledge.

Harvey, D. (1989). *The condition of postmodernity.* Oxford, UK: Basil Blackwell.

Heck, R. (1991). A profile of home-based workers. *Human Ecology Forum, 12,* 15-18.

Heck, R., Owen, A., & Rowe, B. (Eds.). (1995). *Home-based employment and family life.* Westport, CT: Auburn House.

Henry, S. (1978). *The hidden economy: The context and control of borderline criminology.* Oxford, UK: Martin Robertson.

Hisrich, R., & Brush, C. (1986). *The woman entrepreneur.* Lexington, MA: Lexington Books.

Lamphere, L., Zavella, P., Gonzales, F., & Evans, P. (1993). *Sun Belt working mothers: Reconciling family and factory.* Ithaca, NY: Cornell University Press.

Light, I., & Bonacich, E. (1988). *Immigrant entrepreneurs: Koreans in Los Angeles, 1965-1982.* Berkeley: University of California Press.

Lozano, B. (1989). *The invisible work force.* New York: Free Press.

Moallem, M. (1991). Ethnic enterprise and gender relations among Iranians in Montreal, Quebec, Canada. In D. Asgharfathi (Ed.), *Iranian refugees and exiles since Khomeini* (pp. 180-199). Quebec: Mazda Publishers.

Nagel, J. (1994). Constructing ethnicity: Creating and recreating ethnic identity and culture. *Social Problems, 41,* 152-176.

Nelson, M. K. (1990). *Negotiated care: The experience of family day care providers.* Philadelphia: Temple University Press.

Owen, A., Heck, R., & Rowe, B. (1995). Harmonizing family and work. In R. Heck, A. Owen, & B. Rowe (Eds.), *Home-based employment and family life* (pp. 1-14). Westport, CT: Auburn House.

Phizacklea, A., & Wolkowitz, C. (1995). *Homeworking women: Gender, racism, and class at work.* Thousand Oaks, CA: Sage.

Portes, A., & Sassen-Koob, S. (1987). Making it underground: Comparative material on the informal sector in western market economies. *American Journal of Sociology, 102,* 30-61.

Pratt, J. (1987). Methodological problems in surveying the home-based workforce. *Technological Forecasting & Social Change, 31,* 49-60.

Pratt, J. (1993). *Myths and realities of working at home: Characteristics of home-based business owners and telecommuters* (NTIS No. PB93-192862). Springfield, VA: U.S. Department of Commerce.

Prugl, E., & Boris, E. (1996). Introduction. In E. Boris & E. Prugl (Eds.), *Homeworkers in global perspective: Invisible no more.* New York: Routledge.

Reskin, B., & Padavic, I. (1994). *Women and men at work.* Thousand Oaks, CA: Pine Forge Press.

Scase, R., & Goffee, R. (1982). *The entrepreneurial middle class.* London: Croom Helm.

Schumpeter, J. (1934). *The theory of economic development: An inquiry into profits, capital, and credit.* Cambridge, MA: Harvard University Press.

Silver, H. (1989). The demand for homework: Evidence from the U.S. census. In E. Boris & C. Daniels (Eds.), *Homework: Historical and contemporary perspectives on paid labor at home* (pp. 103-129). Urbana: University of Illinois Press.

Simon, R. (1995). Gender, multiple roles, role meaning, and mental health. *Journal of Health and Social Behavior, 36,* 182-194.

Smith, N., McCain, J., & Warren, A. (1982). Women entrepreneurs really are different: A comparison of constructed ideal types of man and woman entrepreneurs. *Proceedings of the 1983 Conference on Entrepreneurship: Frontiers of Entrepreneurship Research.* Unpublished manuscript, Babson College.

Spalter-Roth, R., Soto, E., & Zandniapour, L. (1994). *Microenterprise and women: The viability of self-employment as a strategy for alleviating poverty.* Washington, DC: Institute for Women's Policy Research.

Toffler, A. (1980). *The third wave.* New York: William Morrow.

U.S. Department of Labor, Women's Bureau. (1992). *Facts on working women: Women business owners.* Washington, DC: Government Printing Office.

U.S. Small Business Administration. (1989). *The state of small business: A report to the president.* Washington, DC: Government Printing Office.

Walker, R., & Heck, R. (with Furry, M., Stafford, K., & Haynes, G.). (1995). The hidden hum of home-based businesses. In R. Heck, A. Owen, & B. Rowe (Eds.), *Home-based employment and family life* (pp. 75-106). Westport, CT: Auburn House.

West, C., & Zimmerman, D. H. (1987). Doing gender. *Gender & Society, 1,* 125-151.

How Permanent Was Permanent Employment?

Patterns of Organizational Mobility in Japan, 1916-1975

MARIAH MANTSUN CHENG
ARNE L. KALLEBERG

Job mobility has long been important to social scientists. Most research has focused on occupational mobility as an indicator of a society's openness. Less studied is organizational mobility, which is also an important dimension that shapes an individual's work career. From a macro level perspective, organizational mobility reflects the institutional context of work in a society; differences in rates and patterns of organizational mobility reveal the degree of salience organizations have for structuring labor markets in a particular society.

Organizational mobility studies often look to Japan as an ideal case where few people move from an organization to another. In Japan, reciprocal responsibilities and commitments between employer and employee are felt to lead to stable employment, a perception that dominates many discussions of Japanese employment and managerial systems. The permanent employment system—a guarantee of continuous employment until mandatory retirement, regardless of the company's economic performance—is frequently portrayed as one of the three industrial relations pillars (along with the seniority reward system and enterprise unionism) that enabled Japan's dramatic economic growth, surpassing its Western competitors.

Recent data suggest that Japan's employment system is in transition, perhaps moving away from the permanent employment model. In the 1990s, facing slower growth and keener global competition, Japanese firms had to diversify, internationalize, and rationalize production costs. Midcareer recruitment in large enterprises, even for top executives, grew (Beck & Beck, 1994). With an aging workforce, less-committed young workers, and pressing needs for skilled specialists, employers have had to adjust their permanent employment and seniority reward systems. Workers, especially younger ones, seek greater job mobility (Japan Statistics Bureau, 1990).

To evaluate claims about the nature and development of Japan's permanent employment, we need first to examine its extent over the years. Unfortunately, there is little solid evidence on the extent of permanent employment over time. In this chapter, we try to overcome these limitations of past research by estimating the extent of permanent employment among Japanese men during a large part of the 20th

From *Work and Occupations*, Vol. 24, No. 1, February 1997, pp. 12-32. Reprinted by permission.

century. Our analyses show the magnitude of age, period, and cohort for mobility among Japanese workers; such macrohistorical events as wars and postwar economic developments have clear impacts on the permanent employment system.

RESEARCH ON THE PRACTICE OF PERMANENT EMPLOYMENT IN JAPAN

Although descriptive accounts of the Japanese employment system abound, the origins and development of permanent employment have sparked much debate (Abegglen, 1958; Cole, 1971, 1972, 1973, 1979; Dore, 1973; Levine, 1965; Taira, 1962, 1970). The gist of the debate has been whether the system originates from the feudal past: Is it a continuation of the old, paternalistic, master-apprentice relationship in a familylike setting that became the employer-employee relationship in a modern industrial organization? Although Abegglen (1958) contends that it was an irrational carryover of traditional customs and values, others suggest that it was a rational strategy large companies used to retain skilled workers in the 1920s (Levine, 1965), a postwar managerial innovation for profit maximization (Dore, 1962, 1973), a tactic used to pacify union demands (Cole, 1979), and a way to beat labor shortages during economic expansions in the 1950s (Hashimoto, 1990) and 1960s (Mincer & Higuchi, 1988).

Abegglen's (1958) claim that "labor mobility is virtually nonexistent" (p. 68) in Japan because of the practice of permanent employment has prompted much research. Many of the issues studied center on the historicity and validity of the employment system he describes. We now generally believe that the Japanese permanent employment system was gradually institutionalized before World War I through the post-World War II era. Therefore the system is apparently not a direct legacy from the feudal past but the result of a blend of factors in stages of Japan's industrialization. For Japanese employers, the notion of permanent employment is a practical way to solve labor shortage problems during economic expansions; it represents a managerial ideology, garnished with traditional values and symbols, to counter the pervasion of radical ideas of class struggles and conflicts. For Japanese employees, it provides the job security they had long demanded through their enterprise unionization. The state's historical intervention into economic spheres—notably labor mobilization programs and legal restrictions during World War II and postwar support of permanent employment and seniority wage notions—set the framework for the practices to take root.

ESTIMATING THE EXTENT OF PERMANENT EMPLOYMENT

Studies on the extent of permanent employment occupy three main groups: (a) speculations based on assumptions about divergent employment policies practiced in different types of firms, (b) findings based on cross-sectional surveys showing the proportion of workers who have never changed employers or estimates—calculated from individual- or firm-level labor statistics—of the amount of mobility an average worker would have had in his worklife, and (c) historical analyses. We consider examples of each of these types of studies.

Speculations Based on Employment Policies of Different Firms

Studies of Japanese mobility suggest that implementing the permanent employment system differs by organizational type and size (Cole 1979; Dore, 1973). The odds of a Japanese worker's staying with his first company grow with firm size (Cheng, 1991; Cole, 1979). Some maintain that lifelong employment only applies to regular male employees in large companies or government agencies (Rohlen, 1979). Taira (1962) assumes that lifelong employment is limited to large firms (at least 500 employees), suggesting that under 20% of industrial workers in 1960 took part in the system. Marsh and

Mannari (1971) suggest that only huge firms (more than 1,000 workers) apply the practice extensively, so that only about 16% of manufacturing workers were ensured lifelong employment between 1960 and 1966. Levine (1965) assumes that permanent employment applied only to firms of more than 300 workers, suggesting that a third of workers were covered by the system in the 1960s.

However, whether permanent employment is an exclusive practice of large firms but not small firms is still debatable. Some suggest that permanent employment is not just concentrated in large or government firms (Cole, 1979; Dore, 1973; Hashimoto, 1990; Hashimoto & Raisian, 1985). When economic circumstances allow, small firms might try to guarantee lifelong employment to compete for better workers. Hence estimates that depend on the researchers' judgment as to which firms apply that permanent employment policy are quite speculative. Direct measures of employment stability are needed to evaluate more systematically the extent of permanent employment in Japan.

Findings Based on Cross-Sectional Survey Data and Labor Statistics

Cole's research (1979; Cole & Siegel, 1980) on job-changing patterns in Yokohama and Detroit was the first substantial empirical study to compare job shift patterns between Japanese and American workers. If we interpret the notion of permanent employment as a system under which workers remain with their first employer, Cole's finding shows that about a third of his Yokohama sample had never left their first employer (vs. a seventh in Detroit). Cheng (1991) found similar results among male workers in the 1975 Japanese national Social Stratification and Mobility Survey.

Others find clues in labor statistics. Hashimoto and Raisian's (1985) analysis, based on demographic and labor turnover statistics, suggests that a Japanese man would have had about five jobs by age 65, but the average American worker would have had 11 jobs. Levine (1983) argues that only a small group of workers is likely to stay with one employer throughout their lives. He estimates that a Japanese worker would change employers once every 8 years and make at least three changes in a 30- to 40-year career.

Historical Analyses of Permanent Employment and Job Mobility

Most of the estimates above refer to short periods of time. By contrast, studies by Fruin (1978), Taira (1970), Gordon (1985), and Cole (1979) examine Japanese permanent employment in historical perspective. Fruin (1978) focused on personnel records of managerial employees in a large food industry firm from 1918 to 1976 and found that the extent of permanent employment practice was affected by wars, industrial mergers, economic fluctuations, and wage differentials between firm sectors. Taira (1962, 1970) used labor turnover statistics to challenge Abegglen's (1958) view that permanent employment is a legacy carried over from preindustrial days. He argues that in 1900, probably only 1 in 10 textile and manufacturing workers had been with his current employer more than 4 years, and every industrial worker would have changed employment in that year. He found that two thirds of workers were likely to have shifted companies in each year from 1916 to 1925. Other studies also suggest the nonexistence of lifetime employment among industrial workers at the turn of the 20th century. During the first phase of Japan's industrialization (the Meiji era, 1867-1912), job changing was a typical way for heavy industry workers to acquire skills (Gordon, 1985), and skilled labor was highly mobile (Helvoort, 1979). During World War I (1914-1918), with the upsurge of labor demands in a war-heated economy, Japan's labor market was very fluid. Workers reportedly changed employers on short notice, employers snatched workers from one another (Taira, 1970), job change rates for textile workers (half the industrial workforce) reached 67% annually (Levine & Kawada, 1980), and yearly turnover rates in some industries were as high as 75% (Gordon, 1985). Even large-scale, capital-intensive industries suffered from high turnovers of skilled workers. Only between 1920 and 1935 did job tenures lengthen, but commitment to initial employers (an indication of permanent employment) was still rare. Fewer than a fifth of the new hires in 1924 remained with the same firm until 1933 (Taira, 1970).

The reported lower mobility in the 1920s prompted some to conclude that this was when permanent employment practices were adopted (Levine, 1965). High labor turnover in World War I and increased strike and union activities motivated management to institute a new model of administration. Both the government and employers sought to promote a paternalistic, familial managerial ideology, with benevolence—loyalty, obligation, commitment—defining a harmonious employer-employee relationship (Cole, 1979). Scholars, especially labor economists, see this as evidence of permanent employment being a rational, calculated device for solving practical labor problems during rapid industrialization. Levine (1965) argues that managers of large firms adopted the system in the mid-1920s to lure master craftsmen (*oyakata*) into their administrative control. It functioned to stabilize the workforce, exerting control over the skilled, "footloose" craftsmen (Cole, 1979; Jacoby, 1979; Levine, 1965) and enabling on-the-job training of firm-specific skills needed for the foreign technology introduced (Helvoort, 1979; Levine & Kawada, 1980).

Japan's economy suffered from the worldwide Great Depression from 1929 to 1933. To revitalize the economy and maintain social order, the state resorted to military ultranationalism and imperialism.[1] In the mid-1930s, permanent occupation was widely recognized as an ideal personnel policy. However, in practice, mid-career hiring was said to be common, even among managerial executives (Hirschmeier & Yui, 1981). Although military spending revived the economy, industries suffered from labor shortages because of military drafting. The lack of workers, particularly skilled ones, again increased labor mobility between 1937 and 1939 (Taira, 1970). As the war intensified, the state controlled all economic resources—labor, capital, and material. Laws and ordinances demanding national registration and job mobility restriction were passed.[2] However, Gordon (1985), based on his Nippon Kokan iron and steel company findings, suggests that throughout the war, skilled workers changed employment against legal sanction. Yet others also argue that, at least among managerial executives, mobility was low during the war (Beck & Beck, 1994). That permanent employment was state endorsed and enforced has led some to think that it was actually a wartime product.

Although permanent employment might have existed in some form before or during the war, its profusion might have come only after 1955, concurrent with government-supported productivity enhancement campaigns (Hashimoto, 1990) or, maybe later, in the 1960s, when economic growth was well underway (Mincer & Higuchi, 1988). Labor economists attribute Japan's lower labor turnover (as compared to Western industrial nations) to its more intensive on-the-job human capital formation (Mincer & Higuchi, 1988) and steeper wage-age profile (Hashimoto & Raisian, 1985; Tachibanaki, 1984). The fast-growing postwar Japanese economy conditioned these causal factors.

The prevalence of permanent employment after the mid-1950s seems to be substantiated by empirical evidence. For example, Taira's data (1970) indicate that the percentage of workers having 5 or more years of job tenure nearly doubled between 1939 and 1957 (from 19% to 37%). On average, the portion of manufacturing workers expected to change employers in a certain year also fell from 50% from 1934 to 1936 to about 25% in the 1950s and early 1960s. Such decreases in mobility among production workers coincided with the assertion that, after World War II, the permanent employment privilege was extended from white- to blue-collar regular employees because of union pressures and labor scarcity (Cole, 1979; Gordon, 1985; Jacoby, 1979). However, it is unclear whether white- or blue-collar small-firm employees enjoyed the same privilege because postwar enterprise unionization was highly (positively) correlated with firm size.[3]

Historical studies of permanent employment provide qualitative information and important insights on how it actually might have been practiced and how it interacted with the economy, government, and unions. But these historical analyses are limited by the scatteredness, and often nonrepresentativeness, of the data; they need to be supplemented by empirical evidence based on representative job mobility data.

DATA AND VARIABLES

We used three Japanese national surveys—the 1955, 1965, and 1975 social stratification and mobility (SSM) surveys[4]—to analyze permanent employment practice in recent Japanese history. These representative studies targeted men aged 20 to 69 and consist of 2,014, 2,077, and 2,724 cases, respectively. They are trend mobility surveys with similar research designs—basically representative samples stratified on levels of urbanization (major cities, smaller cities, towns, and villages), with further selection based on electoral blocks and resident registers (Ishida, 1993; Kosaka, 1994). They provide comparable information on respondents' employment histories, including duration, type of job transitions, age and year of each change, and all their unemployment, military service, or reentry to school experiences. Cross-sectionally, when compared to census data, these samples consistently underestimate the proportions of production workers (by about 9%) but overrepresent by 1% to 3% various categories of white-collar workers, and for the 1955 and 1975 SSM surveys, also the farmer category.[5] Cases from these surveys yield personal retrospective work histories covering about six decades. Although the work histories reported in the 1955 survey actually extend to some labor force experiences that occurred as early as 1901, we limit our analyses between 1916 and 1975 to avoid selection bias because of age and the small number of cases reported for these early years.

Although we would have preferred to examine mobility among women as well as men, we do not think that the restriction of our analyses to men is a major limitation. Women employees in Japan are expected to leave their jobs after marriage or the birth of their first child, so they are practically excluded from the system[6] (Brinton, 1993). If mobility data for women were available and included here, we would expect much less permanency in employment overall than the current results show.

Firm size information[7] regarding employment over the worklife is available in the 1965 and 1975 surveys (but not in the 1955 survey). Firm size, cross-classified with occupational type information, serves as the basis for our analyses of employment permanency in different labor market sectors. To identify employment in the large-firm versus small-firm sector, we distinguish private employers with more than 1,000 employees and government agencies from all other smaller firms. We create a white-collar versus blue-collar distinction by separating men in professional, managerial, clerical, and sales occupations from others in service and production work of various skill levels. Leaving one's employer constitutes a change in employment, regardless of the destination status (to another employer, self-employment, unemployment, etc.). We consider employer changes to include across-firm transitions, as well as shifts into other employment or nonemployment statuses. Age and year variables were originally measured in 1-year units but grouped into intervals (5-year interval for rate calculations; 10-year interval for graphic presentations) for current analyses.

RESULTS

We examine the permanency of employment in Japan in three ways. First, using cross-sectional data, we look at employment permanency in 1955, 1965, and 1975. Second, using retrospective data, we compute retention rates of first nonfarm employment as evidence of changes in the practice of permanent employment over time. Third, also based on individual work histories, we calculate employment change rates for different age groups and estimate the total number of employer changes for different cohorts as their careers unfolded throughout time.

Overall Estimate of Permanent Employment

Strictly speaking, the notion of permanent employment implies that companies recruit graduates directly from school, train them, and guarantee their employment until mandatory retirement at around age 55. In a limited sense, the concept pertains only to workers who started nonfarm careers. However, data in the surveys indicate that as late as 1946 to 1950, less than two thirds of Japanese men entered the labor force as nonfarm employees; rather, they entered as self-employed or family employed in the farm or nonfarm sector. The percentage entering the labor force as nonfarm employees increased to 75% by the end of the 1950s, 80% in the 1960s, and 90% between 1971 and 1975. This suggests that permanent employment, defined rigidly, does not even apply to most older workers who began their careers before or immediately after the war.

Given this, we relax this form of the definition of permanent employment and consider the first nonfarm employee episode to be a man's first employment, regardless of prior nonfarm or nonwork experiences. To address the basic permanency question, we examine the percentage of nonfarm employees who spent most of their worklives, say at least 30 years, with their very first employer in 1955, 1965, and 1975. To avoid quits because of mandatory retirement, we further restrict our attention to men younger than 56. If permanent employment was extensive and became prevalent after World War II, we would expect a relatively high percentage of men to still be working for their first employer and this percentage to increase after the war.

We found that among men with 30 to 35 years of experience in the three surveys, about a third (of 39 cases) were still with their first employer in 1955, as were a quarter or so in 1965 (of 57) and in 1975 (of 105). Roughly a quarter of men with 36 to 40 years of experience remained with their first employer in each survey (of 13, 23, and 19 cases). Overall, the proportion of men with 30 or more years of experience who were still with their first employer decreased from 1955 (33% of 52 cases) to 1965 (24% of 80 cases) but was similar between 1965 and 1975 (23% of 124 cases). We also found that among these employees, about two thirds started careers in huge or government firms, yet for those with similar experiences but who no longer worked for their first employer, only a third (in 1965) to less than half (in 1975) began their careers in these large firms. This is consistent with the claim that the permanent employment system is practiced more often in government and large firms. Nonetheless, these results are seriously limited by the small number of cases that fall into our selection criteria (in terms of specific labor force experience and age limit).

Retention Rates as Indicators of Permanence of Employment

We extend our examination of permanent employment to include employees who have not yet completed their worklives by looking at retention rates over the initial 10 years of every respondent's first nonfarm employment. From the retention rates recorded in respondents' work histories, we can assess changes in the practice of permanent employment over time. A widespread practice of lifelong employment should be reflected by very high retention for all these years of initial employment. Fluctuations in implementing the permanent employment practice should be indicated by variations of retention rates at different times. Hence, if permanent employment began around the 1920s and became prevalent around 1955 or 1960, we should see a corresponding increase in retention rates, particularly in Years 5 and 10.

Figure 9.1 indicates that retention rates were generally very high for the first few years of em-

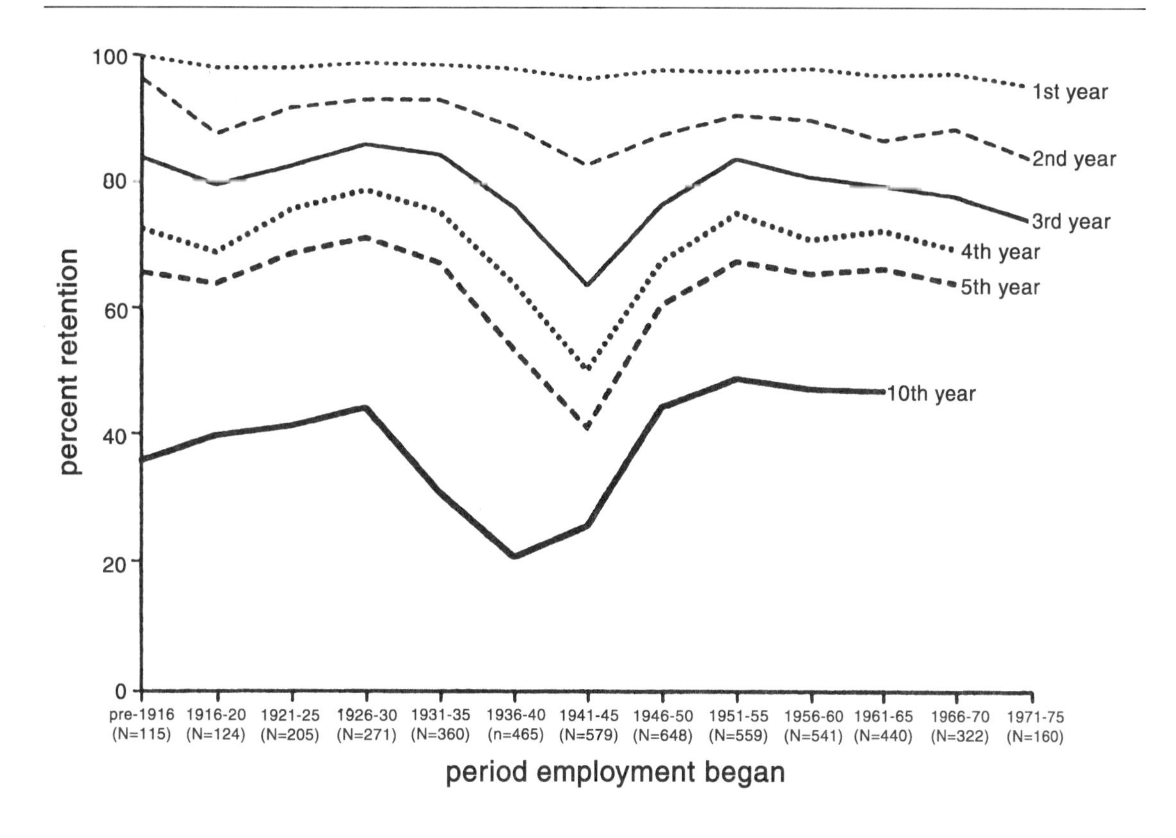

Figure 9.1. Retention Rates for First Nonfarm Employment, by Period
NOTE: *N* = number of cases.

ployment throughout the 20th century. Of workers who began careers between 1916 and 1920, almost all stayed with the same employer for the Year 1, 91% for the next, and down to 44% in Year 10. However, changes in the rates across periods result from macrosocial and economic changes. Percentages slightly increased from 1921 to 1930, giving some support for the idea of stable employment during the 1920s. The effects of World War II are reflected in the considerable drop in percentages for Years 5 and 10 for those who started their employment in the 1931 to 1935 and 1936 to 1940 periods. Among those who began their employment between 1936 and 1940, only 23% remained with their same employer for 10 years. The massive disruptions of careers because of wartime drafting and mobilization are reflected in the declines in retention for employment from 1941 to 1945, particularly for the first 5 years (dropping to 51% retention in Year 4 and to about 42% in Year 5). After 1945, retention rates rose again. For employment that started between 1951 and 1955, about 90% remained until Year 2, and three of four remained until Year 4. Nearly half survived through Year 10.

If permanent employment became extensive in large firms in the 1920s, spreading to small firms after 1955 or 1960, we should also see correspondingly high retention rates among workers (white and blue collar) in these firms during these periods. To examine this hypothesis, we first distinguish nonfarm employment originating in large firms from that beginning in

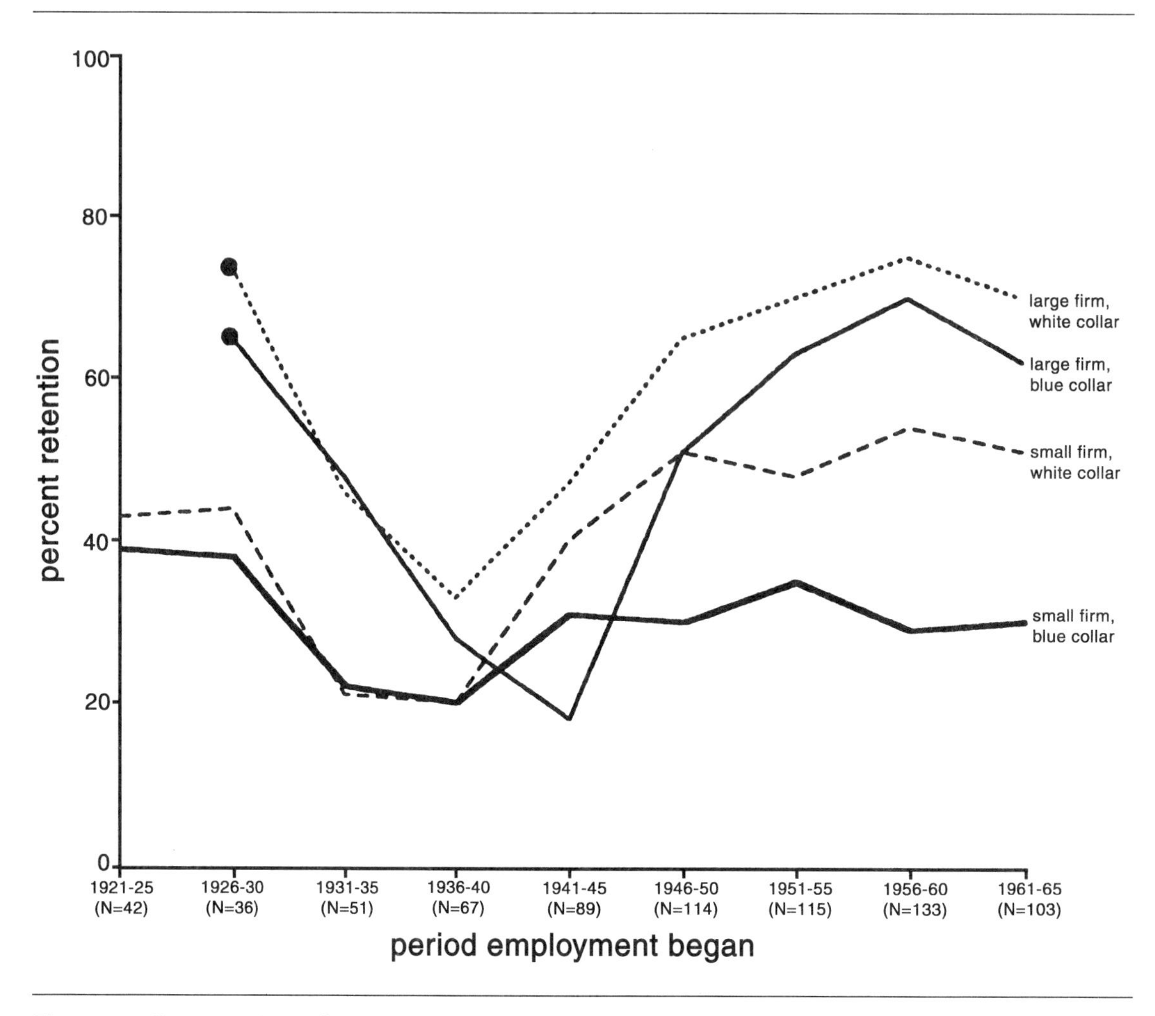

Figure 9.2. Retention Rates for the Initial 10 Years of First Nonfarm Employment, by Firm, Occupation, and Period
NOTE: *N* = average number of cases in each group.

smaller firms, as well as white-collar from blue-collar jobs.

Figure 9.2 shows retention rates of the first 10 years, beginning in different periods. The discrepancy in retention rates between large- and small-firm employees existed as early as 1926, which may be taken as an indication that permanent employment was in place in large firms in the 1920s.[8] Retention rates were about 65% to 75% in the first 10 years, in contrast to about 40% among small-firm employees.

Within each firm sector, white-collar workers consistently had a higher retention rate for first nonfarm employment that started between 1926 and 1930. The difference between white- and blue-collar occupations diminished in the 1930s, but the firm sector difference stayed. The sudden drops in retention between 1931 and 1935 for both large and small firms coincided partly with the Great Depression. The rates for white- and blue-collar employees in large firms continued to fall during the late 1930s. Career disruptions caused by wartime mobilization affected employees in both large- and small-firm sectors. Among employees who started working for large firms between 1936 and 1940, only 28% to 33% remained through Year 10. For small-firm workers, the figures were reduced to about a fifth.

As World War II intensified in the early 1940s and the firm size effect reached its minimum, the retention rates for white- and blue-collar occupations started to diverge. In fact, large-firm blue-collar workers became the least permanent among the groups. Their retention rate of employment from 1941 to 1945 for the next 10 years was the lowest (18%), even lower than small-firm blue-collar workers (31%). The reason is not obvious, though we know from Gordon (1985) that production workers in large heavy industrial enterprises were drafted massively, which consequently also led to high turnover (among others not in the military) despite legal mobility restrictions.

After the war, retention rates rose for employees in all labor market sectors, although the increases were greater for employees of large firms. The differences in employment permanency seemed quite consistent throughout the postwar years: a clear distinction between large and small firms and an evident gap between white- and blue-collar workers within each firm sector. If we take the large-firm white-collar workers as the exemplar of permanent employment in practice, we are looking at a 70% to 75% retention in a 10-year period. If the permanent employment system had extended to blue-collar employees, it was more likely to be the case for those in large firms, not small firms. If we are willing to argue that the system broadened during the time of postwar economic prosperity and extended to small firms, it probably covered only their white-collar employees, not the blue-collar employees. And, in reality, we are looking at retention rates of about 48% to 54% over 10 years. The one group that lagged much behind is small-firm blue-collar occupations, whose retention rates only rose by about 10% after the war, hovering around the 30% mark.

Rates of Employment Change

If permanent employment applies to every nonfarm employee, the employment change rate would be theoretically, on average, very close to 0, and the total number of employers close to 1. Degrees of departure from these figures thus indicate the extent of permanent employment in practice. Moreover, employment change rates computed at different ages indicate mobility tendencies over an entire career and let the analysis go beyond a worker's first nonfarm employment. Thus these rates are useful for assessing the extent of permanent employment practices and also indicate the employment permanency of workers as they progressed in their careers.

Based on work histories, we computed the average employment change per year of labor force exposure by respondents' age and the period to which the data pertained.[9] The high employer change rates during the war (Figure 9.3) echo the low retention rates in Figures 9.1 and 9.2. As we showed earlier, the war affected men's careers at all ages. For every age group, employment change rates began to increase drastically between 1936 and 1940, peaked between 1941 and 1945, and fell to the 1931 to 1935 level between 1951 and 1955. As for the ordering of mobility rates by age, we can see that from the 1920s to 1940s, those aged 16 to 20 had a lower change rate than those aged 21 to 25, and men aged 31 to 40 were less mobile than those aged 41 to 55. However, this order reversed after the war. Except for men aged 56 to 65, who were less mobile than men aged 16 to 25 but higher than the rest, mobility rates correspond neatly with age. Overall, men aged 41 to 55 had the lowest rate, and age 30 seemed to be a critical social age for settling down with a certain employer. Beginning in 1951, we also see an increasing trend of mobility for employees under 26. For men aged 16 to 20, the increase was remarkable, especially in the early 1970s. Simultaneously, we also see increased mobility in the oldest group.

Based on these employment change rates of age groups at a specific period, we can estimate

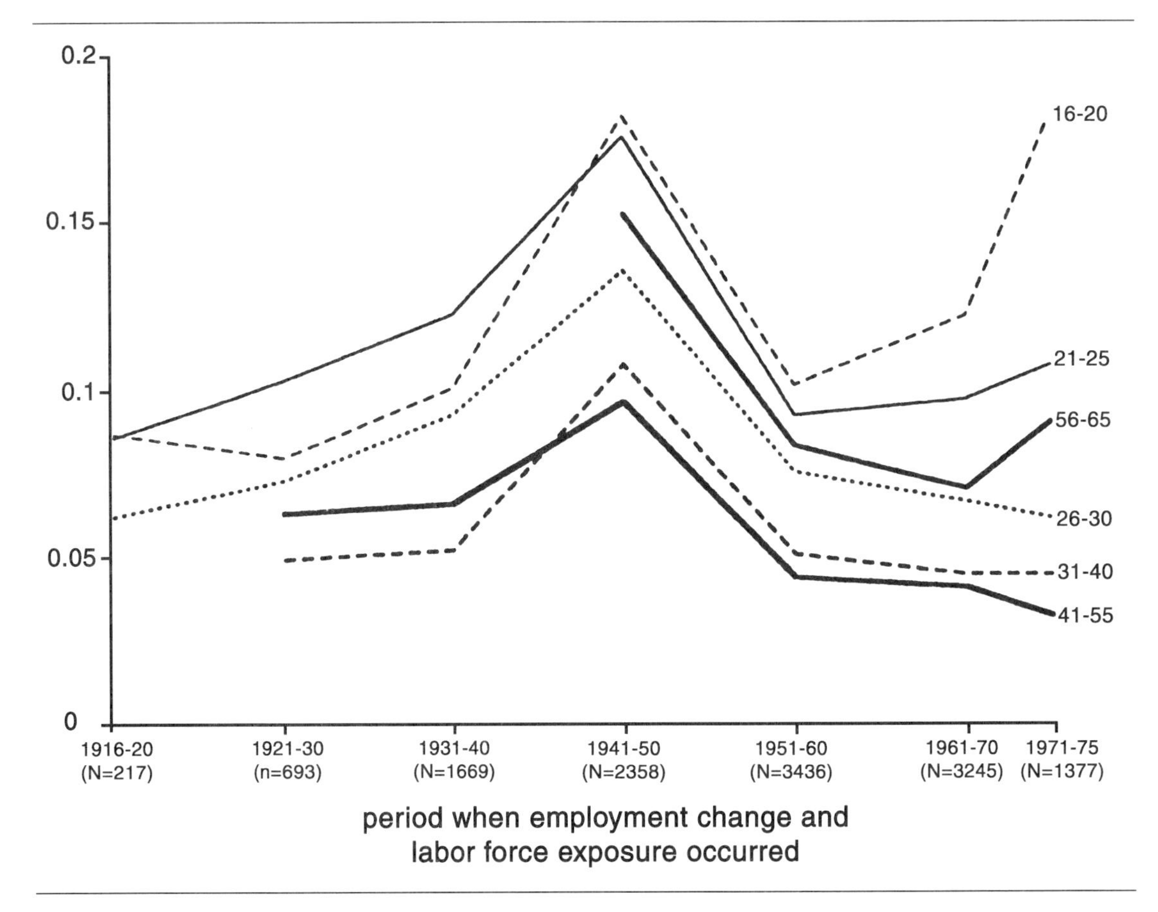

Figure 9.3. Employer Change Rates in Nonfarm Employee Sector, by Age
NOTE: *N* = average number of person-year records in each group.

the number of employers a typical nonfarm worker would have had at various ages and times (see Table 9.1). They are direct functions of the cumulative, estimated number of employer changes experienced over the years as a specific birth cohort age. Alternatively, we can calculate directly the total number of employers a particular age group has had until a certain time. We chose the first method because it is more reliable. Let us take as an example the estimated number of employers a nonfarm employee, who had reached age 65 between 1971 and 1975, would have had (4.93 in Table 9.1). The figure is computed based on the age-specific employer change rates in all corresponding time periods—cumulating rates for ages 16 to 20 between 1926 and 1930, 21 to 25 between 1931 and 1935, and so forth. Because we are looking at work histories of three trend studies, the resultant estimate actually would be based on the nonfarm employee experiences (at the specific age and time) of cases who were 41 to 45 years old in the 1955 SSM survey, 51 to 55 in the 1965 survey, and 61 to 65 in the 1975 survey. However, if we chose the second method, the estimate would have to be based on many fewer cases—only those who were aged 65 between 1971 and 1975 and who had been a nonfarm employee since age 16—and all respondents in the 1955 and 1965 SSM survey would not even be qualified in this particular case.

Data in Table 9.1 suggest that a man who entered the labor force at age 16 between 1926 and 1930 and continuously worked in the nonfarm

TABLE 9.1 Estimated Number of Employers a Nonfarm Employee Would Have at Different Ages and Periods

	Age							
Period	*30*	*35*	*40*	*45*	*50*	*55*	*60*	*65*
1926-1930	2.23	—	—	—	—	—	—	—
1931-1935	2.38	2.41	—	—	—	—	—	—
1936-1940	2.37	2.69	2.73	—	—	—	—	—
1941-1945	2.81	2.98	3.30	3.24	—	—	—	—
1946-1950	3.47	3.29	3.46	3.77	3.71	—	—	—
1951-1955	3.23	3.76	3.58	3.74	4.04	3.98	—	—
1956-1960	2.53	3.45	3.98	3.75	3.91	4.21	4.28	—
1961-1965	2.31	2.76	3.67	4.19	3.96	4.12	4.60	4.67
1966-1970	2.31	2.54	2.98	3.86	4.38	4.16	4.48	4.43
1971-1975	2.46	2.54	2.77	3.15	4.03	4.55	4.60	4.93
Average	2.38	2.94	3.31	3.67	4.05	4.20	4.49	4.68

sector until age 65 (between 1971-1975) would have worked for about five (4.93) employers in his career. Earlier cohorts seemed to have a slightly smaller average number of employers (4.43 and 4.67 for those reaching age 65 from 1966 to 1970 and 1961 to 1965). The cohorts seeming to experience more mobility reached age 21 to 25 in the intense phase of World War II (1941 to 1945) and were 26 to 30 years old when the economy was reconstructed during 1946 to 1950. Compared to the same age group across time, they tend to have experienced more employer changes over the years.

To examine firm sector and occupational differences, Figure 9.4 further breaks down mobility rates by firm and occupational types. The employment change rates pinpoint some interactions among age, firm, and period in the tendency to move. Results show that the often-cited vast mobility difference between large and small firms occurred mainly among employees younger than age 30 (see the top three panels). Young workers aged 16 to 20 in small firms had a much higher mobility rate than those in large firms, especially during the early 1970s. The former had a drastic rise in mobility, and the latter took a plunge. There were considerable differences across firm sectors throughout history in mobility rates among workers aged 21 to 25 and 26 to 30. However, although small-firm employees aged 31 to 40 still consistently had a higher rate, their difference from their large-firm counterparts was much smaller. Those 41 to 55 years old before the war seemed to have slightly lower mobility than large-firm employees. Only after the war was their mobility minimally higher. In the oldest group, large-firm workers had a much higher rate of leaving the employer, reflecting more widespread mandatory retirement implemented in those firms. The difference was dramatic during the 1960s and, to a lesser extent, in the early 1970s. World War II affected all age groups, especially those under 40. Except for large-firm blue-collar workers aged 16 to 20, who were as mobile as other young workers (under age 31) in small firms, large-firm employees still tended to have lower mobility rates throughout the war. In the postwar years, except for small-firm white-collar employees aged 16 to 20, who were more mobile than those in blue-collar occupations from 1971 to 1975, all other blue-collar workers had higher mobility rates than white-collar workers within their firm sector and age group. The only group

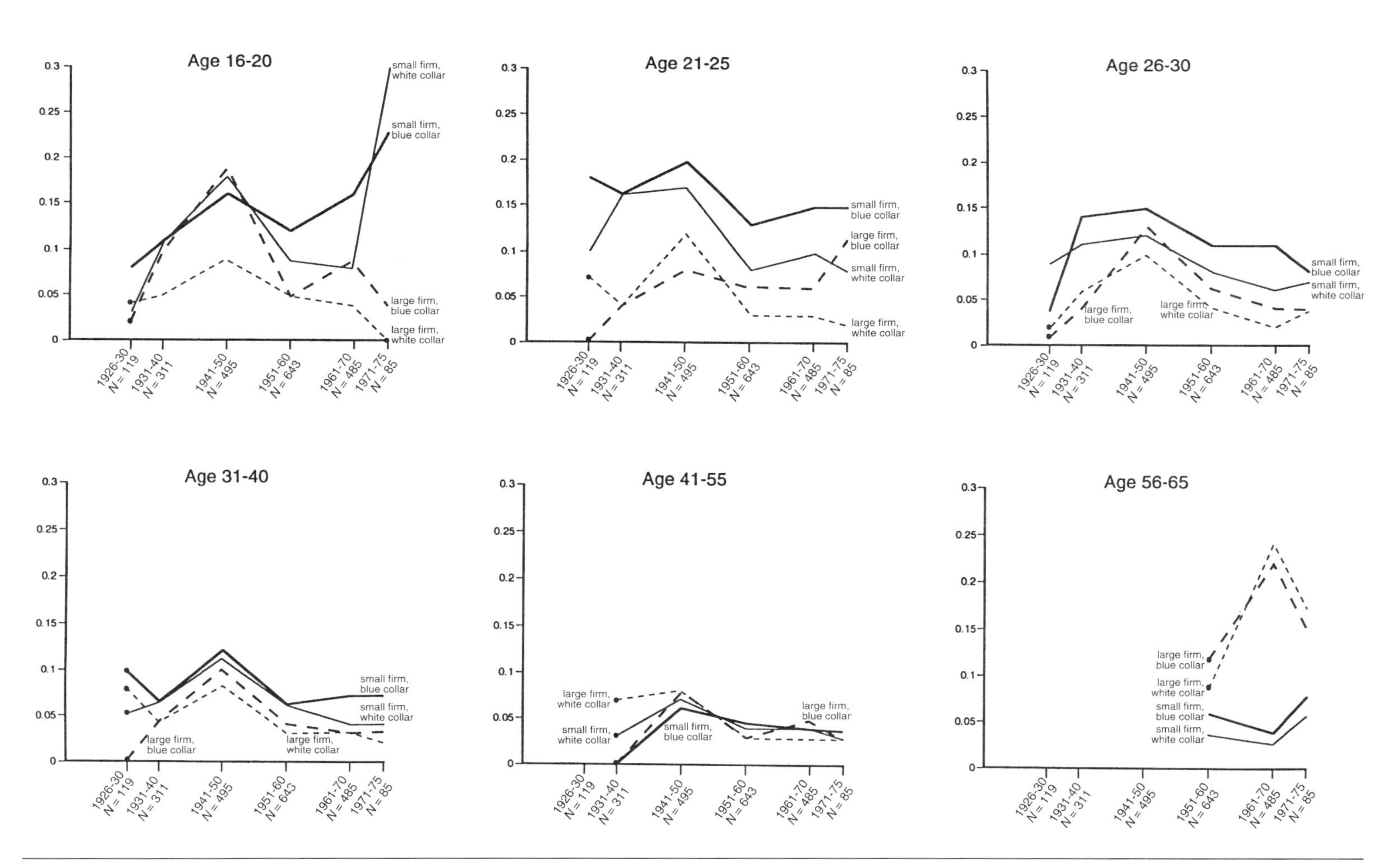

Figure 9.4. Employment Change Rates in Nonfarm Employee Sector, by Age, Firm Size, Occupation, and Period
NOTE: N = average number of person-year records; • = estimate based on less than 30 cases.

of large-firm blue-collar employees that had a slightly higher mobility rate than small-firm white-collars was that aged 21 to 25 between 1971 and 1975.

Applying these mobility rates to worker cohorts, we can estimate the average number of employers a typical white- or blue-collar employee in the large- or small-firm sector would have had at various ages and times. In results not shown here, we estimated that, on average, if a white-collar employee starts his career in a large firm, he would have had about two employers by age 35 and about three employers by age 55. However, a blue-collar worker who started his career in a small firm would have had more than three employers by age 35 and almost five employers by age 55. The difference in the mobility tendency between the two persists until the age of 55, the traditional mandatory retirement age for large-firm employees. As the white-collar, large-firm employee began to experience a much higher propensity of leaving the current employer, the number of employers he and his small-firm counterpart would have had when reaching age 65 is more or less the same—a total of about five.

CONCLUSIONS

In this chapter, we have used work histories derived from three national studies to examine empirically the permanency of employment for Japanese men from 1916 to 1975. In various ways, we have estimated the extent of permanent employment over time and across labor market sectors. At the macro level, this research shows that the implementation of permanent employment varied with societal and economic changes, as well as the importance of structural factors such as firm size and occupational type. Results suggest higher employment retention in large firms (vs. small firms) existed in the 1920s. Largely because wartime mobilization and extensive military drafting struck both sectors similarly, the differences in retention decreased during the late 1930s and early 1940s. However, when retention rates bounced back after the war, the increases in employment permanency were much greater among white- and blue-collar workers in large firms and those in small firms. The gap between large- versus small-firm sectors and between white- and blue-collar occupations within sectors is consistent and obvious. If permanent employment became prevalent during the prosperous years of the 1950s and 1960s, it was probably among employees in big companies and perhaps the white-collar occupations in small firms, but it was very unlikely among blue-collar occupations in small firms.

At the micro level, this research shows how the macro structural factors—the variations of permanent employment practice across labor market sectors over time—intersect with a worker's life at a certain age and, consequently, affect the worker's organizational mobility tendency. Our results suggest that the vast mobility differences among employees in different labor market sectors happen mainly when they are younger than 30. Middle-aged groups had a similar and rather low-mobility tendency. However, when large-firm employees in white- and blue-collar occupations reach mandatory retirement age (around 55), their rates of leaving the current employer are much higher than those of their counterparts in small firms. Therefore, the total number of employers a typical large-firm white-collar worker would have had at the end of his worklife (age 65) would not be too different from the total number a small-firm blue-collar employee would have had—about five employers.

In light of this empirical evidence, we see that permanent employment was influenced by macro societal factors—job mobility patterns changed that were responsive to changing economic and social circumstances. Although we see an overall higher employment retention rate accompanying the rapid postwar economic growth, we also see an increase in mobility among young small-firm workers in white- and blue-collar jobs, suggesting they were responsive to external opportunities as they came along.

By empirically examining the extent of permanent employment in different labor sectors over a fairly long period, we tried to escape from the tradition that focuses mainly on postwar large-firm phenomena, debunking the stereotype of permanent employment as being for all workers at all times. Our analysis is limited to men because we lack comparable data on women. We need studies of women's mobility patterns to expand our understanding of the permanent employment system and examine the extent to which women employees provide a buffer zone for the implementation of permanent employment among men. We hope the 1985 SSM survey will soon be released to non-Japanese scholars because it provides mobility data that would shed light on how the permanent employment system responded to the slower economic growth years in the late 1970s and early 1980s, and its employment data on women can be used to examine female work mobility.

NOTES

1. Japan formally entered World War II in 1941, signing the Axis Pact with Germany and Italy. The Asian phase of the war—the Sino-Japanese War—actually began in 1937.

2. Following the passing of the National General Mobilization Law in 1938, a series of ordinances was issued between 1939 and 1941 (Gordon, 1985). A National Registration System was set up, requiring technical workers in strategic industries to register. Registration was then extended to other sectors and, in 1944, covered all males aged 12 to 59 and single females aged 12 to 39. The revision of the Employment Agency Law in 1938 allowed the state's welfare ministry to control all employment agencies. Heavy and chemical industrial workers could not change employers without the agency's authorization. In 1940, the rule applied to all men aged 14 to 60 in all military-related industries. When the 1941 Labor Turnover Control Ordinance was issued, any employment transition had to be approved by the National Employment Agency.

3. For example, in the 1950s and 1960s, only 2% to 3% of small firms with less than 30 workers were unionized, and about 40% of firms with 100 to 499 workers and 75% of larger firms had enterprise unions (Taira, 1970).

4. The SSM surveys can be seen as responses of the Japanese Sociological Society to the International Sociological Association's 1951 call for cross-national research in social stratification and mobility. The 1955 survey was directed by Kunio Odaka and Shigeki Nishihira, modeled after David Glass's 1949 British mobility survey and funded by the Rockefeller Foundation. It was a representative random survey, stratified on geographical urbanization levels: ku-districts (the six largest cities of Japan—Tokyo, Yokohama, Nagoya, Kyoto, Osaka, Kobe), shi-districts (other smaller cities), and the gun-districts (towns and villages). With the basic research framework and core questions retained, the survey has been replicated every 10 years to gauge the trend of inter- and intragenerational social mobility over the years. The 1965 SSM was led by Saburo Yasuda and Shigeki Nishihira, and the 1975 SSM was led by Ken'ichi Tominaga.

5. Specifically, the 1955 SSM survey overrepresented the professional and sales category by 1% each, and the 1965 SSM survey also overrepresented these categories by 1% and 2%, respectively, plus another 3% for clerks and 1% for managers. In the 1975 SSM survey, representations in professional and sales were exact, but overrepresentation occurred in managerial (by 3%), clerical (2%), and farm (4%) categories. The 1955 SSM also overrepresented farmers by about 7% (see Kosaka, 1994).

6. In response to the 1985 Equal Employment Opportunity Law (EEOL), some large firms created multiple career tracks (instead of the previous single noncareer track) for their young female employees (Brinton, 1992). Yet career prospects for many Japanese women are still grim. First, the EEOL does not evoke penal sanctions for its violation (Bergeson & Oba, 1994). Second, as Brinton (1992) pointed out, "without concomitant changes in the nature of the family and in husbands' expectations that wives bear almost full responsibility for housework and childcare" (p. 102), the barriers Japanese women face in their careers are still substantial.

7. The firm size information pertains to the firm (not plant) in which the employee worked. Names of companies also were asked but were not available for secondary analysis. Different employers' respondents were identified by numbers only. In the surveys, the government firm is one of the response categories in the firm size questions, and no further questions were asked about the size of the particular government agency. For our analysis, government employment was identified by using the firm size variable and information from the industry variable. "Government employment" pertains both to national and local government employment.

8. Distinguishing white-collar from blue-collar workers in each firm sector results in too few cases for reliable estimates before 1921 to 1925. In results not shown here that retain only the firm sector distinction (and thus reliable data extend to earlier periods), we find that from 1916 to 1920, retention rates for the first 5 years were equal for employees in large or small firms. Even for 10-year retention rates, the discrepancy was only 12%. The rates began to diverge between 1921 and 1925. For new workers who entered large firms, then, nearly 90% remained for at least 5 years, and 80% for 10 years. For men in small firms, 80% survived the first 5 years, but only 40% made it to Year 10.

9. Technically, we examine all nonfarm employee experiences reported in the survey work histories. They are counted as "person-year" records, which are the bases for our computation of labor force exposure by period, age, or

labor market sectors. Corresponding to each cross-classification, we also calculate the pertinent number of employer changes reported. The final rate is the employer change rate per each year of labor force exposure pertaining to different combinations of period, age, and labor market sector (large vs. small firms, white- vs. blue-collar workers).

REFERENCES

Abegglen, J. (1958). *The Japanese factory: Aspects of its social organization.* Glencoe, IL: Free Press.

Beck, J. C., & Beck, M. N. (1994). *The change of a lifetime: Employment patterns among Japan's managerial elite.* Honolulu: University of Hawaii Press.

Bergeson, J. M., & Oba, K. Y. (1994). Japan's new equal employment opportunity law: Real weapon or heirloom sword? In P. Burstein (Ed.), *Equal employment opportunity: Labor market discrimination and public policy* (pp. 357-365). New York: Aldine.

Brinton, M. C. (1992). Christmas cakes and wedding cakes: The social organization of Japan's women's life course. In T. S. Lebra (Ed.), *Japanese social organization* (pp. 79-107). Honolulu: University of Hawaii Press.

Brinton, M. C. (1993). *Women and the economic miracle: Gender and work in postwar Japan* (California Series on Social Choice and Political Economy No. 21). Berkeley: University of California Press.

Cheng, M. T. (1991). The Japanese permanent employment system: Empirical findings. *Work and Occupations, 18,* 148-171.

Cole, R. E. (1971). *Japanese blue collar: The changing tradition.* Berkeley: University of California Press.

Cole, R. E. (1972). Permanent employment in Japan: Facts and fantasies. *Industrial and Labor Relations Review, 26,* 615-630.

Cole, R. E. (1973). Functional alternatives and economic development: An empirical example of permanent employment in Japan. *American Sociological Review, 38,* 424-438.

Cole, R. E. (1979). *Work, mobility, and participation: A comparative study of American and Japanese industry.* Berkeley: University of California Press.

Cole, R. E., & Siegel, P. (1980, January). *Alternative job-changing patterns: A Detroit-Yokohama comparison.* Paper presented at the Japan-U.S. Conference on Social Stratification and Mobility, Hawaii.

Dore, R. P. (1962). Sociology in Japan. *British Journal of Sociology, 13,* 116-230.

Dore, R. P. (1973). *British factory, Japanese factory: The origins of national diversity in industrial relations.* Berkeley: University of California Press.

Fruin, W. M. (1978). The Japanese company controversy. *Journal of Japanese Studies, 4,* 267-300.

Gordon, A. (1985). *The evolution of labor relations in Japan: Heavy industry, 1853-1955* (Harvard East Asian Monographs No. 117). Cambridge, MA: Harvard University, Council on East Asian Studies.

Hashimoto, M. (1990). Employment and wage systems in Japan and their implications for productivity. In A. S. Blinder (Ed.), *Paying for productivity: A look at the evidence* (pp. 245-294). Washington, DC: Brookings Institution.

Hashimoto, M., & Raisian, J. (1985). Employment tenure and earnings profiles in Japan and the United States. *American Economic Review, 75,* 721-735.

Helvoort, E. V. (1979). *The Japanese working man: What choice? What reward?* Vancouver: University of British Columbia Press.

Hirschmeier, J., & Yui, T. (1981). *The development of Japanese business, 1600-1980* (2nd ed.). London: Allen and Unwin.

Ishida, H. (1993). *Social mobility in contemporary Japan: Educational credentials, class and the labor market in a cross-national perspective.* Stanford, CA: Stanford University Press.

Jacoby, S. (1979). The origins of internal labor markets in Japan. *Industrial Relations, 18,* 184-196.

Japan Statistics Bureau. (1990). *Japan statistical yearbook 1990.* Tokyo: Management and Coordination Agency.

Kosaka, K. (1994). Introduction. In K. Kosaka (Ed.), *Social stratification in contemporary Japan* (pp. 1-18). London: Routledge & Kegan Paul.

Levine, S. B. (1965). Labor markets and collective bargaining in Japan. In W. W. Lockwood (Ed.), *The state and economic enterprise in Japan: Essays in the political economy of growth* (pp. 633-637). Princeton, NJ: Princeton University Press.

Levine, S. B. (1983). Careers and mobility in Japan's labor markets. In D. W. Plath (Ed.), *Work and lifecourse in Japan* (pp. 18-33). Albany: State University of New York Press.

Levine, S. B., & Kawada, H. (1980). *Human resources in Japanese industrial development.* Princeton, NJ: Princeton University Press.

Marsh, R. V., & Mannari, H. (1971). Lifetime commitment in Japan: Roles, norms, and values. *American Journal of Sociology, 76,* 795-812.

Mincer, J., & Higuchi, Y. (1988). Wage structures and labor turnover in the United States and Japan. *Journal of Japanese and International Economies, 2,* 97-133.

Rohlen, T. P. (1979). "Permanent employment" faces recession, slow growth, and an aging work force. *Journal of Japanese Studies, 5,* 235-272.

Tachibanaki, T. (1984). Labor mobility and job tenure. In M. Aoki (Ed.), *The economic analysis of the Japanese firm* (pp. 77-102). Amsterdam: North-Holland.

Taira, K. (1962). Characteristics of Japanese labor markets. *Economic Development and Cultural Change, 10,* 150-168.

Taira, K. (1970). *Economic development and the labor market in Japan.* New York: Columbia University Press.

The Transformation of the Japanese Employment System

Nature, Depth, and Origins

JAMES R. LINCOLN
YOSHIFUMI NAKATA

Speculation on the demise of Japan's distinctive employment institutions, always popular with the Western business press, has mushroomed with the country's worsening economic circumstances. The "three pillars" of the Japanese system—permanent employment (*shushin koyo*), seniority grading (*nenko joretsu*), and enterprise unions (*kigyo-nai kumiai*)—seem in danger of toppling. Such practices were not widespread, particularly for blue-collar workers, until the 1950s (Cole, 1971; Gordon, 1985). They have nonetheless attained a remarkable degree of acceptance, even sanctity, in Japanese employment tradition.[1] Yet Japanese and foreign commentators alike are now debating whether postwar Japanese work organization—once thought an exotic vestige of Japan's feudal era (Abegglen, 1958), later hailed as the leading edge in worldwide employment trends (Dore, 1973; Lincoln & Kalleberg, 1990)—is perched on the brink of extinction.

Our purpose in this chapter is to give an overview of the restructurings and adjustments now so conspicuously underway. Despite active public discussion in Japan, Western scholars have thus far paid little attention to these issues. Much recent English-language research and writing on Japanese work organization give the impression that the three pillars remain in their rock-solid foundation. The full impact of the socioeconomic changes we discuss will be felt gradually and are difficult to verify with hard data. In the meantime, observers must rely on anecdotal evidence from corporate and union interviews, supplemented by the ample reporting in the business press. A second aim of this chapter is to consider Japanese trends within a conceptual framework that highlights the pressures firms adapting to a new economic environment are under to maintain legitimacy before various constituencies.

Legitimacy Constraints

Our discussion of shifts in Japanese employment practice makes frequent reference to legitimacy constraints on managers' freedom to impose deep, broad, and lasting changes (DiMaggio & Powell, 1983; Lincoln, Hanada, & McBride, 1986). The Japanese view the corporation as a societal institution whose mission goes well beyond mere profit making and share-price appreciation. The doctrine has roots in

From *Work and Occupations,* Vol. 24, No. 1, February 1997, pp. 12-32. Reprinted by permission.

Japan's state-spearheaded late development and in its use of economic growth as a tool in the attainment of national ends (Dore, 1973).

The highly institutional character of Japanese economic organization has drawn much attention over the past two decades. Japanese firms have been celebrated as clans and enterprise communities whose strong cultures bind employees to them in reciprocal lifetime commitments (Fruin, 1992; Lincoln & Kalleberg, 1990; Ouchi, 1981; Peters & Waterman, 1982). Japanese managers routinely extol the spiritual (*seishin*) and "wet" (*uetto*) qualities of Japanese management as opposed to the emotionally dry (*dorai*) and calculative flavor of Western management styles (Beck & McCormick, 1986). The core constituencies of the Japanese firm—labor, local communities, government bureaucrats, partner companies in a *keiretsu* network—are distinct from those (e.g., shareholders) to whom the American corporation is beholden, particularly so in this era of reengineering, where once-paternalistic U.S. companies such as AT&T and IBM have abandoned, in the name of efficiency and competitiveness, their commitments to people for which they were once celebrated (Peters & Waterman, 1982).

Further indicative of legitimacy constraints is the tendency, particularly in turbulent times, for business, labor, and government to seek consensus solutions to economic problems. One established mechanism for doing so is the annual *shunto* (spring offensive) negotiations between labor and management federations that, in the period since the 1973 oil shock, has produced a de facto incomes policy, molding national wage standards to the contours of the business cycle. Also familiar is the administrative guidance that government bureaucracies such as the Ministry of Finance and the Ministry of International Trade and Industry give companies, a process eased by *amakudari*—the "descent from heaven" of officials to corporate board positions. A final example is the large-scale labor market adjustments that Japan's horizontal *keiretsu* networks orchestrated with the support of the government in response to the mid-1980s *endaka* (appreciation of the yen). Thousands of workers were shifted from declining industries such as steel and shipbuilding into such growth sectors as autos and electronics.

Yet a common view of Japan's present economic malaise is that these cozy, corporatist networks are fast unraveling. With them, the fabled competitive strategy of the Japanese firm—subordinate short-term profitability to long-term growth and maximum (human and material) asset deployment—has given way to a new commitment to cost reduction, profit margins, and moderation in investment and product variety. The emerging Japanese corporation thus seems less and less distinct from its American counterpart. Moreover, in sharp contrast with the late 1980s, when U.S. practices were held in broad contempt, the resurgence of American competitiveness has generated renewed interest in American business models and an erosion of respect for Japanese ways.

Corporate restructurings often serve a signalling function, conveying to target audiences information on shifts in a company's strategy and goals. Recent restructurings in Japan seem tailored to satisfy opposing legitimacy constraints. To signal forward-looking adaptation to the new and harsh realities of a volatile business environment, firms proclaim that once-revered ways—permanent employment, seniority promotion—are costly anachronisms and with much fanfare introduce reforms that appear to constitute dramatic breaks with the past. On closer scrutiny, however, these often prove to be cautious and incremental. Concurrently, companies activate all the safety valves available under the traditional system—curtailing recruitment, downsizing employee buffer groups (temporaries and part-timers), shifting surplus workers to affiliated firms—while publicly honoring traditional commitments to job and wage security. How these strategies have been used to weather bad times and pave the way for long-term structural change is the subject of our inquiry.

SOURCES OF CHANGE

Key to grasping the legitimacy-preserving nature of Japanese corporate change is whether the adjustments made are fundamental and structural—accounting for the demise of core labor institutions and their replacement by new ones—or cyclical and transitory, kept within the limits of the current system and apt to give way to tradition once the economy recovers momentum. Japan has gone through cycles of boom and recession before. The causes of earlier downturns—currency appreciation, heightened competition, capital shortages, muddled policy response—are operative again today. They were handled in the past by adjustments that were at times wrenching but not at odds with the established institutional framework. So a case can be made that Japan's present malaise is not unique and that it, too, will pass, leaving intact the economic fundamentals of the Japanese employment system as its underlying legitimacy and consensus.

There is also a credible case to the contrary: Some of the forces for change are unprecedented, and they are opening deep fissures between old and new ways. Included are the so-called hollowing of the economy (*kudoka*) due to offshore production; the diminished competitiveness of Japanese products owing to the inflated yen but perhaps, more important, to the diffusion of Japanese manufacturing techniques (just in time, total quality) to the United States and Europe (Womack, Jones, & Roos, 1990); and the breakdown of the *keiretsu* (interfirm network) system of cross-shareholding and preferential trading among member corporations of a business group (Gerlach, 1992b). The new reluctance of *keiretsu* banks and parent corporations to bail out troubled affiliates has badly tattered the safety net supporting the long-term growth strategy of the Japanese firm and its capacity to insulate employees from downside market risks (Lincoln, Gerlach, & Ahmadjian, 1996).

Deregulation is another relatively unprecedented force for change. It has made Japanese markets more fluid, efficient, and accessible, not only to foreign entrants but to would-be domestic competitors as well. To Japan's powerful export-oriented companies, the deregulatory trend is claimed to be welcome.[2] The lean times notwithstanding, new manufacturing methods and strategic shifts (e.g., from engineering frills and model proliferation to parts standardization and cost minimization) will likely sustain their strong performance records. But in weaker and heretofore protected industries—financial services, distribution, and agriculture—the passing of the regulatory era finds few firms prepared for the onslaught of competition and uncertainty.

Moreover, the aging of Japan's population has obvious implications for corporate human resource practice. Some 25% of the Japanese will be 65 or older in 2020 (Balls, 1993). With an aging workforce, the permanent employment and seniority systems saddle firms with rising numbers of higher-paid and less-productive workers. In past decades, these institutions suited employers because the steep seniority escalator meant that the relatively young workforce was underpaid, and the permanent employment norm spared firms the uncertainties of high turnover.

Finally, as in the United States, the transition to a service economy is reshaping Japan's employment institutions. Although leading-edge manufacturers are still competitive, their contribution to Japanese domestic employment and income is shrinking. Although manufacturing fueled the growth of the 1950s and 1960s, policymakers are pinning their hopes on the service sector as the next great engine of jobs and wealth (Ikeya, 1995). Employment practices typical of sales and service firms depart from those of manufacturing. Their heavily female workforce is younger, more mobile, less committed to work and to the firm. Work organization is less team based in such settings, and individual performance is more easily assessed. Hence occupational skills are valued over firm-specific skills, so that broad job experience rather than loyalty to one employer drives wages and promotions.

THE END OF PERMANENT EMPLOYMENT?

Japanese firms have stretched to the limit the meaning of permanent employment in a frantic

TABLE 10.1 Mean Years of Tenure, by Firm Size (male high school graduates)

Employee's Age	*Large Firm (1990)*	*Large Firm (1994)*	*Small Firm (1990)*	*Small Firm (1994)*
20-24	3.7	3.6	2.6	2.7
25-29	7.8	7.5	4.8	4.8
30-34	12.3	11.6	7.1	7.2
35-39	17.3	16.5	9.4	9.2

SOURCE: Ministry of Labor, Tokyo, Japan (1995).

search for costs savings without formal layoffs. Part and parcel of Japanese employment practice has always been a good deal of built-in flexibility (Dore, 1986). It has allowed Japanese companies to keep their commitment to employees as a corporate value while still reducing workforce size. The American business press (led by the *Wall Street Journal*) has been quick to criticize Japanese companies for their insufficient and fast restructurings compared with U.S.-style slash-and-burn "reengineering." But Japan's postwar record of massive economic adjustments at relatively low direct social cost cautions against too quick a judgment on the wisdom of the Japanese approach (Dore, Bounine-Cabale, & Tapiola, 1989; Taira & Levine, 1985).

Evidence of continuing commitment to the permanent employment principle, even in a time of rapid economic change, comes from a recent survey of directors, personnel managers, and union officials in 308 major Japanese companies by the Japan Productivity Center for Socio-Economic Development (Work in America Institute and The Japan Institute of Labor, 1995). Almost 90% of the respondents indicated that their companies planned to provide workers with continuous employment until retirement. Moreover, 82% of those surveyed called lifetime employment advantageous, but less than 18% called it disadvantageous. Such consensus underscores the enormous legitimacy that permanent employment has accumulated over the postwar era and the constraints on companies' freedom to move quickly to alternative practices.

The steps firms have taken to scale down labor costs while preserving titular commitment to the permanent employment ideal are varied. The Ministry of Labor recently reported that 34% of the establishments it surveyed had done one or more of the following: overtime reduction (23%), cutbacks in the hiring of core workers (13%), intrafirm transfers (10%), outplacements to affiliates and subsidiaries (8%), dismissal of part-time and temporary workers (4%), furloughs and other temporary suspension of work (4%), and voluntary early retirements (2%).[3] (As the following discussion suggests, however, this ordering is likely distorted by differences in the perceived legitimacy of these options and their ease of measurement.) Aggregate data on labor force trends show these measures having some impact. Table 10.1 reveals a notable decline from 1990 to 1994 in the average tenure of male high school graduates employed by large firms. The decline is much less evident in the small-firm sector, no doubt in part because employee tenure was already much lower there.

Buffer Groups

Offsetting the rigidities of the permanent employment system is the use of part-time and temporary labor to "buffer" regular workers from market uncertainties. The practice is expanding in the current Japanese economy. Firms worry about a glut of aging employees, but as temporary or subcontract workers, older people are often welcome. They come cheap. Being past the mandatory retirement age, they have few employment options, and any income they earn is augmented by corporate and state pensions. A 1994 liberalization of the legal restrictions on wages earned by pensioners has encouraged older people to reenter the labor market and companies to take advantage of their services (Koshiro, 1995). Sankyo Engineering recently created a subsidiary, Sankyo Exceed Co., which is staffed primarily with employees over 60. The subsidiary form was dictated by a culturally based legitimacy constraint. "Older staff might resent working under colleagues many years their junior," a company spokesman was quoted as saying ("New Ventures," 1994).

Large numbers of part-time or seasonal workers also have lost their jobs in the drive to cut costs, but following well-publicized U.S. trends, many Japanese companies see a long-term solution in raising the ratio of temporaries to regulars. Temporaries cost less initially but, more important, they free the firm from heavy long-term career commitments. Toyota aims to raise its percentage of temporaries from 10% to 20% while reducing its regular workforce (through hiring cutbacks and attrition) by 20% to 30% ("Toyota Official Hints," 1995).

Also portrayed as a class of "contingent" labor used to buffer regular (male) employees is women. More than 70% of the part-time labor force is women (Work in America Institute and The Japan Institute of Labor, 1995). The Japanese managers we have interviewed generally deny that women in full-time, nonseasonal positions have less job security than men. Typical is the comment that female turnover, high as it may be, is voluntary: They leave to marry and have children. Yet a 1993 survey of corporate personnel officials by the Ministry of Labor reported that less than 5% of currently employed women employees hold regular employee (*sogoshoku*) positions. Moreover, no more than 7% of new female graduates had been offered such positions that year ("Newly Opened," 1994).

The fortunes of women have worsened in the present downturn. Many firms, in flagrant violation of the 1986 Equal Opportunity Law, have dismissed female employees and declined to hire new ones, publicly advertising that only men need apply and justifying these measures on the ground that male heads of households have priority in a time of job scarcity. A recent Ministry of Labor survey reports that the percentage of graduates hired by large companies (1,000 or more) fell 17% among men but 41% among women between 1991 and 1993 (Higuchi, 1995).

"Voluntary" Early Retirement

The line between a forced layoff or dismissal and voluntary early retirement has always been thin in Japan. Regular workers who receive the "tap on the shoulder" (*katatataki*) yet balk at going quietly are rare, but those who exist place the firm in a bind. The firm cannot order them out and maintain the appearance of fidelity to permanent employment norms. What it can do is isolate them from the company, foreclose opportunities within it, and make their lives miserable. The *madogiwazoku* ("sitting by the window tribe") is a standing joke about the Japanese workplace, and in the past a few people have occupied this position more or less indefinitely without undue harassment from the firm. Now, however, firms are more aggressive about dislodging *madogiwazoku* (Ikeya, 1995). A noted consequence is the rising incidence of complaints that workers have taken to the company union, the press, and even to the courts. Litigation has been made easier by the existence of a national organization of left-wing labor lawyers eager, because of ideological reasons, to challenge companies accused of abusing workers' rights ("Scary Trend," 1994).

Moreover, although Japanese unions have made concessions on other issues, they remain vigilant in policing management attempts to dismiss employees. At an interview in July 1994 with *Denki Rengo,* The Japan Federation of Electronics Workers, we heard the interesting case of Hirose Musen, the only unionized store in Akihabara, which is the primary consumer electronics shopping district in Tokyo. The company had closed a store and fired all workers. *Denki Rengo* failed to get the workers reinstated but was able to arrange a generous severance package: the equivalent of one full year of salary and bonus. *Denki Rengo* members went to the president's house, threatened to take the firm to court, stirred up negative publicity about the company, and harassed employees in Hirose's remaining stores.

Another factor limiting freedom to terminate employees is the watchful eye of the Ministry of Labor, which in the recessionary years has come down hard on firms exceeding what the Ministry of Labor views as the limits of acceptable workforce reduction policy. When Pioneer Electric formally laid off a number of employees in 1993, strong objections by the Ministry of Labor, coupled with a storm of criticism in the press, quickly brought a change of corporate heart (Nishimura, 1993). The Ministry of Labor also succeeded in reversing the milder action by Okuma Corporation, a machine tool maker that had reduced its mandatory retirement age from the present norm of 60 to the earlier postwar standard of 55.[4] From the labor perspective, a retreat to the Age 55 mandatory retirement (*teinen*) was a dangerous precedent after years of struggle to establish a consensus on Age 60.

Interfirm Personnel Transfer (Skukko)

To Western observers, perhaps the most mysterious device available to the large Japanese firm for thinning its ranks in a time of business adversity is *shukko,* the transfer of people to affiliates, suppliers, and other partner firms. Facilitated by the *keiretsu* (interfirm network) system (Gerlach, 1992a), the *shukko*ing of excess people from large to smaller firms has escalated in the recession. The practice is particularly conspicuous in mature and cyclical industries such as steel, where companies relocated some 7,400 employees to *keiretsu* affiliates last year ("Blue-Chip Firms," 1995).

The Japanese employee asked to transfer to an affiliated firm has little choice in the matter. Employees are under heavy normative pressure to play by the rules of the permanent employment system and comply with transfers or rotations. Resistance is taken by the firm as a sign of disloyalty with all the adverse implications that Japanese careers can have (Endo, 1994). Moreover, in sharp contrast to the traditions of the American labor movement, postwar Japanese unions largely traded off for permanent employment guarantees their rights to challenge management prerogatives in regard to job design and task assignment (Cole, 1971).

Because wages and benefits vary with the size and stature of the firm and permanent (*tenseki*) transfers are invariably from larger, more prestigious firms to companies of lesser stature, the *shukko* worker stands to lose a good deal. An upside is that owing to the recipient firm's perception that the incoming people are superior to its own, the employee may gain in job status and responsibility (Beck & McCormick, 1986). This is especially true if the parent's motive for the transfer combines labor reduction with control over the affiliate because the incoming manager may displace an officer of the receiving firm. Lesser firms in a *keiretsu* network cannot recruit the quality of labor enjoyed by superordinate corporations. Moreover, the pay discrepancy is reduced by the parent firm covering the difference in wages between the employee's former salary and the wage rate of the new employer. The parent, in turn, may be reimbursed with a variety of government subsidies.[5] Such subsidies exemplify the distinctive Japanese taste for indirect government intervention in the economy: supporting with funds and information private sector initiatives and implementation (Thomson, 1993).

The affiliated firm (*kanren gaisha*) does have some say in the selection of the people it receives ("Fat-Trimming Firms," 1993). A well-placed manager Lincoln interviewed in 1990 at a major Japanese city bank characterized the *shukko* process at his organization in an intriguing way. The people who stay, he said, are the best and the worst: the best because we want to retain them and the worst because our affiliates will not have them. As the recession deepened, large and prestigious parent companies with vast networks of subsidiaries and affiliates (such as the trading company Itochu with more than 800) began encountering opposition to their *shukko* attempts ("Fat-Trimming Firms," 1993). The offshore movement of production, which has meant a considerable loss of business for domestic suppliers and distributors, has contributed to the growing resistance to *shukko*.[6]

The *shukko* system, as noted, serves two functions. Its value to large companies as a way of eliminating surplus employees is clear, but it also facilitates communication and coordination between transacting firms. Some transfers (*zaiseki shukko*) play no role in workforce reduction but are designed to shift expertise and assistance from one organization to another. Our interviews found managers of dispatching firms inclined to stress this function of close communication and know-how exchange over that of permanent workforce reduction (*tenseki shukko*). The latter has a strong connotation of dual-economy asymmetry and exploitation.

The receiving firms or *ukezara* (meaning *saucer*: dish catching the overflow) characterize the process less rosily. Toyota managers defended to us the practice of *shukko*ing employees to its automobile dealerships on the ground that workers would thereby acquire a feel for the customer end of the business. Such people would be motivated to sell, it was argued, because placing products in customers' hands would secure their jobs with the manufacturer (Toyota). However, dealers are frequently unhappy with the *shukko* manufacturing employees they get. The latter are not good at selling, and their manner, factory-bred, does not suit the image dealers wish to project to customers.[7]

That *shukko* workers, in the eyes of *ukezara* firms, are something other than a welcome bequest of top-flight labor from benevolent *oyagaisha* (parent firms) is clear from recent media commentary: "Subsidiaries and affiliates . . . should not be victimized by being forced to accept surplus workers from parent firms, which must assume full responsibility for the welfare of such workers" ("Businesses Should Seek Other Options," 1993). Subcontractor bullying (*shitauke ijime*) has become a sensitive issue in the recession as large firms cut both prices and orders from their *keiretsu* suppliers while foisting excess workers on them (Shirouzu & Williams, 1995).

Why, then, do *ukezara* firms generally comply with *shukko* attempts? They derive some economic benefit in the long run from close and reciprocal relations with large customers. But there is a legitimacy constraint as well. *Shukko* is an entrenched norm by which the steeply hierarchical community of organizations has long abided. Violation risks retribution (e.g., exclusion from long-term trade and lending relations), not only by the parent company but by the larger network in which the *ukezara* firm is embedded.

RECRUITMENT AND CAREERS

Changing Recruitment Practice

Cutbacks in new hiring might seem a simple and painless way to reduce labor costs, and the recession has brought steep reductions in the numbers of people hired.[8] But managers view as formidable the risks to doing so for a protracted spell, for herein lies another legitimacy constraint. Maintaining a stable yearly influx of new graduates reassures the labor market of the stability and trustworthiness of a Japanese firm. Because these qualities in an employer are much prized by Japanese young people, corporations fear that their competitiveness for new talent will be jeopardized by a decline in hiring. The recent memory of tight labor markets and panicky competition for graduates during the Bubble period (1988-1990) still haunt employers.[9]

Most companies would prefer to keep hiring young people while sloughing off older ones. As one bank manager put it,

> It's less effective to reduce new recruits than middle aged workers. Many are unlikely to contribute greatly to the bank since banking services have become increasingly complicated, yet they receive much higher salaries. But banks are

averse to getting rid of aging employees. . . . Such action would deal a significant blow to public confidence in the financial system. ("Businesses Should Seek Other Options," 1993)

The notion that easing out older employees might shake public confidence in the financial system strongly conveys to Americans how different are the audiences Japanese companies play to. At the same time, although firms are constrained from moving fast, there is no mistaking whether they want to go. Toyota's aggressive new CEO, Hiroshi Okuda, likewise has announced his determination to "rejuvenate the company by promoting younger people to management positions; younger people are more competent" (Reitman, 1995).

Beyond the hiring cutbacks that have marked this downturn, there are significant "structural" shifts in how recruitment is done. During the Bubble period, much was made of a breakdown of Japan's traditional recruitment system, whereby inexperienced graduates move directly from school to lifetime careers in one firm. The labor shortage had forced many firms to break with tradition and hire people with prior job experience, particularly in the booming financial sector (Nagashima, 1990). This bid up the price of midcareer labor, motivating a significant number of regular "lifetime" employees to jump ship.[10] With the Bubble's collapse (and with it the prestige and attractiveness of a finance career), the brain drain from manufacturing to financial services slowed. Such trends are evident in Table 10.2.

TABLE 10.2 Entry and Separation Rates in Manufacturing and Finance

	Separation Rate in Manufacturing (%)	*Entry Rate in Finance (%)*
1991	3.1	16.3
1992	2.6	14.3
1993	2.1	12.9

SOURCE: Ministry of Labor, Tokyo, Japan (1994).

Now, however, the system of recruiting inexperienced grads from elite universities is under assault by the manufacturers themselves. A growing number claim an interest in hiring white-collar and technical workers without college degrees. The firms are devising elaborate tests and other screening devices to ensure that the people they select are of high quality, whatever their deficits in academic certification. Sony removed any reference to the name of the job candidate's university from the employment application form, purportedly basing its hiring decisions entirely on test scores and personal interviews. Of Toyota's new hires this spring, 30% to 40% will be made without a college recommendation letter, the traditional device for matching graduates with employers ("Blue-Chip Firms," 1995; "'Exam Hell,'" 1995).

Apart from the potential cost savings of hiring outside the pool of top-flight university grads, a reason for the interest in people with specialized skills is that fast-changing technologies are undermining the traditional system of taking novices and socializing them within the firm. Because microelectronics now is such a large percentage of the value of a car, Toyota is developing in-house capacity in such technologies. However, the company is not yet capable of giving expert training in electrical engineering and is relying on midcareer hires and *shukko* engineers, chiefly from Toshiba (interview at Toyota, July 13, 1994; "'Exam Hell,'" 1995).

How fundamental is this shift in hiring practice? Like other changes we discuss, the reality lags the rhetoric. A recent survey by the human resource firm, Recruit, Inc., found 74% of firms polled in 1994 reporting that they discount university prestige in hiring. Yet a similar poll 10 years earlier found 59% of companies taking that view. The increase is notable, but plainly a professed openness on the part of employers to recruit from nonconventional channels is no startling new development. Such survey results are shaped to some degree by a corporate desire to portray a recruitment strategy as flexible and nonelitist. Yet universities are taking these trends seriously. Worried by the prospect of fewer jobs for their graduates (and its portent of declining enrollments), a consortium of private schools was recently formed to address such concerns.

The Dual-Promotion System

"Reengineering" ideology, albeit less aggressive and ruthless in Japan than in the United States, is nonetheless very much in vogue in Japanese business circles. Interviews we conducted in early 1995 at Toyota headquarters and at the Toyota union repeatedly turned up the phrase "new flat" (*nuufratto*). Toyota is aiming at lower management density, shorter chains of command, and, the company hopes, dampened workforce expectations for upward career mobility.

Especially symbolic of this restructuring agenda is Toyota's much-ballyhooed elimination of the *kacho* (section head) title (White, 1989), a step other large companies (including Nissan) have made as well. The *kacho* is a key position in Japanese formal organization, both as the linchpin role between rank-and-file employees and the executive ranks and as a career achievement with deep symbolic significance in Japanese society (e.g., the ritual invitations to *kacho* to attend weddings, births, and funerals). At Toyota, although far fewer employees now wield the supervisory authority of the traditional *kacho* role, *kacho* persists at a status rank and pay level. Moreover, although neither the practicing managers of former *kacho* rank nor their equivalents in the ability (*shokuno*) status system may use the title *kacho* in on-the-job address, both are permitted to put the title on their *meishi* (business card), largely, one presumes, for the benefit of family and friends but also to clarify relative rank in business dealings with spokespeople for other companies.

The dual-hierarchy regime divorces the pyramid of management titles and responsibilities from that of experience, expertise, and, correspondingly, pay and status. Although an employee of *kacho* rank in the ability or status (*shokuno*) hierarchy has no management role but remains an engineer or staff member, his compensation and status ranking are equivalent to that of true section heads. Seniority, commitment, and ability propel people up the status hierarchy, but only those with a real flair for leading others have a shot at being managers.

Dual-career tracks (like the salary system and other innovations) provide a legitimating bridge between the old ways and the new. They permit firms to flatten hierarchies and downsize management while preserving traditional commitments to employees in career, status, and compensation terms. The system also is designed to change the discourse of the workplace, reorienting corporate culture from slow-moving paternalism to aggressive entrepreneurism, signaling to employees the trajectory on which the firm is embarked. Having redefined the terms of employment relations without much actual shock to the substance of those relations, the company can gradually work at closing the rhetoric-reality gap.

Yet even with such adjustments, Japanese managers will confide their doubts about the restructuring agenda. Reflecting familiar Japanese concerns, they fear the loss of community and commitment that "new flat" may bring about. Denied the prospect of reaching *kacho* status and beyond, will Toyota's recruits pursue their duties with the consuming dedication that distinguished past generations of salaried men and factory workers (Lincoln & Kalleberg, 1990)?

As is often true of the rapid diffusion of new organizational forms in Japanese business, the dual-hierarchy scheme was publicly promoted by government agencies after it was already in place at a number of large companies. Japanese-style regulatory strategy brings together private sector players and government bureaucrats in an effort to ascertain "best practice" and encourage early buy-in and adoption by leading firms. Such consensus building legitimates the innovation and facilitates its spread. The Employment Information Center of the Ministry of Labor in a 1994 report urged companies to create three promotion tracks: true managers administering subordinates, researchers and planners, and skilled workers and technicians ("New Promotion, Wage System," 1994). Within these categories, the Ministry of Labor recommends that workers be ranked according to their abilities, the ranks in turn determining wages. This is precisely the system that our interviews found at Hitachi, Matsushita, NTT, Sanyo, and Toyota ("New Promotion, Wage System," 1994; "Matsushita," 1995).

PAYMENT SYSTEMS

The Demise of Nenko?

The *nenko* system—wherein novice employees who join the firm without experience are paid a low starting wage but look forward to steady raises with advancing age and seniority until an early mandatory retirement (now 60; for many years 55)—has a logic of motivation and control (Cole, 1971; Lincoln & Kalleberg, 1990). In Lazear's (1979) rational choice model, employees in effect post a bond by accepting in their youth wages lower than their productivity but then enjoy wages in excess of productivity late in their careers. Such a scheme assumes permanent employment, because without the guarantee that they will be on hand to receive a return on the early career investment, rational workers would find it unattractive. Likewise, a seniority-based system is efficient only on the assumption that with each passing year the worker acquires skill and experience, thereby enhancing his or her value to the firm. Under permanent employment, the company has an incentive to invest heavily and often in training, without risking the loss of its investment or proprietary knowledge. Moreover, as we discuss later, its contract with the workforce and the union gives it great discretion in rotating and transferring people to offset the system's rigidities. The consequence is that the employee has a long-term stake in the fortunes of the firm and a strong commitment to its survival and success.

Performance and ability have always played a greater role in *nenko* advancement and reward than the system's critics allowed. Beyond the first 10 to 12 years, age and experience become necessary conditions for advancement to the management ranks—that is, no one under 35 can enter the eligible pool for promotion to *kacho*—but only the cream of the cohort is chosen. Moreover, despite general neglect in the English-language literature on Japanese employment, systematic performance appraisal (*satei*) has long been a part of Japanese career advancement and wage determination (Endo, 1994). It complements rather than substitutes for *nenko,* however, in that the qualities prized are less short-term achievements than company commitment (as indexed, say, by perfect attendance, late hours, and sacrifice of vacation time), skill acquisition, and other signs of long-term potential.

A manager at the Hitachi Okima plant, where we conducted 2 days of interviews in early 1995, concluded a lengthy discussion of the company's merit-oriented compensation system with the comment that because performance appraisal is subjective and managers are slow to change their ways, length of service still plays a role in wage determination. Upper-line management, he said, decides how much compensation money to give the section. Then the *jinjibu* (personnel department) distributes the increases. Their assessment of who is meritorious is heavily guided by *ninjo*—human feeling. If a person puts in 30 years at the firm, they conclude he is a loyal and committed employee and therefore deserves a larger salary.

Still, there is considerable evidence that age and seniority do not shape pay and promotion as they did in the past (see Hashimoto & Raisian, 1985; Kalleberg & Lincoln, 1988). A recent article by Koshiro (1995, Figure 7) documents significant declines in the age-earnings profiles for male university graduates between 1980 and 1992. The declines are greatest in the lowest earning and, presumably, least productive classes of employees.

Moreover, despite the close functional and historical linkage between the two, there is a growing tendency in labor circles to sacrifice *nenko* on the altar of *shushuin koyo* (permanent employment). A *Nikkei* editorial called for more flexible, merit-based wage setting to preserve job security. It criticized the current wave of early voluntary retirements, temporary employee dismissals, and *shukko* to affiliates, arguing that a rationalized wage policy would render such moves unnecessary ("Businesses Should Seek Other Options," 1993).[11] *Denki Rengo* recently proposed abandoning *nenko* in exchange for an employment guarantee. This is a noteworthy shift in labor's bargaining stance. Unions fought hard in the early postwar period to establish the *nenko* principle that companies bear the "reproduction costs" of labor by providing seniority wages and family allowances (see Gordon, 1985). *Denki Rengo*'s proposal is indicative of widespread union fears that without givebacks on *nenko* provisions, the weak economy, combined with corporate restructuring fervor, might put an end to permanent employment.

In recent years, growing numbers of companies are explicitly weighting ability and performance over tenure and age in wage and promotion decisions. Yet close scrutiny of the merit pay and performance bonuses now heralded in Japanese corporate publicity reveals that the monetary benefit to the worker is often small. The incentive effect, if there is one, stems much more from the symbolism and acclaim of winning the award. A Hitachi research and development (R&D) manager told us that an engineer who obtained a patent for an innovation might get 5,000 yen (about $50) and a royalty of some percentage of the wholesale price. However, the momentum in Japanese compensation practice is toward larger merit increases. Matsushita last year announced a program to award high performers an annual bonus of 120% of monthly salary on top of wages and the normal biannual bonus.

More significant, at least in terms of long-run impact on Japanese compensation practice, is the now-fashionable "salary system" wherein the employee's annual compensation is fixed at the beginning of each year according to how well he or she has attained company targets (Seike, 1995). The Ministry of Labor released a survey of 5,300 firms conducted in late 1994 with a response rate of 94%. Of the firms surveyed, 4.3% claimed to have adopted the new system. However, the rate was higher for large firms, for executives, and in the financial services sector.

One such system is Fujitsu's "Spirit" incentive program for engineers and researchers. Most experienced only minor changes in compensation. The salaries of 70% of the eligible employees rose, with only 20% receiving unsatisfactory ratings and lower pay. Overall, comments the *Nikkei* reporter, "Fujitsu expects Spirit will cause it to spend more on salaries than before, but it will be paying for performance rather than time at the office" (Sato, 1995). As we observed, much of the hoopla over performance pay schemes, flatter hierarchies, and the like seems calculated not so much to reduce a firm's present cost or bureaucratic structure than to shake up its corporate culture, communicating to employees that leaner times and greater performance demands lie ahead.

The attempt to shift from *nenko* to performance pay illustrates the quandary firms face. Managers worry that the resulting inequities will damage morale and cohesion. Moreover, despite the rhetoric about the obsolescence of *nenko,* most companies remain averse to having younger people supervise older ones. There is further concern that merit pay for individuals will disturb the vaunted Japanese system of team-based production, wherein stronger members assist weaker colleagues to improve the performance of the team as a whole. Shigeru Tanaka, general manager of the Tokyo office of Hay Management Consultants, said,

> Japanese companies are still preoccupied with coordination and harmony among employees and a wage system based on job performance is bound to shake up human relations within these companies. . . . Many of our clients who have shown interest in the performance based pay system conclude that it doesn't suit their organizations. . . I have the impression that managing employees by job performance does not fit Japanese companies. ("Scary Trends," 1994)

A survey conducted in late 1993 by Recruit, Inc. found that only 15.1% of the 629 firms polled had introduced merit pay systems. Despite the pressures of the recessionary economy, this was an increase of just 2.2% over 3 years earlier, when a similar study found 12.9% of firms having merit pay.

CONCLUSIONS

The changes sweeping the Japanese employment system are broad and striking. How fundamental or reversible they are is harder to assess. As our review has shown, caution is warranted in drawing strong conclusions from the casual observation of the shifts attracting so much notice in the business press. Whether the issue is performance pay, the elimination of management titles, or workforce reductions, the evidence is that Japanese companies are easing into new ways, taking care to avoid abrupt or traumatic breaks with the past. Seemingly dramatic and radical adjustments often prove under scrutiny to be less so. "Most companies are phasing in change at a snail's pace," commented a *Nikkei* reporter on Japanese labor trends (Sato, 1995).

The resistance of unions, ministries, and public opinion is one important reason for going slow. But it is not simply a matter of external constraint. Japanese managers have a stronger sense of corporate obligation to provide jobs, income, and security than U.S. companies typically display. They are also more fearful of a breakdown in the postwar consensus and legitimacy surrounding employment practice and industrial relations that has given Japanese firms a highly stable and supportive domestic business environment. What Lincoln and Kalleberg (1990), following Dore (1973), called "welfare corporatism" remains a pervasive organizing principle of the Japanese employment system.

Of course, although restructurings may follow Japanese tradition in being gradual and consensus seeking, in the long run the transformation process could nonetheless prove profound. Japanese companies are constrained from moving quickly, but their tenacity and effectiveness over the long haul often have confounded doubters. Management fads come and go with lesser frequency in Japan because the forces that fan them in the United States (rapid executive succession, financial markets sensitive to any change in corporate strategy or fortunes) are less strong. Indeed, we have argued that the public hype by Japanese corporations of rather cautious substantive reforms is aimed at shaping workforce and community expectations, preparing people for the steady stream of fine adjustments that will culminate in the end of what was once known as the traditional Japanese employment system.

At this stage, even that seems too extreme a scenario. The uncertainty in Japanese management ranks on the appropriate long-term course of action is genuine. Companies would like to secure legitimacy on two fronts: Signal to investors and customers a commitment to greater efficiency while reassuring employees and communities that the adjustments will not prove so disruptive after all. Assuming that real economic recovery takes hold, we envision considerable stabilization of Japanese employment practice, albeit at a higher level of marked-oriented flexibility than the three pillars system has thus far allowed.

FUTURE RESEARCH

Our investigation has been heavily exploratory and anecdotal. In closing, we discuss how systematic research on these topics might proceed. The ideal research design is a large-scale comparative (United States and Japan) plant-and-employee survey of the kind Lincoln and Kalleberg (1990) conducted in the 1980s. This project, consisting of personal interviews with plant and personnel managers in 106 Japanese and U.S. plants and questionnaires from 8,302 of their employees, produced a very rich data set on the organizational structure and employment systems of factories and the attitudes, values, and career experiences of employees.

A comparable survey conducted now might collect similar data on structure and practice but would also address directly the issue of change. First, it would allow comparisons with the Lincoln and Kalleberg baseline survey from the early 1980s—a period of relative stability in Japanese economic history. Second, survey items could be designed to deal with the introduction of new practices. A simple approach is to inquire about the advent of the "salary system," "new flat," and other buzz phrases that currently abound in Japanese business circles. Moreover, the survey would use similar items and scales as the Lincoln-Kalleberg project to measure dimensions of organization, such as decision-making centralization, specialization of functional roles, internal labor market structuring, and scope of employee welfare services, combining them with follow-up probes of how these are evolving over time. The employee-level component of the survey also would address workers' feelings in regard to changing practices: fears of diminishing job security and the degree of acceptance of company claims for the superiority of new ways.

Finally, the data analysis itself would generate evidence on the scope and depth of change. Have the determinants of wages shifted since Kalleberg and Lincoln (1988) modeled them with the Indiana-Kanagawa data, producing strong evidence that age, family obligations, seniority, and on-the-job training were more important in Japan than in the United States? Similarly, have the level and determinants of employee commitment changed since the early 1980s when the Lincoln-Kalleberg data were collected? Indications abound that restructurings and downsizings have taken a heavy toll in corporate loyalty and dedication among American employees. Japanese managers fear a similar erosion of commitment and with it the labor discipline and stability that by all accounts figure in the postwar competitiveness of Japanese industry. These questions are timely and important to an understanding not only of Japanese patterns but of worldwide trends in work organization and employee attitudes and behavior. A survey of the Lincoln-Kalleberg sort is one of few research designs able to address them.

NOTES

1. In contrast to the equally distinctive institutions of codetermination legislation, works councils, and strong central unions in continental Europe, Japanese labor practices have remained relatively uncodified in law and judicial precedent (Lincoln, Kerbo, & Wittenhagen, 1995).

2. Indeed, a highly placed Toyota manager told us that the key tension in the Japanese economy today is no longer between management and labor but rather between the competitive, efficient sectors such as autos and electronics and the protected, *keiretsu*-ridden, oligopolistic sectors such as financial services. Not everyone would agree, of course, that the Japanese auto and electronics industries are untainted by *keiretsu* and protectionism.

3. This was cited in a joint report by the Work in America Institute and The Japan Institute of Labor (1995).

4. A 1990 survey of 6,000 companies by the Ministry of Labor found that 91% of those with 100 or more employees either had or were planning to introduce a mandatory retirement age of 60 or more. For smaller firms, the corresponding rate was 80% ("Most Firms," 1990).

5. The Employment Adjustment Subsidy (*Koyou Chousei Joseikin*) will support up to one half of the wage cost in large firms with 300+ employees and two thirds of the cost in smaller firms. The subsidy is used for three purposes: temporary layoffs, education and training, and interfirm transfer or *shukko.* As of December 1994, a total of 2,099 firms with 446,002 employees had received this subsidy. A new breed of young ministry bureaucrats is opposed to the system of *shukko* and *madogiwazoku* subsidies, preferring the free play of market forces (Robert Cole, personal communication, December 1995).

6. We are indebted to Robert Cole for his thoughts on this point.

7. However, all new college graduates hired by Japanese companies are cross-trained in a variety of functions, including production and sales. Toyota told us that 5 months of sales training is the standard in the Japanese auto industry. We are grateful to Hiromi Shioji of Kyoto University for his observations on this topic.

8. Toyota planned to hire 140 grads in the spring of 1996 as opposed to 20 in 1995. Mazda hired none in 1995 and planned to hire only 50 in 1996. Five major steelmakers planned to hire a total of 500 grads in 1996, 10% less than in 1995.

9. In 1989, the ratio of job offers to seekers was 3.14 for male graduates and 1.98 for females ("Job Offers to Students," 1990).

10. The speculative boom at the time had inflated compensation in financial services, such that technical people in manufacturing could sometimes double their incomes by moving.

11. One form of wage flexibility that sharply differentiates Japanese corporations from their U.S. counterparts is the salary freezes and cuts for managers and executives that are generally a company's first response to hard times ("Executive Salary Cuts," 1992).

REFERENCES

Abegglen, J. C. (1958). *The Japanese factory: Aspects of its social organization.* Glencoe, IL: Free Press.

Balls, E. (1993, December 6). Delayed effects of Japan's demographic time-bomb. *Financial Times.*

Beck, J., & McCormick, J. (1986). *Nippon Motorola (A)* (HBS Case No. 9-487-029). Boston: Harvard Business School Press.

Blue-chip firms tighten hiring, shift workers to subsidiaries. (1995, June 12). *Nikkei Weekly.*

Businesses should seek other options before resorting to personnel cuts. (1993, November 8). *Nikkei Weekly.*

Cole, R. E. (1971). *Japanese blue collar: The changing tradition.* Berkeley: University of California Press.

DiMaggio, P. J., & Powell, W. W. (1983). The iron case revisited: Institutional ismorphism and collective rationality in organizational fields. *American Sociological Review, 48,* 147-160.

Dore, R. (1973). *British factory, Japanese factory: The origins of diversity in industrial relations.* Berkeley: University of California Press.

Dore, R. (1986). *Flexible rigidities.* Stanford, CA: Stanford University Press.

Dore, R., Bounine-Cabale, J., & Tapiola, K. (1989). *Japan at work: Markets, management and flexibility.* Paris: OECD.

Endo, K. (1994). Satei (personnel assessment) and interworker competition in Japanese firms. *Industrial Relations, 33,* 70-82.

"Exam hell" no longer assures career bliss. (1995, May 22). *Nikkei Weekly.*

Executive salary cuts hit broad range of sectors. (1992, May 23). *Nikkei Weekly.*

Fat-trimming firms eye manager glut. (1993, February 8). *The Nikkei Weekly.*

Fruin, M. (1992). *The Japanese enterprise system: Competitive strategies and cooperative structures.* Oxford, UK: Oxford University Press.

Gerlach, M. (1992a). *Alliance capitalism.* Berkeley: University of California Press.

Gerlach, M. (1992b). Twilight of the *keiretsu*: A critical assessment. *Journal of Japanese Studies, 18,* 79-118.

Gordon, A. (1985). *The evolution of labor relations in Japan: Heavy industry, 1853-1955.* Cambridge, MA: Harvard University Press.

Hashimoto, M., & Raisian, J. (1985). Employment tenure and earnings profiles in Japan and the United States. *American Economic Review, 75,* 721-735.

Higuchi, Y. (1995, March 20). New graduates must sell themselves harder: Young entries finding it tough to crack job market. *Nikkei Weekly.*

Ikeya, A. (1995, June 12). Workers corporate cocoons collapsing as yen drives production offshore. *Nikkei Weekly.*

Job offers to students top 1 million. (1990, August 21). *Japan Times.*

Kalleberg, A. L., & Lincoln, J. R. (1988). The structure of earnings inequality in the United States and Japan. *American Journal of Sociology, 94*(Suppl.), S121-S153.

Koshiro, K. (1995). *Company-based collective wage determination in Japan: Its viability revisited amid intensifying global competition* (Discussion Paper No. 95-11). Yokohama, Japan: Yokohama National University, The Center for International Trade Studies, Faculty of Economics.

Lazear, E. (1979). Why is there mandatory retirement? *Journal of Political Economy, 87,* 1261-1284.

Lincoln, J. R., Gerlach, M. L., & Ahmadjian, C. (1996). Keiretsu networks and corporate performance in Japan. *American Sociological Review, 61.*

Lincoln, J. R., Hanada, M., & McBride, K. (1986). Organizational structures in Japanese and U.S. manufacturing. *Administrative Science Quarterly, 31,* 338-364.

Lincoln, J. R., & Kalleberg, A. L. (1990). *Culture, control, and commitment: A study of work organization and work attitudes in the U.S. and Japan.* Cambridge, UK: Cambridge University Press.

Lincoln, J. R., Kerbo, H. R., & Wittenhagen, E. (1995). Japanese companies in Germany: A case study in cross-cultural management. *Industrial Relations, 34,* 417-440.

Matsushita toughens worker ratings. (1995, May 1). *Nikkei Weekly.*

Ministry of Labor. (1994). *Survey on employment trends.* Tokyo: Author.

Ministry of Labor. (1995). *Basic survey of wage structure: 1994.* Tokyo: Author.

Most firms have retirement age over 60. (1990, May 7). *Japan Times.*

Nagashima, H. (1990, August 3). Companies revamp personnel systems to favor specialists. *Japan Times.*

New promotion, wage system urged for white collar staff. (1994, July 18). *Nikkei Weekly.*

Newly opened corporate career paths prove rocky. (1994, February 21). *Nikkei Weekly.*

Nishimura, H. (1993, March 3). System of lifetime jobs resisting change. *Nikkei Weekly.*

Ouchi, W. G. (1980). Markets, bureaucracies, and clans. *Administrative Science Quarterly, 25,* 120-142.

Peters, T. J., & Waterman, R. H., Jr. (1982). *In search of excellence: Lessons from America's best-run companies.* New York: Harper & Row.

Reitman, V. (1995, August 11). Toyota names a chief likely to shake up global auto business: Okuda wants more output from overseas plants, greater sales at home; a finance guy who laughs. *Wall Street Journal.*

Sato, M. (1995, September 25). Firms test competitive tool: Merit pay. Companies take go-slow approach, worry about loss of team spirit. *Nikkei Weekly.*

Scary trend for Japanese managers. (1994, September 9). *Nikkei Weekly.*

Seike, A. (1995, May 15). Annual wage talks still have a meaningful role to play: Instead of being scrapped, process should be revised to reflect changing economic environment. *Nikkei Weekly.*

Shirouzu, N., & Williams, M. (1995, July 25). The big squeeze: Pummeled by giants, Japan's small firms struggle with change. *Wall Street Journal.*

Taira, I., & Levine, S. (1985). Japan's industrial relations: A social compact emerges. In H. Juris, M. Thompson, & W. Daniels (Eds.), *Industrial relations in a decade of economic change* (pp. 247-300). Madison, WI: Industrial Relations Research Association Series.

Thomson, R. (1993, December 19). Tokyo comes to the aid of over-the-hill 40-year-olds. *Financial Times.*

Toyota official hints at big job cuts as output in Japan continues to fall. (1995, July 14). *Wall Street Journal.*

White, J. B. (1989, August 2). Toyota wants more managers out on the line; auto maker to reorganize middle-level positions, offer more to workers. *Wall Street Journal.*

Womack, J. P., Jones, D. T., & Roos, D. (1990). *The machine that changed the world.* New York: Macmillan.

Work in America Institute and The Japan Institute of Labor. (1995). *Employment security: Changing characteristics in U.S. and Japan.* New York: U.S.-Japan Foundation.

PART III

Restructuring and Worker Marginalization

The seven chapters in this section address some of the consequences associated with the degree to which workers are marginalized as a result of workplace restructuring; the final chapter takes a macro perspective on displaced workers. These chapters demonstrate that even workers in stable, relatively permanent, and unionized employment may experience marginalization; in other words, marginalization is *not* limited to workers in casualized employment. These chapters examine a variety of workplaces and of outcomes for workers and use different types of data and analytic techniques. They are well-integrated with one another by dint of their clear focus on the effects of work organization and workplace restructuring on the well-being—and sometimes the very lives—of workers.

Quitting is a common worker response to workplace reorganization and worker marginalization. Kathryn Schellenberg examines this topic in Chapter 11, "Taking It or Leaving It: Instability and Turnover in a High-Tech Firm." Research on internal labor markets is, Schellenberg asserts, based on the assumption that the promise of employment stability elicits employee commitment to firms and limited turnover. This assumption, however, is rarely examined with over-time data. Using data from the accounting, personnel, and payroll records of a single high-tech firm and interviews with 25 firm members, Schellenberg traces the effect of "constant restructuring" on the quit behaviors of male engineers over a 5-year period. Higher pay and longer tenure reduced the chances that an engineer would quit the firm, whereas extensive business travel increased the likelihood of quitting. In the context of workplace restructuring, Schellenberg's key finding is that cumulative change (measured as cumulative reassignments of engineers from one cost center to another over time) resulted in higher quit rates. No single reorganization, no matter how extensive, affected the likelihood that engineers left the firm, but continual change did. As Schellenberg points out in her conclusion, the next step for researchers is to know more about where workers go after they quit and whether they fare better or worse with subsequent employers.

We are more accustomed to thinking of temporary workers than engineers as marginalized by workplace restructuring, as Jackie Krasas Rogers does in Chapter 12, "Just a Temp: Experience and Structure of Alienation in Temporary Clerical Employment." Rogers uses in-depth interviews with 13 clerical workers who were employed through temporary agencies to better understand the social organization of temporary work and the experiences of workers in the temporary sector. In interviews with Rogers, the workers (all women) spoke of their on-the-job experiences and described strategies that they used to cope with alienation from their work, from others, and from themselves. Temporary workers, Rogers finds, rarely have a clear sense of how their activities fit into the firm's larger purpose, or even into a project within the firm. Several women reported that, to maintain interest while on the job, they engaged in alternative activities. (Because the interviews occurred in Los Angeles, many of these had to do with spotting celebrities and reading original TV or movie scripts.) The temporary and clerical nature of their work also isolated these workers from others; for example, temporary workers were often physically separated from other employees during work hours and excluded from on-site and after-hours social events. Temporary workers responded to this form of alienation by attempting to maintain strong ties to one or two temporary agencies and by seeking longer assignments. Finally, temporary workers sometimes had to act as chameleons, changing their dress and hairstyles and managing their emotions to fit their assignments, even concealing extensive education and skills to avoid any threat to permanent employees.

As Rogers points out, members of disadvantaged statuses—particularly women and African Americans—are overrepresented in temporary (and clerical) work. Thus, the expansion of temporary employment (see Hirsch and Naquin's Chapter 23, this volume) has served in part to reproduce the marginal positions of already marginalized workers. Further research might explore the long-term consequences of marginalization: Do workers seek other employment when they experience marginalization, redefine themselves so that employment is not central to their identities, or join forces with coworkers to challenge detrimental work practices and structures?

In Chapter 13, Catherine Ross and Marilyn Wright tackle the question of whether women and men differ in their experiences of and responses to marginalization; the question is complicated by the fact than many women, but few men, work full-time as unpaid homemakers. In "Women's Work, Men's Work, and the Sense of Control," Ross and Wright use data from a national survey to examine gender differences in workers' belief that they have control over both good and bad events in their lives.

Full-time homemaking and part-time wage work share many of the characteristics of temporary employment: Both tend to be more routine and less complex than full-time, permanent wage work and offer few opportunities for interaction with coworkers (or other homemakers). But homemakers often describe their daily work as highly autonomous, citing their decision-making power and freedom from close supervision. In general, Ross and Wright find support for their central premise that women's lower sense of control is attributable to their employment situations rather than to gender differences in responses to similar work conditions. Zero-order gender differences in sense of control disappeared when work characteristics (task variety, opportunity to learn new things, etc.) were included in multivariate analyses. Despite their claims of autonomy, full-time homemakers report a lower sense of control over events, due to limited task variety, opportunity to learn new things, and so forth. This chapter, as well as those by Rogers, Carr, and Jurik, sounds the theme that women's work—whether unpaid or paid, at home or not—is more often marginalized.

Workers can also be viewed as marginalized if they have limited or negative interactions with other workers. The quality of interactions among coworkers is the focus of Chapter 14, "Group Relations at Work: Solidarity, Conflict, and Relations With Management." Here, Randy Hodson tackles an understudied topic in the sociology of work: the impact of relations among coworkers on workers' job satisfaction and on the character of their interactions with management. Hodson points out that sociologists have limited understanding of "lateral relations among coworkers," which are increasingly important in these days of team-based production, quality circles, and the like.

In a novel strategy, Hodson analyzes information on workplace relations coded from 83 book-length ethnographies of workplaces *and* responses to a phone survey of employed adults. (Researchers interested in exploring new angles of long-standing literatures might read Hodson's chapter simply for the description of the selection and coding of the ethnographies.) Most of the multivariate findings from both the survey and the ethnographic analyses square with hypotheses from previous literature: Positive relations among coworkers (worker solidarity) enhanced workers' job satisfaction, whereas poor relations with coworkers (worker conflict) compromised satisfaction. Worker conflict also negatively affected the quality of interactions between workers and managers but—contrary to expectations—coworker solidarity was *positively* linked with the quality of worker relations with management. To the extent that some types of workplace restructuring foster closer and more positive relations among workers, such change holds the possibility of two positive outcomes for workers: greater satisfaction with their work and less contentious relations with management. Drawing from Hodson, sociologists of work can ask, *how* might activists, workers, and progressive employees redesign work to foster employee decision making and positive relations among coworkers? Are there workplace-level "remedies" for the ways in which economic restructuring has attenuated workers' active connection with and participation in their workplace?

Chapters 15 and 16, respectively, address the organization of work in health care settings for nurses caring for AIDS patients and for primary care physicians. Linda Aiken and Douglas Sloane's Chapter 15, "The Effects of Organizational Innovations in AIDS Care on Burnout Among Urban Hospital Nurses," argues, similar to Ross and Wright, that burnout among nurses is less a function of *worker* than of *workplace* traits. This research is also nicely linked to the questions raised by several other chapters about the consequences of workplace structures and practices for the morale of workers. Aiken and Sloane suggest that turnover among nurses—even those in the emotionally wearing specialty of AIDS care—can be reduced if nurses have adequate organizational support with which to do their jobs and if units are organized in ways that maximize nurses' autonomy. To test their assertions, Aiken and Sloane compare survey responses from nurses in three types of settings: dedicated AIDS units within hospitals, scattered-bed units in magnet hospitals, and scattered-bed units in nonmagnet hospitals. (In scattered-bed units, patients with AIDS are housed in various departments of the hospital rather than in a single unit. Magnet hospitals are those identified by the American Academy of Nursing as having low turnover and high satisfaction among nurses.) Perceived organizational support significantly reduced nurses' burnout; net of personal characteristics and organizational support, nurses in AIDS units reported the lowest levels of emotional exhaustion. Aiken and Sloane conclude that alternative organizational designs, if combined with organizational support, are associated with positive staff outcomes. This could well be a conclusion for several chapters in this section: Workers who are denied autonomy, voice, and positive relations with coworkers are more likely to have contentious relations with management, to have a limited sense of control over their lives, to suffer emotional exhaustion and less likely to expend any additional effort to benefit their employers.

Compared to line workers subject to technical control, physicians are often regarded as the epitome of autonomy, outstanding even among professionals. Yet, as Timothy Hoff and David McCaffrey point out in Chapter

16, recent changes in the organization of the health care industry have brought perhaps unprecedented change to the medical profession. In "Adapting, Resisting, and Negotiating: How Physicians Cope With Organization and Economic Change," Hoff and McCaffrey use data from in-depth interviews with 25 primary care physicians. By comparing physicians working in private practices (both solo and group) to those employed in a single HMO, Hoff and McCaffrey are able to examine *intra*profession responses to the restructuring of an entire industry. They argue that much sociological research has focused on *professions* as actors, ignoring variation across practitioners within an occupation.

Hoff and McCaffrey find first that, regardless of work setting, physicians shared similar views of their profession, with the importance of autonomy emerging time and again. By defining autonomy in terms of their interactions with patients in the examining room, even HMO physicians emphasized the high degree of autonomy that medicine afforded them; also, none of the physicians interviewed viewed nonphysicians as threats, either economically or in terms of autonomy. There were clear differences among physicians, however, that Hoff and McCaffrey link to the differences in workplaces. Private practice physicians saw themselves as entrepreneurs and enjoyed the daily competition and personal control over the vitality of their practices; for them, this was a further expression of autonomy. By contrast, HMO physicians viewed the organization as freeing them from administrative details and concerns about fees, permitting them to focus on the well-being of their patients. The paradox, however, lay in the "seepage" of the medical marketplace into their daily activities, which the physicians could resist only by becoming more involved in management of the HMO. The authors' general conclusion is that both private practice and HMO physicians engaged in various forms of negotiation with and resistance to changes resulting from the restructuring of health care delivery.

Chapter 17, by Beth Rubin and Brian Smith, moves us to a macro level of analysis, through examination of the factors that affect displaced workers' time to reemployment. In "Reemployment in the Restructured Economy: Surviving Change, Displacement, and the Gales of Creative Destruction," Rubin and Smith examine alternative theoretical perspectives on large-scale economic restructuring. They contrast the neoclassical outlook—which paints deindustrialization, massive layoffs, and other economic changes as movement toward a postindustrial economy that will benefit skilled workers—with class-based approaches that view these changes as evidence of employers' drive to extract ever more profit from labor and with feminist critiques that argue that restructuring affects women and men differently, and reinforces gender inequality.

Using data from a 1992 survey of workers displaced in the previous 5 years, Rubin and Smith examine the effects of worker characteristics on time to reemployment. (By the time of the survey, about 75% of the displaced workers had found new jobs.) By and large, their results buttress the claims of class-focused and feminist critics of economic restructuring. College graduates and high-wage workers (a proxy for high skill), contrary to neoclassical expectations, took longer to find new jobs, as did older workers, married women, and women with young children. Not only did the highly skilled find themselves vulnerable, so did women, whose household responsibilities, as feminists had predicted, served to disadvantage them even further in the new economy. Unexpectedly, neither the industry nor the region from which the worker was displaced had any net effect on time to reemployment, and this poses questions for future researchers: Beyond worker and job characteristics (such as the availability of group health insurance), what structural factors affect how workers fare after being displaced? Are there ways in which workers might be protected from the brunt of "creative gales of destruction," if economic restructuring of the past two decades is not reversible? Bridging the micro and macro contributions to Part III is this question: How can workers be empowered when workplace and economic restructuring typically have the effect of weakening and destabilizing workers' positions in the labor market?

Collectively, these seven chapters explore ways in which the practices and structures of workplaces (including homes) affect worker behavior and well-being both positively and negatively. Much of the research presented in Part III paints a bleak picture of the long-run consequences of marginalization, and of its uneven effects on different types of workers. Many of the findings, however, also provide powerful suggestions for how workplaces might be structured to minimize worker marginalization and its deleterious effects.

Taking It or Leaving It

Instability and Turnover in a High-Tech Firm

KATHRYN SCHELLENBERG

Labor market theorists claim that the prospects of employment stability and sponsored career mobility via firm-specific internal labor markets (ILMs) reduce turnover in large bureaucratic firms (Althauser, 1989; Baron & Bielby, 1980; Sorenson, 1983). This assertion rests on a largely unstated, untested premise of organizational stability. However, it is now widely argued that pressures arising from globalization, rapid technological change, and general economic volatility have undermined the ability of firms to achieve a state of stable equilibrium (e.g., DiPrete, 1993; Heydebrand, 1989; Wallace, 1989). DiPrete (1993) noted that although uncertainty may lead firms to try and protect their investment in skilled core workers, "the buffering effect of labor market structures . . . is partial at best" (p. 92). Hirsch (1993) went so far as to argue that instability is now so pervasive and severe as to challenge the viability of ILMs and the very notion of long-term reciprocal relationships between firms and workers. He speculates that cynicism, alienation, and interfirm mobility may increase as a result.

Obviously, ILMs are not the sole basis of commitment. Other bureaucratic or "corporatist" incentives include the perception of fairness and legitimacy imposed by formalized systems of rules and regulations (Halaby, 1986) and normative cultures that foster social integration among coworkers (Lincoln & Kalleberg, 1985, 1990). By creating uncertainty over careers and churning coworker relations, however, instability could undermine the commitment derived from these incentives as well.

Despite our lack of knowledge about instability and its effects, the vast majority of labor market and turnover research continues to rely on static cross-sectional designs that fail to take change into account. Few scholars have focused on change as a central issue or examined its impact on how workers view their place in the organization (Briody, Baba, & Cooper, 1995; Thomas, 1994). More to the point, I have not found one study that has examined the effects of firm-level instability on turnover. In this chapter, I attempt to partially fill this gap and draw on a case study of Pendulum Inc. (pseudonym), a high-tech firm, to test the hypothesis that *instability raises workers' propensities to quit their jobs.*

My examination of instability and turnover begins with a background discussion of high-tech firms. This is followed by a brief introduction to Pendulum as a study site, methods of data collection, and a narrative history describing how the firm changed over a period of several years as revealed through employee interviews. I then examine aggregate exit rates for two occupational groups—craft workers and engineers—and present a multivariate, individual-level analysis of quitting by engineers. Finally, I

From *Work and Occupations*, Vol. 23, No. 2, May 1996, pp. 190-213. Reprinted by permission.

discuss some implications of the study and offer suggestions for future research.

HIGH-TECH FIRMS: INSTABILITY AND TURNOVER

High-tech firms have a dual reputation that suggests a possible link between organizational instability and turnover. Whereas the pressures of economic uncertainty are being felt in a wide range of sectors, high-tech firms are seen as especially vulnerable to environmental flux. Numerous accounts portray the normal condition of high-tech firms as one of chronic upheaval related to *constant restructuring,* shifting job demands, and cycles of growth and decline (see Gomez-Mejia & Balkin, 1985; Kaufman, Parcel, Wallace, & Form, 1988; Kunda, 1992; Perrow, 1970; Thomas, 1994). Gomez-Mejia and Balkin state that even people who like change find the upheaval of high-tech work stressful.

It is often observed that high-tech firms tend to rely on normative controls as opposed to bureaucratic incentives to foster commitment. But Kunda (1992) showed that in one large firm, some workers tried to avoid being "swallowed" by the culture, thus casting doubt on the "authenticity of commitment" (p. 222). He (and others) also pointed to no-layoff policies, promotional ladders, and other bureaucratic strategies in some larger firms (e.g., Finlay, 1988; Thomas, 1994; Zenger, 1992). Even so, some workers are more highly valued than others. In times of downturn, for example, firms may try to "hoard" elite technical workers while reducing the employment of other occupational groups (Glasmeier, 1986).

It seems that hoarding efforts are less than successful because, even in prosperous times, high-tech firms have a reputation for high turnover. Delbecq and Weiss (1988) decried the level of (presumably voluntary) labor mobility in high-tech Silicon Valley as "frenzied" and "scandalous." Zenger (1992) described annual turnover rates of 8% to 9% for high-tech engineers as "modest" and 15% to 18% as "quite high." But is organizational instability a factor in why employees decide to leave?

DATA AND METHOD

To address this question, I contacted two firms in which employees I knew had offered to introduce me to potentially supportive members of senior management. One firm declined to be studied; Pendulum, through its human resources department, accepted.

Despite very high cooperation, data collection was difficult, occupying an estimated minimum of 400 hours spread over 8 months. Pendulum has a structure of "fixed" cost centers complemented by an overlapping "matrix" of fluid project teams (Davis & Lawrence, 1977). There were no formal records on former matrix teams, and many other records, including organization charts of the cost center structure, were incomplete, unreliable, or "missing." The best data on firm structure came from accounting lists of cost center names and codes. Changes in the number and structure of the codes over time highlighted structural changes in the organization as a whole.

Other qualitative data were obtained through two types of interviews with employees. The first type involved a purposive sample of approximately 25 individuals selected from a broad range of vantage points with respect to tenure, authority, roles, and knowledge of policies, practices, and events. Interviews lasted about an hour; most took place at the firm's head office or main plant. The second type of interview entailed informal discussions that evolved in the course of seeking information about company records or other data sources. I estimate that about 35 employees participated in such exchanges.

Data on employees and jobs were obtained from human resources and personnel files as well as 25 (microfiche) payroll reports sampled at exact 4-month intervals. The firm provided on-site computer resources so that data could be collected in electronic form. Data on employee characteristics, pay, role demands, and cost center codes were entered into three files that were merged into one integrated data set.

THE CASE OF PENDULUM

Pendulum began as a small entrepreneurial engineering company and quickly grew into a major producer of large-scale, integrated robotics systems controlled by millions of lines of sophisticated software code. Each system is customized; prices range from several hundred thousand to several million dollars. The firm's core occupational groups are skilled craft workers and technical professionals. (Like Kunda, 1992, I refer to this latter group as "engineers," although a large portion have computer science rather than engineering training.) Due to product customization and constant technical innovation, work is nonroutine and workers have considerable autonomy over how they go about their jobs. A high percentage of roles involve travel to customer sites spread across North America and beyond.

Pendulum's early success attracted venture capital backing from Parent Corporation (pseudonym), a diversified multinational conglomerate. Unlike many venture capitalists (Gomez-Mejia, Balkin, & Welbourne, 1990), Parent did not interfere in Pendulum's internal operations; the company retained a strong normative culture based on camaraderie and intense loyalty to the charismatic founder. The founder apparently reciprocated that loyalty. Longtime employees said that when business was slack, he did all he could just to keep people working because "it nearly killed him to have to lay someone off." They recalled the early years with great fondness, saying, "We were like a family" and turnover was low.

With growth, normative controls showed signs of strain. A morale study conducted when the payroll exceeded 400 workers suggested that the organization was out of control. The consultants who conducted the study administered a standard employee satisfaction survey and interviewed 97 employees. They reported that "old-timers" regretted the loss of closeness that had existed when the company was smaller. Also, there were numerous complaints that centered on "promotions from the outside" and a need for logical career ladders, equitable pay and promotion practices, and "proper" job descriptions. Workers also complained about frequent reorganizations. One individual claimed that a series of recent changes had left everyone asking, "Who do we report to now?" Two years later, a follow-up study found unabated frustration over these same issues.

By the second study, however, Pendulum was a wholly owned Parent subsidiary and undergoing sweeping reform. Whereas Parent did not interfere as a venture capitalist, it was an intrusive parent company. As is often the case (DiMaggio & Powell, 1983), it made subsidiaries adopt policies and practices compatible with its own. The reforms imposed on Pendulum took nearly 3 years to implement fully. They included a far more elaborate cost center structure, formal job titles and descriptions, performance reviews, and a policy of hiring at the lowest level and promoting through internal career ladders (i.e., ILMs).

These reforms were based on the Hay System, a widely used point factor analysis (PFA) method of ranking jobs according to the "order and extent of their difficulty and importance" to the organization (Bellak, 1984, p. 5). As such, PFA is designed to impose order and equity. Critics charge that PFA's classic bureaucratic premises of rigid top-down control stifle the ability of high-tech firms to change and use innovations that originate at the bottom of the organization (e.g., Lawler, 1987). But if Pendulum insiders were aware of such criticisms, they were not in position to adopt an alternative system.

Parent did not fully immunize Pendulum against the effects of market reversals and growing competition. This point is illustrated in Figure 11.1, which shows fluctuations in workforce size over a 13-year span *after* Parent became a venture capital partner. (Pendulum did not want exact numbers of employees reported, but I have used 1,000 as an approximate maximum number.) Both large-scale retrenchments occurred during the 1980s, a period when many

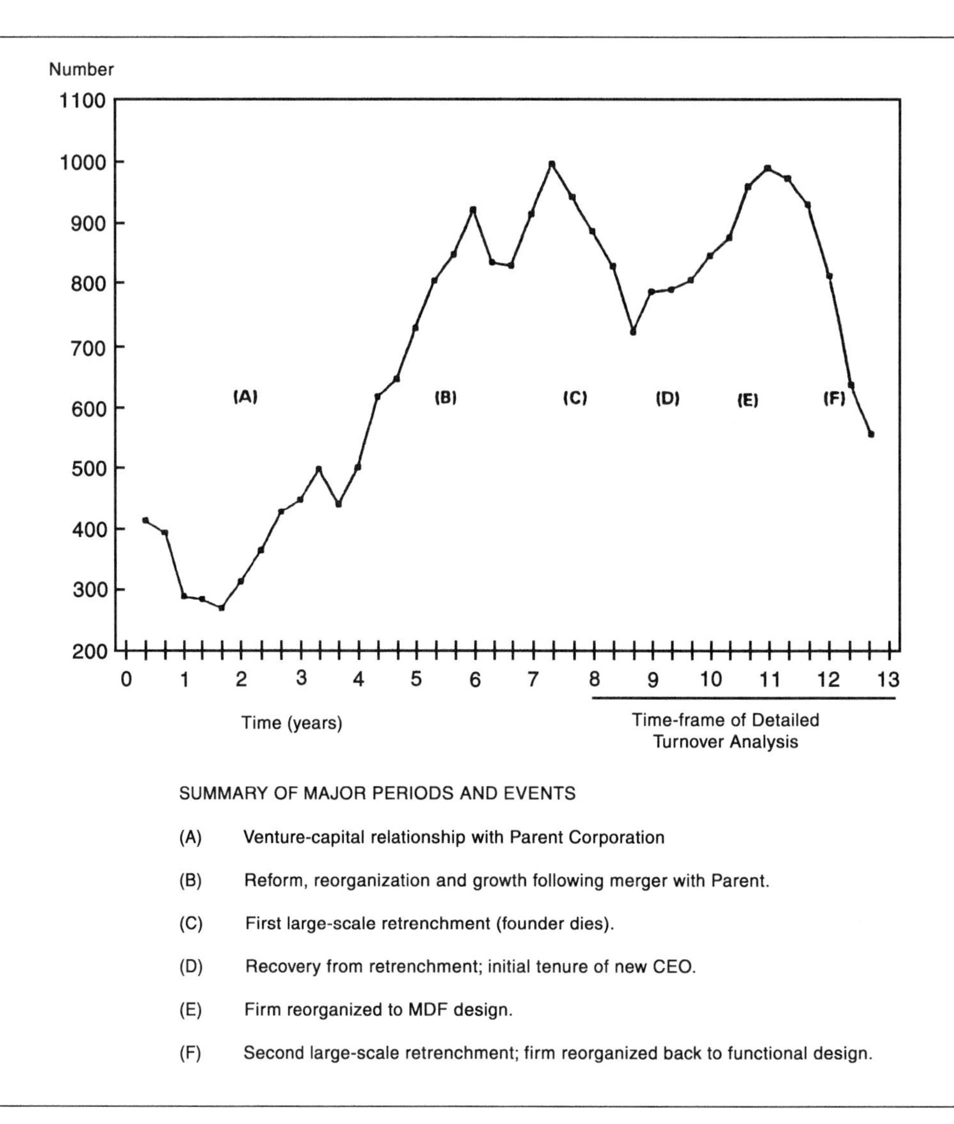

Figure 11.1. Approximate Number of Employees (regular, temporary, and part-time) at Successive 4-Month Intervals Spanning 13 Years

high-tech firms struggled (Finlay, 1988; Kunda, 1992).

The first retrenchment (C in Figure 11.1) began soon after Parent's organizational reforms were in place and continued for more than a year. Manufacturing workers were the most severely affected. Craft workers accounted for 26% of regular employees before the layoffs, whereas technical specialists were less than 20%. Afterward, their positions were reversed: Craft workers were 20% and engineers were 28%. Just as Pendulum was recovering from the decline, the beloved founder died. Parent hired a new chief executive officer (CEO) (D in Figure 11.1).

The CEO was not a technical expert and did not have a high-tech background. His previous employer was a conglomerate bureaucracy like Parent. He made Pendulum more bureaucratic by adding more cost centers, rules, formality, and layers of hierarchy. Most importantly, he reorganized the *nonmanufacturing* units of the firm by converting its functional design (cost centers based on occupational specialty) to a multidivisional form (MDF) of three divisions, each with its own functional cost centers (E in Figure 11.1). Unlike the earlier reforms imposed by Parent, these changes were implemented abruptly.

On paper, Pendulum now appeared to be a mature bureaucracy. Job descriptions included a small section of an organization chart outlining the incumbent's projected career path. Numerous policies defined managerial duties, including the need to make employment, promotion, pay, and reduction-in-force decisions with valid, equitable criteria.

After the MDF reorganization, management continued to reassign workers from one cost center to another. At the same time, a "hiring frenzy" brought many new people into the company. One jaded informant surmised, tongue in cheek, that internal moves "kept two local moving companies in business." For a while, the pace of change was so hectic that human resources staff could not keep track of where everyone worked or who their supervisors were. The firm could not produce an accurate organization chart, and workers grew ever more frustrated over the instability. Notices of mysterious origin began to appear on company bulletin boards. The most poignant read,

> We trained hard . . . but it seemed that every time we were beginning to form into teams we would be reorganized. I was to learn later in life that we tend to meet any new situation by reorganizing; and a wonderful method it can be for creating the illusion of progress while producing confusion, inefficiency, and demoralization. (attributed to Petronius Arbiter, circa 200 B.C.)

The CEO was disliked intensely. Hodson (1988) found that "bad management" is a common problem in high-tech firms, but workers' idealization of the founder contributed to the operation of a "Rebecca Myth" syndrome[1] (Gouldner, 1954) for this CEO. To blue-collar workers, he was aloof, seldom setting foot in the plant. Others said he openly berated people for alleged incompetence and summarized his style as "management by intimidation." Due to his nontechnical background, they questioned his qualifications to run a high-tech firm. They also became irate when he bypassed internal candidates and filled management positions with (firm and industry) outsiders. It was said that hostility grew until everyone became "nasty." It was also widely rumored that everyone "had resumes out."

The CEO promoted a (false) impression of great company success. In truth, the most profitable venture of his tenure came not from the sales of technical systems but from the sale of human capital. A joint venture involving a number of firms had led to the creation of a new high-tech company that had need of the sort of technical expertise at Pendulum. The CEO negotiated a deal that resulted in more than two dozen employees being called to a meeting at which they were "asked" to quit their current jobs and accept offers from the new company. Some were elated and others were incensed; most felt that they had little choice but to comply. They "quit" in unison on a date mutually arranged by the two firms.

Only weeks later, Parent laid off the CEO and several other executives. Because the CEO had perpetuated an image of success, workers were stunned by the news. At first some cheered, but the mood soon turned to shock and panic as it became clear that the firm was in trouble. Massive layoffs ensued, and hundreds lost their jobs. Few workers received advance layoff notices; typically, they were told on a Monday morning and escorted off the premises by noon. The manufacturing sector was again hit the hardest. When the layoffs ended, craft workers accounted for only 15% of a much smaller regular workforce. Some engineers were also laid off, but their share of the regular workforce rose to more than 30%.

On top of these disruptions, the MDF was dismantled and Pendulum swung back to a functional form. This was the third major reorganization during the 8 years following the

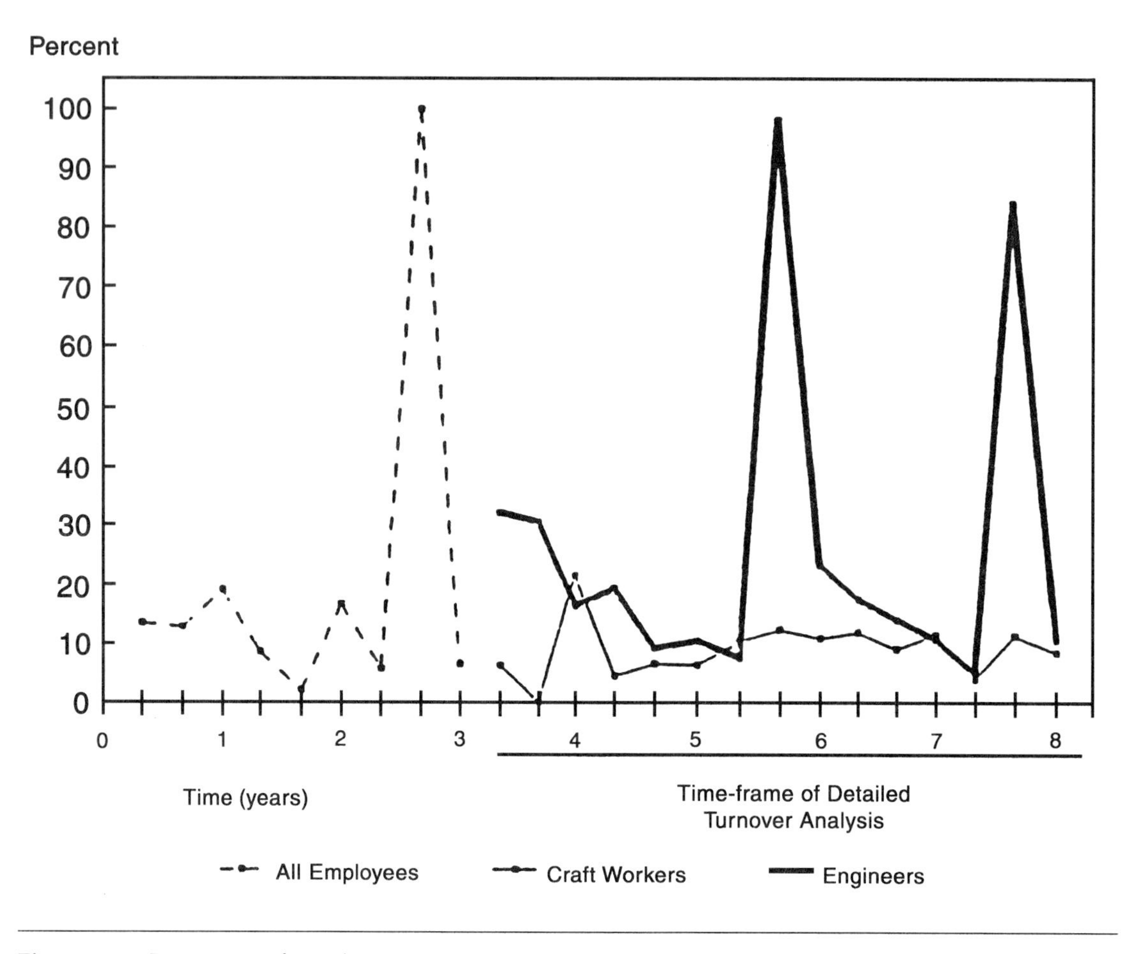

Figure 11.2. Percentage of Employees Assigned Different Cost Center Codes in Successive 4-Month Intervals Spanning 8 Years

merger with Parent. Figure 11.2 highlights these reorganizations by showing the percentage of workers (except new hires) whose cost center codes changed within successive 4-month intervals. The first peak follows the merger and shows when a new coding system went into effect. It exaggerates the upheaval because other changes were phased in gradually. The second peak signals the shift to the MDF and accurately portrays the percentage of technical and craft workers affected. The third spike shows the shift back to a functional design. Some MDF codes were reused, as 16% of engineers got the same cost center code again.

AGGREGATE-LEVEL EXITS OF CRAFT WORKERS AND ENGINEERS

Craft workers and engineers had much in common. Both were highly skilled, and their mean ages at hire (29 and 32 years, respectively) suggest that both brought considerable experience to the firm. Previous research (Schwalbe, 1986) and qualitative interviews support the premise that both had intrinsically satisfying jobs. But, especially for craft workers, Pendulum failed to deliver on the implied bureaucratic promise of employment stability. In the two downsizings, 53% of craft workers were laid off. Others have found that workers who feel in danger of losing their jobs have a higher propensity to quit (e.g., Halaby, 1986). Yet Pendulum's craft workers had the *lowest* 5-year quit rate (22%) in the company.

Like other companies that give preferential treatment to elite technical specialists (Glasmeier, 1986; Kunda, 1992; Thomas, 1994), Pendulum laid off "only" 11% of engineers, who nonetheless had the highest 5-year quit rate (46%) in the firm. Even if those who were asked to quit are classified as layoffs, engineers had the lowest layoff rate and the highest quit rate.

These apparent contradictions reflect disparities between the external labor markets of these two groups. Alternative opportunities are crucial to quit decisions (DiPrete, 1993; Hachen, 1990, 1992; Halaby, 1986; Hirschman, 1970; Price, 1977; Stolzenberg, 1988; Withey & Cooper, 1989). Based on Herbert Simon's theorizing on the link between individual quit decisions and layoff rates, Stolzenberg (1988, p. 112) stated that a firm's quit rate should be positively related to its layoff rate but negatively related to economy or industry rates. DiPrete's findings are consistent with these predictions.

Craft workers had few alternatives. Based on *state* figures (Bureau of Labor Statistics, 1989, table 87), manufacturing employment declined in 3 of the 5 years under study; the 5-year net gain was only 3%. Pendulum craft workers who thought they could find other work doubted that they could match their current jobs for creativity, autonomy, and the chance to work with cutting-edge technology. These workers were viewed as the most "loyal" employees, especially when the firm was in trouble, but the notion of loyalty implies the availability of a substitute (Hirschman, 1970). Therefore, what passed for loyalty may have been closer to "neglect," which Withey and Cooper (1989) defined as "less like . . . support of [the] organization than like resignation and entrapment" (p. 536).

By contrast, engineers were often wooed by headhunters and not seen as particularly loyal to the firm. Reportedly, their only major exit barrier was that a job change might require moving to another state. National figures for electrical and electronic engineers[2] show strong employment growth for the first 4 years of this period and a leveling off in the fifth year (Bureau of Labor Statistics, 1983, table 17; 1989, table 18). The net gain was 45%.

Risk and opportunity are not independent, as firms may take account of labor market conditions when making layoff decisions (Stolzenberg, 1988). Those that can expect high numbers of quits can plan for fewer layoffs and vice versa. Because retrenchments coincided with statewide declines in manufacturing jobs, Pendulum should have expected few quits by craft workers. Thus their limited exit options increased their vulnerability to layoff.

But the picture is more complex than this because laid-off workers received generous severance pay. It would be irrational to quit in the face of poor alternatives and/or a high risk of layoff. This point was made by one worker who, after 16 years, decided he could no longer cope with the chaos. In an exit interview, he confessed he had "hoped" to be laid off and use the severance pay to start a business. When the chance of layoff passed, he quit, noting, "I'm not sure this move is better for my career, but it is better for my life."

Figure 11.3 shows aggregate layoff and quit rates for craft workers. In the first year, the risk of layoff was high but the external sector was weak and remained so during the recovery in the second year. Not surprisingly, the quit rate was very low both years. In the third year and first part of the fourth year, internal opportunities grew, but so did the external market and the quit rate rose correspondingly. When the external sector softened again, the firm was in another decline and quitting fell off to nearly zero.

There was little need to resort to large-scale layoffs of engineers due to their abundant alternatives and higher propensity to quit. As Figure 11.4 shows, quit rates dropped in two retrenchment intervals, but overall there is little correspondence between layoff rates and quit rates. Quits and alternatives both rose over the first 4 years, but quits kept on climbing in the fifth

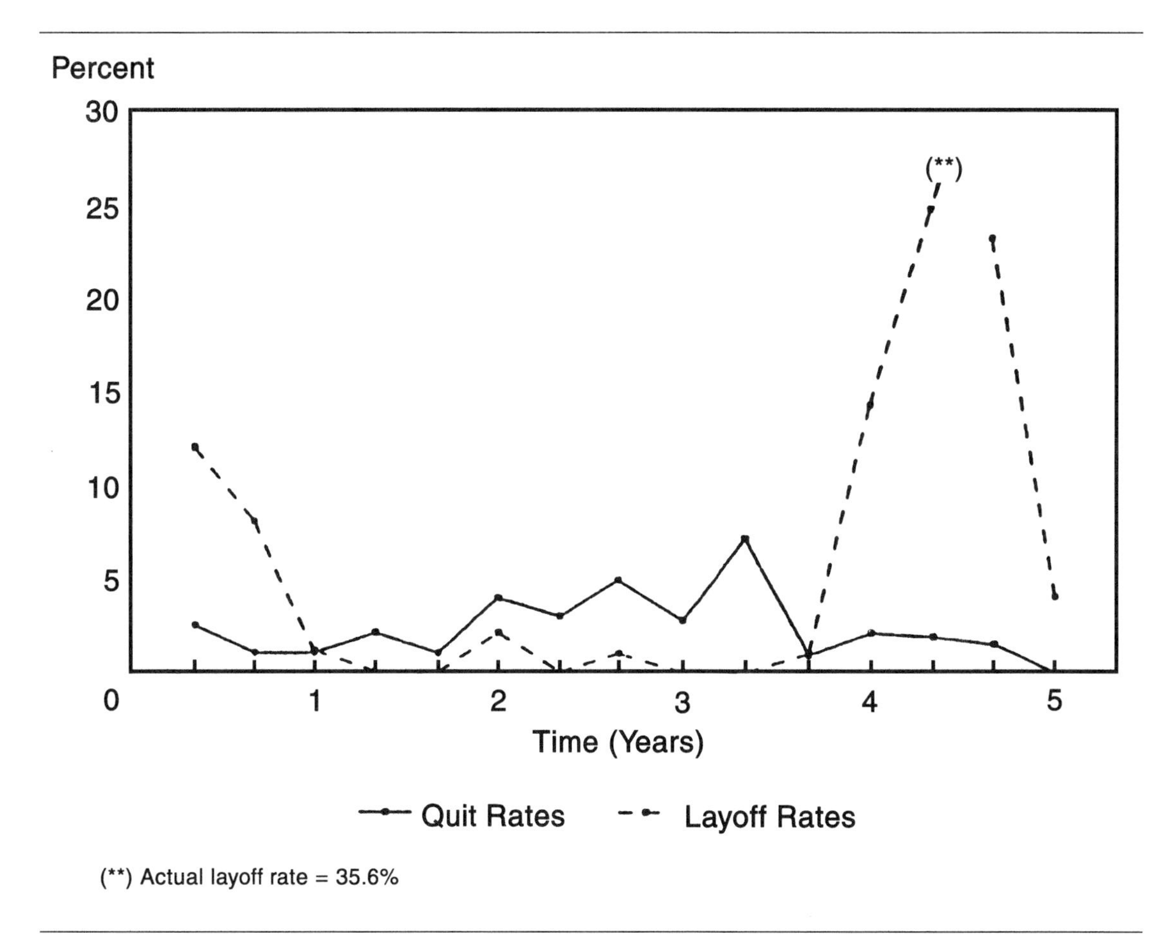

Figure 11.3. Four-Month Quit Rates and Layoff Rates for Craft Workers

year, when the firm was in decline and external job growth was negligible.

Although the availability of alternatives helps to explain why engineers had higher quit rates than those of craft workers, it does not account for why engineers pursued other options. We know, however, that workers' decisions are shaped by factors operating at several levels of analysis (Baron & Bielby, 1980). In the remainder of the article, I examine the impact of organizational, role, and individual factors in engineers' decisions to quit. Craft workers are excluded here due to the constraints on their leaving and because they were largely untouched by the structural reorganizations that are of special theoretical interest here.

MULTIVARIATE ANALYSES

The data set contains all regular, full-time, male, nonmanagement, head office engineers on the payroll during the 5 years under consideration. Females and branch office workers are excluded because of small numbers; earlier time periods are excluded because occupational data are unavailable. This leaves a sample of 283, although the number at any given time ranged from 135 to slightly over 200.

All but two variables—travel demands and local ties—in the model are time-varying covariates. To take account of this variation, and given the discrete nature of the data, "discrete-time hazard rate" (event history) models were

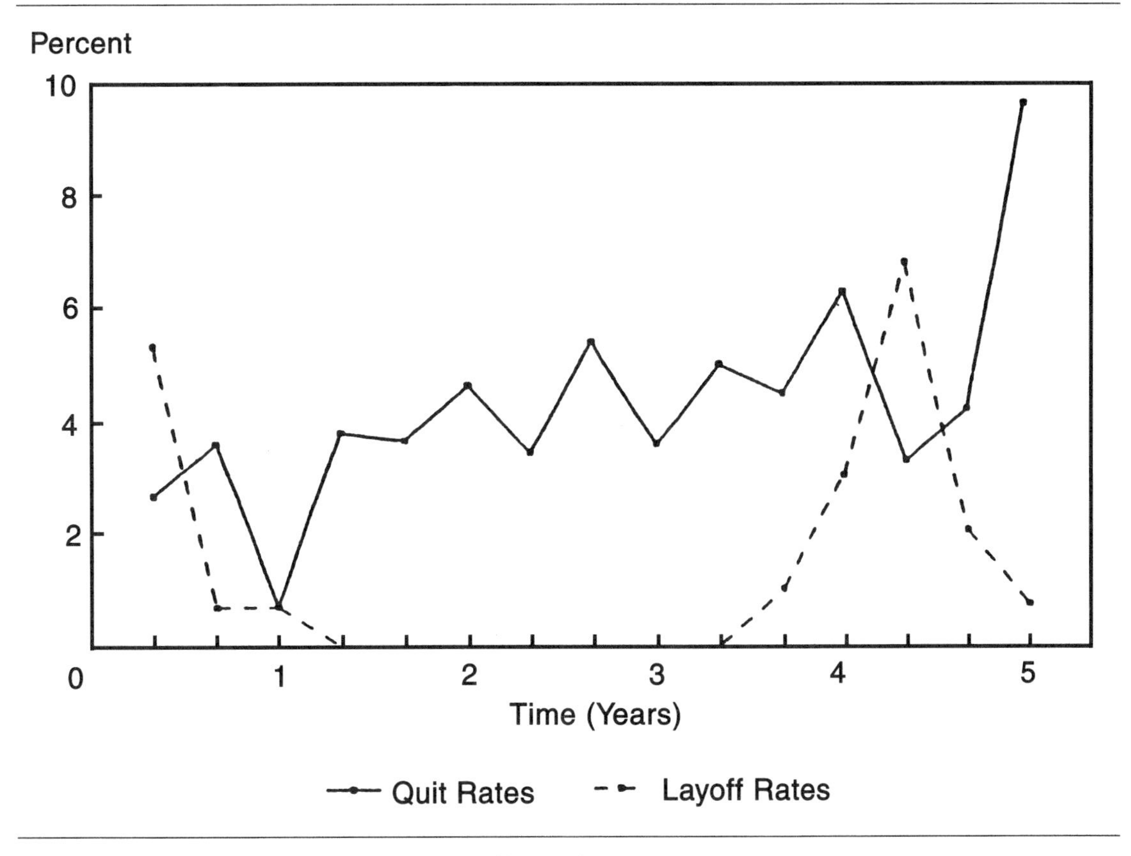

Figure 11.4. Four-Month Quit Rates and Layoff Rates for Engineers
NOTE: Engineers who were asked to quit are not included. If they were coded as voluntary exits, the quit rate at the Year 4 interval would be 17%. If they were coded as involuntary exits, the layoff rate for this interval would be 14%.

constructed (see Allison, 1984; Yamaguchi, 1991). Workers were observed on each variable at 15 4-month intervals. A separate observation unit was created for each interval that a worker was on the payroll. Observations were then pooled, creating 2,506 person-time units. The SPSS logistic regression program was used to estimate the effects of the covariates on the dependent variable. (Logistic regression converts a 0,1 dependent variable to a log-odds ratio, which is transformed to a hazard rate when applied to person-time data.)

The Dependent Variable

The dependent variable is simply whether or not the worker quit. For each time unit, all quits were coded 1 and dropped from the sample. Those who were laid off in the interval were "right censored" and dropped at that point. Those who stayed were coded 0 and, along with new hires, formed the risk set of the following interval.

Operationalizing this variable was problematic because it was not clear whether all quits were voluntary or that all layoffs were involuntary. In the last downsizing, a small number of workers were allowed to "volunteer" for layoff, but few (if any) engineers were affected. The more than 20 engineers who were asked to quit pose a greater concern. Their leaving involved a clear element of coercion, although technically they could have refused (but very few did so).

From Pendulum's perspective, it would have made sense to ask the most expendable workers to resign. Presumably, these individuals would have been layoff candidates in the retrenchment that followed. Besides the monetary payment it received from the "buyer" firm, Pendulum would have avoided the unpleasantness and severance expenses associated with laying them off. However, as the CEO was later taken by surprise himself, it appears there was no sign of a pending layoff. Also, the buyer firm had a say in who was selected, and it wanted some of the same workers Pendulum wanted to keep.

Again, from Pendulum's perspective, it would also have made sense to select those most likely to quit. If "everyone had resumes out," it must have been easy to identify the disaffected. Informants claimed that many of those who were asked were on the job market or thinking about looking elsewhere. It would have been shrewd of Pendulum to get paid for sacrificing workers who wanted to leave anyhow. To reiterate, it would have been logical to ask those at high risk of layoff and/or likely to quit on their own.

A notation in personnel files made it easy to identify these workers and compare them to others on the payroll about the time the transfer occurred. Mean tenure was longer (4.3 years) for those who were asked compared to that for voluntary quitters (3.1 years) but was not as long as mean tenure for those who stayed (5.0 years) or who were laid off (5.7 years). Mean ages (in years) were 33.2 (quits), 36.1 (asked), 36.9 (stayers), and 39.1 (layoffs). In sum, those who were asked to quit were more like quitters than layoffs on tenure and were between quitters and layoffs in age. Because these findings offer weak justification for classifying them one way or the other, separate analyses were conducted with them coded as quits and as layoffs.

Independent Variables: Measurement and Hypotheses

LaFarge (1994) found that, like layoff victims, workers who quit their jobs can feel "pushed out" by organizational circumstances. Most (20 of 31) of the quitters she studied were engineers exiting a high-tech firm despite being asked to stay. My central question is whether Pendulum's engineers were pushed out by the instability associated with structural reorganizations. I define a reorganization as a change in a worker's cost center code from one interval to the next.[3]

Recall that cost centers were, in principle, the *stable* dimension of the dual matrix/cost center structure. They were also an important dimension of the ILM structure, and the kinds of promises suggested by little career path charts attached to job descriptions implicitly assume that structure is fixed. Yet, looking at the last 5 years in Figure 11.2, between 5% and 100% of engineers got new cost center codes in each 4-month interval.

In the eight intervals leading up to the MDF reorganization, 18% of engineers had three or more code changes. In the 15 intervals spanning the 5 years in total, 61% had three or more changes and a handful had six. (By contrast, 22% of craft workers had two or more changes and no one had two until the last downsizing.) Comparing those who were asked to quit to other engineers on the payroll around the same time (and with at least 2 years tenure) reveals that those who were ultimately laid off and stayers had slightly more than two cost center code changes on average; both types of quitters averaged close to three changes.

REORGANIZATION VARIABLES

Briody et al. (1995) found that a reorganization created uncertainty and concern over career paths; when promises were not kept, concern was transformed into disbelief. It is not known how much any one cost center change altered a career path at Pendulum. No doubt some changes had trivial impacts, whereas others demanded major adjustments. But each is presumed to represent a "potentially" unkept (implied) promise (and disruption of social ties). Therefore, my central hypothesis is that *engineers grew more likely to quit as the number of cost center changes mounted.* The *cumulative changes* variable was measured as the total number of cost center code changes that the individual worker experienced prior to each observation of the dependent variable. For those who joined the firm prior to the start of the study, the count begins at the third year in Figure 11.2 (i.e., the variable is left censored).

Two other reorganization covariates are included in the model. The first tests whether a single *recent cost center change* affected the likelihood of quitting. A single change may seem relatively minor, but changes were often unexpected and may have created a need to establish one's place in a new work group. Both factors suggest the hypothesis that *a recent cost center code change increased the likelihood of quitting.* The variable was measured simply as whether the individual was assigned a new cost center code in the interval prior to the current interval (1 = yes).

Davis and Lawrence (1977, p. 18) suggested that the ability to cope with change depends on the magnitude of the disruption it causes. They argued that workers can deal with frequent doses of change so long as it is not the kind of "rare eruption" that causes severe dislocation in the organization. I assume that dislocation is more severe when many persons are affected by a reorganization than it is when few are affected, and I measure *organizational disruption* as the percentage of all engineers who had cost center code changes in the interval prior to the observation of the dependent variable. Values range from 5% to 100%, as shown in the last 5 years in Figure 11.2. The hypothesis is that *the higher the organizational disruption, the higher the likelihood of quitting.*[4]

INTERNAL OPPORTUNITIES AND INCENTIVES

Five covariates tap the effectiveness of internal incentives to stay with the firm. The first is the *demand for engineers* (which mirrored the size of the firm as a whole). It has often been hypothesized that commitment is positively related to firm size. Price's (1977) and Stolzenberg's (1988) reviews of the literature showed that tests of the hypothesis have led to weak, inconsistent findings. Stolzenberg pointed out, however, that, as a proxy for opportunities, growth is probably more important than size per se (also see DiPrete, 1993; Finlay, 1988; Rosenbaum, 1984). Therefore, I hypothesize that *the higher the internal demand (in terms of growth), the lower the likelihood of quitting* (and its converse).

Demand was constructed as the percentage change in the number of engineers over the two intervals (t-2 to t-1) prior to the observation interval (t). Values are relative to a base of 100 to eliminate negative numbers and range from 80 to 118.

The second "incentive" is the *MDF phase* (1 = yes). Whereas previous research has found support for the bureaucratic alienation hypothesis (Lincoln & Kalleberg, 1985, 1990), the bureaucratic/corporatist model suggests that commitment should have been highest when Pendulum was in the MDF phase. The elaborate career structure and added layers of hierarchy, along with high growth in the initial intervals of this phase, should have created a sense of security and high mobility opportunity. And, consistent with the notion of bureaucratic authority and legitimacy (Halaby, 1986, Lincoln & Kalleberg, 1985, 1990; Stolzenberg, 1988; Wallace, 1995), numerous policies and procedures mandated fairness in hiring and promotion. Finally, the CEO issued a stream of (false) messages "confirming" strong company performance over this period. For these reasons, the obvious hypothesis is that engineers were less likely to quit during the MDF.

The qualitative evidence offers little reason to think that this hypothesis will be supported. As Althauser (1989) noted, ILMs (and presumably other bureaucratic incentives) sometimes fail to operate as designed. Pendulum did not operate like a bureaucracy. It was beset with upheaval, career ladders kept shifting, promotion policies were violated, conflict intensified, and the culture got increasingly nasty. As the period progressed, commitment should have been further eroded by the CEO's management-by-intimidation (authoritarian) style (Price, 1977) and growing lack of personal legitimacy as a leader (Halaby, 1986). All things considered, it is quite plausible that engineers were more likely to quit during the MDF.

Technically, the MDF phase spilled over to the last downsizing, but the variable stops short of the retrenchment. It includes the five intervals from the initial reorganization through to the interval when the CEO asked for the special resignations.

The third incentive is the *Hay grade,* which is a proxy for status and degree of job autonomy. Despite debates over PFA's validity, grades are presumed to offer a reasonable indication of the relatve importance of *know-how* (formal knowledge and skill), *problem solving,* and *accountability* within the occupation. Know-how was the biggest component of all jobs, but with each step from the lowest (1) to the highest (4) engineering grade, the weight of problem solving and accountability increased relative to that of know-how. And although they were not managers, higher grade engineers often coordinated or supervised the work of others.

Work and labor market scholars tend to take it as a given that higher grade jobs are better jobs. Status and autonomy are "rewards" that should lower the probability of worker-initiated exits (Hachen, 1990, p. 324). Status is also a "resource" in that it gives holders greater "voice," thus offering an alternative to exit (Hirschman, 1970). Lincoln and Kalleberg (1985, 1990) found that commitment was positively related to higher job complexity (skill, knowledge, and freedom) and managerial/supervisory status (also see Hachen, 1990, 1992). These findings suggest that *engineers in higher grades were less likely to quit.*

On the other hand, the CEO reputedly reacted with unveiled contempt toward those who disagreed with him. If the cost of exercising voice is high, workers are more likely to exit instead (Withey & Cooper, 1989). Also, Halaby and Weakliem (1989) found that workers in high-autonomy jobs were less attached to their employers and speculated that stress and uncertainty associated with autonomy weaken attachment. These factors suggest the alternative hypothesis that *a higher grade raised the propensity of quitting.*

The fourth incentive is whether the employee had a *recent promotion* (i.e., within two intervals prior to the observation period and coded as 1 = yes). Similar to Rosenbaum's (1984) findings, most of these engineers were not promoted, as 26% of engineers (compared to 13% of craft workers) advanced one grade level in 5 years and a few advanced twice. Low mobility may be less important than whether workers believe that they can advance (Finlay, 1988; Lincoln & Kalleberg, 1985, 1990; Wallace, 1995) or that promotions are granted on fair criteria (Halaby, 1986; Wallace, 1995). Both beliefs may have been undermined when the firm filled executive positions with outsiders. In the nonmanagerial ranks, only 22% of engineering hires entered at the lowest grade, whereas 34% started in the top two levels.

If Halaby and Weakliem (1989) are right, a promotion might amplify uncertainty and stress and thus raise the likelihood of quitting. However, a promotion affirms good performance and should boost confidence—at least initially. Because the variable is limited to promotions occurring within the previous two intervals, I assume that negative effects would not have had time to solidify in workers' minds. I also assume that promoted workers have higher perceptions of fairness and legitimacy than do workers who are not promoted, and I hypothesize that *recently promoted workers were less likely to quit.*

The last incentive is *relative pay.* Mueller, Boyer, Price, and Iverson (1994) argued that higher pay is important for its own sake and because it legitimates the authority structure. They claimed that pay is a "key variable" in driving turnover decisions of "economically rational beings" (p. 187). Empirically, the evidence on whether higher pay reduces quitting has been mixed. In a particularly relevant study, Zenger (1992) found that, among high-tech engineers, turnover intentions were lower for high performers who were "well paid" and for poor performers who were "overpaid" (also see Hodson, 1988, p. 267). Although it is not possible to control for performance, I nevertheless hypothesize that *the higher the pay, the lower the likelihood of quitting.* (Pay is a *z* score based on mean hourly pay, controlling for grade and interval, plus a constant to eliminate negative numbers. This formulation is not highly correlated with the Hay grade and allows both variables to be in the model together.)

TRAVEL DEMANDS

In any interval, between 57% and 65% of engineers were in jobs demanding frequent, extensive, often unscheduled, stressful travel. Because travelers spend less time on company premises, this alone could weaken identity with the firm. Perhaps more importantly, it would be harder for those away much of the time to develop strong ties with coworkers. Also, it has often been hypothesized that there is a positive relationship between commitment and social ties outside the workplace (Angle & Perry, 1983; Lincoln & Kalleberg, 1985, 1990; Mueller et al., 1994; Wallace, 1995). Logically, the converse should also apply. Workplace demands that threaten to injure external relationships should weaken commitment to the employer. Finally, travel could increase turnover by raising these boundary spanners' visibility to other firms and providing opportunities to scan the wider job market. Therefore, I hypothesize that *those in high-travel roles were more likely to quit.* (Travel was measured at the level of the role. It is based on the judgment of a human resources specialist who gave each job title an ordinal rating between 1 and 9. Engineering roles tended to cluster around high and low values, and the variable was dummy coded with 1 = high.)

CONTROLS

Tenure and *age* are resources that raise employees' value to current employers (Hachen, 1990) and are proxies for "side bets" that drive up the costs of exit (Becker, 1960). The effects of both variables are conditioned by a worker's age when hired (Krecker, 1994); therefore, I use age at hire (in years) as my measure of age. Tenure is measured as the number of days between the hire date and payroll date divided by 365.25. The hypotheses are that *the longer the tenure or the older the age when hired, the lower the likelihood of quitting.*

Dependents (as claimed for income tax purposes) and *local ties* (a social security number issued in the current state of residence or in a state a few hours' drive away; 1 = yes) also represent side bets limiting mobility options. Previous research using similar controls has produced mixed results (e.g., Angle & Perry, 1983; Mueller et al., 1994; Wallace, 1995), but most findings are consistent with the hypotheses that *higher numbers of dependents and local ties lower the likelihood of quitting.*

External opportunities is included on the theoretical grounds and previous research already discussed. I hypothesize that *the higher the growth in alternative opportunities, the higher the likelihood of quitting.* The variable is measured as the national yearly growth (in thousands) in employed civilian electrical and electronic engineers (Bureau of Labor Statistics, 1983, table 17; 1989, table 18). Values range from 6 to 53.

The last control is whether the worker was *asked to quit* (1 = yes). No hypothesis is offered because it is self-evident that workers are more likely to quit if they are asked to do so.

ANALYSIS AND FINDINGS

Two main equations (and several variants of each[5] were estimated. All equations yielded more or less the same substantive results, as reported in Table 11.1.

The central hypothesis is strongly supported. As shown in both models in Table 11.1, the *cumulative cost center changes* variable has a positive, significant impact on quitting, net of other factors. This is the only significant reorganization variable. Contrary to Davis and Lawrence's (1977) argument, the persistence of instability rather than the magnitude of disruption strained these workers' abilities to cope. The negative, although nonsignificant, sign suggests little difficulty in coping with any single cost center change. It seems clear that as the number of cost center changes mounted, ability

TABLE 11.1 Effects of Covariates on Engineers' Quitting (discrete-time hazard rates: $N = 283$; person-time units = 2,506)

		Model 1[a]		*Model 2*[b]	
Covariate	*Hypothesis*	*b*	*Wald*	*b*	*Wald*
Individual cumulative cost center changes (0 to 5+)	Positive	0.256	6.761***	0.213	4.735**
Recent change in individual cost center code (1 = yes)	Positive	–0.430	2.242	–0.456	2.132
Overall organizational disruption (5 to 100)	Positive	0.003	0.412	0.003	0.550
Demand for engineers in firm (percentage change + constant)[c]	Negative	–0.041	4.760**		
Firm in multidivisional form phase (1 = yes)	Negative[d]	0.120	0.381	0.176	0.718
Hay grade (low = 1, high = 4)	Negative[d]	–0.146	1.187	–0.123	0.740
Recent promotion (1 = yes)	Negative	–0.803	2.290	–0.742	1.947
Relative pay (within Hay grade; *z* score + constant)	Negative	–0.229	5.672**	–0.249	5.362**
Role entails high travel demands (1 = yes)	Positive	0.375	3.238*	0.398	3.079*
Tenure	Negative	–0.075	4.454**	–0.112	7.378***
Age at hire (years)	Negative	–0.017	1.215	–0.022	1.723
Dependents (0 to 20+)	Negative	0.015	0.408	0.021	0.679
Local ties (1 = yes)	Negative	–0.298	2.375	–0.336	2.574
External opportunities (annual growth in thousands)[c]	Positive	0.016	1.729		
Asked to quit (1 = yes)		0.740	7.612***	–6.362	0.818
Constant		2.150	1.579	–0.928	1.573
Model chi-square (Model 1 $df = 15$, Model 2 $df = 13$)			60.554†		51.504†

a. In Model 1, workers who were asked to quit are treated as voluntary exits.
b. In Model 2, workers who were asked to quit are treated as involuntary exits.
c. Covariates were dropped from Model 2 ($p \geq .850$); this had no effect on values of other covariates or total chi-square of the model.
d. Based on the particulars of this case, there are strong grounds for believing that opposing hypotheses may be supported.
*$p \leq .10$ (two-tailed); $p \leq .05$ (one-tailed); **$p \leq .05$ (two-tailed); ***$p \leq .01$ (two-tailed); †$p \leq .0001$ (two-tailed).

or willingness to cope dissipated. These findings hold up whether one, two, or all three reorganization variables are entered into the equation.

Turning to other variables, the two models yielded inconsistent results for internal demand and external opportunities. In Model 1, the quit rate is negatively related to demand and positively related to opportunities, as hypothesized, but only demand is significant. In Model 2, where workers who were asked to quit are coded as layoffs, the coefficients of both covariates are close to zero (p .85). Removing them from the model has virtually no effect on the values of other covariates.

In both models, the findings for these variables are potentially confounded by the artificial exit *timing* of those who were asked to resign. Because they "quit" after the company stopped growing and before the external market softened, their impact on the quit rate for that interval (17%) makes it look like exits soared when internal demand weakened and then waned in sync with external opportunities (in Model 1). Treating them as layoffs (in Model 2) poses different problems. At least *some* of them would have quit anyhow, perhaps in the same interval but more likely in a later interval when the firm was cutting jobs. More exits here would be consistent with the hypothesis of a negative relationship between quits and internal demand but would contradict the hypothesis for external opportunities. These factors make it impossible to come to a conclusion about either covariate.

The coefficients of other variables are similar in both models, making interpretation more straightforward. Three other hypotheses are supported. Higher pay and longer tenure reduce the likelihood of quitting; being in a high-travel job increases it. A recent promotion, age at hire, and local ties all are in the hypothesized negative direction but do not achieve significance. However, the Wald for local ties (Model 2) is right at the edge of significance at $p \leq .05$ for a one-tailed test, suggesting weak support for the hypothesis. (The Wald is a measure of the statistical significance of each independent variable. It is similar to the likelihood ratio statistic and has the same interpretation [see Menard, 1995, pp. 38-43].)

The MDF, Hay grade, and dependents are very weak and nonsignificant. In every equation, the MDF is positive; it is never significant but is stronger when reorganization variables are omitted. If these findings do not let us conclude that bureaucracy raised the propensity to quit, they leave little doubt that it failed to raise commitment. And because the Hay system was part of Pendulum's bureaucratic incentives package, it is not surprising that promotions and grade are not significant. Finally, workers with obligations toward others should prefer a secure, stable employer. Thus it also seems fitting that dependents failed to keep engineers from quitting or even that the sign is positive.

CONCLUSIONS

Pendulum workers wanted fairness, stability, and predictability. Perhaps they believed that their pleas for order, logical career ladders, and equitable promotion policies would be met with the bureaucratic incentives implemented by Parent and the CEO. As the evidence mounted that Pendulum was unlikely to deliver on those incentives, however, the propensity to quit rose. Craft workers' highest quit rates occurred during the bureaucratic MDF phase despite a low threat of layoff and growing internal opportunities during this period. In one MDF interval, their quit rate even exceeded that of engineers. And, judging by the lack of significance, even promotions failed to persuade engineers that the ILMs or other bureaucratic incentives were operating as designed.

Like all case studies, this study has inherent limitations. It should hardly be assumed that these findings can be generalized to both sexes or to other occupational groups, organization types, or industries. However, Pendulum is far from unique in terms of failing to achieve stability or deliver on the benefits of ILMs or other implied bureaucratic promises. Workers in many other firms and industries have undoubtedly felt threatened and frustrated by the kinds of repeated restructurings these craft workers and engineers experienced. It would seem, therefore, that their responses may have relevance well beyond this case. At the very least, they underscore the need to forsake a static image of organizations and examine the implications of instability for workers, the workplace, and labor market processes.

Collectively, these findings raise a number of questions that might be addressed in future research. First, the dilemmas of instability and restructuring involve more than downsizing. The finding that engineers' propensity to quit rose with the number of cost center changes points to the conclusion that instability undermines trust independent of whether or not job security is threatened. And although concerns over layoffs are important, some firms do expand again after episodes of contraction. It would be valuable to know what kinds of change might be viewed as beneficial and to probe more deeply into threatening dimensions of change. Another line of questioning might explore how workers react to threat when leaving is not an option. For those who have alternatives, it would be interesting to know not only how instability affects workers' decisions to quit but *where they go.* More to the point, do they seek out employers who offer more believable claims about employment security or advancement opportunities? If yes, then how can volatile firms that depend on long-term commitments attract and retain qualified employees? Will they do worse if they fail to offer ILMs and other bureaucratic incentives or if they purport to offer them but then fail to deliver?

Postscript

In the aftermath of the turmoil and turnover highlighted here, Pendulum explicitly proclaimed a long-range goal to "create a working environment [that will] attract and *retain* the most qualified people in the industry" (internal communication; emphasis added). At the same time, human resources personnel traded the label of "permanent" in favor of "regular" employees so as to avoid implying false promises. They also acquired self-help materials including a popular audiotape on the subject of "coping with chaos" to help workers deal with unplanned change. The CEO's successor was somewhat more successful in subduing the level and pace of change. Although the effects of these reforms on quitting are unknown, some employees who left during more stressful times came back.

NOTES

1. "Rebecca" was the deceased wife of a widower in a Daphne DuMaurier novel of the same name. Her memory was overly idealized by some of the widower's associates, thus creating a sense of inferiority regarding the widower's second wife.

2. The national number of "electrical and electronic engineers" is a proxy for all technical jobs. Data for other specialties are unavailable. The most important missing specialty is "software" engineering, but Bureau of Labor Statistics (1989, table 18) figures for computer specialists show patterns of employment growth similar to those of electrical and electronic engineers. Therefore, this category is presumed to represent "technical workers" fairly well.

3. If anything, cost center changes understate the instability workers faced because many events such as project turnovers, changes in supervisors, or moving to different offices when the firm grew or shrank would not necessarily be captured by cost center changes.

4. Zero-order correlations for the reorganization variables range from .25 to .62. Although such values are acceptable in standard regression analyses, multiple measures of a concept can weaken effects of individual variables (Gordon, 1968). To test for collinearity effects, multivariate models were estimated with each reorganization variable alone, in combinations of two, and with all three together. The coefficients and signs for these variables and other variables in the model were quite stable, suggesting the absence of collinearity effects.

5. In two equations, the dummy variable identifying those who asked to quit was omitted. In another, these cases were eliminated from the sample. Reorganization variables were deleted in some equations, and others used alternative measures of external opportunities. The results of these additional analyses do not differ substantively from those presented in Table 11.1.

REFERENCES

Allison, P. D. (1984). *Event history analysis: Regression for longitudinal event data* (Sage University Press series on Quantitative Applications in the Social Sciences, Series No. 07-046). Beverly Hills, CA: Sage.

Althauser, R. (1989). Internal labor markets. *Annual Review of Sociology, 15,* 143-161.

Angle, H. L., & Perry, J. L. (1983). Organizational commitment: Individual and organizational influences. *Work and Occupations, 10,* 123-146.

Baron, J. N., & Bielby, W. T. (1980). Bringing the firm back in: Stratification, segmentation, and the organization of work. *American Sociological Review, 45,* 737-765.

Becker, H. S. (1960). Notes on the concept of commitment. *American Journal of Sociology, 66,* 32-40.

Bellak, A. O. (1984). *The Hay guide chart-profile method of job evaluation.* Philadelphia: Hay Group.

Briody, E. K., Baba, M. L., & Cooper L. (1995). A tale of two career paths: The process of status acquisition by a new organizational unit. *Work and Occupations, 22,* 301-327.

Bureau of Labor Statistics, U.S. Department of Labor. (1983). *Handbook of labor statistics.* Washington, DC: Government Printing Office.

Bureau of Labor Statistics, U.S. Department of Labor. (1989). *Handbook of labor statistics.* Washington, DC: Government Printing Office.

Davis, S. M., & Lawrence, P. R. (1977). *Matrix.* Reading, MA: Addison-Wesley.

Delbecq, A. L., & Weiss, J. (1988). The business culture of Silicon Valley: Is it a model for the future? In G. Hage (Ed.), *Futures of organizations: Innovating to adapt strategy and human resources to rapid technological change* (pp. 123-141). Lexington, MA: Lexington Books.

DiMaggio, P. J., & Powell, W. W. (1983). The iron cage revisited: Institutional isomorphism and collective rationality in organizational fields. *American Sociological Review, 48,* 147-160.

DiPrete, T. A. (1993). Industrial restructuring and the mobility response of American workers in the 1980s. *American Sociological Review, 58,* 74-96.

Finlay, W. (1988). Commitment and the company: Worker-manager relations in the absence of internal labor markets. *Research in Social Stratification and Mobility, 7,* 163-177.

Glasmeier, A. K. (1986). High-tech industries and the regional division of labor. *Industrial Relations, 25,* 197-211.

Gomez-Mejia, L., & Balkin, D. B. (1985, December). Managing a high-tech venture. *Personnel,* pp. 31-36.

Gomez-Mejia, L., Balkin, D. B., & Welbourne, T. M. (1990). Influence of venture-capitalists on high-tech management. *High-Technology Management Research, 1,* 103-118.

Gordon, R. A. (1968). Issues in multiple regression. *American Journal of Sociology, 73,* 592-616.

Gouldner, A. W. (1954). *Patterns of industrial bureaucracy.* Glencoe, IL: Free Press.

Hachen, D. S., Jr. (1990). Three models of job mobility in labor markets. *Work and Occupations, 17,* 320-354.

Hachen, D. S., Jr. (1992). Industrial characteristics and job mobility rates. *American Sociological Review, 57,* 39-55.

Halaby, C. N. (1986). Worker attachments and workplace authority. *American Sociological Review, 51,* 634-649.

Halaby, C. N., & Weakliem, D. L. (1989). Worker control and attachment to the firm. *American Journal of Sociology, 95,* 549-591.

Heydebrand, W. V. (1989). New organizational forms. *Work and Occupations, 16,* 323-357.

Hirsch, P. M. (1993). Undoing the managerial revolution? Needed research on the decline of middle management and internal labor markets. In R. Swedberg (Ed.), *Explorations in economic sociology* (pp. 145-157). New York: Russell Sage.

Hirschman, A. O. (1970). *Exit, voice and loyalty: Responses to decline in firms, organizations and states.* Cambridge, MA: Harvard University Press.

Hodson, R. (1988). Good jobs and bad management: How new problems evoke old solutions in high-tech settings. In G. Farkas & P. England (Eds.), *Industries, firms, and jobs* (pp. 247-279). New York: Plenum.

Kaufman, R. L., Parcel, T. L., Wallace, M., & Form, W. (1988). Looking forward: Responses to organizational and technological change in an ultra-high-technology firm. *Research in the Sociology of Work, 4,* 31-67.

Krecker, M. L. (1994). Work careers and organizational careers: The effects of age and tenure on worker attachment to the employer relationship. *Work and Occupations, 21,* 251-283.

Kunda, G. (1992). *Engineering culture: Control and commitment in a high-tech corporation.* Philadelphia: Temple University Press.

LaFarge, V. (1994). The ambivalence of departing employees: Reactions of voluntary and involuntary exiters. *Journal of Applied Behavioral Science, 30,* 175-197.

Lawler, E. (1987, January). What's wrong with point-factor evaluation. *Personnel,* pp. 38-44.

Lincoln, J., & Kalleberg, A. (1985). Work organization and workforce commitment: A study of plants and employees in the U.S. and Japan. *American Sociological Review, 50,* 738-760.

Lincoln, J., & Kalleberg, A. (1990). *Culture, control and commitment: A study of work organizations and work attitudes in the United States and Japan.* Cambridge, UK: Cambridge University Press.

Menard, S. (1995). *Applied logistic regression analysis* (Sage University Paper series on Quantitative Applications in the Social Sciences, Series No. 07-106). Thousand Oaks, CA: Sage.

Mueller, C. W., Boyer, E. M., Price, J. L., & Iverson, R. D. (1994). Employee attachment and noncoercive conditions of work: The case of dental hygienists. *Work and Occupations, 21,* 179-212.

Perrow, C. (1970). *Organizational analysis: A sociological view.* Belmont, CA: Wadsworth.

Price, J. L. (1977). *The study of turnover.* Ames: Iowa State University Press.

Rosenbaum, J. E. (1984). *Career mobility in a corporate hierarchy.* New York: Academic Press.

Schwalbe, M. L. (1986). *The psycho-social consequences of natural and alienated labor.* Albany: State University of New York Press.

Sorenson, A. B. (1983). Sociological research on the labor market: Conceptual and methodological issues. *Work and Occupations, 10,* 261-287.

Stolzenberg, R. M. (1988). Job quits in theoretical and empirical perspective. *Research in Stratification and Mobility, 7,* 99-131.

Thomas, R. J. (1994). *What machines can't do: Politics and technology in the industrial enterprise.* Berkeley: University of California Press.

Wallace, J. E. (1995). Corporatist control and organizational commitment among professionals. *Social Forces, 73,* 811-839.

Wallace, M. (1989). Brave new workplace: Technology and work in the new economy. *Work and Occupations, 16,* 363-392.

Withey, M., & Cooper, W. H. (1989). Predicting exit, voice, loyalty, and neglect. *Administrative Science Quarterly, 34,* 521-539.

Yamaguchi, K. (1991). *Event history analysis.* Newbury Park, CA: Sage.

Zenger, T. R. (1992). Why do employers only reward extreme performance? Examining the relationship among performance, pay, and turnover. *Administrative Science Quarterly, 37,* 198-219.

12

Just a Temp

Experience and Structure of Alienation in Temporary Clerical Employment

JACKIE KRASAS ROGERS

Both sociologists and management theorists seem to agree that the world of work is changing in the United States. Whether that world is changing for better or for worse is up for debate. One way in which the work world is changing is through increasing "flexibilization" of labor. Flexible strategies run the gamut from increasing the range of workers' skills, to rotating jobs, to decreasing employer obligation through the use of temporary and contract workers. Joan Acker (1992) cautions that changes in the organization of work often result in a polarization of skill, security, and autonomy and that this polarization is inflected by race, class, and gender.

This study looks at the ways in which workers experience temporary employment, one of several strategies employers use to increase their flexibility. So on one level, this is an ethnographic account of the daily struggles of temporary workers; however, it also analyzes the social organization of temporary work as it shapes those experiences and struggles.

How do workers experience temporary work? How does the organization of temporary work empower or constrain workers?

In what ways is gender embedded in the organization of temporary work?

What are the implications of the increasing use of temporary workers for social equality? As more and more people in the United States find themselves in temporary work arrangements, a sociological understanding of these arrangements becomes more imperative.

Both the popular press and human resource management texts discuss the boom in temporary employment (see, for example, Castro, 1993; Morrow, 1993). These sources relate how companies are finding temporary workers to be a less expensive alternative to increasing their staffs, especially because access to such workers has become relatively easy with the proliferation of temporary agencies (National Association of Temporary Services, 1992). Parker (1994) demonstrates how temporary-help firms' public relations efforts portray temporary work as an exchange beneficial to both the employer and the temporary employee. Therefore, the reader should keep in mind that this study is set against a dominant discourse of flexibility and cost reduction that largely reflects employers' realities and interests. This study seeks to establish a new discourse that places the worker at the center of inquiry.

From *Work and Occupations,* Vol. 22, No. 2, May 1995, pp. 137-166. Reprinted by permission.

TEMPORARY EMPLOYMENT AND THE CONTINGENT ECONOMY

Temporary clerical workers are part of what is called the contingent economy. The term *contingent economy* covers a diverse array of work arrangements, including part-time employment, temporary employment, employee leasing, job sharing, and domestic day work (Polivka & Nardone, 1989). The growth in this sector has outpaced overall employment growth, demonstrating that this phenomenon is less cyclical than in the past and more incorporated into usual business strategies. For example, temporary employment has grown at three times the rate of overall U.S. employment since 1982 (Callaghan & Hartmann, 1991) and currently stands at approximately 1.4 million (Senate Committee on Labor and Human Resources, 1993). This is about 1% of the U.S. workforce, but the proportion of temporary workers is predicted to continue growing. Indeed, noncyclical (i.e., does not rise and fall with recession and recovery periods) continued growth of the temporary workforce was cited in the 1993 congressional subcommittee meetings on contingent labor (Senate Committee on Labor and Human Resources, 1993). By 1989, between 25% and 30% of the American workforce could be classified as contingent workers (Belous, 1989). Yet social scientists have only recently attempted to understand this growing phenomenon.

Certain segments of the contingent economy have received more attention than others. For example, there seems to be a fair amount of attention to part-time work (Beechey & Perkins, 1987; Negrey, 1993; Tilly, 1990), whereas other portions of the contingent economy, such as temporary work, remain relatively unexamined.

MANAGERIAL AND LABOR PERSPECTIVES ON TEMPORARY EMPLOYMENT

Research about temporary employment to date can be categorized into two dominant streams, the managerial perspective and the labor perspective. Congressional hearings on temporary employment in 1988 and 1993 (House Committee on Government Operations, 1988; Senate Committee on Labor and Human Resources, 1993) reveal this same distinction, with business leaders, managers, and the temporary industry generally championing the former view while workers, social reformers, and some labor leaders champion the latter. For its proponents, temporary employment is a functional phenomenon or a market exchange. It allows the flexibility necessary for competition in the global marketplace. In fact, a term previously reserved for money-saving inventory control systems has been adopted to describe this new workforce: "just-in-time." When managers speak in terms of flexibility and just-in-time, they seldom ask, "flexible for whom?" or "just in time for whom?" The worker is conceptualized as a work input and is managed in much the same way as inventory or machines. This attitude is revealed in one simple statement, "In fact, in certain cases, [contingent labor] may be the most important control mechanism that management has in the short run, given that management often can treat labor as a variable cost while other costs usually are fixed" (Belous, 1989).

Such an understanding of temporary employment reveals a managerial bias that obfuscates the realities of those not in the position to manage or control their work. There is a parallel here between managerial postures of temporary work and Taylor's discussion of scientific management. Braverman's (1974) criticism of Taylor's notion of a fair day's work illustrates this point, "Why a 'fair day's work' should be defined as a physiological maximum is never made clear" (p. 97). In other words, a fair day's work for whom? Taylor's work was conducted purely from a managerial perspective without the least concern for the realities of the worker. Callaghan and Hartmann (1991) begin to expose the bias in a managerial perspective:

> If, however, the impetus for change [to contingent employment] is only to meet the evolving needs

of the work environment, then we would not expect to see the lower wages and lack of fringe benefits which are currently part of the price of being a contingent worker. (p. 1)

In contrast to the managerial perspective, the labor perspective has provided a much more illuminating analysis of the situation of temporary workers. The congressional hearings in 1988 and 1993 brought many economic and legal labor issues to the forefront. On the whole, contingent workers:

- are paid less
- have fewer fringe, health, and retirement benefits
- are unlikely to be unionized
- have little or no long-term security
- have a more difficult time qualifying for unemployment and workers' compensation
- often "slip through the cracks" with regard to labor legislation, specifically OSHA, ERISA, and Wage & Hours Standards (House Committee on Government Operations, 1988; Senate Committee on Labor and Human Resources, 1993)

Callaghan and Hartmann (1991) identify several alarming trends in contingent employment. Recent increases in contingent employment have occurred at the expense of workers who would otherwise prefer to be employed full-time. Thus employers are not merely accommodating workers' desires for greater flexibility. The phenomenon appears to be employer-driven rather than worker-driven, as employer-demand variables are better predictors of growth in temporary employment than labor-supply variables (Golden & Appelbaum, 1992). As a result, contingent workers experience uncertainty regarding the duration or regularity of their work and are unlikely to receive on-the-job training or to be considered for promotional opportunities. Callaghan and Hartmann (1991) summarize:

Low wages and a lack of benefits result in economic hardship and poverty for contingent workers more often than for other workers. Involuntary part-time workers have a poverty rate of 16.5 percent, which is slightly higher than unemployed people who are out of work and seeking a job (15.3 percent), and much higher than for full-time workers (2.7 percent). (p. 15)

Finally, Callaghan and Hartmann (1991) offer a precautionary note regarding the extent to which temporary employment has become "business as usual." They view the change in temporary employment to a noncyclical phenomenon as evidence that employers are avoiding "long-term commitments, wage growth, and substantial fringe benefits" as well as occupational safety and health protections (p. 28).

Labor perspectives such as those given in the 1988 and 1993 congressional hearings and those given by Callaghan and Hartmann (1991) provide a substantial, but incomplete, picture of temporary work. In addition to the material consequences of temporary jobs cited by labor perspective advocates, temporaries experience the social and interpersonal consequences of their work. This area in the literature is underdeveloped. We need an understanding of the day-to-day challenges contingent workers face and how they deal with those challenges in order to round out a labor perspective, which focuses mainly on economic drawbacks and legal loopholes in contingent work arrangements.

RACE, GENDER, AND THE CONTINGENT WORKFORCE

Callaghan and Hartmann (1991) and Tilly (1990) have demonstrated the overrepresentation of women and people of color in various sectors of the contingent economy. Women and African American[1] workers are overrepresented in the temporary workforce. For example, a survey by the National Association of Temporary Services (1992) estimates that 80% of member-agency temporaries are female,[2] and

Belous (1989) estimates that more than 64% of the entire temporary workforce is female, and more than 20% is Black. The corresponding figures for the general workforce are 45% and 10%, respectively. Thus the problems associated with temporary employment are disproportionately the problems of women and African Americans. And the numbers of Americans being introduced to these working arrangements is increasing every year.

Many social scientists have demonstrated that men and women often perform different work. Cynthia Cockburn (1985) tells us that "women may push the buttons but they may not meddle with the works" (p. 12). Furthermore, men tend to be located in capital-intensive jobs, whereas women tend to be located in labor-intensive jobs (Acker, 1990; West, 1990); part-time work (which has been shown to intensify the labor process) is largely gendered as female (Beechey & Perkins, 1987; West, 1990).

At the occupational level, many have detailed the persistence of occupational segregation and the male-female wage gap (Reskin & Roos, 1990; Sokoloff, 1992) and Black-White wage gap (Sokoloff, 1992) within and across occupations. Job queues and labor queues are influenced by a broad array of factors, ranging from job autonomy and working conditions to sex composition of a job and gender ideology of employers (Milkman, 1987).

Race/ethnicity and gender are also implicated in the structuring of the secondary labor market (Amott & Matthaei, 1991). Jobs in the secondary labor market are marked by low wages, poor working conditions, little stability or opportunity for advancement, and minimal benefits, if any. Furthermore, these labor markets are a primary mechanism in reproducing racial/ethnic and gender inequality, although they do not do so in isolation from other social institutions.

Smith (1993) and Acker (1992) build upon the notion that gender is implicated in the structuring of labor markets by examining how gender affects the organization of "flexible" work arrangements. Not all flexible labor strategies are created equal. Smith characterizes some as "enabling" (those that upgrade labor processes and employment relationships) and others as "restrictive" (those that downgrade labor processes and employment relationships). In manufacturing, gender ideology largely delineates the contingent from the permanent jobs, as women's jobs are turned into temporary or part-time jobs in order to support a "core" of male workers. Smith points to institutional foundations of gender inequalities that occur when an entire sector, such as clerical work, is increasingly organized as contingent. Thus, to fully understand the effect of contingent work on the workers, gender and race must be part of the analysis. To help organize such an analysis, I have employed the concept of alienation.

ALIENATION: A CONTESTED TERM

Alienation is a complex concept, the terms of which are often contested by social scientists. Nevertheless, alienation can be a useful heuristic device for understanding temporary workers' experiences. As I use the term, *alienation* signals a lack of control, a certain powerlessness felt by the individual and derived from the structure of social relations. It is the lack of power to direct one's work, to maintain satisfactory work relationships, and to create a self-definition rather than have it imposed.

Some of the literature on alienation characterizes it as a subjective psychological or emotional state to manage (see Kohn & Schooler, 1983; Rizzo, House, & Lirtzman, 1970; Seeman, 1959) and as highly individualistic in orientation. In contrast, Marxist interpretations view alienation as an outgrowth of the social relations of capitalist production, sometimes seemingly removing the individual from analysis entirely. These two orientations are not mutually exclusive.

One can employ the concept of alienation in such a way that it attends to individual psychological and emotional states and broader structural factors related to the organization of capitalist production. Such a concept of alienation would link individuals' experiences of alienation to the way in which their work is organized as alienating. Israel (1971) suggests a useful application of alienation to demonstrate a series of social relations "that present a link between the sociological and the psychological conditions" (p. 15). Analysis must be structural as well as subjective. Schmitt and Moody (1994) suggest the concept of alienation is a useful tool of social criticism when its use demonstrates how social organization exacerbates alienation *when it need not.* Therefore, the alienating aspects of temporary employment are contrasted to more traditionally organized work, which in itself may be considerably alienating.

In integrating experience and structure in the discussion of alienation and clerical temporary work, I follow three broad Marxist categories: alienation from work, alienation from others, and alienation from self. I will address each of these aspects of alienation more closely in the empirical sections on alienation that follow.

Furthermore, as Schmitt and Moody (1994) note, any discussion of alienation is incomplete without examining resistance as well. In examining resistance, we glean a more accurate understanding of the ways temporary workers attempt to shape their own world in the face of enormous constraints. Attention to resistance reveals the contested character of the temporary worker's terrain. Temporary work is not a mutual exchange between employer and worker.

Some feminist writings on women and work (Bookman & Morgan, 1988; Ward, 1990) implement a broad view of women's resistance that includes more subtle forms of resistance than are usually considered in more traditional studies of work. Forms of resistance range from subtle (crying and "female" problems; Ong, 1987) to overt (those means traditionally labeled resistance, such as sabotage and union organizing; Bookman & Morgan, 1988). I will follow a broad conceptualization of resistance to include both subtle and overt forms. This is particularly important when studying work that affords little opportunity for traditionally conceived worker resistance, particularly unionization. Because temporary work separates temporary workers from each other, temporary workers from "regular" workers, and temporary workers from union workers,[3] unionization for temporary workers is unlikely at this time. This broad conception of resistance also creates space to explore the contradictory nature of much resistance. Resistance in one realm may make workers complicit in their own subordination in another realm (Ong, 1987), or it may reinforce damaging stereotypes. Nevertheless, temporary workers do resist, sometimes effectively and sometimes not. In this article, I will explore the multitude of ways temporary workers resist, attempting to understand this resistance in light of the constraints temporary work places on that resistance.

METHOD

This research is based on in-depth interviews with 13 women who have been employed[4] as temporary clerical workers and with the branch managers of two temporary-services firms in Los Angeles. I obtained the interviews through a variety of sources: responses to a letter of introduction given to the workers at a temporary agency I work through,[5] personal contact with other temporaries while working as a temporary, responses to a flier posted at a local gym requesting interviews, and referrals from friends and previous interview subjects (snowballing). Collecting data from such diverse means is preferable to relying solely on self-selection or on the personal recommendation of the temporary agency personnel. In this way, I avoided drawing solely on people who "have an axe to grind," who are comfortable responding to a letter written on university letterhead, or whom the agency wishes to represent them.

The data represent a diverse group of respondents, including subjects from 23 to 60 years old, both married and single women, high school as well as college graduates, and two African American women, two Latino women, one Filipino woman, and eight White women. In addition, the respondents' experience with temporary work ranges from several months to over 10 years and includes experiences with over 20 different temporary agencies; most have worked through at least two temporary agencies.

Each semistructured interview lasted between 1 and 2 hours and followed three trajectories:

1. the relationship of the worker to her work,
2. the relationship of the worker to others in the workplace, and
3. the feelings of the worker about herself in relation to her work.

The interviews with the branch managers focused on the business of temporary employment, relationships with clients, and relationships with temporary workers. Using interview guides structured around these themes lends consistency to the interviews while still affording flexibility in following interesting topics. All names and places in the text are pseudonyms.

I transcribed each interview and employed both methodological and theoretical memo writing, open coding, axial coding, and selective coding (Strauss, 1987) in the development of an emergent theory (Glaser & Strauss, 1967). In this case, the emergent theory corresponded closely to the sociological concept of alienation; therefore, I employed the concept of alienation as the underlying theme of analysis, fleshing out the ways in which alienating experiences are related to the organization of temporary work.

ALIENATION FROM WORK

In the classical Marxist depiction, alienation from work has at least two components. Workers are alienated not just from the product of their work, but from the work process as well: "alienation shows itself not only in the result, but also in the act of production, inside productive activity itself" (McLellan, 1977, p. 80). With temporary work, labor is twice alienated from its product. The worker's labor belongs not only to the company for whom she works but also to the temporary agency that receives a fee for her services. For example, the company that hires a temporary may pay the agency $10 an hour for her services; however, the temporary worker may only receive $7 an hour. Thus, the alienation Marx depicted is taken one step further through the subcontracting relationship that exists in temporary employment.

More important for this analysis is the fact that temporary workers also are alienated from the labor process. This type of alienation is characterized by temporaries' lack of control over their work, their lack of control over the conditions of their work, and their lack of understanding of the purpose of their work. Certainly, these conditions are not unique to temporary employment. As Braverman (1974) illustrated, clerical work has become degraded in much the same manner as factory work through the separation of conception and execution.

> Typists, mail sorters, telephone operators, stock clerks, receptionists, payroll and timekeeping clerks, shipping and receiving clerks are subjected to routines, more or less mechanized according to current possibilities, that strip them of their former grasp of even a limited amount of office information, divest them of the need or ability to understand and decide, and make of them so many mechanical eyes, fingers, and voices whose functioning is, insofar as possible, predetermined by both rules and machinery. (p. 340)

To an even greater extent than the workers Braverman described, clerical temporaries are seldom provided with enough information for them to understand the purpose of the work that they perform. Little time is invested in instruction regarding the task to be performed, particularly for short-term assignments. When asked about their tasks, the temporaries I interviewed were seldom able to describe the purpose of their work. One woman who was doing temporary work after losing her "permanent" job stated:

> I still don't know what it was that I was doing. I just sat there and entered, I think they were coordinates or something. It's some kind of program

that builds a building. They just gave me the coordinates to punch in. (Julie Grovers, 30-year-old White woman)

Another temporary described the purpose of her filing "hundreds of boxes" over a period of 3 to 4 weeks:

For some reason they were redoing all their files because they changed something, they changed the districts or something like that. Whatever, I don't really know. (Irene Pedersen, 25-year-old White woman)

The temporary nature of the work deprives the temporary worker of even the most limited realization of the finished product of her work. This happens even on longer-term assignments, because once the work is finished, the temporary moves on to another assignment. Seldom do temporaries complete subsequent stages of a project, which would provide them with a sense of continuity. In fact, one temporary described a situation in which the speedy completion of her work resulted in the termination of the assignment, rather than progression to the next phase of the project.

She had estimated that this job would take 3 days. Well it turns out that my partner and I worked quickly together. The woman that hired us was surprised that a 3-day job got finished in a day. And she goes, that's fantastic, here's your reward, I'll cut the assignment short. I mean you're told it's going to be a 3-day assignment and you arrange your schedule, but it gets pulled from you. (Cheryl Hansen, 23-year-old White woman)

Later, reflecting on that experience and its lack of purpose Cheryl said, "It's not like you're in there to clean up, it's not like you're in there to say well, 'I think that we need to improve this, and I think we need to improve that.'"

Thus, while clerical work has wrested understanding from the hands of workers, temporary work has done so more dramatically. This analysis can be taken further if one looks at the labor process more closely. For temporaries, alienation from work is partially due to the organization of clerical work. However, the particular organization of temporary work exacerbates the situation. First, the work is often the least desirable of all the clerical work. Temporaries consistently report being assigned to "shit work," "scut work," or "dreg work." They expressed an awareness that this particular type of work was allocated to temporaries over "regular" employees: "You end up doing the stuff that nobody else wants to do, or has time to do. And when I worked at that bank, I ended up doing. . . . It was just too monotonous, too boring" (Jean Masters, 34-year-old African American woman).

In many cases, temporaries described long periods of monotonous filing, stuffing envelopes, copying, or even proofreading address labels. They described their work as monotonous, mindless, and even robotic. One temporary who once had to work 23 consecutive hours offered this explanation for the monotony and intensity of her work:

It's because you are a temp. They sort of look at you as a sort of disposable factor. You're in there, you get all the dirty work, because nobody wants to do the filing or the xeroxing for 2 hours at a time. Nobody wants to do any of this stuff so you get it. (Cheryl Hansen)

Another woman describes her experience at a bank,

I worked in a bank and stuffed envelopes for 5 days straight. It was terrible, it was so monotonous. He delegated me these huge boxes of stuff, so like I would only have to go to him 2 days later. I'd just go to him when I ran out of stuff to stuff. (Sarah Tilton, 26-year-old White woman)

Others described work being piled on them in a never-ending fashion. One woman described her temporary work experience in a manner reminiscent of the sorcerer's apprentice in the Disney movie, *Fantasia.* Just as Mickey Mouse is confronted by an army of uncontrollable brooms, Irene is confronted by her own uncontrollable workload:

All I could do was come home and think about these boxes piling up. And then I remember one day, I had just finished filing like all these *fuckin' boxes* and this humongous UPS truck comes in, or whatever it was, this truck with this man, he just unloaded like 50 more. So it was almost like I didn't do anything! So yeah, I had a lot of anxiety about these boxes. (Irene Pedersen)

Although temporaries often perform their tasks at an intensified rate when compared with regular employees, there is a second, contradictory tendency in the work experience of temporaries. They are often left for long periods of time without any work to do.

You know, you're hired as a receptionist and the phone rings like twice. . . . I had a temp job I think for 2 weeks. I was covering for a secretary and the bosses were all out of town, but they needed somebody just to be there and to cover the phones. (Ludy Martinez, 36-year-old Filipino woman)

Fifty percent of the time, there was absolutely very little to do, with just answering the phone or taking messages. (Ellen Lanford, 38-year-old White woman)

Often, the difference between feast and famine lies in the nature of the assignment. According to the interviews, feast conditions usually occur when temporaries are brought in to complete a special assignment (for example, a company might be recoding all its files; rather than have regular employees perform this work, they hire three temps for 2 weeks) and famine conditions usually occur when a temporary is brought in to substitute for a regular employee.

However, temporaries in substitute positions occasionally do report being assigned projects that have been sitting around the office. For example, one company wanted to use this temporary's time efficiently by having her complete a filing project while she was substituting for the receptionist.

Oh my Lord, this woman wanted me to work. You're doing the phone, OK. You're filing. And it's not like next to each other. The phones are right here, and the filing cabinet is all the way in Siberia . . . the job was too much. Using you, not paying you. They want you to do this, to do that . . . the inventory, the filing, the telephone. I was doing so many things. What else? What else? (Shari Jensen, 31-year-old African American woman)

In addition, substitute temporaries can be assigned to help out everyone in the office in the absence of a regular employee. Work is intensified by increasing the number of supervisors one must serve: "It's like you know when I got here and you said I'm working for two people. Well, I'm working for four" (Ludy Martinez).

In summary, temporary workers are alienated from the product of their work as well as from the labor process. They have little control over their work and often experience periods of intense labor or a complete lack of activity. Quite often, temporaries have little understanding of the purpose of their work, and they are seldom around to see the finished product because they are, after all, "only temporary."

ALIENATION FROM OTHERS

Alienation from others derives from the relational characteristics particular to temporary clerical employment. Temporary workers are structurally constrained from forming satisfactory relationships in the workplace. There are several factors unique to temporary employment that foster alienation from others. The transitory relationship of the temporary to both the agency and the companies she works for engenders social isolation. First, temporaries are isolated from other temporaries employed by the same agency. Temporaries from the same agency rarely know each other unless the assignment happens to require the placement of two individuals at a single location. For example, Katie Hallaway, a 60-year-old White woman, reported attending a "holiday party" for the temporaries given by the agency; the only person she knew was the woman who sent her on assignments.

The only in-person contact most temporaries report with the agency is for the initial application and on subsequent paydays. One woman even reported faxing her time cards and receiving her paycheck through the mail, the only contact with the temporary agency being the initial application. Therefore, temporaries find it difficult to form lasting relationships with agency personnel. In addition, several of the women I interviewed identified turnover in the agencies as problematic for them.

> At the agency, they changed faces too many times. I mean, the only person who was stable there was their marketing person. It's great if they know you, but then the next thing you know every couple months, they change supervisors on you. (Jean Masters)

> The agencies have massive turnover too. And it was amazing because they would jump from agency to agency. You get somebody different like every 2 months. (Ludy Martinez)

Further complicating the ability to form relationships with the agency is the fact that nearly all of the women I interviewed used multiple agencies to ensure that they would have enough work to pay their bills. Several of them used more than five agencies: "I used, oh I don't know, eight agencies for some reason. You know, sometimes I even took it personal. It's like, is it me? You don't have anything for *me* or you just don't have anything?" (Shari Jensen).

Second, temporary employees are socially isolated from regular employees at the worksite. The transitory nature of temporary work discourages all but the necessary social interaction. Temporary workers felt that their coworkers did not think they were worth getting to know on a personal level.

> That's what can be really hard. Because most people don't really wanna get to know the temps . . . because they figure you're not worth the investment. You're not gonna be there that long. That was probably one of the biggest frustrations. People just don't want to get to know you. (Ludy Martinez)

> You know, as a matter of how much they were interested in knowing about me . . . more often than not, they wouldn't ask any questions. Or they'd be too busy or not interested. (Ellen Lanford)

> I think since they don't see you as being permanent they sort of dismiss you as being expendable, like you're not worth it. I don't know. . . . I find that now even as a permanent worker I create a distance between myself and temps, you know. It's like you don't want to get too close to them because you know they're leaving. (Carol Ketchum, 29-year-old White woman)

Temporaries reported being left to do their work while regular employees socialized. One temporary mentioned that other employees would go out for drinks while she stayed at the office and worked. I asked her if she ever got invited along and she responded,

> Well, it's like a small community, everybody has their friends, and to break into that circle of friends is . . . when you're just about ready to break into the circle of friends, they actually invite you out on a Friday night for drinks with everybody else . . . you leave. (Cheryl Hansen)

This particular type of social isolation is not unique to short-term assignments. One temporary relayed the following story about a temporary job where she and others had worked for several months.

> And there was no Christmas present for you under the tree like the rest of the company would get. . . . There were some places where it was just blatant, just terribly blatant. Whenever there was going to be a company party or something, the temps had to stay and work. You know, cover the

phones so the regular people got to go. You could tell where the second-class citizenship started. (Ludy Martinez)

Third, in cases where the workload is extremely heavy and monotonous, actual physical isolation accompanies and exacerbates social isolation. Often, work takes place in an unobtrusive location where temporaries cannot easily be seen. Arlene Kaplan Daniels (1987) described the different types of "invisible work" that women perform as volunteers or domestic workers. Temporary work, although paid work, is invisible in that it is often undervalued and performed behind the scenes.

The nature of the tasks and the intensity of much of the work, which several women characterized as "grunt work," often resulted in temporaries being relegated to the "back office," out of the sight of visitors and other workers.

They kind of separated us from the permanent employees. But I didn't care, it was only temporary. (Linda Mejia, 31-year-old Latina woman)

She was really gung ho about giving me all this grunt work to do, and I spent the entire time back there typing in things while she was pigging out on Doritos and what not. And I think I was really supposed to be answering the phones all the time, but she ended up doing the phones and I ended up back there typing and stuff. (Irene Pedersen)

I had this little room to myself. I brought in my walkman and listened to tapes all day. . . . I was very removed. I mean I didn't deal with anyone because I was there for 1 week and I had to report to one person who delegated the work to me. There was no interaction whatsoever. (Sarah Tilton)

Sometimes, temporaries who are hired to do office work are used for more personal services, which more directly resemble women's unpaid work in the home.

I mean the job that I just left . . . they had temps taking the bosses' cars to car washes. And one temp was going shopping for the boss's Christmas party at his house. (Ludy Martinez)

People just take advantage of you and they get in that habit. They say, "Let's go out for a drink and have her still work, she's happy." It's kind of like being a housewife, I guess. It might start off being appreciated, but then after a while if you keep doing it, it's taken for granted. (Cheryl Hansen)

Finally, the low status of the temporary clerical worker and the gender of the worker engenders nonperson treatment. Even when temporaries are physically visible, they are assigned the role of nonperson, an interactionally invisible role. Goffman (1959, p. 151) described the discrepant role of a nonperson as someone who is present during a performance, and may actually be part of the team, but who is considered "not there" by both the performers and the audience. The role of nonperson is usually reserved for those of low status, such as waiters or children (I would also add women to Goffman's gender-blind approach).

As a nonperson, the temporary employee is treated much like a waiter or a child. This treatment occurs particularly when they are given tasks to perform inconspicuously in conspicuous places. For example, the temporaries I spoke with reported working in well-trafficked hallways, behind the receptionist while she answered phones, at filing cabinets in the way of other employees, and in a conference room while a meeting was proceeding. In all these cases, interaction was kept to a minimum. The temp is interactionally invisible.

I could tell she'd been temping for years. She knew when to shut up. She knew when to be invisible. She knew when to make herself known. And it was like, yes, she had been a servant in a master's house before. (Ludy Martinez)

This woman came out of her office and said [about the temporary worker sitting there], "I didn't want *HER*! I told the agency not *HER*. No, send her home." (Bernice Katz, 36-year-old White woman)

> The guy who was in charge of the office was also not very . . . he kind of didn't treat me like I was a person. He was like, well, he didn't treat me like a human being. He was condescending to me. He would tell me, "Oh, type that up," and not talk to me like I was a human with a brain, like I was a machine, and that I was a woman, lower than he was. He didn't talk to me. He never formally talked to me and said, "You're going to be here today and my name is so and so." (Irene Pedersen)

> I don't object to getting coffee for someone, but what I do object to is. . . . "Coffee!" [points, snaps fingers]. And I've gotten that. I just thought, "OK if I was the vice president would you have done that?" See, what I don't like in this whole thing is that you're really looked on as low class. . . . You're just in another world. (Cheryl Hansen)

Temporary workers are alienated from others because they have no longevity on which to base satisfactory relationships, because they are sometimes physically isolated from other employees, and because their low status in the workplace engenders nonperson treatment.

ALIENATION FROM SELF

The temporary employee is also alienated from herself through her labor. This type of alienation occurs through emotional labor and identity struggles. Arlie Hochschild (1983) revealed the costs of emotional labor that women perform as flight attendants: "The worker can become estranged or alienated from an aspect of self—either the body or the margins of the soul—that is *used* to do the work" (p. 7). As she further points out, women are overrepresented in jobs that require this type of emotional labor, particularly in the service sector. Temporary clerical employees experience similar demands for emotional labor in their assignments (Henson, in press).

The agency relationship creates a greater need for emotional labor in two ways. First, the temporary worker actually has two jobs: one as a clerical worker at the hiring company and another as a representative of the temporary agency. Temporary workers are highly aware that they are considered representatives of the temporary agency that sent them on the assignment, even though they may work through several other agencies. They are also aware that their job may depend upon their accommodation of the clients.

> You need flexibility . . . and a strong ego. And calm, I mean you're being hired to be calming, not enervating. And that's what a lot of times would be commented on . . . that you're just so calm. (Ellen Lanford)

> I don't usually have a problem with anybody. Usually, I do well with adjusting. She's the type of person that probably needed a 2-month vacation because she was too nervous. You know and because of that you had to either tune her out or you got involved in that same nervous attitude. (Jean Masters)

> I think you need to be first of all, very friendly. And very nice, and very, well you have to be I think very, very easy-going. Because you're not going to stay in one place. Today you're here, the next day you're . . . you know. You always gotta be nice, I think. (Shari Jensen)

The temporary workers' perceptions accurately reflect what I was told by the temporary agency representatives when I asked what qualities were important for a temporary.

> Friendly, friendly. That always works. Happy, um, helpful. Based on personality if I get a friendly applicant I think has a great personality and they're warm and they're fuzzy and they're friendly. Warm and fuzzy is always a good quality. If they're warm and fuzzy I may choose that over technical ability. If I can tell a client, you know what I've got someone who's hard-working, she's willing to try, she's got a great personality, she'll mesh with the people in the office . . . as opposed to someone who types 102 words a minute and is very stoic and has no personality. I'd rather send the warm and fuzzy

that types 40 or 50 words a minute. As long as they can get the job done, I think that works better in the long run. (Sandy Mathers, a 28 year-old African American woman)

Second, temporary workers feel the need to perform emotional labor to secure future assignments. This ranges from putting on a happy face for the agency to tolerating abusive work situations. Temporaries are instructed to maintain a pleasant demeanor in the face of conflict at the work location and to report problems with the assignment to the agency only. For example, temporaries report taking the blame for mistakes they did not make.

I know my boss has blamed me on this assignment for a lot of things that he's misplaced, that he's screwed up, and he goes, "Well, you see, Sarah didn't get it in on time" or "Sarah lost it." And it's really embarrassing because he asks me in front of people like, "Sarah, where did you put this?" And I know full well that he didn't give it to me. This has happened 3 days in a row now. After a while you just go, "Well, you know, I'm just really sorry. I guess I just really screwed up." (Sarah Tilton)

They also report taking abusive comments without responding. The following incident occurred when one woman's "boss" could not get the copier to work.

So I said [in a child's voice], "Oh gosh, do you want me to give it a shot?" And he goes to me, like I am a little girl, "Well, I really don't think you can make it work." So I looked around and pushed the "ON" button. And he threw a fit. He called me a smart this and an f'in that. (Sarah Tilton)

If they treat you badly on the job. . . . I have never figured out what to do. Because I'm afraid if I complain to the agency they'll just pull me off the assignment and then I have to wait for the next one and you never know when that's gonna come. . . . If I complained they'd just think I was a complainer. I knew this was a great account for them. (Cindy Carson, 38-year-old White woman)

Emotional labor is a significant component of temporary work. Temporary workers are required to use emotional labor to gain favor with the agency and to manage difficult situations on the job.

The second way temporary workers are self-alienated arises because of the organization of temporary work as something that is brief and intermittent, and it is also related to the low status of the temporary worker both as a temp and as a woman. Here alienation from self arises from the worker's inability to satisfactorily create a self-definition (Schmitt & Moody, 1994). Aspects of their identity are imposed from the outside, and these often conflict with the worker's ideas about who she is.

The women I interviewed reported consistently that when people did interact with them, they did so on a very superficial level and often resorted to employing negative stereotypes of temps in their interactions.[6] Women's responses to these negative stereotypes repeatedly took the form of identity struggles and identity manipulation.

You just felt like a moron. And if you weren't thinking like a moron, you weren't going to get the job done. So you have to train yourself to be a moron, and then you feel like you're becoming a moron. But it's in your best interest to be a moron. (Irene Pedersen)

There were some days when I thought this is ludicrous. I am so miserable. I can't believe I'm however many years old and I am making 9,000 copies of this script or something. I have two master's degrees. (Ellen Lanford)

Another woman volunteered to bring in a computer book for her supervisor, who was having trouble with a complicated software package. The following account reveals frustration with being stereotyped:

He asked why I had this book. I go, "Because it's on my machine at home." His expression was just so, I mean he was really blown away. Did anybody bother to ask me? I mean it's on my resume.

People look at me and say you must not really be that capable . . . because I'm a temp. (Sarah Tilton)

Other temporaries report changing their behavior and their dress from assignment to assignment to fit into the image required. One woman who used to work full-time in an insurance office reported that she often had to "dress down." So rather than wear her suits from her previous job, she went to Kmart and bought what she felt were unobtrusive and nonthreatening clothes.

That temps must manipulate their identity became evident throughout the interviews. When asked what qualities were important in a temp, Cheryl Hansen summarized:

I think you have to have a pretty strong personality so that you can be *adaptable,* and you really have to be *political.* I mean you have to be very *pliable* so that you can just automatically just *mold* to any situation. It just sort of demands that you *blend* in.

Another form of identity struggle concerns the substitution of "the temp" for one's name. I found that not only do employers call temporaries, "the temp" or "the temporary," but women frequently report self-naming as "the temp." One woman even used a different name in her temporary assignments so that she could be remembered. Although her name was not unusual, she found that it helped to provide people with a simple way to remember her name, even if it wasn't her real name: "All you do is introduce yourself as 'Jill, as in Jack and . . . 'and people never forget. So that's the name I use when I'm temping." (Sarah Tilton).

Women report changing their voices, their names, their personalities, and even their histories on a regular basis. In fact, temporary agencies encourage identity manipulation by telling temporaries how to dress, how to act, and how to "sell" themselves to the client.

She would really go so far as to tell us, "On this job, please do not smoke, or please do not wear those kinds of clothes, because these are not those kinds of people. So if that makes a difference to you, if you have to dress like that, then don't take this assignment please." (Ludy Martinez)

Before each assignment they give you instructions on how to dress for that company, whether it's very conservative and wear a suit or casual, wear nice slacks and a blouse or whatever. (Bernice Katz)

One woman with a college education reported denying anything more than a high school diploma in order to feel like she could get along in her assignments. She quickly learned to keep her education and aspirations "under wraps," as she put it

If I told them, people would look at me like I had an attitude. And if I ever expressed a desire to go on to something else, they sort of squashed you down. So I keep that under wraps. (Cheryl Hansen)

They saw my resume, which has two master's degrees, and they said take all that stuff out. That's going to scare people. You're never going to get work that way. Just put the secretarial experience you have down. So that's what I did. I rewrote my resume for them because they felt they could pitch me better. (Ellen Lanford)

Thus temporaries tend to keep their "other" self out of the workplace. Just as "a grocer who dreams is offensive to the buyer because such a grocer is not wholly a grocer" (Sartre, 1966, p. 102), the temp must be wholly a temp or she is offensive.

RESISTANCE TO ALIENATION

Although temporaries regularly experienced alienation from work, from others, and from themselves, they actively resisted alienation in a variety of ways. As used here, the concept of resistance encompasses a broad range of strategies, going beyond worker organization (Ward,

1990) to include more subtle forms such as reminding oneself that "it's only temporary," as well as more overt forms such as leaving an assignment and even sabotage. It is also important to recognize that resistance often occurs in a context of constraint that shapes what modes of resistance are employed. Resistance can be more or less effective and can even bring contradictory results, such as reproducing stereotypes about temporary workers. However, the fact remains that temporary workers do not merely experience alienation, they actively resist it.

Resistance to Alienation From Work

Some temporaries employed strategies to minimize or resist alienation. In the case of monotonous work, they reported shifting their interest from the tasks that they were performing to the objects on which they performed the task or to other aspects of the work environment. In the Los Angeles entertainment industry, temps have an advantage in this aspect. One temporary worker who was filing studio memorabilia for 4 months found a lot of interest in the old pictures and scripts that she was filing.

> We were handling a lot of neat things, like original scripts and stills and things from some of these television shows like *Dr. Kildare, I Spy, I Spy* with Bill Cosby. Oh, *Get Smart, Get Smart.* We were handling the original scripts and that was pretty exciting. (Bernice Katz)

Another temporary described her favorite assignment as one in which the monotony was broken by watching celebrities come in and out of the offices at her worksite.

> Yeah, I still think that the movie company comes to mind. 'Cause I found it intriguing and interesting and I had never been exposed to anything in the entertainment business. And I ran into Marilu Henner one day. That was good. (Carol Ketchum)

Even in nonentertainment companies, temporaries find some interest in their work to alleviate the monotony. For example, one woman who was doing transcriptions found interest in the content of the material she was transcribing.

> It's like piecework. That's when I would make a game of it. You know it's like sewing machine work. You sit there and you do it. You get paid by the hour. You take a break. You have to be able to do spelling. And you can get kind of interested in some of what you're doing. I was doing these transcriptions of death row inmates. And I was sitting there saying "Oh my God!" Same thing with personal injury cases. But then the other stuff could be just incredibly dull. You just sort of get through. (Ludy Martinez)

In cases of too little work, temporaries found their greatest latitude for resistance. Although they could not control the flow of work coming to them because temporaries (especially on the shorter-term assignments) typically do not possess enough organizationally specific knowledge to seek additional work tasks, they could surreptitiously control the use of their time at the worksite. So rather than sitting and staring at the wall, some temporaries "cruised," slept, or did other work.

> I realized that I tended to be real fast, and rather than slow myself down and socialize, I could work real fast and take a lot of breaks. I call it cruising. (Carol Ketchum)

> Very bored! I'm telling you. . . . I used to sleep there. Yes there's nothing to do. I always bring my book. When I get sick and tired of reading, I sleep. And I wake up and take the phone calls. Sometimes, OK, you're not supposed to make phone calls, but what am I gonna do with 8 hours? OK, you can only read so much. After that, you sleep. You're going to wake up because it's not in your bed. OK. And then after that, you make some calls. (Shari Jensen)

> There were times when somebody, another office worker, would say listen you really can't be reading. And so I'd put my book away and I wouldn't read and I would just do whatever. Sometimes I

would play computer games if I felt I could get away with it. Depending on how much supervision I had, if I felt comfortable working on my own stuff. I just can't sit and not do anything. And oftentimes I would hide what I was doing under something associated with work. But I also felt responsible to the temp agency. . . . I didn't want anybody complaining about me back to the temp agency. (Ellen Lanford)

Although the work was alienating, the temporaries I interviewed strategized to find interest in or have control over their work. In cases where temporaries had too little work, their resistance might be misinterpreted to reinforce stereotypes of temporaries as "flaky" or lazy. However, when viewed from the temporary's perspective and in the context of the organization of temporary work, these actions represent temporary workers' resistance to otherwise alienating forms of labor.

Resistance to Alienation From Others

One way temporaries resist social isolation is by taking longer-term assignments when available. Temporaries felt that at least part of their isolation came from the transitory nature of temporary work. Seeking out less transitory assignments (i.e., a duration of several months) was one effective way to combat social isolation. However, as mentioned earlier, a long assignment does not guarantee social integration.

Basically when you work long-term assignments, after a while everything gets to be yours so to speak. You know where you're going every day. You know, maybe you're working through the agency, but you're going through one agency so that's all you have to deal with. (Jean Masters)

A second way I found that temporaries resisted social isolation was through restricting their work to one or two agencies. Although turnover in the agencies, or lack of available assignments, can limit the effectiveness of this strategy, one woman got around the problem by following her representative to a new agency. In addition, temporaries often work very hard at maintaining relationships with agency personnel. For example, frequent phone calls and "check-ins" help the agency get to know a temporary. This relationship work, a type of emotional labor, often serves an economic purpose as well, because some temporaries feel that an agency is more likely to give them more work if they know them better.

I do think that being known to them helps. I mean there are temps who sign up with an agency and never call them again . . . it doesn't work that way. You've got to be a presence. When I went out of town I sent them postcards and I was a presence, even when I'm not there. It helped. The people they know, the people who show the real desire to work, are the ones who get the jobs. (Bernice Katz)

Temporaries resisted nonperson treatment in two ways. The first was to remind oneself that "it's only temporary" and that one should not take things personally. Here's what Ellen Lanford did when someone treated her poorly.

I would just shut down and I would do the work and I would be in my own space in my head. I'd be writing my own story in my head. Because when someone treats me badly I know that they've got their own problems. . . . I mean I'm a temp, I have nothing to do with any of their problems, and so I don't let that stuff bother me.

In fact, Ellen is able to use her status as a temporary to reject internalizing any poor treatment that does occur. However, not all temporaries frame their experiences in this way. Each assignment may be temporary; however, for the worker, temporary work may be not-so-temporary and may go on long after a particular assignment has ended.

Others resist nonperson treatment more directly through office sabotage. Carol Ketchum felt that she was not considered for a permanent job opening because she was a temp, even though she had already been doing the job for a month: "I wondered . . . if they didn't like me or whatever. So I got back at them, this is an entertainment company, by stealing one of their screenplays. I showed them" [laughs].

On several occasions, Bernice Katz had an assignment end abruptly and was not informed by either the agency or the client so that she could seek additional work elsewhere. Bernice was resentful of the way she was treated and told me what she did.

> I had a little revenge with it too because they had these cabinets that you locked, and I had the key, you know. While I was there another employee had given it to me. And in it I stored things, my coffee cup, a couple of work tools. So I locked it and there I had the key with me. So they had to break their cabinet open. I was not gonna go all the way back there just to give them their key back. They had made such a big deal about don't lose the key, I guess they had to break it. Which is fine with me.

Once again, temporaries' resistance offers contradictions. The relationship work that temporaries use to combat social isolation is a form of emotional labor that engenders alienation from self. There is also the possibility that more overt acts of resistance, such as stealing a screenplay, can be used to justify both the marginal position of temporary workers and even greater social control of temporaries via the agency. For that reason, I was concerned that portraying some acts of resistance would reveal temporaries' "secrets." However, I emphasize again that all acts of resistance must be placed in the context of women's struggles to survive and derive a sense of control over otherwise alienating work.

Resistance to Alienation From Self

Temporaries resist emotional labor through seeking out assignments that are less likely to require emotional labor. "Back office" jobs such as filing are less likely to require emotional labor on the job than "front office" jobs such as executive secretary or receptionist. For example, Shari preferred filing jobs to receptionist jobs because filing jobs can often be done with minimal contact or supervision. After telling me about a bad experience with a supervisor, Shari Jensen told me that she came to prefer filing assignments because everyone left her alone to do her own work: "I like computer filing. That was my favorite because, you know, nobody told me what to do. I used to start there at 7 a.m. Nobody bothers you."

Temporaries also resist emotional labor by leaving an agency or an assignment. Although this option is not often used and is dependent upon the worker's financial circumstances, it does often represent an effective immediate strategy. Temporaries may actually walk out of an assignment, but it is more likely that they will just tell the agency that they are not available for further assignments. Here again, the worker can invoke her status as temporary to her advantage. In areas with an abundance of temporary agencies, this may represent a more effective strategy than in areas where temporary agencies are few, because the worker has more agencies available to her.

Another way temporaries resist alienation from self is by reminding themselves that they are not "just a temp." Interestingly this is the opposite of the strategy of claiming "just a temp" or "it's only temporary" in order to get by.

> It's important to keep in mind why you're doing it, because if you're treated badly you can have something to hold onto and keep your self-esteem up. Try to be assertive if you're called "the temp" or if you're picked on. Try to be clear about what your skills are and keep your long-term goals in mind. (Carol Ketchum)

> I was happy to redefine in my mind that I was only there temporarily, and to let everyone know that I was only there temporarily . . . and let everyone know that that wasn't my life. (Irene Pedersen)

This response works most easily for temps who have something "going on the side," but it can work in other cases as well. Temporaries may do this by using skills that coworkers were not aware that they possessed as a way of setting themselves apart from "just temps." For example, both Linda Mejia and Ludy Martinez surprised coworkers and supervisors with their ability to speak two or more languages. Cheryl Hansen and Jean Masters showed they were capable of using complicated computer software from previous job experience and education. As a result, each of these women was given additional job duties that made her feel better about her work and herself. It is a way to reject the negative stereotypes about temporary workers. The women I interviewed often reported that they were not like the "bad temps" we all here stories about. In fact, they often told me that employers or agencies told them "bad temp" stories as well.

The agencies don't really like it when you flake out that way and don't show up. They told me about these people. In fact, when I first signed up, they warned me about this kind of thing. And I'm there, like, "No, people really do that?" They're like, "Yeah." They've had people just flake out. They didn't feel like going to work that day, or had an audition that day. (Bernice Katz)

I think they expected a less competent person. I think they expected someone who wasn't . . . they definitely expected a less competent person from a temp agency. I think that's the stereotype. (Sarah Tilton)

Nothing surprises me in this industry any longer. Applicants when they don't show, when they have excuses. And then we're dealing with people and human nature. And you would think that these are responsible adults we're hiring, but not all the time. . . . They don't show up, they're 2 hours late, they leave for lunch and don't come back. (Sandy Mathers)

Temporaries who compare themselves favorably with "bad temps" are successful in resisting internalizing the negative identity themselves; however, this does leave the broader stereotypes intact. They are, in effect, stereotyping other temps. Although this may not be in their best interest in the long run, it reaffirms their sense of self today, even if they receive neither additional compensation nor permanent employment from the use of these special skills. In addition, the "bad temp" stories coming from the agency or the client seem to operate as a mechanism of social control, reinforcing temporaries' marginality. It serves as a warning and conveys expectations about what is deviant.

CONSTRAINTS ON RESISTANCE

Even though temporary workers found room for resistance at the worksite, this resistance occurs within a context of constraint. The constraint on resistance is largely due to temporary workers' marginal position in the workforce. Temporary workers' relationships with the agencies is one of dependence. Temporaries feel they must please the agency in order to continue to receive assignments. This often means tempering or forgoing one's resistance to alienation. Bernice was asked to take an assignment at a company where she had previously had a bad experience.

Oh, I said, put it this way. If they really needed someone and I didn't have a job that day. . . . I mean it's a job for the day. But it's not my first choice. . . . So I did it and they were pleased with me. (Bernice Katz)

Once Ludy complained about being overworked on an assignment. She told me about the agency's response.

It was just you know, they said, "If you're not *happy* on that assignment, well we'll take you off and put somebody else on." And if I couldn't afford it, then I'd just stay there. But I noticed that most agencies, even when they knew I was being taken advantage of, they wouldn't go to bat for you. . . . They very often wimped out. They wanted to keep the accounts or whatever, "Just accommodate them." What does that mean, "accommodate them"? (Ludy Martinez)

Cindy Carson was angry when the paychecks were delayed, and "stomped" out of the office when she learned she could not get her check until the next day: "And I stomped out of the office. And I thought, 'OK, I guess when this assignment ends that'll be then end of me.' I figured I'd be canned or something just for expressing myself. I'm not sure."

Indeed, temporary employees' perceptions of their position vis-à-vis the temporary agency are confirmed by my interviews with temporary agency personnel. Both agency representatives expressed an unwillingness to continue relationships with temporaries they considered "flaky" or bothersome. Joe Harcum, a branch manager, said he is less likely to place someone who "won't work with him." Similarly, Sandy Mathers told what happened when a temp does something that displeases the agency or the client: "You don't get too many opportunities to do that. One strike. I give just one strike. After the first one, that's it for me."

For some temporary workers, dependence appeared to be less of a factor. They actually felt empowered to resist, stating that they could leave their agency and use other agencies instead. Indeed, at least in Los Angeles, the proliferation of agencies seems to offer some chance for temporaries to break the dependency relationship. "And I said if she ever screamed at me, I'm out of there. And she did it once. And that's when I thought, I mean you don't pay me enough. . . . I'm not permanent. So I left" (Linda Mejia).

However, these measures are tempered by the financial constraints each temporary faces individually. One temporary worker summarized:

In a way you have to be better than the regular people. You have to behave better. You have to be more on time. You have to not take personal calls. You have to be more straight and narrow because you're a temp. They can dump you tomorrow. . . . I've seen other secretaries sitting and knitting on the phone. If you could figure out how much these people can get away with that might be acceptable for you. Usually it wasn't because they'd get back to the agency and that could jeopardize your getting an assignment when you really needed it or something like that. (Ludy Martinez)

Shari Jensen told me what happened after a particularly bad work experience. Although Shari supports herself, she shares an apartment with her mother and sister who also work. Breaking the relationship with one temporary agency did not pose a great financial threat to her, even though she consequently went several weeks without finding work.

I called the agency and told them what happened. So what, you're not gonna give me another assignment. Am I gonna die? No, I'm not gonna die. I will survive. So and after that, they never gave me another assignment. I don't care. I knew they were gonna do that but I don't care.

In addition, leaving one agency means greater reliance on other agencies (since many temporary workers use more than one) or cultivating relationships with new temporary agencies. Jean Masters initially fought a pay decrease, but eventually ended up taking the cut and going to a different agency.

I went from $17 to $12. It was too hard to get a job that was even $13 an hour then. And then they wanted to cut me down from that to $11. I think I was getting like $12. I know whatever it was that I fought it. In those cases with unemployment, if someone called you for an assignment you had to have a really good reason not to accept that assignment, otherwise unemployment will cut you off. So basically you had to accept the job. But when they wanted to go to that second pay cut, I fought it. You know, because if I accepted it, that means I'd have to accept jobs from now on at that pay scale.

Even though temporary workers manage to resist alienation from work in a variety of ways, this resistance occurs within a context of constraint that includes the availability of work at other agencies and the temporary worker's financial situation. Although resistance occurs in a variety of ways, it is more likely to occur surreptitiously than overtly. Modes of resistance are shaped by the organization of temporary work and can have contradictory and unintended results. Nevertheless, temporary work should be described as a struggle rather than an exchange.

CONCLUSION

These experiences, related by the women I interviewed, increase the understanding of the everyday experiences and struggles of temporary clerical employment. This research adds another dimension to labor studies that focus on the economic and legal issues of temporary employment. The comments of the women I interviewed demonstrate an astute understanding of the ways in which temporary workers are alienated, not only from their work, but from themselves and others. My analysis, along with the voices of the workers, poses a challenge to managerial analyses by asking, "What are the human costs of flexibility and who bears those costs?" Unfortunately, the answer is that the temporary worker bears the costs in the form of alienation from work, alienation from others, and alienation from self.

Examining the organization of temporary work in conjunction with these experiences provides understanding of the structural basis for this alienation. This structural basis is found not only in the capitalist work relations from which temporary work arises, but also in women's often marginal position in the labor market. Despite overwhelming constraints, women do resist alienation in its various forms, with results that range from favorable to contradictory. It is clear that temporary work should be characterized in more conflictual than consensual terms.

The implications of the alienating effects of temporary employment for the organization of work in the United States should not be understated, especially considering the demographic composition of this group of workers. Recall that groups that are already marginalized in this society, such as women and African Americans, are overrepresented in the temporary workforce. Temporary work as it is now organized serves to reproduce and reinforce marginality. With nearly one third of the U.S. workforce (Belous, 1989) employed in work characterized as contingent, these implications are serious.

Finally, as management consultants continue to espouse the benefits of temporary employment for business, even in times of economic recovery, the phenomenon of temporary employment is expected to grow. As temporary employment of all kinds grows, so does the number of us who will be incorporated into working arrangements similar to those analyzed in this study. We must ask ourselves if this is a wave of the future that we want to ride.

NOTES

1. Unfortunately, the available data do not include adequate racial/ethnic breakdowns. The figures here only indicate percentages for White and Black workers.

2. Keep in mind that the agencies that compose the National Association of Temporary Services largely focus on temporary clerical work, where the proportion of women is considerably higher than in temporary industrial work. Belous's (1989) figures include all temporary workers.

3. Recall the 1994 Teamsters strike, in which the increasing use of contingent workers was one of the main issues. Currently, union leaders seem to oppose contingent work (House Committee on Government Operations, 1988) because it threatens what remaining power unions do have in the United States.

4. Of the women interviewed, five were not currently working as temporaries when I interviewed them; however, they had worked as a temporary in the past 2 years. Having the input of both current and previous temporary workers decreases the likelihood that my data are unbalanced in favor of those who are staying with temporary work for one reason or another. It is also quite common for people to move in and out of temporary work over a peri-

od of time; therefore, these interviews help capture that experience as well.

5. I have worked on and off as a temporary employee in the Los Angeles area over the past 3 years. My interest in temporary work came before my employment as a temporary worker. My experience as a temporary worker has helped me to formulate effective questions, to gain access to interview subjects, and to have better rapport with my interview subjects.

6. There have been several excellent examples of the stereotypes associated with temporary employees that have appeared on television or in films. For example, in a recent episode of NBC's new drama series, *ER*, a temporary employee sat filing her nails while chaos ensued all around her. She then interrupted emergency surgery to have her time card signed. Most of the stereotypes the women I interviewed encountered portrayed temporaries as incompetent and unintelligent.

REFERENCES

Acker, J. (1990, June). Hierarchies, jobs, bodies: A theory of gendered organizations. *Gender and Society, 4*, 139-158.

Acker, J. (1992). The future of women and work: Ending the twentieth century. *Sociological Perspectives, 35*(1), 53-68.

Amott, T., & Matthaei, J. (1991). *Race, gender, and work: A multicultural economic history of women in the United States.* Boston: South End Press.

Beechey, V., & Perkins, T. (1987). *A matter of hours: Part-time work and the labor market.* Minneapolis: University of Minnesota Press.

Belous, R. (1989). *The contingent economy: The growth of the temporary, part-time and subcontracted workforce.* Washington, DC: National Planning Association.

Bookman, A., & Morgan, S. (1988). *Women and the politics of empowerment.* Philadelphia: Temple University Press.

Braverman, H. (1974). *Labor and monopoly capital: The degradation of work in the twentieth century.* New York: Monthly Review Press.

Callaghan, P., & Hartmann, H. (1991). *Contingent work.* Washington, DC: Economic Policy Institute.

Castro, J. (1993, March 29). Disposable workers. *Time*, pp. 43-47.

Cockburn, C. (1985). *Machinery of dominance: women, men, and technical know-how.* Boston: Northeastern University Press.

Daniels, A. K. (1987). Invisible work. *Social Problems, 34*(5), 403-415.

Glaser, B., & Strauss, A. (1967). *The discovery of grounded theory.* Chicago: Aldine.

Goffman, E. (1959). *The presentation of self in everyday life.* New York: Doubleday.

Golden, L., & Appelbaum, E. (1992). What was driving the 1982-88 boom in temporary employment: Preferences of workers or decisions and power of employers? *American Journal of Economics and Society, 51*(4), 473-494.

Henson, K. D. (in press). *Just a temp: The disenfranchised worker.* Philadelphia: Temple University Press.

Hochschild, A. R. (1983). *The managed heart: Commercialization of human feeling.* Berkeley: University of California Press.

House Committee on Government Operations, 100th Congress. (1988). *Rising use of part-time and temporary workers: Who benefits & who loses?* Washington, DC: Government Printing Office.

Israel, J. (1971). *Alienation from Marx to modern sociology.* Boston: Allyn & Bacon.

Kohn, M., & Schooler, C. (1983). *Work and personality: An inquiry into the impact of social stratification.* Norwood, NJ: Ablex.

McLellan, D. (1977). *Karl Marx: Selected writings.* New York: Oxford University Press.

Milkman, R. (1987). *Gender at work: The dynamics of job segregation by sex during World War II.* Chicago: University of Illinois Press.

Morrow, L. (1993, March 29). The temping of America. *Time*, pp. 40-41.

National Association of Temporary Services. (1992). *Report on the temporary help services industry.* New York: DRI/McGraw-Hill.

Negrey, C. (1993). *Gender, time, and reduced work.* Albany: State University of New York Press.

Ong, A. (1987). *Spirits of resistance and capitalist discipline: Factory women in Malaysia.* Albany: State University of New York Press.

Parker, R. E. (1994). *Flesh peddlers and warm bodies: The temporary help industry and its workers.* New Brunswick, NJ: Rutgers University Press.

Polivka, A., & Nardone, T. (1989, December). On the definition of contingent work. *Monthly Labor Review*, pp. 9-16.

Reskin, B., & Roos, P. (1990). *Job queues, gender queues.* Philadelphia: Temple University Press.

Rizzo, J., House, R. J., & Lirtzman, S. I. (1970). Role conflict and ambiguity in complex organizations. *Administrative Science Quarterly, 15*, 150-163.

Sartre, J.-P. (1966). *Being and nothingness.* New York: Washington Square Press.

Schmitt, R., & Moody, T. E. (1994). *Alienation and social criticism.* Atlantic Highlands, NJ: Humanities Press.

Seeman, M. (1959). On the meaning of alienation. *American Sociological Review, 26*, 753-758.

Senate Committee on Labor and Human Resources, 103rd Congress. (1993). *Toward a disposable work force: The increasing use of "contingent labor."* Washington, DC: Government Printing Office.

Smith, V. (1993). Flexibility in work and employment: The impact on women. In *Research in the sociology of organizations* (pp. 195-216). Greenwich, CT: JAI.

Sokoloff, N. (1992). *Black women and White women in the professions.* New York: Routledge.

Strauss, A. L. (1987). *Qualitative analysis for social scientists.* New York: Cambridge University Press.

Tilly, C. (1990). *Short hours, short shrift.* Washington, DC: Economic Policy Institute.

Ward, K. (1990). *Women workers and global restructuring.* Ithaca, NY: ILR Press.

West, J. (1990). Gender and the labor process. In D. Knights & H. Willmott (Eds.), *Labor process theory* (pp. 244-273). London: Macmillan.

13

Women's Work, Men's Work, and the Sense of Control

CATHERINE E. ROSS
MARYLYN P. WRIGHT

Is women's work more alienating than men's? In this study, we examine gender differences in work alienation and the ways in which work alienation shapes subjective powerlessness versus control. We focus on two ways in which women's work differs from men's. First, the employment status of men and women differs. Women are more likely than men to be unpaid domestic workers, and if employed, women are more likely than men to work part-time. Second, the characteristics of men's and women's work differ. We propose that women's work is more routine, less autonomous, less fulfilling, and more isolated than men's. Together these constitute work alienation. We argue that women's work is more objectively alienating than men's, which produces subjective alienation, and explains the effects of homemaker status and part-time employment on subjective alienation.

Our propositions fit a differential exposure perspective (Loscocco & Spitze, 1990; Pugliesi, 1995). Because women are more likely to be unpaid domestic workers and part-time workers, they are exposed to more alienating work conditions, which affect their sense of personal control. In contrast, a differential vulnerability perspective claims that work has a different impact on men than on women (Schooler, Miller, Miller, & Richtand, 1984). Blauner (1964), one of the early proponents of the latter perspective, concluded that women faced more objectively alienating work—they had less decision-making autonomy and less freedom from supervision—but the psychological consequences were not as negative for women as for men. In contrast, we hypothesize that women, like men, suffer the subjective consequences of work alienation (Feldberg & Glenn, 1979). One consequence of women's differential exposure to alienating work at home and in the paid economy may be a lower sense of control over their lives.

Of all the beliefs about self and society, one's sense of control over one's own life may be the most important (Mirowsky & Ross, 1989). Perceived control versus powerlessness represent two ends of a continuum, with the belief that one can and does master, control, and shape one's own life on one end of the continuum, and

From *Work and Occupations*, Vol. 25, No. 3, August 1998, pp. 333-355. Reprinted by permission.

the belief that one's actions cannot influence events and outcomes at the other (Mirowsky & Ross, 1989). Perceived powerlessness is the major form of *subjective* alienation (Seeman, 1959, 1983). Concepts related to the sense of personal control appear in a number of forms with various names, notably instrumentalism (Wheaton, 1980), personal efficacy (Downey & Moen, 1987; Gecas, 1989), mastery (Pearlin, Menaghan, Lieberman, & Mullan, 1981), internal locus of control (Rotter, 1966), psychological self-direction (Kohn & Schooler, 1982), and personal autonomy (Seeman, 1983). The effects of perceived powerlessness versus control are far-reaching and include depression, anxiety, malaise, physical illness, alcoholism, and mortality (Elder & Liker, 1982; Gecas, 1989; Mirowsky & Ross, 1989, 1990; Pearlin et al., 1981; Rodin, 1986; Seeman & Anderson, 1983; Seeman & Lewis, 1995; Wheaton, 1980). Past evidence indicates that women have a lower sense of control than men (Mirowsky & Ross, 1984; Thoits, 1987), although sometimes the difference is insignificant (Ross & Bird, 1994; Ross & Mirowsky, 1992).

Research on the psychological consequences of work alienation for individuals typically does not compare men's work to women's. Most studies include only men (Kohn, 1976; Kohn, Naoi, Schoenbach, Schooler, & Slomczynski, 1990; Kohn & Schooler, 1973, 1982; Kohn & Slomczynski, 1993), one includes only women (Miller, Schooler, Kohn, & Miller, 1979), and some include both men and women but still focus on social class, not gender (Link, Lennon, & Dohrenwend, 1993; Schwalbe & Staples, 1986). In his review of this research, Spenner (1988) found only two studies comparing men to women. On the other hand, most research that does compare men's work to women's is silent on the topic of alienation (e.g., England, 1992; England, Farkas, Kilbourn, & Dou, 1988; Reskin & Hartmann, 1986). Furthermore, both of these research traditions usually focus on the paid economy, with little attention to unpaid domestic work. Only a few studies, which we soon discuss, examine the subjective consequences of gender differences in work alienation among people in and out of the paid economy.

SUBJECTIVE CONSEQUENCES OF ALIENATING WORK

Workers who are alienated have little control over their own work, find little fulfillment in work, and have few connections to others. Their work is routine, nonautonomous, unfulfilling, and isolated. On the nonalienating end of the continuum, work is autonomous, nonroutine, fulfilling, and socially integrated. Whatever the terms used to indicate nonalienating work—freedom, control, commitment, connectedness, identity—they are the positive characteristics of work of interest to many sociologists (Blauner, 1964; Erikson, 1986; Hodson, 1996; Lincoln & Kalleberg, 1990).[1]

In his theory of alienation, Marx (1884/1964) emphasized whether or not workers owned the means of production because he believed that owning the means of production usually meant control over the labor process. Control over one's own work is indicated by nonroutine work and autonomy (Kohn & Schooler, 1982). Nonroutine work involves doing a variety of tasks and having the opportunity to solve problems. It gives workers the chance to use thought and independent judgment in doing different things in different ways. In contrast, workers engaged in routine work do the same thing in the same way over and over, with no chance to use their skills or solve problems. Autonomous work gives workers the freedom to make their own decisions rather than being told what to do and how to do it by their supervisor. It includes participation in decision making and the freedom to disagree with one's boss. In nonautonomous work, workers are closely supervised, decisions are imposed from above, and workers do not participate in decision making.

Kohn and his colleagues do not distinguish autonomous from nonroutine work, instead calling the two occupational self-direction. Among employed men, occupational self-direction, or control over one's own work—rather than ownership of the means of production or control over the labor of others—increases psychological self-direction and the sense of personal control (Kohn, 1976; Kohn et al., 1990; Kohn & Schooler, 1982; Seeman, Seeman, & Budros, 1988).

Ross and her colleagues distinguish autonomous from nonroutine work. Autonomous work, as indicated by freedom from close supervision and participation in decision making—more than authority over others, job prestige, or the opportunity for promotion—increases perceived control (Ross & Mirowsky, 1992). When both are included in multivariate analyses, autonomous and nonroutine work have independent, significant positive effects on personal control among both paid and unpaid workers (Bird & Ross, 1993). For Kohn's purposes, it probably was not crucial to distinguish autonomous from nonroutine work, since both have positive, independent effects on personal control when examined separately. However, as Lennon (1994) argues and we will show, when gendered work is the focus, it is important to distinguish autonomous from nonroutine work.

Fulfilling work is enjoyable and provides intrinsic gratification (Mirowsky & Ross, 1989). It gives people the opportunity learn new things and develop as a person through work. Its opposite, work estrangement, is the feeling that there is nothing inherently gratifying about work; it is done only for the extrinsic rewards. Like nonautonomous and routine work, the importance of estranged work appears in Marx's discussion of alienated labor. Marx (1884/1964) believed that paid work for others was a means of satisfying certain needs rather than being fulfilling in itself; external rather than part of the worker's nature, imposed rather than voluntary (Schwalbe, 1986). Fulfilling versus estranged work is rarely directly measured by researchers or correlated with the sense of control.[2] Exceptions include Kobasa, Maddi, and Courington (1981) and Bird and Ross (1993), both of whom found an association between work fulfillment and the sense of personal control. In contrast, Greenberg and Grunberg (1995) and Seeman et al. (1988) found no effect of engaging, interesting, challenging work on perceived powerlessness among mill workers or in a representative sample of employed White males.

Social interaction at work involves positive communication and interaction with others, including peers, friends, coworkers, supervisors, students, clients, and so on. In isolated work, on the other hand, the person is separated from positive interaction with others. Social isolation was not central to Marx's concept of work alienation. However, it fits the general definition of alienation as any kind of social detachment or separation (Mirowsky & Ross, 1989). Blauner (1964) considered it to be a major form of work alienation, as does Leiter (1985) in his reassessment of work alienation in the textile industry, and Seeman et al. (1988) include social isolation versus integration as a dimension of work alienation. No previous research examines the association of social interaction at work with the sense of control versus powerlessness. Theoretically, positive social interaction might increase control over work by allowing workers to work together efficiently and effectively, but, alternatively, it could substitute for fulfilling, nonroutine, and autonomous work.

DIFFERENCES IN WOMEN'S AND MEN'S WORK

Women are more likely to work full-time in the home doing unpaid domestic work, and women who work for pay are more likely than men to work part-time. Full-time unpaid domestic workers, almost 99% of whom are women, provide services for the family, including cleaning, cooking, shopping, doing laundry, budgeting, managing, and taking care of children (Bergmann, 1986). Part-time employment is the second-most female-dominated work. Almost 70% of part-time workers are women, and women's overrepresentation in part-time work also partly reflects the fact that they are responsible for domestic work (Rubery, Horrell, &

Burchell, 1994). What characterizes unpaid domestic work and part-time paid work?

Paid and Unpaid Work

Unpaid domestic worker is the most female-dominated occupation and would be the largest occupation if it were counted (Andre, 1981; Bergmann, 1986). In 1990, 26.5 million women and 541,000 men made their living by keeping house (U.S. Bureau of Labor Statistics, 1990). Compared to unpaid domestic work, employment is associated with status, power, economic independence, and noneconomic rewards for men and women (Bird & Ross, 1993; Gove & Tudor, 1973). For women who are exclusively homemakers, domestic work is done without economic rewards, without the opportunity for advancement or promotion for work well done, and, because it is often invisible, devalued, and taken for granted, without psychological rewards (Bergmann, 1986; Gove & Geerken, 1977; Gove & Tudor, 1973; Oakley, 1974). Work done without rewards produces a sense of disconnection between efforts and outcomes, and those doing such work typically are economically dependent. Theoretically, both decrease the sense of control among unpaid domestic workers compared to paid workers, and some empirical evidence indicates that employed persons have a higher sense of control than the nonemployed overall (Ross & Mirowsky, 1992), and that the employed have a higher sense of control than homemakers specifically (Bird & Ross, 1993). Elder and Liker (1982) found that elderly women who had taken jobs 40 years earlier, during the Great Depression, had a higher sense of self-efficacy and lower sense of helplessness than women who remained homemakers.

Can homemakers' low sense of control be explained by alienating work conditions? Is homemaking more estranged, more routine, less autonomous, and more isolated than paid work? Marx (1884/1964]) believed that wage labor is estranging. Yet, most unwaged work for the household—including most child care—consists of housework; and cleaning, doing the dishes, shopping, vacuuming, doing laundry, and chauffeuring children are typically described as ungratifying, unfulfilling, nonenjoyable tasks that do not give a person a chance to learn or develop as a person (Berk & Berk, 1979; Gove & Tudor, 1973; Hill & Stafford, 1980). Only cooking and caring for children are rated as enjoyable by homemakers (Berheide, 1984; Kahn, 1991). Just because this work is unpaid does not make it inherently more enjoyable, and one comparative study found that wage laborers report significantly *higher* levels of work fulfillment than unpaid domestic workers (Bird & Ross, 1993).

Unpaid domestic work is described as routine, monotonous, and repetitive (Berheide, 1984; Bernard, 1972; Gove & Tudor, 1973; Oakley, 1974), and the evidence shows that full-time unpaid domestic work is more routine than paid work (Bird & Ross, 1993; Lennon, 1994) and that the housework done by both the employed and nonemployed is more routine and less complex than paid work (Schooler et al., 1984).

Unpaid domestic work is also portrayed as isolating (Bernard, 1972; Gove & Tudor, 1973), but to our knowledge, no one has measured social interaction in paid and unpaid work and compared them. Over 20 years ago, Gove and others proposed that being isolated in the home, without the opportunity for positive social interaction with other adults, is one of the most negative aspects of full-time homemaking as compared to employment, but to date the isolation theory remains untested.

In contrast to the other aspects of work alienation, unpaid domestic workers may have a high level of autonomy. Homemakers report that lack of supervision, setting their own schedules, and organizing their own work are the most valued aspects of housework (Andre, 1981; Berheide, 1984; Kibria, Barnett, Baruch, Marshall, & Pleck, 1990). Only two studies compare homemaking to employment, and both find that housework is more autonomous than paid work when measured in terms of freedom from close supervision and decision-making autonomy (Bird & Ross, 1993; Lennon, 1994).

Alternatively, however, some argue that the decisions homemakers make are trivial "pseudochoices"—such as which laundry detergent to use—and do not indicate real control over one's work (Rosenberg, 1984).

Part-Time and Full-Time Paid Work

Women are more than twice as likely as men to work in part-time jobs (26% of women compared to 10% of men in the employed civilian labor force), and about 70% of all part-time workers are women (Tilly, 1991; U.S. Bureau of Labor Statistics, 1988). Women who work part-time do so over the life course starting as young adults with children, and 33% of employed women with children work part-time (Beechey & Perkins, 1987; England, 1992; Mirowsky, 1996). Men who work part-time, in contrast, typically do so after the age of 60—after retiring from a full-time job—and only 7% of employed men aged 25-60 work part-time (Quinn & Burkhauser, 1994; Siegel, 1993). In the representative national sample used here, 80% of part-time workers under the age of 60 are women. Part-time work pays 58% of the hourly pay of full-time work; is even more segregated than full-time work; and offers less training, lower returns to experience, less authority, fewer chances for advancement, and fewer benefits (Holden & Hansen, 1987; Reskin & Padavic, 1994; Rubery et al., 1994; Tilly, 1991).

Part-time work may be associated with a low sense of personal control because many part-time jobs are low skilled, routine, unsteady, and involuntary (Reskin & Padavic, 1994; Tilly, 1991). Although most part-time workers report that they prefer part-time work, involuntary part-time work (where workers would prefer full-time work) accounts for most of the growth of part-time work since 1970, and part-time work typically benefits employers, not employees (Pfeffer & Baron, 1988; Tilly, 1991). Work that is not chosen theoretically produces a sense of powerlessness over one's life outcomes. Some part-time work is contingent work in which workers lack an explicit or implicit contract for long-term employment or in which the number of working hours fluctuate unsystematically (Polivka & Nardone, 1989). This uncertainty theoretically leads to a sense of powerlessness. Compared to full-time work, the uncertainty, lack of choice, restricted opportunity for advancement, and economic marginality of much part-time work, combined with the routine and unfulfilling characteristics of the work itself, may produce a sense that one is not in control of one's own life. However, to date, no research has examined these issues empirically.

HYPOTHESES

In this study, we examine three propositions. First, women are exposed to more routine, less autonomous, less fulfilling, and more isolated work than men. Second, these work characteristics shape individual perceptions of personal powerlessness versus control. And third, work characteristics explain the effects of homemaker status and part-time employment—in which women are disproportionately represented—on perceived powerlessness.

SAMPLE

Our analyses use the 1995 survey of Aging, Status, and the Sense of Control (ASOC). The ASOC is a national telephone probability sample of United States households. The National Institute on Aging supported the data collection. Sampling, pretesting, and interviewing were conducted by the Survey Research Laboratory of the University of Illinois. Respondents were selected using a prescreened random digit dialing method that decreases the probability of contacting a business or nonworking number and decreases errors compared to the standard Mitofsky-Waksberg method while producing a sample with the same demographic profile (Lund & Wright, 1994; Waksberg, 1978). The ASOC survey has two subsamples, designed to produce an 80% oversample of persons 60 years or older. The survey was limited to English-speaking adults. The main sample draws from all households; the oversample draws only from households with one or more seniors. In the main sample, the adult (18 years or older) with the most recent birthday was selected as respondent, and in the oversample the senior (60 years or older) with the most recent birthday was selected (O'Rourke & Blair, 1983). Up to 10 callbacks were made to select and contact a respondent, and up to 10 to complete the interview once contact was made. Interviews were completed with 71.6% of contacted and eligible persons: 73.0% for the main sample and 67.3% for the oversample. The final sample has 2,592 respondents ranging in age from 18 to 95. Because the survey oversampled respondents 60 years or older by 1.8, we weighted the sample using a weighting variable equal to 1 if 59 years or younger and 1/1.8 if 60 years or older. In the weighted sample, 1,841 respondents are under 60, and 751 are 60 or older.

The following weighted statistics compare the demographic characteristics of the ASOC sample to those of the U.S. population as a whole (U.S. Bureau of the Census, 1995). For ASOC and the U.S. population, respectively, the percentage female is 56.2 and 51.2, the percentage White is 85.1 and 82.9, the percentage married is 55.7 and 55.0, and the mean household size is 2.67 and 2.59. For persons 25 years or older, the percentage with a high school degree is 85.1 and 80.9, and the percentage with a college degree is 25.6 and 22.2. The mean household income is $43,949 and $41,285.

MEASUREMENT

Gender compares females (1) with males (0).

Employment status is a series of dummy variables in which part-time employees, homemakers, retired persons, the unemployed, people in school, and people unable to work because of disability or poor health are compared to full-time employees, the omitted category in the regression analyses. Inability to work because of disability or illness is included to control for the selection of some people out of the labor force because of illness. Some people with problems associated with low perceived control, such as physical disabilities, may not work, therefore creating an association between work and control that is due to selection of persons with low control out of the workforce. By adjusting for the inability to work, we can examine whether paid work is associated with high perceived control, holding selection effects constant to some extent.

To assess the degree of *work alienation,* we asked employed and nonemployed persons to describe the work, tasks, or activities they most frequently do during the day. Respondents were then asked about the degree of routinization, enjoyment, freedom, the chance to learn new things and develop as a person, and so on, in their primary daily work, paid or unpaid. Nonalienating work is defined here as nonroutine, autonomous, fulfilling, socially integrated work. Nonroutine work includes doing different things in different ways and solving problems. Autonomous work includes decision-making autonomy and freedom from supervision. Fulfilling work is enjoyable and gives people the chance to learn and develop as a person. Integrated work provides positive social interaction. When we use the term *objective work alienation,* it is only to distinguish it from its subjective, or psychological, consequences. All information is based on self-reports (see appendix for questions and coding).

Sense of control is measured by the Mirowsky and Ross (1991) 2 × 2 index that balances statements claiming or denying control over good or bad outcomes. The measure is conceptually similar to the personal control component of Rotter's (1966) internal = external locus of control scale (modified for community surveys by using Likert-type scale responses rather than forced-choice responses) and to Pearlin et al.'s (1981) mastery scale. The major difference is that it balances statements claiming control against those denying it, and statements about good outcomes against those about bad outcomes. The balanced 2 × 2 design eliminates defense and agreement bias from the measure of personal control (see the appendix for questions and coding).

Sociodemographic controls include age and education, coded in number of years; race, which contrasts Whites (1) and non-Whites (0); and marital status, which contrasts married persons (1) and nonmarried persons (0).

RESULTS AND DISCUSSION

Differences in Women's and Men's Work

Compared to men's, women's work is routine. It provides less of a chance to do different tasks in different ways and less of a chance to solve problems (see Table 13.1). Women's work provides less of an opportunity to learn new things but is not significantly less enjoyable overall than men's. Women's work provides more of a chance for positive social interaction, and is more autonomous overall. Are these differences due to the fact that women are more likely than men to be homemakers? Less than 1% of men report that they are homemakers compared to 19% of women in our sample. Compared to employed persons, full-time homemakers' work is routine: It does not involve doing a variety of tasks in different ways and it does not involve as much problem solving. Homemaking is less fulfilling than paid work: It is not associated with learning new things and it is not as enjoyable. Homemaking is more isolated, involving less positive social interaction with others than paid work. However, homemaking is more autonomous than paid work: There is more decision-making autonomy and more freedom from close supervision. Thus, part of the reason that women's work is more autonomous overall is because women are much more likely to be homemakers. However, homemaking cannot explain the fact that women in general report more positive social interaction because homemakers are more isolated than paid workers.

Compared to employed men, employed women engage in routine work that does not allow for problem solving or engaging in a variety of tasks. However, employed women's work is just as enjoyable as men's, and provides the same opportunity to learn new things. Employed women report more positive interaction with others than do their male counterparts. Employed women report less freedom from close supervision, but no less decision-making autonomy. Thus, compared to employed men, employed women face routine work and close supervision. On the other hand, employed women report more positive social interaction and equal levels of fulfillment. Thus, some of the reason that women face more alienated work conditions overall is that they are more likely to work full-time in the home doing unpaid domestic work. When they work for pay, some but not all of these disadvantages are mitigated. However, employed women still face routine work and close supervision. Is this due to the fact that women are much more likely than men to work part-time?

Women are much more likely to work part-time. Thirteen percent of all women work part-time compared to 5% of all men, and 25% of employed women work part-time compared to 8% of employed men in our sample. Very few men work part-time, especially during middle age. Only 6% of employed men under the age of 60 work part-time, and 22% of employed women under the age of 60 work part-time. Part-time work is more routine than full-time work, is less fulfilling, and provides less decision-making autonomy (see Table 13.1). Part-time work is associated with more freedom from supervision than full-time work, a result that required further investigation in light of its other alienating characteristics. It turns out that male, but not female, part-time workers report freedom from supervision. Part-time female employees are not free from close supervision. Although there are only 59 male part-time workers (despite our oversample of seniors), it is their very low levels of supervision that produce the overall effect shown in Table 13.1. Some of these men may be retired from their full-time jobs and working part-time out of their home on a consulting or contingent work arrangement with little direct supervision. This appears to be an interesting

TABLE 13.1 Differences in Men's and Women's and Homemakers' and Employed Persons' Work Characteristics

	Female *Male*	*Homemaker* *Employed*	*Employed Female* *Employed Male*	*Employed Part-Time* *Employed Full-Time*
Nonroutine work				
Task variety	<	<	<	<
Solve problems	<	<	<	<
Fulfilling work				
Learn new things	<	<	n.s.	<
Enjoyable work	n.s.	<	n.s.	<
Social interaction	>	<	>	n.s.
Autonomous work				
Decision-making autonomy	>	>	n.s.	<
Freedom from supervision	>	>	<	>

NOTE: Mean differences significantly greater or less than noted with > and <; insignificant differences noted with n.s. (.05 level, two-tailed test). Because less than 1% of men are homemakers, we do not show them separately. Male and female full-time employees show the same patterns as shown above for employed. Male and female part-time workers differ significantly on three work characteristics: females score significantly higher on social interaction and enjoyable work, and males score significantly higher on freedom from supervision. Although there are only 59 male part-time workers, it is their high scores on freedom from supervision that produce the overall effect of part-time work shown in the table.

group of older male part-time workers that requires further investigation; but their situation should not obscure the fact that women are much more likely to work part-time than are men; work that is routine, unfulfilling, and provides little latitude in decision making.

Homemaking and part-time work are performed predominantly by females. Homemakers, almost all of whom are women, work without supervision, make their own decisions, and overall have more autonomous working conditions than those who work for pay. These benefits are offset by the fact that homemakers report that their work is routine, provides little chance for solving problems or learning new things, is not intrinsically gratifying, and is socially isolated. In contrast to employed women, homemakers' work does not provide positive interactions with peers. Homemaking is more alienating work than paid work on three of the four dimensions of alienation. Part-time work is more alienating than full-time work, too. It is more routine and provides less decision-making autonomy and less fulfillment. Part-time female workers are less free from close supervision than full-time women employees, although part-time male workers are freer than full-time workers.

Work and the Sense of Control

Women's disproportionate representation in homemaking and part-time employment explain women's low personal control. Equation 1 of Table 13.2 shows that women report a lower sense of control over their lives than do men. Adjustment for employment status in Equation 2 renders the effect of gender insignificant. Compared to full-time employees, part-time employees, homemakers, retired persons, unemployed persons, and those unable to work because of disability have a lower sense of control over their lives. In contrast, people in school have a higher sense of control than do full-time workers. Women are more likely than men to be

TABLE 13.2 Sense of Control Regressed on Gender (Equation 1) Employment Status (Equation 2), Work Characteristics Favoring Employed (Equation 3), and Homemakers (Equation 4) (N = 2,498)

	Equation 1	*Equation 2*	*Equation 3*	*Equation 4*
Female	–.045*	–.024	–.029	–.028
	(–2.275)	(–1.157)	(–1.448)	(–1.404)
Employment				
Homemaker[a]		–.133**	–.055	–.105**
		(–3.950)	(–1.624)	(–2.848)
Retired[a]		–.132**	–.070*	–.106**
		(–3.829)	(–2.016)	(–2.935)
Unemployed[a]		–.125*	–.063	–.112†
		(–2.119)	(–2.016)	(–1.871)
In school[a]		.183**	.188**	.155**
		(3.542)	(3.692)	(2.992)
Unable to work[a]		–.479**	–.355**	–.402**
		(–8.627)	(–6.348)	(–7.007)
Employed part-time[a]		–.109**	–.058†	–.054
		(–3.197)	(–1.706)	(–1.604)
Work characteristics				
Task variety			.026*	.024*
			(2.219)	(2.070)
Solve problems			.079**	.077**
			(4.828)	(4.748)
Learn new things			.018	.016
			(1.111)	(0.987)
Enjoyable work			.050**	.045**
			(2.815)	(2.547)
Social interaction			.044**	.043**
			(2.656)	(2.635)
Decision-making autonomy				.037*
				(2.011)
Freedom from supervision				.022*
				(2.055)
Sociodemographics				
Age	–.005**	–.002**	–.003**	–.003**
	(–8.358)	(–3.170)	(–3.843)	(–4.368)
White	.116*	.110**	.090**	.088**
	(4.275)	(4.136)	(3.405)	(3.361)
Education	.054**	.048**	.039**	.039**
	(14.510)	(12.895)	(10.576)	(10.293)
Married	.078**	.081**	.069**	.069**
	(3.952)	(4.075)	(3.523)	(3.550)
Constant	.054	.077	–.466	–.574
R^2	.134	.170	.204	.207

NOTE: Metric coefficients (with t values in parentheses) are shown.
a. Compared to full-time employment.
†p < .10; *p < .05; **p < .01 (two-tailed).

homemakers and, if employed, to work part-time. Women and men are equally likely to be retired (18% for both) and to be in school (4% for both), and are about equally likely to be unable to work (4% of women and 3% of men). Women are less likely to be unemployed (2% of women and 4% of men). Thus, only homemaking and part-time employment can explain women's lower sense of control over their lives. Do the alienating work characteristics associated with homemaking and part-time employment affect personal control and account for the associations?

Work characteristics positively associated with paid employment are added in Equation 3. Nonroutine work in which a person does a variety of tasks and solves problems, enjoyable work, and work in which one interacts with people one likes are all significantly associated with high perceived control. Adjusting for these work characteristics renders the effect of being a homemaker insignificant. However, homemaking is not uniformly negative. Equation 4 adds autonomous work, more characteristic of homemaking than paid work. Decision-making autonomy and freedom from close supervision are significantly associated with high personal control. Adjustment for all work characteristics in Equation 4 shows a significant effect of homemaker status once all work characteristics are in the equation. In sum, homemakers have a lower sense of control over their lives than do employed persons in part because their work is more routine, less fulfilling, and more isolated. However, their work is more autonomous, which offsets the negative aspects somewhat. Adjusting for all work characteristics shows that at the same level of nonalienated work, homemakers have a lower sense of control than employed persons, so something over and above the characteristics of homemakers' work (possibly lack of pay) also contributes to their low sense of control.

Part-time workers have a lower sense of control than full-time workers because their work is more routine, provides less of an opportunity to solve problems, is less enjoyable, provides less of a chance to learn new things, and affords less decision-making autonomy. Adjusting for all these work characteristics in Equation 4 renders the effect of part-time employment insignificant.

If women achieved the same levels of paid employment as men, their work would be less alienating overall. Paid employment is less routine, more fulfilling, and less isolated than is unpaid domestic work. These benefits of paid employment, compared to full-time homemaking, in part explain women's sense of control. The one benefit of homemaking is autonomy, which is associated with high perceived control. Part-time employment explains the rest of women's low sense of control over their lives. Part-time work is routinized, unfulfilling work that provides little latitude in decision-making. It is these characteristics of the labor, rather than part-time employment per se, that affect the sense of control. Adjusting for them shows no independent effect of part-time employment on personal control.

Does work have the same effect on men as it does on women? To address the differential vulnerability perspective, we test interactions of all dimensions of work alienation with gender to see if work affects men's sense of control differently than it does women's. We tested interactions one at a time. None was significant. The p values of gender by task variety, solve problems, learn new things, enjoyable work, social interaction, decision-making autonomy, and freedom from supervision were .65, .94, .91, .13, .65, .17, and .26, respectively. Only the interaction of gender with enjoyable work was close to significant ($p = .13$), and it showed that enjoyable work has less of an effect for women. The nonsignificant interaction between gender and social interaction is especially noteworthy, since some have claimed that connections with others are more psychologically important to women than to men. To examine further whether employment affects men's sense of control differently than it does women's, we test the interaction of employment status with gender. We substituted full-time employment in comparison to all other employment statuses. The interaction of employment by gender has a nonsignificant p value of .74, indicating that full-time employment is associated with high perceived control for both men and women. What differs is the allocation of men and women to different kinds of work, not the effects of work on men's and women's perceived control. Paid employment and nonalienating work are both equally beneficial to men and women.[3]

CONCLUSION

In this study we find significant effects of work alienation on the sense of control. Nonroutine work in which people solve problems and engage in a variety of tasks, enjoyable work, work that provides positive interaction with others, and autonomous work in which people have decision-making autonomy and freedom from close supervision all significantly and positively affect the sense of control over life, adjusting for all other work conditions and for age, race, education, and marital status.

Women's work is more alienating than men's work. Homemaking exposes women to routine, unfulfilling, isolated work; and part-time employment exposes them to routine, unfulfilling work, with little decision-making autonomy. Compared to full-time employees, part-time workers have a lower sense of control because their work is more routine, less enjoyable, and less autonomous. Compared to full-time employees, homemakers have a lower sense of control in part because their work is more routine, less enjoyable, and more isolated.

Does the lower sense of control among homemakers and part-time workers reflect selection of persons with low personal control into this kind of work? Put another way, does the higher sense of control among full-time employees compared to the retired, unemployed, part-time employees or homemakers reflect the selection of persons with high personal control into full-time employment? It seems unlikely that people retire, become unemployed, work part-time, or perform unpaid domestic work full-time largely because of low personal control. Structural causes like age stratification, high unemployment rates among those without a college education, gender-based responsibilities for domestic work, or a lack of child care in the community likely affect retirement, unemployment, part-time employment, and the decision to stay home as much or more than psychological causes. It seems unlikely that women's lower sense of control over their lives leads them to work in the home without pay or to work part-time, and most sociologists do not think that sex segregation in work is due to psychological attributes of women (e.g., Reskin & Hartmann, 1986). Kohn and Schooler (1982) find that work has an large effect on psychological self-direction (in part by way of distress and lack of problem-solving flexibility), which in turn has a smaller effect on work choices. We expect a similar process here. We do not claim that there are no reciprocal effects between work and the sense of control. However, given our causal order assumptions, we find empirical support for our theory that work alienation, faced disproportionately by women, is associated with low perceived control. Longitudinal data are necessary to examine reciprocal effects.

We find that, overall, women's work is more alienating than men's work, with two exceptions. First, as expected, homemakers have more autonomy than paid workers. Second, less expected, women's paid work is more socially integrated than men's. Compared to male workers, female employees report more positive social interaction with others at work (in contrast to women who work in the home, who report high levels of isolation).[4] We conceptualized the opposite of isolation as positive social interaction, consistent with our theme of nonalienating work. Others have found that women employees also spend more time working with people, somewhat more time in public interactions with clients and customers, and probably more time in negative social interactions, since women's jobs involve more work with difficult clients (Bulan, Erickson, & Wharton, 1997; Erickson & Wharton, 1997; Jacobs & Steinberg, 1990). However, contrary to expectations about the harmful effects of interactive service work, Erickson and Wharton found that interacting with the public had no effect on depression, and total time spent interacting with others was associated with lower levels of depression. More empirical evidence about the subjective consequences of positive and negative interactions with other employees and, especially, with clients and customers is needed, as more and more workers are employed in the service sector.

On the whole, homemaking and part-time employment are characterized by work alienation, and women's overrepresentation in these statuses accounts for women's lower sense of control over their lives. What might the future bring for women's perceptions of personal control? A decline in homemaking as a full-time job may increase American women's sense of control over their own lives, but a growth in part-time work may reduce it.

APPENDIX

Measurement of Nonalienating Work and the Sense of Control

NONROUTINE WORK

Task variety. Whether the work or daily tasks involve (1) "Doing the same thing in the same way repeatedly," (2) "Doing the same thing in a number of different ways," or (3) "Doing a number of different kinds of things."

Solving problems. "In my work (daily activities), I have to figure out how to solve problems." Responses are coded (1) (*strongly disagree*), (2) (*disagree*), (3) (*agree*), and (4) (*strongly agree*).

FULFILLING WORK

Enjoyable work. "My work (daily activities) give me a chance to do things I enjoy." Responses are coded (1) *strongly disagree*, (2) *disagree*, (3) *agree*, and (4) *strongly agree*.

Learning. "My work (daily activities) give me a chance to develop and to learn new things." Responses coded (1) *strongly disagree*, (2) *disagree*, (3) *agree*, and (4) *strongly agree*.

AUTONOMOUS WORK

Decision-making autonomy. "Some people have supervisors or someone else who tells them what to do, while others make their own decisions. Who usually decides *how* you will do your work (daily activities)? Who usually decides *what* you will do in your work (daily activities)?" Responses to the two questions coded (1) *someone else decides*, (2) *you and someone else decide about equally*, and (3) *you decide* and summed.

Freedom from supervision. "How free do you feel to disagree with the person who supervises your work (daily activities)?" Responses coded (1) *not at all free*, (2) *somewhat free*, (3) *largely but not completely free*, (4) *completely free*, and (5) *no one supervises my work*.

SOCIAL INTERACTION

"My work (daily activities) give me a chance to interact with people I like." Responses coded (1) *strongly disagree*, (2) *disagree*, (3) *agree*, and (4) *strongly agree*.

SENSE OF CONTROL

Claiming Control Over Good Outcomes

(1) "I am responsible for my own successes."
(2) "I can do just about anything I really set my mind to."

Claiming Control Over Bad Outcomes

(3) "My misfortunes are the result of mistakes I have made."
(4) "I am responsible for my failures."

Denying Control Over Good Outcomes

(5) "The really good things that happen to me are mostly luck."
(6) "There's no sense planning a lot—if something good is going to happen it will."

Denying Control Over Bad Outcomes

(7) "Most of my problems are due to bad breaks."

(8) "I have little control over the bad things that happen to me."

Responses to control questions (1 through 4) are coded –2 = *strongly disagree*, –1 = *disagree*, 0 = *neutral*, 1 = *agree*, 2 = *strongly agree*. Responses to lack of control questions (5 through 8) are coded in reverse. From these responses, a mean score perceived control index was created, coded from low sense of control (–2) to high sense of control (2) (α = .68, mean = .669).

NOTES

1. Others have looked at characteristics like heavy lifting; working in hot, cold, or humid conditions; and other physical dimensions of work (in addition to control and social interaction) (Szafran, 1996). As Schwalbe (1986) points out, dirty, risky, or physically demanding labor is not a dimension of alienated labor. It could be nonalienating or alienating. Gardening, building homes, sculpting, fighting forest fires, clearing land, caring for large animals, and so on could be hot and dirty, and require heavy lifting, stooping, and so on, and still be nonalienating work. The concept of work alienation provides a theoretical unity to an otherwise nonconceptual list of work characteristics.

2. The few that measure fulfillment, or lack of it, do so by assessing the amount of agreement with questions such as "I find it difficult to imagine enthusiasm for my work" and "I find it hard to believe people who actually feel the work they perform is of value to society" (Kobasa et al., 1981) and, on the other end of the continuum, "My work gives me a chance to do things I enjoy," "My work gives me a chance to develop and learn new things" (Bird & Ross, 1993), "My job lets me use my best abilities" (Leiter, 1985), "In my job I can be creative," and "My work is meaningful and interesting" (Lowe & Northcott, 1988). We argue that satisfaction versus dissatisfaction does not measure fulfillment versus estrangement. Dissatisfaction results from deprivation *relative to one's expectations* (Mirowsky & Ross, 1989). Many workers are satisfied with their jobs because they provide adequate pay and security, and because they do not expect much more. To many satisfied workers, the idea that work is enjoyable, that one would feel good about the work done, or that work allowed one to learn and develop would be incomprehensible. Thus, workers could be satisfied with work and still not find fulfillment in it (Lincoln & Kalleberg, 1990; Mirowsky & Ross, 1989; Spenner, 1988). In *Alienation and Freedom*, Blauner (1964) reported that women textile workers had less autonomy and less freedom from supervision than men, but that women did not suffer self-estrangement as a result. However, Blauner measured self-estrangement as dissatisfaction, so the finding that women were not less satisfied than men could simply be due to lower expectations among women.

3. We also tested interactions of work characteristics with employment status. In order to ensure that the meanings of the seven work characteristics were the same in paid employment as in unpaid work, we created a dummy variable for all employed persons (part- and full-time) and tested its interaction with each work characteristic, one at a time. None was significant.

4. Glass and Camarigg (1992) found that women were more likely than men to report that they had supportive supervisors and coworkers, although Loscocco and Spitze (190) found no gender differences in agreement with the statement "people in my work unit are friendly and helpful" or in satisfaction with coworkers, and Leiter (1985) found no gender differences in social isolation from coworkers.

REFERENCES

Andre, R. (1981). *Homemakers: The forgotten workers.* Chicago: University of Chicago Press.

Beechey, V., & Perkins, T. (1987). *A matter of hours. Women, part-time work and the labour market.* Cambridge, MA: Polity.

Bergmann, B. (1986). *The economic emergence of women.* New York: Basic Books.

Berheide, C. W. (1984). Women's work in the home: Seems like old times. In B. B. Hess & M. B. Sussman (Eds.), *Women and the family: Two decades of change* (pp. 37-55). New York: Hawthorne Press.

Berk, R. A., & Berk, S. F. (1979). *Labor and leisure at home.* Beverly Hills, CA: Sage.

Bernard, J. (1972). *The future of marriage.* New York: Bantam.

Bird, C. E., & Ross, C. E. (1993). Houseworkers and paid workers: Qualities of the work and effects on personal control. *Journal of Marriage and the Family, 55,* 913-925.

Blauner, R. (1964). *Alienation and freedom.* Chicago: University of Chicago Press.

Bulan, H. F., Erickson, R. J., & Wharton, A. S. (1997). Doing for others on the job: The affective requirements of service work, gender, and emotional well-being. *Social Problems, 44,* 235-256.

Downey, G., & Moen, P. (1987). Personal efficacy, income and family transitions: A longitudinal study of women heading households. *Journal of Health and Social Behavior, 28,* 320-333.

Elder, G. H., & Liker, J. K. (1982). Hard times in women's lives: Historical influences across forty years. *American Journal of Sociology, 88,* 241-269.

England, P. (1992). *Comparable worth: Theories and evidence.* New York: Aldine de Gruyter.

England, P., Farkas, G., Kilbourn, B. S., & Dou, T. (1988). Explaining occupational sex segregation and wages: Findings from a model with fixed effects. *American Sociological Review, 53,* 544-558.

Erickson, R. J., & Wharton, A. S. (1997). Inauthenticity and depression. Assessing the consequences of interactive service work. *Work and Occupations, 24,* 188-213.

Erikson, K. (1986). On work and alienation. *American Sociological Review, 51,* 1-8.

Feldberg, R. L., & Glenn, E. N. (1979). Male and female: Job versus gender models in the sociology of work. *Social Problems, 26,* 525-535.

Gecas, V. (1989). The social psychology of self-efficacy. *Annual Review of Sociology, 15,* 291-316.

Glass, J., & Camarigg, V. (1992). Gender, parenthood and job-family compatibility. *American Journal of Sociology, 98,* 131-151.

Gove, W. R., & Geerken, M. R. (1977). The effect of children and employment on the mental health of married men and women. *Social Forces, 56,* 66-76.

Gove, W. R., & Tudor, J. (1973). Adult sex roles and mental illness. *American Journal of Sociology, 78,* 812-835.

Greenberg, E. S., & Grunberg, L. (1995). Work alienation and problem alcohol behavior. *Journal of Health and Social Behavior, 36,* 83-103.

Hill, C. R., & Stafford, F. P. (1980). Parental care of children: Time diary estimates of quantity, predictability, and variety. *Journal of Human Resources, 15,* 202-239.

Hodson, R. (1996). Dignity in the workplace under participative management: Alienation and freedom revisited. *American Sociological Review, 61,* 719-738.

Holden, K. C., & Hansen, W. L. (1987). Part-time work, full-time work, and occupational segregation. In C. Brown & J. A. Pechman (Eds.), *Gender in the workplace* (pp. 217-238). Washington, DC: Brookings Institution.

Jacobs, J. A., & Steinberg, R. J. (1990). Compensating differentials and the male-female wage gap: Evidence from the New York State Comparable Worth Study. *Social Forces, 69,* 439-468.

Kahn, R. L. (1991). The forms of women's work. In M. Frankenhaeuser, U. Lundberg, & M. Chesney (Eds.), *Women, work and health* (pp. 65-83). New York: Plenum.

Kibria, N., Barnett, R. C., Baruch, G. K., Marshall, N. L., & Pleck, J. H. (1990). Homemaking-role quality and the psychological well-being and distress of employed women. *Sex Roles, 22,* 327-347.

Kobasa, S. E., Maddi, S. R., & Courington, S. (1981). Personality and constitution as mediators in the stress-illness relationship. *Journal of Health and Social Behavior, 22,* 368-378.

Kohn, M. L. (1976). Occupational structure and alienation. *American Journal of Sociology, 82,* 111-130.

Kohn, M. L., Naoi, A., Schoenbach, C., Schooler, C., & Slomczynski, K. M. (1990). Position in the class structure and psychological functioning in the United States, Japan, and Poland. *American Journal of Sociology, 95,* 964-1008.

Kohn, M. L., & Schooler, C. (1973). Occupational experience and psychological functioning: An assessment of reciprocal effects. *American Sociological Review, 38,* 97-118.

Kohn, M. L., & Schooler, C. (1982). Job conditions and personality: A longitudinal assessment of their reciprocal effects. *American Journal of Sociology, 87,* 1257-1286.

Kohn, M. L., & Slomczynski, K. M. (1993). *Social structure and self-direction. A comparative analysis of the United States and Poland.* Cambridge, MA: Blackwell.

Leiter, J. (1985). Work alienation in the textile industry: Reassessing Blauner. *Work and Occupations, 12,* 479-498.

Lennon, M. C. (1994). Women, work, and well-being: The importance of work conditions. *Journal of Health and Social Behavior, 35,* 235-247.

Lincoln, J. R., & Kalleberg, A. L. (1990). *Culture, control, and commitment.* Cambridge, UK: Cambridge University Press.

Link, B. G., Lennon, M. C., & Dohrenwend, B. P. (1993). Socioeconomic status and depression: The role of occupations involving direction, control, and planning. *American Journal of Sociology, 98,* 1351-1387.

Loscocco, K. A., & Spitze, G. (1990). Working conditions, social support, and the well-being of female and male factory workers. *Journal of Health and Social Behavior, 31,* 313-327.

Lowe, G. S., & Northcott, H. C. (1988). The impact of working conditions, social roles, and personal characteristics on gender differences in distress. *Work and Occupations, 15,* 55-77.

Lund, L., & Wright, W. E. (1994, June). *Mitofsky-Waksberg vs. screened random digit dial: Report on a comparison of the sample characteristics of two random-digit-dialing survey designs.* Paper presented at the Center for Disease Control's 11th Annual Behavior Risk Factor Survey Conference, Atlanta.

Marx, K. (1964). Economic and philosophical manuscripts. In *Karl Marx: Early writings* (T. R. Bottomore, Trans. & Ed.). New York: McGraw-Hill. (Original work published 1884)

Miller, J., Schooler, C., Kohn, M. L., & Miller, K. A. (1979). Women and work: The psychological effects of occupational conditions. *American Journal of Sociology, 85,* 66-91.

Mirowsky, J. (1996). Age and the gender gap in depression. *Journal of Health and Social Behavior, 37,* 362-380.

Mirowsky, J., & Ross, C. E. (1984). Mexican culture and its emotional contradictions. *Journal of Health and Social Behavior, 25,* 2-13.

Mirowsky, J., & Ross, C. E. (1989). *Social causes of psychological distress.* New York: Aldine de Gruyter.

Mirowsky, J., & Ross, C. E. (1990). Control or defense? Depression and the sense of control over good and bad outcomes. *Journal of Health and Social Behavior, 31,* 71-86.

Mirowsky, J., & Ross, C. E. (1991). Eliminating defense and agreement bias from measures of the sense of control: A 2 × 2 index. *Social Psychology Quarterly, 54,* 127-145.

Oakley, A. (1974). *The sociology of housework.* New York: Pantheon.

O'Rourke, D., & Blair, J. (1983). Improving random selection in telephone surveys. *Journal of Marketing Research, 20,* 428-432.

Pearlin, L. I., Menaghan, E. G., Lieberman, M. A., & Mullan, J. T. (1981). The stress process. *Journal of Health and Social Behavior, 22,* 336-356.

Pfeffer, J., & Baron, J. N. (1988). Taking the workers back out: Recent trends in the structuring of employment. *Research in Organizational Behavior, 10,* 257-303.

Polivka, A. E., & Nardone, T. (1989). On the definition of contingent work. *Monthly Labor Review, 112,* 9-16.

Pugliesi, K. (1995). Work and well-being: Gender differences in the psychological consequences of employment. *Journal of Health and Social Behavior, 36,* 57-71.

Quinn, J. F., & Burkhauser, R. V. (1994). Retirement and labor force behavior of the elderly. In L. G. Martin & S. H. Preston (Eds.), *Demography of aging* (pp. 50-101). Washington, DC: National Academy Press.

Reskin, B., & Hartmann, H. (Eds.). (1986). *Women's work, men's work: Sex segregation on the job.* Washington, DC: National Academy Press.

Reskin, B., & Padavic, I. (1994). *Women and men at work.* Thousand Oaks, CA: Pine Forge Press.

Rodin, J. (1986). Aging and health: Effects of the sense of control. *Science, 233,* 1271-1276.

Rosenberg, H. G. (1984). The home is the workplace: Hazards, stress, and pollutants in the household. In W. Chavkin (Ed.), *Double exposure. Women's health hazards on the job and at home* (pp. 219-245). New York: Monthly Review Press.

Ross, C. E., & Bird, C. E. (1994). Sex stratification and health lifestyle: Consequences for men's and women's perceived health. *Journal of Health and Social Behavior, 35,* 161-178.

Ross, C. E., & Mirowsky, J. (1992). Households, employment, and the sense of control. *Social Psychology Quarterly, 55,* 217-235.

Rotter, J. B. (1966). Generalized expectancies for internal vs. external control of reinforcements. *Psychological Monographs, 80,* 1-28.

Rubery, J., Horrell, S., & Burchell, B. (1994). Part-time work and gender inequality in the labour market. In A. M. Scott (Ed.), *Gender segregation and social change* (pp. 205-234). Oxford, UK: Oxford University Press.

Schooler, C., Miller, J., Miller, K. A., & Richtand, C. N. (1984). Work for the household: Its nature and consequences for husbands and wives. *American Journal of Sociology, 90,* 97-124.

Schwalbe, M. L. (1986). *The psychosocial consequences of natural and alienated labor.* Albany: State University of New York Press.

Schwalbe, M. L., & Staples, C. L. (1986). Class position, work experience, and health. *International Journal of Health Services, 16,* 583-602.

Seeman, M. (1959). On the meaning of alienation. *American Sociological Review, 24,* 787-791.

Seeman, M. (1983). Alienation motifs in contemporary theorizing. *Social Psychology Quarterly, 46,* 171-184.

Seeman, M., & Anderson, C. S. (1983). Alienation and alcohol: The role of work, mastery, and community in drinking behavior. *American Sociological Review, 48,* 60-77.

Seeman, M., & Lewis, S. (1995). Powerlessness, health and mortality: A longitudinal study of older men and mature women. *Social Science and Medicine, 41,* 517-525.

Seeman, M., Seeman, A. Z., & Budros, A. (1988). Powerlessness, work, and community: A longitudinal study of alienation and alcohol use. *Journal of Health and Social Behavior, 29,* 185-198.

Siegel, J. S. (1993). *A generation of change. A profile of American's older population.* New York: Russell Sage.

Spenner, K. I. (1988). Social stratification, work, and personality. *Annual Review of Sociology, 14,* 69-97.

Szafran, R. F. (1996). The effect of occupational growth on labor force task characteristics. *Work and Occupations, 23,* 54-86.

Thoits, P. A. (1987). Gender and martial status differences in control and distress. *Journal of Health and Social Behavior, 28,* 7-22.

Tilly, C. (1991). Reasons for the continuing growth of part-time employment. *Monthly Labor Review, 114,* 10-18.

U.S. Bureau of Labor Statistics. (1988). *Labor force statistics derived from the Current Population Survey, 1948-1987* (Bulletin 2307). Washington, DC: Government Printing Office.

U.S. Bureau of Labor Statistics. (1990). *Employment and earnings* (37/2). Washington, DC: Government Printing Office.

U.S. Bureau of the Census. (1995). *The statistical abstract of the United States 1995.* Washington, DC: Government Printing Office.

Waksberg, J. (1978). Sampling methods for random digit dialing. *Journal of the American Statistical Association, 73,* 40-46.

Wheaton, B. (1980). The sociogenesis of psychological disorder: An attributional theory. *Journal of Health and Social Behavior, 21,* 100-124.

Group Relations at Work

Solidarity, Conflict, and Relations With Management

RANDY HODSON

Coworkers can make a job a blessing or a curse. Yet, studies of coworkers have held at best a secondary role in the analysis of the workplace, lagging far behind sociotechnical systems, labor process control, and individual attitudes. As a result, our knowledge of vertical relations of authority and power at the workplace and our knowledge of individual attitudes about work far outweigh our knowledge of lateral relations among coworkers. Coworker relations include all interpersonal relations, both positive and negative, within bounded task groups at work. Such social relations constitute an important part of the "social climate" at work (Moos, 1986, p. 14) and provide a setting in which workers experience meaning and identity (Gabarro, 1987, p. 174). Coworker relations are important for humanizing the workplace (Walton & Hackman, 1986, p. 191) and in so doing have significance well beyond what have been termed "prosocial" behaviors or "organizational citizenship" behaviors (Schnake, 1991, p. 737).

Increased interest in group processes and coworker relations has been spurred in recent years by the movement toward team-oriented systems of production. Interest in coworker relations also has been heightened by increasing diversity in the workplace, which further highlights the importance of coworker relations (Jackson & Ruderman, 1995; Morrison, Ruderman, & Hughes-James, 1993). The movement toward team forms of work organization has expanded outside manufacturing and has gained a significant presence in most sectors of the economy, from services to sales to government (Applebaum & Batt, 1994; Trice & Beyer, 1992). Team-based organizations of work are seen by many as the leading component of the "postbureaucratic" organization of work (Barker, 1993, p. 408) and as being essential for efficiency and competitiveness in the global economy (Tausky & Chelte, 1991). Although much faddishness accompanies these developments, it is widely recognized that team-based organizations of production are essential in an economy based on increasing complex technological and organizational processes of production and on an increasingly skilled and educated labor force (Reich, 1987).

A lack of sustained research on the roles and significance of coworkers, unfortunately, has left the field with few verified constructs and established relationships on which to build new theories helpful for understanding the dynamics of an increasingly team-oriented workplace. Related literatures in sociology and in management studies are useful but do not address coworker relations as a central focus or are incomplete in their analysis.

The literature on occupational communities and occupational self-control burgeoned in the 1960s and 1970s. This literature includes both studies of blue-collar craft communities and

From *Work and Occupations,* Vol. 25, No. 3, August 1998, pp. 333-355. Reprinted by permission.

studies of professional occupational control (see Van Maanen & Barley, 1984). Insights based on this literature have been instrumental in fueling developments in the study of professional autonomy (Abbott, 1988). Studies of occupational self-control, however, gradually have moved toward becoming a subfield of the sociology of the professions and have drifted away from their roots in the study of coworker relations among craft and factory workers. As a result, a generalizable line of research on coworker relations has not resulted from studies of occupational self-control.

In the 1980s, studies of occupational self-control in blue-collar workplaces turned to the investigation of resistance, theft, and sabotage as strategies by which workers seek to attain at least some personal freedom and some minimum of symbolic control. Such strategies appear to be especially prevalent in systems that are tightly controlled by management. For instance, Mars (1982) published an enduring work on the adaptive roles that workers assume in their efforts to gain occupational control. In the vision of Mars and other students of workplace resistance, workers' creative strategies enable them to obtain at least some semblance of control under almost any management system (Jermier, Knights, & Nord, 1994). These studies have included some consideration of coworker relations but, more typically, the focus is on vertical relations of power and the "struggle for control."

Studies analyzing the nature and consequences of the rise of management-initiated, team-organized forms of production also have burgeoned in recent decades (Lillrank & Kano, 1989; Walton & Hackman, 1986). Much of the management literature on teams is unabashedly delighted about the control functions performed by teams. For example, Walton and Hackman (1986) note that "probably the most pervasive and powerful influence on compliance is influence from one's coworkers" (p. 172). They further note that such peer influence is essential for the success of the modern organization based on high levels of commitment.

Other, more critical research has highlighted ways in which teams manipulate workers according to implicit management agendas. For instance, Graham (1995) illustrates how managers in a Japanese automobile assembly plant in the Midwest manipulated workers through team pressure: "Unkind acts toward team members were not necessarily discouraged by management and, at times, they were even encouraged" (p. 99). This new form of control is labeled "concertive control" by Barker (1993):

> This form represents a key shift in the locus of control from management to the workers themselves, who collaborate to develop the means of their own control. Workers achieve concertive control by reaching a negotiated consensus on how to shape their behavior according to a set of core values, such as the values found in a corporate vision statement. (p. 411)

Such critically oriented studies argue that management is generally successful in enforcing consensus in work groups around management-defined values (see also Garrahan & Stewart, 1992; Grenier, 1988; Parker & Slaughter, 1994).

Other observers, however, remain optimistic that new systems of workplace control with greater worker and team involvement also allow new possibilities for the realization of goals and values put forward by workers themselves. "An analysis of participative experiments suggests that these new systems produce new contradictions engendering worker expectations and entitlements for democracy in the workplace" (Derber & Schwartz, 1983, p. 61). Based on a systemic study of worker involvement programs, Juravich, Harris, and Brooks (1993) arrive at the conclusion that there is a wide gap in expectations between workers and managers about what can be expected from worker involvement programs. This gap in expectations is seen as providing an opening in which workers' agendas can be introduced in self-managing teams (Hodson, 1996).

It is widely acknowledged that teams and coworker relations have become increasingly important for understanding the contemporary workplace. Coworker relations are taking on an ever-increasing role, not just in the realms of productivity and vertical relations of control but also in determining the experience of work and its meaning. The horizontal dimension of interactions among coworkers—in both its supportive and conflictual aspects—has been all too frequently missed or minimized by studies of the contemporary workplace. Studies that take the role of coworker interactions as a central focus have only recently begun to appear in the published literature (see, e.g., Smith, 1996).

FUNCTIONS OF COWORKER RELATIONS

Our understanding of the dynamics of coworker relations and the consequences of team-organized forms of production is in its infancy due in part to the limited nature of the data available on these topics. Much of the information available on coworker relations is based on case studies, and this knowledge has been difficult to synthesize into verifiable conclusions. Coworker relations are a recurrent phenomenon of observation in organizational ethnographies, although their analysis is seldom identified as a key contribution of this methodology. Ethnographic observations reveal at least four major functions of coworker relations: (a) occupational socialization, (b) solidarity and mutual defense, (c) resistance to authority and role distancing, and (d) the affirmation of class and gender identities at work.

In a classic ethnographic study of occupational socialization, Haas (1972) demonstrates how kidding and ridicule are crucial components of the initiation process for apprentice ironworkers. Teasing and ridicule serve as tests to determine whether apprentice workers will be willing to accept occupational training on the job from the journeymen. More senior workers reason that apprentices who are unwilling or unable to respond with good-natured repartee to personal barbs also may be unwilling to accept important hints and suggestions concerning work tasks. Such apprentices are considered a hazard in the dangerous world of high steel and are quickly ostracized. In this craft setting, coworkers constitute an important screen through which workers must pass to become members of the occupation.

Joking relationships and their role in establishing and affirming core work group values of friendship and generosity also are a central focus in Halle's (1984) ethnography of a chemical plant. These values are important for the workers in Halle's study as they strive to humanize their environments against the forces of technology and bureaucracy and as they work to maintain the solidarity necessary for collective protection of their hard-won privileges as relatively well-paid blue-collar workers.

Group solidarity in the workplace is based on the willingness of workers to defend each other in the face of challenges, most generally from management but also sometimes from other groups of workers or from customers (Fantasia, 1988; Jermier et al., 1994). Solidarity also can help mitigate feelings of alienation that arise from meaningless work (Tausky, 1992). The foundation of solidarity is "shared experiences at work" and the "sense of involvement and attachment" that arises from these shared experiences (Goffee, 1981, pp. 475, 488). Group activities involving solidarity provide the basis on which workers "gain the experience and create the conditions which make possible a transformation of the labor process" (Clawson & Fantasia, 1983, p. 676). Workers' goals can include oppositional elements that focus on resistance to management practices as well as more mundane task-related elements that do not directly oppose management but that still provide a basis for workers to shape a collective identity separate from management (Hodson, 1995; Jermier et al., 1994).

The use of resistance and role distancing to secure "personal space" at work is illustrated in the following excerpt from an ethnography of a cigarette factory:

> In leaving the workplace without official permission, the rules on "loitering" in corridors or toi-

lets, on the use of the specified toilet, and on smoking were all broken. Gradually whole groups, not always young girls but also older women, emerged as the "non-conformists" who met each other "out in the back." The toilets became centres of mild rebellion. They came to represent a place of refuge for a smoke and a chat—a potential forum for informal communication and organization. (Pollert, 1981, p. 147)

Supportive coworker relations are crucial for maintaining even such modest agendas of resistance to authority.

Besides being fundamental to the maintenance of solidarity and resistance to authority, coworker relations also can be important for affirming group identities including gender identities. Westwood (1984, pp. 94-96) notes how elaborate rituals concerning birthdays, weddings, and births evolved among a largely female workforce in a knitting mill. These rituals created solidarity through shared activities and the exchange of gifts. The rituals were important to the women involved because they displaced time, focus, and resources from the mill work to their own agendas. Worker resistance in this setting focused on symbolic distancing from management agendas and on the creation of alternative, positive, gender-based self-identifications. Similarly, in a study of male factory workers, Collinson (1988) notes how sexual banter among male workers helped to reaffirm masculinity as a parameter of work identity separate from the formal job description (see also Linhart, 1981; Spencer, 1977).

The importance of coworker relations is not limited to blue-collar settings. Kunda (1992, p. 154) illustrates how groups of engineers develop emergent strategies of role distancing to deal with demands for highly visible forms of allegiance and loyalty under new "participatory" workplace relations. Similarly, top executives often are thought of as "loners"; however, in a study of top managers in an American company, Morrill (1991) finds an elaborate "code of honor" among managers and detailed "rules of the game" even for the fiercely competitive world of top management.

In summary, there is substantial evidence that coworker relations are crucial for the quality of work life and fulfill a variety of functions. I focus on two aspects of coworker relations as centrally important. First, coworker relations can provide or fail to provide a foundation for solidarity and collective resistance to management. This solidarity can be an important basis for trade unionism and other organized collective actions as well as for other, more mundane forms of struggle (Fantasia, 1988; Hodson, 1995; Molstad, 1988). Second, coworker relations can be conflictual or harmonious, leading to feelings of alienation and distress or affinity and comfort. The ethnographic evidence suggests that solidarity and peer conflict, as principal dimensions of coworker relations, are crucially important for job satisfaction, meaningful work, and relations with management.

Hypotheses

Existing knowledge on coworker relations and their implications for the nature of worklife suggests a series of four propositions.

Hypothesis 1: *Solidarity among coworkers will increase job satisfaction.* Mutual defense and feelings of solidarity with coworkers have been noted from the early years of industrial sociology as a principal determinant of positive affect at work (Tannenbaum & Kahn, 1958).

Hypothesis 2: *Solidarity among coworkers will be associated with increased conflict between workers and managers.* This hypothesis is grounded on the observation that mutual aid and solidarity among coworkers are necessary for effective resistance to the demands of management (Burawoy, 1979; Fantasia, 1988).

Hypothesis 3: *Conflict among coworkers will decrease job satisfaction.* This hypothesis is derived from the important role of supportive relations among coworkers for a positive experience of worklife (Hurlbert,

1991, p. 415; Moos, 1986, p. 26; Schnake, 1991, p. 740).

Hypothesis 4: *Conflict among coworkers will be associated with increased conflict between workers and managers.* This hypothesis is derived from the observation that anomic workplaces generate conflict among all actors. By contrast, more normatively based workplaces encourage relatively positive relations among the various actors (Hackman, 1986, p. 96). An opposite expectation for this relationship can be derived from the work of Burawoy (1979, pp. 62-67), who argues that modern forms of management displace conflict from authority relations to lateral relations among workers. Burawoy's argument suggests that heightened conflict among coworkers will be associated with relatively peaceful worker-management relations. Burawoy's observations provide part of the evidence suggesting Hypothesis 2. However, I believe this argument fails to distinguish between coworker solidarity as mutual defense and more generally conflictual or harmonious relations among coworkers. Burawoy's argument is thus more relevant to the relationship between coworker solidarity and relations with management than it is to the relationship between levels of general conflict among coworkers and relations with management.

Three objective job characteristics are used in parts of the analysis as controls. These job characteristics are skill, autonomy, and participation. Prior research suggests that skill, autonomy, and participation have positive effects on job satisfaction (Greenberg, 1986; Kalleberg & Berg, 1987; Spenner, 1990). The effects of these variables on good relations with management also are expected to be positive.

A ROLE FOR MULTIPLE METHODS

Coworker relations have been considered in ethnographic studies of workplaces more often than in survey-based research, which has tended to focus on job attitudes and structural characteristics of the workplace. Even though theories of the workplace have underplayed the role of coworker relations, researchers in the field have found that these relations often are central to workers' experiences. A multimethod approach is particularly important for the study of coworker relations at this point in the development of the field because so few findings have been confirmed across different methods. Workplace studies are all too frequently divided into nonoverlapping domains of survey-based analyses and ethnographic analyses. The lack of systematic cross-referencing of findings between these two methods has resulted in few findings being reliably confirmed across methods.

In the chapter, I use data both from ethnographic methods and from survey-based methods to confirm the effects of coworker relations on job satisfaction and on good relations with management. Both data sets used include (a) measures of solidarity and conflict among coworkers, (b) indicators of the two concepts that serve as dependent variables (job satisfaction and good relations with management), and (c) measures of objective job characteristics.

THE ETHNOGRAPHIC DATA

The analysis presented in this chapter is based in part on data collected from book-length workplace ethnographies. Organizational ethnographies are constructed from sustained observation of workplaces and workplace relations, a depth of observation considered by ethnographers to be essential for getting sufficiently behind the scenes to accurately perceive patterns of workplace relations. The coding of information from these ethnographies allows the development of in-depth measures of workers' behaviors as well as measures of the contexts in which these behaviors occur. A similar analytic strategy, using the Human Relations Area Files, has been used for several decades by cultural anthropologists. The wealth of ethnographic data on organizations, however, has not previously been organized and analyzed in this manner.

Workplace ethnographies typically have a stylized format. This format can be traced jointly to the work of cultural anthropologists and industrial sociologists. The format includes mandatory coverage of a fixed set of topics including organizational characteristics, worker characteristics, management style, coworker relations, and sociotechnical relations. This standard format allows data from the ethnographies to be coded into consistent sets of indicators without generating a data set with large areas of missing data. In this regard, workplace ethnographies are more obliging for the sort of analysis undertaken in this chapter than are anthropological studies of primitive societies, which range across a broader set of topics and contain wider areas of omission.

The data set was generated by reading and coding information from the existing published set of English-language workplace ethnographies. Many thousands of titles were examined in a three-phase procedure to locate appropriate ethnographies. First, likely titles were generated by computer-assisted searches of existing archives and by perusal of the bibliographies of ethnographies already located. These titles were screened on the basis of the information provided in on-line computer archives or on the basis of perusals of the books themselves as they were selected from the shelf. Repeated application of these procedures constitutes what I believe was an exhaustive search; eventually, the pursuit of new leads produced only titles already considered. This process yielded a final pool of 373 titles as candidates for inclusion.

These 373 books underwent additional scrutiny. During this second phase of selection, either reviews of the books were located and read or, if reviews were not available, the books themselves were secured and examined directly. The criteria for inclusion were as follows. First, the book had to be based on direct ethnographic methods of observation over a period of at least 6 months. Second, the locus of the observations had to be within a single organization. Third, the book had to include a focus on a clearly identifiable group of workers. During this stage, 193 books were excluded as inappropriate. Most of these were occupational rather than organizational studies. These books report on an occupation as a whole without focusing on a particular organizational context. For example, an occupational ethnography might focus on secretaries in New York City without focusing on a particular work site. Without an extended investigation and presentation on a specific work site, such books did not provide data on the organizational and work group covariates that are essential for the current analysis.

During the third phase of selection, the remaining 180 books were perused in detail. Of the books that survived to this final selection stage, 83 were retained as appropriate for analysis and 97 were excluded for various reasons. The majority of the excluded books were studies of various industries as a whole rather than single organizations. Other exclusions included company histories, executive biographies, community studies of factory towns, and studies of planned job redesign projects.

No book was excluded categorically if it failed to meet a particular criterion. Rather, each book was examined in detail to see whether it met the overall model for inclusion. In some cases, a book was relatively weak on one criterion, but the depth of its material in other areas allowed its inclusion. Thus, sometimes a book with a fairly broad occupational focus was included if it had excellent material on the organization and on the labor process in several occupations. When coding material from such books, an explicit decision was made about which occupational category would be the focus, and only material about that occupation was coded. For instance, sometimes books contained information about both skilled machinists and assembly workers. Or, other books might contain information about both waitresses and their managers. In a book involving the latter situation, two cases from the same book were coded—one for waitresses and one for managers (Spradley & Mann, 1975). Multiple cases were coded from a total of 12 books. In a few cases where the labor process material was particularly strong, books based on observations across several organizations also were included. This option was considered only where the organizations involved were discussed in detail and were highly similar; in these cases, organizational characteristics were coded based on a composite.

Application of the preceding criteria generated a set of 108 cases based on 83 separate published ethnographies. These ethnographies constitute the population of published English-language ethnographies that focus on a single workplace and on an identifiable occupation within the workplace and that provide relatively complete information on the workplace and the nature of the labor process taking place there. The average time spent in the field was well over a year for each ethnography. Writing time was at least as great. This population of workplace ethnographies thus represents more than 200 years of Ph.D.-level labor and is a resource potentially worth exploring for its implications.

The coding instrument for the ethnographies was developed by a team of four researchers. First, a list of relevant concepts was generated, and preliminary response items and categories were developed. Second, over a period of 6 months, a set of eight ethnographies were read and coded by each of the four researchers. After each ethnography was completed, the researchers met from 3 to 5 hours to discuss their respective codings. At these meetings, decisions were made about the retention or removal of items and the development of new response categories and new coding protocols. The goal was to refine an instrument that could be completed for each ethnography with high reliability by trained interviewers.

The ethnographies were read and coded by the same team of four researchers and by the eight members of a graduate research practicum. All coders initially were trained on a common ethnography and met twice weekly as a group to discuss ongoing questions and issues. Coders recorded up to three page numbers identifying the passages used for coding each variable. If multiple instances of a behavior were found, then the coder was instructed to review all previous passages cited, reconcile inconsistencies between the passages, and record the best answer along with all relevant page numbers. After completing a book, the primary coder was debriefed by a member of the research staff to check the accuracy of the codings. At this time, the codings were reviewed in detail. One book was selected as a reliability check and was coded independently by three reviewers. The reliability coefficient for these codings was .92, indicating a high degree of intercoder reliability. The coding of data from this population of ethnographies allows the depth of observation embodied in ethnographic accounts to be systematically analyzed toward the goal of understanding coworker relations.

THE SURVEY DATA

A telephone survey of a random sample of 371 employed adults living in a midwestern state was undertaken in the spring of 1992, simultaneous with the compilation of the ethnographic data. The collection of similar variables in the ethnographic data and the telephone survey of workers allows the evaluation of a common model of coworker relations across two very different methods of observation. The telephone interviews were approximately 35 minutes in length and included both open-ended and closed questions.

Because survey methodology uses standardized and widely understood procedures, only a brief description of these procedures is provided here. The survey design, implemented through computer-assisted random digit dialing, sampled telephone exchanges throughout the state and included cities, small towns, and rural areas. Screening was conducted at each household contacted to determine whether any household member was at least 18 years of age and currently working for pay (excluding individuals who were self-employed or who worked without pay in a family farm or business). If more than one adult member of the household was working for pay, then the appropriate respondent was computer selected. Interviewing was monitored regularly by supervisors, with each interviewer monitored at least twice during each 4-hour shift. The response rate for the survey was 70%. Systematic overlap between the questions included in the survey and the data collected from the organizational ethnographies was planned into the survey instrument.

VARIABLES

The variables for the analysis of the effects of coworker relations on job satisfaction and good relations with management are listed in Table 14.1. The analogous ethnographic and survey variables are listed in separate columns. The wordings of the questions and the response categories also are included. Similar concepts are measured in the two data sets. For scaled concepts, however, the number of items in the scales sometimes varies between data sources. The number of response categories for variables also sometimes differs between the two data sets. Most of the survey questions use a 4-point Likert scale, as is standard practice in survey instruments. The ethnographic questions use more customized response categories. These response categories were developed through the reading and coding of several ethnographies as described in the methods section. The response categories were selected to most accurately and reliably portray the characterizations typically made in the ethnographic accounts. These characterizations do not necessarily fit well into 4-point Likert scales. Accordingly, although concepts are identical between data sources, the exact items and the number of response categories vary according to the dictates of each method. In the results section, standardized coefficients are used to remove differences in scale between variables from the two data sets.

The content of the survey variables is revealed by the question wordings. Many of the ethnographic variables also are self-explanatory. Several of the variables from the ethnographic data, however, require further explanation. In the following subsections, I present examples of the ethnographic material behind the coding of these variables that help to reveal their content and meaning.

Job Satisfaction

An example of low job satisfaction among workers is evidenced in an ethnography of work in a large factory on the East Coast:

> He had learned to expect nothing from his job but money. He treated the company the way the company treated him, coldly and with calculation. . . . He didn't appreciate being treated like a child by the company, but he didn't fight back or complain much any more. He just hung in there, doing his job, earning his bread and regularly refilling the refrigerator he had at home reserved exclusively for beer. (Pfeffer, 1979, pp. 78-79)

Conversely, high job satisfaction is suggested in an ethnography of a construction site:

> Most oilers are nearly invisible, fueling and lubricating their rigs before the day begins for the rest of us, vanishing to God knows where during the bulk of the day, reappearing at 4:00 to preside over putting the rig to bed. Beane, however, was not of that stripe. He fussed over the crane like a stage mother, constantly wiping away puddles of oil or grease, touching up scratches with fresh paint. (Cherry, 1974, p. 166)

Relations With Management

A good example of *abusive management* can be seen in an ethnography of an automobile assembly plant in France:

> [The foreman is] a red-faced alcoholic and treats immigrants . . . with scorn and hatred. . . . When he prowls around a shop . . . conversations stop

TABLE 14.1 Variable Definitions

Ethnographic Data	*Survey Data*
Dependent variables	
Job satisfaction	
1 = very low, 2 = moderately low, 3 = average, 4 = high, 5 = very high	"I am satisfied with my job as a whole." (4-point Likert-type scale)
Good relations with management	
Little abuse: 1 = constantly, 2 = frequently, 3 = sometimes, 4 = rarely, 5 = never	Respect: "My supervisor consistently treats me with respect." (4-point Likert-type scale)
Leadership: 1 = catastrophic, 2 = marginal, 3 = adequate, 4 = good, 5 = exceptional	Satisfaction with supervisor: "Overall, I am satisfied with my immediate supervisors." (4-point Likert-type scale)
Organization of production: 1 = catastrophic, 2 = marginal, 3 = adequate, 4 = good, 5 = exceptional	
Little conflict with managers: 1 = constant, 2 = frequent, 3 = average, 4 = infrequent, 5 = never	
Little conflict with supervisors: 1 = constant, 2 = frequent, 3 = average, 4 = infrequent, 5 = never	
Coworker relations	
Solidarity	
Mutual defense: 1 = little or none, 2 = average, 3 = strong	Mutual defense: "People in my work group stick up for each other if someone gets in trouble with a supervisor." (4-point Likert scale)
Discipline enforced by workers: 1 = never, 2 = occasionally, 3 = frequently	Help others: "People in my work group often help each other out in order to get the work done." (4-point Likert-type scale)
Leadership within the group: 1 = little or none, 2 = average, 3 = strong	Absence of bickering: "There is a lot of bickering among the people I work with." (4-point Likert-type scale, reverse coded)
Group cohesion: 1 = absent, 2 = infrequent, 3 = average, 4 = widespread, 5 = pervasive	Satisfaction with coworkers: "Overall, I am satisfied with my coworkers." (4-point Likert-type scale)
Conflict with coworkers	
Conflict between groups: 1 = nonexistent, 2 = occasional, 3 = frequent	Special treatment: "Some people at my workplace receive special treatment because they are friendly with supervisors." (4-point Likert-type scale)
Gossip between groups: 0 = no, 1 = yes	Incompetence: "The work in my department is often more difficult than it needs to be because people in other departments do not do their jobs the best they could." (4-point Likert-type scale)
Interference between groups: 0 = no, 1 = yes	Work avoidance: "People at my workplace sometimes put off finishing tasks so that they do not get assigned additional work." (4-point Likert-type scale)
Conflict within group: 1 = nonexistent, 2 = occasional, 3 = frequent	Unfair credit: "People at my workplace sometimes get credit for doing more than they actually do. (4-point Likert-type scale)
Gossip within group: 0 = no, 1 = yes	
Interference within group: 0 = no, 1 = yes	
Job characteristics	
Participation	
Solicitation of worker involvement: 1 = never asked, 2 = informal, 3 = formal	Participate: "My job allows me to participate in important decisions that concern my organization." (4-point Likert-type scale)
	Opinion asked: "My supervisor frequently asks for my opinion on work-related matters." (4-point Likert-type scale)

(Continued)

TABLE 14.1 Continued

Ethnographic Data	*Survey Data*
Skill	
Job-required skill: 1 = speed and dexterity only, 2 = some complexity, 3 = highly complex	High skill required: "My job requires a high level of skill." (4-point Likert-type scale)
	Use full abilities: "My job allows me to use my full abilities." (4-point Likert-type scale)
	Repetitious: "My job is very repetitious." (4-point Likert-type scale, reverse coded)
	Learn new things: "I often get to learn new things on my job." (4-point Likert-type scale)
Autonomy	
1 = none, 2 = little, 3 = average, 4 = high, 5 = very high	"I can set priorities about the order in which I do required tasks." (4-point Likert-type scale)

abruptly, the men fall silent, and the only noise to be heard is that of the machines. . . . Inside the works you're in an accepted police state. (Linhart, 1981, p. 64)

An example of exceptionally good *organization of production* is provided by an ethnography of a bank:

In the bank, the reorganization that was effected when Mr. Davis came to the branch a year ago is acclaimed by everybody in the situation as a great success. The efficiency and productivity of the tellers has been increased . . . "This is much better; the day doesn't seem so hectic and disorganized. . . . I go home in the afternoon, [and] I don't feel like collapsing like I used to." (Kusterer, 1978, p. 172)

Workers in an apparel factory evidence a pattern of frequent *conflict with management.* Following the delivery of a new baby garment to be sewn, the workers objected because of the low piece rate attached to the work:

"Every time the minutes are given they get worse, they want more from us every time. Well it won't work. I can't do that target. . . .

Some sat defiantly with arms folded while others talked together in small groups. The unit had disintegrated. . . . Gillian [the supervisor] was looking distraught and said: "I hate this minutes thing; it's the worst part of my job. I feel sick, I've got a headache.". . . . Lisa, the assistant supervisor, was also looking very worried as the fury from the women grew. (Westwood, 1984, p. 51)

Solidarity

Solidarity is defined in part as *mutual defense,* as the willingness of workers to put themselves at risk to defend fellow workers. Strong solidarity is evidenced in an ethnography of an underground mine. The ethnographer reports the following episode during which a lead worker and his men gather at the head of a shaft to search for coworkers trapped by fire:

Suddenly Jimmie Isom picks up a mask from the jeep. "Put one on me, Dan," Jimmie says. Dan stares at his friend with the deep-etched lines from his heart attack. Dan usually works Jimmie on the outside crew these days, afraid of working him inside. Now Jimmie is volunteering to go into the smoke. Dan doesn't know how to turn him down. (Vecsey, 1974, p. 190)

Discipline enforced by coworkers is evidenced in an ethnography of a defense industry subcontractor:

Many of the winders did poke fun at Danny Watt in a mean-spirited way. Much of it concerned Watt's "boy scout" image and his righteous religious pose. But the real focus of their taunts was his rapid work pace. (Seider, 1984, p. 44)

Group discipline also can arise in the process of socializing new workers, as the following example from an ethnography of ironworkers illustrates:

He did everything wrong, of course. . . . He was forever on the wrong side of the pieces, and it still amazes me that he wasn't knocked over the side. . . . Jiggs continually screamed at him to be careful. Several times I pulled and held pieces away from him and told him I wasn't going to let him have his end unless he stopped bouncing around. (Cherry, 1974, p. 186)

An example of *leadership within groups* is provided by an ethnography of construction work:

Informal leaders emerge through reputations based on skills, knowledge, and personality. Channels of communication are established for work, social, and other matters. Social interaction takes place at work, during lunch time, and after work at the local bar or bowling alley. All of this activity builds group feeling. (Applebaum, 1981, p. 96)

The same ethnography also provides evidence of high levels of *group cohesion:*

On one feed we had during the sewer plant project, the men used concrete blocks and an oxyacetylene torch to make a stove. Several men brought in their favorite dishes, and during lunch time, instead of the usual sandwiches, we all had a hot gourmet meal. Another time, the men organized a "wild meat" feed, which featured only meat from animals that had been hunted. The meal was accompanied by hunting stories full of frustration, comic situations, and triumphs. This activity—the kidding and horseplay, the storytelling and feeds—contributes to group cohesion and produces in the men feelings of fellowship and affinity. (Applebaum, 1981, p. 34)

An example of group cohesion in direct sales work is provided by an ethnography of Tupperware distributors. For these workers, regular company meetings are important occasions for sharing information on how new products are selling and which sales techniques are most effective for these products. These meetings also are important for developing social cohesion: "Meetings become an important social occasion as well as a business function for many. . . . One Tupperware dealer, for example, said, 'Rally is every Monday morning. I wouldn't miss it. I'd kill to go to Rally'" (Biggart, 1989, p. 152).

Conflict With Coworkers

An example of high levels of *conflict between groups* at work is provided by an ethnography of a hospital:

Between the house officer group and the private doctors there is a fundamental and constantly arising conflict of interests. . . . It is in the private physician's interest (in matters of finance, personal convenience, and legal self-protection) to admit and keep all of his sick patients in the hospital and to administer a cautious and complete battery of diagnostic tests and treatments. On the other hand, the interests of the residents and interns are best served by admitting only a select portion of these patients (those with interesting diseases), by learning and practicing challenging diagnostic procedures on these patients, and by getting them released from the hospital as soon as possible after the diagnosis is made. (Millman, 1976, pp. 61-62)

Gossip between groups is evidenced in an ethnography of temporary clerical workers:

Not only were individual temps the butt of contemptuous and often bitchy remarks made by the permanents, but the whole group of us were sometimes subject to generalised insults and cool behavior. Temps were often discussed by the permanent staff. This usually happened when all the temps had left at 4.30 p.m. (McNally, 1979, p. 169)

Job Characteristics

Worker participation is indicated by formal structures that actively incorporate workers in operating decisions. Formal participation is clearly evidenced in an ethnography of a plywood manufacturing cooperative:

> Central to life in the cooperatives is the sense that the worker-shareholders are in charge, that they run the enterprise, are responsible for what goes on in it, and have the opportunity, within certain boundaries, to make of their environment what they will.
>
> "If it comes down to it, the stockholders have absolute rule down there. . . . If things get too bad, the stockholders can just say, 'Wait a minute. . . . We are going to change this.'" (Greenberg, 1986, pp. 36-37)

An example of highly *skilled* work is provided by an ethnography of railroad engineers:

> The learning experienced by enginemen may be classified into at least four broad areas. The first is manual operative skills coupled with technical knowledge. . . .
>
> The second area is codified knowledge of rules and guidelines for operating procedures. It comes from intensive study, practical application, and constant interpretation and restudy of various written sources. . . .
>
> The third area is on-the-job judgment, apart from the skills noted in the previous two areas. This area cannot be readily taught and cannot always be easily learned. . . .
>
> The fourth area is learning the railroaders' code of etiquette. Here a rail internalizes the mores or values governing interpersonal relations within the railroad social system. . . . A good rail excels in all four areas. (Gamst, 1980, pp. 42-44)

Autonomy measures the degree of control over decisions about one's own work tasks. On the 5-point scale, 1 = *none* indicates that workers' tasks are completely determined by others, by the machinery, or by organizational rules; 2 = *little* implies that workers occasionally have the chance to select among procedures or priorities; 3 = *average* implies regular opportunities to select procedures or to set priorities but the existence of definite limits on these choices; 4 = *high* implies significant latitude in determining procedures and setting priorities; and 5 = *very high* implies that significant interpretation is needed to reach broadly stated goals. An example of restricted autonomy (Level 2) is provided by an ethnography of an insurance company:

> I'm in a framework, a corporate framework, where I have to abide by their rules and regulations for everything, which gets to me because of all the bureaucratic junk that I have to go through to complete something. I know there's a faster way to do something, but I have to follow their ways, which is frustrating sometimes. (Burris, 1983, p. 157)

Analysis Strategy

Both dependent variables (job satisfaction and good relations with management) are interval-level measures. Ordinary least squares (OLS) regression is thus appropriate for the analysis.[1] Tables 14.2 and 14.3 report the range, mean, and standard deviation for each explanatory variable taken from the ethnographic and survey data sets. Because the analysis is based on the *population* of published ethnographic case studies of the workplace, and because these case studies do not constitute a representative sample of all workplaces, reported levels of statistical significance for the ethnographic data should be interpreted as suggestive only. In interpreting the results, I thus consider general patterns as well as the statistical significance of coefficients. Cases to be analyzed were selected on the basis of having data present for both dependent variables. Mean values were substi-

TABLE 14.2 Variable Means, Ranges, and Standard Deviations for Ethnographic Data (N= 108)

Variable	*Range*	*Mean*	*Standard Deviation*
Dependent variables			
Job satisfaction	1-5	2.89	1.08
Good relations with management (alpha = .70)	Scaled	0.00	1.00
Little abuse	1-5	3.54	1.00
Leadership	1-5	3.15	0.90
Organization of production	1-5	3.11	0.99
Little conflict with managers	1-5	3.26	0.89
Little conflict with supervisors	1-5	3.03	0.92
Coworker relations			
Solidarity (alpha = .78)	Scaled	0.00	1.00
Mutual defense	1-3	2.20	0.77
Group discipline	1-4	2.40	0.96
Group leadership	1-3	1.93	0.69
Group cohesion	1-5	3.47	1.00
Conflict with coworkers (alpha = .71)	Scaled	0.00	1.00
Conflict between groups	1-3	2.05	0.55
Gossip between groups	0, 1	0.76	0.30
Interference between groups	0, 1	0.48	0.36
Conflict within groups	1-3	1.95	0.49
Gossip within groups	0, 1	0.85	0.28
Interference within groups	0, 1	0.48	0.37
Job characteristics			
Participation	1-3	1.88	0.75
Skill	1-3	1.96	0.73
Autonomy	1-5	2.79	1.24

tuted for missing data for independent variables, resulting in a conservative estimation of effects.

RESULTS

Results from the regression of job satisfaction on coworker relations are presented in Table 14.4. Solidarity has a significant positive effect on job satisfaction in both the ethnographic and survey data. These effects provide support for Hypothesis 1. Hypothesis 3, predicting a negative effect of coworker conflict on job satisfaction, also receives partial support. The estimated effects of coworker conflict on job satisfaction are negative in both data sets but are significant only in the survey data.

An example of high levels of coworker solidarity in association with high levels of job satisfaction is found in a study of a cocktail bar in which the waitresses are observed to quickly become "like members of a family" (Spradley & Mann, 1975, p. 16). Some of the waitresses are particularly close and are "often inseparable," even in their lives outside the bar. This social cohesion provides a basis for mutual support in the face of difficult work situations. For instance, when a group of eight (potentially rowdy) members of the local college football

TABLE 14.3 Variable Means, Ranges, and Standard Deviations for Survey Data (N = 371)

Variable	*Range*	*Mean*	*Standard Deviation*
Dependent variables			
Job satisfaction	1-4	3.29	0.86
Good relations with management (alpha = .80)	Scaled	0.00	1.00
Management respectful	1-4	3.53	0.71
Satisfaction with supervisor	1-4	3.42	0.78
Coworker relations			
Solidarity (alpha = .62)	Scaled	0.00	1.00
Mutual defense	1-4	2.89	0.88
Help others	1-4	3.57	0.64
Absence of bickering	1-4	2.88	1.02
Satisfaction with coworkers	1-4	3.48	0.62
Conflict with coworkers (alpha = .72)	Scaled	0.00	1.00
Special treatment	1-4	2.43	1.15
Incompetence	1-4	2.51	1.07
Work avoidance	1-4	2.18	1.08
Unfair credit	1-4	2.36	0.96
Job characteristics			
Participation (alpha = .71)	Scaled	0.00	1.00
Participate	1-4	2.89	1.01
Opinion asked	1-4	3.11	0.94
Skill (alpha = .70)	Scaled	0.00	1.00
High skill required	1-4	3.13	0.94
Use full abilities	1-4	3.09	0.91
Not repetitious	1-4	2.30	1.10
Learn new things	1-4	3.35	0.74
Autonomy	1-4	3.40	0.88

team come in, "Sue glances at Denise and catches her eye, an instant message of sympathy hidden to everyone else. Sue nods her head at the clock and Denise shakes her head in agreement: 'Its a long time until closing'" (p. 49). Similarly, the "waitresses are especially supportive of one another when it comes to dealings with the bartenders and usually unite against direct 'attack' concerning their collective ability or intelligence" (p. 74). The waitresses voice high levels of job satisfaction, and their social cohesion and mutual support appear to be important foundations for their satisfaction on the job (p. 16).

Conversely, an ethnography of a bank reveals low job satisfaction in combination with high levels of conflict among coworkers. "A secretary who has been with the bank for seven years comments: 'Am I satisfied with my work? It's a job—just that. How many people do you know that are really *into* work?'" (Jackall, 1978, p. 95). Workers in this bank live in a social world of invidious comparison and backbiting, and this experience contributes significantly to their low levels of job satisfaction:

> Each individual knows that she herself may become an object of criticism. This creates an enervating apprehensiveness of others' judgements. An analysis clerk, when asked if she was staying for a branch party, expresses a widely felt anxiety: . . . I stay because if I don't, they'll talk about me."

TABLE 14.4 Regression of Job Satisfaction on Coworker Relations and Job Characteristics Using Ethnographic and Survey Data (standardized coefficients)

	Ethnographic Data		*Survey Data*	
Variable	*Model 1*	*Model 2*	*Model 1*	*Model 2*
Coworker relations				
Solidarity	.299*	.148***	.215*	.107**
Conflict with coworkers	–.060	–.068	–.185*	–.152*
Job characteristics				
Participation		.108		.234*
Skill		.188***		.186*
Autonomy		.422*		.081
R^2	.095*	.446*	.113*	.263*
N	101	101	371	371

*$p \leq .01$; **$p \leq .05$; ***$p \leq .10$ (two-tailed *t* tests).

[Another worker reports:] "Everyone is two-faced, and you have to watch out for yourself." [A third reports:] "They're a bunch of phoneys. . . . They are snotty. I feel awful if I'm around any of them." (Jackall, 1978, pp. 121-122)

Model 2 in Table 14.4 adds three job characteristics as predictors of job satisfaction.[2] Participation has a large positive effect, but only in the survey data. Autonomy has a large positive effect on job satisfaction, but only in the ethnographic data. The coworker variables remain significant under these controls. The general pattern of effects for the coworker variables and the job characteristics lends support to the hypothesis that coworker relations are an important determinant of job satisfaction. The coworker effects are generally significant, replicated across methods, and stable under controls.

Table 14.5 reports results from the analysis of good relations with management. Conflict among coworkers is negatively and significantly related to good relations with management in both the ethnographic and survey data. These findings provide support for Hypothesis 4. It appears that the sort of anomic conditions at the workplace classically associated with worker-manager conflict also produce substantial conflict among coworkers. In contrast to the expectation of Hypothesis 2, however, coworker solidarity is positively associated with good relations with management. In other words, high solidarity among workers leads to better relations with management. This finding is replicated across both methods but is significant only in the survey data. Our understanding of coworker solidarity as an inherently anti-management phenomenon may be mistaken. Supportive coworker relations appear to lessen rather than increase conflict with management. The positive relationship of coworker solidarity and good relations with management may derive in part from the generally positive effects of normatively organized workplaces.

An example of the pattern of good relations with management in combination with high levels of solidarity among workers is provided by an ethnography of a factory producing home tableware. The ethnographers describe the workers as evidencing a strong sense of cohesiveness (Savage & Lombard, 1978, p. 118). This cohesiveness includes supportive relations between senior and junior workers (p. 127) and the existence of strong leadership roles within the work group on topics ranging from work rules to relations with management (pp. 67, 120). Within this context, rate breaking (i.e., producing more than the informal norm) was effectively discouraged (pp. 91, 125) and workers

TABLE 13.5 Regression of Good Relations With Management on Coworker Relations and Job Characteristics Using Ethnographic and Survey Data (standardized coefficients)

	Ethnographic Data		*Survey Data*	
Variable	*Model 1*	*Model 2*	*Model 1*	*Model 2*
Coworker relations				
Solidarity	.128	.093	.342*	.228*
Conflict with coworkers	–.346*	–.343*	–.268*	–.260*
Job characteristics				
Participation		.141		.359*
Skill		.200		–.075
Autonomy		–.093		.110**
R^2	.137*	.188*	.266*	.402*
N	101	101	371	371

*$p \leq .01$; **$p \leq .05$; ***$p \leq .10$ (two-tailed *t* tests).

were able to maintain an effective and pleasant working environment. The company was profitable, and the manager's role was made easier and less conflictual by this context:

In the plant, [the manager] discussed production problems and passed the time of day with groups of workers. He appeared alert and attentive and obviously enjoyed conversation with everyone. ... Talking with people and listening to them was what he did best. (p. 59)

Poor worker-management relations in combination with high levels of conflict among workers are evidenced in a study of a steel mill. The ethnographer reports on numerous episodes of abusive actions on the part of management. For example, aggravated by a minor complaint from a worker, a supervisor "flew into a rage and shouted, "Get back on your job. You don't know what in hell you're talking about. I've been watching you, and you've been sitting on your [expletive] all morning" (Spencer, 1977, p. 171). In this abusive setting, there was considerable animosity and jealousy among workers in different departments (p. 158). Conflict among workers in the same department also was common. For example, millwrights were secretive in their knowledge and were unwilling to share it with apprentices:

Steve [the apprentice] was beginning to boil over, and one morning when the millwright was thumbing over a blueprint, holding it purposely out of Steve's view as though it were personal and confidential, he popped off,. . . . "I'm gonna' learn everything there is to know about this [expletive] job, no matter what you think." (p. 64)

Model 2 adds the three job characteristics as predictors of good relations with management. The effects of coworker relations on management relations are relatively stable under these controls. The effects of the job characteristics on good management relations, by contrast, are relatively weak. Participation increases good management relations. This effect, however, is significant only in the survey data. None of the effects of the job characteristics on good management relations is significant in the ethnographic data.[3]

The most robust determinant of good management relations across the ethnographic and survey data is coworker conflict. This finding provides additional support for the hypothesis that coworker relations have been underestimated as a determinant of important workplace outcomes.

DISCUSSION

The effects of coworker relations on job satisfaction and on good relations with management are substantial, often equaling or exceeding in magnitude those of job characteristics. In addition, these effects are generally consistent across ethnographic and survey methods of observation. Coworker conflict and infighting are associated with lower job satisfaction and poorer relations with management. Conversely, worker solidarity is associated with greater job satisfaction. Solidarity among coworkers also is positively associated with good relations between workers and managers—the opposite of what was predicted.

This latter finding suggests that our understanding of the role of coworker relations in the workplace still is quite limited. Mutual defense and other supportive coworker relations appear to be part of a normative environment with positive implications for hierarchical relations as well as for lateral ones. Decades ago, Tannenbaum and Kahn (1958, pp. 133, 149) presented a similar finding in their study of participation in union locals. They found that union participation (analogous to solidarity in our terms) was based not on a basic antipathy to management but rather on commitment to the organization and on a desire to make it a better place.

The finding that coworker solidarity is associated with good management relations contrasts sharply with theoretical propositions that describe workplace solidarity and resistance as social relations hardened in the fire of conflict with management (Fantasia, 1988). The norms of solidarity do not appear to be as much hardened in the fires of conflict as formed in the process of identifying with a job and deciding it is worth defending. Such norms of solidarity do not appear to be solely oppositional in origin or content (Hodson, Welsh, Rieble, Jamison, & Creighton, 1993).

These findings suggest the possibility that coworker solidarity should be conceptualized differently than it has been in the past. Solidarity appears to be not so much a result of conflict with management as a precondition for good relations between workers and managers. This may result in part from managers being more careful to be civil in their relations with workers when workers can count on mutual support among themselves than when they cannot. In this sense, prosocial organizational citizenship behaviors can be expected to flow from solidaristic settings and perhaps to be, at least in part, dependent on solidarity rather than impeded by it. Good worker-management relations appear to flow from workers experiencing solidarity with their peers rather than disunity, distrust, and conflict that erode a general atmosphere of positive relations at work.

These findings suggest that we may need to reconceptualize the nature of coworker relations, particularly in modern team-oriented production systems. This new conceptualization would include a greater role for coworker cohesion and solidarity as foundations for smoothly functioning workplaces. These findings also suggest that managers may want to be careful not to use team production systems to undermine worker cohesion and group solidarity; it could be a strategy with negative consequences for the maintenance of a normatively integrated and smoothly functioning workplace.

CONCLUSIONS

Infighting among workers is associated both with lower job satisfaction and with poorer relations between workers and managers. Conversely, coworker solidarity is associated with higher job satisfaction and better relations with management. These findings are supported in separate analyses based on two distinct methodologies: survey data and a systematic analysis of workplace ethnographies. The findings suggest an underdeveloped role for the analysis of coworker relations in studies of organizational behavior.

Our findings also suggest a possibly fruitful line of research that conceptualizes the workplace as a normative environment and then investigates deviations from this normative environment. This image stands in contrast to the often implicit image that fuels many, if not most, workplace studies—the image of a conflictual workplace in which the principal antagonists are workers and managers and in which peaceful relations are tantamount to capitulation.

NOTES

1. A binary measure of job satisfaction contrasting those most satisfied with all others also was analyzed using both OLS and logistic regression specifications. The results were substantively identical to the analysis using an interval-level measure of job satisfaction and OLS regression.

2. Gender also was examined as a control in all the equations estimated and was in no case significant.

3. The fact that the coefficients from the ethnographic data sometimes are similar in size to those from the survey data but less often are significant, or are significant only at a lower level, suggests that their statistical insignificance may result in part from a smaller N in the ethnographic data.

REFERENCES

Abbott, A. (1988). *The system of professions.* Chicago: University of Chicago Press.

Applebaum, E. R., & Batt, R. (1994). *The new American workplace.* Ithaca, NY: ILR Press.

Applebaum, H. (1981). *Royal blue: The culture of construction workers.* New York: Holt, Rinehart & Winston.

Barker, J. R. (1993). Tightening the iron cage: Concertive control in self-managing teams. *Administrative Science Quarterly, 38,* 408-437.

Biggart, N. (1989). *Charismatic capitalism: Direct selling organizations in America.* Chicago: University of Chicago Press.

Burawoy, M. (1979). *Manufacturing consent.* Chicago: University of Chicago Press.

Burris, B. H. (1983). *No room at the top: Underemployment and alienation in the corporation.* New York: Praeger.

Cherry, M. (1974). *On high steel: The education of an ironworker.* New York: Quadrangle.

Clawson, D., & Fantasia, R. (1983). Beyond Burawoy: The dialectics of conflict and consent on the shop floor. *Theory and Society, 12,* 671-680.

Collinson, D. L. (1988). "Engineering humour": Masculinity, joking and conflict in shop-floor relations. *Organization Studies, 9,* 181-199.

Derber, C., & Schwartz, W. (1983). Toward a theory of worker participation. *Sociological Inquiry, 53,* 61-78.

Fantasia, R. (1988). *Cultures of solidarity.* Berkeley: University of California Press.

Gabarro, J. J. (1987). The development of working relationships. In J. W. Lorsch (Ed.), *Handbook of organizational behavior* (pp. 172-189). Englewood Cliffs, NJ: Prentice Hall.

Gamst, F. C. (1980). *The hoghead: An industrial ethnology of the locomotive engineer.* New York: Holt, Rinehart & Winston.

Garrahan, P., & Stewart, P. (1992). Management control and a new regime of subordination. In G. N. Gilbert, R. Burrows, & A. Pollert (Eds.), *Fordism and flexibility* (pp. 107-117). London: Macmillan.

Goffee, R. (1981). Incorporation and conflict: A case study of subcontracting in the coal industry. *Sociological Review, 29,* 475-497.

Graham, L. (1995). *On the line at Subaru-Isuzu: The Japanese model and the American worker.* Ithaca, NY: ILR Press.

Greenberg, E. S. (1986). *Workplace democracy.* Ithaca, NY: Cornell University Press.

Grenier, G. J. (1988). *Inhuman relations: Quality circles and anti-unionism in American industry.* Philadelphia: Temple University Press.

Haas, J. (1972). Binging: Educational control among high steel ironworkers. *American Behavioral Scientist, 16,* 27-34.

Hackman, R. (1986). The psychology of self-management in organizations. In M. Pallak & R. Perloff (Eds.), *Psychology and work* (pp. 89-136). Washington, DC: American Psychological Association.

Halle, D. (1984). *America's working man.* Chicago: University of Chicago Press.

Hodson, R. (1995). Worker resistance: An underdeveloped concept in the sociology of work. *Economic and Industrial Democracy, 16*(1), 79-110.

Hodson, R. (1996). Dignity in the workplace under participative management: *Alienation and Freedom* revisited. *American Sociological Review, 61,* 719-738.

Hodson, R., Welsh, S., Rieble, S., Jamison, C. S., & Creighton, S. (1993). Is worker solidarity undermined by autonomy and participation? Patterns from the ethnographic literature. *American Sociological Review, 58,* 398-416.

Hurlbert, J. S. (1991). Social networks, social circles, and job satisfaction. *Work and Occupations, 18,* 415-430.

Jackall, R. (1978). *Workers in a labyrinth: Jobs and survival in a bank bureaucracy.* Montclair, NJ: Allanheld & Osmun.

Jackson, S. E., & Ruderman, M. N. (1995). *Diversity in work teams.* Washington, DC: American Psychological Association.

Jermier, J. M., Knights, D., & Nord, W. R. (Eds.). (1994). *Resistance and power in organizations.* London: Routledge.

Juravich, T., Harris, H., & Brooks, A. (1993). Mutual gains? Labor and management evaluate their employee involvement programs. *Journal of Labor Research, 14,* 165-185.

Kalleberg, A. L., & Berg, I. (1987). *Work and industry.* New York: Plenum.

Kunda, G. (1992). *Engineering culture: Control and commitment in a high-tech corporation.* Philadelphia: Temple University Press.

Kusterer, K. (1978). *Know-how on the job: The important working knowledge of "unskilled" workers.* Boulder, CO: Westview.

Lillrank, P., & Kano, N. (1989). *Continuous improvement: Quality circles in Japanese industry.* Ann Arbor: University of Michigan Center for Japanese Studies.

Linhart, R. (1981). *The assembly line* (M. Crosland, Trans.). Amherst: University of Massachusetts Press.

Mars, G. (1982). *Cheats at work.* London: Unwin.

McNally, F. (1979). *Women for hire.* New York: St. Martin's.

Millman, M. (1976). *The unkindest cut: Life in the backrooms of medicine.* New York: William Morrow.

Molstad, C. (1988). Control strategies used by industrial brewery workers: Work avoidance, impression management and solidarity. *Human Organization, 47,* 354-360.

Moos, R. H. (1986). Work as a human context. In M. Pallak & R. Perloff (Eds.), *Psychology and work* (pp. 9-48). Washington, DC: American Psychological Association.

Morrill, C. (1991). Conflict management, honor, and organizational change. *American Journal of Sociology, 97,* 585-621.

Morrison, A. M., Ruderman, M. N., & Hughes-James, M. (1993). *Making diversity happen.* Greensboro, NC: Center for Creative Leadership.

Parker, M., & Slaughter, J. (1994). *Working smart: A union guide to participation programs and reengineering.* Detroit, MI: Labor Notes.

Pfeffer, R. M. (1979). *Working for capitalism.* New York: Columbia University Press.

Pollert, A. (1981). *Girls, wives, factory lives.* London: Macmillan.

Reich, R. B. (1987). Entrepreneurship reconsidered: The team as hero. *Harvard Business Review, 65*(3), 77-83.

Savage, C. H., Jr., & Lombard, G. F. F. (1986). *Sons of the machine.* Cambridge: MIT Press.

Schnake, M. (1991). Organizational citizenship: A review, proposed model, and research agenda. *Human Relations, 44,* 735-759.

Seider, M. (1984). *A year in the life of a factory.* San Pedro, CA: Singlejack.

Smith, V. (1996). Employee involvement, involved employees: Participative work arrangements in a white-collar service occupation. *Social Problems, 43*(2), 166-179.

Spencer, C. (1977). *Blue collar: An internal examination of the workplace.* Chicago: Lakeside.

Spenner, K. I. (1990). Skill: Meaning, methods, measures. *Work and Occupations, 17,* 399-421.

Spradley, J. P., & Mann, B. J. (1975). *The cocktail waitress: Woman's work in a man's world.* New York: John Wiley.

Tannenbaum, A. S., & Kahn, R. L. (1958). *Participation in union locals.* Evanston, IL: Row, Peterson.

Tausky, C. (1992). Work is desirable/loathsome: Marx versus Freud. *Work and Occupations, 19,* 3-17.

Tausky, C., & Chelte, A. F. (1991). Employee involvement: A comment on Grenier and Hogler. *Work and Occupations, 18,* 334-342.

Trice, H. H., & Beyer, J. M. (1992). *The cultures of work organizations.* Englewood Cliffs, NJ: Prentice Hall.

Van Maanen, J., & Barley, S. R. (1984). Occupational communities: Culture and control in organizations. In B. M. Staw & L. L. Cummings (Eds.), *Research in organizational behavior* (Vol. 6, pp. 287-365). Greenwich, CT: JAI.

Vecsey, G. (1974). *One sunset a week: The story of a coal miner.* New York: E. P. Dutton.

Walton, R. E., & Hackman, J. R. (1986). Groups under contrasting management strategies. In P. S. Goodman & Associates (Eds.), *Designing effective work groups* (pp. 168-201). San Francisco: Jossey-Bass.

Westwood, S. (1984). *All day every day: Factory and family in the making of women's lives.* London: Pluto.

Effects of Organizational Innovations in AIDS Care on Burnout Among Urban Hospital Nurses

LINDA H. AIKEN
DOUGLAS M. SLOANE

Increased penetration of profit-making firms directly into medical services and the growth of managed care have resulted in higher levels of external control over health services including hospitals (Robinson, 1996). Use of inpatient settings has been reduced, leading to excess capacity, greater price competition, and financial instability for hospitals (Reinhardt, 1996). Organizational restructuring is widespread as hospitals reposition themselves to survive in a changing environment. Hospitals are labor intensive, and much of the focus of restructuring is on human resource management (Aiken, Sochalski, & Anderson, 1996). Concurrently, the AIDS epidemic presented multiple challenges to urban hospitals in the form of growing numbers of comparatively young patients from stigmatized groups with a fatal, potentially contagious disease needing acute care. Hospitals' responses have been varied and sometimes innovative (Fox, Aiken, & Messikomer, 1990). The AIDS epidemic has, in effect, created a natural experiment in hospital care and work redesign that offers the potential not only to understand how to improve AIDS care but also to inform restructuring initiatives presently sweeping the hospital industry.

In this chapter, we are interested in whether the organization of nursing in hospitals affects the extent to which nurses report being "burned out" or emotionally exhausted by their work. We compare how three different models for organizing hospital care affect burnout among nurses caring for AIDS patients. We go an important step further than most previous studies on burnout by demonstrating empirically that organizational features that support nurses' professional autonomy and control over their work mediate job-related emotional exhaustion.[1] We discuss the implications of our findings for the organization of inpatient AIDS care and for hospital redesign initiatives.

Burnout

The concept of burnout was first introduced into the academic literature by Freudenberger (1974) more than 20 years ago. Since that time, the term has become widely popular and the number of scholarly articles devoted to it has grown exponentially. In 1982, Perlman and Hartman (1982), in what was reported to be "a complete review of the field of burnout" (p. 293), counted 48 writings on the topic. A computer search of four data banks by Duquette, Kerouac, Sandhu, and Beaudet (1994) uncovered more than 300 documents published

From *Work and Occupations,* Vol. 24, No. 4, November 1997, pp. 453-477. Reprinted by permission.

by 1990. By 1995, according to Schulz, Greenley, and Brown (1995), there were more than 2,500 publications on the topic of burnout.

In the early stages of burnout research, there was a lack of agreement about what burnout was and how it should be measured. As originally conceived by Freudenberger (1980), burnout was "a state of fatigue or frustration brought about by devotion to a cause, way of life, or relationship that failed to produce the expected reward" (p. 13). Over time, burnout increasingly has become associated with work, and in particular with those who do "people-work" (i.e., who work in human service professions), and the use of the Maslach Burnout Inventory (MBI) to measure work-related burnout has gained widespread acceptance (Schaufeli & Van Dierendonck, 1993). The MBI (Maslach & Jackson, 1981) measures three related components of burnout: emotional exhaustion (i.e., feelings of being emotionally overextended and exhausted by one's work), depersonalization (i.e., an unfeeling and impersonal response to clients), and lack of personal accomplishment (i.e., dissatisfaction with personal accomplishment at work).[2]

In spite of the volume of research on the subject and the convergence on the MBI as the preferred measure of burnout for human service workers, there remains a lack of consensus about what causes individuals to experience burnout and what can be done to ameliorate it. Part of the problem is that the number of variables that have been studied as causes or correlates of burnout has produced, as Einsiedel and Tully (1981) described it, an "unwieldy universe." Schaufeli (1990) listed more than 100 factors that have been associated with burnout. The factors studied have included a broad range of demographic characteristics of workers such as sex (Williams, 1989), age (Cordes & Dougherty, 1993), education (Pines & Maslach, 1978), length of time in their current jobs (Maslach & Florian, 1988), and workers' personality characteristics including their expectations (Stevens & O'Neill, 1983), motivations (Anderson & Iwanicki, 1984), and coping strategies (Chiriboga & Bailey, 1986). The factors studied in relation to burnout also have included a large number of workplace characteristics, among them role ambiguity and conflict (Firth, McKeown, McIntee, & Britton, 1987), workload (Maslach and Jackson, 1984), social support (Hare, Pratt, & Andrews, 1988), and job autonomy or control (Landsbergis, 1988; Maslach, 1982). Our reading of the substantial literature on the topic of burnout leads us to conclude that burnout has more to do with characteristics of the workplace than with characteristics of the worker. This view is supported by the work of Pearlin and Schooler (1978), who argued that individual coping skills are more effective in ameliorating stress in close interpersonal role areas such as family and child rearing, where individual actions are more likely to modify the problem conditions, than in occupational settings, where, in the absence of structural change, individuals are relatively powerless through their own actions to correct the source of their frustration.

In this chapter, we focus on nurses, and in particular on nurses who provide care to patients with AIDS. Because of the physically and emotionally exhausting nature of AIDS care, the high death rate of comparatively young patients, the social stigma associated with AIDS, and the risk of occupational transmission of HIV, nurses caring for AIDS patients in large numbers could be expected to experience high burnout and job turnover. A growing body of research suggests that there are many stresses inherent in the caring role of nurses including the limited capabilities of medical science to cure disease and prevent death and the need to make critical decisions with ambiguous or incomplete information. Yet, nurses' negative attitudes about their jobs and the high resulting job turnover appear to have less to do with the challenges of caring for sick people than with the structured inequalities and organizational rigidities that characterize nurses' roles within hospitals (Hinshaw & Atwood, 1984; Maslach & Jackson, 1982). For example, nurses in intensive care units have *lower* levels of stress than do nurses in general medical units, where there are fewer life-and-death decisions but there is less autonomy and control over their practice (Gray-Toft & Anderson, 1981). Similarly, nurses who work on specialized oncology and hospice units, where most patients have poor prognoses, are in pain, and/or are terminally ill, have greater autonomy in both clinical decision making and unit management and, concomitantly, report lower perceptions of job-related stress (Gray-Toft & Anderson, 1981).

In the analyses reported subsequently, we consider and control for the effects of selected nurse characteristics on emotional exhaustion, but our principal interest involves whether the likelihood of being emotionally exhausted, among nurses who provide care to AIDS patients, is affected by the organizational form in which the care is rendered. We compare nurses in dedicated AIDS units to nurses in scattered-bed units and, among the latter group of nurses, distinguish between those who work in "magnet" hospitals and those who work in nonmagnet hospitals. Dedicated AIDS units, as the name suggests, are units that are dedicated solely to the care of HIV/AIDS patients, whereas scattered-bed units are conventional, multidiagnosis medical units that often have a diverse patient mix. Magnet and nonmagnet hospitals are distinquished less by definition than by designation. As we describe in the next subsection, magnet hospitals were so designated, in a study by the American Academy of Nursing, because they possessed organizational attributes that nurses found attractive, most notably the integration of nursing in the management and operations of the institutions. Only a handful of studies have looked at the effect of differing forms of hospital organization on burnout.

Hospital Organization and Outcomes

In the 1980s, the American Academy of Nursing conducted a study designed to identify hospitals across the nation that were successful in recruiting and retaining nurses even during national nursing shortages (McClure, Poulin, Sovie, & Wandelt, 1983). Some 41 such hospitals were identified and studied. These hospitals had high nurse satisfaction, low job turnover, and low nurse vacancy rates even when hospitals in close proximity were experiencing nursing shortages, and they came to be designated as magnet hospitals because of their success in attracting and keeping nurses. Research conducted at these hospitals confirmed that they shared a set of common organizational attributes including that (a) the nurse executive was a formal member of the highest decision-making body in the hospital, signifying the high priority hospital management placed on nursing; (b) nursing services were organized in a flat organizational structure with few supervisory personnel as opposed to a pyramid structure with many supervisors between the staff nurses and the nurse executive; (c) decision making was decentralized at the unit level, giving nurses on each unit as much discretion as possible in organizing care and staffing in a manner most appropriate to the needs of their patients; (d) the management structure in hospitals supported nurses' decisions about patients; and (e) good communications existed between nurses and physicians (Kramer & Schmalenberg, 1988, 1991).

A definitive history of the hospital response to the AIDS epidemic is yet to be written. However, in broad outline, we note the following features that characterized the first decade of the epidemic. First, there was an early period in which AIDS patients were relatively rare, the disease was not well diagnosed or understood, and patients were, for the most part, treated in general medical units. Second, understanding of the infectious nature of the disease increased. This coincided with a magnification of concern about infection among the public and health professionals alike. Third, in 1983, the nation's first specialized unit for AIDS patients was established at San Francisco General Hospital. It was organized primarily for nursing rather than medical care (Morrison, 1987). Although this unit has become well known for, among other things, its part in an integrated, community-wide response to the health and welfare needs of persons with AIDS, its creation was motivated by a desire on the part of the hospital to segregate AIDS patients from other patients and to segregate the majority of staff from AIDS patients (Pogash, 1992). Fourth, the success of the San Francisco General unit, as perceived by patients, doctors, and nurses alike, led to a rapid diffusion of specialized (or dedicated) AIDS units across the urban United States. By the end of 1988, 40 U.S. hospitals were operating specialized inpatient acute care AIDS units (Taravella, 1989).

A detailed look at the San Francisco General unit reveals a confluence of factors that made it a model for specialized AIDS units. First, the task of organizing the unit was given to a nurse rather than to a physician or hospital administrator. Second, the unit was established in a city where the high incidence of AIDS and the comparatively strong organization of the community most afflicted by the epidemic had led to the creation of a community-based health care system with relatively little professional hierarchy. The attendant ideology of community and personal control over illness and its care fostered a demand for a range of services—and not merely medical services—that extended to treatment of persons with acute AIDS in a hospital setting. The fact that San Francisco General is a city-owned hospital may well have made it more responsive to community preferences regarding how health care would be provided. Third, health care personnel who came to be associated with the unit had long-standing experience with the patient population. There was a core of physicians who had specialized interests in infectious diseases that predated the epidemic and that were rapidly transformed into a primary interest in AIDS care. Of course, not all these features were unique to San Francisco General, and prior to the AIDS epidemic, San Francisco General was not particularly noted for organizational innovation, especially in nursing.

Thus, as specialized units spread as an organizational form of AIDS care, it was plausible, but by no means certain, that new units would embody the features of the original San Francisco General unit responsible for the perceived success of that unit. Some of the reason for the rapid spread of this organizational form was doubtless a desire to imitate a success; for example, it was quickly apparent that San Francisco General was having no trouble recruiting nurses for, and retaining nurses on, its specialized AIDS unit. At the same time, the factors that originally motivated the San Francisco General unit—more and more patients with AIDS, a skittish non-AIDS patient population, and worries that a reluctance among nurses to treat patients with AIDS would exacerbate long-standing problems of recruitment and retention—still were important factors in the adoption of this innovation (Taravella, 1989; van Servellen, Lewis, Schweitzer, & Leake, 1991, p. 26).

What do magnet hospitals and dedicated AIDS units have in common that might reduce the likelihood of nurse burnout? Both organizational models promote greater autonomy for nurses to act within their areas of professional expertise, greater nurse control over the support services and personnel necessary to provide high-quality care (e.g., transport services, social services, discharge planning), and better communication structures between nurses and physicians that are well understood and result in better relationships (Aiken, Smith, & Lake, 1994). Magnet hospitals achieve these organizational outcomes because hospital management grants greater autonomy and control to nurses than is common in most hospitals. This is the magnet hospital model. Specialized units achieve these organizational outcomes by devolving more autonomy, control, and status to nurses as a result of providing them with an opportunity to practice within their specialties and to assume greater command of the knowledge base and technology. In these specialized AIDS units, nurses reside in a somewhat more equal position to physicians than is the case elsewhere, in part because the needs of AIDS patients, in the absence of a cure, are more in line with what nurses do best than with the curative medical model practiced by physicians.

There has been no research on differences between magnet and nonmagnet hospitals in terms of nurse burnout. Also, there has been little research on the impact of working in different unit types on nurse burnout, and what research has been done suggests little difference. Harris (1984) found no difference in burnout between nurses in general medical units and those in intensive care units; Cronin-Stubbs and Rooks (1985) found no relationship between burnout and nurses working in intensive care, operating room, psychiatry, and/or medical units; and Chiriboga and Bailey (1986) found no differences in comparing nurses in medical-surgical units to those in critical care units. These studies, however, selected units for comparison on the basis of perceived differences in type of care provided, type of patient, or degree of client illness severity. None selected units that were clearly different in terms of organizational characteristics that might be presumed to affect burnout. The only studies that looked at differences in burnout in dedicated AIDS units as opposed to scattered-bed units were done by van Servellan and Leake (1993) and Oktay (1992), who considered samples of nurses and social workers, respectively. Both found that working in a dedicated AIDS unit was associated with higher emotional exhaustion.

In this chapter, we specifically consider how, in units and hospitals where AIDS care is given, nurses in specialized AIDS units differ from nurses in general medical units, as well as how nurses in magnet hospitals differ from those in nonmagnet hospitals, with respect to burnout. Our primary interest is in emotional exhaustion because it is here that the links among theory, measurement, and phenomenology are greatest; that is, the organizational stressors noted previously are assumed to wear people down, the items measuring emotional exhaustion appear to have high face validity, and it is the sense of being drained and beleaguered that best captures what one observes viscerally in a setting characterized by frustration and strain.

DATA AND METHODS

Our primary interest here is whether the organization of nursing care affects the extent to which nurses report being emotionally exhausted by their work. Three basic models of nursing organization are compared: (a) general scattered-bed units in nonmagnet hospitals, (b) specialized or dedicated AIDS units in nonmagnet hospitals, and (c) general scattered-bed units in magnet hospitals. There were no dedicated AIDS units in magnet hospitals either in our sample or in the broader population of hospitals that we sampled.

Hospital Sample

Nurses in 20 hospitals were surveyed. The 20 hospitals consisted of 10 hospitals with dedicated AIDS units and 10 comparison hospitals without such units. The universe of hospitals with dedicated AIDS units was defined by a census conducted in 1988 that enumerated 40 hospitals with dedicated units. Of these hospitals, 22 met the following inclusion criteria: nonprofit, nonfederal hospitals with dedicated AIDS units of 10 beds or more, located in one of the 25 cities with the highest cumulative total of AIDS cases in 1988. Of these 22 hospitals, 10 (45% of eligible hospitals) were selected for study on the basis of the following considerations: geographic distribution in all four census regions, a mix of public and private hospitals, a mix of teaching and community hospitals, and the proximity of a matched hospital with a substantial AIDS census but no AIDS unit.

The 10 comparison hospitals were selected on the basis of their match with dedicated AIDS unit hospitals on the following dimensions: ownership, teaching status, size, location, average AIDS census, and estimated proportion of AIDS patients who were injecting drug users. Although our original intention was to match hospitals in 10 pairs, we ultimately determined that 9 matched hospital groupings—the 7 matched pairs and 2 matched triplets of hospitals shown in Table 15.1—yielded groups of hospitals that were more alike on factors that we thought might affect patient outcomes and nurse outcomes than were the original set of 10

TABLE 15.1 Numbers of Nurses Surveyed on Dedicated AIDS Units and Scattered-Bed Units in 20 Study Hospitals, by Matched Groups

		Nurses Interviewed		
Group	*Hospital*	*Dedicated AIDS Units*	*Scattered-Bed Units*	*Total*
A	New York I[a]	12	20	32
	New York II	0	36	36
B	New York III[a]	12	15	27
	New York IV	0	44	44
C	New York V	23	0	23
	New York VI	0	22	22
D	Baltimore[a]	12	15	27
	Boston[b]	0	72	72
	Chicago I[b]	0	71	71
E	Miami[a]	23	25	48
	Dallas	0	28	28
F	New Orleans[a]	13	43	56
	Atlanta	0	40	40
G	Chicago II[a]	10	8	18
	Chicago III[a]	14	8	22
	Philadelphia	0	36	36
H	San Francisco I[a]	25	29	54
	Los Angeles I	0	35	35
I	Los Angeles II[a]	24	29	53
	San Francisco II[b]	0	76	76

a. Hospital in our restricted sample that has nurses in both a dedicated AIDS unit and scattered-bed units.
b. Magnet hospital.

hospital pairs. A series of preliminary one-way analyses of variance (not shown) revealed that 70% to 80% of the variation across the 20 hospitals included in our study—in average daily census, nurse-to-patient ratio, payroll-to-beds ratio, mortality rate, and high technology index—involved variation between the 9 groups of matched hospitals and that only 20% to 30% of the variation was within the 9 matched groups.

Included among those comparison hospitals having only scattered-bed units were three magnet hospitals known for their organizationwide integration of nursing in the management and operation of the institutions. All three magnet hospitals have been the subject of research demonstrating a common set of organizational attributes associated with high institutional priority on clinical nursing care, high job satisfaction among nurses, and better patient outcomes (Christman, 1978; Kramer & Schmalenberg, 1988; McClure et al., 1983).

Hospital units. In each study hospital, two units were selected. In hospitals with dedicated units, we selected, in addition to the dedicated unit, the one other general medical unit with the highest average AIDS census. There was one exception to this: One New York hospital had two dedicated AIDS units and no AIDS patients in scattered-bed units, so the two dedicated AIDS units were selected. In hospitals with only scattered-bed units, the two units with the highest average daily AIDS census were selected.

these, 145 (43%) were in dedicated AIDS units, and 192 (57%) were in scattered-bed units.

Nurse Sample

We attempted to survey all 955 of the registered or licensed practical nurses who worked at least 16 hours per week in the 40 study units. Data were collected in two waves between September 1990 and December 1991. Each nurse was asked to complete a 21-page self-administered questionnaire designed to elicit information on the nurse's background (personal, educational, and employment characteristics), job satisfaction, job-related stress and burnout, assessments of the presence of various organizational attributes and practices on the nurse's unit, perceptions of the nurse's relations with physicians and of the adequacy of support services, and attitudes and behaviors toward AIDS patients and persons with AIDS.

As a result of an intense regimen of reminders, follow-ups, and financial incentives, we were able to obtain responses from 820 nurses—an 86% response rate. Given this high response rate, it is not surprising that respondents and nonrespondents did not differ on a variety of characteristics that could be reported by others and/or obtained from administrative records. There were no significant differences in age, sex, race, nursing degree, work shift, work status (staff, float, per diem, or agency nurse), or level of nurse satisfaction (as reported by the head nurse of the nursing unit).

Table 15.1 shows the numbers of nurses surveyed in the various study hospitals, and is further classified by whether they worked in dedicated AIDS units or in scattered-bed units. In the full sample of 820 nurses in the 20 study hospitals 168 nurses (20%) worked in dedicated AIDS units, and the remaining 652 (80%) worked in scattered-bed units. Of the 652 nurses working in scattered-bed units, 219 (34% of the nurses in that type of unit, or 27% of the full sample of nurses) were in the 3 magnet hospitals. The sample of nurses in hospitals with both types of units involves a total of 337 nurses; of

Measures and Methods

Emotional exhaustion, the dependent variable in our analyses, was measured by the frequently used summated scale that is a subscale of the MBI (Maslach, 1982; Maslach & Jackson, 1982, 1986). It was derived by summing responses to nine items: (a) "I feel emotionally drained from my work," (b) "I feel used up at the end of the workday," (c) "I feel fatigued when I get up in the morning and have to face another day on the job," (d) "Working with people all day is really a strain for me," (e) "I feel burned out from my work," (f) "I feel frustrated by my job," (g) "I feel I'm working too hard on my job," (h) "Working with people directly puts too much stress on me," and (i) "I feel like I'm at the end of my rope." The response categories for each of the nine items originally were scored 0 = *never,* 1 = *a few times a year or less,* 2 = *once a month or less,* 3 = *a few times a month,* 4 = *once a week,* 5 = *a few times a week,* and 6 = *every day.* Preliminary work suggests that the scale that results from these nine items is quite reasonable; Cronbach's alpha is .89, and the average interitem correlation is .47. The left panel of Figure 15.1 shows the distribution of nurses' scores on this scale, which were near normally distributed with a mean of 24.3, a median of 23.0, and observed values ranging from 0 to 52. As coded, higher scores reflect higher levels of emotional exhaustion.[3]

The independent variable of most proximate interest to us is the model or type of nursing organization, which we measure, as noted previously, by contrasting dedicated AIDS units in nonmagnet hospitals, scattered-bed units in nonmagnet hospitals, and scattered-bed units in magnet hospitals. Our comparison of the emotional exhaustion of nurses in dedicated AIDS units and scattered-bed units in nonmagnet hospitals is made both using the restricted sample of nurses who worked in the nine hospitals that had both types of units and

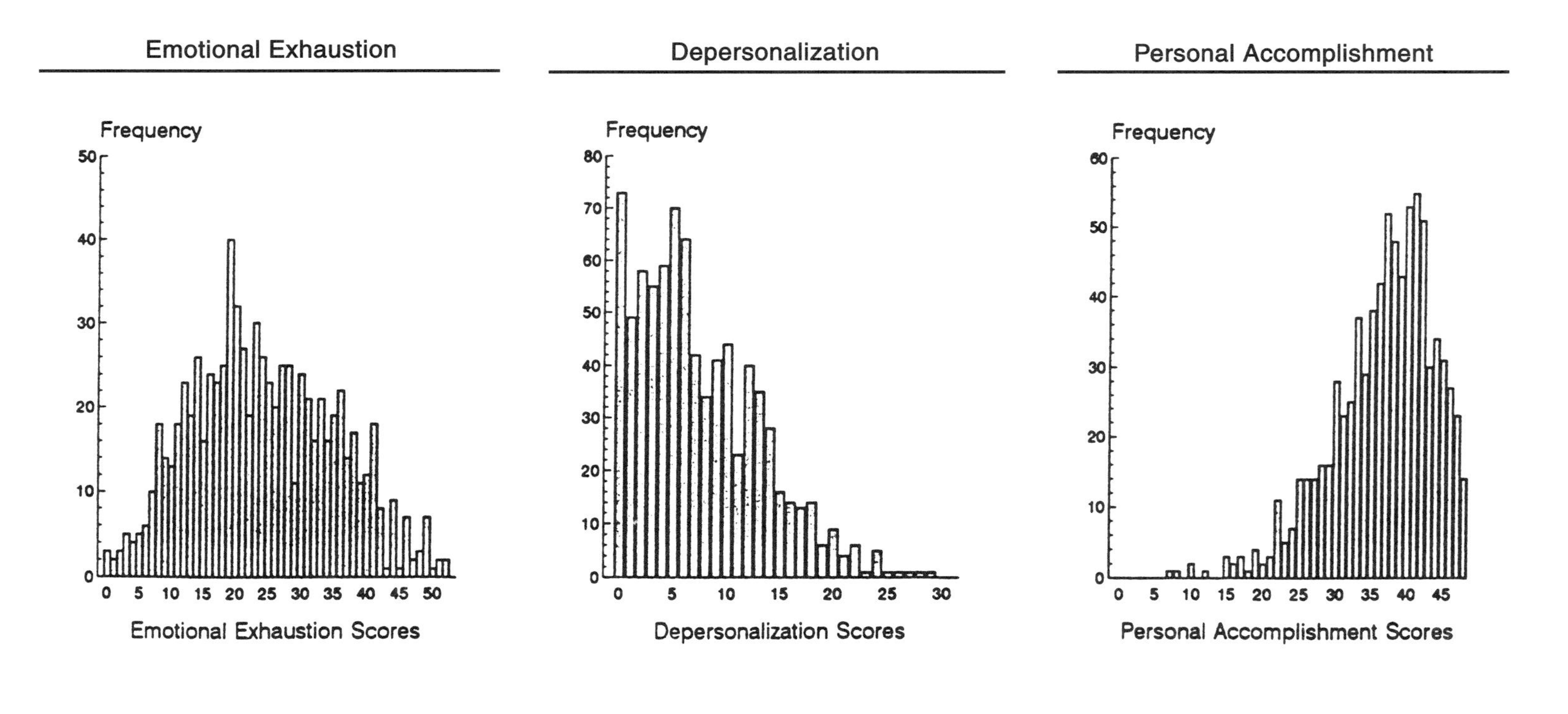

Figure 15.1. Distributions of Burnout Subscale Scores

using the full sample of nurses. The comparison of those two groups of nurses to nurses in scattered-bed units in magnet hospitals is done using the full sample.

We suspected that differences in emotional exhaustion between nurses in these different types of units and/or hospitals would be accounted for to some extent by differences across types of units or hospitals in organizational support. This factor was measured by a summated scale derived from 10 items that were found to vary quite substantially across the three types of nursing organization we compared. The 10 individual items asked nurses whether they *strongly disagreed, disagreed, agreed,* or *strongly agreed* that the following organizational characteristics were present in their current job situations: (a) "Adequate support services allow me to spend time with my patients," (b) "Physicians and nurses have good relationships," (c) "Nursing controls its own practice," (d) "Enough time and opportunity to discuss patient care problems with other nurses," (e) "Enough registered nurses on staff to provide quality patient care," (f) "A head nurse who is a good manager and leader," (g) "Freedom to make important patient care and work decisions," (h) "Not being placed in a position of having to do things that are against my nursing judgment," (i) "A lot of teamwork between doctors and nurses," and (j) "Patient care assignments that foster continuity of care (i.e., the same nurse cares for the patient from one day to the next)." The scale derived from these 10 items also showed reasonable psychometric properties, yielding an alpha of .84 and an average interitem correlation of .34.

We recognize that, in estimating the difference between nurses in dedicated AIDS units and those in scattered-bed units in the restricted sample, whatever aggregate (or overall) difference we find in emotional exhaustion could reflect differences in emotional exhaustion across different hospitals as well as differences across the two types of units given that the relative numbers of nurses in the two types of units vary by hospital. As such, in those analyses, we estimate unit type differences both before and after controlling for interhospital differences, using eight dummy variables to represent the differences in emotional exhaustion across the nine hospitals. In our analyses using the full sample, where certain interhospital differences (i.e., differences between nurses in magnet hospitals and those in nonmagnet hospitals) are part of what we are trying to estimate, we cannot employ dummy variables to represent individual hospitals. In the full-sample analyses, therefore, we control for interhospital differences that do not necessarily have anything to do with the magnet/nonmagnet distinction by using eight dummy variables to represent the nine matched groups (pairs or triads) of hospitals.

We also recognize that the selection of nurses to a particular type of unit within a hospital and/or to a particular type of hospital may not occur at random. It may be that nurses who are attracted to, and working in, dedicated AIDS units or magnet hospitals are better suited to the work they are doing and, as a result, are less likely to be emotionally exhausted from that work (see Williamson, 1996, for a discussion of this, which frequently is referred to as the job fit hypothesis). As such, variation in emotional exhaustion across unit or hospital types may result not only from the differences in nursing organization that those three distinct unit/hospital types represent but also from differences in the characteristics of nurses who are attracted to the different types of units or hospitals. We show subsequently, for example, that nurses in dedicated AIDS units are more likely to be male, White, gay or bisexual, older, and more experienced. We also know, from preliminary analyses not shown, that a number of these characteristics are related to emotional exhaustion. Non-White and foreign-born nurses exhibit higher levels of emotional exhaustion than do other nurses, whereas older and more experienced nurses exhibit lower levels. For that reason, in our analyses, we also control for certain nurse characteristics that we found to vary across dedicated AIDS units and scattered-bed units or across magnet and nonmagnet hospitals. These include a nurse's sex, race, country of origin, religion, religious intensity, education, sexual preference, age, nursing experience, and time spent on present unit.

RESULTS

The upper panel of Table 15.2 shows the mean levels of emotional exhaustion and organizational support for nurses in dedicated AIDS units, and in scattered-bed units, for the nine hospitals in the restricted sample that had nurses in both types of units. The zero-order differences across unit types in both measures are statistically significant and quite sizable. The mean emotional exhaustion score for nurses in the dedicated AIDS units was some 4 points lower than that for nurses in the scattered-bed units. In this restricted sample, the Emotional Exhaustion subscale has a standard deviation of approximately 11, so the difference of more than 4 points on the scale implies a difference of roughly four tenths of a standard deviation. In the middle of a normally distributed variable such as the Emotional Exhaustion subscale, this corresponds (approximately) to the difference between the 35th and 65th percentiles. The relative size of the difference in organizational support across units is only slightly smaller (i.e., about one third of a standard deviation). In these hospitals with both types of units, nurses in dedicated AIDS units have substantially lower levels of emotional exhaustion and higher levels of organizational support.[4]

The results in the bottom panel of Table 15.2, which are derived from the full sample of nurses, suggest a similar and (roughly) equally sizable difference in emotional exhaustion between the nurses in the dedicated AIDS units and those in the scattered-bed units in nonmagnet hospitals. We also find, in the full sample of nurses, that nurses in scattered-bed units in magnet hospitals exhibit lower levels of emotional exhaustion than do those in scattered-bed units in nonmagnet hospitals. Moreover, we find that nurses in magnet hospitals have greater organizational support than do those in dedicated AIDS units, who in turn have greater organizational support than do nurses in scattered-bed units in nonmagnet hospitals. One-way analyses of variance reveal that although all three groups of nurses differ significantly in terms of organizational support, the only significant differences in emotional exhaustion involve the differences between nurses in scattered-bed units in nonmagnet hospitals and the other two groups. (Nurses in dedicated AIDS units and those in scattered-bed units in magnet hospitals do not differ from one another.[5])

As already noted, we suspect that at least some of the difference in emotional exhaustion seen in Table 15.2 is due to differences across units and hospitals in organizational support. Table 15.3 shows, for the full sample of nurses, how differently nurses in dedicated AIDS units and nurses in scattered-bed units in magnet and nonmagnet hospitals responded to each of the 10 individual items that we used to derive our Organizational Support subscale.[6] The three columns of numbers in Table 15.3 are odds ratios that indicate how much higher (or lower, in the case of the one odds ratio that is less than 1.0) the odds on reporting that these characteristics were present in their jobs were for nurses in dedicated AIDS units than for nurses in scattered-bed units in nonmagnet hospitals (D vs. S in the table), for nurses in scattered-bed units in magnet versus nonmagnet hospitals (M vs. S), and for nurses in scattered-bed units in magnet hospitals versus nurses in dedicated AIDS units in nonmagnet hospitals (M vs. D).

These odds ratios reveal that differences abound and that many are quite sizable. In all cases, nurses in the dedicated units, and in the scattered-bed units in magnet hospitals, were more likely than nurses in scattered-bed units in nonmagnet hospitals to indicate that these characteristics were present in their jobs. Also, with one exception (having a head nurse who is a good manager and leader), nurses in scattered-bed units in magnet hospitals were more likely to indicate that these characteristics were present than were nurses in dedicated AIDS units in nonmagnet hospitals. Likelihood ratio chi-square tests indicated that in the large bulk of comparisons made, the differences were signifi-

TABLE 15.2 Emotional Exhaustion and Organizational Support Among Nurses in the Restricted Sample of Nurses in Nonmagnet Hospitals With Both Dedicated AIDS Units and Scattered-Bed Units and in the Full Sample of Nurses, by Unit/Hospital Type (means and standard deviations)

Sample	*Emotional Exhaustion*	*Organizational Support*
Unit type (restricted sample)		
Dedicated AIDS unit (n = 143)	21.1	30.0
	(11.0)	(5.5)
Scattered-bed unit (n = 186)	25.3	28.1
	(11.3)	(6.1)
Unit/hospital type (full sample)		
Dedicated AIDS unit (n = 166)	21.5	29.5
	(10.9)	(5.4)
Scattered-bed unit, nonmagnet (n = 422)	26.7	27.4
	(11.2)	(6.1)
Scattered-bed unit, magnet (n = 218)	21.9	32.8
	(9.6)	(3.9)

NOTE: Standard deviations are in parentheses. The Emotional Exhaustion and Organizational Support subscales are described in the text. All pairwise differences between mean scores for both measures are statistically significant with the exception of the difference in emotional exhaustion between nurses in dedicated AIDS units and nurses in scattered-bed units in magnet hospitals in the full sample.

TABLE 15.3 Odds Ratios Indicating the Differences Between Nurses in Dedicated AIDS Units, General Scattered-Bed Units, and Scattered-Bed Units in Magnet Hospitals in the Odds on Indicating Certain Characteristics Were Present in Their Jobs

Dependent Variable	*D vs. S*	*M vs. S*	*M vs. D*
Adequate support services allow me to spend time with my patients	2.34*	5.46*	2.33*
Physicians and nurses have good relationships	1.49	2.20*	1.48
Nursing controls its own practice	1.08	6.41*	5.94*
Enough time and opportunity to discuss patient care problems with other nurses	2.20*	8.70*	3.95*
Enough registered nurses on staff to provide quality patient care	2.03*	12.04*	5.93*
A head nurse who is a good manager and leader	1.53*	1.38	0.90
Freedom to make important patient care and work decisions	1.64*	6.03*	3.68*
Not being placed in a position of having to do things that are against my nursing judgment	1.14	2.13*	1.87*
A lot of teamwork between doctors and nurses	1.61*	3.99*	2.48*
Patient care assignments that foster continuity of care (i.e., the same nurse cares for the patient from one day to the next)	1.96*	2.91*	1.48

NOTE: Odds ratios indicate differences in the odds on nurses indicating that these characteristics are present in their jobs, across nurses in dedicated AIDS units (D), general scattered-bed units (S), and scattered-bed units in magnet hospitals (M). Nurses were given the list of characteristics above and asked whether they agreed or disagreed that these were present in their current job situations.
* Significant at the .05 level.

cant at the .05 level. We also know from additional analyses (not shown) that higher organizational support, measured by a summary scale derived from these items, is associated with lower levels of emotional exhaustion. In the full sample of nurses, the correlation between the two measures is –.34, and a simple bivariate regression of emotional exhaustion on organizational support yields a significant negative coefficient of –.63.

Some of the differences in emotional exhaustion between nurses in the different types of units and hospitals, however, may be due to differences in the characteristics of nurses who work in dedicated AIDS units versus scattered-bed units or who work in magnet hospitals versus nonmagnet hospitals. Table 15.4 shows that a number of differences do exist. In both the restricted sample and the full sample, nurses in dedicated AIDS units are significantly more likely than nurses in scattered-bed units to be male, White, gay or bisexual, older, and more experienced as well as less likely to be of foreign origin, Catholic, and devoutly religious. They also, on average, have spent less time in their present units than have nurses in scattered-bed units. In the full sample, we find, moreover, that among the nurses in scattered-bed units, those in magnet hospitals are more likely than those in nonmagnet hospitals to be White and Catholic, to have college degrees, and to be younger and less experienced as well as less likely to be devoutly religious.

Tables 15.5 and 15.6 reveal what happens to the estimated differences in emotional exhaustion between the nurses in these different types of units and/or hospitals when, using ordinary least squares regression procedures, we adjust for interhospital differences not related to the magnet/nonmagnet distinction and for differences in nurse characteristics and organizational support.[7] The first column of coefficients in Table 15.5 gives the unadjusted difference between nurses in dedicated AIDS units and those in scattered-bed units in the restricted sample of nurses in hospitals that have both types of units (i.e., the significant 4.2-point difference we observed in Table 15.2).

The second, third, and fourth columns of coefficients in Table 15.5 are estimated coefficients from models that sequentially adjust for interhospital differences, then nurse characteristics, and then organizational support. Whereas the coefficients in the second column indicate that the nurses in the different hospitals in our restricted sample are, in a number of cases, significantly different with respect to emotional exhaustion, controlling for such differences increases our estimate of the difference between nurses in dedicated AIDS units and those in scattered-bed units (from 4.2 to 4.7 points). The third column shows that controlling for nurse characteristics, including the significantly negative effects on emotional exhaustion of being Black, Hispanic, and Catholic as well as the significantly positive effect of time (in years) on present unit, diminishes the size of the difference between nurses in dedicated AIDS units and those in scattered bed units by only 0.5 point. The final column shows, however, that controlling for the highly significant effect of organizational support—that is, each unit increase in organizational support is associated with a 0.5-point decrease in emotional exhaustion—diminishes the dedicated AIDS unit effect from a difference of 4.2 points to a difference of 3.1 points. The adjusted R^2 for this final model, given in the last row of Table 15.5, indicates that it accounts for some 19% of the variance in emotional exhaustion among nurses. The effect of organizational support, net of all the other factors, accounts for roughly 5% of that variance. (Note the increment in R^2 between Models 3 and 4.)

Table 15.6 shows the results of a parallel analysis, using the full sample, in which the effects of working in a dedicated AIDS unit and in a magnet hospital are considered simultaneously. Again the coefficients for the first model, given in the first column of the table, reproduce the differences between these types of nursing organization that we saw in Table 15.2. Nurses in the dedicated AIDS units and in the scattered-bed units in magnet hospitals have emotional exhaustion scores that are some 5.3 and 4.8 points lower, respectively, than those for

TABLE 15.4 Selected Nurse Characteristics in the Restricted Sample of Nurses in Nonmagnet Hospitals With Both Dedicated AIDS Units and Scattered-Bed Units and in the Full Sample of Nurses, by Unit/Hospital Type

	Unit Type (restricted sample)		*Unit/Hospital Type (full sample)*		
Nurse Characteristic	*Dedicated AIDS Unit*	*Scattered-Bed Unit*	*Dedicated AIDS Unit*	*Scattered-Bed Unit (nonmagnet)*	*Scattered-Bed Unit (magnet)*
Male	24.7*	3.2	23.0*	3.5	3.2
White (non-Hispanic)	58.9*	24.1	57.1*	28.8	81.9*
Black	24.1*	40.8	22.7*	38.2	7.9*
Asian	7.1*	27.2	10.4*	26.7	7.4*
Hispanic	9.2	5.2	9.2	4.5	1.4
Other race	0.7	2.6	0.6	1.9	1.4
Foreign origin	25.3*	51.2	27.1*	44.9	11.1*
Protestant	32.4	29.3	32.3	31.4	28.8
Catholic	35.3*	52.4	39.2*	46.7	55.2*
Jewish	2.2	1.6	1.9	0.9	3.3
Other religion	30.2*	16.8	26.6*	21.0	12.7*
Devoutly religious	9.4*	18.4	11.8*	19.0	10.6*
College degree	34.3	36.7	36.1	40.9	81.5*
Gay or bisexual	27.3*	1.7	24.5*	3.0	6.1
Age (years)	38.7 ± 9.0*	35.9 ± 9.5	38.9 ± 9.3*	35.7 ± 9.5	29.4 ± 7.1*
Experience (years)	12.0 ± 9.5*	10.1 ± 8.3	12.3 ± 9.7*	10.3 ± 8.6	6.0 ± 6.8*
Time on present unit (years)	2.6 ± 2.6*	4.8 ± 5.1	2.7 ± 2.5*	4.2 ± 4.5	3.3 ± 3.7

* In the second and fourth columns, difference between dedicated AIDS units and nonmagnet scattered-bed units significant at .05 level; in the last column, difference between magnet and nonmagnet scattered-bed units significant at .05 level.

nurses in the scattered-bed units. These differences are largely unaffected by controlling for interhospital differences using dummy variables for eight of the nine matched blocks of hospitals but are slightly diminished by adjusting for differences in the various nurse characteristics—by 1.0 point in the case of the dedicated AIDS unit effect and by 0.5 point in the case of the magnet hospital effect.

Again, however, controlling for the pronounced effect of organizational support diminishes our estimate of the effect of being in a dedicated AIDS unit by roughly one third (from 4.6 to 3.1 points) and diminishes our estimate of the magnet hospital effect by more than two thirds (from 4.7 to 1.4 points). The effect of organizational support that we estimate in this full sample is very similar to what we obtained in the restricted sample (–0.6 vs. –0.5) and accounts for some 7% of the overall 17% of variance in emotional exhaustion that is explained by the full set of factors.

CONCLUSIONS

This analysis indicates that burnout among hospital nurses, or at least the emotional exhaustion component of burnout, is decidedly lower among those who work in dedicated AIDS units than among nurses who work in multidiagnosis medical units where AIDS patients constitute portions of the patient populations. This finding is counter to the conventional wisdom holding that nurse burnout and job turnover will be highest in practice settings where nurses are in-

TABLE 15.5 Coefficients Indicating the Effects of Different Factors on Emotional Exhaustion Under Various Specifications

Factor in the Model[a]	*Model 1*	*Model 2*	*Model 3*	*Model 4*
AIDS unit	–4.2***	–4.7***	–4.2***	–3.1**
Hospital effects				
New York I		8.3***	6.5**	6.2**
New York III		6.8***	5.6*	6.7**
Baltimore		5.3***	0.3	0.9
Miami		0.7	1.3	3.3
Chicago II		9.3***	7.8***	8.1**
Chicago III		3.8	0.5	1.4
San Francisco I		3.1	–1.9	1.1
Los Angeles I		4.4**	2.3	3.3
Nurse characteristics				
Male			1.9	1.7
Black			–5.4***	5.0***
Asian			1.7	2.9
Hispanic			–4.7*	–4.6*
Foreign born			0.3	–0.7
Protestant			0.1	0.2
Catholic			–3.2*	–2.9*
Devoutly religious			0.6	0.7
College degree			0.9	1.7
Gay or bisexual			3.2	2.3
Age (years)			–0.2*	–0.2*
Experience (years)			–0.1	–0.04
Time on present unit (years)			0.4**	0.4**
Organizational support				–0.5***
Constant	25.3	21.8	29.0	41.9
Adjusted R^2	.03	.07	.14	.19

NOTE: The coefficients in the table are standardized, ordinary least squares regression coefficients.
a. Eight dummy variables were used in the regression models to contrast the hospitals listed to the omitted hospital (New Orleans). All of the nurse characteristics except for age, experience, and time on present unit were categorical and also were dummy coded in the regressions, with 1 assigned to the categories listed in the table and 0 assigned to the omitted categories (i.e., females, Whites, nonforeign born, other religion, not devoutly religious, no college degree, heterosexual).
* Significant at .01 level; ** significant at .05 level; *** significant at .10 level.

volved in full-time AIDS care. Indeed, the widespread concern that nurse burnout and turnover would be so great in dedicated AIDS units as to make it unlikely that adequate staffing levels could be maintained has been an important deterrent to the establishment of a greater number of dedicated AIDS units. We have demonstrated empirically that the AIDS unit effect on lower burnout cannot be explained by the differences in the characteristics of nurses who choose to work in these units. Moreover, we have provided what we believe is convincing evidence that the lower burnout is due to the organizational attributes of the units themselves. Our first comparison of dedicated AIDS units to scattered-bed units demonstrated that organizational differences at the unit level are associated with differences in nurse burnout. In

TABLE 15.6 Coefficients Indicating the Effects of Various Factors on Emotional Exhaustion Under Various Specifications Using the Full Sample of Nurses

Factor in the Model[a]	*Model 1*	*Model 2*	*Model 3*	*Model 4*
AIDS unit	–5.3***	–5.6***	–4.6***	–3.1**
Magnet hospital	–4.8***	–5.2***	–4.7***	–1.4
Hospital effects				
Group A		6.1***	6.1***	4.1**
Group B		6.5***	4.5**	3.0
Group C		8.8***	7.5***	3.7
Group D		5.1***	2.1	0.8
Group F		2.6	3.9**	0.7
Group G		7.1***	5.3***	3.1*
Group H		3.7**	1.1	1.5
Group I		4.3**	2.3	0.9
Nurse characterisics				
Male			2.9	2.4
Black			–1.1	–1.2
Asian			3.1*	2.5
Hispanic			–1.6	–1.2
Foreign born			–0.7	–0.4
Protestant			–0.2	0.2
Catholic			–1.8	–1.3
Devoutly religious			0.7	0.8
College degree			1.2	1.8**
Gay or bisexual			–0.5	–0.8
Age (years)			–0.2**	–0.2**
Experience (years)			0.01	0.03
Time on present unit (years)			0.07	0.08
Organizational support				–0.6***
Constant	26.7	22.3	25.6	42.9
Adjusted R^2	.05	.08	.10	.17

NOTE: The coefficients in the table are standardized, ordinary least squares regression coefficients.
a. Eight dummy variables were used in the regression models to contrast the groups of hospitals listed to the omitted hospital group (Group E). The nurse characterisics were coded as described in Table 15.5.
* Significant at .01 level; ** significant at .05 level; *** significant at .10 level.

our magnet hospital comparations, we demonstrated that magnet hospitals can achieve equally low nurse burnout without the establishment of specialized units that segregate AIDS patients because the organizational attributes common to dedicated AIDS units are achieved through the hospitalwide organizational form implemented within the magnet hospitals that influences how nurses on all units experience their work.

Our research is consistent with the conclusion of Pearlin and Schooler (1978) that supportive organizational structures are central to the successful adaptation of workers. This is especially true for workers in service occupations such as hospital nurses, whose jobs are inherently stressful and whose responses to their clients sometimes may make the difference between life and death but almost always will matter to the comfort and well-being of those for whom they care. Whereas this chapter was concerned with the relationship between organization form and nurse outcomes, there also is a body of research linking hospital organizational structure, nurses, and patient outcomes, and our research has application to that literature as well. Scott, Forrest, and Brown (1976, p. 88), for example, showed that registered nurses influence the quality and outcomes of hospital care not only through their direct patient care efforts but also through the medium of the ward organizations they create. Dedicated AIDS units are very much the creation of nurses (Morrison, 1987), as are magnet hospitals (McClure et al., 1983). In other research, we have shown that the same organizational features associated with lower nurse burnout also are associated with a safer work environment for nurses in terms of lower rates of needlestick injuries (Aiken, Sloane, & Klocinski, 1997), greater patient satisfaction with care (Aiken, Sloane, & Lake, 1996), and lower mortality (Aiken et al., 1994).

Our findings have important implications for the widespread restructuring of hospitals currently taking place nationally in response to predictions of diminishing hospital revenue growth. Our research confirms that alternative organizational designs are associated with positive staff outcomes so long as the organizational form selected provides the critical organizational support. In the case of AIDS care, our results suggest that hospitals caring for consistently large numbers of AIDS patients should consider the benefits of dedicated AIDS units. However, and hopefully, many communities never will have sufficient numbers of patients with AIDS to justify specialized units. Our findings suggest that, in such communities, nurse well-being can be enhanced by instituting hospitalwide organizational structures that support nurses' professional autonomy and control over their work. Aggregation of similar patients into specialized units is effective but is not the only strategy for reducing job-related emotional exhaustion among hospital nurses.

Our findings also demonstrate that unit-level reform can achieve positive outcomes even if institutionwide restructuring is not feasible. Our study of AIDS units provides a particularly strong test of the effectiveness of unit-level reform given that AIDS is a worst-case scenario in many respects. As noted previously, AIDS care is physically exhausting, emotionally draining, and hazardous. In addition, many of the hospitals at the center of the AIDS epidemic that have dedicated AIDS units are financially and organizationally distressed institutions not known to be attractive places to work. That nurses on reorganized units within such hospitals have lower burnout than nurses on conventionally organized units in the same hospitals, or in conventionally organized units in matched hospitals, adds strong support to the value of unit reorganization even when the climate for hospitalwide reform is not favorable.

A promising area for future research suggested by our findings is the positive AIDS unit effect on reducing nurse burnout that is not as fully explained by our measure of organizational support as is the positive magnet hospital effect. The unexplained positive effect of dedicated AIDS units may have to do with an imperfect operationalization of organizational support, or it may be due to an unmeasured variable in our model such as unit culture. Tolbert (1988) investigated and succinctly described how organizational cultures emerge and are transmitted in institutions, and Meyerson (1994) showed how such cultures influence workers' experiences of stress, ambiguity, and burnout. Much more is known about the relationship between organizational structure and worker outcomes than is known about the operant mechanisms by which organizations affect outcomes. Organizational research on worker burnout could be advanced substantially by greater focus on the operant mechanisms that link organizations and outcomes. Until we understand *how* organizational form affects outcomes, we stand the risk of replicating successful organizational models without reproducing the desired outcomes (Flood, 1994).

NOTES

1. Koeske and Koeske (1993) provide references to literature on occupational stress and burnout that has considered what they refer to as the "buffering" role of social support. Most of that literature, however, has conceived of and measured social support somewhat differently than we do here, and, as Koeske and Koeske observe, results have been inconsistent and confusing.

2. Another widely employed burnout scale, especially for subjects or respondents who are not in the human services professions, is the Burnout Measure (BM) developed by Pines & Aronson (1988), which is unidimensional and strongly related to the Emotional Exhaustion and Depersonalization subscales of the MBI.

3. Figure 15.1 also shows the distribution of nurses' scores on the two other subscales from the MBI, which measured depersonalization and personal accomplishment. Both of those scales were severely skewed, with the nurses in our sample being, in general, quite low on the Depersonalization subscale and quite high on the Personal Accomplishment subscale. Analyses of those subscales revealed that neither was greatly or significantly affected by the organizational attributes (unit and hospital type) of interest to us here.

4. The magnitude of the difference in emotional exhaustion between nurses on the two types of units in the restricted sample also is indicated by the individual item from the Emotional Exhaustion subscale that reads, "I feel burned out from my work." Fully 29% of the nurses on the scattered-bed units, but only 10% of those on the dedicated AIDS units, indicated that they felt that way a few times a week or daily. The other individual items reveal similar differences.

5. In the full sample as well, the individual items that comprise the Emotional Exhaustion subscale indicate similar differences. For example, 33% of the nurses on scattered-bed units in nonmagnet hospitals reported feeling burned out a few times a week or daily; the same is true of only 11% of the nurses on scattered-bed units in magnet hospitals and only 12% of the nurses on dedicated AIDS units.

6. We also estimated differences in these reported characteristics for nurses in dedicated AIDS units and scattered-bed units in the restricted sample of nurses in hospitals with both types of units. Because those differences were essentially the same as those we report for the full sample, we suppress those results.

7. Given the modest sample size, and because of our concern that ordinary least squares estimates might be affected by a small number of aberrant cases (or outliers), we also estimated these differences or effects using robust regression techniques in which cases with large deviations from the fitted model were successively downweighted in a series of weighted least squares regressions. Results were virtually identical and are suppressed.

REFERENCES

Aiken, L. H., Sloane, D. M., & Klocinski, J. (1997). Hospital nurses' risk of occupational exposure to blood: Prospective, retrospective, and institutional reports. *American Journal of Public Health, 87,* 103-107.

Aiken, L. H., Sloane, D. M., & Lake, E. T. (1996, August). *Satisfaction with inpatient AIDS care: A national comparison of dedicated units and scattered-beds.* Paper presented at the annual meeting of the American Sociological Association, New York.

Aiken, L. H., Smith, H. L., & Lake, E. T. (1994). Lower medicare mortality among a set of hospitals known for good nursing care. *Medical Care, 32,* 771-787.

Aiken, L. H., Sochalski, J. A., & Anderson, G. F. (1996). Nursing workforce and U.S. hospitals: Current status and future implications. *Health Affairs, 15*(4), 88-92.

Anderson, M. B., & Iwanicki, E. F. (1984). Teacher motivation and its relationship to burnout. *Educational Administration Quarterly, 20,* 109-132.

Chiriboga, D. A., & Bailey, J. (1986). Stress and burnout among critical care and medical surgical nurses: A comparative study. *Critical Care Quarterly, 9,* 84-92.

Christman, L. (1978). A micro-analysis of the nursing division of one medical center. *Hospitals, 41,* 83-87.

Cordes, C. L., & Dougherty, T. W. (1993). A review and an integration on job burnout. *Academy of Management Review, 18,* 621-656.

Cronin-Stubbs, D., & Rooks, C. A. (1985). The stress, social support and burnout of critical care nurses: The results of research. *Heart and Lung, 14,* 31-39.

Duquette, A., Kerouac, S., Sandhu, B. K., & Beaudet, L. (1994). Factors related to nursing burnout: A review of empirical knowledge. *Issues in Mental Health Nursing, 15,* 337-338.

Einsiedel, L., & Tully, J. (1981). Methodological considerations in studying the burnout phenomenon. In J. Jones (Ed.), *The burnout syndrome: Current research, theory, and interventions.* Park Ridge, IL: London House.

Firth, H., McKeown, R., McIntee, J., & Britton, P. (1987). Professional depression, burnout and personality in long stay nursing. *International Journal of Nursing Studies, 24,* 227-237.

Flood, A. B. (1994). The impact of organizational and managerial factors on the quality of care in health care organizations. *Medical Care Research Review, 51,* 381-428.

Fox, R. C., Aiken, L. H., & Messikomer, C. M. (1990). The culture of caring: AIDS and the nursing profession. *Milbank Quarterly, 68,* 226-256.

Freudenberger, H. J. (1974). Staff burnout. *Journal of Social Issues, 30,* 159-165.

Freudenberger, H. J. (1980). *Burnout: The high cost of high achievement.* New York: Doubleday.

Gray-Toft, P. A., & Anderson, J. G. (1981). Stress among hospital nursing staff: Its causes and effects. *Social Science and Medicine, 15,* 639-647.

Hare, J., & Pratt, C. C., & Andrews, D. (1988). Predictors of burnout in professional and paraprofessional nurses working in hospitals and nursing homes. *International Journal of Nursing Studies, 25,* 105-115.

Harris, P. L. (1984). Burnout in nursing administration. *Nursing Administration Quarterly, 8,* 61-70.

Hinshaw, A. S., & Atwood, J. R. (1984). Nursing staff turnover, stress, and satisfaction: Models, measures, and management. *Annual Review of Nursing Research, 1,* 133-153.

Koeske, G., & Koeske, R. D. (1993). A preliminary test of a stress-strain-outcome model for reconceptualizing the burnout phenomenon. *Journal of Social Service Research, 17*(3/4), 107-135.

Kramer, M., & Schmalenberg, C. (1988). Magnet hospitals: Institutions of excellence. *Journal of Nursing Administration, 8,* 13-24.

Kramer, M., & Schmalenberg, C. (1991). Job satisfaction and retention: Insights for the 90's. *Nursing, 91,* 50-55.

Landsbergis, P. A. (1988). Occupational stress among health care workers: A test of the job demands-control model. *Journal of Organizational Behavior, 9,* 217-239.

Maslach, C. (1982). Understanding burnout: Definitional issues in analyzing a complex phenomenon. In W. S. Paine (Ed.), *Job stress and burnout* (pp. 29-40). Beverly Hills, CA: Sage.

Maslach, C., & Florian, V. (1988). Burnout, job setting, and self-evaluation among rehabilitation counselors. *Rehabilitation Psychology, 33,* 85-93.

Maslach, C., & Jackson, S. E. (1981). The measurement of experienced burnout. *Journal of Occupational Behavior, 2,* 99-113.

Maslach, C., & Jackson, S. E. (1982). The burnout syndrome in the health professions: A social psychological analysis. In G. Sanders & J. Suls (Eds.), *Social psychology of health and illness* (pp. 227-247). Hillsdale, NJ: Lawrence Erlbaum.

Maslach, C., & Jackson, S. E. (1984). Patterns of burnout among a national sample of public contact workers. *Journal of Health and Human Resources Administration, 7,* 189-212.

Maslach, C., & Jackson, S. E. (1986). *Maslach Burnout Inventory manual.* Palo Alto, CA: Consulting Psychologists Press.

McClure, M. L., Poulin, M. A., Sovie, M. D., & Wandelt, M. A. (1983). *Magnet hospitals: Attraction and retention of professional nurses.* Kansas City, MO: American Academy of Nursing.

Meyerson, D. E. (1994). Interpretations of stress in institutions: The cultural production of ambiguity and burnout. *Administrative Science Quarterly, 39,* 628-653.

Morrison, C. (1987). Establishing a therapeutic environment for patients with AIDS. In J. Durham & S. Cohen (Eds.), *The person with AIDS: Nursing perspective.* Philadelphia: Springer.

Oktay, J. S. (1992). Burnout in hospital social workers who work with AIDS patients. *Social Work, 37,* 432-439.

Pearlin, L. I., & Schooler, C. (1978). The structure of coping. *Journal of Health and Social Behavior, 19,* 2-21.

Perlman, B., & Hartman, E. A. (1982). Burnout: Summary and future research. *Human Relations, 35,* 283-305.

Pines, A. M., & Aronson, E. (1988). *Career burnout: Causes and cures.* New York: Free Press.

Pines, A., & Maslach, C. (1978). Characteristics of staff burnout in mental health settings. *Hospital and Community Psychiatry, 29,* 233-237.

Pogash, C. (1992). *As real as it gets: The life of a hospital at the center of the AIDS epidemic.* New York: Birch Lane Press.

Reinhardt, U. E. (1996). Spending more through "cost control": Our obsessive quest to gut the hospital. *Health Affairs, 15*(2), 145-154.

Robinson, J. C. (1996). The dynamics and limits of corporate growth in health care. *Health Affairs, 15*(2), 155-167.

Schaufeli, W. B. (1990). *Opgebrand: Over de Achtergronden van Werkstress bij Contactuele Beroepen—Het Burnout Syndroom* (Burnout: About the job stress in the human service professions—The burnout syndrome). Rotterdam, Netherlands: Ad. Donker.

Schaufeli, W. B., & Van Dierendonck, D. (1993). The construct validity of two burnout measures. *Journal of Organizational Behavior, 14,* 631-647.

Schulz, R., Greenley, J. R., & Brown, R. (1995). Organization, management, and client effects on staff burnout. *Journal of Health and Social Behavior, 36,* 333-345.

Scott, W. R., Forrest, W. H., & Brown, B. W. (1976). Hospital structure and postoperative mortality and morbidity. In S. Shortell & M. Brown (Eds.), *Organizational research in hospitals* (pp. 72-89). Chicago: Blue Cross Association.

Stevens, G. B., & O'Neill, P. (1983). Expectation and burnout in the developmental disabilities field. *American Journal of Community Psychology, 11,* 615-627.

Taravella, S. (1989). Reserving a place to treat AIDS patients in the hospital. *Modern Health Care, 19,* 32-39.

Tolbert, P. S. (1988). Institutional sources of organizational culture in major law firms. In L. Zucker (Ed.), *Institutional patterns and organizations* (pp. 101-114). Cambridge, MA: Ballinger.

van Servellan, G. M., & Leake, B. (1993). Burnout in hospital nurses: A comparison of acquired immunodeficiency syndrome, oncology, general medical, and intensive care unit nurse samples. *Journal of Professional Nursing, 9,* 169-177.

van Servellan, G. M., Lewis, C. E., Schweitzer, S. O., & Leake, B. (1991). Quality and cost of AIDS nursing care as a function of inpatient delivery systems. *Journal of Nursing Administration, 21,* 21-28.

Williams, C. A. (1989). Empathy and burnout in male and female helping professionals. *Research in Nursing and Health, 12,* 169-178.

Williamson, D. A. (1996). *Job satisfaction in social services.* New York: Garland.

Adapting, Resisting, and Negotiating

How Physicians Cope With Organizational and Economic Change

TIMOTHY J. HOFF
DAVID P. MCCAFFREY

The health care industry is in the midst of profound change. New financing arrangements and the expansion of managed care, specifically through the development of health maintenance organizations (HMOs), deeply affect physicians' work. HMOs are expected to provide health care to 25% of the U.S. population by the end of 1997, doubling their patient membership in less than 10 years. This growth is expected to continue at a double-digit rate for at least the next 5 years (Interstudy Publications, 1995). Reimbursement for physicians' services is now made before services are even delivered rather than retrospectively. This has caused a dramatic shift in doctors' emphasis from the revenue to the expense side of the balance sheet. As a result, competition within the health care market has become based on cost control (as opposed to revenue generation), with providers trying to provide the best service at the most reasonable price and still make a profit. The medical profession, at the center of the production and delivery of health services, is generally viewed as a group facing long-term, substantial change.

Yet we know almost nothing of how individual physicians are attempting to cope with and respond to these organizational and economic changes on a daily basis. Traditional sociological theories of professions focus on physicians as a collective entity, debating the outcomes of structural changes such as these in terms of the continued dominance, deprofessionalization, or proletarianization of the profession *as a whole.* Although valuable in gaining insight into how professions shape and are shaped by other stakeholders in society, these perspectives understate the extent to which individual practitioners deal actively with their surrounding environments. This individual action is defined by everyday strategies of resistance, adaptation, and negotiation, all within varying work settings.

This chapter uses qualitative data gathered from physicians in two of these settings—self-employment in solo or group practice and salaried in a large HMO—to examine how doctors deal with large-scale changes in financing and organization. Two research questions are addressed. First, how do professionals attempt to maintain central elements of professionalism, such as autonomy, while coping with situations demanding new types of work, beliefs, and controls? Second, how do aspects of the specific work setting and employment relationship mediate professional adaptation? These questions

From *Work and Occupations,* Vol. 23, No. 2, May 1996, pp. 165-189. Reprinted by permission.

reflect a larger need to incorporate practitioner-level data back into the professions literature to gain a better sense of how larger developments play out in the workplace.

Bringing Individuals Back Into the Literature on Professions

Since the early 1970s, research on professions has been guided mainly by the professional dominance paradigm (Freidson, 1970a, 1970b). This view maintains that professions control their work conditions and content through political and legal action. The majority of this writing focused on physicians. Freidson said that professionals' authority over the medical division of labor, and their legal monopoly of licensing and credentialing, allowed such control. Similarly, writers such as Larson (1977) focused on professional power based on esoteric knowledge and technical competency.

The "deprofessionalization" and "proletarianization/corporatization" perspectives (again, focused primarily on physicians) responded directly to the dominance view in different ways. The deprofessionalization view put forth the "alternative hypothesis" that an increasingly knowledgeable consumer and rapidly developing information technology would weaken professional dominance and undermine values such as autonomy (Haug, 1973; Starr, 1982). The notion of proletarianization (McKinlay, 1982; Navarro, 1976) saw capitalist forces deskilling professionals in the workplace, just as these forces had earlier deskilled craft workers (see Braverman, 1974). The corporatization view emphasized similar dynamics, although focusing less on the ownership of the means of production and more on managerial tendencies to erode professional discretion regardless of organizational ownership (McKinlay & Stoeckle, 1988)

During the 1970s and 1980s, research elaborated the theoretical debates among supporters of these views, less frequently examining professions in specific work settings (Freidson, 1985; Hafferty & Wolinsky, 1991; Hall, 1988). This was partly because the perspectives encouraged the full development of theoretical debate at the expense of data collection. The professional dominance view seeks to explain how a profession collectively maintains its position through legal and political activity; studies of practitioners arguably do not illuminate broader legal and political action. The deprofessionalization and proletarianization perspectives focus on workplace processes but do so largely through theoretical essays and discussion of broad societal forces, possibly because they have developed in dialogue with professional dominance theorists.

As a result of this emphasis on structure and professions as powerful corporate entities, these theoretical debates did not require data on individual professional behavior, and so few data were collected. However, it is striking to remember that Freidson's (1970a, 1970b) detailed study of physicians' behavior, which provided much of the foundation for the professional dominance model and concepts such as autonomy, was an early landmark in the field. Despite this promising beginning, the literature on professions gradually moved away from directly studying everyday workplace activity. Left were competing deterministic views of how professionals either dominated others (and maintained collective control over their work) or were increasingly subservient to managers and/or clients.

A similar trend has been noted in industrial sociology (Hodson, 1995; Simpson, 1989; Smith, 1994). In its focus on the ways in which management practices and organizational structure controlled workers, the field forgot about "the possibility that workers could reshape, appropriate, and temper modes of managerial control," often leading "employers and managers to adopt particular control strategies in the first place" and creating "new terrains of contestation" (Smith, 1994, p. 406). The major point made in this literature is directly relevant for the professions literature: that making sense of the workplace requires attention to how structural forces *and* individuals' activities jointly shape the labor process and the nature of work. In this chapter, we reintroduce that same perspective to the study of physicians facing major organizational and economic changes in health care.

New Forms of Health Care Financing and Organization

Prospective payment systems, providing a fixed schedule of payments to providers for services that have not yet been delivered, have become the standard in response to health care inflation. Health care costs increased dramatically over the past few decades because of the development and use of expensive medical technology, emphasis on costly specialty medicine, and greater expectations for improved medical outcomes (Starr, 1982; U.S. General Accounting Office, 1992). Under traditional retrospective payment systems, physicians had little incentive to keep patients out of the office or deny them the most sophisticated treatment available. The measure of economic success for the individual doctor under this system was in how much could be earned, not in how much could be saved.

Systems of managed care grew with the shift to new methods of financing. Whereas hospitals have always been the traditional corporate enterprise in health care, the rise of HMOs occurred primarily since the mid 1980s. The term HMO refers to a number of organizational settings within which a physician is either a salaried worker (staff model), a hybrid of self-employed and salaried worker (group and network models), or a fully self-employed worker contracting with a number of different HMOs through contractual agreements while maintaining some level of fee-for-service practice. As the number of HMOs has increased and the managed care philosophy has become more popular, competition for market share (i.e., patients) has become intense, leading to greater concentration and networking of both organizations and physicians to take advantage of economies of scale. As a result of these financing and organizational changes, physicians now practice within contexts that are diverse, competitive, and increasingly regulated.

METHODOLOGY

This chapter draws mainly on interviews with 25 primary care physicians (defined as family practitioners, pediatricians, or internists). Of the 25 respondents, 14 were salaried employees in the staff model part of an HMO and the remaining 11 were self-employed in either a solo or a group practice setting. The majority of physicians were family practitioners (19 of 25). The geographic area for the study was a mid-sized (more than 100,000 population) urban area with numerous suburbs and rural areas surrounding it. The managed care market in this area could be characterized as growing and increasingly competitive (especially in terms of the number of new HMOs entering the market). Data were collected using semistructured interviews lasting 45 to 75 minutes. Physicians were selected using a purposive, quota-driven strategy to ensure an approximately equal number of doctors on the two dimensions of the variable work setting (i.e., self-employed vs. salaried setting). A total of 28 physicians were asked to participate, yielding a response rate of 89% (25 of 28). Following the initial 25 interviews, 5 additional interviews were conducted with three full-time physician managers within the HMO under study. None of these 5 were part of the original sample of 25 physicians. These extra 5 interviews were conducted only to provide additional information on the level of input available in the HMO to salaried physicians in areas of management and administrative decision making. Obtaining this information was necessary to fully contextualize the findings for salaried physicians and took place only after analysis of the original 25 interviews.

All 25 interviews were conducted between July and September 1994, and the 5 additional interviews of full-time physician-managers were conducted during May and June 1995. The questions centered on the following issues: (a) activities involved in the physicians' "normal" workday and how these might be changing; (b) what physicians liked most and least about their work settings; (c) how physicians in one work setting viewed those in other settings; (d) values contributing to the physicians' own feelings of job satisfaction and professionalism, particularly as they related to their work settings; (e) liability concerns; and (f) how the physicians felt about new developments in the health care setting such as the move to managed care, the use of clinical practice guidelines (CPGs), and the increased role played by allied health professionals. The interview questionnaire is included in the appendix. All the interviews were tape-recorded and transcribed verbatim. An inductive approach to data analysis was then used on the transcripts, using the coding framework developed by Strauss (1987), to identify and link together the major themes and categories in the data.

SIMILARITIES ACROSS WORK SETTINGS

The interviews suggested five views shared by primary care physicians in both the self-employed and salaried work settings. These involved (a) the notion of medicine as art, (b) the appeal of primary care as a field of work, (c) definitions and levels of autonomy, (d) views of nonphysician providers, and (e) fears about malpractice.

Medicine as an Art Form

Although the traditional role of physician as scientist was important, participating physicians saw themselves as "artists" in their total role as professionals. The artist role is seen as the ability to use one's intuition, experience, and past training to diagnose and treat each patient given a limited amount of time and information. This view of medicine provided a strong context within which physicians viewed important new tools such as CPGs, designed to routinize physicians' work. Generally, the strongest proponents of the art of medicine were the most adamantly opposed to CPGs; for them, the method implied a standardized approach to care that undermined the unique combinations of artistic elements needed for each individual patient. A few doctors were more accepting of a role for CPGs for one primary reason: their interest in obtaining "concrete" data on various approaches to care so that they could be more confident of their professional judgments. They felt that new medical knowledge was outpacing their ability to process it. Almost all physicians expressed the paradoxical view of being afraid to make a mistake yet also unwilling to accept any guideline that would restrict and regulate their own styles of practice. The following two statements from different physicians show each side to this tension.

> One of my biggest fears since medical school is being in that room with the patient and telling that patient something that's totally wrong. I'm not going to know and they're not going to know.

> The idea that medicine is going to become one big algorithm where we can push a button on a computer and the computer can diagnose something . . . that's not what I went into the field of medicine for and I'll be upset if I'm forced to become computerized mentally in how I practice medicine.

This latter statement was typical of the reasoning used to support all 25 physicians' views that guidelines must be second to physician discretion at all times. Generally, they saw CPGs as a part of the medical "toolbox" but maintained that they should decide when and how to use them.

The Appeal of Primary Care as a Specialty

Almost all physicians liked the field of primary care because of the opportunity for close, long-term relationships with patients and the scope of knowledge required. In both self-employed and salaried work settings, however, physicians saw these close relationships threatened by a managed care philosophy emphasizing primary care medicine as a cost-control strategy. This created high levels of patient demand for their services and workdays where patients were seen in short (less than 15-minute) intervals, undermining physicians' ability to get to know patients—as persons and in terms of their ailments. Physicians were within two different settings, but the same economic pressure was finding its way increasingly into workdays in both places. The flip side to the increased demand, as almost half of the 25 physicians recognized, was the economic benefit managed care would bring to the field of primary care, increasing their incomes and prestige relative to those of other specialties.

In this day and age, it's nice to be wanted. It's nice to get letters asking me to join practices all over the country. I can only see primary care becoming more in demand, and it's nice to be in demand.

Definitions and Levels of Autonomy

Physicians in the two work settings, when asked directly, defined their professional autonomy in similar ways.

Autonomy would be the ability to practice medicine as I was trained and developed through experience, with minimal constraints on who I can consult, what kinds of procedures I could order, etc.

To me, it's the ability to make clinical judgments based on a patient's presentation and complaints and to direct a diagnosis and treatment the way I see fit.

Almost all the responses resembled definitions of technical and clinical autonomy first proposed by Freidson (1970a); however, physicians did not distinguish between the two types. Of the 25 physicians, 8 could not articulate a definition of the term when asked to do so. The 17 physicians responding with definitions were asked whether their actual levels of autonomy met their definitions. Of these, 16 did not expect their definitions to be completely fulfilled in the present health care environment, yet they indicated that they had a satisfactory amount of control over their *daily work.* Even those 8 who did not provide definitions of autonomy stated that they maintained a satisfactory level of control.

Complaints about both settings suggested that physicians were working under increased restrictions. But physicians emphasized that in deciding diagnoses and treatments, they felt in almost total control. They seemed to ignore the fact that these decisions were not necessarily final; they could be easily modified by administration, government, or insurers at a later point in time. This reveals a subtle yet important type of coping mechanism that both groups of doctors used during their workday to help make them feel like they had an adequate level of autonomy. They focused more on preserving technical autonomy at the moment of the initial physician-patient encounter than they did on whether this autonomy was undermined at a later point in time. This resulted in a perceived level of control among these physicians that was greatest at the instant when their clinical skills were being used.

For me, the freedom is in the [examination] room, when I am with that patient and they are describing those symptoms and I am making the diagnosis. That is the ultimate freedom. The freedom ends when you walk out of that room. When you walk out of the room, the fun is over. Then all the other difficulties begin.

Views of Nonphysician Providers

All 25 physicians acknowledged the useful roles that nonphysician providers (e.g., nurses and physician assistants) served for the medical profession and the health care system. But almost all physicians thought these roles had strict limits and should always be managed by doctors.

They're [physician extenders] useful up to a point. Nine out of 10 sore throats may be the same, but it's the difficult one that needs the physician. . . . There's something unique about a physician's training that others don't have.

Both groups of physicians interviewed—self-employed and salaried employees—saw increased use of these providers in the future as the result of economic imperatives. But no physician perceived them as a real threat to their own livelihoods. Instead, they were viewed as another tool to use at physicians' discretion, helping to make their daily lives less complicated and pressured. Many physicians felt that patients provided a check on the growth of these providers. As one doctor put it, "If you had a problem, wouldn't you want to go to someone with the most training?" Their personal belief in physicians' superior education and training was the major reason for a lack of concern about the market's growing use of nurses and physician assistants.

Fears About Malpractice

Fear of being sued reportedly entered into all physicians' decision making at least part of the time. However, it was difficult to discern from the respondents the impact of this fear on their decision making. Yet the interviews suggested two related themes. First, physicians were more likely to practice "defensive medicine" if they had been sued or had experienced the "horrors" of a malpractice trial.

> Ten years ago, I was a witness at a [malpractice] trial, and I got criticized for not doing a blood count on a patient. The lawyer made me look like an idiot. You can bet that every patient over the next 6 months got a blood count, whether he needed it or not.

Second, a majority of the physicians practiced defensive medicine especially when diagnosing patients' problems.

> Yes, it [liability fears] affects my decision making, mostly in the diagnostic phase. For instance, I'll get a patient with a headache. I don't want to miss something, so I'll order a CAT [computerized axial tomography] scan.

These physicians were more afraid of missing diagnoses than they were of using the wrong treatments. Many admitted that their training experiences had sensitized them to the reality that patients accepted the notion of the treatment phase containing greater uncertainty but had little tolerance for uncertainty in the diagnostic phase. They also knew that, as a result, misdiagnosis was the most common reason for initiating a malpractice suit. In this instance, physicians were clearly aware of the public expectations regarding the work they performed.

Table 16.1 presents the degree of consensus among the respondents about the five views of their work. These views reflect the traditional model of professionalism (Larson, 1977; Parsons, 1954). They are an important ingredient in creating what Sonnenstuhl and Trice (1991) call a "strong group occupation" (p. 303), and they play an important role in establishing a group identity and culture for physicians that is stable and persistent (Trice, 1993). This identity finds its roots in the medical training and socialization process (Freidson, 1970a). How physicians perceived and responded to change within two diverse work settings is the focus of the following two sections.

SELF-EMPLOYED PHYSICIANS: MERGING ENTREPRENEURIAL AND BUREAUCRATIC ROLES

All 11 self-employed physicians thought of themselves as entrepreneurs, responsible for their economic survival through the financial success of their practices. They defined entrepreneurship as having three components: (a) producing a quality product (i.e., being a competent doctor), (b) working harder and taking risks, and (c) gaining increased financial reward in return. The following statements reflect this ideology.

TABLE 16.1 Degree of Consensus for Select Views Among 25 Primary Care Physicians

Issue	*Shared View*	*Consensus*
View of medicine	Art form as important as science	25/25 (100%)
Clinical practice guidelines	"Tool" under physician control	25/25 (100%)
Best aspect of primary care	Intimate physician-patient relationship	21/25 (84%)
	Range and scope of knowledge required	20/25 (80%)
Definition of autonomy	Similar to either Freidson's technical or clinical	17/25 (68%)
Level of autonomy or control	Decreased but satisfactory	24/25 (96%)
Physician extenders	Useful for "routine" patients	25/25 (100%)
	"Tool" under physician control	23/25 (92%)
Fear of liability	Plays dominant role in diagnostic phase	17/25 (68%)

There's flexibility for physicians in private practice; if one wants to work harder or work less, their income will be adjusted to reflect that. I like the fact that I get compensated when I'm working a little harder.

If I'm going to take all the risks, I should be at the top financially [compared with other primary care physicians].

For the majority, the appeal of being entrepreneurs was not realized until after they had been in the employment setting for some time (contrary to the idea that physicians would self-select into self-employed practice because of an overt desire to run their own businesses). Their responses revealed that they did not begin their medical careers eager to own their practices. Most stated that this never even crossed their minds; they had been too busy trying to become trained physicians. They talked about "falling into" this type of employment situation, almost by accident, encouraged by circumstances such as helping out other colleagues, the desire to stay close to home, or being actively recruited by other physician-entrepreneurs. (A similar pattern is found in studies of entrepreneurs generally [Carroll, 1993].) They learned "on the job" about the rewards associated with being self-employed, and they adapted to this role accordingly.

Competitiveness and Control

Competitiveness and control were the dominant themes revealed in discussing the benefits of being a physician-entrepreneur. The theme of competitiveness was best summed up by one doctor as follows.

I like the competitiveness of being in private practice. If I can't give my patient something, I'm out of business. You are responsible for your own actions and service. If you do it bad, you're out of business.

Competitiveness in this way referred to physicians' ability to provide quality care and keep patients satisfied. Like any business owner, these physicians believed that the product they offered must be one that the patient, as a consumer, valued over another physician's product. If not, they would be out of business. There was general agreement that the patient was no longer the only consumer; external third parties now paying for the majority of the product needed to be satisfied as well.

Another value of being self-employed was the added control it gave these physicians in their everyday work. For example, they liked controlling decisions involving staffing, office design, equipment purchases, service provision, and the types of patients seen in the practice. This control increased physicians' work satisfaction. Finally, although all saw that entrepreneurship was becoming more challenging and risky, they believed it was the best employment situation for maintaining autonomy and economic freedom. The alternative of being a salaried employee was not a serious option for any of them. In their opinion, the trade-off of a guaranteed income for less control and independence was too great.

> An employed physician must do it the company's way or find a new job. You give up your individuality. Your loyalties are to the employer and not to the patient.

Self-employed physicians had been transformed over time into entrepreneurs as well as practicing clinicians. The entrepreneurial role had been reinforced through interaction with a supportive health care market. It forged a view of professionalism that included building a successful business and tying profit to effort. Yet these doctors realized that the market was becoming more hostile to their business interests. New challenges were requiring them to take on a new role. The physician-entrepreneur of the past and present was being forced to also become the administrator and manager of tomorrow.

Resisting the Integration of Entrepreneurial and Bureaucratic Roles

Physicians who held firm to the ideal-type notion of entrepreneurship described here (5 of 11) expressed extreme anger and resentment at the organizational and financing changes occurring within the health care market. The delivery of health services through large corporate enterprises and new payment systems meant an increased role played by external third parties such as the government and insurers. They viewed this role as interfering with the physician-patient *economic* relationship, which they defined as follows.

> My practice is an oral contract between me and my patient. My patient comes to me, we discuss the diagnosis and treatment, and I give them my professional judgment. In the past, patients dug down into their pockets and paid for that service. If they didn't like it, they were free to leave and go to someone else.

These doctors viewed cost control through new prospective payment structures such as capitation (a fixed fee per year for a patient subscriber regardless of the number of visits or procedures) as transforming the physician-patient relationship from a mutually beneficial one to an adversarial one. They were convinced that their primary loyalties under such a system would shift from the patient to the third party, who would reward them for being cost-effective. They would no longer be able to function as entrepreneurs because their economic fate would depend on complying with the rules of external stakeholders and executive fiat rather than with the laws of the free market mechanism. In effect, they would lose an important part of their professional freedom: the economic autonomy that was important to them.

> I think at one point in my life, if you had said to me, "Are you in private practice?" I would have said, "Yes I am in private practice, it's my own business." Now if you ask me, I will tell you, "I have a private practice, but I am basically an employee of the insurance company and it is their doctrine I need to follow." I no longer feel that I am a private enterprise.

Given this skepticism, it was not surprising that they seemed much more likely than other physicians in the study to employ strategies of resistance in their daily work. This resistance mainly took the form of game playing, where the physicians devised ways to circumvent insurers or the government and maintain some degree of economic control (see Fielding, 1990; Notman et al., 1987).

> I do pretty much what I want, and I'll be creative in the way I bill for it. I'll explain it to the patient.

If they [the insurance company] balk and don't pay for it, the next time the patient comes in I'll bill for something else that costs the same. I won't saddle the patient with it. I can play the game, too.

The findings suggest that these physicians were reluctant to adapt because they adhered to a strong ideology of entrepreneurialism and were unwilling to accept less economic autonomy (and, in the short run at least, loss of profit) in a more regulated market. They spoke of "getting out" before things got any worse and of not becoming doctors if given the choice again.

No, I would not go into medicine today. I think there are intellectual things I could have been interested in without the government and without the liability, the regulations, and all the pressures.

The Increased Challenge of Being an Owner: Adapting to the Role of Administrator-Manager

The remaining six self-employed physicians, many of whom were younger and had been in private practice for less time than the five "resistors," were not as hostile about these changes and the increasing involvement of external stakeholders in the physician-patient economic relationship. They reluctantly accepted the need to make new trade-offs to ensure their economic survival.

The business side of medicine was never something of high interest to me. . . . It's a necessary evil that I'm learning and need to know, and I work to do the best job I can at it. But it's not something I love to do, that's for sure.

When I'm doing my reading, I might spend some percentage of time studying about the new stuff in medicine. But I spend at least as much time now, maybe more, reading about finance, management, negotiating skills, and planning.

These physicians talked repeatedly about daily pressures from increased business responsibilities and activities such as (a) monitoring expenses and overhead within their practices (acting as financial managers), (b) negotiating complex contractual agreements with multiple insurers (acting as salesmen and negotiators), (c) developing internal pricing mechanisms to allocate costs to activities in the workday (acting as accountants), and (d) shifting their practice philosophy from one of generating revenue to a focus on holding down costs (acting as strategic planners). Physicians were forced to become more conscientious business owners who had to make fiscally sound and informed managerial choices *on a daily basis* or risk going out of business. The traditional entrepreneurial focus on maximizing patient revenue in a given workday was no longer suitable. The organizational and financing changes described here were producing a change in thinking and a new, nonmedical role for the physicians.

Acceptance of the administrator-manager role and the development of new management-oriented beliefs were evident in the examples provided by physicians when discussing economic pressures in more detail. For instance, one physician discussed the decision-making process he and his partners had recently completed to better align their practice with the economic incentives provided under managed care and a capitated payment structure. His description of this process revealed the proactive nature of their activity as well as the belief that this activity was now a necessary part of their daily job responsibilities.

I made my rounds to all the insurance companies that we were dealing with and I had a little slide show presentation with me. I said to them, "Look, this is where we're at [the practice], and we need help or we're not going to be able to continue to be in business." And they responded.

The six physicians in this "adaptive" group never gave any indication that they were happy about the changes occurring in health care. But they seemed to realize that the rules of the game were different because of these changes and that being an entrepreneur was no longer enough. They would have to learn the fine details about managing a medical practice, and this would require additional time out of their workday. But doing this would enable them to understand and manipulate the economic environment. This in turn would preserve autonomy and keep them entrepreneurs. They saw resistance as self-destructive and adaptation as the only choice.

PHYSICIANS AS EMPLOYEES: A PROTECTIVE ROLE HINDERING ADAPTATION

The tension evident in self-employed physicians' struggle to accept and adapt to a new role of administrator-manager was absent when speaking to salaried physicians in a large HMO. Salaried physicians had no direct or immediate economic stake in the HMO's business decisions. Being practicing clinicians was their only role. These doctors fully understood that they were employees of the organization. Much of the sociological literature regards this employment relationship as a loss of status for physicians (and professionals in general), who presumably relinquish too much autonomy in becoming economically dependent in a corporate marketplace. Yet almost none of these physicians regarded his or her position unfavorably.

> I think it's easier to work here than when you own your own practice. There's less bullshit and I get paid OK. There are wonderful things about being an employee.

The Benefits of Professional Employment

The interviews revealed four benefits of salaried practice: (a) freedom from worrying about patients' financial or insurance situations, (b) freedom from time-consuming administrative and managerial issues, (c) the security of a guaranteed income (i.e., "a steady paycheck"), and (d) more free time to devote to the nonmedical areas of their lives such as family and recreation.

A first benefit was that these physicians did not have to attempt to understand or take into account a patient's financial situation at the time of the visit. They felt relieved that these issues were addressed by other parts of the organization before a patient arrived in their examination room. This provided them with an ongoing sense of freedom to deliver services as they felt appropriate.

> One thing I find very satisfying is that I think there is a lot of freedom in knowing that your patients are not financially strapped to be diagnosed and treated, that my work is not going to cost them more than the $10 copay.

> You don't have to think about bringing a patient back for a recheck because it's only going to cost them their copay. You don't have to think about finances. It allows you to practice quality medicine. You don't have to hold back because they can't afford it.

Nonetheless, these physicians worked with an understanding that there were certain "rules of the game" that the organization required them to follow. For example, a commonly discussed rule was the need to prescribe only medications on the HMO's approved list, known as a drug formulary. Physicians acknowledged that at times this interfered with their practice styles in that certain high-cost drugs believed to be more effective in treating a condition were not part of the formulary. Yet these were minor trade-offs that seemed fair because of their realization that the HMO needed to have ways of controlling costs. In return for playing by these rules, the organization guaranteed that physicians would not have to concern themselves with the patient's ability to pay for services.

A second benefit was the freedom from administrative paperwork and managerial issues. Except for several doctors who voluntarily became involved in management, physician-employees were *much* less involved with administration than were self-employed doctors. Some of the tasks described as administrative or managerial included complying with government regulations, handling personnel decisions, monitoring the balance sheet, negotiating reimbursement and insurance contracts, and marketing their services to the public. These tasks, so vital to self-employed physicians' continued economic survival (thus forcing the adaptation we discussed), were handled by the administrative structure of the HMO. Salaried physicians liked the fact that working overtime would mean attending to clinical issues, not administrative or managerial issues.

> The organization pulls its weight in that [administrative-management issues] sense. It takes its responsibility there and doesn't feel that it lays with the physicians, which I think is appropriate.

Third, the security of a guaranteed income in a volatile and competitive market was valuable to them. The majority felt relieved to avoid the entrepreneurial role in that they were not dependent for their livelihoods on attracting patients or negotiating favorable reimbursement contracts. They could count on a steady paycheck every 2 weeks while the organization worried about how payroll demands would be met. Unlike self-employed physicians, they did not mind completely trading off economic autonomy and other types of control for increased financial security. This only increased their job satisfaction.

> There's a financial security [working here]. I know what I'm going to earn this year, and I can plan around it.

> I really have no desire to work 90 hours a week or squish millions of patients into a very short period of time. I think you would lose a lot of the pleasurable interaction with patients.

Several physicians went even further, believing that one's attention to practicing medicine was distracted by the pressure of having to compete directly for patient business. One doctor stated,

> I don't have to be political and I don't have to sell myself. If I'm in private practice, I've gotta play the game. I've gotta meet and greet, I've gotta be available, I've gotta compete for the business because it's directly related to my income. I don't have to do that here.

Finally, a fourth benefit was the increased time that salaried physicians felt they had to concentrate on other parts of their lives. They did not mind being accountable to the HMO for 40 or 50 hours a week, but knowing that they had consistent free time to devote to other concerns increased the satisfaction and vigor with which they approached their workday.

> I like the lifestyle. I go home at night and, if I'm not covering the hospital, I don't get a phone call. I don't have to worry about being bugged. You can't beat that. I can invest my energies in other things.

Professional Employment and Enhanced Professional Status

What did these benefits mean to physicians in their daily lives, and how did they influence personal beliefs about their work? Surprisingly, it appeared that freedom from the entrepreneurial and bureaucratic role had the following effect: *These physicians felt that their status as professionals was enhanced to the degree they were left alone to do their jobs.*

> In the HMO, I get to spend more time doing what I'm trained to do and less time on the things I'm not trained to do. All that other stuff I would just as soon leave to someone else.

These physicians truly believed that the organization buffered them from a health care market that would demoralize and distract them from their "true" mission of practicing medicine. Thus the utility of the HMO to physicians was in insulating their work from external market demands (see Whalley, 1990, for a similar process with corporate engineers). The enhanced sense of professionalism has been found in other studies (see Gross & Budrys,

1991), and it contradicts images of salaried physicians as deprofessionalized or proletarianized.

Salaried physicians, however, were worried that this enhanced status was being threatened by the organization's need to increasingly monitor and control their workday to remain profitable and competitive. This "seepage" of the health care marketplace through the organization and into physicians' lives was becoming more visible, leading to heightened tensions within the work setting.

Environmental Seepage and the Threat of Deprofessionalization

Competition within the HMO service area was becoming fierce. The number of HMOs had increased from three to eight since 1988. Of these eight, seven were currently freezing or reducing premiums to gain new customers and retain existing ones. Patient enrollment in the HMO had increased from 75,000 to 340,000 over a 10-year period (353%), whereas the number of physicians working either as employees or as independent contractors had increased from 1,500 to almost 5,000 (233%) during the 18 months preceding the start of the study. Along with growth, the HMO was bureaucratizing through formalization of policies and rules and centralization of authority in top management units. Physicians saw the implications of these changes.

> When I came here 8 years ago, it [the HMO] was relatively small and decisions affecting overall policy were made more by consensus. Increasingly, the organization is getting larger and larger, and many decisions now don't involve physicians.

For physician-employees, increased competitive pressures and internal controls contained the seeds of decreased job satisfaction and a feeling of deprofessionalization. They realized that, as the most important asset of the HMO, they were prime targets of decisions aimed at maintaining market share and controlling costs. One example of these pressures affecting them involved the patient scheduling process. Most of our interviewees feared losing the control of their own schedules and that the greater number of patients subscribing to the HMO would force shorter visits with patients and more "assembly-line medicine," resulting in an alteration of practice styles.

> I am so prescheduled that if I want to do something like counseling about life issues or stress management, I won't get the chance to do it except for about a minute.

> I have 15-minute appointments now for patients. If I have complex patients that I really need to spend time with, I have to develop several 15-minute appointments at different times to address all their problems.

Unlike self-employed physicians, these doctors had no direct financial rewards offsetting the decreased flexibility and satisfaction caused by an increased patient load. Being insulated from administrative and entrepreneurial pressures meant that these physicians would not receive anything in return (such as increased compensation) for sacrificing something good about their work (i.e., close relationships with patients). Another example of environmental seepage was increased monitoring of physician work behavior through new, formal precertification and utilization management policies. For instance, almost all physicians mentioned newly written policies for precertification of select surgical procedures as the tip of what would become a huge regulatory iceberg. There was a subtle but growing resentment among the physicians that the organization was changing the rules of the game without their input. The evidence of this resentment was in physician references to the "good old days" and in their framing almost every regulation and monitoring issue within the organization as an "us versus them" situation, with "them" being upper management.

Addressing Seepage: The Management Option

The only way for these physicians to deal with this increasing feeling of alienation was to get more involved in decision making and policy formulation through formal management roles. There were several levels of physician management within the organization, from the medical director down to frontline physician coordinators working part-time within each department and satellite office. This structure paralleled the administrative structure of the HMO. The medical director was part of a "management team" that was (and had always been) responsible for making major business and policy decisions for the entire organization. The other levels of the physician management structure traditionally had been concerned with clinical as opposed to business issues. Several physicians in the HMO recently had assumed newly formed, full-time executive roles as regional and associate medical directors. Clearly, a formal structure for physician input was in place and growing. However, several of these upper level physician-managers talked about the "fire alarm" approach that had always characterized physicians' collective involvement in organizational decision making within the HMO.

> It [physicians' interest in decision making and policymaking] varies over time. Any time the physicians felt nonphysician administration was getting too much in control, then there would be a resurgence. They'd want to get back into the idea of being heard as opposed to just seeing patients. It really is an up-and-down cycle.

There appeared to be both organizational and cultural barriers that limited physicians' ability to become more involved in management. One organizational barrier was the fact that all the physicians, under their employment contract with the HMO, saw patients for at least 30 hours per week. Much of their remaining time was devoted to office time needed for dictation, callbacks to patients, and other clinically related peripheral tasks that went along with the practice of medicine. Even existing physician coordinators had only a few hours per week set aside for their management tasks. The increasing number of new patient subscribers to the HMO, and a shortage of primary care physicians in the local labor market, prevented the organization from allowing physicians to become more involved in decision making and management.

Another organizational barrier to increased physician involvement in decision making was the lack of internal training available to physicians interested in management-type roles. The HMO offered physicians few educational opportunities in finance, marketing, billing, accounting, management, and other subjects important to understanding how an HMO operates. Instead, physician coordinators received on-the-job training. One commented,

> If they [the HMO] want me to manage, they better teach me how to manage. C'mon! I mean, I don't know what I'm doing when it comes to budgeting and stuff like that.

Cultural barriers to greater involvement in organizational policy and decision making stemmed from both the medical socialization process and physicians' salaried status. For instance, these physicians gave a higher priority to preserving their personal autonomy in patient care than they did to having input into decisions affecting physicians collectively. Their loyalty, instilled in them when training to become physicians, was to their own patients first. One physician, who had been with the HMO since it first opened in 1977, put it succinctly.

> I'm loyal to the core to the HMO. But my first and foremost responsibility is to my patients and to a lesser extent my colleagues and the HMO. The organization is just an umbrella overseeing us.

Salaried employment status within a large organization had provided a number of benefits (as we have discussed) that served to enhance physicians' own sense of professionalism. But many of these benefits, such as the freedom from administrative tasks and increased time to spend on other nonprofessional activities, were contrary to the ingredients necessary to have greater input into organizational policy and decision making. To gain a larger share of control within the HMO for the entire medical subculture, physicians would need to compromise beliefs they had grown to value in their occupational setting over time. They would need to modify their existing ideology to incorporate new responsibilities and roles, responsibilities that would inevitably detract from what they currently saw as their true mission of practicing medicine. They would need to expose themselves to market-related issues from which the organization had buffered them in the past. Once again, they were in the same position as self-employed physicians (with respect to facing similar external pressures); only those physicians had larger incentives (i.e., remaining self-sufficient entrepreneurs) currently pushing them to adapt and take on new responsibilities.

DISCUSSION

These data suggest three points about the relationship between professionals, their work, and the specific organizational setting in which this work is performed. First, self-employed and salaried physicians visualized their work as an art form; defined and assessed the value of autonomy in similar ways; viewed important practice issues such as malpractice, clinical practice guidelines, and the use of allied health professionals almost identically; and liked the same things about their work in primary care. That these two physician groups shared such beliefs about important aspects of their work, even in the midst of external change, suggests that the professional socialization and training process continues to be an important source of homogeneity within the profession. Medicine's strong occupational culture appeared to shape physician views in longlasting ways.

Second, the two physician groups nonetheless harbored different views of the professional role because of their interaction over time with the rewards and barriers of specific work settings. The self-employed doctors enjoyed being entrepreneurs and the control and economic autonomy this role afforded them. Salaried physicians enjoyed practicing medicine within the context of what Stoeckle (1988) has referred to as "a good job" in which the demands extraneous to "true" medical work could be avoided. The HMO insulated salaried physicians from external market pressures, freeing them to pursue their professional roles and maximize their technical autonomy (see Kornhauser, 1962, and Whalley, 1990, for similar findings related to corporate engineers). In return, salaried doctors agreed to conform to certain managerial rules. Each group appeared to create a different professional image for itself, suggesting the negotiated character of professionalism (see Nelson & Trubek, 1992, for a similar finding with respect to lawyers).

Third, characteristics of the specific work and employment context must be considered when looking at the process and forms that these negotiations take. For example, both groups were conscious of the need to renegotiate the terms of their work given changing circumstances. However, one group's employment situation allowed the physicians to be more immediately proactive (in both positive and negative ways) in their renegotiation than was the case with the other physician group. Self-employed physicians were concerned with protecting their economic autonomy vis-à-vis large employers and insurers. They pursued two separate strategies: resistance through work-related games played on insurers and adaptation to new business and management responsibilities. The salaried physicians, due to their employee status, were having difficulty overcoming threats to their technical autonomy (which was really the only autonomy they had left) from new organizational controls. At present, they could only react to the HMO as it adapted itself structurally to changing conditions in its environment.

CONCLUSION

The two groups of physicians studied here simultaneously resisted, accommodated, and adapted their aspirations in adjusting to organizational and economic encroachments. Examining such individual behavior is central to understanding how change plays out in a given setting, especially in industries such as health care where new developments currently are rapid and unpredictable. Members of professions, especially ones such as medicine and law, have various resources and talents they can use to limit the negative effects that this change will have on their work and autonomy. Professionals are not passive victims of change; they are "active agents" (as Hodson, 1995, proposes) trying to shape their future work conditions.

Studies of professionals should investigate both individual- and group-level processes to see how professions and other stakeholders with different interests, skills, and leverage attempt to negotiate and maintain *new* types of organizational and professional arrangements in the midst of larger developments. Increased use of longitudinal study would be one means by which to examine these processes. The physicians in this study were involved in an ongoing process, and although the snapshot taken here can intimate the nature of that process, it cannot describe it fully. Longer term ethnographies and case studies of everyday professional life and experiences, much like those that Hughes (1959) advocated in studying professional socialization and work, would also be well suited to this approach. The sociology of work in other areas has benefitted from this type of approach; the sociology of professions can benefit as well.

Individual action does not take place in a vacuum, however, and the work setting itself substantially influences professional adaptation. The number of contexts within which professional work gets performed is more varied than the self-employment versus salaried situations described here. Physicians today work in numerous settings: self-employment in small practices, medium-sized group practices, and very large networks of independent practitioners; salaried employment in hospitals, HMOs, academic medical centers, and government-owned facilities. They commonly are paid through a combination of self-employment and salaried labor in any of these arrangements. These varied contexts provide a major influence on professionals' ability to adapt to and negotiate change. Comparative study of the same profession in two or more settings will increase our knowledge of the interplay between organizational structure and worker behavior, a critical element in understanding the relationship between professions and organizations (Abbott, 1991; Barley & Tolbert, 1991).

This study also raises some interesting questions related to the internal stratification of professions. For example, in the self-employed physician group, two subgroups pursued different strategies to deal with the economic change facing them. Those who resisted were older than those who chose to take on new bureaucratic responsibilities. The older group was much less able to compromise their view of professionalism, most likely because they had been trained and socialized at a time when the prestige, respect, and autonomy accorded physicians was at an all-time high. This difference among doctors in the same type of work context indicates how intraprofessional variables influence the form of individual adaptation. An individual- and group-based approach to studying professions will increase the likelihood that the effects of such variables will be sorted out.

The sociology of professions could benefit from a renewed emphasis on individual professionals and their everyday actions. Traditional theories of professions have not paid enough attention to the professional as agent. Instead, they have pointed to structure as the overwhelming factor explaining dominance, deprofessionalization, proletarianization, or corporatization. The picture becomes much more complicated than these perspectives suggest when we look at professional life in detail. For this reason, the integration of these perspectives with the theme of individual agency would generate new and useful ideas in the field of professional studies.

APPENDIX

Interview Questionnaire

When did you decide on primary care? When did you decide on the type of employment setting?

There's been a good deal written in the health services literature about what activities physicians are actually involved in but little effort in trying to understand from doctors themselves about their work. Describe to me, briefly, how your time during the day is broken up, for example, into patient time, administrative time, and so on.

Could you state the three things you like most about (1) working in the primary care field and (2) working in this particular employment arrangement? Do other colleagues mention the same things or different things? Were these things you most like always the same or have they changed over time in any way?

Many physicians say that what they like least about their jobs is the amount of paperwork with which they have to contend. Do you agree with this? What exactly is it about paperwork that creates this dislike? What are some other things you like least about working in this particular employment arrangement?

What do you see as the most important difference(s) between working as a salaried physician in an organization and working as a physician in a private or group practice? What do you feel you have either gained or sacrificed, in terms of control, by working in your particular setting?

One important aspect of people's work is the amount of freedom that they feel they have to do their job. What does this freedom mean to you in terms of being a physician and working where you do? How would you define a word like *autonomy* as it relates to your work? Can you tell me about some of the times, throughout the course of your normal day, when you feel you have the freedom to do your job the way you want or need to? Are there ever any times when you feel you do not have the freedom to do your job the way you want to? If you had to name one thing you think affects this freedom the most, what would it be?

Would you make all the same choices over if you had to do it again? In all this change people talk about, what do you think are the one or two most important freedoms or are as of control that physicians must protect or not compromise? On what do you think the profession as a whole can or should compromise?

Do liability concerns ever affect your decision making in any way?

There are others who are also involved in delivering primary care, for example, nurses and physician assistants. What do you think their role should be in the future health care system? Should they be given more responsibility and independence in delivering primary care?

REFERENCES

Abbott, A. (1991). The future of professions: Occupation and expertise in the age of organization. In S. Barley & P. S. Tolbert (Eds.), *Research in the sociology of organizations: Vol. 8. Organizations and professions* (pp. 17-42). Greenwich, CT: JAI.

Barley, S., & Tolbert, P. S. (1991). At the intersection of organizations and occupations. In S. Barley & P. S. Tolbert (Eds.), *Research in the sociology of organizations: Vol. 8. Organizations and professions* (pp. 1-13). Greenwich, CT: JAI.

Braverman, H. (1974). *Labor and monopoly capital.* New York: Monthly Review Press.

Carroll, G. (1993). A sociological view on why firms differ. *Strategic Management Journal, 14,* 237-249.

Fielding, S. (1990). Physician reaction to malpractice suits and cost containment in Massachusetts. *Work and Occupations, 17,* 302-319.

Freidson, E. (1970a). *Professional dominance: The social structure of medical care.* New York: Atherton.

Freidson, E. (1970b). *Profession of medicine.* New York: Dodd, Mead.

Freidson, E. (1985). The reorganization of the medical profession. *Medical Care Review, 42,* 11-35.

Gross, H., & Budrys, G. (1991). Control over work in a prepaid group practice. In J. A. Levy (Ed.), *Current research on occupations and professions* (Vol. 6, pp. 279-295). Greenwich, CT: JAI.

Hafferty, F. W., & Wolinsky, F. (1991). Conflicting characterizations of professional dominance. In J. A. Levy (Ed.), *Current research on occupations and professions* (Vol. 6, pp. 225-249). Greenwich, CT: JAI.

Hall, R. H. (1988). Comment on the sociology of the professions. *Work and Occupations, 15,* 273-275.

Haug, M. (1973). Deprofessionalization: An alternate hypothesis for the future. *Sociological Review Monograph,* No. 20, 195-211.

Hodson, R. (1995). The worker as active subject: Enlivening the "new sociology of work." In D. B. Bills (Ed.), *The new modern times: Factors reshaping the world of work* (pp. 253-280). Albany: State University of New York Press.

Hughes, E. C. (1959). *Men and their work.* Chicago: Free Press.

Interstudy Publications. (1995). *The competitive edge industry report.* Minneapolis, MN: Author.

Kornhauser, W. (1962). *Scientists in industry: Conflict and accommodation.* Berkeley: University of California Press.

Larson, M. S. (1977). *The rise of professionalism: A sociological analysis.* Berkeley: University of California Press.

McKinlay, J. B. (1982). Toward the proletarianization of physicians. In C. Derber (Ed.), *Professionals as workers: Mental labor in advanced capitalism* (pp. 37-62). Boston: G. K. Hall.

McKinlay, J. B., & Stoeckle, J. D. (1988). Corporatization and the social transformation of doctoring. *International Journal of Health Services, 18,* 191-205.

Navarro, V. (1976). *Medicine under capitalism.* New York: Prodist.

Nelson, R. L., & Trubek, D. M. (1992). Arenas of professionalism: The professional ideologies of lawyers in context. In R. L. Nelson, D. M. Trubek, & R. L. Solomon (Eds.), *Lawyers' ideals/lawyers' practices: Transformations in the American legal profession* (pp. 177-214). Ithaca, NY: Cornell University Press.

Notman, M., Howe, K. R., Rittenberg, W., Bridgham, R., Holmes, M. M., & Rovner, D. R. (1987). Social policy and professional self-interest: Physician responses to DRGs. *Social Science and Medicine, 25,* 1259-1267.

Parsons, T. (1954). *Essays in sociological theory.* New York: Free Press.

Simpson, I. H. (1989). The sociology of work: Where have all the workers gone? *Social Forces, 67,* 563-581.

Smith, V. (1994). Braverman's legacy: The labor process tradition at 20. *Work and Occupations, 21,* 403-421.

Sonnenstuhl, W. J., & Trice, H. M. (1991). Organizations and types of occupational communities: Grid-group analysis in the linkage of organizational and occupational theory. In S. B. Bacharach (Ed.), *Research in the sociology of organizations* (Vol. 9, pp. 295-318). Greenwich, CT: JAI.

Starr, P. (1982). *The social transformation of American medicine.* New York: Basic Books.

Stoeckle, J. (1988). Reflections on modern doctoring. *Milbank Quarterly, 66*(Suppl. 2), 76-91.

Strauss, A. (1987). *Qualitative analysis for social scientists.* New York: Cambridge University Press.

Trice, H. M. (1993). *Occupational subcultures in the workplace.* Ithaca, NY: ILR Press.

U.S. General Accounting Office. (1992). *Hospital costs: Adoption of technology drives cost growth* (GAO Publication No. HRD 92-120). Washington, DC: Government Printing Office.

Whalley, P. (1990). Markets, managers, and technical autonomy. In S. Zukin & P. DiMaggio (Eds.), *Structure of capital: The social organization of the economy* (pp. 373-394). New York: Cambridge University Press.

17

Reemployment in the Restructured Economy

Surviving Change, Displacement, and the Gales of Creative Destruction

BETH A. RUBIN
BRIAN T. SMITH

Capitalism has, from its origins, been an economic system characterized by instability and change. Recent debates about the nature of those changes have reached little consensus on whether or not these changes have been positive or negative for workers. On one hand, massive deindustrialization and the displacement of previously secure, skilled, and unionized workers, the decline of unions, and the apparent loss of good jobs have devastated lives, households, and communities (Bluestone & Harrison, 1982; Perrucci, Perrucci, Targ, & Targ, 1988). Many view such changes pessimistically as portents of an economy that provides shrinking opportunities, declining wages, and insecure futures for the majority of American workers. On the other hand, downsizing and worker displacement might well be viewed as characteristic of capitalism's "gales of creative destruction" (Schumpeter, 1976). Here, optimists see a new, information-based, postindustrial economy that seeks and rewards skilled workers, and then provides them with interesting, challenging, flexible, and team-based work.

Underlying these two views of the economy are radically different theoretical perspectives linking workers to jobs. The optimistic view is rooted in 19th-century stage theories of economic growth (Tilly, 1984; Wallerstein, 1991). Those theories conceptualize change and economic transformation as linear, progressive processes in which countries grow increasingly differentiated, complex, and technologically mature while their populations grow increasingly educated, healthy, and long-lived. Consistent with, and narrower than, these macro level theories of change are neoclassical economic theories of the processes matching workers to jobs. Rational actors with full information trying to maximize their utilities populate the neoclassical world. Their actions and choices reflect preferences; thus employment outcomes represent some equilibria between workers' and employers' preferences. The optimism derives from the assumption that choices and preferences, rather than systematic barriers and entrenched inequalities, shape outcomes.

Critical analysts of the new economy reject both the optimism and the assumptions of neoclassical models and focus, instead, on relations of domination and exploitation. From this theoretical stance, changes in employment practices emerge out of the continual struggles between labor and capital over the labor process and outputs of that labor. Within a class framework, current changes in the job-worker matching process reflect capitalists' efforts to restructure employment in the face of constraints on accumulation. Employers' efforts to rejuvenate accumulation processes and reclaim past rates of profit growth require deepening workers' exploitation, minimizing labor costs, and removing constraints on future profit growth. Class theorists explicitly recognize workers' "short-sided" and employers' "long-sided" power (Bowles & Gintis, 1993).

Similarly, feminist scholars have also claimed that the advantages of economic restructuring are not shared equally by men and women. From their perspective, restructured employment continues to reinforce male privilege by relying on gendered employment queues (Acker, 1992; Reskin & Roos, 1990). The pessimistic view is rooted, then, in a claim that current conditions create widespread power inequities in employment relations. In particular, these conditions deepen *workers'* vulnerability to employers' preferences.

The purpose of this chapter is to adjudicate between these theoretical views of contemporary economic transformations by focusing on the absorption of displaced workers in the restructured economy. In particular, we examine the speed of their reemployment and the determinants of that speed. We develop hypotheses derived from these two perspectives and assess the extent to which each theory predicts the reemployment process. We begin with a brief discussion of previous research on workers' displacement and job acquisition in the new economy.

DISPLACEMENT AND REEMPLOYMENT

The deindustrialization and overall restructuring of the American economy emerged out of profitability crises in the early 1970s (Bowles, Gordon, & Weisskoph, 1983; Ranney, 1993; Rubin, 1995), which occurred primarily in manufacturing industries in the economic core. The response, slow and piecemeal, took a variety of forms: active union busting (Goldfield, 1987), domestic and international relocation (Harvey, 1989), and disinvestment in the nation's productive core and reinvestment in more flexible outlets such as finance capital. In the search for revitalized profitability, employers have shifted investment from manufacturing industries to service-based industries, closing or relocating plants in the historical Rustbelt and shifting them to the rising Sunbelt, Mexico, or overseas. This spatial reorganization allowed employers to seek out nonunion, or relatively low-unionized, workers and probusiness policies as well as displace thousands of previously costly, unionized workers (Bluestone & Harrison, 1982; Grant & Wallace, 1994; Storper & Walker, 1989).

With that displacement has come increased hardship for American workers across the economy and throughout the occupational structure. Wage polarization (Bernhardt, Morris, & Handcock, 1995; Danzinger & Gottschalk, 1993), unstable work resulting from the growth of contingent employment (Belous, 1989; Henson, 1996; Rubin, 1995, 1996; V. Smith, 1997a, 1997b; Tilly, 1996), and community devastation (Dudley, 1994; Perrucci et al., 1988) are just some of the consequences. Some accounts of the near future make even more dire predictions, anticipating a jobless future (Aronowitz & DiFazio, 1994) and the end of work (Rifkin, 1995). This research, as well as the *New York Times* (1996) summary report, *The Downsizing of America*, presents a grim future for workers in the new economy, *especially for those who have been displaced.*

Not all accounts of the new economy are, however, so grim. While recognizing the depth of disruption in the 1980s, some argue that it was a temporary and healthy stage in which bloated organizations and unproductive businesses were forced to "cut the fat" and develop more efficient and productive technologies and labor strategies. Out of that restructuring, such optimists argue, emerged a newly competitive and successful economy, in which skilled workers are valued and employable, education is the coin of the realm, and incompetence and sloth have been relegated to the ashbin of history (see, for instance, Arthur & Rousseau, 1996; Kenney & Florida, 1993; Womack, Jones, & Roos, 1990).

This perspective on the current economic transformation has its roots in Daniel Bell's (1973) *The Coming of Post-Industrial Society.* The newly emergent economy, increasingly information based, values intellect and skill over brawn, shifts the axes of power from property to knowledge, creates opportunities for creative and entrepreneurial thinkers, and frees workers and managers alike from the rigidities of bureaucratic organizations (see V. Smith, 1997a, for a succinct review of much of this literature). Importantly, this vision of the restructured economy, with its dynamically flexible workforce (Colclough & Tolbert, 1992), is a vision that sees expanded, enriched, and meaningful jobs for *educated* workers (Womack et al., 1990).

An additional component of the new economy within this view is that workers, both blue- and white-collar, are no longer *stuck* in a single organization throughout their working lives and have far more opportunities to maximize their utilities through job change. Each job that a worker takes, presumably, adds to the worker's skill repertoire, *allowing* that individual to move on to the next, exciting growth opportunity (Arthur & Rousseau, 1996). Thus, consistent with stage theories of growth and economic progress, worker displacement, while temporarily unsettling, is viewed as an opportunity. In fact, a January 1998 newspaper article by Carol Smith claims that "in all the hand-wringing about layoffs and downsizing . . . one thing that has gone quietly unnoticed is that a lot of people like their lives better than before" (p. C4). The article cites a recent survey's conclusion that "one of the biggest myths about downsizing is that it damages employees careerwise" (p. C4).

By and large, however, scholarly research on the fate of displaced workers provides little reason for optimism and challenges notions of change as both linear and progressive. Studies of more recent plant closings and worker displacement tell relatively grim stories, though sometimes providing some thin streams of optimism. Perrucci and colleagues' (1988) now classic study of the RCA plant closing provides, for instance, a bleak picture of the fate of displaced electronics workers. Workers, particularly older and female workers, had difficulty finding new jobs, and typically, the quality was considerably below that of their lost jobs. Overall, the consequences for these workers went beyond job and income loss; they lost their benefits, security, political integration, and communities.

Other case studies echo these findings. Both Dudley (1994) and Milkman (1997), in recent rich examinations of workers displaced from the automobile industry, document the loss of income, benefits, security, and opportunity that many workers experienced. There are, however, key differences in the findings of these two studies (as there are key differences in their foci). For Dudley, who studied workers displaced from an auto plant in Kenosha, Wisconsin, the vision is consistently desolate. For older workers, male and female, many of whom have a high school diploma at best, the loss of their jobs in the auto plant meant economic and psychic devastation. Whereas the high-school-educated workers displaced from Kenosha had few employment opportunities, occasionally younger college-educated men fared somewhat better, though not always. For most workers, however, downward mobility was the norm.

Milkman's (1997) study of workers at the restructured auto plant in Linden, New Jersey, compares workers who stayed at Linden after workplace reorganization with those who accepted the company buyout. The buyout-takers were unique among displaced workers, Milkman argued, for their relative postdisplacement well-being. Generally, the workers were satisfied with their decision to take the buyout rather than stay at the plant. More important for our purposes, all were reemployed; some even started their own businesses. The college-educated among them did particularly well. A quarter of the buyout-takers relocated to another state, and interestingly, these workers tended to regret taking the buyout as they did not fare as well as other workers. The privileged position of many of the buyout-takers among the displaced stemmed, Milkman shows, from a number of factors: They self-selected, they were in a region with low unemployment, and, most important, they were young (p. 130).

Her account is not completely positive, however. African Americans (male and female) and White female buyout-takers fared less well than others. These were the groups that experienced the greatest downward mobility and wage loss, a finding that Milkman points out (p. 133) is consistent with Wilson's (1996) claims about the particularly damaging impact of deindustrialization on the well-being of African Americans. In fact, many African American workers were more likely to rethink their choices as they faced entrenched race-based labor market inequalities; they also took the buyout at lower rates than did White workers in recognition of those inequalities (Milkman, 1997, pp. 95, 107).

In addition to these rich case studies of displaced workers, Moore (1992, 1996) has conducted several studies of the Census Bureau's *Displaced Worker Survey,* the data we use in our study, as have a number of economists (Flaim & Sehgal, 1985; Howland & Peterson, 1988; Podgursky & Swaim, 1987). These studies have done much to demonstrate, using aggregate data, the wage costs of displacement, particularly for less skilled and older workers. One important and consistent finding in this body of work, and one that undergirds our interpretations below, is that the *neoclassical* model of *job search* fails to explain the duration to reemployment after displacement. From the neoclassical perspective, which undergirds optimistic readings of the new economy, the duration to reemployment is a function of *workers'* preferences as they "search" for the best job at the best wage, given their human capital. Any cash reserves allow workers to hold out for an optimum job. The rejection of this assumption is crucial for our analysis since we suspect the reemployment experience of displaced workers is shaped alternatively by employers' preferences and class pressures.

Despite the contributions of these studies, there are some limitations. By and large, the sociological studies of reemployment have relied on case study methods, which, while rich in detail, are limited in their generalizability. They do not provide enough information about the more aggregate reemployment experience of displaced workers. Second, prior aggregate-level research on the reemployment of displaced workers was conducted within nonsociological paradigms; thus they excluded from serious consideration much that is of interest to sociologists (e.g., power, gender, and household division of labor). As a result, although this research has begun to challenge neoclassical models of reemployment processes, it speaks to a limited set of concerns. Third, much of the scholarship on the reemployment process has neglected to consider the gendering of these relationships (for exceptions, see Rubin & Smith, 1999; Spalter-Roth & Deitch, 1998); we attempt to address those issues seriously in the research presented here.

In an earlier work, using aggregate data, we focused on a single component of the reemployment process: human capital (Smith & Rubin, 1997). The major concern in that article was to test arguments about the employment-enhancing effects of human capital and experience in the new economy. We found little support for these arguments and concluded that workers were relatively unprotected by education and were thus *hyperexploitable,* that is to say, factors such as maleness, credentials, and skill no longer privilege workers the way they used to. We introduced the argument that an alternative understanding of the impact of restructuring on workers and their employability is rooted in class relations and the ability of employers to restructure the ways in which they exploit workers to further enhance profitability.

That work, however, represented only an initial foray into our line of reasoning. Here we further explore the utility of this theoretical view by paying stricter attention to the spatial and gendered elements underlying processes of reemployment. While doing so, we retain consideration of the role of human capital in the present analysis in order to gauge whether our class-based, hyperexploitability argument holds up in the face of claims made by human capital proponents.

HYPOTHESES

In the analysis presented here, we build on this body of qualitative and quantitative research so as to explore further the speed with which displaced workers are reemployed and the determinants of that speed. In so doing, we intend to further adjudicate between contemporary perspectives of the reemployment process that, like 19th-century theories of social change, view the dynamics of economic transformation as linear and progressive, in contrast to class and feminist approaches to the reemployment of displaced workers that emphasize their short-sided power and vulnerability in the new economy.

As a jumping-off point, we refer back to the uniqueness of the workers in Milkman's (1997) case study. Remember that the workers who took the buyout did far better, she claimed, than the typical displaced worker. This finding suggests some of the characteristics that should hasten the reemployment of displaced workers.

We examine the impact of age on the reemployment of displaced workers since one of the most important determinants in reemployment success in Milkman's research (1997) as well as Dudley's (1994) was workers' age. Those who fared well in the new economy seem to be younger, highly educated workers (who reported expectations of jobs as short-term phenomena), a finding consistent with progressive, stage-based views of current economic transformations. These case study findings are also consistent with class theories that see capitalist development as a process creating larger and larger pools of redundant and expendable labor (i.e., a process that favors youth over age). Such theories predict that older displaced workers obtain new jobs more slowly than do their younger counterparts. Neoclassical arguments, however, highlight age as an indicator of labor market experience and thus predict more rapid reemployment for older workers (vis-à-vis younger).

Similarly, Milkman found that for those workers who accepted the buyout the benefits were unequally distributed by race. This in conjunction with Wilson's (1996) claims about the impact of deindustrialization points to the continuing disadvantages of race in the new economy. In addition to the efforts to minimize costs, past research suggests that African American workers are simply lower in the hiring queue than are White workers (Leiberson, 1980; Reskin & Roos, 1990). Thus, a class perspective predicts that African American workers will obtain new jobs more slowly than do White workers. Neoclassical theories suggest that, given comparable levels of education, employers should not prefer one race over another; thus race should neither hamper nor enhance workers' efforts to obtain new jobs.[1]

Education and skill are perhaps the most important factors determining the fate of displaced workers in the new economy within the neoclassical framework (Kenney & Florida, 1993; Womack et al., 1990). Both Dudley and Milkman point out that in their samples most workers have a high school degree at best, and both argue that this contributes to their postdisplacement success or lack thereof (also see Moore, 1996). Both studies also argue quite strongly that college-educated White men fared better than any other group. Thus, these case studies in conjunction with the neoclassical view of the postindustrial economy suggest that those with a high school diploma or more should find reemployment more rapidly than those with less than a high school education. Similarly, those with a college degree should also be reemployed more rapidly than those without, as the new economy quickly reabsorbs such human-capital-rich workers.

In contrast, consistent with class analyses of contemporary changes, our prior research claimed that the new economy widens the pool of what we called *hyperexploitable workers* (see Smith & Rubin, 1997). That is, we argued that current conditions deepened employees' vulnerability to their employers, and, in particular, we found that the current economy does not privilege human-capital-rich workers. That earlier study and class models of employment relations in general predict that these workers will not be reemployed more rapidly than their less educated counterparts. In fact, in their efforts to replace skilled with unskilled labor, employers might well avoid highly educated workers, an argument that hypothesizes a negative effect.

Neoclassical theory implies that not only will more *educated* workers fare better in the new economy but so too will more *skilled* workers. Thus, skilled displaced workers should be reemployed more rapidly. Class theories, however, argue that in a highly competitive global market, employers seek to cheapen and deskill workers whenever they can (Braverman, 1974; Shaiken, 1984). Too costly workers would be an anathema to employers and thus lower in the hiring queue as contemporary employers are less willing to, and have little reason to, pay these skilled individuals what they want or expect (see Harrison & Bluestone, 1988; Wallace & Rothschild, 1988). Thus, the expected effect of being a high-skill worker, from a class perspective, is to slow the rate of reemployment.

Neoclassical theories, because of their focus on individual preferences, are silent about the impact of macrostructural factors on the reemployment process. Such factors are crucial, however, in class analyses that situate the employment process in the context of capitalist development. To that effect, we consider two such factors: the industry and region of the country from which workers were displaced. At the center of class-based theories of deindustrialization is the denuding of basic industry in the Northeast and in America's heartland. The dismantling and relocating of basic production facilities in automobile assembly (Milkman, 1997), electronics (Perrucci et al., 1988), and steel (Bluestone & Harrison, 1982), among others, have generated similar employment declines not only in these industries but, through ripple effects, in other industries as well (e.g., retail sales and services). While many companies subsequently shifted their investment from goods to service-based production, that shift has not been accompanied by comparable shifts in employment growth. This strategy has revitalized corporate profitability, yet there are few instances of similarly revitalized communities, incomes, and employment stability. Moreover, while the initial growth of services was accompanied by expanded employment in the early 1980s, that process has slowed as employers have sought to further streamline and rationalize the production of services (J. Smith, 1987; Leidner, 1993). Thus, class theories predict that workers displaced from the old monopoly sector of the economy should be the most redundant of workers and thus less rapidly reemployed than are other workers.

Equally important for understanding the dynamics of deindustrialization and economic transformation, for class analysts, has been the spatial transformation of the American economy. Besides global relocation, internal relocation has been a dramatic component of economic change (Storper & Walker, 1989). In their efforts to avoid powerful and entrenched unions in the North, those manufacturers who retained their manufacturing enterprises often reduced costs and improved production by leaving their antiquated production facilities in the old industrial cities and developing new plants, drawing on the lean production techniques and flexible technologies borrowed from the Japanese (Kenney & Florida, 1993; Womack et al., 1990). The South and West attracted new production facilities by providing strong probusiness climates with favorable tax laws, union-free workforces, and/or weak regulatory constraints (Grant & Wallace, 1994; Perrucci, 1994; Storper & Walker, 1989). Class-based theories suggest, therefore, that workers displaced in Rustbelt (Grant & Wallace, 1994) and Frostbelt (Bluestone & Harrison, 1982) states should be reemployed more slowly than those workers displaced in Sunbelt states, where many manufacturers relocated.

At the core of class analysis of economic change, however, are employers' constant efforts to increase capital accumulation and decrease worker power and expense. Thus, such research focuses on employers' efforts to revitalize profitability at the expense of workers' well-being. As employers seek to cut costs and minimize the extent to which workers make demands, benefits have been one of the casualties of the the new economy, an economy increasingly characterized as one in which workers lack health insurance and other benefits (Bluestone & Harrison, 1982; Doeringer, 1991). Our preceding discussion of employers' motivations for displacing workers pointed to efforts to minimize workers whose wage demands and benefit expectations render them expensive. Thus, while neoclassical arguments have less to say in this regard, class arguments suggest that displaced workers whose prior employment was "benefit rich" will be reemployed more slowly than will less expensive workers.[2]

Gender scholars have taken both class and neoclassical research to task for their gender-blind analysis. Little of the research on displacement and reemployment considers the gendered nature of social relations despite the well-documented impact of worker (and employer) sex on a whole host of outcome variables. We draw on those arguments in our examination of reemployment.

Neoclassical arguments eschew gender-based discrimination in the hiring process as fundamentally irrational on the part of employers and would suggest that dynamically flexible information-based workplaces should no longer privilege men over women. Sullivan (1989), Acker (1992), V. Smith (1993), and Rubin and Smith (1999) all show that the new economy remains polarized along gender lines and that women continue to experience differential returns to their human capital. Likewise, Milkman's (1997) case study also showed that women workers obtained lower status and lower wage jobs than did male workers who took GM's buyout, although there the women expressed less dissatisfaction and were more likely to drop out of the labor force.

Class theorists have long argued that employers draw employees from raced and gendered queues. In the same vein, in contrast to neoclassical claims, gender scholars argue that employers rank women below men in their hiring queues (Reskin & Roos, 1990) and so to understand the reemployment rates of women relative to men we must consider the role played by patriarchy and discrimination.

Feminist critiques of neoclassical theory have also pointed out that while many workplaces are indeed more flexible, the household division of labor has changed little over the years (Hochschild, 1989; Presser, 1989). Women maintain their responsibility for the household, and particularly for child care (Brayfield, 1995). As a result, women's household responsibilities continue to be a drag on their full labor force participation. In contrast, accounts of the "informated" (see Zuboff, 1988), flexible economy suggest that new information technologies ought to lessen the burden of those responsibilities (Applebaum & Batt, 1994). Moreover, in this view, team-based flexible workplaces, allowing varying work schedules, should further alleviate the burden on women. Even if women do continue to sustain primary responsibility, according to these arguments, these flexible workplaces should allow accommodating schedules so that women may better negotiate the demands of work and family.

Yet absent in much of the *quantitative* research on worker displacement has been a consideration of household constraints on reemployment. Where prior research on duration to reemployment has typically included "head of household" as "a measure of the family responsibilities that encourage more active job search" (Moore, 1992, p. 682), we think a more relevant measure of those household responsibilities is child care. The former is a particularly gendered notion of responsibility but captures less the real drag on reemployment. We consider two such factors: whether there are children under age 6 in the household and whether the effect of young children is particularly consequential for women. Feminist theories would anticipate that both of these factors would slow the acquisition of a new job after displacement, particularly for women.

Research on displaced workers has focused not only on income losses but on consequences for the family well-being (Perrucci et al., 1988). In their study of the RCA plant closings,

Perrucci and colleagues (1988) tested the job search arguments that married women, sheltered from market pressures, would take longer to find new employment. Like other tests of job search theory, they found little support. We argue instead that married *male* displaced workers will find employment more rapidly than their unmarried counterparts as familial pressure is greater and marriage, at least for male employees, is usually deemed a sign of a stable (and reliable) worker. We thus hypothesize a positive relationship between being married and male and speed of reemployment. Since female workers have the culturally approved option of full-time homemaking, and thus may drop out of the labor market or delay reemployment following displacement, we expect married women to be reemployed more slowly.

One of the factors that played a role in the fate of Milkman's (1997) workers was whether or not they moved after taking the buyout. In her case, she found that those workers who moved fared less well; she acknowledges, however, that the New Jersey auto plant was unlike many plants in that it was situated in a strong local economy. Those displaced workers who left may have relocated to communities with less viable economies. Similarly, those who move also lose their extant social networks. These arguments suggest that moving will slow reemployment. Spatialization arguments, however, focusing on the mobility of capital would suggest the opposite: that workers who move should be reemployed more rapidly than those who stay.

Past research has consistently shown the importance of basic worker protections in explaining reemployment rates. Of particular importance, and one place in which we have to account not only for employer preferences but worker preferences as well, is the impact of nonmarket wages. Unemployment benefits provide workers with a nonmarket wage in the period between jobs. This wage allows workers leeway in their job search. Importantly, however, workers can receive these benefits for only, at most, 24 weeks. In fact, federal laws only mandate provision of these benefits for 13 weeks; states can extend them for up to 24 weeks. Roughly half of the displaced workers examined here received unemployment insurance. Those who did were, on average, reemployed 10 weeks later than those who did not receive such benefits. Thus, we anticipate a negative relationship between receipt of unemployment insurance and reemployment. We also include a control for aggregate economic conditions. A key variable facilitating post-buyout reemployment in Milkman's (1997) analysis was the health of the local economy. Although we have no measure of the displaced workers' *local* economy, we expect to observe the reemployment-enhancing effects of a growing national economy.

Given the preceding, in the analysis that follows we examine the independent effects of ascriptive characteristics (age, race, sex), human capital (education, skill), industrial structure, region, family constraints (marital status, presence of young children), and economic conditions (health insurance, aggregate wage growth, unemployment benefits) on the speed with which displaced workers find reemployment. The results of these analyses should throw further weight behind one of the two competing images of the new economy.

ANALYSIS

Data

The data we use in this study are from the January 1992 Displaced Workers Survey that supplemented that month's *Current Population Survey* (U.S. Department of Commerce, Bureau of the Census, 1992). These supplemental questions were asked of all persons 20 years of age or older who reported being displaced from their job in the past 5 years. For these individuals, the survey provides data on reasons for their displacement, characteristics of their former job, the nature of the displaced worker's ensuing job search, as well as selected comparative information concerning the displaced worker's current job (if there is one).

All individuals who lost jobs are not necessarily displaced. We consider only those who reported losing their job prior to January 1992 due to a plant closing, slack work, or because their position or shift was abolished. Thus, our specific research question dictates that our analysis excludes self-employed individuals whose businesses failed or those who lost their job due to the seasonal nature of their employment. Since we are concerned here with reemployment, we also restrict our analysis to those displaced workers under 64 years of age.[3] There were 6,526 such cases. Approximately 75% of these displaced individuals were reemployed at the time of the survey.

Analytic Technique

Empirical tests of hypotheses concerning differences in the duration to reemployments are achieved via PROC LIFETEST in SAS© that evaluates the null hypothesis that the times to reemployment are the same for all groups of displaced workers examined. Three different test statistics result from this procedure, each of them an examination of the deviations of observed numbers of events from expected numbers.[4]

Although these procedures are useful for preliminary analyses of the data and for testing simple hypotheses about differences in reemployment times across groups, they are not adequate for examining the effects of variables controlling for other covariates. Thus, since we are interested in how the speed of the reemployment process differs by theoretically relevant micro and macro characteristics of the displaced workers, we use partial-likelihood estimation of proportional hazards models to estimate their effect on the duration to reemployment after displacement. This procedure (PROC PHREG in SAS©) is particularly well suited to capturing the dynamic nature of the reemployment process as it enables the specification of beta coefficients without having to specify any particular baseline hazard functions (as do the often used Exponential, Weibull, or Gompertz specifications associated with analyses of survival data). Such a model takes the following form:

$$h_i(t) = \alpha_0(t)\exp\{\beta_1 x_{i1} + \beta_i x_{jk}\},$$

where the "risk of reemployment" for displaced worker *i* at time *t* is the product of two factors: $\alpha_0(t)$, an unspecified, (possibly) time-dependent hazard function, which affects the rate of reemployment of every individual in the same way, and $\beta_1 x_{i1} + \ldots \beta_i x_{jk}$, a linear function of a set of *k* fixed covariates, which is then exponentiated.[5] The exponentiation is necessary because although such models do not require specification of the hazard function α_0 they do require parametric assumptions about the temporal dependence of the second component. The customary assumption is that the rate of interest here is a log-linear function of the current values of observed variables; that is to say, it is assumed that the time-dependence affects the rates of all members of the population in the same multiplicative way (Tuma & Hannan, 1984, pp. 234-264).

Measures

DEPENDENT VARIABLE

Our dependent variable in this analysis is the estimated risk of reemployment. Changes in this risk can be conceptualized as an indicator of the speed with which a displaced worker is reemployed. Our interest is in how the individual's human capital, structural and familial characteristics, controlling for a number of other covariates, accelerate or slow that rate.[6]

INDEPENDENT VARIABLES

Age. We include a measure of the displaced worker's age at the time of the survey. Because the data exclude all workers younger than 20 and older than 64 we do not have to specify beyond that. In preliminary analyses, we examined a squared-age term under the assumption that the effect was curvilinear; that variable was not significant, so we keep the linear specification as have others in this literature.

Race. We include an indicator of the race of the displaced worker by assigning a value of 1 to workers who are African American.

Sex. We include an indicator of the sex of the displaced worker, assigning the value of 1 to women.

Human capital. Our preceding discussion suggests that it is important to consider different measures of human capital. Many of the displaced workers have a high school education and no more.[7] With this in mind, we examine the effect of the displaced worker's education, paying particular attention to the salience of a high school degree. The first of two indicators examines the effect of a displaced worker's educational background by examining the speed to reemployment for those workers with less than high school graduation and for those with any amount of post-high school education, relative to the speed to reemployment of those having *only* a high school degree. Since, however, many of the assumptions about who will fare well in the new economy stress the importance of college, we also examine an indicator of whether the displaced worker was a college graduate, in order to test the hypothesis that the new economy will reward (i.e., rapidly reabsorb) college-educated workers.

Skilled high-wage worker. The Displaced Workers Survey data do not include a direct measure of skill. Because wages are often skill proxies (see, for instance, Wallace & Kalleberg, 1982), we therefore identified as "high-wage workers" the more "costly" of the displaced by classifying those workers who, when displaced, were making more than one standard deviation above the national mean hourly wage *for their occupational group.*[8]

Health coverage. To tap those workers who came from "benefit rich" jobs, which arguably adds an additional perceived expense, we include an indicator of whether or not workers were displaced from jobs in which they were included in a group health plan.

Industrial structure. Research on industrial transformation focuses on the particularly detrimental impact of the decline of manufacturing on workers. However, we argue that the deindustrialization argument goes beyond manufacturing and entails a shift from previously monopoly-sector to service-sector industries. Thus, although we examine the impact of being displaced from manufacturing industries we examine as well the effect of being displaced from monopoly-sector industries.[9]

Region. Following Grant and Wallace (1994), we include an indicator of having been displaced from Rustbelt or Sunbelt states. We also examine displacement from Frostbelt states (Bluestone & Harrison, 1982).[10]

Familial responsibilities. We include four measures of family responsibilities: marital status, coded 1 if the displaced worker is married with spouse present; an interaction term between marital status and sex; children, coded 1 if there are children 6 years of age or under in the household; and an interaction term specifically indexing women with children under age 6.

Macroeconomic conditions. We control for the percentage change in aggregate earnings from the previous year as a global measure of the health of the national economy (Howland & Peterson, 1988). Rising overall wages indicate an expansionary economy that would arguably reabsorb workers more quickly than would a contracting economy.

Worker protections. We control for the receipt of unemployment benefits.

We turn now to the results of our analysis.

RESULTS

In Table 17.1, we present descriptive information about the displaced workers whose reemployment we are examining. Most are White between 25 and 48 years of age, 42% are women, and 3% live in households with young children. Seventeen percent are college graduates, with a similar number, at best, having finished high school. Half of the displaced workers lost jobs in the monopoly sector, and the Frostbelt and Sunbelt states contributed equally to the ranks of the displaced.

The statistics reported in Table 17.2 show the results of our analysis of tests of hypotheses concerning the duration of time to reemployment for selected groups of displaced workers. There were no significant differences in the speed with which displaced men and women found reemployment (Panel A of Table 17.2). On average, displaced men found new work within 14 weeks and displaced women within 15 weeks.

There also were no significant differences in the speed with which workers of different races were reemployed (Panel B of Table 17.2). The statistics do indicate, however, that there *might* be "early" versus "late" differences; that is to say, one of the three empirical tests (the log-likelihood ratio) is particularly sensitive to such differences and it is this test that suggests significant differences. Thus, there is reason to suspect that the race of the displaced worker may affect the speed with which that person finds reemployment, *depending on the time since displacement.*

There were significant differences in the speed of reemployment when examined by the standard *BLS* 4-categorization of Northeast, Midwest, South, and West (Panel C of Table 17.2). In general, displaced workers in the western states found work more slowly than others. As expected, the times to reemployment for displaced workers in Sunbelt states (in which the western states are included), were significantly different (i.e., shorter) than those experienced by their counterparts in Frostbelt and Rustbelt states (Panels D and E of Table 17.2).

TABLE 17.1 Means and Standard Deviations of Major Variables

Variable	*Mean*	*SD*
Age (years)	37.3	11.1
Black (%)	10.8	29.7
Female (%)	41.6	49.1
Education (%)		
Less than high school	16.4	37.1
High school or higher	43.6	49.6
College graduate	17.4	37.9
High wage worker (%)	27.2	44.5
Married male (%)	58.0	49.0
Married female (%)	21.7	41.2
Children ≤ age 6 (%)	2.8	16.4
Female with child ≤ age 6 (%)	1.0	9.7
Monopoly (%)	49.6	50.0
Rustbelt (%)	30.4	46.0
Frostbelt (%)	48.2	50.0
Sunbelt (%)	51.8	50.0

Anecdotal and journalistic accounts suggest that displaced workers typically experience downward mobility (see, e.g., the 1996 *New York Times* report titled *The Downsizing of America*). The following data address this question. Did displaced workers regain employment in the same fields from which they were displaced? Did those who found work most quickly do so by being rapidly reemployed into the industries and occupations from which they were displaced? To address these questions, we examine the degree to which displaced workers found reemployment in the same industrial sector (i.e., monopoly or competitive) as that from which they were displaced (Table 17.3).

For the most part, reemployment occurred in the sector of displacement. Among those displaced in the monopoly sector, 72% were reemployed in the same sector when surveyed. Of the remaining, all but 2% found reemployment in competitive sector industrial locations.

TABLE 17.2 Tests of Hypotheses Concerning Differences in the Duration to Reemployment

Panel A: $H_0 = S_{male}(t) = S_{female}(t)$ for all *t*.

Sex	*Log-Rank*	*Wilcoxon*
Male	44.38	148119
Female	–44.38	–148119

	Chi-Square	*Pr > Chi-Square*
Log-Rank	2.01	0.1562
Wilcoxon	2.68	0.1010
–2Log(LR)	2.369	0.1272

Panel B: $H_0 = S_{white}(t) = S_{black}(t) = S_{asian}(t) = S_{other}(t)$ for all *t*.

Race	*Log-Rank*	*Wilcoxon*
White	31.96	118410
Black	–35.70	–131330
Asian	7.93	20053
Other	–4.19	–7133

	Chi-Square	*Pr > Chi-Square*
Log-Rank	5.185	0.1590
Wilcoxon	6.9942	0.0721
–2Log(LR)	7.5853	0.0554

Panel C: $H_0 = S_{northeast}(t) = S_{midwest}(t) = S_{south}(t) = S_{west}(t)$ for all *t*.

Region	*Log-Rank*	*Wilcoxon*
Northeast	–131.34	–398847
Midwest	61.27	199277
South	13.44	25607
West	56.63	173963

	Chi-Square	*Pr > Chi-Square*
Log-Rank	24.0780	0.0001
Wilcoxon	28.1293	0.0001
–2Log(LR)	37.5971	0.000

(Continued)

A similar number of displaced competitive sector workers (71%) "stayed" in the sector from which they were displaced; of the remainder, 17% were reemployed in the monopoly sector. Looking *within* the competitive sector only at service workers, we see a similar pattern; 73% of displaced service workers remained in the competitive sector, while 15% found new work in the monopoly sector. Among former service workers, 61% were reemployed in the service sector.

We examined a similar table at the occupational level (Table 17.4). Here we are interested in the same issue. Did displaced workers find reemployment in jobs similar to those they lost? Using the Office of Management and Budget's (OMB) Standard Occupational Classification system, we see that, by and large, the answer was yes. With few exceptions, the majority of reemployed workers were working in the same occupation group from which they were displaced. Reemployment in the same occupational group, however, does not necessarily indicate reemployment in the same job; a lawyer reemployed as a preschool teacher would be a "stayer" in Table 17.4, yet clearly someone who experienced a certain degree of job movement.

In 5 of the 13 occupational categories, over 50% of the workers were reemployed in the

TABLE 17.2 Continued

Panel D: $H_0 = S_{sunbelt}(t) = S_{frostbelt}(t)$ for all t.

Region	*Log-Rank*	*Wilcoxon*
Sun Belt	–70.06	–199570
Frost Belt	70.067	199570

	Chi-Square	*Pr > Chi-Square*
Log-Rank	4.833	0.027
Wilcoxon	4.694	0.030
–2Log(LR)	8.796	0.003

Panel E: $H_0 = S_{sunbelt}(t) = S_{rustbelt}(t)$ for all t.

Region	*Log-Rank*	*Wilcoxon*
Sun Belt	77.90	178226
Rust Belt	–77.90	–178226

	Chi-Square	*Pr > Chi-Square*
Log-Rank	7.895	0.0050
Wilcoxon	7.520	0.0061
–2Log(LR)	13.5983	0.0002

TABLE 17.3 Industrial "Movement" (in percentage) of Displaced Workers[a]

	Monopoly	*Competitive*	*Service*
Monopoly	72.2	25.8	12.9
Competitive	17.1	70.9	34.0
Service	15.3	73.0	61.1

a. Service sector workers are a subset of competitive sector workers. Monopoly *N* + Competitive *N* + *Public Sector* = 100%.

same fields. In only 3 of the remaining categories did the percentage of workers that "stayed" in the occupation from which they were displaced fall below 40%, and in 1 of the 3 (private household service), the number of workers in the sample is too small to consider.

These results led us to ask about those who were not reemployed in the same fields.[11] We assessed the degree to which the displaced workers' current job shifted within this classification system. As one would expect, there was considerable downward movement at the top end of the classification system and considerable upward movement at the bottom. For example, almost 54% of displaced executives, administrators, and managers were reemployed as something other than an executive, administrator, or manager. Although we suggest that these workers probably experienced downward mobility, we make no claims about the relative position of those in some of the other categories. For instance, almost 40% of displaced transportation and material moving equipment workers were reemployed to a category above them (which might, if they ended up in protective service, be downward mobility), and only around 8% moved to the category of handlers and to similar occupations. While these data provide clues about where displaced workers end up following displacement, they do not inform us about the process leading to those jobs. For that information we turn to the results of our multivariate analysis in Table 17.5.

We remind the reader that the coefficients estimate effects on the risk of reemployment, which we treat as an indicator of the relative speed with which displaced workers obtain new jobs. Thus, we interpret positive coefficients as indicators of factors enhancing/speeding reemployment and negative coefficients as factors retarding reemployment. Equations 1 through 6 of Table 17.5 differ in the measure of human capital (either high school related indi-

TABLE 17.4 Occupational "Movement" (in percentage) of Displaced Workers

Occupational Group	*Categories Above*	*Stayers*	*Categories Below*
Executive, Administrative, Managerial	0.0	46.4	53.6
Professional Specialty	8.8	66.8	24.4
Technicians	16.5	45.6	37.9
Sales	19.6	48.5	31.9
Administrative Support	25.6	57.4	17.0
Private Household Service	33.0	33.3	33.0
Protective Service	25.9	44.4	29.7
Other Services	29.2	57.5	13.3
Precision Production, Craft, and Repair	21.4	57.8	20.8
Machine Operators, Assemblers, and Inspectors	48.5	38.4	13.1
Transportation and Material Moving Equipment	39.3	52.3	8.4
Handlers, Equipment Cleaners, Helpers, and Laborers	75.5	22.7	1.8
Farming, Forestry, and Fishing	65.6	34.4	0.0

cators or college graduation) and regional indicators (Rustbelt, Frostbelt, or Sunbelt). Since the effects of the covariates are stable across models, we discuss our findings in terms of the specific covariates across the models.[12]

Older displaced workers were reemployed more slowly than younger ones. In general, the rate at which African American workers were reemployed did not differ significantly from that of other workers. While it is the case that a low level of statistical significance was attained *when college graduation was the educational variable indexed,* we suspect that this effect is an artifact attributable to the small number of African American college graduates in this sample (less than 1% of all the displaced workers surveyed). Being female does not slow the rate of reemployment. In Equations 1, 3, and 5, neither of the indices of education *relative to high school* attain levels of significance (although they are appropriately signed). Having a college degree consistently slows the speed to reemployment (Equations 2, 4, and 6). Relative to those without a college degree, degree holders spent more time without work prior to reemployment. More expensive workers (and thus presumably more skilled, or unionized, or both; we simply cannot tell with these data) attained new jobs more slowly than their lower-wage counterparts, and because these are relatively rather than absolutely high wages, this is *not* strong evidence that high wages enable workers to "hold out" longer.

Married workers were reemployed more rapidly than single workers. However, the interaction term indicates that married *female* workers were reemployed more slowly than were other workers.[13] Similarly, the presence of young children did not affect the reemployment rate of displaced workers, *except when the displaced worker is a woman.* Women with young children found new jobs less quickly. At no time are any of the regional variables, nor the indicator of displacement from the monopoly sector, statistically significant.[14] The failure of any indicator of region or industry from which the worker was displaced is surprising and something to which we return in our concluding remarks.

Turning to the impact of having been displaced from a job with a group health plan, we find that these workers are reemployed more slowly than are workers who were not members of a group health plan. Workers who moved since displacement found jobs more rapidly than those who did not. Similarly, our two controls act consistently as expected; an expanding economy, indicated by the direction and magnitude of movement in aggregate earnings, is con-

TABLE 17.5 Estimated Effects on the Risk to Reemployment of Displaced Workers[a]

Variable	*(1)*	*(2)*	*(3)*	*(4)*	*(5)*	*(6)*
Age	–.010***	–.010***	–.010***	–.010***	–.010***	–.010***
	(.001)	(.001)	(.001)	(.001)	(.001)	(.001)
Black	–.079	–.095*	–.077	–.093*	.077	.093*
	(.055)	(.055)	(.055)	(.055)	(.055)	(.055)
Female	.066	.061	–.068	.063	–.068	.063
	(.046)	(.046)	(.046)	(.046)	(.046)	(.046)
Education						
Less than high school	–.061	—	–.058	—	–.058	—
	(.046)		(.047)		(.047)	
High school or higher	.047	—	.047	—	.047	—
	(.032)		(.032)		(.032)	
College graduate	—	–.069*	—	–.072*	—	–.072*
		(.038)		(.038)		(.038)
High wage worker	–.147***	–.152***	–.148***	–.053***	–.148***	–.153***
	(.035)	(.035)	(.035)	(.035)	(.035)	(.035)
Married male	.160***	.151**	.162***	.154**	.162***	.154***
	(.040)	(.040)	(.040)	(.040)	(.040)	(.040)
Married female	–.255***	–.245***	–.254***	–.245***	–.254***	–.245***
	(.061)	(.061)	(.061)	(.061)	(.061)	(.061)
Children ≤ age 6	.035	.042	.033	.040	.033	.040
	(.104)	(.104)	(.105)	(.104)	(.104)	(.104)
Female with child ≤ age 6	–.464*	–.505**	–.463*	–.503**	–.463*	–.503**
	(.193)	(.193)	(.193)	(.193)	(.193)	(.193)
Monopoly	–.002	–.010	.004	–.011	.004	–.011
	(.030)	(.030)	(.030)	(.030)	(.030)	(.030)
Rustbelt	–.034	–.031	—	—	—	—
	(.033)	(.033)				
Frostbelt	—	—	.015	.021	—	—
			(.030)	(.030)		
Sunbelt	—	—	—	—	–.015	–.021
					(.030)	(.030)
Health insurance	–.065**	–.088**	–.064*	–.087**	–.064**	–.087**
	(.032)	(.033)	(.032)	(.033)	(.032)	(.030)
Move since displaced	.200***	.185***	.195***	.179***	.195***	.179***
	(.038)	(.038)	(.038)	(.038)	(.038)	(.038)
% Change in earnings	.105***	.107***	.107***	.109***	.107***	.109***
	(.022)	(.022)	(.022)	(.022)	(.022)	(.022)
Unemployment benefits	–.733***	–.740***	–.736***	–.744***	–.736***	–.744***
	(.032)	(.032)	(.032)	(.032)	(.032)	(.032)

a. Standard error in parentheses.
***$p \leq .001$; **$p \leq .01$; *$p \leq .10$.

sistently associated with more rapid reemployment whereas the receipt of unemployment insurance is consistently associated with slower reemployment rates.

DISCUSSION

We first conducted a descriptive analysis (Tables 17.1 through 17.4); those data tend to support arguments that view the new economy in a relatively positive light. The majority of displaced workers find reemployment relatively quickly in the industries and occupations from which they've been displaced, a finding that is consistent with claims that the period of the later 1970s and 1980s was one of disruption and transformation that has settled into a new, reindustrialized economy able to reabsorb the temporarily dislocated workers.

The multivariate analyses in Table 17.5 fail, however, to support the claims derived from stage theories of economic transformation and, more narrowly, neoclassical theories about the job-worker matching process. By and large, the findings support class and feminist theories about the reemployment process with one exception. That older workers were reemployed more slowly is consistent with the hypotheses derived from class analyses. In contrast, to some extent, the effects of race were consistent with *neoclassical* arguments; African Americans' reemployment rates did not differ *substantially* from those of other workers (see above).

The human capital effects are consistent with class theories and challenge directly the human capital argument that education is the ticket to success (see Bell, 1973; Smith & Rubin, 1997). Even human-capital-rich workers find themselves highly vulnerable, or hyperexploitable, in the restructured economy. Also consistent with the class perspective is the effect of being a high wage worker. High wage workers were, for example, 14% less likely to obtain new jobs than their lower-wage counterparts. In contrast to the workers in Milkman's (1997) study but consistent with class theories, we find that those workers who moved since displacement were reemployed 19% more rapidly than those who did not.

The absence of a slower rate of employment of women workers at first seems to challenge expectations. It is, however, consistent with our earlier arguments (Smith & Rubin, 1997) that the hyperexploitability of workers in the new economy diminishes some of the advantages of sex per se. Nonetheless, the findings overall are consistent both with class and feminist analyses. The effects for married women and women with children are consistent with feminist analyses of women's position in the new economy (Acker, 1992; Rubin & Smith, 1999; Sullivan, 1989). Specifically, women with children under age 6 were 38% less likely to obtain new jobs at the speed of other workers. Married female workers were reemployed 23% more slowly than others.

The one major analytic surprise was the failure of either industry or region to attain statistically significant levels as class theories predicted. We think, however, that this "nonfinding" is important and address it in our conclusions that follow.

CONCLUSION

The purpose of this chapter was to adjudicate between two theoretical views of contemporary transformations by focusing on the reabsorption of displaced workers in the restructured economy. The results of this study challenge neoclassical approaches to the reemployment process and highlight the necessity for future scholars to consider seriously the gendered nature of employment and reemployment in the context of economic and workplace restructuring.

We consider our insignificant region and industry findings important and reflective of the new terrain that future research must explore. The 1970s and early 1980s were characterized by massive displacement of blue-collar workers; by the late 1980s, white-collar workers had joined their ranks. Similarly, although downsizing began in manufacturing, it became a dominant managerial strategy across the economy by the late 1980s. By the 1990s, all workers are relatively vulnerable to displacement processes regardless of region of residence or industry of employment. These findings are consistent with the most dire predictions about a new economy with a shrinking number of jobs. Although it is true that 75% of the workers were reemployed by the end of the survey, 25% *still had not been reemployed.* The fate of these workers is still unknown. Future research needs to better follow the job trajectories of the long-term unemployed.

Finally, our research points to the ongoing dynamics of capitalist transformation. As capitalism once again renews its profitability, workers pay the price. In the absence of strong unions and proworker political actors, workers can continue to anticipate becoming redundant, expendable, and increasingly vulnerable to the gales of creative destruction. What's more, in the new millennium, for capitalists, the rules for survival remain the same: Concentration, centralization, and innovation lead to profitability. For workers, however, while their potential vulnerability may remain, the rules for their survival, what protects them and gives them security, are changing.

NOTES

1. One could argue that employers have a "taste to discriminate" (Becker, 1957). Nonetheless, seminal studies focusing on Black-White differences in a variety of workplace outcomes did not resort to tastes for discrimination but, rather, focused on human-capital differences (Doeringer & Piore, 1971; Thurow, 1969, 1972). More recently, see Borjas (1994) and Holzer (1996).

2. By and large we have focused on employer preferences as these are our major theoretical concern. In the case of this variable, it is difficult for us to untangle worker and employers preferences, and an equally plausible argument is that workers who had health coverage were more likely to be in a unionized plant or in one that mimics some of the characteristics of a unionized plant. One might expect these workers to obtain new jobs more slowly than other workers because such workers may "hold out" for protections similar to those associated with the job they last held. We are less confident that this explanation holds because prior research has so convincingly debunked such "search"-based explanations.

3. One might argue that we should right-censor these data at some earlier age in order to take into consideration the idea that, depending on their age, elderly workers may not seek work after displacement. Although displacement might have opened retirement doors for some, we assume that for most (if not all) of these workers the displacement was involuntary and unwelcome and hence the desire to return to work as soon as possible was utmost.

4. Allison (1995) argues that two of these, the log-rank test and the Wilcoxon test, are particularly good for analyses such as ours. The likelihood-ratio test, according to Allison, is inferior to the other two due to its dependence on the "typically implausible assumption" that the risk of reemployment is constant for all groups, an assumption that implies a particular form of time dependence in the risks (p. 37).

5. A characteristic feature of partial likelihood estimation is the absence of an intercept term. The intercept is part of $\alpha(t)$, the unspecified hazard function. This value cancels out of the estimating equations. As Allison (1995) discusses, not specifying a baseline hazard function means that these estimates are not fully efficient, but in most cases, the loss of efficiency is small, and "what you gain in return is robustness because the estimates have good properties regardless of the actual shape of the baseline hazard function" (pp. 112-117). Tuma and Hannan (1984) concur that such parameters "have excellent statistical properties, assuming that the postulated proportional rate model is valid" (p. 263).

6. The effects of indicator variables in such a model, e^{β}, can be interpreted as the ratio of the estimated "risk of reemployment" for those with a value of 1 to the estimated "risk" for those with a value of 0 (controlling for the other covariates). For variables with n categories, $n - 1$ covariates (and parameters) are included in the model. The factor e^{β} is then the risk associated with membership in the particular category *relative* to the omitted category. For quantitative covariates, the estimated percentage change in the "risk of reemployment" for each 1-unit increase in the covariate is obtained by subtracting 1.0 from e^{β} and multiplying by 100 (Allison, 1995).

7. For example, in this sample, 52% of displaced manufacturing workers had a high school degree or less, and displaced manufacturing workers constitute 29% of the sample.

8. To identify these "high-wage workers," we compared displaced workers' earnings at the time of their displacement with the mean earnings of their counterparts in each of the five major occupational groups for each year of this analysis. To clarify: The mean weekly earnings reported by workers displaced from managerial and professional specialty occupations in 1987 was $559 (standard deviation = $383). Those workers who were displaced from managerial and professional specialty occupations in 1987 who reported predisplacement weekly earnings of greater than $942 were coded "high-wage." We initially included a measure of the displaced workers' predis-

placement wage. Its effect was identical to that of normative wage-deviation variable. We present the latter because, while broad, it is the theoretically richer variable. That is, it best measures the costs that employers are seeking to avoid.

9. We coded the following as monopoly sector industries: Mining, Construction, all Durable Goods Manufacturing (with the exception of Lumber and wood products and Furniture and fixtures), Nondurable Goods Manufacturing (with the exception of Textile mill products and Leather and leather products), Transportation, Communications, Utilities and Sanitary Services, Banking and Other Finance, and Insurance and Real Estate.

10. In Bluestone and Harrison's (1982) analysis, the Frostbelt includes New England, Mid-Atlantic, and northeastern states; the Sunbelt includes South Atlantic, East South Central and West South Central states (see their table A.1). Grant and Wallace (1994) define the Rustbelt as being made up of the northeastern and midwestern states.

11. Our conceptualization of "up" and "down" is heuristic at best; the only reason to call movement up or down reflects positioning on the OMB list. These are essentially unranked categories. What is most important for our purposes is the "Stayers" category and the sense of movement. Clearly, the outcome of the displacement process warrants further research.

12. The reader is reminded that the dependent variable in this analysis is the risk of reemployment for displaced worker$_i$ at time$_t$. A positive (negative) effect on this risk suggests a shorter (longer) duration to reemployment *relative* to those displaced workers who do not share the trait under consideration.

13. For ease of presentation, we have omitted the models that include the "married male" since all other coefficients were relatively identical to those presented. We did find, however, that displaced married men found reemployment 26% more rapidly than did others.

14. We experimented with other measures of industry such as whether the worker was displaced from a manufacturing or service sector and we did not observe any differences. We also explored the specific impact of occupation of the displaced workers on their reemployment rate and examined whether being displaced from craft, managerial, professional, technical, sales, and administrative support occupations, service occupations, and production positions (all coded as indicator variables) differed in their rates of reemployment. We found significant effects only for (a) craftwork and (b) technical, sales, and administrative support occupations. Craftworkers were reemployed more rapidly than others and technical, sales, and related support occupations were reemployed more slowly. Although the craft occupational effect is consistent with human-capital-based arguments, it belies the image of postindustrial arguments as does the failure of technical workers to obtain jobs more rapidly.

REFERENCES

Acker, J. (1992). The future of women and work: Ending the twentieth century. *Sociological Perspectives, 35*(1), 53-68.

Allison, P. D. (1995). *Survival analysis using the SAS system: A practical guide.* Cary, NC: SAS Institute.

Appelbaum, E., & Batt, R. (1994). *The new American workplace.* Ithaca, NY: ILR Press.

Aronowitz, S., & DiFazio, W. (1994). *The jobless future.* Minneapolis: University of Minnesota Press.

Arthur, M. B., & Rousseau, D. M. (1996). *The boundaryless career.* New York: Oxford University Press.

Becker, H. S. (1957). *The economics of discrimination.* Chicago: University of Chicago Press.

Bell, D. (1973). *The coming of post-industrial society.* New York: Basic Books.

Belous, R. S. (1989). *The contingent economy: The growth of the temporary, part-time and subcontracted workforce.* Washington, DC: National Planning Association.

Bernhardt, A., Morris, M., & Handcock, M. S. (1995). Women's gains or men's losses? A closer look at the shrinking gender gap in earnings. *American Journal of Sociology, 101*(2), 302-328.

Bluestone, B., & Harrison, B. (1982). *The deindustrialization of America.* New York: Basic Books.

Borjas, G. J. (1994). The economics of immigration. *Journal of Economic Literature, 32,* 1667-1717.

Bowles, S., & Gintis, H. (1993). The revenge of *Homo economicus*: Contested exchange and the revival of political economy. *Journal of Economic Perspectives, 7*(1), 83-102.

Bowles, S., Gordon, D. M., & Weisskoph, T. E. (1983). *Beyond the wasteland: A democratic alternative to economic decline.* Garden City, NY: Doubleday.

Braverman, H. (1974). *Labor and monopoly capital.* New York: Monthly Review Press.

Brayfield, A. (1995). Juggling jobs and kids: The impact of employment schedules on fathers' caring for children. *Journal of Marriage and the Family, 57,* 321-332.

Colclough, G., & Tolbert, C. J. (1992). *Work in the fast lane.* Albany: State University of New York Press.

Danzinger, S., & Gottschalk, P. (1993). *Uneven tides: Rising inequality in America.* New York: Russell Sage.

Doeringer, P. B. (1991). *Turbulence in the American workplace.* New York: Oxford University Press.

Doeringer, P. B., & Piore, M. J. (1971). *Internal labor markets and manpower analysis.* (Reprint). Lexington, MA: D. C. Heath.

Dudley, K. M. (1994). *The end of the line.* Chicago: University of Chicago Press.

Flaim, P. O., & Sehgal, E. (1985, June). Displaced workers of 1979-83: How well have they fared? *Monthly Labor Review,* pp. 3-16.

Goldfield, M. (1987). *The decline of organized labor in the United States.* Chicago: University of Chicago Press.

Grant, D. S., & Wallace, M. (1994). The political economy of manufacturing growth and decline across the American states, 1970-1992. *Social Forces, 73*(1), 33-64.

Harrison, B., & Bluestone, B. (1988). *The great U-turn: Corporate restructuring and the polarizing of America.* New York: Basic Books.

Harvey, D. (1989). *The condition of postmodernity.* Oxford, UK: Basil Blackwell.

Henson, K. D. (1996). *Just a temp.* Philadelphia: Temple University Press.

Hochschild, A. (1989). *The second shift: Working parents and the revolution at home.* New York: Viking.

Holzer, H. J. (1996). *What employers want: Job prospects for less-educated workers.* New York: Russell Sage.

Howland, M., & Peterson, G. E. (1988). Labor market conditions and the reemployment of displaced workers. *Industrial and Labor Relations Review, 42*(1), 109-122.

Kenney, M., & Florida, R. (1993). *Beyond mass production.* New York: Oxford University Press.

Leiberson, S. (1980). *A piece of the pie: Blacks and White immigrants since 1880.* Berkeley: University of California Press.

Leidner, R. (1993). *Work in the fast lane.* Berkeley: Univesity of California Press.

Levinson, H. (1962). *Men, management and mental health.* Cambridge, MA: Harvard University Press.

Milkman, R. (1997). *Farewell to the factory.* Berkeley: University of California Press.

Moore, T. S. (1992). Racial differences in post-displacement joblessness. *Social Science Quarterly, 73*(3), 674-689.

Moore, T. S. (1996). *The disposable work force.* New York: Aldine de Gruyter.

New York Times. (1996). *The downsizing of America.* New York: Time Books.

Perrucci, C., Perrucci, R., Targ, D., & Targ, H. (1988). *Plant closings.* Hawthorne, NY: Aldine de Gruyter.

Perrucci, R. (1994). *Japanese auto transplants in the heartland.* Hawthorne, NY: Aldine de Gruyter.

Podgursky, M., & Swaim, P. (1987). Duration of joblessness following displacement. *Industrial Relations, 26*(3), 213-226.

Presser, H. B. (1989). Can we make time for children? The economy, work schedules and child care. *Demography, 26,* 523-524.

Ranney, D. C. (1993). Closing of Wisconsin Steel. In C. Craypo & B. Nissen (Eds.), *Grand designs* (pp. 65-91). Ithaca, NY: ILR Press.

Reskin, B., & Roos, P. (1990). *Job queues, gender queues.* Philadelphia: Temple University Press.

Rifkin, J. (1995). *The end of work.* New York: Putnam.

Rubin, B. A. (1995). Flexible accumulation, the decline of contract and social transformation. *Research in Social Stratification and Mobility, 14,* 297-323.

Rubin, B. A. (1996). *Shifts in the social contract: Understanding change in American society.* Thousand Oaks, CA: Pine Forge Press.

Rubin, B. A., & Smith, B. T. (1999, August). *Gendered processes: Reemployment of displaced workers in the new economy.* Paper presented at the annual meeting of the American Sociological Association, Chicago.

Schumpeter, J. (1976). *Capitalism, socialism and democracy.* New York: Harper & Row.

Shaiken, H. (1984). *Work transformed.* New York: Holt, Rinehart & Winston.

Smith, B. T., & Rubin, B. A. (1997). From displacement to reemployment: Job acquisition in the flexible economy. *Social Science Research, 26*(3), 292-308.

Smith, C. (1998, January 6). Laid-off workers find the up side of downsizing. *Times-Picayune,* p. C4.

Smith, J. (1987). Transforming households: Working class women and economic crisis. *Social Problems, 34*(5), 416-436.

Smith, V. (1993). Flexibility in work and employment: The impact on women. *Research in the Sociology of Organizations, 11,* 195-216.

Smith, V. (1997a). New forms of work organization. *Annual Review of Sociology, 23,* 315-339.

Smith, V. (1997b). *Theorizing power, participation and fragmentation in the contemporary workplace: The case of the temporary worker.* Unpublished manuscript, University of California, Davis.

Spalter-Roth, R., & Deitch, C. (1998, August). *"I don't feel right-sized—I feel out of work sized": The unequal effects of downsizing on women in the workforce.* Paper presented at the annual meeting of the American Sociological Association, San Francisco.

Storper, M., & Walker, R. (1989). *The capitalist imperative.* New York: Blackwell.

Sullivan, T. (1989). Women and minority workers in the new economy. *Work and Occupations, 16,* 393-415.

Thurow, L. (1969). *Poverty and discrimination.* Washington, DC: Brookings Institution.

Thurow, L. (1972, Summer). Education and economic inequality. *Journal of Public Interest, 28,* 66-81.

Tilly, C. (1984). *Big structures, large processes, huge comparisons.* New York: Russell Sage.

Tilly, C. (1996). *Half a job: Bad and good jobs in a changing labor market.* Philadelphia: Temple University Press.

Tuma, N. B., & Hannan, M. T. (1984). *Social dynamics.* London: Academic Press.

U.S. Department of Commerce, Bureau of the Census. (1992). *Current Population Survey, January 1992: Displaced workers* [Computer file]. Washington, DC: U.S. Dept. of Commerce, Bureau of the Census [producer], 1992. Ann Arbor, MI: Inter-University Consortium for Political and Social Research [distributor], 1994.

Wallace, M., & Kalleberg, A. (1982). Industrial transformation and the decline of craft: The decomposition of skill in the printing industry, 1931-1978. *American Sociological Review, 47*(3), 307-324.

Wallace, M., & Rothschild, J. (1988). Plant closing, capital flight, and worker dislocation: The long shadow of deindustrialization. *Research in Politics and Society, 3,* 1-36.

Wallerstein, I. (1991). *Unthinking social science: The limits of nineteenth-century paradigms.* Oxford, UK: Polity.

Wilson, W. J. (1996). *When work disappears.* New York: Knopf.

Womack, J. P., Jones, D. T., & Roos, D. (1990). *The machine that changed the world: The story of lean production*. New York: Harper Collins.

Zuboff, S. (1988). *The age of the smart machine*. New York: Basic Books.

PART IV

Comparative Labor Responses to Global Restructuring

The five chapters that follow consider an important but often overlooked aspect of economic restructuring. Labor's responses to restructuring in an age of global competition and corporate flexibility have been given little attention in the restructuring literature, and yet there exists a myriad of questions that can be asked about workers and their organizations and actions in this context. The authors presented here take a variety of approaches, ranging from study of individual workers' responses to reactions of whole union movements. And, as many of the following authors note, this is an area of research that presents rich possibilities for further study.

In Chapter 18, Axel van den Berg, Anthony Masi, Michael Smith, and Joseph Smucker, in "To Cut or Not to Cut: A Cross-National Comparison of Attitudes Toward Wage Flexibility," consider that workers' willingness to accept pay cuts to preserve their jobs is influenced by national levels of employment and income security. To explore this possibility, the authors compare workers in Canada and Sweden. The Swedish economy offers workers far greater job and wage security than does the Canadian economy largely because of Sweden's expansive welfare state. Van den Berg and his colleagues predict that because of this, Swedish workers will be less willing than their Canadian counterparts to accept corporate demands for wage reductions. The protective state policies in Sweden are believed to strengthen the resistance of the Swedish workers to corporate cutbacks. Indeed, the authors find that the Swedish workers are less likely to accept wage flexibility. Although van den Berg et al. find that their measures of national employment and income security are not predictors of the workers' different responses, they speculate that the very different levels of state protection of worker security explain the differences in labor's willingness to resist.

The larger question raised by van den Berg and his collaborators is an important one, concerning the impact of state policy on worker responses to corporate strategies designed to counter global competition. At the end of their chapter, these authors state that more systematic, comparative research is needed to understand the impact that Social Democratic governments and state protection more generally can have on workers' willingness and ability to resist threats to their employment and incomes. Researchers should even consider broadening this question to ask what factors in addition to political circumstances strengthen workers' ability to refuse corporate demands for wage reductions or layoffs. This is an area of research on restructuring that is rife with possibilities.

In Chapter 19, "Globalization and International Labor Organizing: A World-System Perspective," Terry Boswell and Dimitris Stevis observe that in an era of economic internationalism, labor movements, for the most part, remain immersed in national rather than international organizations with national instead of global agendas. Boswell and Stevis examine in this chapter the existing international labor organizations and their strengths and weaknesses, and the prospects for national labor movements of greater internationalism in the future. In addition, Boswell and Stevis discuss important exceptions to the lack of global orientation on the part of labor, most notably perhaps, the International Labor Organization and the International Confederation of Free Trade Unions. Finally, these authors suggest that regional forms of transnational governance such as that occurring in the European Union and through the North American Free Trade Agreement (NAFTA) offer opportunities for national labor movements to strategize ways of building cross-national organizations.

A crucial direction for future research, then, is to examine the organizations and strategies pursued by various national labor movements as they attempt to become more globally oriented. Moreover, researchers should work to uncover why some movements choose to embark upon such strategies and why others do not. Furthermore, they should investigate why some of labor's approaches are more successful in building international organizations and implementing change in global labor politics than others. Boswell and Stevis offer a detailed conclusion to their chapter that addresses such research possibilities. This is a thoughtful discussion that should not be missed by readers.

Richard Hyman's focus in Chapter 20, "Trade Unions and European Integration," is on labor's role in shaping the emerging economic unity of the western European nations. He tells us, though, that labor has played only a minimal role in the development of the European Union. The European Trade Union Confederation, the western European regional labor organization, has been for the most part a weak player in integration negotiations in part due to its underfunding by constituent groups and its small size. But the real culprit that Hyman points to echoes the arguments of Boswell and Stevis. Hyman tells us that the unions in western Europe have a national focus, and this greatly impedes attempts to build regional organizations with regional or international focus.

Hyman calls upon researchers to engage in more study of the ways in which the European trade unions are responding to European integration. Thus, many of Boswell and Stevis's appeals for research into labor's successful strategies of organizing and acting more broadly can be repeated here. But Hyman's chapter draws attention to a particular issue: the need to understand the circumstances that lead labor movements to think and act more globally, because, as both Hyman's and Boswell and Stevis's chapters conclude, for labor to be a player and influence global restructuring, an important step lies in adjusting its own organizational and issue orientation.

Chapter 21, by Roy Adams, is titled "The Impact of the Movement Toward Hemispheric Free Trade on Industrial Relations." Adams considers the effects of two international trade agreements on the economies and labor movements in some of the countries governed by the treaties. Mainly, he examines the impact of the 1989 Canadian-U.S. Free Trade Agreement (FTA) and the 1993 NAFTA on the labor movements in the United States and Canada. Both the Canadian and U.S. workers' movements opposed the FTA, although the Canadians did so more heartily. They feared a loss of jobs and other benefits as American companies' responsibilities to Canadian workers were restricted by the agreement. Again, both movements also opposed the NAFTA; this time, however, U.S. workers opposed the treaty more vociferously. But again, the focus by U.S. workers was on potential job loss; they feared that with the agreement in place companies would move operations to Mexico. Adams tells us that the literature is mixed in terms of establishing the impact of the FTA on the Canadian economy. Studies thus far suggest that the NAFTA is having an overall positive impact on the U.S. economy but that high-wage workers often benefit in terms of job security and wages at the expense of low-wage workers. Another interesting outcome that Adams points out as a result of these treaties is that whereas the FTA put distance between the Canadian and U.S. labor movements, the NAFTA has drawn them closer together by fostering shared interests.

Adams's work draws our attention again to the importance of considering the effects of international trade agreements on international trade union relations. This echoes the concerns expressed by Boswell and Stevis and Hyman in earlier chapters in Part IV. The impact of these agreements, as can be seen in Adams's work, is not uniform. The nature of the agreement, considered in the context of international market relations, can have varying effects on the ties between and among national labor movements.

In an era when such cross-national agreements are seemingly increasingly common, their effects not only on worker organization and action within nations but on labor organization relations across nations is an important focus for new research. Adams's finding that the NAFTA helped to build closer ties between the U.S. and Canadian movements suggests that such treaties, under certain circumstances, may provide an opportunity for a more international perspective among labor movements.

Frederic Deyo in Chapter 22, "Labor and Post-Fordist Industrial Restructuring in East and Southeast Asia," provides a detailed look at the circumstances affecting labor movements in Hong Kong, South Korea, Malaysia, Singapore, Taiwan, Thailand, and the Philippines. Although these countries have industrialized rapidly in recent decades, organized workers remain a relatively small part of the labor force and often are without significant political and economic power. Deyo's analysis reveals that labor's weakness in these countries is due not only to political factors, including labor legislation hostile to labor and, at times, outright repression, but is also fostered in important ways by economic factors, particularly moves by many companies to institute flexible production systems to counteract growing international competition. This restructuring of workplaces by greater reliance on contract labor, outsourcing, and temporary workers, for instance, has added to labor's weakened position in the Asian economies. Deyo reports that, thus far, unions have been unable for the most part to resist such changes.

Deyo's work provides a complement to van den Berg and his colleagues' research into the willingness of Swedish and Canadian workers to accept wage cuts. Deyo, like van den Berg and the others, finds that when states offer less protection to workers, labor movements are weakened. However, Deyo goes beyond these political factors to reveal that, in the case of East and Southeast Asia, economic factors matter as well. An important direction, then, for additional research is to determine which economic circumstances in particular are most detrimental to attempts by labor to organize and act collectively. Knowledge of this can specify to labor where the crucial battles to resist corporate practices lie.

The chapters in Part IV represent a variety of approaches to an understudied area. In the face of the massive changes in the global economy, examining labor's response is an important avenue for future research. Not only can researchers consider the newly emerging political and economic circumstances that labor faces in a global economy, but they can also investigate how labor chooses and is sometimes compelled to respond to these momentous changes.

18

To Cut or Not to Cut

A Cross-National Comparison of Attitudes Toward Wage Flexibility

AXEL VAN DEN BERG
ANTHONY C. MASI
MICHAEL R. SMITH
JOSEPH SMUCKER

In recent years, there has been much talk, in public as well as scientific debates, about the paramount importance of economic flexibility in the current era of increasingly intensified competition due to economic globalization (see, e.g., Bélanger, Edwards, & Haiven, 1994; Drache & Gertler, 1991; Piore & Sabel, 1984; Porter, 1991; Stafford, 1989). The flexibility of labor markets is often singled out as especially crucial in this context (see Casey, Dragendorf, Heering, & John, 1989, p. 449; "The OECD and Jobs," 1994, p. 64; Organization for Economic Cooperation and Development [OECD], 1994; Osterman, 1988, p. 129). It is widely held that international competitiveness depends to no small degree on the speed and ease with which labor is allocated (or reallocated) from one place, employer, skill level, occupation, technology, or job, to another.

According to one perspective, primarily advocated by neoclassical economists and those on the political Right, wage flexibility is the most effective means of generating allocative efficiency in the labor market. In turn, wage flexibility is only likely to be maintained under highly competitive conditions. Any interference with the free functioning of the competitive labor market, such as various income security programs, governmental regulation of the relations between labor and management, elaborate labor market policies, and strong unions, invariably shields labor from the discipline of the market, producing wage rigidity and thereby reducing the most important incentive to adjust to change.

In this vein, the chronically high levels of unemployment on the European continent are often blamed on the alleged rigidity of labor markets there. Left-of-center European governments and powerful unions, it is argued, have indulged in a variety of overly generous job and income security programs that have shielded already employed workers from the effects of changes in demand, technology, and competition. In contrast, the argument continues, Japan and the United States have more flexible wages and, consequently, unemployment is much lower (Adnett, 1989, pp. 47-50; "A Chart-Breaking Affair," 1995, p. 70; Forslund, 1994; Graafland, 1989; Lindbeck & Snower, 1988; OECD, 1994).[1]

From *Work and Occupations,* Vol. 25, No. 1, February 1998, pp. 49-73. Reprinted by permission.

Note that this kind of argument rests on a basic social-psychological assumption about the relationship between labor market security (or insecurity) and wage flexibility. According to that assumption, a certain amount of insecurity with respect to one's employment prospects is necessary to induce the requisite willingness to accept wage flexibility. Conversely, it is assumed that excessive labor market and/or income security renders workers more resistant to such flexibility, or at least to the downward variety.[2] The present chapter reports on a part of a Swedish-Canadian comparative research project intended to test this basic assumption (see also Smith, Masi, van den Berg, & Smucker, 1995).[3] For several reasons, Canada and Sweden make good comparative cases for this purpose.

After many decades of almost uninterrupted social democratic government, Sweden has become one of the most generous welfare states among advanced industrial countries, with far-reaching job security and worker codetermination legislation, the highest rate of unionization in the world, and, until recently, persistently low levels of unemployment.[4] Moreover, the celebrated Swedish Model was intended specifically to help stiffen workers' resolve to resist wage concessions to relatively inefficient employers to save their jobs.[5] The complex package of interrelated (solidaristic) wage, fiscal, and active labor market policies, originally framed by Landsorganisationen I Sverige (LO)[6] economists Gösta Rehn and Rudolf Meidner, were quite deliberately designed to produce high levels of income and employment security (but not job security with the present employer),[7] which, it was thought, would strengthen workers' resistance to wage flexibility but weaken their support for protectionism and resistance to technical change and labor market mobility (see, e.g., Esping-Andersen, 1985; Esping-Andersen & Korpi, 1987; Öhman, 1974; Ramaswamy, 1992; Rehn, 1984; van den Berg & Smucker, 1992).[8] In all these respects then, especially as far as the factors presumably conducive to wage flexibility are concerned, Sweden provides an extreme case of the protective state that is so often criticized by neoclassical theorists.

By contrast, Canada has traditionally been closer to the free-market end of the public policy spectrum, with modest income support programs, relatively little job security, not much legal interference in the labor market, strong individual unions in some industries but a weak union movement, and finally, traditionally high levels of unemployment (see, e.g., Johnson, McBride, & Smith, 1994; McBride, 1992; Muszynski, 1985). At the same time, however, the two countries are quite similar in terms of the overall structure of their economies, with strong, internationally competitive industries concentrated in the resource-based industries, engineering and telecommunications, and similar degrees of overall dependence on international trade (around 30% of gross national product [GNP] in both). These similarities should help to minimize confounding factors stemming from differences in these former respects.

WAGE CUTS, WORRIES, AND FLEXIBILITY: TWO HYPOTHESES

Thus, in terms of the independent variable, employment and income security (or insecurity), the contrast between the two countries is as great as one could reasonably expect for the purpose of testing the aforementioned assumption about the relationship between labor market security (or insecurity) and wage flexibility. If the assumption has any validity at all, one would then expect to find pronounced differences in the dependent variable, wage flexibility.

In this chapter, we operationalize wage flexibility as workers' stated willingness to accept a pay cut to save their current jobs. Thus, our dependent variable is both attitudinal and hypothetical. We are aware, of course, of the potential problems in inferring behavior from such attitudes but note that the assumption to be tested posits a social-psychological mechanism whereby labor market security leads to intransigence with respect to wage change. There appears to be no more direct way of tapping that mechanism than by way of attitudinal information.

On the basis of the above discussion, we can briefly formulate two specific hypotheses regarding such attitudes. The first hypothesis simply applies the assumption to be tested to our two cases.

> Hypothesis 1: Canadian workers should be significantly more willing to accept pay cuts to save their jobs than Swedish workers.

Given the differences between the two countries just outlined, the argument is that Sweden's overly generous income security and welfare state programs, restrictive job security provisions, powerful unions, and left-leaning interventionist governments enable those Swedish workers who have a job to reject any pay cuts without fear of detrimental consequences to themselves.

Our second hypothesis directly addresses the main reason for the expected difference in willingness to accept a pay cut as formulated in Hypothesis 1. Swedish workers should be less disposed to accept a pay cut because they have less to fear from the consequences of such a refusal. Put differently, Swedish workers need to worry less about the alternative income and employment options open to them and are, for this reason, less willing to accept wage reductions to save their present jobs. This leads to our second hypothesis.

> Hypothesis 2: The difference between Canadian and Swedish workers' willingness to accept pay cuts should, to a considerable degree, be explained by the significantly higher levels of anxiety about alternative labor market prospects among Canadian workers.

In the following sections, we address these hypotheses in turn. We begin with a brief description of our data and methods, followed by a presentation of our main variables. This also allows us to present data that test directly (and lend support to) our first hypothesis. We then go on to present our major findings concerning the second hypothesis. Finally, we briefly speculate, based on somewhat circumstantial evidence from our data, on alternative explanations of our main results.

DATA, VARIABLES, AND BIVARIATE ANALYSIS

Data

As part of a larger project aimed at testing alternative general assumptions about the relationship between labor market security (or insecurity) and flexibility, we commissioned two parallel surveys from the national statistical agencies of Sweden and Canada (Statistiska Centralbyrån [SCB] and Statistics Canada [StatsCan], respectively). The research design called for representative samples in each country to be asked a number of questions concerning issues of labor market flexibility, anxiety, and adjustment. To this end, we designed a supplementary questionnaire consisting of some 30 items that were asked of subsamples from one of the regular monthly labor force surveys in each country. The supplementary surveys were conducted in each country at approximately the same time. In addition to the flexibility, anxiety, and adjustment items, our questionnaire asked about recent experiences with change in the workplace, background characteristics, and other attitudes.

In the analyses that follow, we report only on one segment of the national subsamples, namely, those individuals who at the time of the surveys, Fall 1992 to Winter 1993, were employed as blue-collar workers in the manufacturing sector of their respective economies. Both statistical agencies selected individuals to be interviewed for our special surveys on the basis of their labor-force status. Individuals were identified as eligible for inclusion if they were employed as blue-collar workers in the manufacturing sector. In Canada, of 1,000 selected individuals, 903 were eligible for the survey. Of the 903 individuals eligible for the survey, 779 completed interviews, yielding a response rate of just over 86%. For our Swedish blue-collar manufacturing workforce, the response rate was just under 90% (1,205 completed interviews out of 1,345). The statistical agencies reported no significant response rate bias for the samples; thus, we were left with a total blue-collar manufacturing sample of 1,984 individuals. However, not all respondents provided valid answers to all questions. For the analyses reported below, we chose a very conservative selection procedure—we deleted in a listwise fashion all cases that were missing information on even 1 of the more than 20 variables we used in our statistical analyses. As a consequence, the final sample consisted of 1,096 individuals (399 Canadians, 697 Swedes).[9]

There are several reasons why we have chosen to concentrate only on the blue-collar manufacturing sector workforces of Canada and Sweden in this chapter. The most important is that blue-collar workers represent a crucial group for testing our theory. As already noted, much of the Swedish Model has been formulated by economists and officials of the country's powerful blue-collar union central, the LO, and is specifically meant to apply to blue-collar workers in the manufacturing sector (see, e.g., Martin, 1984). The LO has also been much more consistent and resolute in its opposition to wage concessions than its white-collar counterparts. Moreover, much of the burden of adaptation in the current round of globalization is said to fall precisely on blue-collar manufacturing workers, the main victims of the widely noted deindustrialization allegedly afflicting the advanced industrialized countries (Bluestone & Harrison, 1982; Crandall, 1993; Masi, 1989; Masi & Del Balso, 1991; Noponen, Graham, & Markusen, 1993). Finally, restricting the samples to blue-collar manufacturing workers implicitly controls for factors such as class, occupational status, and industrial sector that might otherwise confound the analysis. This is particularly important because, whereas the two countries' manufacturing sectors have much in common, their service sectors are very different indeed.[10]

Dependent Variable: Refusal to Accept a Pay Cut

Our principal dependent variable is labeled *mrfuscut* (refusal to take a pay cut). Table 18.1 provides the exact wording of the corresponding survey question (in English) as well as the respective percentage response breakdowns for the Swedish and Canadian samples. Table 18.2 shows the zero-order difference between the Canadian and Swedish samples when the variable is dichotomized into mrfuscut, with "would not accept any pay cut" coded as 1 and all other valid response categories coded as 0.

As can be seen from Table 18.1, just over 2 in 5 Swedes (42.4%) but just 1 in 5 Canadians (20.5%) would refuse to take a pay cut of any magnitude to save their present jobs. In addition, those among the Swedes who would accept a pay cut tend toward more modest cuts than do their Canadian counterparts. Although less than 1 in 10 Swedes (7.6% + 0.8% = 8.4%) would accept a cut of 11% or more, just under 1 in 4 Canadians would do so (18.9% + 4.1% = 23.0%).

In Table 18.2, we have transformed the response pattern of the question into a dichotomy (i.e., mrfuscut, coding value 1 [refusal to take a pay cut] as 1, and categories 2 through 4 as 0). We have excluded the 13.0% of Canadians and 7.4% of Swedes who, as can be seen from the table's top panel, responded "don't know," "no answer or not stated," or who "refused to answer." It would have been, we think, reasonable to assume that at least some of these respondents would in fact refuse to take a pay cut even if it were the only way to save their jobs. But, had we coded them as 0 (i.e., including them in the category of those who did not say outright that they would refuse such a cut), it would have made the interpretation of the difference between the two groups who stated an opinion somewhat more difficult. To put it slightly differently, we deliberately isolated those respondents who clearly and explicitly stated that they

TABLE 18.1 Zero-Order Differences Between Swedes and Canadians on "Refusal to Take a Pay Cut" Variable

Value/Label	*Sweden*	*Canada*	*Difference*
1. No, I would not accept any pay cut	42.4%	20.5%	21.9%
2. Yes, 1% to 10%	49.2%	56.4%	–7.2%
3. Yes, 11% to 15%	7.6%	18.9%	–11.3%
4. Yes, more than 25%	0.8%	4.1%	–3.3%
7. Don't know			
8. Refused			
9. No answer, not stated			
Sum of "missing categories" (7, 8, 9)	7.4%	13.0%	–5.6%
Valid cases (categories 1-4)	1,116	677	
Original sample sizes	1,205	779	

NOTE: Survey question = If your workplace was threatened with closure, would you accept a pay cut if it were the only way to save your job? If yes, please indicate how big a percentage of your present wage.

TABLE 18.2 Dichotomized Difference of Proportion *t* Test With a Listwise Deletion of Cases Based on All Variables in Subsequent Analyses

	Sweden N = 697	*Canada* N = 399	*Difference*
Mean	0.389	0.186	
SD	0.488	0.390	
SE	0.019	0.018	
Difference			–0.203
SE of difference			0.027
t test			–7.538
p value of *t* test			0.000
95% confidence interval for difference			0.1498-0.2553

NOTE: "Would Not Accept Any Pay Cut" coded as 1; all valid categories coded as 0.

would refuse to accept a pay cut from those who said that they would accept such a cut (although to varying degrees) because this is the group of greatest theoretical interest to us. By excluding the missing cases using a list, we lost a large number of cases from our samples that might otherwise have been preserved.[11]

We followed this same logic for all of the independent variables (see below) that tapped attitudes or opinions as well as for those individuals for whom we did not have valid responses on objective variables (such as income, firm size, etc.). They were simply excluded from the analyses reported here.

Table 18.2 presents the results of a simple *t* test of the difference of the proportions of outright refusers who refuse to accept a pay cut in the two countries. The statistical results are highly significant, with the 95% confidence interval for the difference between the two countries estimated to be between 14.9% and 25.5%. Thus, we can say with considerable statistical confidence that our first hypothesis is amply supported by our data. As predicted by the theory that links intransigence to relative employment and income security, Swedish blue-collar manufacturing workers are about twice as likely as their Canadian counterparts to refuse to accept a pay cut of any magnitude to safeguard their jobs.

But, is this difference in the level of reluctance to accept wage adjustments mostly, or to some considerable extent, due to a tendency on the part of Swedish workers to be less worried or insecure about their labor market prospects than Canadian workers? To address this question (our second hypothesis), we will first explore

TABLE 18.3 Independent Variables That the Two Theories Argue Should Account for the Variance in Flexibility (or Inflexibility)

Variables	*Descriptions for Ordinal Variables or Value = 1 for Dummy-Coded Responses*
Level of (in)security and anxiety	
mworrune	Worries about becoming unemployed (1 = very worried to 3 = not worried)
mjobloss	Likelihood that present job will be lost (1 = very unlikely to 5 = very likely)
mbecmune	Likelihood that he or she will become unemployed (1 = very unlikely to 5 = very likely)
mfindtuf	Difficulty in finding an equivalent job (1 = very easy to 5 = very difficult)
mlabxpor	Perception of functioning of government employment offices (1 = very well to 5 = very poorly)
Experiences with workplace changes	
mfirmdwn	Change in number employed at workplace (1 = increased a lot to 5 = decreased a lot)
mchngmac	There have been changes in machinery at the workplace (1 = yes)
mchngwrk	There have been machinery changes affecting own job (1 = yes)
mchngtsk	There have been changes in tasks assigned to respondent's job (1 = yes)
mlaidoff	Respondent has experienced being laid off from principal job at any time during the past 3 years (1 = yes)
Collectivist versus individualist attitudes for responsibility in the labor market	
dresungv	Believes that government is primarily responsible for unemployment (1 = yes)
dredungv	Believes that unemployment can be reduced by government action (1 = yes)
Labor relations and unions	
mfirmsiz	Size of respondent's workplace (1 = < 20 to 9 = 5,000+)
mbargunt	Respondent is a member of a bargaining unit (in Sweden of the Landsorganisationen I Sverige [LO]) or has a contract that is collectively bargained even if individual is not a member (1 = yes)
msomsay	Workers' say or influence in the implementation of technological changes in the workplace (1= much to 3 = no say)
mirgood	Opinion concerning workplace industrial relations (1 = very good to 5 = very bad)
Sociodemographic background factors	
age	Respondent's age category (1 = 15-16 to 7 = 55-64)
woman	Respondent is a woman (1 = yes)
bott2_5	Respondent is located (approximately) in the bottom two fifths of the respective country sample's income distribution (1 = yes)

several major differences between our two samples in terms of measures of labor market security (or insecurity) as well as a number of important control variables that potentially might help to explain differences in labor market flexibility.

Independent and Control Variables

Table 18.3 lists the major independent and control variables considered here, along with abbreviated versions of the questions that were asked in the surveys.[12] The variables are arranged in groups that correspond to different theoretic concerns.

The first group of five variables is intended to tap the respondents' level of security (or insecurity) and anxiety with respect to his or her employment prospects: *mworrune* (worries about becoming unemployed), *mjobloss* (likelihood that present job will be lost), *mbecmune* (likelihood that such a loss will lead to unemployment), *mfindtuf* (difficulty in finding an equivalent job), and *mlabxpor* (whether government employment offices are perceived as ineffective in helping people find job opportunities). These are the primary independent variables for the purpose of testing our second hypothesis.

The remaining items in Table 18.3 are intended to be control variables. Although we are primarily interested in the anxiety variables of the first group, we know that many other factors on which Canadians and Swedes differ might directly or indirectly affect their propensities to refuse to take a pay cut. Thus, for instance, the argument has in effect been that for any given level of change actually experienced, strong unions, social security, active labor market policies, and so on, generate higher or lower levels of anxiety, which, in turn, determine flexibility. However, should there be systematic differences between our samples in the amount of change workers have actually experienced themselves, then this might have a direct effect of its own on flexibility patterns. Hence, it is necessary to try and control for the most obvious of these. Similar reasoning justifies the inclusion of the other control variables discussed below.

The second series in Table 18.3 contains five variables intended to gauge the extent to which respondents have actually been exposed to change in their workplaces or have actually experienced various forms of change themselves: *mfirmdwn* (change in establishment's workforce), *mchngmac* (changes in machinery and equipment at the establishment), *mchngwrk* (changes in equipment for one's present job), *mchngtsk* (organizational changes in the way in which the job is done), and *mlaidoff* (respondent was laid off at some time in the past 3 years).

Our next two control variables are dummy-coded indicator variables that deal with collectivist (as opposed to individualist or fatalist) attitudes regarding responsibility for coping with employment (or unemployment): *dresungv* (government is primarily responsible for unemployment), and *dredungv* (government action can reduce unemployment).

Organizational aspects of employment and labor relations are measured by the next group of four variables: *mfirmsiz* (ordinal scale of the size of workplaces in which our respondents are employed), *mbargunt* (a dummy-coded indicator variable to measure whether an individual is covered by a contract negotiated by the LO in Sweden or any trade union in Canada), *msomsay* (an ordinal scale indicating the extent to which workers have a say in or influence the implementation of technological change), and *mirgood* (an ordinal assessment of labor-management relations at the plant level).

The final three variables provide sociodemographic background controls: *age* (ordinal scale of seven age groups between the ages of 15 and 64), *woman* (dummy code for the sex of the respondent), and *bott2_5* (individual's earnings are in the lower two fifths of the distribution).

CANADA-SWEDEN DIFFERENCES ON THE INDEPENDENT AND CONTROL VARIABLES

Table 18.4 provides the descriptive statistics and *t*-test results for the differences between the means of the two national samples on the independent and control variables just outlined. Many of the statistically significant differences are as one might expect from a general knowledge of the two countries. Canadians are more likely to expect to become unemployed in the near future than Swedes (mbecmune; $p = 0.089$) and are more prone to worry about the prospect (mworrune; $p = 0.000$). This may be partly because they have more experience with being laid off than Swedes (mlaidoff: 33.5% of Canadians compared to 19.5% of Swedes). Canadians also expect less from governments (dresungv and dredungv). By extension, they appear to favor more individual efforts in the fight against unemployment than the Swedes do.[13] Canadian blue-collar manufacturing workers are much less densely unionized than their Swedish counterparts (mbargunt),[14] and they feel that they have less say in managing the workplace than the Swedish workers do (msomsay).

Table 18.4 does offer a few minor surprises, however. For instance, it turns out that Swedes are just as likely to think that their present jobs are at risk in the near future as their Canadian counterparts are (mjobloss) and considerably more likely to think that it would be difficult to find an equivalent job if they lost their present one (mfindtuf). These results, no doubt, reflect the recent and unprecedented employment crisis in Swedish manufacturing.[15]

Somewhat surprisingly, also, a slightly higher proportion of Swedes than Canadians thought their country's employment offices did a poor job (mlabxpor) of finding work for the unemployed—although this may well be the product of higher Swedish expectations rather than worse actual performance. Also, contrary to the oft-repeated clichés of Sweden as the land of consensus and Canadian labor relations as chronically strife torn, about equal proportions of workers report that labor relations at their workplaces are very good or rather good (mirgood),[16] and the two country samples do not differ significantly on this *t* test.

Finally, there are some statistically significant differences on the workplace change and sociodemographic variables. Although these are not great or very surprising,[17] they suffice to justify controlling for them in any attempts to explain the differences found in willingness to accept a pay cut between the two samples.

To sum up then, there is enough evidence of difference in the degree of concern about labor market prospects between our Canadian and Swedish samples to render an attempt to test our second hypothesis feasible. At the same time, controlling for a number of possible confounding factors will be necessary.

MULTIVARIATE ANALYSES AND FINDINGS: LABOR MARKET SECURITY (OR INSECURITY) AND WAGE FLEXIBILITY (OR INFLEXIBILITY)

To what extent, then, does the relatively low level of Swedish workers' concern about their employment prospects account for their greater propensity to refuse a pay cut as compared to Canadians? Table 18.5 shows the results of a series of logistic response models, regressing mrfuscut on successive layers of the independent and control variables outlined above (and entered in that order), for a combined sample of Canadians and Swedes. Our primary interest here is in the contribution that the labor market security (or insecurity) variables make in accounting for the difference between the Swedish and Canadian responses with respect to refusal to take a pay cut to save one's job (mrfuscut; 1 = *refuse*; 0 = *all others*). Specifically, we want to see whether, and to what extent, the national difference, captured by a dummy variable labeled *swedish* (1 = *Swedish*; 0 = *Canadian*), diminishes in importance as other predictor variables are added to the model.[18] Below, we limit our discussion to the statistical significance of the raw logistic regression coefficients and make no attempt to exponentiate the values into probabilities. Because, as noted above, most of the variables are either ordinal or indicator dummies (i.e., coded 1 or 0), the size and statistical significance of these coefficients permit straightforward interpretation of their relative contribution also. We did not think it essential to compute any of the various pseudo-R^2 measures, but we do note the predictive efficacy of the various models (see Aldrich & Nelson, 1984; Menard, 1995).

Two features are immediately apparent in Table 18.5. First, as one would anticipate from the bivariate analysis in the preceding section, swedish is by far the single most important determinant of the refusal to accept a pay cut (mrfuscut). Second, the statistically significant difference between Canadians and Swedes on the mrfuscut variable, reported in Table 18.1, re-

TABLE 18.4 Descriptive Statistics and t Tests for Independent Variables That Theories Argue Should Account for the Variance in Flexibility (or inflexibility)

	Canadian Sample (N = 399)			*Swedish Sample (N = 697)*						
	Mean	*SD*	*SE*	*Mean*	*SD*	*SE*	*Difference*	*Variance*	*t Test*	*p*
Level of (in)security and anxiety										
mworrune*	2.293	0.805	0.040	2.515	0.652	0.025	–0.223	unequal	–4.983	0.000
mjobloss	2.374	1.402	0.070	2.386	1.321	0.050	–0.011	equal	–0.134	0.893
mbecmune	2.394	1.488	0.074	2.307	1.321	0.050	0.087	unequal	0.087	0.314
mfindtuf*	4.013	1.299	0.065	4.313	0.975	0.037	–0.299	unequal	–4.007	0.000
mlabxpor	3.385	0.978	0.049	3.481	0.968	0.037	–0.096	equal	–1.572	0.116
Experiences with workplace changes										
mfirmdwn*	3.212	1.261	0.063	3.752	1.133	0.043	–0.539	unequal	–7.067	0.000
mchngmac	0.589	0.493	0.025	0.531	0.499	0.019	–0.058	unequal	1.863	0.063
mchngwrk*	0.438	0.497	0.025	0.336	0.473	0.022	0.102	unequal	3.341	0.001
mchngtsk*	0.374	0.484	0.024	0.303	0.460	0.017	0.071	unequal	2.384	0.017
mlaidoff*	0.335	0.473	0.024	0.195	0.397	0.015	0.140	unequal	4.988	0.000
Collectivist versus individualist attitudes for responsibility in the labor market										
dresungv*	0.642	0.480	0.024	0.852	0.355	0.013	–0.210	unequal	–7.635	0.000
dredungv*	0.586	0.493	0.025	0.712	0.453	0.017	–0.126	unequal	–4.174	0.000
Labor relations and unions										
mfirmsiz	3.680	2.230	0.112	3.917	2.145	0.081	–0.236	equal	–1.730	0.084
mbargunt*	0.642	0.480	0.024	0.920	0.272	0.010	–0.278	unequal	–10.640	0.000
msomsay*	2.312	0.736	0.037	2.115	0.653	0.025	0.197	unequal	4.433	0.000
mirgood	2.294	1.235	0.062	2.309	1.069	0.041	–0.015	unequal	–0.199	0.843
Sociodemographic background factors										
age	4.842	1.074	0.054	4.852	1.222	0.046	–0.009	unequal	–0.140	0.889
woman*	0.150	0.360	0.018	0.220	0.420	0.016	–0.071	unequal	–2.988	0.003
bott2_5	0.410	0.493	0.025	0.352	0.478	0.018	0.059	unequal	1.915	0.056

NOTE: See Table 18.3 for descriptions of variables.
* $p \leq .01$.

mains large (indeed virtually unchanged, in terms of the difference in predicted values) and strong, even in the presence of a variety of factors that theoretically should help account for the difference between the two countries as we move from Model 1 (the constant and country dummy) to Model 6 (constant, country, level of anxiety, and all of our control variables: experiences with change, individualist/collectivist attitudes, labor-management factors, and socio-demographic characteristics). Third, note that the extent of worry about the prospect of becoming unemployed (mworrune), perhaps the variable most straightforwardly measuring anxiety about labor market prospects, is, except in one of the equations, the next strongest variable after swedish. However, it remains a distant second to it even in the final regression model (where mirgood has a larger and more statistically significant coefficient).

TABLE 18.5 Logistic Regression Models for the Swedish-Canadian Sample

	Model 1	*Model 2*	*Model 3*	*Model 4*	*Model 5*	*Model 6*
Constant	−1.4744****	−2.4862****	−3.0972****	−3.3032****	−4.2148****	−4.9332****
	(.1285) (.0000)	(.5112) (.0000)	(.5607) (.0000)	(.5811) (.0000)	(.6353) (.0000)	(.6993) (.0000)
swedish	1.0221****	1.0000****	0.9555****	0.9332****	0.9997****	1.0980****
	(.1502) (.0000)	(.1545) (.0000)	(.1602) (.0000)	(.1653) (.0000)	(.1771) (.0000)	(.1807) (.0000)
mworrune		0.2557*	0.3246**	0.3434**	0.3970***	0.3562**
		(.115) (.0218)	(.1141) (.0045)	(.1151) (.0028)	(.1179) (.0008)	(.1191) (.0028)
mjobloss		0.0002	−0.0230	−0.0108	−0.0318	−0.0258
		(.0941) (.9979)	(.0946) (.8078)	(.0945) (.9090)	(.0963) (.7410)	(.0964) (.7893)
mbecmune		0.1330	0.0960	0.0881	0.0680	0.0603
		(.0919) (.1477)	(.0928) (.3013)	(.0925) (.3409)	(.0943) (.4707)	(.0946) (.5235)
mfindtuf		−0.0601	−0.0596	−0.0674	−0.0509	−0.0685
		(.0627) (.3378)	(.0635) (.3478)	(.0637) (.2902)	(.0654) (.4367)	(.0669) (.3060)
mlabxpor		0.0969	0.0873	0.0920	0.0679	0.0908
		(.0693) (.1620)	(.0700) (.2123)	(.0704) (.1910)	(.0716) (.3430)	(.0731) (.2144)
mfirmdwn			0.1704**	0.1709**	0.1500*	0.1140
			(.0610) (.0052)	(.1709) (.0053)	(.0632) (.0177)	(.0645) (.0769)
mchngmac			−0.1930	−0.1862	−0.1445	−0.1402
			(.1596) (.2265)	(.1602) (.2450)	(.1643) (.3793)	(.1656) (.3973)
mchngwrk			0.0088	−0.0149	0.0121	0.0312
			(.1642) (.9574)	(.1649) (.9282)	(.1672) (.9422)	(.1683) (.8529)
mchngtsk			0.1207	0.1093	0.1508	0.1548
			(.1509) (.4237)	(.1515) (.4708)	(.1548) (.3298)	(.1562) (.3219)
mlaidoff			0.3613*	0.3662*	0.4087*	0.4536**
			(.1663) (.0298)	(.1669) (.0283)	(.1702) (.0163)	(.1724) (.0085)
dresungv				−0.1268	−0.1670	−0.1496
				(.1752) (.4693)	(.1795) (.3524)	(.1821) (.4112)

An important consideration here is that the statistical weight of mworrune in accounting for mrfuscut actually increases in the presence of the other variables included in this analysis, up to the inclusion of the sociodemographic factors in Model 6, when the raw logistic regression coefficient for mworrune reduced slightly as compared to Model 5. This could be interpreted as indicating that one major motivation for declaring oneself willing to take a pay cut in Sweden as well as in Canada is fear. The effects of all other labor market security (or insecurity) variables are negligible (i.e., not statistically significant).

Thus, relative lack of confidence about one's labor market prospects, at least as measured by mworrune (ordinal scale), does seem to make one more reluctant to refuse a pay cut both in Canada and in Sweden.[19] But, to what extent do the differences in anxiety about one's own labor market prospects help to explain the difference between Swedish and Canadian workers' will-

TABLE 18.5 Continued

	Model 1	*Model 2*	*Model 3*	*Model 4*	*Model 5*	*Model 6*
dredungv				0.4161**	0.4061**	0.3872*
				(.1521) (.0062)	(.1551) (.0089)	(.1563) (.0132)
mfirmsiz					–0.0906**	–0.0798*
				(.0347) (.0090)	(.0354) (.0242)	
mbargunt					0.2402	0.1767
				(.2191) (.2729)	(.2212) (.4242)	
msomsay					0.2441*	0.2498*
					(.1113) (.0468)	(.1124) (.0263)
mirgood					0.2142**	0.2452***
					(.0655) (.0011)	(.0667) (.0002)
age						0.1710**
						(.0618) (.0056)
woman						–0.4560*
						(.1967) (.0204)
bott2_5						0.0951
						(.1626) (.5584)
Predictive efficiency	68.50%	68.68%	69.04%	69.41%	70.96%	71.60%
–2 Log likelihood	1315.479	1303.833	1288.323	1280.577	1253.298	1240.752
Goodness of fit	1096.329	1090.826	1088.280	1098.306	1116.085	1114.827
Model χ^2	50.725	11.637	15.510	7.745	27.280	12.546
df	1	5	5	2	4	3
Significance	.0000	.0401	.0084	.0208	.0000	.0057

NOTE: N = 1,096; dependent variable = wrfuscut; independent variables interval, ordinal, or indicator dummies as per Table 18.3; standard errors and exact p values in parentheses below regression coefficients; initial log likelihood function = 1366.195; p values based on Wald statistic: $W_k^2 = (b_k/\text{s.e. of } b_k)^2$ following a chi-square distribution.
* $p < .05$; ** $p < .01$; *** $p < .001$; **** $p < .0001$.

ingness to accept wage reductions when their jobs are at risk? In other words, by how much does the country difference in refusal to take a pay cut decline when one controls for such anxiety? To see this, we need to look at the impact of the inclusion of the other variables on the effect of swedish on mrfuscut. If the Swedes' relative lack of worries about their labor market prospects is really behind their greater reluctance to accept pay flexibility, then the effect of swedish should decrease considerably as we control for variables purporting to measure that lack of worries. But, as Table 18.5 shows, controlling for all the anxiety variables (Model 2) and an increasing number of control factors (Model 3 through Model 6) has virtually no impact at all on the effect of swedish. After all these controls, the difference between Swedes and Canadians in their refusal to take a pay cut is just as large and significant as it was before. In addition, the predictive efficiency of Model 1 (constant and country dummy) is 69.50%, whereas that of

Model 6 (which adds 19 additional variables) is only 71.60%.

Our second hypothesis, namely, that the difference in willingness to take a pay cut is to a considerable degree explicable by the difference in anxiety about labor market prospects, seems to be roundly refuted by our evidence. Swedes clearly are more likely to refuse to take a cut than Canadians. They are also less worried about the alternatives available to them. But, as the raw logistic regression coefficients indicate, it is not this relative carefree attitude on the part of the Swedes that explains the difference in attitudes toward pay cuts.

The most complete regression model is presented in Model 6. It tells the following story. Swedish workers are more likely than their Canadian counterparts to refuse a pay cut. This is true even though being worried about unemployment reduces this propensity. Workers who believe government labor exchanges do not work well and those who work in firms that have been downsizing or have themselves been laid off recently appear to become more rigid in the face of potential pay cuts. The same is true of older workers. Women seem more flexible than men, having some say in technological changes in the workplace is almost as important as fear and anxiety in reducing the probability that workers will refuse a pay cut, and good local industrial relations is, in fact, more statistically significant. Yet, none of this explains away any of the original country difference in propensity to reject a pay cut.

CONCLUSION

Let us briefly recapitulate. There is a widely held belief that a strong sense of security with respect to employment and earnings prospects stiffens workers' resistance to wage flexibility, in particular of the downward variety. On the basis of this assumption and some knowledge of the very different labor market regimes characteristic of Canada and Sweden, we formulated two predictive hypotheses with respect to willingness to accept a wage cut to save one's job among workers in these two countries. Our first hypothesis was that Canadian workers should be considerably more willing to take a pay cut to save their jobs than Swedish workers. Second, we hypothesized that the difference in willingness to take a pay cut between the two countries' workers should, to some considerable degree, be explained by the differences between them in terms of labor market security (or insecurity).

Our data, taken from samples of Canadian and Swedish manual manufacturing workers, provided strong support for the first hypothesis but very little for the second. We found a considerable difference in the predicted direction between Canadians and Swedes in the propensity to refuse to take a pay cut to save one's job. We also found some evidence that labor market insecurity leads to greater willingness to accept such a cut. However, none of the difference between Canadian and Swedish workers' willingness to take a pay cut was explained by the difference in the levels of employment and earnings security (or insecurity) of the two samples. Nor is the difference explained away to any appreciable degree by a host of other possibly relevant variables on which the two samples differed significantly.

In view of these negative findings, one is tempted, however reluctantly, to look for more macro level explanations of the difference between Swedes and Canadians on this score. One such explanation has to do with the general sociopolitical culture of the two countries. According to many observers (e.g., Einhorn & Logue, 1989; Esping-Andersen, 1985; Heclo & Madsen, 1987; Milner, 1989; Smucker & van den Berg, 1991), the long reign of social democracy and the dominance of the LO have had a profound effect on Swedish norms and values, generally shifting the entire political spectrum toward the Left.

A sizable comparative literature on workers' attitudes, with respect to political, economic, and social issues, tends to confirm that Swedish workers have absorbed the social democratic image of society (Castles, 1978) to a significantly greater extent than workers in any other Western country (see, e.g., Korpi 1978, 1983; Scase, 1977; Svallfors, 1993, 1995; van den Berg & Szulkin, 1994; Wright, 1985; Wright & Cho, 1992; Wright & Shin, 1988). In fact, even the Swedish elite seems to have been somewhat infected with the sociopolitical values preached by the Swedish labor movement (see Verba et al., 1987).

In light of this, one could interpret the refusal to accept a pay cut to save one's job as a part of this broader social democratic image of society absorbed by Swedish workers over many years of social democratic dominance in Swedish politics. In other words, a sizable proportion of Swedish manufacturing workers may simply have come to take it for granted that no worker should have to put up with pay cuts to save his or her job as a matter of general principle, quite irrespective of their own individual labor market situations.

We are not in a position to test directly this alternative explanation here. But, there are some indications that render it at least plausible. First, as noted, there is the Swedish labor unions' long-standing opposition to pay cuts as a way of subsidizing inefficient companies. Second, there is some indirect evidence in our data to suggest that there may be something to this interpretation. In our preliminary analyses in preparation for our logistic regressions, we found that some of the variables in the collectivist versus individualist attitudes group, which were omitted from the present analyses to avoid problems of multicollinearity (i.e., the variables most obviously related to the alleged social democratic view of society), to some degree share variance with our Swedish dummy in accounting for mrfuscut.

Such rather circumstantial evidence does not, of course, settle the matter, nor does it tell us anything about the magnitude of the effect of general political culture. But it does suggest some fruitful avenues for further research. For instance, a comparison between Sweden and other European countries, many of which have similarly highly developed income and employment security programs without the long-standing political dominance of social democracy, should help to sort out the effects of political culture from those of labor market security (or insecurity).

Also, other forms of work-related flexibility, such as willingness to retrain, adopt new technology, change jobs, and so on might be compared. Some of these are surely less subject to major differences in general political culture than others, at least among the most advanced industrialized countries.

Finally, some caveats seem to be in order. Most obviously, our data refer to what people say they would do under hypothetical circumstances rather than to what they actually do. Clearly, any direct extrapolation from the former to the latter is problematic. However, data on actual pay cuts in conjunction with individual-level data on attitudes and personal concerns, such as those we want to examine, are rather hard to come by. Moreover, as Blanchflower (1991) has shown, there is some empirical evidence linking such attitudes and concerns with actual pay level, even when controlling for a host of human capital and contextual variables.

Another possible objection might be that we failed to tap the right attitudes or that our measures of them are flawed in one way or another. Perhaps some other set of determinants would succeed in explaining the difference between Canadian and Swedish attitudes toward wage flexibility. Perhaps our security (or insecurity) variables do not really gauge the true extent of personal anxiety about one's prospects. We certainly would not rule out either of these possibilities or many others, and we look forward to receiving suggestions along these lines. Until we do, however, our main findings stand. In particular, the fact that none of a number of putative measures of labor market security (or insecurity) helps to explain the large difference in resistance to pay cuts in our two countries seems to us rather a robust one. It certainly justifies casting about for explanations of wage rigidities other than those now most widely on offer. We have suggested local factors, such as the quality of industrial relations, as well as global factors, such as a country's overall political culture, as possible alternatives. Further, cross-national comparisons, involving countries with different political traditions, social security systems, and industrial relations, would be needed to test these as well as lend support to our main findings.

NOTES

1. For a forceful argument along these lines with respect to regional differences within the United States, see Crandall (1993).

2. To the best of our knowledge, no one has ever suggested that a sense of security would lead workers to resist pay rises.

3. Actually, the research was designed to test two alternative theories of the relationship between labor market security (or insecurity) and resistance to workplace and employment change, one underlying the neoclassical economic approach referred to here and the other supporting a more institutionalist approach that has much influenced Swedish policymakers and labor movement theorists (see van den Berg, Furåker, & Johansson, 1997; cf. Tilton, 1991). But, with respect to the issue of wage flexibility addressed in this chapter, because the two approaches yield quite similar predictions, we do not elaborate on our comparison of them in any detail here.

4. Until 1992, postwar average annual unemployment rates had never exceeded 3.5%. But since then, Sweden has suffered its worst economic crisis since the Great Depression, with unemployment rates soaring to more than 8%, even as an additional 4% to 5% of the labor force has been employed in various labor market programs (mostly training and relief work or subsidized jobs). The data we report on in this chapter were gathered in 1993, just as the current crisis had set in. Although this may have influenced our findings somewhat, we assume that they still mostly reflect Sweden's historically highly secure labor market conditions. We also have parallel data collected in Sweden in 1991. Initial comparisons between these and the 1993 findings support our assumption. In future work, we will report in detail on the extent to which the Swedish economic crisis appears to have affected Swedish workers' attitudes.

5. Despite the powerful pressures in the opposite direction generated by the recent serious crisis in the Swedish economy, this remains official Landsorganisationen I Sverige (LO) policy (for a relatively recent restatement, see "Say No to Wage Reductions," 1992).

6. LO is the powerful blue-collar union central of which more than 90% of Swedish blue-collar workers are members and which has traditionally had close ties with and a strong influence over the long-ruling social democratic party.

7. The original idea was that workers could be made to move more readily between specific jobs and employers as long as they could be assured of some more or less equivalent employment. This principle of employment but not job security was to some extent abandoned with the introduction of the job security legislation of the early 1970s (see Smucker & van den Berg, 1992, p. 29).

8. Although the framers of the Swedish Model shared the basic assumption about the relation between labor market security (or insecurity) and wage flexibility examined here with their neoclassical counterparts, they rejected the related claim that wage flexibility was the only or best way to ensure efficient allocation (or reallocation) of labor. Quite to the contrary, based on their more institutionalist analysis of labor markets, they deliberately set out to forgo wage flexibility to elicit other, and in their view more important, forms of flexibility from Swedish workers (see also van den Berg, Furåker, & Johansson, 1997; Note 3 above).

9. According to the specifications provided by the Statistiska Centralbyrån (SCB), the Swedish sample is representative of the desired subgroup. Statistics Canada (StatsCan) provided a weighting factor that we have used to ensure that the Canadian sample can be considered representative of the blue-collar manufacturing workforce at the time of the survey. We modified the Canadian weighting factor so it would redistribute the relative value of the observations in a nonreplicative fashion, so as not to change the value of *N*. Thus, this procedure can be considered as neutral with regard to statistical inference. There is some controversy surrounding the use of fractional or nonreplicative weights in the interpretation of tests of statistical inference. SPSS and SYSTAT, two widely used statistical packages in social science research that are owned by the same company, take completely different stands on the issue, with the former allowing fractional values for weighting variables and the latter accepting only integer values for replicative weighting of cases. We have used the former statistical package and approach. For complete details on the weighting procedures, contact the authors (see also, SPSS, 1990, pp. 720-721; SYSTAT, 1989, p. 52).

10. Canada has a much higher proportion of service workers in private-sector wholesale and retail trade than Sweden, whereas Swedish service workers are much more heavily concentrated in public-sector community, social, and personal services. One would certainly expect the labor market experiences, concerns, and attitudes of these two types of service workers to be very different indeed. Consequently, their uncontrolled inclusion in the sort of analysis we are attempting here is likely to seriously confound the results. We plan to do additional analyses of flexibility and its related components dealing with other parts of the labor forces of these two countries.

11. The results reported here on the basis of this attenuated sample are virtually identical to those obtained in the analysis with all 1,984 cases. Of course, we tested for the effects of missing information and ran our analysis strategies with different case-selection procedures. When we treated "don't know" and "no opinion" cases as valid, we placed them either in the reference group for dichotomized variables or in the neutral category for ordinal scales. For interval variables, we employed mean substitution (or left such cases out of the analysis). We also performed these analyses excluding all nonresponses for only the dependent variable but treating the independent variables as in the full sample case. The results for this subsample of 1,786 cases were, once again, exactly the same as in the present analysis. In short, we feel that this consistency in the findings indicates that we could have used a more case-preserving selection method because these are obviously robust relationships.

12. A great deal of effort had gone into translating and back-translating the questions so that they would have the same valence in the three languages of the surveys: English, French, and Swedish. Moreover, in some cases, we had to make compromises on the actual form of the questions to obtain the agreement of the statistical agencies to ask the questions. In short, we are aware that the questions contain many shortcomings, but we are reasonably confident that we have done as well as was possible, given the time and budget constraints of this international research project, in obtaining meaningful and truly comparable responses from the two countries' samples. A copy of the questionnaire is available from the authors on request.

13. Somewhat surprisingly, about one fifth of both samples are rather fatalistic with regard to this question, believing either that "there is not much anyone can do about unemployment" or electing to endorse none of the alternatives offered. Again, perhaps recent events had already begun to take their toll on the traditional Swedish confidence in the government's ability to effectively keep unemployment at minimal levels. The data are not shown in the table but are available on request.

14. Because we restricted Swedish union membership to affiliation with the LO only, the Swedish unionization rate of more than 92% may actually slightly underestimate the true rate of unionization there.

15. This interpretation is supported by a comparison with an earlier survey of Swedish manufacturing workers taken just before the onslaught of the present crisis (see van den Berg, Furåker and Johansson, 1997, chap. 8).

16. Swedish workers do not necessarily have greater confidence in union leadership than Canadians. In fact, based on additional survey questions not analyzed here, Swedish workers are more likely to feel that national union leaders are primarily concerned with "getting along with politicians and employers" and less likely to think their primary concern is with "looking after members' interests" than Canadian workers. On the other hand, and perhaps somewhat more surprisingly (but, see Kjellberg, 1983), Swedish workers are more inclined to believe local union leaders are primarily concerned with looking after their members' interest (as opposed to the country's long-term interests or getting along with employers and politicians) than Canadian workers (see also Masi, van den Berg, Smith, & Smucker, 1995). These data are available on request and will form the basis of a future article.

17. The fact that slightly fewer Swedes than Canadians end up in the bottom two fifths of their respective earnings distributions is, of course, not the result of Swedish egalitarianism but merely a statistical artifact. For our earnings data, we had to rely on the existing methods of the national statistical agencies in each country. This provided a series of categories that proved somewhat difficult to manage given exchange rate or purchasing power parity equivalents. Therefore, we decided to use a relative position measure and to dummy code the bottom two fifths of the earners in each sample. However, as indicated by the mean values, the coding schemes meant that a dummy value of 1 had to be assigned to about 43% of Canadians but to only 37% of Swedes.

18. We also carried out analyses of variance with a multiple classification analysis on these data and arrived at substantially the same conclusions as presented here. Given that the split in proportions on the criterion variable were not as extreme as 80:20, such conformity in findings is hardly surprising. Although the multiple classification analysis (MCA) interpretation (deviations from the grand mean, presented for dummy variables as percentages) is very straightforward for the purposes of the hypotheses at hand, it is not as frequently employed in the literature as logistic regression of the sort presented in the text. On the advice of one of *Work and Occupations'* reviewers, we therefore opted for the latter instead.

19. This conclusion is also supported by the results of the separate ordinary least squares (OLS) and logistic regression equations and MCAs that we ran on the two national samples (data not shown here). In addition, the separate analyses indicate that the effect of worries about becoming unemployed is appreciably stronger in Canada where institutional supports are noticeably less well developed.

REFERENCES

Adnett, N. (1989). *Labour market policy*. London: Longman.

Aldrich, J. H., & Nelson, F. D. (1984). *Linear probability, logit, and probit models* (Sage University Paper Series on Quantitative Applications in the Social Sciences, Series No. 07-045). Beverly Hills, CA: Sage.

Bélanger, J., Edwards, P. K., & Haiven, L. (Eds.). (1994). *Workplace industrial relations and the global challenge*. Ithaca, NY: Cornell University Press.

Blanchflower, D. G. (1991). Fear, unemployment, and pay flexibility. *Economic Journal, 101,* 483-496.

Bluestone, B., & Harrison, B. (1982). *The deindustrialization of America: Plant closings, community abandonment, and the dismantling of basic industry.* New York: Basic Books.

Casey, B., Dragendorf, R., Heering, W., & John, G. (1989). Temporary employment in Great Britain and the Federal Republic of Germany: An overview. *International Labour Review, 128*(4), 449-466.

Castles, F. G. (1978). *The social democratic image of society: A study of the achievements and origins of Scandinavian social democracy in comparative perspective.* London: Routledge & Kegan Paul.

A chart-breaking affair. (1995, May 20). *The Economist,* p. 70.

Crandall, R. W. (1993). *Manufacturing on the move.* Washington, DC: Brookings Institution.

Drache, D., & Gertler, M. S. (1991). *The new era of global competition.* Montreal,: McGill-Queen's University Press.

Einhorn, E. S., & Logue, J. (1989). *Modern welfare states: Politics and policies in social democratic Scandinavia.* New York: Praeger.

Esping-Andersen, G. (1985). *Politics against markets.* Princeton, NJ: Princeton University Press.

Esping-Andersen, G., & Korpi, W. (1987). From poor relief to institutional welfare states: The development of Scandinavian social policy. In R. Erikson, E. J. Hansen, S. Ringen, & H. Uusitalo (Eds.), *The Scandinavian model: Welfare states and welfare research* (pp. 39-47). Armonk, NY: M. E. Sharpe.

Forslund, A. (1994). Wage setting at the firm level—insider versus outsider forces. *Oxford Economic Papers, 46,* 245-261.

Graafland, J. J. (1989). Can hysteresis explain different labour market operations between Europe and the United States? *Applied Economics, 21*(1), 95-111.

Heclo, H., & Madsen, H. (1987). *Policy and politics in Sweden: Principled pragmatism.* Philadelphia: Temple University Press.

Johnson, A. F., McBride, S., & Smith, P. J. (Eds.). (1994). *Continuities and discontinuities: The political economy of social welfare and labour market policy in Canada.* Toronto, Canada: University of Toronto Press.

Kjellberg, A. (1983). *Facklig organisering i tolv länder [Trade union organization in twelve countries].* Lund, Sweden: Arkiv.

Korpi, W. (1978). *The working class in welfare capitalism: Work, unions, and politics in Sweden.* London: Routledge & Kegan Paul.

Korpi, W. (1983). *The democratic class struggle.* London: Routledge & Kegan Paul.

Lindbeck, A., & Snower, D. J. (1988). *The insider-outsider theory of employment and unemployment.* Cambridge: MIT Press.

Martin, A. (1984). The shaping of the Swedish model. In P. Gourevitch, A. Martin, G. Ross, C. Allen, S. Bornstein, & A. Markovits (Eds.), *Unions and economic crisis: Britain, West Germany, and Sweden* (pp. 190-359). London: Allen and Unwin.

Masi, A. C. (1989). Deindustrialization, economic performance, and industrial policy: British and American theories applied to Italy. In R. E. Folgesong & J. D. Wolfe (Eds.), *The politics of economic adjustment: Pluralism, corporatism, and privatization* (pp. 127-152). New York: Greenwood.

Masi, A. C., & Del Balso, M. (1991). Restructuring: The experiences of Italy and Canada. In R. Cagiano de Azevedo (Ed.), *Le Società in transizione: Italiani ed Italo-Canadesi negli anni ottanta* [Societies in transition: Italians and Italian-Canadians in the 1980s] (pp. 451-372). Milan: Franco Angeli.

Masi, A. C., van den Berg, A., Smith, M. R., & Smucker, J. (1995, August). *Technological change and industrial relations: A comparison of the Swedish and Canadian patterns in three industries.* Paper presented at the annual meeting of the American Sociological Association, Washington, DC.

McBride, S. (1992). *Not working: State, unemployment, and neoconservatism in Canada.* Toronto, Canada: University of Toronto Press.

Menard, S. (1995). *Applied logistic regression analysis* (Sage University Paper Series on Quantitative Applications in the Social Sciences, Series No. 07-106). Thousand Oaks, CA: Sage.

Milner, H. (1989). *Sweden: Social democracy in practice.* Oxford, UK: Oxford University Press.

Muszynski, L. (1985). The politics of labour market policy. In G. B. Doern (Ed.), *The politics of economic policy* (pp. 251-305). Toronto: University of Toronto Press.

Noponen, H., Graham, J., & Markusen, A. R. (Eds.). (1993). *Trading industries/trading regions.* New York: Guilford.

The OECD and jobs: Adapt and survive. (1994, June 11). *The Economist,* p. 64.

Öhman, B. (1974). *Landsorganisationen I Sverige (LO) and labour market policy since the second world war.* Stockholm: Prisma.

Organization for Economic Cooperation and Development [OECD]. (1994). *The OECD jobs study: Evidence and explanations: Part II. The adjustment potential of the labour market.* Geneva, Switzerland: Author.

Osterman, P. (1988). *Employment futures: Reorganization, dislocation, and public policy.* Oxford, UK: Oxford University Press.

Piore, M., & Sabel, C. (1984). *The second industrial divide.* New York: Basic Books.

Porter, M. E. (1991). *Canada at the crossroads: The reality of a new competitive environment.* Ottawa: Government of Canada and the Business Council on National Issues.

Ramaswamy, R. (1992). Wage bargaining institutions, adaptability, and structural change: The Swedish experience. *Journal of Economic Issues, 26*(4), 1041-1061.

Rehn, G. (1984). *Cooperation between the government and workers' and employers' organizations on labour market policy in Sweden.* Stockholm: The Swedish Institute.

Say no to wage reductions! (1992, February 14). *LO Tidningen*, p. 2.

Scase, R. (1977). *Social democracy in capitalist society: Working-class politics in Britain and Sweden.* London: Croom Helm.

Smith, M. R., Masi, A C., van den Berg, A., & Smucker, J. (1995). External flexibility in Sweden and Canada. A three industry comparison. *Work, Employment, and Society, 9*(4), 689-718.

Smucker, J., & van den Berg, A. (1991). Some evidence of the effects of labour market policies on workers' attitudes toward change in Canada and Sweden. *Canadian Journal of Sociology, 16*(1), 51-74.

Smucker, J., & van den Berg, A. (1992). Labor markets and government interventions: A comparison of Canadian and Swedish labor market policies. *International Journal of Contemporary Sociology, 29*(1-2), 9-46.

SPSS, Inc. (1990). *SPSS reference guide.* Chicago: Author.

Stafford, B. (1989). De-industrialization in advanced economies. *Cambridge Journal of Economics, 13,* 541-554.

Svallfors, S. (1993). Dimensions of inequality: A comparison of attitudes in Sweden and Britain. *European Sociological Review, 9,* 267-287.

Svallfors, S. (Ed.). (1995). *In the eye of the beholder: Opinions on welfare and justice in comparative perspective.* Umeå, Sweden: Impello Säljsupport.

SYSTAT, Inc. (1989). *SYSTAT: The system for statistics for the PC.* Evanston, IL: Author.

Tilton, T. (1991). *The political theory of Swedish social democracy: Through the welfare state to socialism.* Oxford, UK: Clarendon.

van den Berg, A., Furåker, B., & Johansson, L. (1997). *Labour market regimes and patterns of flexibility: A Canadian-Swedish comparison.* Lund, Sweden: Arkiv.

van den Berg, A., & Smucker, J. (1992). Labor markets and government interventions: A comparison of Canadian and Swedish labor market policies. *International Journal of Contemporary Sociology, 29*(1-2), 9-46.

van den Berg, A., & Szulkin, R. (1994). Sweden: Still the model? In A. Gottlieb, E. Yuchtman-Yaar, & B. Strümpel (Eds.), *Socioeconomic change and individual adaptation: Comparing East and West* (pp. 159-192). Greenwich, CT: JAI.

Verba, S., Kelman, S., Orren, G. R., Miyake, I., Watanuki, J., Kabsahima, I., & Ferree, G. D., Jr. (1987). *Elites and the idea of equality: A comparison of Japan, Sweden, and the United States.* Cambridge, MA: Harvard University Press.

Wright, E. O. (1985). *Classes.* London: Verso.

Wright, E. O., & Cho, D. (1992). State employment, class location, and ideological orientation: A comparative analysis of the United States and Sweden. *Politics and Society, 20*(2), 167-196.

Wright, E. O., & Shin, K. Y. (1988). Temporality and class analysis: A comparative study of the effects of class trajectory and class structure on class consciousness in Sweden and the United States. *Sociological Theory, 6*(1), 58-84.

Globalization and International Labor Organizing

A World-System Perspective

TERRY BOSWELL
DIMITRIS STEVIS

Considering . . . that the emancipation of labour is neither a local nor a national, but a social problem, embracing all countries in which modern society exists, . . . this International Association and all societies and individuals adhering to it, will acknowledge truth, justice, and morality, as the basis of their conduct towards each other, and towards all men, without regard to color, creed, or nationality.

—From "Inaugural Address and Provisional Rules of the International Working Men's Association" by Karl Marx, 1864

More than 130 years after the founding of the First International, the benefits of transnational organization are greater than ever, and increasing. Yet, the unity of political purpose and shared vision of a better world among workers and other progressive forces are perhaps at an all-time low. Why is this? The full answer is long and complex but one key reason is certain: Success for progressive movements has largely come from compelling states to enforce equal standards and to enact programs that raise standards. Although most organizing takes place at work or in the community, rather than in politics, labor movements require a state that can fairly enforce contracts and spread benefits to the unorganized. The national state, however, has lost efficacy with the increase in neoliberal world integration and lost legitimacy as its programs falter. As the state's ability to manage its share of the world economy declines, movements that rely on state power suffer as well. Few who loathe government or think it incompetent will rally behind those dedicated to expanding state programs.

Four factors—world market integration, decline of the welfare state, flexible specialization, and emerging forms of multistate governance—pose major challenges for labor movements. In the first part of this chapter, we overview these challenges from a world-system perspective (Chase-Dunn, 1989; Wallerstein, 1974), informed by historical structuralism (Cox, 1987). This perspective starts with viewing the world economy as the unit of analysis, which has its own systemic trends and cycles that are discernable over the long term. The world's major inequality is between the industrial core in North America, Western Europe, and Japan, and the underdeveloped periphery of the core's

From *Work and Occupations,* Vol. 24, No. 3, August 1995, pp. 288-308. Reprinted by permission.

former colonies, with an industrializing semiperiphery in between. This perspective tells us that transnational organizing and international politics are necessary to any solution to labor's woes. As the decline of labor union strength is intertwined with the decline of the welfare state, then its revival must be found in an international labor politics that contests labor's role in the newly emerging forms of global and regional governance.[1] In the second part of this chapter, we profile the limitations and possibilities of international labor politics, focusing on North America. We conclude with an outline of prospects and a set of suggestions for further research.

GLOBAL ECONOMIC INTEGRATION AND THE WELFARE STATE

The opening statement above from the most prominent international labor organization of the 19th century embodies two different progressive agendas; liberty and equality (with solidarity being a source of both). Although the International played but a small role, in the 130 years since its founding, the global trend has been of working-class success in both agendas (Rueschemeyer, Stephens, & Stephens, 1992). One of core labor's major successes was in delivering the welfare state (Esping-Andersen, 1990). By setting a national floor on living standards, the welfare state shifted labor market competition away from lower wages and toward greater productivity. Following World War II, rapidly increasing technological and human capital productivity in the core countries paid for both high wages for industrial workers and a slowly rising national floor.

Labor movements were crucial to the development of the welfare state (Hicks, 1988), and the extent of success is clear when compared to the rapacious market despotism that characterized the 19th century. Through state enforcement of welfare, labor movements, by which workers pursue their political interests in labor-affiliated parties and civic organizations as well as in unions, have succeeded in raising living standards for all workers more than unions succeeded in raising wages through membership. In fact, success has been sufficient to forestall revolutionary socialism in favor of reform wherever strong labor movements can make the state guarantee a class compromise (Boswell & Dixon, 1993; Przeworski, 1985). The problem for the 21st century is that market despotism is making a rather impressive comeback.

During the last quarter of the 20th century, the welfare side of the progressive agenda came under increasing attack and experienced steady reversal (Cox, 1987; The Group of Lisbon, 1995). The inefficacy of the welfare state has its source in the remarkable increase in the pace of world integration, or "globalization," and associated industrial restructuring that has occurred over the last few decades. With globalization has come a neoliberal world order in which economic growth and welfare states are increasingly at odds. Manifestations of this conflict are evident in stagnant wages, high unemployment, industrial transformation, government deficits—and declining unions. Despite wide national differences in politics and culture, unions declined in nearly every core country in the 1980s and early 1990s, and scattered evidence from the semiperiphery and periphery reported declines outside the newly industrializing countries (Galenson, 1994, chap. 1).[2]

From a world-system perspective, world integration is a continuous and cumulative process of at least 500 years duration. However, the pace of this integrative process has accelerated markedly since the mid-1970s as a global response, and a solution, to an uneven and stagnant world economy. The world economy has gone through long phases of stagnation ("K-waves"), the solution to which are new social structures of accumulation (Gordon, Edwards, & Reich, 1982; Kondratieff, 1926/1979). Each solution is different. The current phase involves a rapid increase in world integration, in part because of the concurrent decline in U.S. hegemony and the previous decolonization of core empires. These factors eliminated vast political barriers to global competition and capital mobility. The Soviet collapse was perhaps the most striking recent dissolution of political barriers, which has further hastened the pace of integration. In a cumulative process, even a small increase in growth rates soon has large effects. The result is a conspicuous qualitative shift in political structures within a single generation that accompanies the less perceptible ongoing changes. What is the result of a long-term process thus appears to be a novel phenomenon because adaptation to the process now elicits integral rather than incremental change.

A major result of heightened integration is that mass production technology is increasingly commonplace. Firms using low-skill labor more easily move investment to the (semi)periphery where workers are less expensive and more oppressed, especially women workers. With high capital mobility, American workers in the rust belt experienced deindustrialization (Bluestone and Harrison, 1982), whereas newly industrializing countries (NICs) in East Asia rose into the semiperiphery. Core production cannot compete with the (semi)periphery simply in terms of labor costs. A growing portion of core workers are now in direct competition with semiperipheral labor, a situation resembling the period preceding the second industrial revolution at the end of the 19th century. Hardest hit have been unionized industrial and service workers. Unemployment has remained high for low skilled and less educated workers even when economic growth has been robust, a central factor in union declines (Galenson, 1994, ch. 3). In contrast, highly skilled and professional workers still fare well as their skills are even more valuable in a rapidly changing market and technological environment. These valued employees increasingly differ from their more easily replaceable brethren, increasing unemployment rates and income inequality levels (Piore & Sabel, 1984). As a result, the welfare state's floor of national living standards has cracked and is crumbling.

For the large transnational corporations, these changes required restructuring to focus on highly skilled and educated workers who could employ innovative (high) technology to produce nonstandard (specialized) goods not available in the (semi)periphery (Hearn, 1987; Piore & Sabel, 1984). Innovation has dramatically advanced the pace of product obsolescence, making the long production runs of a uniform product an increasingly risky core investment. This is especially true in a more integrated world market where few products are protected from alternatives. Although firms have adopted various accumulation innovations, a commonality among the most successful has been "flexibility" or "flexible specialization." Flexible organizations include variable batch production runs, rapid adoption of new technology, increased scientific and technical input, decentralized management, higher skilled and more autonomous technical workers, and lesser benefits and increased temporary contracts for low skill workers (Hearn, 1987, Piore & Sabel, 1984). The institution of this new flexible accumulation regime is causing social upheaval against the social rigidities of mass production, mass consumption, bureaucratic organization, government regulation, and welfare dependency from both the New Left and the New Right.

Globalization and Governance

One popular response to increased globalization and resulting inefficacy of the state has been nationalist. The burst of new states in Central and Eastern Europe is but the most visible manifestation of a rise of nationalist fervor throughout the world. Many labor unions have also responded to globalization with support for national protectionism, but any such attempt is undermined by the increased pace of world market integration (McNally, 1990).

The irony is that the surge of nationalism is driven, in no small part, by the very process of globalization that makes state power less potent. In the face of world integration, dominant ethnic groups demand reinforcement of their national identity and the competitive advantage nationals have within it. Subordinate ethnic populations with identifiable territories (i.e., nations) increasingly seek their own sovereign states as they gain less from having a voice within an increasingly ineffectual and nationalist state and more from interstate relations (Lapid & Kratochwil, 1996). The result has been a massive outpouring of both xenophobia and ethnic separatism within what had previously been stable multination states. A further irony is that the breakdown into smaller sovereignties makes each more dependent upon the world market and permeable to world integration.[3]

Deepening integration and neoliberal competition have thus engendered centrifugal processes of declining sovereignty yet rising nationalism. The combination of state proliferation and world economic integration also increases dramatically the importance of international governance. The rise of international governance follows a basic principle of contracting. Any voluntary contract requires precontractual agreement on definitions and standards, and postcontractual third-party negotiation, adjudication, and enforcement. The greater the number of states, the greater the need for international authorities to define standards, adjudicate conflicts, and otherwise regulate exchange (Boswell & Chase-Dunn, in press). This is happening at two levels, global and regional.

Of growing importance is the geometric rise in the number of international organizations, both governmental (IGOs) and nongovernmental (INGOs) (Boli & Thomas, in press). The phenomenal growth in INGOs largely serves the precontractual function, whereas the IGOs are haltingly being driven to become the postcontractual third-party enforcers (Boswell & Chase-Dunn, in press). The primary thrust of these efforts is the standardization and enforcement of rules, products, and codes for everything from intellectual property rights to the hormones acceptable in cow's milk (Loya & Boli, 1995).

At the regional level, we have witnessed a deepening of political projects of economic coordination (Smith, 1993). Most prominent are the regional blocs and future hegemonic contenders, the European Union (EU) and its American offspring, the North American Free Trade Agreement (NAFTA). Lagging behind, but nevertheless important are regional groupings in East Asia.[4] These regional blocs account for the overwhelming majority of the world's product, and their interactions are central to governance of the world economy. Regional integration, however, also contains the potential for conflict between blocs. Such potential can be seen in the immigration policies debated in both the EU and North America, the strategic trade moves of the United States vis-à-vis Asia, and the disputes between the United States and the EU over use of the International Monetary Fund. Interregional competition is a little acknowledged specter over the world economy.

These new forms of global and regional governance affect the prospects for international labor politics by creating institutions that can enforce transnational standards. Although domestic strategies will remain central to labor politics, a dimension which we must only touch upon in passing, our focus is on globalization. By setting common standards across borders, international governance benefits transnational capital by reducing trading costs and further eases the shift of capital to lower cost suppliers and lower wage labor. The EU is bringing lower costs throughout Europe. NAFTA has yet to offer major benefits but in principle it should head in the same direction. If capitalists benefit from and are rapidly pursuing international standards and governance, why not labor?

International Labor Politics

Labor unions have a long history of international politics (for background, see Windmuller, 1980). However, the current problematic hails from the labor radicalization of 1968 to 1973. During that period, labor leaders raised the question of an international labor strategy to match the profusion of organized international capital (Levinson, 1972). Not surprisingly, the corporate response was overwhelmingly negative (Northrup and Rowan, 1979). Opposition also came from some national unions. For instance, the International Confederation of Free Trade Unions, under pressure from the American Federation of Labor and Congress of Industrial Organization (AFL-CIO), could not formulate a strategy of collaboration with communist unions (Busch, 1983, pp. 182-187). Some analysts at the time thus argued that labor internationalism would not be a direct by-product of the transnationalization of capital (Cox, 1972; Olle & Scholler, 1977/1987).

Decades later, the critics for the most part have been proven right. Despite deepening integration, labor movements have not yet produced resilient strategies and efficacious organizations. This does not mean that labor politics has stood still or that labor organizations have been unaware of these developments (International Confederation of Free Trade Unions, 1979; Levinson, 1972). A number of initiatives and innovations have enriched the repertoire of tactics and strategies, and alert us to the potential for transborder collaboration. What are the principal current attempts by labor movements to organize internationally?

GLOBAL GOVERNANCE OF LABOR RELATIONS

The preeminent global forum for labor affairs is the International Labor Organization (ILO). Social Democrats prior to World War I conceived of an ILO as a supranational entity controlled by labor unions. The final product, however, was a tripartite IGO whose membership involves state, capital, and labor, with states dominating. Although it has produced a fairly comprehensive set of conventions, their adoption and implementation is in the hands of recalcitrant states (Swepton, 1994). With the specter of communism being swept away, their recalcitrance is likely to grow without new sources of pressure.

The recently established World Trade Organization (WTO), on the other hand, is likely to grow in importance and power. The WTO, successor to the General Agreement on Trade and Tariffs, is designed to be an arbitrator of trade disputes, enforcer of contracts, and forum for establishing common world standards (Ruggiero, 1996). Although WTO decisions will surely affect workers worldwide, it does not yet provide a means for dealing with labor matters or any process for unions to initiate action. As WTO Director General Renato Ruggiero admits, "Beyond the built-in agenda, issues which have been proposed by some countries include trade and labor standards (the most potentially controversial of all these subjects)" (Ruggiero, 1996, p.1).

At a global level, therefore, there are no strong mandatory arrangements protecting workers or warranting labor rights. Yet, IGOs are increasingly involved in standardization and regulation of the world economy, such that the organizational means for pursuing labor's global interests exist in principle. Some analysts and activists, particularly from the periphery, argue that labor movements should push to upgrade the ILO's role in monitoring and enforcing international labor rights and standards (see Compa, 1995). In their view, the ILO is best suited to represent the interests of the less developed world because its decision-making structure includes unions and because it does not connect trade and labor matters. This strength in terms of representing the interests of workers and states in the periphery is a weakness, however, in terms of enforcement (a weakness for which the ILO is famous). In contrast, the decision-making mechanisms and the rules of the WTO render it likely that core states will use it as a forum and consent to its decisions. We thus conclude that contesting the nature and practices of only the ILO would be a mistake, and addressing the WTO should be part of international labor politics.

Global Labor Federations

Addressing international governmental organizations and organizing globally requires some means of international coordination by labor unions. Three union federations have traditionally promoted global policies: the International Confederation of Free Trade Unions (ICFTU), the World Federation of Trade Unions, and the World Confederation of Labor (for background, see Devin, 1990). We deal here only with the ICFTU because it is the largest of the three and because the future of the second largest, the communist-led World Federation, is questionable.

The ICFTU brings together socialist and trade-unionist national unions from all continents. Its organization is confederal, with limited political scope and power over constituent units (see Bendiner, 1987, pp. 35-42). The ICFTU has had a regular presence in IGOs and has helped members organize in their respective countries, rather than organize itself, something that would have met governmental resistance and is beyond its confederal nature. Historically, the ICFTU's policies have been constrained by the dynamics of the Cold War. Today, two challenges confront the ICFTU. First, how should it reorganize in light of the end of the Cold War and, second, how can it overcome the potential divisions between social democratic and trade-unionist orientations.

The latter challenge is most pressing because of the development of NAFTA and the AFL-CIO's long-standing ambivalence toward international labor organizations, including social democratic ones (for background, see Busch, 1983). The AFL-CIO essentially operates its own "foreign policy," as do a number of other national unions (Devin, 1990; Harrod, 1972; Sims, 1992). During the 1950s and 1960s, the AFL-CIO participated in the ICFTU, mostly to enforce anticommunism. The ICFTU's movement toward detente, led by German unions, prompted the AFL-CIO to withdraw from the confederation from 1969 to 1981 (Busch, 1983, chap. 9). On balance, the influence of the ICFTU outside Europe has been historically limited as a result of AFL and later AFL-CIO resistance. On the other hand, the AFL-CIO has had a historical role in supporting noncommunist European unions after World War II (for a debate over the AFL-CIO's foreign policy see Garver, 1989; Kahn, 1989). More recently, it has played an important role in the success of Poland's Solidarity, and with it, the unraveling of East European communism. This success has not as yet translated into greater transnational organizing, but a more activist AFL-CIO administration is currently in the process of reorganizing its foreign policy, including the removal of strong "Cold Warriors." Such developments hold the prospect of a vitalized ICFTU, provided that the AFL-CIO and the European unions deal with long-standing organizational and ideological issues that the Cold War helped contain.

International Trade Secretariats

The International Trade Secretariats are 15 loose confederations with limited organizational authority that bring together unions in broad sectors of the world economy (Windmuller, 1995). The AFL-CIO has historically been closer to the secretariats than the ICFTU, and some secretariats are active in the Americas in providing information and contacts with unions around the world (Banks, 1993; Cohen, 1993).

For the most part, the secretariats have mainly functioned to facilitate the exchange of information. Beginning in the 1960s, the International Metalworkers' Federation and later the International Federation of Chemical, Energy and General Workers' Unions, two of the largest secretariats, took the leadership in creating World Company Councils, the first four of which were formed in 1966 (Bendiner, 1987). The councils were intended to bring together all the unions of a single transnational corporation to achieve transnational collective bargaining. At most, the councils managed to assist local unions by providing information and limited material support. Corporate opposition and unresolved differences between unions have, however, undermined the council effort (see Northrup & Rowan, 1979, for an overview). A recent variant of the council strategy are corporate campaigns that turn a particular transnational corporation into the focal point for international action (Cohen, 1993). These corporate strategies have the potential to unite core and (semi)peripheral unions, and to spread beyond already organized workers. To do so, they need to develop an agenda that can coordinate the varied interests of national labor unions and, more generally, of workers in countries at different levels of economic development.

REGIONAL POLITIES AND LABOR POLITICS: THE NAFTA CASE

The prospects and the debates over NAFTA reintroduced questions of international labor politics to the Americas that had long been dormant. In the process, it clearly demonstrated the lack of coordination between the top labor federations of the three countries (Carr, 1995; Hecker, 1993). The AFL-CIO opposed NAFTA for lacking any type of funding similar to the European Social Fund and especially for want of strong and binding labor regulations (Donohue, 1991). They wanted regulations to be enforced either through U.S. government agencies or through a trinational arrangement. The Canadian Congress of Labor also opposed NAFTA, but the federations failed to mount a coordinated campaign (Robinson, 1995). In fact, the two movements have moved away from their historical transnationalism. Canadian unions have increasingly become independent, partly as a result of the difficulties of transnational collective bargaining and partly as a result of the nationalist turn of the Canadian left (McNally, 1990).

In Mexico, the Confederation of Mexican Workers strongly supported NAFTA and opposed any coordinated system of industrial relations (Cowie, 1995). The relations between the AFL-CIO and the Mexican Confederation are extremely superficial despite (and because of) a long history of AFL involvement with Mexican labor. Although the AFL-CIO has a permanent representative at the confederation's offices, the two federations have not built any programs of collective action. The confederation objected to any unilaterally or even trinationally imposed regulation of Mexican labor. Although the AFL-CIO's reasons for opposition are self-evident, the confederation's rationale may be less apparent. They argued that Mexican labor laws were sufficient, and given the history of U.S.-Mexican relations, they had good reason to fear outside interference. Also important was the confederation's traditional support of the ruling political party and a possible personal understanding between Fidel Velasquez (the confederation's leader) and then President Salinas de Gortari (Cook, 1995a). In general, the Mexican union and government thought that NAFTA would be advantageous for attracting foreign capital and for easing migration to the United States (Grayson, 1995).

What success the opposition had in affecting NAFTA can be found in the North American Agreement on Labor Cooperation. The agreement calls for each country to enforce its own labor laws (agreement article 1.f, International Legal Materials [ILM], 1993). It also allows for the enforcement of "technical labor standards" through the processes of the agreement (Article 49). The technical standards include labor protection for children and youth; minimum employment standards, such as minimum wages and overtime pay; and prevention of and compensation for occupational injuries and illnesses. The standards also include elimination of employment discrimination, equal pay for men and women, and protection of migrant workers. However, as violations of the technical standards must be trade related and covered by mutually recognized laws (Annex 23.1), it is debatable if the latter standards are enforceable through the procedures of the agreement (but see Cowie & French, 1993-1994). Overall, although better for labor than the silence offered by the WTO, the agreement provides no mechanisms for transnational enforcement or for collaborative union action (see Cook & Katz, 1994).

Since implementation, the agreement has been tested by both U.S. and Mexican unions. Three things have become apparent. First, there are state elements that disagree with the limitations of the agreement; second, the implementation of the agreement is subservient to stronger economic and political priorities; and third, the opportunities offered to labor unions by the agreement are quite limited and costly, relegating them to mainly tactical use (Mumme &

Stevis, 1996). Nevertheless, NAFTA has invigorated strategic transborder collaboration among several individual labor unions and their allies. Some of the most active have had long-standing critical views of neoliberal trade policies (La Botz, 1994). We group examples of these initiatives below according to their emphasis and depth, from common organizing across borders to only informational exchanges, with some cases falling in between.[5]

A case that involves common organizing and transnational bargaining with a long history is that of the Farm Labor Organizing Committee (Velasquez, 1995). A more recent, similar example of common organizing is an alliance of the United Electric Workers and the Frente Autentico del Trabajo. The alliance, signed in 1992, is for collaborative activities in Mexican plants of companies that the United Electric Workers have organized in the United States. So far, the two have collaborated in a General Electric plant in Juarez and a Honeywell plant in Chihuahua (Alexander & Gilmore, 1994). This alliance does not mean that the two unions will unite, but it builds long-term collaboration and avoids turf wars. In both of these cases, the emphasis is on organizing as the road to political influence rather than trying to change politics from the top down.

Workers in the communication sector provide an example of a strategic alliance that does not involve common organizing (see also developments in the trucking industry, McGinn, 1996). In 1992, the Communications Workers of America (CWA), the Communications Workers of Canada, and the Mexican Telecommunications Workers signed a formal alliance (Pattee, 1995). One important result has been an innovative use of the North American Labor Agreement. Although the first three cases of labor violations involved U.S. unions complaining of violations in Mexico, the fourth case involved an innovative complaint by the Mexican union of violations of U.S. labor law.

During 1994, the Sprint Corporation decided to close its San Francisco-based subsidiary, Conexion Familiar, and fired about 180 Spanish-speaking employees whom the CWA had been trying to unionize. On February 9, 1995, the Mexican union brought a complaint to the Mexican National Administrative Office on behalf of the CWA. The Mexican Office found that U.S. law had been violated. In June, Mexico's Labor and Welfare Secretary requested consultations with his counterpart in the United States (the second step in the process) (*Labor Relations Reporter,* 1995, pp. 211-213). Ministerial consultations concluded in mid-February 1996 that "As part of an action plan agreed upon by the three Labor Ministers [including the Canadian Minister] the Secretariat [of the Commission for Labor Cooperation] was requested to conduct a study of the effects of a sudden plant closing on freedom of association and the right of workers to organize in the three countries" (*Bulletin of the Commission for Labor Cooperation,* 1996, p. 10.). The study was to be available by the end of 1996. The case has been successful to the degree that it led to a commitment by the U.S. Department of Labor to study organizing rights as part of NAFTA. In addition, the Postal, Telephone and Telegraph International Trade Secretariat played an active role by informing and raising support from unions outside North America. As such, this case provides one example of how a secretariat can connect regional struggles to the rest of the world.

A labor union that has had a long interest in international labor politics is the United Auto Workers. Its record, however, has been marred by serious problems, such as the dissociation of its Canadian component. In recent times, various autoworker locals within U.S. and Mexican unions have played a leading role in establishing closer contacts with each other (Moody & McGinn, 1992). These contacts involve visits and symbolic acts of solidarity as well as more regular channels for the exchange of information and the promotion of unionization (personal communication, Julio Cesar Guerrero, Transnational Information Exchange, June 12, 1996). What is significant in this case is that the leadership has been taken by grassroots elements. In fact, there are enough instances of locals or even plant organizations seeking to reach across boundaries that we can expect this grassroots action to prompt more attention to international labor politics at the highest levels (Moody & McGinn, 1992).

We should also mention the role of various religious, civic, environmental, and women's groups in promoting labor standards and rights, often in collaboration with labor activists (La Botz, 1994). Such examples include the Coalition for Justice in the Maquiladoras and the *Comite Fronterizo de Obreras* (Border Committee of Working Women) initiated by the American Friend Service Committee's Maquiladora Project. What is significant about these initiatives is that they broaden the labor agenda in a strategic rather than tactical fashion by paying attention to issues of gender, environment, and community. In so doing, labor movements mobilize support beyond their union base for establishing and enforcing international standards, especially for standards that span core and periphery.

Finally, we should note the contrast between the limited labor provisions found in NAFTA with that found in the EU. The differences in regional agreements are no more, and are perhaps less, than the existing national differences between the United States and most European countries. Although the EU does mandate many more standards than NAFTA, it does not give labor unions commensurate political voice (Rhodes, 1995).[6] On balance, the EU industrial relations system is inferior to most, perhaps all, national level systems in Western Europe. Implementing the EU agenda has thus provoked widespread labor protests.

This was nowhere more evident than during the month of massive strikes by public workers in France in late 1995 (*La Grande Revolté Française*," 1996). The French state faced an EU requirement that it drop its deficit from 5% to 3% of gross domestic product by 1997 to join the single currency union of the "Euro." France's conservative government designed the cuts to come mainly from the constituency of its opposition, public workers, but such rapid deficit reduction would cause significant pain throughout French society. Failure to join the Euro, on the other hand, would mean a lost opportunity to discard costly and nonproductive currency and other transactions. France's economic growth is intermixed with continuing European integration, so that reversal would also cause severe economic dislocation. As a result, despite a huge outpouring, government concessions were small and designed to give in only where it would not derail the overall goal. Look for similar protests to come in Germany, followed by Italy and elsewhere, with similar results.

ORGANIZING PROSPECTS AND RESEARCH DIRECTIONS

Labor movements face formidable tasks. The world economy is moving increasingly in a neoliberal direction that diminishes domestic welfare provisions without replacing them with regional or international ones. On balance, we note that some labor provisions have been attached to regional agreements. Arguably, this is better than the WTO's silence and the ILO's weakness. However, these provisions reserve for labor unions a role that is inferior to the one held in most industrial countries. Altogether, this is a regressive precedent that foreshadows worsening conditions for labor movements in the immediate future. Tilly's (1995) review of the effects of globalization on labor rights, for instance, draws rather pessimistic conclusions. We differ in suggesting that regional and global integration brings with it forms of transnational governance that directly affects unions and provides them with incentives and opportunities for action. Successful organization in the EU and North America would greatly enhance the global power of labor unions, and would facilitate global coordination and collaboration. To make use of this potential, labor movements require a strategy of transnational organizing that secures labor rights in the emerging multistate polities.

In comparing NAFTA and the EU, the potential for coordinated action is far better within the EU. This is not surprising given the political forum for coordination and the greater resources of European unions. What is important from a world-system perspective is that the EU offers a prime training ground for how to coordinate among diverse nations and serves as an institutional model to other potential blocs (including NAFTA). This has proven to be to its advantage in global forums where the EU is supplanting the United States as the initiator of global standardization in many technical and commercial fields (Loya & Boli, 1995). If political integration is successful, then the EU could offer a real alternative to U.S. hegemony, although that contest probably remains at least a generation away (Boswell & Chase-Dunn, in press). In the meantime, there is the potential for labor union success within the EU to cascade throughout the world economy. Such a spillover, however, will not take place unless unions and allied organizations actively engage the challenge of internationalism.

The lack of coordination among the labor federations of the three NAFTA countries we have described illustrates the difficulties in transnational organizing (Carr, 1995; Hecker, 1993). Having said that, we can also say that a number of unions, locals, and other groups in North America are actively seeking to build transnational labor politics. These forces can play leading and perhaps even catalytic roles. On one hand, they can invent appropriate strategies for international labor politics. On the other hand, they can refocus the priorities of their own unions and federations.

Successful regional strategies do not guarantee a successful global strategy. To the contrary, the regional dynamics of the contemporary world economy could lead to increased divisions and conflicts. In this regard, the ICFTU, as well as the International Trade Secretariats, can play a positive role even without changing into a strongly federal type of organization. They can provide fora for the international exchange of information and communications. Additionally, they can be the fora where proposals for a global agenda can be aired, discussed, and agreed upon. Overall, they can be a means for keeping regional and sectoral efforts from degenerating into competition and for enhancing the bargaining environment between unions and regional polities. It seems to us that such an expanded role could be now and should be in the future an important function of the ICFTU and the secretariats. To accomplish these functions, however, they will require more resources and decision-making power to at least guarantee understandings among unions as well as resolve jurisdictional disputes among them. In this vein, labor unions can draw some useful lessons from the development of private dispute resolution in commercial affairs (Loya & Boli, 1995). Labor organizations, however, will have to move beyond dispute resolution and towards imaginative and democratic programs of collaboration.

What of labor movements outside the regional blocs of the core, in the (semi)periphery where it is most oppressed? Although this has not been our focus, some have placed their hopes in the new unionism of the Third World (Boyd, Cohen, & Gutkind, 1987). Most of these movements are ideologically or programmatically nationalist. In our view, there is no a priori reason to believe that national radicalization will translate into global radicalization. In the absence of international mechanisms of collective action, even potentially internationalist labor movements will focus on national development and protection. Such a trend can be reinforced by various core union policies that stress nationalism, protectionist regionalism, or the established worker.

The long-term solution is for core labor movements to support those developmental policies in the periphery that will increase human productivity. As Amsden (1995) points out, global standards that simply raise peripheral labor costs without raising productivity would cause capital flight from poor countries. In this vein, we think the best hope lies in "social movement unionism," whereby unions ally with other social movements such as women's, human rights, and environmental organizations (Waterman, 1993). This has often been a source of expansion and rejuvenation of the organizational and programmatic repertoire of labor movements. Social movement organizing also has great potential to affect the world polity directly (rather than mediated through states). It is not, however, a substitute for organizing people as workers. Alliances will be strongest where the social movement goals are also issues of work. Complementarily, unions cannot expect that all issues can be reduced to workplace concerns. The women's movement is an important example. Women's limited rights in the (semi)periphery is a prime source of their miserable wages and working conditions, which drag down all wages. Although cultural heritages divide women on many issues, transnational corporations provide common ground on issues of work.

RESEARCH DIRECTIONS

International labor politics has not been a byproduct of transnational processes; it will require commitment of resources and priorities. Thus, we call for a broad research agenda that focuses on connections between the long-term context and the strategic characteristics of historical conjunctures. An exemplary beginning is offered by Silver, Arrighi, and Dubofsky (1995), who contend that labor conflicts in several core countries over the past 100 or more years show patterns that reflect in part the historical dynamics of the world system. Research along those lines is invaluable in its diachronic, systemic emphasis. Such research can be complemented and enhanced in two ways. The nature and intent of global processes cannot be fully understood from aggregating domestic factors; diachronic research, therefore, would be enriched by collecting data and forming hypotheses that seek to capture the nature and intent of international organizations and practices themselves (i.e., Boli & Thomas, in press). Further, diachronic research would greatly benefit from linked case studies and comparisons of particular critical moments. Such focused studies and comparisons could alert us to the reasons why labor organizations opted for particular choices, and what were the lasting political and institutional impacts.

The combination of diachronic research with comparative case studies can help us investigate the following important questions: Why do some labor organizations respond to global pressures with transnational organizing, whereas others resort to nativism or fail to act altogether? How do labor organizations become involved in international labor politics? What are the distinct characteristics of the successful cases? Explaining why labor organizations get involved in international politics likely will not be an easy task, because labor politics are contested both internally and externally (Logue, 1980). Revealing how they are involved may be more manageable, but leads to a series of related research questions (Visser & Ebbinghaus, 1992). How do their internal operations adjust to accommodate international organizations and practices? What international organizations do they choose? How much power and resources, monetary or other, do they transfer to them? How are these international organizations organized internally? Do they generate knowledge and techniques or do they simply react to external stimuli? Answers to these questions will reflect, in part, the reasons why national unions got involved internationally in the first place. Additionally, however, they will open to empirical investigation the institutional strengths and weaknesses of existing international organizations and practices.

Although these questions can provide us with information regarding international labor politics, we must also identify those organizations and practices that have been more resilient and successful in changing international labor politics. What are the characteristics of such organizations? How have those organizations, alliances, or contacts been crafted internally? What resources have they had at their disposal or generated themselves? What have been their goals? How have they collaborated with other social movements? Such a research agenda can benefit from the developing literature on transnational social movement organizations which has, so far, drawn from peace, ecological, women's, and civic groups rather than labor organizations (Smith, Pagnucco, & Romeril, 1995). A good start would be to compare the strategies of the international labor organizations we have discussed to those global organizations formed by other social movements.

We will close with a caution that ought to temper conclusions from research on labor. The long, bitter, and glorious history of labor politics can easily lead one to dismiss past international practices or organizational forms because of their actual or presumed failures. In an area that has been so contested it is to be expected that evaluations of the past have been colored by the sound and fury of these contestations. Yet, as we have emphasized herein, the world system is undergoing concentrated changes in political and social relations. Is it not possible that old strategies, properly adjusted, may produce different results now than in the past? The global conditions that defeated past attempts at internationalism have themselves been the subject of change with the increasing development of global governance. Should we not be looking to labor's past to gather possibilities as well as lessons?

NOTES

1. We recognize that global transformations do not totally explain the limited transborder collaboration among unions or the lack of transnational labor movements. Nor do we portend that union decline is solely related to global dynamics and associated processes. Comparison of national labor movements inevitably points a second finger at organizational factors internal to unions, especially their lack of unity and their difficulties in attracting minorities and women (Galenson, 1994).

2. Union density rates declined from 1.4% in Canada to over 36% in France from 1980 to 1988, with most countries showing continued decline or no change going into the 1990s. The decline began in the 1970s for many core countries, with the United States and Britain showing the largest overall losses. Only the Scandinavian countries appeared immune to decline in the 1980s, but unions have stagnated even there during the 1990s (Galenson, 1994).

3. From a global perspective, "sovereignty" is defined by the world order that emanates from interstate relations. That world order is the set of agreed-upon institutions, treaties, rules and unwritten norms that govern relations between states, ranging from U.N. peacekeeping forces to proper diplomatic etiquette (Meyer et al., 1996). Whatever the origins of a state, its definition and survival as sovereign depends on recognition from other states as a compliant member in interstate relations. Prior to 1945, admission was primarily limited to imperial states. Since that time, entry has been institutionalized by the United Nations and is potentially open to any nation that can militarily control a territory. We have seen a geometric increase in the number of states produced by decolonization and by the break-up of multination states.

4. For an overview of regional bloc formation, see Gibb and Michalak (1994).

5. There are as yet no attempts at creating transnational unions similar to those of the Congress of Industrial Organizations or the Industrial Workers of the World nor any strategic alliances involving peak associations.

6. The major, but not unique, forum for coordinating union efforts in the European Union (EU) is the European Trade Union Confederation, formed in 1972. Although not yet a strong federation, it has helped create the rudiments of a common agenda and has brought together unions from all political ideologies (Visser & Ebbinghaus, 1992). We expect the confederation (or like organization) to grow in importance within the EU, and to be a potent global actor—but space and focus prevent further discussion here.

REFERENCES

Alexander, R., & Gilmore, P. (1994). The emergence of cross-border labor solidarity. *NACLA Report on the Americas, 28*(1), 42-48,51.

Amsden, A. H. (1995). Hype or help? *The Boston Review. XX*(6), pp. 3-6.

Banks, A. (1993). Taking on the global boss: An interview with Paul Garver of the IUF. *Labor Research Review, 21,* 57-69.

Bendiner, B. (1987). *International labour affairs: The world trade unions and the multinational companies.* Oxford, UK: Clarendon.

Bluestone, B., & Harrison, B. (1982). *The deindustrialization of America.* New York: Basic Books.

Boli, J., & Thomas, G. (in press). *World polity formation since 1875: World culture and international non-governmental organization.* Stanford, CA: Stanford University Press.

Boswell, T., & Chase-Dunn, C. (in press). The future of the world-system. *International Journal of Sociology and Social Policy.*

Boswell, T., & Dixon, W. (1993). Marx's theory of rebellion: A cross-national analysis of class exploitation, economic development, and violent revolt. *American Sociological Review, 58*(5), 681-702.

Boyd, R. E., Cohen, R., & Gutkind, P. C. W. (Eds.). (1987). *International labour and the Third World: The making of a new working class.* Aldershot, UK: Avebury.

Bulletin of the Commission for Labor Cooperation. (1996, August). Vol. 1, No. 2.

Busch, G. K. (1983). *The political role of international trades unions.* New York: St. Martin's.

Carr, B. (1995). Labor internationalism in the era of NAFTA: Past and present. *Latin American Labor Occasional Paper #14.* Center for Labor Research and Studies, Florida International University.

Chase-Dunn, C. (1989). *Global formation.* Cambridge, MA: Basil Blackwell.

Cohen, L. (1993). Mobilizing internationally: Global employee network pressures multinational to reverse anti-union strategy. *Labor Research Review, 21,* 47-55.

Compa, L. (1995). . . . And the twain shall meet? A North-South controversy over labor rights and standards. *Labor Research Review, 23,* 51-65.

Cook, M. L. (1995a). Mexican state-labor relations and the political implications of free trade. *Latin American Perspectives, 22*(4), 77-94.

Cook, M. L. (1995b). National labor strategies in changing environments: Perspectives from Mexico. *Latin American Research Paper #18.* Center for Labor Research and Studies, Florida International University.

Cook, M. L., & Katz, H. C. (Eds.). (1994). *Regional integration and industrial relations in North America.* Ithaca, NY: ILR Press.

Cowie, J. R. (1995). The search for a transnational discourse for a North American economy: A critical review of U.S. labor's campaign against NAFTA (with the Robinson/Cowie debate). *Latin American Labor Occasional Paper #22.* Center for Labor Research and Studies, Florida International University.

Cowie, J., & French, J. (1993-1994). NAFTA's labor side agreement: A textual analysis. *Latin American Labor News,* No. 9, 5-8.

Cox, R. (1972). Basic trends affecting the location of decision-making powers in industrial relations. In H. Gunter (Ed.), *Transnational industrial relations* (pp. 5-14). London: Macmillan.

Cox, R. (1987). *Production, power, and world order: Social forces in the making of history.* New York: Columbia University Press.

Devin, G. (Ed.). (1990). *Syndicalisme: Dimensions internationales.* La Garenne Colombes, France: Editions Européennes ERASME.

Donohue, T. R. (1991). The case against a North American Free Trade Agreement. *Columbia Journal of World Business, 26*(2), 92-96.

Esping-Andersen, G. (1990). *The three worlds of welfare capitalism.* Princeton, NJ: Princeton University Press.

Galenson, W. (1994). *Trade union growth and decline: An international study.* New York: Praeger.

Garver, P. (1989). New directions for labor internationalism. *Labor Research Review, 13,* 61-71.

Gibb, R., & Michalak, W. (Eds.). (1994). *Continental trading blocs: The growth of regionalism in the world economy.* Chichester, UK: Wiley.

Gordon, D., Edwards, R., & Reich, M. (1982). *Segmented work, divided workers.* Cambridge, UK: Cambridge University Press.

Grayson, G. (1995). *The North American Free Trade Agreement: Regional community and the new world order.* Lanham, MD: University Press of America.

The Group of Lisbon. (1995). *Limits to competition.* Cambridge: MIT Press.

Harrod, J. (1972). *Trade union foreign policy.* New York: Anchor.

Hearn, F. (1987). *The transformation of industrial society.* Belmont, CA: Wadsworth.

Hecker, S. (1993). U.S. unions, trade and international solidarity: Emerging issues and tactics. *Economic and Industrial Democracy, 14,* 355-367.

Hicks, A. (1988). National collective action and economic performance: A review article. *International Studies Quarterly, 32*(2), 131-154.

International Confederation of Free Trade Unions. (1979). *Trade unions and the transnationals: A handbook for negotiators.* Brussels: Author.

International Legal Materials. (1993). *North American Agreement on Labor Cooperation,* No. 1499 (32).

Kahn, T. (1989). Beyond mythology. *Labor Research Review, 11,* 72-79.

Kondratieff, N. D. (1979). The long waves in economic life. *Review, 11,* 519-562. (Original work published 1926)

Labor Relations Reporter. (1995, June 12). Pp. 211-213.

La Botz, D. (1994, August). Making links across the border. *Labor Notes, 185,* 7-10.

La grande revolté française contre L'Europe liberale. (1996, January). *Le Monde Diplomatique,* p. 502.

Lapid, Y., & Kratochwil, F. (Eds.). (1996). *The return of culture and identity in IR theory.* Boulder, CO: Lynne Rienner.

Levinson, C. (1972). *International unionism.* London: Allen and Unwin.

Logue, J. (1980). *Toward a theory of trade union internationalism.* Kent, OH: Kent Popular Press.

Loya, T., & Boli, J. (1995, August). *Standardization in the world polity: Technical rationalization over power.* Paper presented at the annual meeting of the American Sociological Association, Washington, DC.

McGinn, M. (1996). Solidarity goes international as truckers set NAFTA action plan. *Labor Notes, 206,* 3-4.

McNally, D. (1990). Beyond nationalism, beyond protectionism: Labor and the Canada-US Free Trade Agreement. *Review of Radical Political Economics, 22*(1), 179-194.

Meyer, J., Boli, J., Ramirez, F., & Thomas, G. (1995, August). *Theories of culture: Institutional vs. actor-centered approaches—The case of world society.* Paper presented at the annual meeting of the American Sociological Association, Washington, DC.

Moody, K., & McGinn, M. (1992). *Unions and free trade: Solidarity vs. competition.* Detroit: Labor Notes.

Mumme, S., & Stevis, D. (1996). *Comparing international social policies: Lessons from NAFTA.* Manuscript available from the authors.

Northrup, H. R., & Rowan, R. (1979). *Multinational collective bargaining attempts: The record, the cases and the prospects* (Multinational Industrial Relations Series, No. 6). Philadelphia: Industrial Research Unit, The Wharton School, University of Pennsylvania.

Olle, W., & Scholler, W. (1987). World market competition and restrictions upon international trade union policies. In R. E. Boyd, R. Cohen, & C. W. Gutkind (Eds.), *International labour and the Third World: The making of a new working class* (pp. 26-47). Aldershot, UK: Avebury. (Original work published 1977)

Pattee, J. (1995). Sprint and the shutdown of La Conexion Familiar: A union-hating multinational finds nowhere to run. *Labor Research Review, 23,* 13-21.

Piore, M. J., & Sabel, C. F. (1984). *The second industrial divide: Possibilities for prosperity.* New York: Basic Books.

Przeworski, A. (1985). *Capitalism and social democracy.* Cambridge, UK: Cambridge University Press.

Rhodes, M. (1995). A regulatory conundrum: Industrial relations and the social dimension. In S. Leibfried & P. Pierson (Eds.), *European social policy: Between fragmentation and integration* (pp. 78-112). Washington, DC: Brookings Institution.

Robinson, I. (1995). The Canadian labor movement against free trade: An assessment of strategies and outcomes. *Latin American Labor Occasional Paper #15.* Center for Labor Research and Studies, Florida International University.

Rueschemeyer, D., Stephens, E. H., & Stephens, J. D. (1992). *Capitalist development and democracy.* Chicago: University of Chicago Press.

Ruggiero, R. (1996). *The road ahead: International trade policy in the era of the world trade organization* (Report by the Director-General of the WTO, May 28, 1996). WTO website: http://www.unicc.org:80/wto/welcome.html; wto/whats_new/press49.html

Silver, B., Arrighi, G., & Dubofsky, M. (Eds.). (1995). Labor unrest in the world economy. *Review, 17,* 1.

Sims, B. (1992). *Workers of the world undermined: American labor's role in U.S. foreign policy.* Boston: South End Press.

Smith, J., Pagnucco, R., & Romeril, W. (1995). Transnational social movement organizations in the global political arena. *Voluntas, 52,* 121-154.

Smith, P. (Ed.). (1993). *The challenge of integration: Europe and the Americas.* New Brunswick, NJ: Transaction Publishing.

Swepton, L. (1994). The future of ILO standards. *Monthly Labor Review, 117*(9), 16-23.

Tilly, C. (1995). Globalization threatens labor's rights. *International Labor and Working-Class History. 17,* 1-23.

Velasquez, V. (1995). Don't waste time with politicians—Organize. *Labor Research Review, 23,* 45-49.

Visser, J., & Ebbinghaus, L. (1992). Making the most of diversity? European integration and transnational organization of labour. In J. Greenwood, J. R. Grote, & K. Ronit (Eds.), *Organized interests in the European community* (pp. 206-237). London: Sage.

Wallerstein, I. (1974). *The modern world-system* (Vol. 1). New York: Academic Press.

Waterman, P. (1993). Social-movement unionism: A new union model for a new world order? *Review, 16*(3), 245-278.

Windmuller, J. P. (1980). *The international labor movement.* Boston: Kluwer.

Windmuller, J. P. (1995). *International trade secretariats: The industrial trade union international.* Washington, DC: U.S. Department of Labor, Bureau of International Labor Affairs.

Trade Unions and European Integration

RICHARD HYMAN

European (economic) integration is a project with major implications for trade unions and for national systems of industrial relations: This much is undisputed. However, the precise nature of the impact is far from clear and is heatedly debated. Understandably, opinions within European labor movements are certain and divided. Partly for this reason, labor has been only a marginal actor in the shaping of an integrated Europe.

In this chapter, I first outline the institutional framework of what is now known as the European Union (EU) and the regional organization of trade unionism, the European Trade Union Confederation (ETUC). The next section explains how the hegemony of market forces has been central to the acceleration of integration since the mid-1980s. I then discuss the nature and limits of the "social dimension," the implications of the Maastricht Treaty, and the process that culminated in the enactment of a Directive on European Works Councils (EWCs). In conclusion, I consider the role of trade unions in the development of EU social policy, the prospects for future trade union influence within the EU, and the more general implications of European experience. Can labor movements develop the international solidarity essential to countering the strategic might of transnational capital and the anarchic and destructive force of global markets? European experience is scarcely encouraging but not wholly negative.

THE INSTITUTIONAL FRAMEWORK OF EUROPEAN INTEGRATION

The notion of "Europe" has become a concept with many shades of meaning: Its significance is intensely debated. Distinct economic and sociopolitical conceptions of European identity underlie conflicting visions of cross-national integration. The definition of Europeanization involves a clash of interests and the mobilization of substantial material and ideological resources. The current EU, unlike other "free trade areas," represents more than an essentially negative project of eliminating obstacles to cross-national economic transfers and movements—much more? The most obvious distinctive feature is the existence of a complex framework of political/administrative institutions with the ability to make and apply supranational law.[1] However, its jurisdiction is closely confined and any proposals to enlarge its powers have always provoked immense contention: The idea that the EU is a superstate in the making is much exaggerated (Schmitter & Streeck, 1992). The dialectic between national politics and the possibility of transnational regulation is a key theme in the difficult experience of the evolution of European industrial relations.

The original European Economic Community (EEC) comprised the six nations signatory to the Treaty of Rome in 1957: France, Germany, Italy, and the smaller "Benelux" countries of

From *Work and Occupations*, Vol. 24, No. 3, August 1997, pp. 309-331. Reprinted by permission.

Belgium, the Netherlands, and Luxembourg.[2] The initiative reflected a complex of pressures and motives: a belief (certainly shared by the American architects of the Marshall Plan) that cross-national economic liberalism was the recipe for reconstruction and growth; a desire to lock Germany into an institutional order which would prevent any resurgence of aggressive nationalism; and more idealistic aspirations for international cooperation. The British government remained aloof, opposing any supranational constraints on national sovereignty, and in 1959, it joined with six other western European countries to establish the European Free Trade Association (EFTA).

The coexistence of two rival transnational economic blocs was relatively short-lived. In 1973, Britain joined the EEC with Denmark and Ireland, Greece followed in 1981, and Spain and Portugal in 1986. EFTA survived as a rump organization, which in 1992 agreed with the 12 members of the EC to establish a European Economic Area (EEA) within which many of the provisions of EC law would apply. In consequence, EFTA countries became subject to key elements of the EC legislative process, which they had no role in shaping. Most recently, in 1995, Austria, Finland, and Sweden became part of what is now known as the EU. The 15 EU members represent virtually every country of Western Europe. Of those outside, only Norway and Switzerland are of significant (population) size.

The constitution of the EU rests on the Treaty of Rome and subsequent amendments, most notably the Single European Act (SEA) of 1986 and the Treaty on European Union agreed at Maastricht in 1991. There are two central decision-making institutions, each of which possesses some of the characteristics of national governments. The Commission of the European Communities[3] consists of 20 members nominated by the member states for a 4-year term of office; each heads one or more of the 24 administrative departments known as Directorates-General (DGs). It has the exclusive power to initiate legislation but has no decision-making authority. This is the prerogative of the Council of Ministers, composed of the heads of the member governments. Its business is managed under the presidency of each member state in rotation; functional councils (for example, the Social Affairs Council responsible for employment issues[4]) consist of specialist ministers from the member states and there is a permanent multinational civil service (the Committee of Permanent Representatives) paralleling that of the commission. Traditionally, the approval of any legislation required unanimity within the council. The SEA introduced the principle of qualified majority voting (QMV) on some issues, permitting a decision on a majority of just over two thirds with the larger countries possessing a greater number of votes; this procedure was extended under the Maastricht Treaty.

There is also a European Parliament, with a 4-year term of office. Though its powers were extended under the SEA, it is a far weaker body than most national parliaments. On some key issues, it may exercise a veto but, in general, its function is more consultative and advisory than legislative. The EU in addition possesses a judicial arm, the European Court of Justice, with a role somewhere between that of a constitutional court and a normal judiciary. Perhaps because its key function is to adjudicate complaints by the commission indicating that a member state is in breach of EU law—a significant issue, because the most important instrument of EU legislation, the Directive, specifies the outcome to be achieved but leaves member states the discretion to draft national law prescribing the means of attainment.

THE EUROPEAN TRADE UNION CONFEDERATION

European trade unions have from the outset adopted conflicting attitudes toward the process and institutions of transnational integration.[5] To some extent, these differences were a predictable reflection of the familiar political divisions within European labor movements. Those unions and confederations affiliated with the World Federation of Trade Unions (WFTU)—

that, after the split in the international labor movement in 1949, consisted primarily of "official" Eastern-bloc unions and communist organizations in the West and the Third World—denounced the original EEC, and the moves toward closer integration in the 1980s and 1990s, as the institutional expression of the interests of large-scale capital. Conversely, social democratic and Christian democratic unions linked, respectively, to the International Confederation of Free Trade Unions (ICFTU) and the World Confederation of Labor (WCL) tended to adopt a more positive position. National specificities were also important. For example, the British Trades Union Congress (TUC) continued to oppose British membership of the EC up to 1988, even though the Labour Party had abandoned its opposition several years before. Conversely, in Germany the *Deutscher Gewerkschaftsbund* (DGB) expressed a commitment to European integration even before the formation of the EEC, whereas the Social-Democratic Party (SPD) was skeptical at that stage.

Hierarchical differences have played a role also. For example, in many of the Nordic countries, the top union leaderships, in the main, have supported membership of the EC/EU, whereas opinion at the grassroots level has been more hostile. Although some of the differences have reflected sectoral economic interests—for example, between public and private employees, or workers in "exposed" and "sheltered" industries—the major line of differentiation has probably reflected that between an orientation to a narrow "industrial relations" agenda and a concern with broader issues of macroeconomic policy and political exchange. In any event, to the extent that debates within and between European unions often have focused on the actual principle of economic integration, this may well have reduced attention to the policy issues internal to the integration process.

Organizationally, a forum for the development of common perspectives and policies exists within the ETUC. It was formed in 1973 through the integration of separate secretariats for ICFTU affiliates in the EEC and EFTA countries, and the following year embraced the European affiliates of the WCL, which had previously maintained their own organization (Visser & Ebbinghaus, 1992, pp. 219-220). Its geographical scope covers all Western European countries (as well as "peripheral" movements from Cyprus, Malta, and Turkey); several union organizations from Eastern and Central Europe have been admitted also.

Postcommunism also has extended the membership to most former Western European affiliates of WFTU, which has all but collapsed now. The Italian *Confederazione Generale Italiana di Lavoro* (CGIL), which, in the 1970s, distanced itself from a Communist Party that itself had moved away from Moscow orthodoxy, was admitted in 1974.[6] Its acceptance of the ideologically diffuse concept of Euro-Communism was followed, more slowly and to varying degrees, by its counterparts in most other Western European countries. Acceptance of more orthodox communist unions was long resisted for political reasons by the DGB and by rivals within their own countries. This policy changed with the acceptance of the Spanish *Comisiones Obreras* in 1990, followed in 1995 by the Portuguese CGTP-Intersindical. The French *Confédération Générale du Travail* (CGT) remains the only significant political outsider.

Thus, today, the ETUC is a highly encompassing representative of European labor.[7] It has a dual structure: As well as national confederations from 22 countries, its affiliates include 15 European Industry Committees (EICs), which, in most cases, are closely linked to (or regional subsidiaries of) International Trade Secretariats. The national centers affiliated at the beginning of 1995 claimed a total of 46 million members (in many cases, without a doubt considerably inflated) and the EICs, 34.4 million (for the most part, these workers will also have been represented by the national bodies). Thus, the ETUC notionally represents about 30% of all employees in Western Europe (just over 150 million) and the large majority of all trade union members.[8]

Despite a high public profile and the status associated with its role as a "social partner" at the European level, the ETUC is, however, a relatively powerless organization. Affiliates are parsimonious both in funding the confederation and in ceding any of their own autonomy in the interests of authoritative supranational decision making. (And indeed, most affiliates lack significant authority over their own member unions.) Its bureaucracy is small: seven senior officials and support staff, plus those employed in four subsidiary institutes (European Trade Union Institute [ETUI], Trade Union Technical Bureau [TUTB], European Trade Union College [ETUCO], and *Association de Formation Européene des Travailleurs dans la Technologie* [AFETT]). Its capacities would be even more limited without substantial subsidies from the EU Commission (for example, its research arm, the ETUI, receives 95% of its budget from this source). This financial support reflects the commission's own interest in fostering representative institutions at the European level in interaction with which it can reinforce its own status.

THE SINGLE MARKET: THE BIAS TO ECONOMIC LIBERALISM

Despite some of the accoutrements of a federal political system, the dominant rationale of West European integration has been the creation of a frontierless economic space. This was evident from the original title of European *Economic* Community and by the familiar terminology of the "Common Market." In the 1980s, the Brussels authorities quietly determined to signal a more encompassing identity by adopting the shorter title European Community (EC). However, the priority of free trade was simultaneously reasserted through the Single Market project.

After the enthusiasm and idealism that in part underlay the early moves to integration within the EEC, there ensued a phase in which the national interests of individual member states; buttressed by the threat or use of the veto within the council, ensured institutional stasis or "Eurosclerosis." Proposals for social regulation were largely stalled and the community functioned in effect primarily as an agency for transfer payments to agricultural interests (the Common Agricultural Policy accounting for roughly two thirds of the total EEC budget).

A new phase of integration took effect with the commission that assumed office in 1985 under the presidency of Jacques Delors. Like the original creation of the EEC, the new dynamic reflected a complex of political and economic motives. Delors—a French technocrat and former minister with close links to the Mitterrand government and a background with the Catholic trade union confederation, *Confédération Française des Travailleurs Chrétiens* (CFTC)— articulated a strong internationalist commitment. However, his vision of an increasingly authoritative European regime with a significant social and political responsibility for developments within the member states encountered firm resistance from national politicians (among whom Thatcherite conservatives in Britain were the most vocal, but certainly not unique) hostile to any "federalist" encroachments (Pérez-Díaz, 1994). Opposition to the ideal of a European superstate was encapsulated in the notion of "subsidiarity"—that the EU should regulate nothing that could be effectively handled at lower level (i.e., by national governments). The general assent to this principle within the council in the late 1980s served to reaffirm the bias against Euroregulation.

The outstanding exception was the Single Market project. This initiative was launched, many argue, by the European Round Table of Industrialists, a semiformal "club" of the heads of leading European-based multinational companies (Middlemas, 1995, p. 138). Their common view was that far greater economic integration was essential if European firms were to respond adequately to the competitive challenges of the United States, Japan, and the emergent Asian economies. The EEC was a genuine free-trade area in the sense that tariff barriers between member states no longer existed but, for at least three reasons, did not constitute a unified economic space: First, the physical barriers of frontier posts and customs inspection imposed costs on cross-border trade; second, governments tended to favor domestic producers in the award of public contracts; and third, a vast variety of regulations concerning product quality and technical specifications differed between member states so that, for many commodities and services, the national markets remained considerably differentiated in practice.

The program for the "Completion of the Single Market" was essentially a project of EU-driven deregulation. Responsibility for developing this initiative was assigned to Lord Cockfield, Thatcher's trade secretary until appointed to the commission in 1985. His blueprint (in a white paper approved in June 1985) for establishing "the free movement of goods, persons, services and capital" by the end of 1992 became the basis for the SEA and ensured that the priority for the subsequent role of the EU would be the elimination of nation-specific restraints on market mechanisms. Cockfield (1990, p. 8) later clearly set out the sequence accepted by both the commission and the council: "After the Single Market will come the single currency; and after the single currency will come the single economy; and after the single economy will come the European union"—economics first, politics to follow.

Closer European union was thus primarily driven by the monetarist and deregulationist principles that increasingly informed the policies of member states in the late 1970s and the 1980s. This was made explicit in the report on the economics of 1992, coordinated by Commissioner Paolo Cecchini, which developed the thesis that intensifying competitive forces within Europe—by instituting a regime of "supply-side shocks"—was the key to strengthening external competitiveness:

> Rigorous maintenance of the Community's competitive processes is the central regulator of the market's machinery for technology innovation, product quality and good management. . . . The White Paper programme, a sort of political guarantee of European commercial risk, requires rapid enactment. More than this, governments need to show that the legislation it contains is irreversible once enacted. (Cecchini, 1988, pp. 105-106)

The revisions to the treaty contained in the SEA—most notably, Article 100a, which introduced the principle of QMV—were specifically directed to accelerating the process of irreversible market liberalization. It is against this economic bias that the notion of a European social dimension must be critically evaluated.

THE SOCIAL DIMENSION AND THE MAASTRICHT TREATY

The evolution of EC/EU social policy has involved a number of distinct phases displaying relative activism and stasis (Gold, 1993; Hall, 1994; Mosley, 1990). As already noted, the original EEC project was explicitly economic in orientation. Nevertheless, the treaty included a deeply ambiguous clause (Article 117), which declared that

> member states agree upon the need to promote improved working conditions and an improved standard of living for workers. . . . They believe that such a development will ensue not only from the functioning of the common market, which will favour the harmonisation of social systems, but also from the procedures provided for in this Treaty and from the approximation of provisions laid down by law, regulation or administrative action.

This embodied the conflicting assumptions that have underlain debate on social policy ever since: on one hand, that economic liberalization would itself bring an upward convergence of social and employment conditions; on the other, that intervention and regulation were necessary to achieve this outcome. The clause was followed by Article 118, which required the commission to promote "close cooperation between member states in the social field," and Article 119, which prescribed that "men and women should receive equal pay for equal work."

In the early years of the EEC, the commission attempted to interpret the treaty as the basis for wide-ranging intervention in the social policy area—which, in the process, would have enhanced its own role and authority. Member governments—particularly the French, highly sensitive to possible encroachments on its national autonomy—resisted such aspirations and, in the 1960s, the council ensured that social intervention was narrowly confined, in particular, that involving the detailed regulation of health and safety.

In the 1970s, partly because of the enlargement of the EEC and partly because of political shifts to the left within member states, the social agenda was broadened. As it became clear that the common market, far from bringing social convergence, was in some respects leading to increased disparities in social and employment standards, so the council itself recognized the need for a more active social program.

A number of directives on gender equality were adopted, extending regulation beyond the specific issue of equal pay identified in the treaty to broader questions of equal treatment; the EC's role in this area was further enhanced by several keynote judgments by the European Court. Another set of directives laid down a requirement for employers to consult worker representatives before imposing collective redundancies and defined rights for employees of firms whose ownership changed as a result of takeovers or other transfers. The commission also issued draft directives—none of which was adopted—with implications for employee participation in company decision making. The European Company Statute, proposed in 1970, envisaged a structure for large transnational companies involving a European works council and employee representation on a supervisory board. Adoption of this structure—closely modeled on the German company system—would have been voluntary but the proposal was fiercely resisted by employers' organizations that feared that it might offer a precedent for later compulsory measures. In 1972, the commission produced what was known as the draft Fifth Directive, which would have required mechanisms of employee participation (chosen from a menu of forms) in all firms with over 1,000 employees. This, too, was blocked. At the end of the decade, a third initiative emerged, the draft Vredeling Directive (named after the then Commissioner for Social Affairs). This initiative would have obliged all large firms with complex structures to establish procedures for employee information and consultation, but it was equally unsuccessful.

By the end of the decade, the agenda had become more restrictive. The election of the Thatcher government in Great Britain was the extreme example of a more widespread swing to the right in European politics, and even supposedly socialist or social democratic governments became increasingly sympathetic to the doctrines of monetarist economics and labor market deregulation. Although the commission continued to produce drafts of new regulation on employment matters, these faced growing opposition within the council, and the British government became notorious for its willingness to exercise a veto over even modest compromise measures. The outcome was an impasse in EC social policy (Hepple, 1987).

After Delors assumed the presidency of the new commission in 1985, the situation changed once more, but in ways that were complex and contradictory. An enthusiast for the Single Market, Delors also insisted that accelerated European integration must possess a social dimension (*espace social*).[9] This reflected at least three assumptions: first, that in a new period of institutional dynamism at the EC level the community should assume responsibility for social intervention and regulation long taken for granted at national level in most member states; second, that economic integration of what were now 12 member states, with substantial differences in standards of living, could well result in a "two-speed Europe" in the absence of a systematic program designed to encourage convergence; and third, that the Single Market project would fail to attract popular support unless it developed a "human face" (Grant, 1994; Rhodes, 1992).

The treaty revisions contained in the SEA offered some recognition of this perspective. A new article, 118a, called on member states to pursue "improvements, especially in the working environment, as regards the health and safety of workers"; Article 118b instructed the commission "to develop the dialogue between management and labor at European level"; and Article 130a committed the community to "the strengthening of economic and social cohesion," in particular by measures "reducing disparities between the various regions and the backwardness of the least favoured regions," with subsequent subclauses defining the role of the various structural funds in the emerging EC regional policy.

On the other hand, however, Article 100a, which introduced the possibility of QMV, explicitly precluded the use of this procedure for measures relating to "the rights and interests of employed person." In effect, this reemphasized the primacy of liberalization of trade and left social policy subject to the veto of any individual member state.

The precarious basis of the social dimension was demonstrated with the evolution of the Community Charter of the Fundamental Social Rights of Workers, more commonly and simply known as the Social Charter. In 1987, as the SEA came into effect, the Belgian presidency of the council called for a communitywide platform (*socle*) of minimum social rights to accompany the completion of the Single Market at the end of 1992. A draft of the Social Charter was produced by the commission and covered a broad agenda but was diluted in successive versions during 1989 in an attempt to achieve consensus within the council—most notably, excluding any concrete proposals on the particularly contentious questions of trade union rights and minimum wages. Despite all efforts to secure a compromise, the British government refused to accept the charter, which was adopted by the remaining member states as a "solemn declaration" (in other words, lacking any legal force). The adoption of the charter was accompanied by an Action Programme, issued by the commission, setting out a list of measures to be introduced in the field of employment regulation. Of the 47 measures specified, however, only 17 explicitly involved the adoption of directives—in other words, legislation binding on member states—and of these, the majority involved relatively technical issues of health and safety (and were presumably already in the commission pipeline).

On major issues of employment regulation, the next period saw continued deadlock. The commission drafted a number of directives on sensitive topics such as working time, the rights of atypical workers,[10] parental leave, and most notably for the creation of EWCs in transnational companies, which predictably failed to escape the British veto. These initiatives could perhaps be seen as "transitional demands" in that they exposed the limitations of the EC constitutional procedures and might encourage pressure for reform (Hall, 1994, p. 297). But on occasion, the commission also stretched the interpretation of Article 118a to exploit the QMV route: Contentious draft directives on maternity leave, working time, and paid holidays were all tabled on this basis (Addison & Siebert, 1992).[11]

This formed part of the background to the Maastricht revisions to the treaty. These followed two intergovernmental conferences (IGCs), which throughout 1991 addressed the broad themes of economic and monetary union (with the eventual aim of creating a single European currency) and of political union. These resulted in twin drafts of amendments to the EC Treaty; that on political union contained a social chapter that extended the scope of QMV over industrial relations questions—most notably, concerning employee rights of information and consultation. The British government proved totally intransigent in its opposition to such a change, whereas the other 11 member states refused to drop the initiative. The outcome was a constitutionally bizarre compromise: the "UK opt-out." Under the terms of the Protocol on Social Policy agreed on at the Maastricht summit of the council in December 1991, all 12 governments agreed to permit the 11 to "continue along the path laid down in the 1989 Social Charter." This would enable them to adopt legislation—either by QMV within the new areas in which this applied, or by unanimity among the 11 on other questions—which would not be binding on the British government. The protocol also created the possibility for direct input into the legislative process by the joint agreement of the European representatives of employers and workers.

In February 1992, the Maastricht agreements were integrated into a single Treaty on European Union. Its implementation was to face several unexpected obstacles. Three countries—Denmark, France, and Ireland—submitted the agreement to national referenda. In the Danish vote, in June 1992, a narrow majority rejected the treaty (a decision reversed in May 1993, after the other member countries agreed to minor changes). In France, in September 1992, a bare majority voted in favor. In Germany, a challenge in the Constitutional Court delayed the signature of the treaty, which finally took effect in November 1993. All these setbacks indicated the extent to which European integration has become perceived as an elitist project that has failed to achieve popular support. This was apparent also in the most recent phase of enlargement. In Switzerland, a referendum in December 1992 rejected membership of the EEA. Two years later, whereas the Austrians voted heavily for EU membership and the Finns by a comfortable majority, in Sweden the vote in favor was close. In Norway—where a special congress of the main trade union confederation, LO, agreed to campaign against entry despite the recommendations of the leadership—there was a narrow majority against. These controversies involved very complex political alignments and confrontations (urban/rural, populist/elitist, nationalist/Europhile), which cut across simple left/right divisions or differences of class interest. In most countries, indeed, the strongest critics were to both the left and the right of a centrist consensus supporting integration.

Though the controversy over the social chapter attracted most attention, this was arguably a subsidiary aspect of the Maastricht agreement (Lange, 1993). As with the Single Market project, the central dynamic was economic: the progress toward economic and monetary union (EMU). It was agreed to adopt a phased program of integration involving the creation of a European Central Bank and the replacement of national currencies by a single European currency. The British government reserved its position on whether to proceed to this final stage of integration, as did the Danes. Conversely, the agreement specified that only those countries that had achieved "a high degree of convergence of economic performance" would be admitted to the completion of EMU. Five criteria were specified: To join EMU, a country's inflation rate should be no more than 1.5 percentage points above the lowest in the community; there should have been no significant devaluation for at least 2 years; long-term interest rates should be no more than 2% above the lowest; public debt should be under 60% of gross domestic product (GDP); and current public deficits should be under 3% of GDP.

EMU has two crucial implications for the future development of employment regulation. The first is to reinforce the prospect of integration based on variable geometry, already inherent in the operation of the exchange rate mechanism (ERM) pegging the relationship between the currencies of participating states.[12] The prospects of an inner core of member states (headed by France and Germany) willing and able to pursue closer integration, and a periphery of second-league members, became a plausible scenario. But second, the convergence criteria related essentially to monetary indicators rather than real economic performance; proposals for an employment criterion were rejected. The emphasis on low inflation and curbing public deficits reinforced pressures toward a (competitive) deflationary regime, recognized in the most recent period as an aggravating factor in Europe's increasingly severe unemployment crisis.

SOCIAL POLICY AFTER MAASTRICHT AND THE EUROPEAN WORKS COUNCILS DIRECTIVE

The social protocol route to EU legislation is complex and entails that the United Kingdom, being exempt, may derive an unfair advantage through its opt-out. In this respect, the British position appears to confirm the fears of those—notably in the trade unions—who, in campaigning for a strong Social Charter, expressed the fear that economic liberalization would otherwise encourage what was termed *social dumping*.[13] This concept encapsulated the argument that without communitywide enactment of labor standards, countries with low wages, weak employment protection, and/or inferior social benefits would gain market benefits that would encourage a competitive undercutting of workers' conditions (Reder & Ulman, 1993; Streeck, 1991, 1992; Teague, 1989). Though many commentators regarded this argument with skepticism (Adnett, 1995; Erickson & Kuruvilla, 1994), the decision in 1993 of the Hoover Company to transfer production from France to Britain, citing labor costs and flexible working practices as the main rationale, seemed to lend some credence.

In any event, the commission, in the main, has relied primarily on the normal route of legislation to be adopted by the full council of 12 (now 15) members rather than the social protocol procedure, resorting to the latter only when the former method has irrevocably failed and the latter seems to offer positive prospects. The most notable instance has been the protracted saga of the EWC directive: the first concrete outcome of the initiatives on employee participation, outlined earlier, which commenced over a quarter of a century ago (Danis & Hoffmann, 1995). After the whole process had stalled during the 1980s, the issue of information and consultation was revived in 1989 and a new draft directive was issued in 1991. This was opposed vehemently by the British government and by the employers' organization *Union des Industries de la Communauté Européenne* (UNICE), and in particular its U.K. affiliate. Eventually, this was resubmitted to the 11 member states covered by the Maastricht social protocol and was adopted in September 1993.

The directive—which now extends to the new members of the EU and to other members of the EEA—applies to companies with at least 1,000 employees in the member states covered, including at least 150 in each of two different countries, and specifies an elaborate procedure for creating a forum in which management will meet employee representatives at least annually for purposes of information and consultation (Hall, Marginson, & Sisson, 1995). Even before the directive was adopted, unions in a number of transnationals had reached voluntary agreements to create such institutions, and the pace has accelerated. However, the earliest date at which a recalcitrant company could be obliged to establish such a body is April 2001. Moreover, EWCs will have no real powers—hence, they are far weaker than works councils in Germany, for example, and the title is thus something of a misnomer. Also, the notion that they may act as precursors of transnational collective bargaining seems far-fetched. Their main significance is that they will provide a forum for cross-national management-employee consultation, certainly but more important, will allow employee (normally trade union) representatives from different countries to meet each other at the company's expense. The British opt-out affects the number of companies covered by the directive (estimated at between 1,000 and 1,500), because only employees outside the United Kingdom count toward the size threshold. However, some British companies have reached voluntary EWC agreements, and it seems inconceivable that many employers would exclude British representatives from an EWC, once created.

In other respects, the process of employment regulation seems to have largely stalled. The current social affairs commissioner, Pádraig Flynn, and commission president, Jacques Santer, lack the dynamism of their predecessors. After a largely unsuccessful effort in 1993 to "clear the decks" of a wide range of outstanding social policy measures, the commission has proceeded with far greater caution and has developed few significant new initiatives. The explicit perspective toward social policy is now one of consolidation and of reflection and analysis rather than radical action (Commission of the European Communities [CEC], 1995a, pp. 5-6).

Meanwhile, the issues of employment and unemployment have become central to the European industrial relations agenda. European experience since 1980 contrasts starkly with that in other major industrial countries. The official unemployment rate in Japan has risen but remains under 3%; in the United States, although substantially higher, the rate has fluctuated considerably and has fallen significantly from the 1985 peak of 10%. In the 15 countries of the EU, however, there has been a sustained increase (with improvement only in the latter part of the 1980s) from 5% to 12% (CEC, 1995b, pp. 8-9).

The key policy debate has thus become a confrontation between supporters of further labor market deregulation, those calling for a reversal of the trend to liberalization and those seeking to combine elements of a liberal and a regulatory regime. In part, this involves a confrontation between the interests of labor and (transnational) capital, but it also involves a political division in which many of the representatives of Christian democracy share with socialists a commitment to collective social regulation of market relations. Distinctive national economic interests also play an important role: What is viewed in the higher-wage economies of Northern Europe as social dumping may be seen in the poorer South as a necessary basis for gaining a fair share of the European market.[14] The 1993 Delors white paper (CEC, 1994) on growth, competitiveness, and employment was a political compromise that followed the third option. In this respect, it reflected what has been discerned as a contradiction within Delors's own economic thinking: a simultaneous commitment to planning and to market liberalism (Grant, 1994, p. 150).

The subsequent continuing deterioration in the labor market, together with the entry to the EU of new members with a tradition of active labor market policy and (in the case of Finland and Sweden) the experience of dramatic recent increases in unemployment, seems to have shifted the agenda. The December 1994 summit, held under the German presidency of the council (it is significant that unemployment in Germany has also risen rapidly in the 1990s), defined employment creation as a central priority. This issue has, in turn, become one of the themes in the current IGC originally scheduled to address a limited range of institutional questions but now also is concerned with broader policies.[15] As well as issues of greater accountability in decision making—reducing what is euphemistically termed the *democratic deficit,* inter alia, by strengthening the role of the European Parliament—demands to be addressed are the systematic entrenchment of social and citizenship rights and the framing of economic strategies to combat unemployment. In this context, the EMU convergence criteria will almost inevitably require reconsideration: not least because Luxembourg is the only country to have consistently satisfied all the criteria agreed at Maastricht. Certainly, the ETUC has been pressing strongly for a change of course, with a detailed set of proposals set out in its 1995 congress statement, "Jobs and Solidarity at the Heart of Europe" (European Trade Union Confederation, 1995; Yuste & Foden, 1995). Whether demands for a switch to Euro-Keynesianism will achieve any effect remains doubtful but no longer, perhaps, totally inconceivable.

DILEMMAS OF TRADE UNIONS IN THE PROCESS OF EUROPEAN INTEGRATION

Trade unions are institutions that emerged in most countries as representatives of sectional, often locally based, collective interests and developed only slowly into more encompassing organizations. In their modern form, they have become established, with varying degrees of effectiveness, as bodies that aggregate and defend the interests of workers at a national level. Even here, their structures and strategies often fail to overcome divisive particularisms, reinforcing rather than transcending differentiations based on skill, gender, ethnicity, sector of employment, type of employment contract, and so on.

Despite the familiar rhetorics of internationalism, unions are rooted in national terrains and, in any attempt to build transnational organization, such problems are amplified and compounded. This has been evident in Europe where the interests and perspective of national unions differ considerably, not only because of contrasting ideological traditions but also, for example, between high- and low-wage countries, between those with advanced industries and those with more archaic structures of production, between those with well-established welfare states and systems of employment regulation and those without them. As noted above, what is social dumping for trade unions in one set of countries may represent an expansion of job opportunities for those elsewhere (Lanzalaco & Schmitter, 1992, p. 210). Common programmatic declarations typically paper over such divisions.

Unions are, in one sense, handicapped by their representative and democratic rationale. The agents of transnational capital can implement policies in a direct and authoritative manner. Representatives of labor must engage in processes of vertical and horizontal negotiation to establish any meaningful policy objectives—reconciling different national, sectoral, and occupational interests but also winning support and understanding at the grassroots level. These processes are at least potentially contradictory. The history of international trade union relations is replete with paper agreements between top-level bureaucrats remote from the memberships in whose name they are presented.

These are familiar problems that are all too evident in the record of the ETUC. Lecher (1994) comments that "the ETUC needs to develop into a trade union with a living connection to its members" (p. 14). As Ebbinghaus and Visser note (1996), "Similar to Brussels technocracy, the ETUC remains by and large the affair of national union leaders meeting sporadically, and of some union leaders serving permanently in Brussels. Everything is far removed from the ordinary member or even national union." For these authors, the pursuit of a hierarchical ordering of national trade union interests and actions is futile. More promising is a network strategy through which the ETUC would act as facilitator of cooperative links at company, sectoral, and regional levels.[16]

The issue of organizational form links to that of purpose: How far can meaningful common policies be crafted for the European labor movement, and what strategies are most appropriate for their attainment? The ETUC has tended to oscillate between three approaches. The first involves the formulation of broad policy goals and lobbying within EU institutions in their support. In this process, it faces enormous disadvantages. The EU is not a coherent supranational actor but an arena of conflicting interests and projects. The counterpart of the ETUC on the employers' side, UNICE, is far better resourced in defending the interests of capital, whereas all major transnational companies have their own lobbyists in Brussels. They enjoy greater potential for private access to decision makers and a more sympathetic hearing in most of the EU apparatus. Whereas a single DG has responsibility for employment issues, there are half a dozen with at least partly an economic brief, headed for the most part by free-market enthusiasts. And the ETUC is pushing for change, change which, for the most part, contradicts the liberalization project of the Single Market (the EU is an institution par excellence adapted to inhibiting change).

The second approach involves the familiar Continental European notion of social partnership. This concept, embraced by Christian and Social Democrats alike, implies that capital and labor enjoy more common than conflicting interests and that the former can be made an effective basis for policy consensus. One of the institutions of the original EEC was the Economic and Social Committee (ECOSOC), an unwieldy body containing representatives of employers, labor, and of consumer and other economic interest groups. It is consulted during the legislative process (normally at a late stage) and is also able to issue opinions in its own right. Participation in ECOSOC absorbs considerable energy on the part of leading European trade unionists, with little effect. It has served, for many years, in the words of one commentator (Middlemas, 1995, p. 386), "as a framework for largely ritual encounters."

An important by-product of the ideology of social partnership is what is known as the *social dialogue* (Carley, 1993). This concept came into vogue with the Single Market initiative and the call for a social dimension to European integration. The SEA established a new article in the treaty, Article 118b, which prescribed that "the Commission shall endeavour to develop the dialogue between management and labor at European level which could, if the two sides consider it desirable, lead to relations based on agreement." This was amplified in the Maastricht protocol. Here, following a last-minute agreement between ETUC and UNICE, a clause was adopted that "should management and labor so desire, the dialogue between them at Community level may lead to contractual relations, including agreements"; and that any such agreement, if both sides so wished, could enter the legislative process and be adopted by QMV.

Not surprisingly, the process of social dialogue has achieved little except, again, to make considerable demands on the resources of European trade unionism. For many years, the various summit discussions between the peak confederations on each side yielded little beyond a handful of joint opinions on such issues as vocational training (Jensen, Madsen, & Due, 1995). The sectoral social dialogue involving the EICs and such employer-side counterparts as exist has been more productive, but not much. The Maastricht agreement—when UNICE conceded for the first time the principle that it might conceivably reach a collective agreement with ETUC—was hailed as a major breakthrough. More skeptical observers have viewed it as introducing the principle of "double subsidiarity," which constitutes a further obstacle to legal regulation, because before commencing on the legislative route, the commission may now feel obliged to allow the social partners to explore the possibility of voluntary agreement (Streeck, 1994). In the case of the EWC directive, for example, this allowed UNICE to delay progress toward legislation. The one positive achievement to date was the (extremely modest) agreement on parental leave reached at the end of 1995 and subsequently enacted as a directive.

The third option is to mobilize rank-and-file support for trade union demands at the European level. This has rarely been used—indeed, there is only one significant example. In April 1993, the ETUC convened a "day of action," which was marked by meetings and demonstrations, and in some countries by token strikes. This was described by the ETUC as "an outstanding success." However, although certainly attracting some media attention, it did not evidently achieve its aim of stimulating an effective European policy for employment generation, and it is unclear how widespread an impact it achieved even among trade union members themselves. This exercise was consistent with the tradition of top-down publicity action and has not been repeated.

A very different, and perhaps more effective, instance of mobilization was achieved by what is perhaps the weakest (in terms of percentage of the workforce unionized) movement in Europe: the movement in France. The mass strikes and demonstrations at the end of 1995 against cuts in social security benefits and loss of benefits and jobs in the public sector attracted widespread popular support and forced the government to make some concessions. The proposals of the Juppé government were explicitly presented as essential to bring France into line with the EMU convergence criteria, and the unrest caused evident alarm among EU policy makers. As preparations for EMU lead other governments to squeeze public welfare and public employment, the French example may well be widely imitated. Such a trend would add force to the ETUC's demands, but it is difficult to envisage the ETUC being willing or able to lead such a movement.

CONCLUSIONS

It is difficult to argue that trade unions have been influential actors in the process of European integration. They are reacting, belatedly, to a transformation in economic relations that is already set firmly on course. It is uncertain whether they are able to transcend their own internal differences of interest and orientation, and if they can, whether their organizations at the

European level can achieve the strategic capacity to affect those decisions that remain open.

Against this background there is, however, a polarization of views. One position is deeply pessimistic: A liberal economic regime provides a terrain on which transnational capital can divide and rule, opting for those national labor market regimes offering the best prospects for accumulation and encouraging a competitive undercutting of national collective bargaining and national welfare states (Altvater & Mahnkopf, 1993; Ramsey, 1991). An effective EU structure of employment regulation might limit such pressures, but seems scarcely attainable (Streeck, 1992, 1994). Whatever paper declarations may have been achieved within the EU system, their real value has proved negligible (Silvia, 1991).

An alternative position, although not necessarily optimistic, is less dismissive. Goetschy (1994), for example, has emphasized that subsidiarity has encouraged the development of a strong regional dimension within the EU, creating new space for labor movement intervention. In addition, the various programs covered by the EU structural funds have an important redistributive role, doing something to offset the dynamic of uneven development. Ross (1994) likewise cautions against "Europessimism." He argues that the achievements of the social dimension are modest but not insignificant. Were the national trade union movements to allow the ETUC more resources and greater authority, in principle, more could be achieved. Leibfried and Pierson (1992) have likewise insisted that there exists room for maneuver (as national governments find their own discretion limited by supranational economic forces, they are likely to be more willing to enhance the role of regulation at EU level).

Although some of these differences reflect ideological idées fixes that are not necessarily amenable to evidence, many of the debates reflect uncertainties that could be clarified by further experience and information. To this extent, the issues discussed in this chapter suggest possible themes and directions for future research. The first is the impact of economic liberalization in Europe on established national industrial relations institutions and employment conditions. Is the Single Market encouraging a destructive process of regime competition as some have predicted? Second, what is the practical effect of those measures of social regulation adopted by the EU? How have they been applied at national level and how far have they counteracted the first set of tendencies? Third, how are the supranational institutions of European trade unionism evolving, both in organizational form and in modes of action? Is European labor developing the strategic capacity to influence its own fate? This in turn links to a fourth question: In what ways can programmatic commitments to international solidarity be made relevant to the everyday experiences and aspirations of workers and union members whose main perspectives are set within national, or more localized, parameters? The fight for a social Europe requires that Europeanization be transformed from an elitist to a popular project, and the ideological preconditions for such a transformation have as yet been barely investigated.

In any event, it is possible to conclude that there exists some space for a potentially greater influence by European labor. The external obstacles are immense: the liberalizing dynamic already in train, the more effective impact of the employer's side, the built-in constitutional obstacles to progressive EU initiatives. The internal obstacles to constructing a cohesive and effective European trade unionism are similarly imposing. Yet, paradoxically, if the pessimistic scenario holds true and if the scope for effective trade union action at the national level becomes systematically reduced, the pressures for effective transnationalism will intensify. There exists some space for strategic intervention.

NOTES

1. For information on the institutional framework, see Dinan (1994) or Nugent (1994).

2. This was foreshadowed by the Treaty of Paris signed by the same six countries in 1952 and establishing

the Coal and Steel Community. In 1957, it was also agreed to set up a third agency, Euratom. All three "European Communities" constitute, in effect, a single supranational entity.

3. The Commission of the European Communities (*Commission des Communautés Européennes*) is headed by a president, appointed by the unanimous decision of the Council of Ministers.

4. In the language of the EU, the term *social* tends to refer primarily to labor market and employment issues.

5. For a useful overview of the background of interunion relations in Europe and trade union policies towards the EEC/EU, see Lecher (1994) and Visser and Ebbinghaus (1992).

6. Much more recently, in 1992, it has been admitted to the ICFTU.

7. Some white-collar and professional confederations outside the ETUC are members of two separate European confederations, though the ETUC claims that its own subsidiary organization EUROCADRES is far more representative.

8. There is a lack of reliable membership data for many European countries but it is reasonable to suppose that ETUC affiliates cover about 85% of the total. See, for example, Ebbinghaus and Visser (1996).

9. This view had also been articulated by the French president, François Mitterrand (in whose government Delors had served before his appointment to the commission).

10. In other words, part-time or temporary employees.

11. The commission is able to select the "treaty base" on which draft legislation is submitted (an important ingredient in the complex politics of commission-council relations). The British government formally complained to the European Court that the commission's use of Article 118a as the basis for the working time directive (finally adopted in November 1993) was in breach of the treaty; its complaint was rejected in November 1996.

12. The UK did not join when the ERM was established in 1979, entering only in 1990, and was forced (with Italy) to suspend its membership with the currency crisis of 1993. Of the new Southern European members of the EU, Greece did not join, and Spain and Portugal did so only after some delay. Italy rejoined in late 1996.

13. This concept was originally developed by the German trade unions.

14. In this respect, the British government has aligned itself with Southern Europe. The decision of Hoover Europe, in 1993, to close a French factory and shift production to Scotland provoked an outcry in continental Europe but was welcomed by the British government as a sign of the advantages of an unregulated labor market (*European Industrial Relations Review*, 1993, pp. 14-20).

15. The council established a "reflection group" of national representatives to receive submissions and develop proposals in advance of the IGC. Progress during 1996 was slow, partly because of British obstructionism, and discussions were put on hold to await the 1997 UK general election, widely expected to result in a change of government. Labor was, indeed, elected in May 1997—with a landslide majority—and is committed to ending the Maastricht opt-out. However, despite its more positive orientation to the EU, the new Labor government seems unenthusiastic toward many of the commission proposals for social regulation and by "opting in" may actually delay further progress.

16. The adoption of the EWC directive has given a boost to company-level linkages. The EICs provide the framework for sectoral trade union interchange and cooperation. The third regional level is particularly important in areas where production activities and labor markets cross national frontiers (for example, Saarland, Lorraine, Luxembourg). In the 1980s, the ETUC established a structure of Inter-Regional Trade Union Councils and their numbers expanded rapidly in the 1990s and, in some cases, bridged EU countries and eastern Europe; 22 such councils were reported at the 1995 ETUC congress.

REFERENCES

Addison, J. T., & Siebert, W. S. (1992). The social charter: Whatever next? *British Journal of Industrial Relations, 30*, 495-513.

Adnett, N. (1995). Social dumping and European economic integration. *Journal of European Social Policy, 5*, 1-12.

Altvater, E., & Mahnkopf, B. (1993). *Gewerkschaften vor der europäischen Herausforderung (Trade unions confront the challenge of Europe)*. Münster, Germany: Westfälisches Dampfboot.

Carley, M. (1993). Social dialogue. In M. Gold (Ed.), *The social dimensions* (pp. 105-134). London: Macmillan.

Cecchini, P. (1988). *The European challenge: 1992*. Aldershot, UK: Wildwood.

Cockfield, Lord. (1990). The real significance of 1992. In C. Crouch & D. Marquand (Eds.), *The politics of 1992* (pp. 1-8). Oxford, UK: Basil Blackwell.

Commission of the European Communities (CEC). (1994). *Growth, competitiveness, employment*. Luxembourg: OOPEC.

Commission of the European Communities (CEC). (1995a). *Medium-term social action programme 1995-97*. Luxembourg. OOPEC.

Commission of the European Communities (CEC). (1995b). *Employment in Europe 1995*. Luxembourg: OOPEC.

Danis, J.-J., & Hoffmann, R. (1995). From the Vredeling Directive to the European Works Council Directive. *Transfer, 1*, 180-187.

Dinan, D. (1994). *Ever closer union? An introduction to the European Community.* London: Macmillan.

Ebbinghaus, B., & Visser, J. (1996). *European labor and transnational solidarity: Challenges, pathways and barriers.* Mannheim, Germany: MZES.

Erickson, C. L., & Kuruvilla, S. (1994). Labor costs and the social dumping debate in the European Union. *Industrial and Labor Relations Review, 48,* 28-47.

European Trade Union Confederation. (1995). *Jobs and solidarity at the heart of Europe.* Brussels, Belgium: Author.

Goetschy, J. (1994). A further comment on Wolfgang Streeck. *Economic and Industrial Democracy, 15,* 477-485.

Gold, M. (1993). Overview of the social dimension. In M. Gold (Ed.), *The social dimension* (pp. 10-40). London: Macmillan.

Grant, C. (1994). *Delors: Inside the house that Jacques built.* London: Brealey.

Hall, M. (1994). Industrial relations and the social dimension of European integration. In R. Hyman & A. Ferner (Eds.), *New frontiers in European industrial relations* (pp. 281-311). Oxford, UK: Basil Blackwell.

Hall, M., Marginson, P., & Sisson, K. (with M. Carley & M. Gold). (1995). *European Works Councils: Planning for the directive.* London: Eclipse Group/IRRU.

Hepple, B. (1987). The crisis in EEC labour law. *Industrial Law Journal, 16,* 77-87.

Jensen, C. S., Madsen, J. S., & Due, J. (1995). A role for a pan-European trade union movement? *Industrial Relations Journal, 26,* 4-18.

Lange, P. (1993). Maastricht and the social protocol. *Politics and Society, 21,* 5-36.

Lanzalaco, L., & Schmitter, P. C. (1992). Europe's internal market, business associability and the labour movement. In M. Regini (Ed.), *The future of labour movements* (pp. 188-216). London: Sage.

Lecher, W. (Ed.). (1994). *Trade unions in the European Union: A handbook.* London: Lawrence and Wishart.

Leibfried, S., & Pierson, P. (1992). Prospects for social Europe. *Politics and Society, 20,* 333-366.

Middlemas, K. (1995). *Orchestrating Europe: The informal politics of the European Union.* London: Fontana.

Mosley, H. G. (1990). The social dimension of European integration. *International Labour Review, 129,* 147-164.

Nugent, N. (1994). *The government and politics of the European Union.* London: Macmillan.

Pérez-Díaz, V. (1994). *The challenge of the European public sphere.* ASP Research Paper 4(c), Madrid, Spain.

Ramsey, H. (1991). The commission, the multinational, its workers and their charter. *Work, Employment and Society, 5,* 541-566.

Reder, M., & Ulman, L. (1993). Unionism and unification. In L. Ulman, B. Eichengreen, & W. T. Dickens (Eds.), *Labor and an integrated Europe* (pp. 13-44). Washington, DC: Brookings Institution.

Rhodes, M. (1992). The future of the "social dimension." *Journal of Common Market Studies, 30,* 23-49.

Ross, G. (1994). On half-full glasses, Europe and the left. *Economic and Industrial Democracy, 15,* 486-496.

Schmitter, P. C., & Streeck, W. (1992). From national corporatism to transnational pluralism: Organized interests in the single European market. In *Social institutions and economic performance* (pp. 197-231). London: Sage.

Silvia, S. J. (1991). The social charter of the European Community. *Industrial and Labor Relations Review, 44,* 626-643.

Streeck, W. (1991). More uncertainties: German unions facing 1992. *Industrial Relations, 30,* 317-349.

Streeck, W. (1992). National diversity, regime competition and institutional deadlock. *Journal of Public Policy, 12,* 301-330.

Streeck, W. (1994). European social dialogue after Maastricht. *Economic and Industrial Democracy, 15,* 151-177.

Teague, P. (1989). Constitution or regime? The social dimension to the 1992 project. *British Journal of Industrial Relations, 27,* 310-329.

Visser, J., & Ebbinghaus, B. (1992). Making the most of diversity? European integration and transnational organization of labour. In J. Greenwood, J. Grote, & K. Ronit (Eds.), *Organized interests and the European Community* (pp. 206-237). London: Sage.

Yuste, A. R., & Foden, D. (1995). Labour market, unemployment and employment policy. *Transfer, 1,* 499-519.

The Impact of the Movement Toward Hemispheric Free Trade on Industrial Relations

ROY J. ADAMS

The passage of the North American Free Trade Agreement (NAFTA) and its associated side agreements on the environment and labor has heightened the sensitivity of researchers and teachers in all three affected countries—Mexico, Canada, and the United States—to practice in the other countries. In doing so, it has the potential to significantly affect not only practice on the ground but also the subject matter and organization of research and teaching in the three countries. The object of this chapter is to consider the implications of hemispheric free trade for both the practice and study of industrial relations, an interdisciplinary field that focuses on a wide range of labor issues. The effects of the move toward freer trade on the North American labor movements and union-management relations, labor policy, and the functioning of the labor market will be reviewed with a view toward eliciting an agenda for future research.

EFFECTS OF THE CANADA-U.S. FREE TRADE AGREEMENT

The proposal in the mid-1980s for a Canada-U.S. free trade agreement set off a major national debate in Canada in which the trade unions played a very significant part. That proposal called for the elimination of tariffs over a 10-year period on a wide range of goods produced in both countries. It also established bilateral codes with regard to agriculture, wine and spirits, energy, automotive products, government procurement, investment, and services. Although completely free trade was not achieved with respect to these issues, many impediments to cross-border activity were removed. The initiative for this agreement came from the Canadian federal government and was strongly backed by business in both Canada and the United States. Approximately 80% of Canadian exports go to the United States, and fear in the Canadian business community of rising protectionist sentiments in the United States led to this Canadian initiative. However, free trade with the United States has been a very contentious issue in Canada throughout most of its history. Those in favor have emphasized the potential economic benefits of freer trade, whereas those against have pointed to the likely political costs in terms of lost sovereignty and perhaps independence. As in the past, the issue in the most recent round led to considerable political upheaval before narrowly being approved (Adams & White, 1989; Glyde, 1993).

The Canadian Labour Congress (CLC), the major labor union federation in the country, joined with a number of other social groups (including human rights, environmental, anti-poverty, consumer, senior citizen, farmer,

From *Work and Occupations*, Vol. 24, No. 3, August 1997, pp. 364-380. Reprinted by permission.

women's, aboriginal, and religious organizations) in opposition to the proposed agreement (see, e.g., Bleyer, 1992; Doern & Tomlin, 1991; Robinson, 1994a). The concerns expressed by the coalition established something of a research agenda. Key issues relevant to industrial relations were:

1. Loss of jobs. The tariff wall, which had existed throughout the 20th century, required American-based manufacturers to establish branch plants in Canada if they wanted to sell their goods at competitive prices. With that wall gone, labor feared, companies would rationalize production by shutting down Canadian plants and consolidating production in the United States. They also feared that low wages and labor standards in the U.S. South would act as a magnet, drawing investment away from Canada (see, e.g., Campbell, 1993b).
2. Increased ease of movement to the United States would enhance management bargaining power, resulting in poorer collective agreements for the unions (see, e.g., Betcherman & Gunderson, 1990; Gunderson & Verma, 1993, 1994).
3. Pressure would be exerted on Canadian legislatures to harmonize labor relations policy to institute a "level playing field." Since Canadian social and labor legislation is generally more favorable to labor than it is in the United States, harmonization would mean a reduction in Canadian standards (see, e.g., Adams & White, 1989).

There were many other concerns expressed by Canadian labor (e.g., loss of sovereignty by Canadian governments), but those listed above were the issues most relevant to industrial relations. Although opinion polls in Canada indicated that the electorate was about evenly divided in its support of or opposition to the proposed trade deal, when the Progressive Conservative Party was returned to power in November 1988, it quickly moved to finalize the Canada-U.S. Free Trade Agreement (FTA). Political opposition in the United States was minor and the agreement came into existence in January 1989 (Adams & White, 1989). Since then, the Canadian Labour Congress has kept a running total of Canadian plants that have shut down and moved to the United States (White, 1993). However, as its critics note, Congress has not kept a list of new plants that have been established in Canada or of businesses that have expanded as a result of opportunities created by the FTA; and it is clear that in some industries, United States investment in Canada has increased, in part, because the value of the Canadian dollar, after initially appreciating, has declined significantly compared to its U.S. counterpart.[1] Shortly after the FTA came into existence, Canada entered into a deep and long recession, which complicated analysis of the effects of the agreement. As a result, there is no consensus on the general impact of the FTA on jobs in Canada (see, e.g., Campbell, 1993b; Cavitt, 1993).

One Canadian study looked at the specific effects of the FTA on the steel industry. Storey (1993) concluded that, contrary to expectations, the Canadian steel industry had been a loser from free trade largely because the agreement did not provide the promised free access to the U.S. market. On the other hand, the FTA rules did work in favor of the import of U.S. steel into Canada, and U.S. firms had captured a significantly larger part of the market to the detriment of Canadian employment.

As to enhanced management bargaining power, certainly the terms negotiated by Canadian unions in the period since the passage of the FTA in 1989 have not been generous, but the main factor influencing collective bargaining in Canada during the first part of the 1990s was the long recession.[2] It was also a period of major restructuring during which many "union" jobs were lost. To what extent enhanced competition due to trade liberalization added to this effect is still a subject of debate. Most analysts agree that corporate restructuring, especially in manufacturing, has been significantly influenced by the increase in worldwide competition that has been taking place for at least a few decades. The

FTA and NAFTA are generally considered to enhance the effects of that broader development.[3] At a micro level, there are many examples of companies using the threat of moving as a bargaining tactic (Campbell, 1993a; White, 1993). On the other hand, some labor organizations—of which the Canadian Auto Workers Union is an outstanding case—used the fact that overall labor costs were lower in Canada than in the United States, in part due to the availability of universal health care in the former country, as part of its strategy in withstanding demands by the auto companies for givebacks and contract restructuring.[4] In short, investment advantage is not all in one direction.

Gunderson and Verma (1993) attempted to delineate the likely broad effects of trade liberalization on collective bargaining. Since there almost certainly would be adjustment consequences, the parties, they reasoned, would have to negotiate clauses on such issues as "advance notice, severance pay, seniority for layoffs and recalls, subcontracting, and retraining" (p. 131). They also expected pressure to downsize via "such mechanisms as early retirement, attrition worksharing, and leaves of absence." Continuing pressure for wage concessions and new demands by management for the institution of human resource practices, such as broad job categories and multiskilling with less emphasis on seniority, were also seen to be likely outcomes. Their empirical research, however, showed only modest changes in Canadian collective agreements in the expected directions (see also Betcherman, McMullen, Leckie, & Caron, 1994). Research in both Mexico and the United States on the developments in the 1980s suggested movement toward workplace change caused by the liberalization of the Mexican economy from the early 1980s and in the United States by the apparent success that many enterprises, and particularly Japanese-owned organizations, had with techniques such as multiskilling and broad job classifications (see e.g., Cook, 1995; de la Garza, 1994; Levine, 1995). Since Canada was affected sooner than Mexico by freer North American trade and was supposed to have been affected more strongly than the United States because of its smaller size, one might have expected a greater reaction there than in either Mexico or the United States, but the available evidence does not support that proposition.

Since the passage of the FTA, there have been many changes in labor law, which, in Canada, is a provincial responsibility. They have not moved in any obvious direction nor have the key changes been modeled on the United States. Instead, they have mostly stemmed from the ideological position of the political parties that have initiated them. Left-leaning New Democratic Party governments in British Columbia and Ontario enacted "prolabor" legislation that would be welcomed by U.S. unions, whereas less labor-friendly governments have put forth changes over union protests in some cases more like U.S. practice (see; e.g., Carter, 1995; Jain & Muthuchidambaram, 1995, 1996; Thompson, 1993). For example, social democratic governments in both British Columbia and Ontario enacted provisions greatly restricting the use by companies of strikebreakers. The Ontario legislation was repealed in 1995 after a very short life when a right-wing government was elected in that year. That government, following the example of a few others, also introduced the U.S. practice of requiring a majority vote for a union to be certified as the bargaining agent of a relevant group of employees. Most Canadian provinces require only that the union demonstrate, by written proof of membership or support, that the majority of the relevant employees want the union to represent them. The requiring of a vote is generally seen by labor to be inimical to its interests because it enables employers more easily to engage in illegal intimidatory tactics to thwart unionization. However, even in those jurisdictions where a vote is required, Canadian practice is to require labor relations agencies to hold a vote shortly after receiving a certification request—commonly within a week or two. As a result, unfair labor practices occur less frequently and unions win a much higher percentage of such votes than they do in the United States (Martinello, 1996).

In accord with the fears of the anti-free-trade camp, there certainly has been a general reduction in Canadian social standards. For example, there have been cutbacks in support to unemployment insurance, pensions, and health insurance (Robinson, 1996; White, 1993). These cutbacks, however, have been the result primarily of governmental fiscal problems and, if there is a link between those problems and the institution of the FTA, they are indirect and difficult to trace. Robinson (1996) attributes these cutbacks not to the FTA per se, but rather to the broader global movement toward market deregulation that has been evident during the past few decades.

In both Canada and the United States, governments promised adjustment assistance to workers made redundant as a result of freer trade, and the effectiveness of the relevant schemes has been a focus of research. Generally, the programs in both countries have been criticized as inadequate (Decker & Carson, 1995; Faux & Lee, 1993; O'Grady, 1993). The United States introduced a specific NAFTA trade adjustment assistance program for workers made redundant as a result of NAFTA-induced cutbacks by U.S. firms. As of June 1996, 75,020 workers had been certified as being qualified for benefits (Teamsters Research Department, 1996). The scheme has been criticized both because of the inadequacy of its provisions and for its exclusion of many workers indirectly affected by trade-related employment decisions. Service workers who do not produce a tradeable good, for example, are excluded from coverage. Canada did not introduce a special trade-related benefits scheme because of the difficulty of separating out redundancies caused by trade from those brought on by more general economic forces. The governmental pledge was to provide good general labor market adjustment programs. However, due to budget deficits, general labor market adjustment programs were the target of cutbacks during the 1990s.

A long-standing theory in industrial relations holds that union structure and strategy generally follow the market. The theory leads to the expectation that the FTA should have strengthened Canadian and American ties (Thompson, 1993). However, although there have been some calls for greater international labor solidarity, the North American reality is that the Canadian and U.S. movements have been growing further apart rather than closer together during the past few decades. Several Canadian sections of American unions (including, for example, communication workers, broadcast employees, brewery workers, and auto workers) have broken away to form independent Canadian unions. In addition, where a unitary structure has been maintained, the Canadian section has typically been accorded more freedom to act autonomously within that structure (Craig & Solomon, 1996; Thompson & Blum, 1983). This trend goes back to the 1960s when a crescendo of nationalist fervor surrounding the celebration of Canada's centennial led to a reexamination of the international union link (Adams, 1976). In many cases, the Canadian sections of North American unions found that they were receiving inadequate service (e.g., research focused on U.S. issues and neglected Canadian concerns), and were subject to policies considered inappropriate in the Canadian context (e.g., many U.S.-based unions have a constitutional injunction against local union involvement with party politics). Heightened Canadian nationalism led to the conclusion that Canadian unionists should be able to establish their own appropriate policies and that they should be able to elect their own leaders either independently or as the result of decentralized decision making in the context of international unionism (see, e.g., Craig & Solomon, 1996, pp. 183-190).

EFFECTS OF NAFTA

Like its Canadian counterpart, the U.S. labor movement opposed the passage of the FTA but, compared to the Canadian movement, its efforts were very muted (Adams & White, 1989; Robinson, 1994a). The reaction of U.S. labor to the NAFTA proposal was entirely different. Its reaction in opposition to NAFTA was as great, if not greater, than Canadian labor's response. In the United States, labor's concern was primarily focused on the impact on jobs. The fear was that

NAFTA would induce U.S. firms to move to Mexico to take advantage of lower wage rates and lax enforcement of social and labor legislation. Unlike the Canadians with respect to the FTA, U.S. unionists did not express concern that Mexican approaches to labor legislation would be imported into the United States. Nor should they have, since the export of approaches to social and labor policy is usually from larger (metropolitan) countries to smaller (peripheral) countries.[5] Moreover, Mexican labor legislation is formally much more favorable to labor in many regards. For example, in the United States, employers may discharge unorganized employees without notice or reason and unionized employers may employ permanent strikebreakers. In Mexico, on the other hand, workers may not be legally dismissed without just cause and it is illegal to discriminate against employees for making use of their right to strike (Befort & Cornett, 1996).

Much research to date has focused on the jobs-and-wages effect of freer trade without conclusive results. A review of more than 75 studies by Gunderson (1993) on the overall effects of trade liberalization estimated that the total impact was likely to be positive but small in Canada and the United States, although having a larger positive effect in Mexico. These studies indicate that there will be substantial labor market disruption and that high-wage workers (in Canada and the United States) will benefit at the expense of those earning low wages with the result that income differentials between the high- and low-paid will become more uneven. Gunderson's review also led to the conclusion that an increase in exports would create jobs, whereas an increase in imports would result in job loss. Although carried out before the Mexican financial crisis in the winter of 1994 to 1995, his conclusion is relevant to the outcome of that development. As a result of the peso devaluation, Mexican exports to the United States soared and U.S. exports to Mexico took a nosedive (AFL-CIO Task Force on Trade, 1995b).

Strategies used by labor in Canada and the United States toward NAFTA have attracted considerable attention. Contrary to forces leading to the weakening of formal U.S.-Canadian union links, the struggle against NAFTA did bring Canadian and American unionists closer together as they coordinated their efforts to scuttle that initiative. The struggle also led to social coalitions in both countries between labor and other groups in opposition to free trade. As Robinson (1994a) notes, in both countries, these coalitions in addition to labor organizations included

> a substantial part of the environmental movement, consumer protection organizations, organizations of retired persons, anti-poverty groups, farmer organizations, the women's movement, Aboriginal peoples' organizations, religious organizations, human rights groups, international development organizations, elements of the peace movement, student organizations, and progressive policy think tanks. (p. 676)[6]

Common Frontiers, a body formed in Canada in the early 1990s to coordinate Canadian and Mexican labor efforts, evolved into a trinational organization with the mission of coordinating opposition in all three affected countries to proposals for a North American free trade agreement (Bleyer, 1992; Hecker, 1994; Robinson, 1994a).[7] The most ambitious proposal to date for trinational labor cooperation is for the creation of a North American Trade Union Confederation (Barrett & Laster, 1995).[8] However, that proposition does not yet seem to have attracted a great deal of support.

In both Canada and the United States, unions devoted most of their efforts to stopping the passage of NAFTA and very little on the achievement of a social clause that would regulate the impact of the agreement on labor (Cowie, 1994; Robinson, 1994a). With the election of Democrat Bill Clinton, however, the social dimension was placed back on the table. Although Clinton refused to oppose NAFTA, he did agree to seek a trinational accord designed to protect labor interests and the result was the North American Agreement on Labor Cooperation that became effective in 1993 (Government of Canada, 1993). This accord generated considerable academic discussion. Many observers considered it to be very weak and likely to be ineffective (Cook, 1994; Cowie & French, 1994; Robinson, 1994b). Nevertheless, a few analysts suggested that although the enforcement procedures are weak, the principles to which the three governments have bound themselves are sound and it is up to labor to parlay that public commitment into effective action (Adams & Singh, 1997; Adams & Turner, 1994; Bensusán Areous, 1994; Compa, 1996; Crandall, 1994; Murphy, 1995).

Although NAFTA itself generated some increase in cross-border union contacts (Cook, 1994), the advent of the side accord gave unions additional motivation to coordinate their efforts. It brought into existence new institutions that have now begun to function. To date, their actions suggest that side-accord mechanisms may be more effective than their detractors suggested. The North American Agreement on Labor Cooperation (NAALC) required each country to establish a National Administrative Office (NAO) whose major functions are to publicize the terms of the agreement and to process complaints that one of the other countries is not living up to its commitments under the agreement. There was considerable general skepticism about the likely effectiveness of the agreement. Although each country committed itself to promote in its own fashion a set of 11 labor rights principles (including, for example, freedom of association and the right to strike), violation of only a small subset of those principles (systematic violation of laws regulating occupational health and safety, child labor, and minimum wages) would result in formal sanctions. Contrary to expectations, the U.S. National Administrative Office has been liberal in its acceptance of cases. Over the objections of employer representatives, the office agreed to hear cases submitted by unions and labor rights groups involving the freedom of association and the right to organize, thus placing Mexican practice with respect to these issues under a spotlight (Adams & Singh, 1997; U.S. National Administrative Office [NAO], 1994, 1995). Complaints filed by unions in the United States against companies operating in Mexico and by a Mexican union against a company operating in the United States, under the terms of the side accord, were coordinated with counterpart unions in the other country (Adams & Singh, 1997; Compa, 1996). Meetings were held bringing together unionists from all of the covered countries to consider strategies designed to maximize the usefulness of the NAALC. A few unions have begun to coordinate organizing and political activities on a cross-border basis (Davis, 1995; Interhemispheric Resource Center, 1996).

That the Mexican government is sensitive to attention from the United States is indicated by its reaction to the Chiapas rebellion (negotiation instead of suppression) and to its placing labor law reform on the back burner when labor policy became an issue after Clinton's election (Cook, 1995; Nassif, 1994). The recent American bailout of the Mexican government after the financial crisis of 1994 to 1995 has made Mexico more dependent on the United States and, thus, more likely to be sensitive to American pressure. Because of the relative success of early union efforts to make use of the side accord, more efforts are likely to be forthcoming and the nature of the procedures are such that cross-border cooperation is a practical necessity.[9]

In their analysis of the NAFTA labor side accord, several researchers have drawn upon the development of the social dimension in Europe in the context of the emergence of a single European market (e.g., Adams & Turner, 1994; Jacek, 1994). Moreover, at the same time that NAFTA and the labor side accord were becoming a subject of research and debate in the United States, the relationship between trade and labor standards became the focus of a broader worldwide discussion (Perez-Lopez, 1995). Proposals were made at the International Labour Office that access to international trade agreements generally should be made contingent upon nations agreeing to commit themselves to the vigorous implementation of a core of labor standards (Hansenne, 1994). This initiative, in turn, raised howls of protest from Third World governments complaining that charges of lax labor standards would be used by advanced countries as a device to exclude goods from poorer countries from their markets (Compa, 1995; Steil, 1994). The general result of these developments is that the relationship between trade and labor is currently a very hot issue for research and debate on the broader world stage (Organization for Economic Cooperation and Development, 1996). Very recently, U.S. and Canadian trade unionists have been exploring joint approaches with leaders of other hemispheric labor movements toward developing a common approach toward trade and labor (Hecker, 1994; Labor Summit, 1995).

That the subject of trade and labor is attracting more attention recently is indicated by the appearance of several books focused on the topic (e.g., Bognanno & Ready, 1993; Cook & Katz, 1994; Grinspun & Cameron, 1993; Lemco & Robson, 1993) with more soon to be published.[10] It is also indicated by the establishment of projects such as the one on "Labor, Free Trade and Economic Integration in the Americas" administered by the Duke-University of North Carolina Program in Latin American Studies (see Smith & French, 1995).

IMPACT ON ACADEMIC INTERCHANGE AND TEACHING

One likely impact of freer trade on the field of industrial relations in the Americas is that it will become more international. There has already been a large increase in interaction between Canadian, U.S., and Mexican labor researchers and those ties will almost certainly strengthen and become broader in future. New initiatives by the executive of the Industrial Relations Research Association, such as the establishment of a special committee to follow NAFTA developments as well as a newly established International Section, are likely to involve researchers from all three countries in the gatherings and debates of the U.S.-based organization.[11] The growing use of the Internet will also increase knowledge of and contacts between researchers and teachers from countries throughout the Americas. Labor-oriented discussion groups such as the International Employee Relations Network (IERN-L) and the Forum on Labor in the Global Economy (Labor-L) have had many postings during the past few years on free trade and labor and on Latin American labor issues more generally.[12] To date, though, there has been very little participation in Internet discussions on labor issues by Latin Americans.

The closer social bonding between the three North American countries will also, no doubt, have an impact on teaching. Already, Canadian and U.S. textbooks are beginning to incorporate observations on the impact of freer trade and on the nature of Mexican industrial relations (see, e.g., Adams, 1995; Mills, 1994). A broad theme in both independent industrial relations departments and in labor relations and human resource departments in business schools over the past decade has been internationalization of the curriculum. At least one university to date (Wayne State) has redesigned its master's degree in industrial relations (IR) program so that its courses address hemispheric IR issues.[13] One very likely result of this trend will be the incorporation of material drawn from all three countries into what were previously domestic IR courses, in contrast to the present in which such material is typically relegated to comparative IR courses.[14] That need should stimulate the production of new texts that draw on material from all three countries. The appearance of such texts in turn will stimulate a demand for more research and for more attention to be paid to international comparisons at professional meetings. Additional information will be made available as a result of the work of the North American Commission on Labor Cooperation and the National Administrative Offices set up in each country under the terms of the Labour Side Accord. A major function of that commission is to carry out research into the labor relations and labor market activities in all three countries. In 1995, it initiated comparative investigations into labor law and practice, into the operation of labor markets in each country, and into the introduction of innovative work practices in manufacturing in companies "that respect labor laws, labor standards and the role of trade unions." (Commission on Labor Cooperation, 1996, p. 18). The NAOs organized several information meetings on issues such as health and safety, equality in the workplace, and labor law and freedom of association.

Some labor researchers have already turned their attention further afield in the Americas. The development of MERCOSUR and the labor effects of that freer trade agreement has begun to be addressed.[15] The potential extention of NAFTA to Chile has also attracted attention (see, e.g., M. Anderson, 1995).

As always, in the (more or less) laissez-faire research regime that exists in North American universities, researchers will pursue whatever issues interest them and, of course, for which they can attract research funding. Because the labor aspect of freer trade should continue to be of policy relevance and because governments are the prime sources of research money, the future for research in this area looks bright. This picture could change, however, if those funding sources discover, and are convinced by, a paper by Thompson (1993). His working proposition was the null hypothesis that movement toward freer trade has little or no effect on major components of IR systems such as trade unions, employer organizations, collective bargaining, and labor policy. After reviewing several incidents of movement toward freer trade, he concluded that he could not confidently reject that null hypothesis. IR institutions, he suggested, tend to persist despite forces that should in theory alter them radically. Like the lyric in the old labor song, they seem to be declaring that "Like a tree standing by the water, we shall not be moved."

NOTES

1. See AFL-CIO Task Force on Trade (1995a), *NAFTAmath, the First Year,* Washington, D.C.: AFL-CIO, in which the large expansion of the auto industry in Canada is noted and lamented.

2. Unemployment went from under 7.5% in 1989 to over 11% in 1993. During the same period, wage increases fell from an average of 5.2% annually to 0.7%. Job losses in manufacturing were particularly severe. From 1989 to 1992, net losses from restructuring amounted to over 20% of the job base (see Craig and Solomon, 1996, and J. Anderson, 1996).

3. Indeed, some authors argue that freer trade agreements are an inherent element of the neoliberal trend toward deregulation of global markets, which has been evident since at least the early 1980s. For a forceful statement of that position, see Robinson (1996).

4. As a result of the recession of the late 1970s and early 1980s, U.S. auto companies pressured the United Auto Workers Union (VAW) to accept contingent compensation schemes such as lump-sum payments and profit sharing. Canadian rejection of this model, after the UAW had agreed to it in the United States, led to the split of the Canadian section of the union and the establishment of the Canadian Auto Workers Union in 1985. In its bargaining with the Big Three auto companies throughout the 1980s and 1990s, that union has rejected contingent pay and has argued at the bargaining table that the auto companies have cost-effective operations in Canada because of a number of differences, of which state provision of medical insurance is the dominant factor. See Kumar and Meltz (1992) for details.

5. There are many examples of this phenomenon. Industrial relations (IR) practices in ex-British and ex-French colonies have much in common with those of the colonial power (see, e.g., Adams, 1993; Kassalow, 1969). The labor policy framework in many Caribbean countries was first modeled on that in Britain and in more recent years on that of the United States (Antoine, 1992). Canada also imported the U.S. Wagner-Act model. On the other hand, there is little evidence that Britain, France, or the United States has borrowed much from smaller countries closely associated with them.

6. Robinson presents an exhaustive list of American and Canadian organizations in opposition to the North American Free Trade Agreement (NAFTA). Examples in Canada include the Canadian Human Rights Foundation, the Canadian Environmental Law Association, Canadian Council on Social Development, the National Pensioners' and Senior Citizens' Federation, the National Farmers' Union, the National Action Committee on the Status of Women, the Assembly of First Nations, the Ecumenical Coalition for Economic Justice, OXFAM-Canada, Canadian Peace Alliance, Canadian Federation of Students, and the Canadian Centre for Policy Alternations. In the United States, the coalition included the International Labor Rights Education and Research Fund, the Sierra Club, the Rainbow Coalition, the National Consumers' League, the National Family Farm Coalition, Women for Economic Justice, the American Friends Service Committee, the Development Group for Alternative Policies, and the Centre for Ethics and Economic Policy.

7. Some elements of the Mexican labor movement as well as other social groups in Mexico also became involved in the anti-NAFTA campaign, and Common Fron-

tiers coordinated efforts in all three countries. However, the largest Mexican labor federation has close ties with the ruling party and it supported NAFTA. Many Mexican unionists saw NAFTA as the source of more efficiency and more jobs and, thus, were uninterested in cooperating with Canadian and U.S. unionists to stop it. Canadians and Americans tried to convince the Mexicans that NAFTA would not be good for Mexican workers but instead would result in the "Maquiladorization" of the Mexican economy. Research on Mexican conditions generally suggested that they were better in domestic industries than they were in the Maquilas. The story of the coordination between labor and other social groups representing, for example, senior citizens, antipoverty groups, farmers, women's and aboriginal organizations, human rights groups, student organizations, and progressive policy think tanks, is told in most detail by Robinson (1994a).

8. Dave Barrett, senior author of the proposal, was New Democratic Party premier of British Columbia during the 1970s and had previously been an active member of the teachers' union in that province. During the 1980s, he ran unsuccessfully for the leadership of the national New Democratic Party. The proposal for a North American Trade Union Confederation is sketchy on details. The basic proposition is that labor in all three countries should systematically and formally coordinate its efforts in response to the impact of free trade.

9. Relative success is, of course, an evaluative phrase. The entire process as well as the early experience still has some strong critics. The current state of the debate is reviewed in Adams and Singh (1997).

10. Conferences that focused on aspects of free trade and labor relations were held at Duke University, Michigan State University, and Rutgers in 1994 and 1995, and books based on papers presented at those conferences are scheduled to be published.

11. See Verma et al. (1996). The International Section of the IRRA was invited by the executive of that association to propose two sessions for the 1997 annual meeting. One of them will focus on labor and trade liberalization in the Americas.

12. The address of the International Employee Relations Network is iern-l@ube.ubalt.edu. The subscription address is listserv@ube.ubalt.edu. Forum on Labor in the Global Economy is at labor-l@yorku.ca. The subscription address is listserv@yorku.ca.

13. This imformation comes from a discussion with Tom Reed, director of the master's degree program in IR at Wayne State.

14. In fact, Mexico was often not considered in comparative courses taught in Canada and the United States. In Canada, the United States was more often considered in the context of domestic courses than in comparative courses. In the United States, Canada was more typically treated as a foreign country and thereby discussed in comparative courses rather than in domestic courses. These observations are based on a set of comparative IR course outlines that I have been assembling over the years, as well as on discussions with colleagues in the Untied States and Canada. For a general report on that survey, see Adams (1991).

15. This issue was taken up, for example, at the interdisciplinary conference on Labor and Free Trade in the Americas, which was held at Duke University in August 1994 (see *Global Perspectives* (Duke University), Fall 1994, and in another meeting sponsored by the Canadian Labour Congress held early in 1996. See also Aparicio Valdez (1993) and Smith (1995). MERCOSUR, the Common Market of the South, includes Argentina, Brazil, Uruguay, Paraguay, and Bolivia. Chile has been accepted as an associate member.

REFERENCES

Adams, R. J. (1976). Canada-U.S. labor link under stress. *Industrial Relations, 15*(3), 295-312.

Adams, R. J. (1991). An international survey of courses in comparative industrial relations. In M. Bray (Ed.), *Teaching comparative industrial relations* (pp. 43-51). Sydney: Australian Centre for Industrial Relations Research and Teaching at the University of Sydney.

Adams, R. J. (1993). Regulating unions and collective bargaining: A global, historical analysis of determinants and consequences. *Comparative Labor Law Journal, 14*(3), 272-301.

Adams, R. J. (1995). Canadian industrial relations in comparative perspective. In M. Gunderson & A. Ponak (Eds.), *Union-management relations in Canada* (3rd ed.). Ontario, Canada: Addison-Wesley.

Adams, R. J., & Singh, P. (1997). Early experience with NAFTA's labour side accord. *Comparative Labor Law Journal, 18*(2), 161-181.

Adams, R. J., & Turner, L. (1994). The social dimension of freer trade. In M. Cook & H. Katz (Eds.), *Regional integration and industrial relations in North America* (pp. 82-104). Ithaca, NY: ILR Press.

Adams, R. J., & White, J. (1989). Labor and the Canada-U.S. free trade agreement. *ILR Report, 27*(1), 15-21.

AFL-CIO Task Force on Trade. (1995a). *NAFTAmath: The first year.* Washington, DC: AFL-CIO.

AFL-CIO Task Force on Trade. (1995b). *After peso devaluation in Mexico: A tale of two countries.* Washington, DC: AFL-CIO.

Anderson, J. (1996). Trade, technology and unions: The theory and practice of free trade and its implications for unions. In C. Craypo (Ed.), *Impact on workers and unions of the free trade agreement involving Canada, the U.S. and Mexico* (pp. 136-185). South Bend, IN: Higgins Labor Research Center, University of Notre Dame.

Anderson, M. (1995, June 21). *Statement submitted on behalf of the Labor Advisory Committee for Trade Negotiations and Trade Policy to the Subcommittee on Trade of the Committee on Ways and Means on Accession of Chile to the North America Free Trade Agreement.* Washington, DC: AFL-CIO.

Antoine, R. (1992). *The CARICOM labour law harmonization report.* Cave Hill, Barbados: University of the West Indies.

Aparicio Valdez, L. (1993). Los aspectos laborales de la integración. *Proceedings of the Second Industrial Relations Congress of the Americas.* Valencia, Venezuela: University of Carabobo.

Barrett, D., & Laster, M. (1995, October). *The North American Federation of Trade Unions: A response to NAFTA.* Paper presented at the Southern Labor Studies Conference, Austin, Texas.

Befort, S., & Cornett, V. (1996). Beyond the rhetoric of the NAFTA treaty debate: A comparative analysis of labor and employment law in Mexico and the United States. *Comparative Labor Law Journal, 17*(2), 269-313.

Bensusán Areous, G. (1994). The Mexican model of labor regulation and competitive strategies. In M. Cook & H. Katz (Eds.), *Regional integration and industrial relations in North America* (pp. 52-65). Ithaca, NY: ILR Press.

Betcherman, G., & Gunderson, M. (1990) Canada-U.S. free trade and labour relations. In J. Burton (Ed.), *Proceedings of the 1990 Spring Meeting of the Industrial Relations Research Association* (pp. 454-459). Madison, WI: IRRA.

Betcherman, G., McMullen, K., Leckie, N., & Caron, C. (1994). *The Canadian workplace in transition.* Kingston, Ontario, Canada: IRC Press.

Bleyer, P. (1992). Coalitions of social movements as agencies of social change: The Action Canada Network. In W. Carroll (Ed.), *Organizing dissent: Contemporary social movements in theory and practice* (pp. 102-117). Toronto: Garamond.

Bognanno, M., & Ready, K. (1993). *The North American Free Trade Agreement: Labor, industry and government perspectives.* Westport, CT: Praeger.

Campbell, B. (1993a). *Free trade destroyer of jobs: An examination of Canadian job loss under the FTA and NAFTA.* Kingston, Ontario: Canadian Centre for Policy Alternatives.

Campbell, B. (1993b). A Canadian labor perspective on a North American Free Trade Agreement. In M. Bognanno & K. Ready (Eds.), *The North American Free Trade Agreement: Labor, industry and government perspectives* (pp. 61-68). Westport, CT: Praeger.

Carter, D. (1995). Collective bargaining legislation, In M. Gunderson & A. Ponak, *Union-management relations in Canada* (3rd ed.). Ontario, Canada: Addison-Wesley.

Cavitt, W. (1993). Reaction panel remarks made at the conference on North American free trade: Labor, industry, and government policy perspectives. In M. Bognanno & K. Ready (Eds.), *The North American Free Trade Agreement: Labor, industry and government perspectives* (pp. 77-80). Westport, CT: Praeger.

Commission on Labor Cooperation. (1996). *1995 annual report.* Dallas, TX: Author.

Compa, L. (1995). . . . And the twain shall meet? A North-South controversy over labor rights and trade. *Labor Research Review, 23*(Spring/Summer), 51-68.

Compa, L. (1996, May). *Another look at the NAFTA labor accord.* Paper prepared for presentation at a conference on International Labor Rights and Standards After NAFTA, Rutgers University, New Brunswick, New Jersey.

Cook, M. (1994). Regional integration and transnational labor strategies under NAFTA. In M. Cook & H. Katz (Eds.), *Regional integration and industrial relations in North America* (pp. 142-166). Ithaca, NY: ILR Press.

Cook, M. (1995). *National labor strategies in changing environments: Perspectives from Mexico* (Latin American Labor Occasional Paper No. 18). Miami: Florida International University, Center for Labor Research and Studies.

Cook, M., & Katz, H. (1994). *Regional integration and industrial relations in North America.* Ithaca, NY: ILR Press.

Cowie, J. (1994). *The search for a transnational labor discourse for a North American economy: A critical review of U.S. labor's campaign against NAFTA* (Duke-UNC Program in Latin American Studies Working Paper No. 13). Durham, NC: Duke University.

Cowie, J., & French, J. (1994). *NAFTA's labor side accord: A textual analysis* (Duke-University of North Carolina Program in Latin American Studies Working Paper No. 11). Durham, NC: Duke University.

Craig, A. W. J., & Solomon, N. A. (1996). *The system of industrial relations in Canada* (5th ed.). Scarborough, Ontario, Canada: Prentice Hall.

Crandall, E. (1994, Spring). Will NAFTA's North American agreement on labor cooperation improve enforcement of Mexican labor law? *Transnational Lawyer, 7,* 166-195.

Davis, T. (1995, Spring/Summer). Cross-border organizing comes home: UE and FAT in Mexico and Milwaukee. *Labor Research Review, 23,* 23-29.

Decker, P., & Carson, W. (1995). International trade and worker displacement: Evaluating the Trade Adjustment Assistance Program. *Industrial and Labor Relations Review, 48*(4), 758-774.

de la Garza, E. (1994). Industrial democracy, total quality, and Mexico's changing labor relations. In M. Cook & H. Katz (Eds.), *Regional integration and industrial relations in North America* (pp. 19-36). Ithaca, NY: ILR Press.

Doern, G. B., & Tomlin, B. (1991). *Faith and fear: The free trade story.* Toronto: Stoddart.

Faux, J., & Lee, T. (1993). The road to the North American Free Trade Agreement: Laissez-faire or a ladder up. In M. Bognanno & K. Ready (Eds.), *The North American Free Trade Agreement: Labor, industry and government perspectives* (pp. 97-115). Westport, CT: Praeger.

Glyde, G. (1993). Canadian labor and the free trade agreement. *Labor Studies Journal, 17*(4), 3-23.

Government of Canada. (1993). *North American agreement on labor cooperation.* Ottawa: Author.

Grinspun, R., & Cameron, M. (Eds.). (1993). *The political economy of North American free trade.* Montreal: McGill-Queen's University Press.

Gunderson, M. (1993). *Labour market impacts of free trade.* Vancouver, Canada: Fraser Institute.

Gunderson, M., & Verma, A. (1993). The impact of free trade on the collective agreement. In M. Bognanno & K. Ready (Eds.), *The North American Free Trade Agreement: Labor, industry and government perspectives* (pp. 128-136). Westport, CT: Praeger.

Gunderson, M., & Verma, A. (1994). Free trade and its implications for industrial relations and human resource management. In M. Cook & H. Katz (Eds.), *Regional integration and industrial relations in North America* (pp. 167-179). Ithaca, NY: ILR Press.

Hansenne, M. (1994, June). The new paths toward social justice. *World of Work,* pp. 4-6.

Hecker, S. (1994). United States union strategy after NAFTA. In S. Deutsch & R. Broomhill (Eds.), *Recent developments in U.S. trade union strategies* (Research Paper Series No. 3, pp. 45-60). Adelaide, Australia: University of Adelaide Center for Labour Studies.

Interhemispheric Resource Center. (1996). Post-NAFTA labor solidarity advances shakily. *BorderLines, 4*(6).

Jacek, H. (1994, June). *Public policy and the North American free trade area: The role of organized business interests and the labour movement.* Paper prepared for delivery at the annual meeting of the Canadian Political Science Association, University of Calgary, Calgary, Alberta.

Jain, H., & Muthuchidambaram, S. (1995). *Ontario labour law reform.* Kingston, Ontario, Canada: IRC Press.

Jain, H., & Muthuchidambaram, S. (1996). Ontario labour law reforms: A comparative study of Bill 40 and Bill 7. *Canadian Labour and Employment Law Journal, 4,* 311-330.

Kassalow, E. (1969). *Trade unions and industrial relations: An international comparison.* New York: Random House.

Kumar, P., & Meltz N. (1992). Industrial relations in the Canadian automobile industry. In R. Chaykowski & A. Verma (Eds.), *Industrial relations in Canadian industry* (pp. 39-86). Toronto: Dryden.

Labor Summit. (1995). *A call for justice and equity in the hemisphere.* A joint statement of ORIT, the Inter-American Regional Organization of Labor, the AFL-CIO and the American Institute for Free Labor Development.

Lemco, J., & Robson, W. (1993). *Ties beyond trade, labor and environmental issues under the NAFTA.* Toronto: C. D. Howe Institute and National Planning Association of Washington, DC.

Levine, D. (1995). *Reinventing the workplace.* Washington, DC: Brookings Institution.

Martinello, F. (1996, May). *Certification and decertification in Canadian jurisdictions.* Paper prepared for presentation at the annual meeting of the Canadian Industrial Relations Association, Brock University in St. Catherines, Ontario, Canada.

Mills, D. (1994). *Labor-management relations* (5th ed.). New York: McGraw-Hill.

Murphy, B. (1995). NAFTA's North American agreement on labor cooperation: The present and the future. *Connecticut Journal of International Law, 10,* 403-426.

Nassif, A. (1994). The Mexican dual transition: State, unionism and the political system. In M. Cook & H. Katz (Eds.), *Regional integration and industrial relations in North America* (pp. 132-141). Ithaca, NY: ILR Press.

O'Grady, J. (1993, June). *NAFTA and labour issues in Canada.* Paper presented at a conference on North American Free Trade: Pro and Con, Park Plaza Hotel, Toronto.

Organization for Economic Cooperation and Development (OECD). (1996). *Trade, employment and labour standards: A study of core workers' rights and international trade.* Paris: Author.

Perez-Lopez, J. (1995). The promotion of international labor standards and NAFTA: Retrospect and prospects. *Connecticut Journal of International Law, 10,* 427-474.

Robinson, I. (1994a). NAFTA, social unionism and labour movement power in Canada and the United States. *Relations Industrielles, 49*(4), 657-693.

Robinson, I. (1994b). How will the North American Free Trade Agreement affect worker rights in North America? In M. Cook & H. Katz (Eds.), *Regional integration and industrial relations in North America* (pp. 105-131). Ithaca, NY: ILR Press.

Robinson, I. (1996). NAFTA and neoliberal restructuring in Canada. In C. Craypo (Ed.), *Impact on workers and unions of the free trade agreement involving Canada, the U.S. and Mexico* (pp. 202-237). South Bend, IN: University of Notre Dame, Higgins Labor Research Center.

Smith, R. (1995, October). *Labor issues in MERCOSUR.* Paper presented at the Southern Labor Studies Conference, Austin, Texas.

Smith, R., & French, J. (1995, June 2). *Labor, free trade, and economic integration in the Americas: Selected materials.* Document prepared for a special seminar on Latin and Interamerican dimensions of industrial relations held at the World Congress of the International Industrial Relations Association, Washington, DC.

Steil, B. (1994). Social correctness is the new protectionism. *Foreign Affairs, 73*(1), 14-20.

Storey, R. (1993). Making steel under free trade? *Relations Industrielles, 48*(3), 712-731.

Teamsters Research Department. (1996). *Two years of NAFTA: Job impacts in the U.S.* Washington, DC: United Brotherhood of Teamsters.

Thompson, M. (1993). Industrial relations and free trade. In H. Lucena (Ed.), *Proceedings of the 2nd Industrial Relations Congress of the Americas* (pp. 387-404). Valencia, Venezuela: University of Carabobo. (A revised version of the paper under the same title was presented at a Joint Session of the North American Economics and Finance Association and the Industrial Relations Research Association, January 4, 1994, Boston, MA.)

Thompson, M., & Blum, A. (1983). International unionism in Canada: The move to local control. *Industrial Relations, 22*(1), 71-86.

U.S. National Administrative Office (NAO) North American Agreement on Labor Cooperation. (1994, October 12). *Public report of review: NAO submission #94001 and #94002*. Washington, DC: U.S. Department of Labor.

U.S. National Administrative Office (NAO) North American Agreement on Labor Cooperation. (1995, April 11). *Public report of review: NAO submission #94003*. Washington, DC: U.S. Department of Labor.

Verma, A., Smith, R., Sandver, M., Ready, K., Gunderson, M., Compa, L., & Chaykowski, R. (1996). *Free trade, labor markets and industrial relations: Institutional developments and the research agenda. 1995 report of the IRRA NAFTA Committee.* Madison, WI: Industrial Relations Research Association.

White, R. (1993). *Submission on the North American Free Trade Agreement to the Sub-Committee on International Trade of the Standing Committee on External Affairs and International Trade.* Ottawa: Canadian Labour Congress.

Labor and Post-Fordist Industrial Restructuring in East and Southeast Asia

FREDERIC C. DEYO

Labor movements in East and Southeast Asia pose something of a paradox. On one hand, several economic, social, and political transformations across the region would seem to favor an enhancement of the bargaining power and political influence of workers and trade unions. These transformations include continued industrialization; rapid expansion of a waged, urbanized, organizationally concentrated, and increasingly settled industrial proletariat; rising levels of literacy and education; democratic reforms in many countries; tightening labor markets; and growing international pressure for fuller observance of labor and human rights.

Despite these favorable socioeconomic and political changes, organized labor remains politically marginalized and ineffectual across the region, as seen most notably in the inability of workers and unions to substantially influence the economic strategies adopted by states and firms, contest the sometimes negative labor consequences of those strategies, or seize new opportunities generated by democratic reforms. This chapter seeks to explain this anomaly by referring to the adverse labor impact of enterprise and state-level economic strategies. Such strategies undercut organized labor in two important ways. First, the labor policies associated with East Asian economic strategies have both reflected and further compromised the already weak position of labor across the region. This is particularly true of earlier export-oriented industrialization strategies (EOI) and more recent enterprise efforts to enhance production flexibility. Second, with a few important exceptions, the unique timing and sequencing of these strategies have, in many cases, preempted independent organizational efforts on the part of East Asian workers, thus further diminishing their bargaining power during recent years of industrial restructuring.

Industrial Transformation and Labor Response

By global standards, East Asia has achieved remarkable rates and levels of industrialization over the past few decades. This rapid economic transition is especially apparent in South Korea, Taiwan, Singapore, and Hong Kong—the most industrially advanced developing countries in the region. It is now evident as well in a rapidly industrializing second tier of Asian countries—led by Thailand and Malaysia, in turn followed by China, Indonesia, and Vietnam. Confining attention to the most industrially advanced countries in the region, it is clear from Table 22.1 that these countries have very substantial industrial and manufacturing sectors that employ a significant portion of their workforces.

From *Work and Occupations,* Vol. 24, No. 1, February 1997, pp. 97-118. Reprinted by permission.

Second, and again to varying degrees, these countries boast high levels of literacy (see Table 22.1), a useful predictor of social awareness and political participation. Third, in South Korea, Taiwan, Thailand, and, arguably, Hong Kong, democratization and political liberalization have provided new opportunities for organized labor. Democratic reforms generally have been associated with a liberalization of previously restrictive labor laws and regimes, thus providing new political space for labor organizing and collective action. These democratic reforms have been urged and reinforced by growing international pressure for a fuller observance of labor and human rights. The United States in particular has linked preferential developing country trade status and other forms of economic cooperation to improved human rights in Asia. Similarly, international trade union organizations, the International Labour Organization (ILO), and a number of international nongovernmental organizations have continued to publicize and attack violations of labor rights in the region.

But despite these various, favorable socioeconomic and political changes, organized labor remains politically marginalized and ineffectual across the region, even in these six rapidly industrializing countries. Trade union densities, ranging from a high of 18% in South Korea to a low of roughly 5% in Thailand, provide one indicator of such marginalization. In all cases, densities actually have declined over recent years, even in South Korea and Taiwan, where industrial development and democratic reforms have progressed farthest. Following sharp increases during 1987 to 1990, South Korean unionization rates dropped from 23% to 18% during the 1990s (Song, 1993). Similarly, Taiwanese union membership increased by more than 50% from 1986 to 1989, thereafter falling gradually (Frenkel, Hong, & Lee, 1993). Singapore's union density declined from 24.5% in 1979 to the level of roughly 17% by 1988, and Malaysia's dropped from 11.2% in 1985 to 9.4% in 1990 (Kuruvilla, 1995) and from 18% to about 14% of the nonagricultural workforce over the 1980s. Union density in Malaysia's private sector is especially low, at only about 7% (Arudsothy & Littler, 1993). Although during the 1980s unionization rates in Thailand's private sector grew slowly from a very low base (roughly 5% during the late 1980s), the forced dissolution of unions in the highly organized state enterprises following the 1991 military coup brought a sharp overall union decline and subsequent stagnation in the private sector, extending into the postcoup restoration of democratic rule. In Hong Kong, an overall density of about 17% by the late 1980s was well below the 23% to 24% levels of a decade earlier (Chiu & Levin, 1993).

The marginal role of collective bargaining provides further evidence of the weakness of organized labor in the region. Collective bargaining is virtually nonexistent in major manufacturing industries in Hong Kong and is confined largely to what Chiu and Levin term *defensive economism.* Collective agreements, they note, cover only about 4% of the workforce and contain only very general regulative language. In Taiwan, about 9% of manufacturing employees work under collective agreements, which cover only 5% of all enterprises (Frenkel et al., 1993). Similarly ineffectual and circumscribed is collective bargaining in South Korea (H.-J. Kim, 1993), Malaysia (where private sector bargaining declined in the mid-1980s) (Arudsothy & Littler, 1993), and Thailand (Brown & Frenkel, 1993).

Labor's participation in national-level economic governance presents a more mixed picture. In Singapore, a long-standing state commitment to co-opted union participation in tripartite national decision making ensures labor representation in wage recommendations, labor dispute arbitration, and a broad range of social policy deliberation. In Hong Kong, democratic reforms have been associated with enhanced participation in public policy, especially through worker representation on the Labor Advisory Board and in a more socially inclusive legislative council. Such increased representation has eventuated in government legislative efforts to raise labor standards and to regulate and restrict local reliance on immigrant labor

TABLE 22.1 Industrial and Social Indicators (in percentages)

	Industry[a] *(1993)*	*Manufacturing*[a] *(1993)*	*Heavy Industry*[b] *(1992)*	*Industrial Employment*[c] *(1998-1993)*	*Urban Population*[a] *(1993)*	*Literacy*[d] *(1994)*	*Wage Employment*[e] *(1988-1993)*
Republic of Korea	43	29	40	33	78	96	70
Taiwan	39[f]	30[f]	NA	39[d]	75[e]	90	—
Hong Kong	21	13	23	30	95	88[f] (1990)	89
Singapore	37	28	63	34	100	87	86
Malaysia	NA	NA	45	28	52	80	80
Thailand	39	28	45	14	19	89	63
Philippines	33	24	23	16	52	88	65

NOTE: NA = not available.
a. As a percentage of GDP (World Bank, 1995 [except Taiwan]).
b. Chemicals, machinery, and transport equipment as a percentage of total manufacturing value added (World Bank, 1995 [except Taiwan]).
c. Mining, manufacturing, construction, and utilities (ILO, 1995b).
d. *World Almanac* (1994), except Hong Kong.
e. As a percentage of nonagricultural total (Frenkel, 1993, p. 18).
f. *The Europa World Yearbook* (1995).

(Chiu & Lui, 1994). In South Korea, the growth of an increasingly assertive and independent labor movement has reinforced existing government commitment to improved labor standards, including expanded pension and medical insurance plans and, most recently, a new unemployment insurance program (Lee & Park, 1995). In Thailand, democratic reforms and political liberalization, beginning in the mid-1980s and resuming after the collapse of interim military rule in 1992, have been accompanied by increased labor influence in national policy making, as seen in the success of a long-standing campaign by organized labor for the enactment of important new social security legislation in 1990 and of a parallel drive to slow privatization programs.

But having said this, it is clear that the economic gains enjoyed by East Asian workers have generally flowed less from labor's political or organizational presence than from labor market pressures associated with growing labor scarcities in critical skill areas. Hong Kong's colonial government, strongly committed to nonintervention in labor and economic affairs, has been strongly adverse to labor market regulation. In Taiwan, wage rates are determined largely by market forces (Lee & Park, 1995). In both Hong Kong and Taiwan, labor standards legislation is poorly enforced among the many small- to medium-sized firms that dominate both economies (Chiu & Lui, 1994). In South Korea, the dramatic political gains on the part of increasingly independent trade unions from 1987 to 1990 were stopped and partly reversed following negative public reaction to labor and student activism after 1990. In Thailand and Malaysia, labor standards enforcement is uneven and ineffectual.

In the case of Thailand, labor department inspectors are under strong pressure not to prosecute firms that violate minimum wage, safety, and other labor laws, fearing that increased costs may undercut the competitive position of firms.[1]

It is primarily in Singapore that one finds a credible case of positive state intervention in labor markets and effective enforcement of labor standards, safety and health, and other labor legislation. But there, as in South Korea and Taiwan until the late 1980s, the peak labor organization has been more an instrument of state policy than of labor representation. For this reason, Singapore's progressive record of labor safeguards is more realistically understood as a pillar of a larger system of developmental paternalism than as an outcome of labor pressure (Deyo, 1992).

THE POLITICAL SOURCES OF LABOR'S WEAKNESS

The discussion thus far suggests the importance of political factors in undercutting Asian labor. Indeed, political explanations have received the lion's share of attention in efforts to understand the weak position of regional labor movements. In several countries, strict union registration procedures have provided an effective deterrent to oppositional unionism while bolstering officially sanctioned unions and union federations. This is especially true in Singapore and South Korea, where state-supported labor federations, the National Trades Union Congress (NTUC) and the Federation of Korean Trade Unions (FKTU), respectively, enjoy political protection from emerging oppositional federations. Similarly, in Malaysia, the ruling coalitional party has sought to support a new labor federation, the Malaysian Labour Organization, over an older, larger oppositional federation, the Malaysian Trades Union Congress. Such government-sponsored unionism, particularly in Singapore, compromises the capacity of unions to effectively represent rank-and-file membership at enterprise or political levels.

In Malaysia and Singapore, labor relations legislation strictly precludes collective bargaining issues such as work assignment, recruitment, retrenchment, and dismissal, all defined as within the purview of "management discretion," thus eliminating altogether a number of topics of considerable interest to workers (Begin, 1995). Similarly, governments across the region, even under democratic regimes, circumscribe labor activities by strictly proscribing union political activities other than those permitted within state-sponsored corporatist structures. Such depoliticization ensures labor's continuing political marginalization under democratization and a corresponding inability to press for favorable economic or social policy. In South Korea, efforts to contain and destroy independent, "democratic" trade unions and their national-level federation, the National Alliance of Trade Unions, which was created in 1990 to push for industrial unionism and an enhanced political role for labor, partially define the institutional boundaries of political liberalization (Song, 1993).

Malaysian workers in the strategic electronics sector were denied union rights for many years, and union leaders have been periodically harassed and even jailed for union-related activities (Kuruvilla, 1995). In Thailand, it was noted that a 1991 military coup was followed by a banning of unionism and collective bargaining in state enterprises. Given that Thai state enterprise unions have played a lead role in Thai unionism, the elimination of these unions effectively decapitated the national labor movement (Brown & Frenkel, 1993). In Taiwan, unions and union leadership selection processes have historically been monitored and controlled by the ruling Kuomintang Party.

As important as restrictive political controls is the lack of positive support and protection for workers and their trade unions, a historically critical prerequisite for effective trade unionism in the West. Even in the context of democratic reforms, labor regime liberalization has largely been confined to deregulation, a process that, if unattended by corresponding measures to strengthen trade unionism, eventuates in increased employer domination at the enterprise level and heightened union factionalism and conflict. The governments of Thailand, Singapore, Malaysia, and South Korea, for example, have yet to ratify ILO convention #87 guaranteeing the right of workers to freely organize (ILO, 1995a). The Malaysian and Thai governments have ratified only 11 of the ILO's labor conventions, and South Korea only 4 (ILO, 1995b). In Thailand, Malaysia, Hong Kong, and elsewhere, it was noted that government enforcement of existing labor standards legislation has been lax, thus effectively subjecting workers to capricious managerial domination, attacks on unions, and noncompliance with minimum wage, health, and safety legislation (Brown & Frenkel, 1993). In Thailand, union organizers receive no legal protection during organizational drives up until the date of official union registration, thus discouraging unionization drives. In Hong Kong, collective agreements enjoy no legal standing and are thus outside the purview of the state (Chiu & Levin, 1995).

Even in cases where workers have mounted effective political movements, often during democratic transitions, workers have generally played a largely subordinate role, mobilized by and allied to elite, middle-class, or student leadership. In Thailand, the relatively successful labor resistance to ongoing privatization during the 1980s was in part rooted in cross-class support from military and bureaucratic elites who benefitted politically and economically from the continuance of important state enterprises. In Taiwan, efforts by independent political parties and factions to garner electoral support have provided a critical base for new organizing efforts there (Frenkel et al., 1993). In South Korea, labor insurgence and organizational gains were strongly supported by student and middle-class groups.

But if cross-class coalitional support sometimes benefits workers and unions, the resulting dependency of labor on such nonworking class support creates attendant vulnerabilities. Loss of bureaucratic and military support for Thai state enterprise unions encouraged the 1990 military coup, following which these unions were banned. Growing middle-class apprehension about labor militancy in South Korea, it was noted, encouraged a harsher government response to strikes after 1990.

It is clearly impossible to account for the weakness of Asian labor movements without understanding the unfavorable political context within which these movements operate. But having said this, it is nonetheless important to note a critical problem with purely political explanations. During recent years, regional labor movements have, if anything, declined in membership and effectiveness. Yet this decline has, with a few exceptions, occurred in an absence of heightened political controls. Indeed, in many cases it has proceeded despite continuing democratic reforms and a progressive liberalization of labor regimes. In part, this decline may be understood by the reference to the form such liberalization has taken, with its greater emphasis on deregulation than protection. But the larger issue remains. In the context of rising levels of education, literacy, urbanization, and waged employment, democratic reforms might be expected to enhance labor movements, especially in expanding industrial sectors. Conversely, labor movements in several countries in Latin America and elsewhere have remained viable and effective during interludes of labor repression, which have been as severe as the ones in capitalist Asia.

Such anomalies suggest the need for greater attention to other nonpolitical factors in understanding the decline of Asian labor movements. Of particular importance are East Asian economic strategies and their associated structural consequences. Indeed, the importance of such economic factors has become ever more central to our understanding, even of political controls themselves, as state labor regimes have become dissociated from earlier anticommunist campaigns and ever more attentive to the imperatives of economic development.

THE ECONOMIC-STRUCTURAL DEMOBILIZATION OF LABOR

Light export-oriented industrialization (EOI) in South Korea, Taiwan, and Singapore in the 1970s and in Malaysia and Thailand in the 1980s was associated with the emergence of a relatively transitory labor force comprising large numbers of young women in unstable, low-skill jobs with little career opportunity. The difficulty of organizing such an unstable workforce into effective unions continues to undercut union-organizing efforts in the large export-manufacturing sectors of Thailand, Malaysia, and other lower-tier East Asian industrializers. Compounding such difficulties were the efforts on the part of regional governments to hold labor costs down and ensure labor peace to attract domestic and foreign investment into labor-intensive export manufacturing (Deyo, 1989).

Second, international pressures to further open domestic markets to foreign imports, often associated with ongoing regional and global trade agreements, have subjected firms to intensified competition in both domestic and international markets. In East Asian developing countries, with their relatively labor-intensive, export-oriented industrial structures, managers have sought to meet these new competitive pressures through cost-cutting measures directed in large part at reducing labor costs. Such measures have in turn both reflected and reinforced a weakened bargaining position on the part of labor. Competitive pressures in particular have created a credible threat of shutdowns, retrenchments, and the relocation of production to cheaper labor sites in the absence of effective labor cost containment. The increasing international mobility of capital, along with a heightened global integration of the production strategies of multinational enterprises, has had the further effect of adversely affecting the ability of governments to enact and enforce labor legislation. Globalization, notes the ILO (1995a), gives "governments an incentive to dilute, or fail to enact, measures intended to protect the welfare of workers, or to turn a blind eye to infringements of legislation with this in mind" (pp. 72-73). This same report also notes an increased erosion of the quality of formal sector employment through reduced job security, the declining significance of local or national-level collective bargaining, new policies of "firm-centric cooperation," union-avoidance strategies, promotion of company unions, and reduced union bargaining leverage at the local level.

In addition, some cost-cutting measures, including the increased use of temporary and contract labor and greater outsourcing of production, have directly undercut union power while addressing a second set of competitive requirements, discussed later, stemming from the globalization of post-Fordist flexible production systems.

Asian Labor and Flexible Production

Production flexibility is an important component of new, globally ascendant, post-Fordist production systems. *Flexibility* here refers to the ability to quickly, efficiently, and continuously introduce changes in a product and process. Such flexibility yields a superior capacity to respond to intensified pressures of liberalized trade, world market volatility, market fragmentation, rapid technological change, and heightened demand for just-in-time production and continuous improvements in productivity and quality (Friedman, 1988; Womack, Jones, & Roos, 1990).

A useful distinction is often made between static and dynamic forms of flexibility (Colclough & Tolbert, 1992). *Static flexibility*, which focuses on short-term adaptability and cost cutting, is the predominant managerial approach in the labor-intensive export sectors that have figured so prominently in many of Asia's developing economies. The reasons for this competitive choice are clear. Intensified global competition under trade liberalization places firms under extreme pressure to cut costs in the short term. Risky long-term investments in training, research and development, and organizational development may be eschewed where they seem to place a firm at a short-term disadvantage vis-à-vis other firms that do not make these investments.

Static flexibility, along with its negative consequences for labor, predominates in many countries and industrial sectors in the region. There is evidence of increased use of subcontracting, casualization, and contract labor (numerical flexibility) in the large export sectors of the Philippines (Ofreneo, 1994) and Thailand (Deyo, 1995). Standing (1989) similarly documents increasing numerical flexibility and casualization in electronics and other export sectors in Malaysia, as do Chui, Levin, and Lui in Hong Kong (Chiu & Levin, 1993; Chiu & Lui, 1994). Indeed, even in industrially advanced

Singapore, Begin (1995) reports continued reliance on static numerical flexibility (see also Rodgers & Yit-Yeng, 1995). In many cases, employers adopt such labor strategies in part explicitly to undercut unions or unionization drives because these strategies have the known effects of creating an insecure, floating workforce and of encouraging a further dispersal of production to small contracted firms and households. By consequence, unions throughout the region have fought strenuously to institute legislative restrictions on the employment of temporary workers and related practices (Charoenloet, 1993; Ofreneo, 1994).

Dynamic flexibility strategies, although less prevalent, are pursued in product niches requiring high levels of quality, batch versus mass production, and continued adoption of improved process and product technologies. Such strategies are most likely to be undertaken by large, resourceful firms that are able in part to create their own support infrastructure and operate in relatively protected or oligopolistic markets where there is less immediate competitive pressure (Deyo, 1995). As noted later, they are encouraged where states underwrite a supportive social infrastructure of training, education, and R&D; where they enforce adequate labor standards; and where they provide incentives to firms to invest in training and organizational development. For these various reasons, dynamic flexibility strategies tend to occur in the upper-tier Newly Industrializing Countries (NICs) with developmentally active states (Singapore, South Korea, Taiwan) and among dominant firms in semiprotected industrial sectors across the region.

Most research on dynamic flexibility has focused on the experience of innovative industrial firms in the developed countries of Japan, Europe, and North America. In these settings, dynamic flexibility generally has been associated with enhanced worker welfare and security, as well as with increased worker participation in organizational decision making, because firms have sought both to increase worker commitment and loyalty and encourage workers to assume increased responsibility for enterprise success (Friedman, 1988; Kenney & Florida, 1993; Womack et al., 1990). A distinction has been drawn in this regard between the "bargained" forms of flexibility that are associated with strong, independent unions and high levels of participation in instituting and operating new production systems, as well as "participative" flexibility, characterized by captive, enterprise unions and more circumscribed forms of worker participation, confined largely to shop floor problem solving (Herzenberg, 1996). This body of research generally seems to suggest that the instituting of dynamic flexibility, whether of bargained or participative forms, would have a similarly salutary effect for workers and perhaps unions in developing Asia. In fact, it does not.

In the higher value-added market niches, where technological and product quality requirements preclude continued reliance on low-skill temporary workers and static flexibility, Asian firms are pressed to make long-term investments in worker training, product development, organizational restructuring, and other programs supportive of enhanced dynamic flexibility. In addition, such firms may sometimes institute suggestion systems, quality circles, labor management councils, and other means of mobilizing worker involvement in quality and productivity improvements (on Malaysia, see Rasiah, 1994). But even such instances of "dynamic flexibility," typically accompanied by improved wages, benefits, and other measures to enhance the stability and commitment of workers, rarely permit the level of worker decision-making involvement found even under participative flexibility. Indeed, improvements in compensation levels and working conditions are as often introduced to avoid unions as to foster long-term organizational improvements (see, e.g., Deyo, 1995). In general, flexibility-enhancing organizational reforms are overwhelmingly attentive to managerial agendas driven by competitive economic pressures, to the exclusion of the social agendas of workers and unions. In many cases, such strategies, along with their relatively benign labor welfare policies, are confined to a few critical production processes, thus fostering internal labor market dualism between core, stable workers, on one hand, and casual or contract workers, on the other (Deyo, 1995).

The suggestion that East Asian dynamic industrial flexibility is substantially more autocratic than its counterparts in more industrially advanced countries is supported by numerous case studies indicating that regional firms adopting flexible production systems more fully tap their human resource base than other firms, but that they are far more likely to employ systems of individual and informal consultation than collective forms of participation, such as labor management councils or team-based decision making, in eliciting worker ideas. Frenkel (1993) notes increased reliance on informal consultation but little encouragement of group-based worker participation in his study of a pharmaceutical firm in Taiwan. T. Kim (1995) reports the restriction of the activities of quality circles to narrowly defined duties and responsibilities in South Korean firms, a finding reflected in Deyo's (1995) study of automobile companies in Thailand. Kuruvilla (1995) notes the autocratic character of recent work reforms in Malaysian industry. Rodgers and Yit-Yeng (1995), reviewing the evidence from an extensive survey of industrial firms in Singapore, report only minimal development of quality circles, a finding confirmed by Begin (1995), who estimates that Quality Control Circles (QCCs) include only about 5% of Singapore's industrial workers and are severely limited in scope and influence.

Why are East and Southeast Asian patterns of flexible production predominantly static in nature and, where dynamic, more autocratic than their counterparts in industrially more advanced countries? To adequately address this question, it is necessary to understand patterns of economic governance across the region.

Economic Governance, Labor, and the Institution of Flexible Production

As noted earlier, static forms of flexibility are encouraged in product niches characterized by large economies of scale, stable markets and technology, and intense competition. In addition, they tend to be pursued in the absence of governance institutions that encourage long-term investments in organizational reform, technology, human resources, and R&D. The following discussion focuses primarily on the way in which governance factors influence those aspects of enterprise-level competitive strategies that impinge most directly on labor.

Most important, perhaps, is the role of the state in providing requisite collective goods, directly influencing competitive strategies, creating a level playing field for firms, and empowering labor to participate in enterprise strategies. *Collective goods* refer in this context to those elements of the economic infrastructure that are both essential to dynamic flexibility strategies and unlikely to be provided by individual firms. These would include not only physical infrastructure (roads, ports, telecommunications) but, as important, technology support (R&D institutes, public funding for private sector R&D) and human resource development (education, vocational, and technical training). That provision of this foundation infrastructure is unlikely to be provided by individual firms follows from the externalities associated with such investments and the strong probability that competitors will benefit from them.

States also directly influence the nature of competitive strategies and related labor policies. Encouragement and financial support may be offered for long-term strategies of research and development, organizational and work reforms, and the acquisition of new technologies. Incentives may be extended for training programs and the institution of quality circles and worker participation schemes. Firms may be encouraged to cooperate among themselves in the provision of collective goods through joint training programs, cooperative R&D and marketing, and other forms of mutual assistance (Sabel, 1995).

States also can ensure a level playing field such that long-term, risky, firm-level investments in, say, R&D, training, and work reorganization, do not place firms at a severe cost disadvantage vis-à-vis other firms that do not incur such costs. Similarly, the establishment of minimal labor standards, adequate wages and benefits, and fair labor practices discourages firms from competing through labor cost containment and union avoidance, encouraging, instead, greater effort to enhance employee skills, productivity, and work involvement. Finally, states play an important role in empowering workers and labor organizations to participate more fully in instituting competitive strategies, thus ensuring that those strategies benefit workers as well as firms (Cole, 1989; Hollingsworth & Streeck, 1994).

It is clear that governments in the more industrially advanced Asian countries (Singapore, South Korea, and Taiwan) have played a more forceful developmental role in these and other areas than in Thailand, Malaysia, and the newer industrializers of the region. In Singapore, South Korea, and Taiwan, substantial public commitment to education in general and to technical and vocational education in particular provides a solid foundation for in-company employee training. Singapore, like Malaysia and now South Korea, has instituted a skills development payroll tax under which companies contribute to a government-controlled training fund that they can draw on only for approved employee training programs (Begin, 1995). Such a levy strongly encourages company training as a way of realizing benefits from a collective good to which all firms contribute, thus effectively reversing the collective goods dilemma of "who will pay for everyone's benefit?" to "who will benefit from everyone's contribution?"

Similarly, Singapore and, to a lesser degree, South Korea and Taiwan (Lee & Park, 1995) enforce basic labor standards to reduce the incentive for firms to view such standards as a competitive cost factor. Where such labor standards are less effective in moderating managerial practices, as in Thailand, Malaysia, Hong Kong, and among smaller firms in South Korea and Taiwan, high rates of employee turnover and weak enterprise commitment undercut training and other human resource programs necessary for dynamic flexibility.

If the static flexibility strategies of firms in the region, especially in Hong Kong, Thailand, and Malaysia, and among small firms in most countries, can be attributed in part to an absence of supportive state policy, they flow as well from failures of collective governance in the private sector. A burgeoning literature on flexible specialization and industrial districts (the "Italian" model) suggests the importance of interfirm cooperation for the provision of collective goods and for the minimization and pooling of risk necessary for flexibility-enhancing investments and innovations (Sabel, 1989; Scott, 1992). A parallel literature on flexible production within firms and among hierarchically organized clusters of large firms and their suppliers (the "Japanese" model) demonstrates the importance of trust-based, enduring relations among firms for high-quality, diversified production (Doner, 1991; Streeck, 1990). Both models suggest that stable associational bonds both within and among firms provide an essential foundation for long-term strategies of dynamic flexibility. Taiwan provides the classic East Asian case. In Taiwan, family and associational bonds underwrite cooperation, the pooling of capital, collective investment in costly new technology, trust-based market relations, and incentives to provide employee training, thus discouraging short-term cost cutting in favor of longer-term organizational investments. It also should be noted in this regard that the state may play a critical, if indirect, role in encouraging such private sector cooperation. In Taiwan, for example, the state has instituted a center-satellite program under which larger firms or assemblers organize large numbers of suppliers among whom R&D, planning, procurement, and other functions are jointly achieved.

The important role of labor relations and institutions should be noted. At some risk of oversimplification, labor movements in the region may be characterized as weak and ineffectual (Hong Kong, Thailand, Malaysia), state co-opted (Singapore, pre-1987 South Korea), enterprise co-opted (Taiwan), and strong though vulnerable (post-1987 South Korea) (see Frenkel, 1993). In all but the latter case, organized labor was incapable of substantially influencing the direction of new managerial flexibility strategies during the 1980s and early 1990s. In the absence of labor pressure, firms instituted strategies of static flexibility without substantial labor opposition to increased reliance on contract labor, outsourcing, and use of temporary workers (Levin & Chiu, 1993). These strategies in turn further undermined labor influence, thus perpetuating a vicious circle between labor weakness and labor-undercutting managerial strategies. This same vicious circle, it should be noted, accounts in part as well for the autocratic forms of dynamic flexibility found across the region. Here we see most clearly the way in which the political resources and effectiveness of labor determine institutional outcomes that reinforce existing power inequalities.

Finally, it should be noted that strategies of static flexibility, prevalent in countries and sectors characterized by institutionally "thin" governance (especially Hong Kong and Thailand), present a long-term developmental cost through the lack of encouragement of industrial restructuring into high value-added production and a corresponding continuation of an ultimately losing battle to compete in low-cost, low value-added market niches. Whether autocratic forms of dynamic flexibility engender corresponding developmental costs is less certain. To this question we now turn.

Autocratic Flexibility and Learning-Based Industrialization

It has been noted that East Asian strategies are more autocratic and less participatory than those in the industrially advanced countries, where they are more prevalent. In part, the explanation for this difference is found in the incapacity of unions to discourage or resist instituting forms of flexibility that preclude an effective collective voice on the part of workers. As elsewhere, Singapore provides an important exception to this pattern. There, local union affiliates of the Peoples Action Party-backed (PAP) National Trades Union Congress have effectively pushed for greater training and employee involvement in both local firms.

In some cases, too, autocratic flexibility is an outcome of political constraint: indirectly through the undercutting of union power and directly through an underwriting of managerial authority. As noted earlier, in both Singapore and Malaysia, autocratic flexibility is encouraged through legislative exclusion from collective bargaining of such matters as job assignment and work transfers, which are important elements of "labor flexibility." Correspondingly, multinational corporations often insist on operating in a union-free environment (Kuruvilla, 1994; Rasiah, 1994), an insistence to which states may readily accede in their efforts to attract foreign investment.

Second, it may be that worker participation and empowerment are less critical to the success of programs of dynamic flexibility in Asia than in industrially mature economies. Following Amsden (1989), we may distinguish between innovative and learning-based industrialization. *Innovative industrialization* relies on the development of a stream of new products and technologies for changing markets. *Learning-based industrialization,* by contrast, relies on the local adoption of technologies and products developed elsewhere. It may be suggested that insofar as newly developing countries pursue technology-dependent, learning-based industrialization, employers may seek to institute forms of flexibility that minimize worker participation in favor of unchallenged managerial control over production. This is so because learning-based industrialization depends mainly on local adaptation and implementation of already debugged production processes and products, thus minimizing the need for the extensive involvement of workers in solving shopfloor production problems. In such a context, engineers and production managers assume the primary role in reorganizing production around imported technologies. Thus more autocratic forms of flexibility are adequate to the demands of industrialization. Given that multinational firms, whose investments provide a major conduit for technology transfer and diffusion to Asian firms, are reluctant to relocate major R&D functions to foreign subsidiaries in developing countries, the perpetuation of learning-based industrialization into future years may imply a long-term stability of such autocratic forms of flexibility and a corresponding discouragement of union or worker empowerment at the workplace level. In such a context, human resource mobilization will continue to confine collective forms of shopfloor participation to co-optive, officially sanctioned, and closely circumscribed deliberative forums, such as quality circles and labor management councils, and to more generally eschew collective participation in favor of suggestion systems, informal consultation, merit-based incentives, job ladders, and other individualized modalities of worker participation and involvement in organizational development.

THE IMPACT OF DEVELOPMENTAL TIMING

Despite the political and economic constraints facing organized labor across Asia, there have been historical moments of dramatic labor activation. These include, most visibly, the period from the mid- to late 1980s in South Korea, Taiwan, and the Philippines. To understand the origins of these episodes, it is necessary to consider the temporal context of the economic strategies and corresponding structural changes discussed earlier. In particular, how has the developmental and historical timing of Asian industrialization influenced its consequences for labor? We start with the Philippines, a country we have not yet considered because of its regionally unique developmental history.

The Philippines differs from the other countries in this discussion in its continuing economic and industrial stagnation and relatively higher levels of unemployment—powerful impediments to strong labor movements. In such an inhospitable setting, it is not surprising to find low and declining overall union densities (currently 10% in the nonagricultural sector), negligible unionism in many industries, and collective agreement coverage for only about 5% of all wage workers (Kuruvilla, 1995). It is important to recognize, however, that the growing economic crisis of the 1980s precipitated what Ofreneo (1995) refers to as a "rise in militant unionism whose depth and breadth has no parallels in the country's history" (p. 2). In part, this militancy, which preceded the "democratic coup" of 1986, can be attributed to a sustained and successful process of domestic, market-oriented industrialization, which sets the Philippines off from other countries in the region and parallels more closely the experience of several Latin American countries that pursued similar development strategies during the 1950s and 1960s. The "Philippine exception" underscores the importance for labor movements of differences in the "developmental sequencing" of the economic strategies discussed earlier.

Early Latin American industrialization (1940s-1950s) was based on import-substituting industrialization (ISI) and the encouragement of domestic, market-oriented local industry through policies of trade protection and state assistance, but that which occurred more recently (in the 1960s-1970s) in Asia was more strongly rooted in export-oriented industrialization (EOI) (Gereffi, 1990). Latin American ISI sought initially to defuse a growing political crisis occasioned by the collapse of primary export-based development by fostering industrial growth, employment, and labor peace under policies of economic nationalism and by building corporatist political coalitions that encompassed strong trade union federations. Protection of local companies from foreign competition permitted sustained industrial development as well as ever higher wages and social benefits for politically supported trade unions in key economic sectors. Indeed, rising industrial wages were seen as supportive of continued industrial growth by increasing consumer demand for local products.

The Philippines, like these ISI-based Latin American countries, entered a sustained ISI phase during the 1940s and 1950s that combined successful import substitution with labor regimes—in this case more liberal than corporatist, which encouraged unionization and collective bargaining. In response to a balance of payments crisis associated with the collapse of the early 20th-century primary-commodity export strategy, protective tariffs and foreign exchange controls marked a shift toward ISI-led development. This shift was in turn associated with the enactment of new labor legislation that greatly enhanced worker welfare and union security in the formal sector of manufacturing (Kuruvilla, 1994; Ofreneo, 1995). Especially important was new minimum wage legislation in 1951 and the Industrial Peace Act of 1953, subsequently dubbed the "Magna Carta of Labour," which was patterned after the U.S. National Labor Relations Act of 1935 in providing protection for trade unions and encouraging effective collective bargaining at the enterprise level (Ofreneo, 1995). This "misplaced" Latin American experience, rooted in part in a cross-regionally shared U.S. influence, eventuated in the emergence of strong local unions that, under subsequent years of martial law and state repression (1972-1986), sustained a latent, community-based opposition movement. This movement may be seen as having provided the essential foundation for labor mobilization and militancy during the economic and political crises of the mid-1980s.

The Philippines case contrasts strongly with the developmental sequencing of political regimes and economic strategies elsewhere in the region. Early industrialization in most countries of the region was accompanied by authoritarian state controls that sought to either repress or coopt organized labor. Such political controls were in turn rooted in a need to hold down labor costs and reduce the power of organized labor to compete in world markets under an EOI development strategy. Foreign assembly plants operating in the export-processing zones in Taiwan and South Korea and, more recently, in Thailand, Malaysia, and the Philippines have often insisted on operating in a union-free or union-restrained environment and have been supported in this requirement by the respective governments. Effectively demobilized or coopted at the outset of sustained industrialization, most East and Southeast Asian labor movements lacked the political capacity to shape new labor relations institutions in the early years of industrial development, thus ensuring their weakness during subsequent years of industrial development except under exceptional periods of political mobilization, such as the late 1980s in South Korea and Taiwan (Deyo, 1989).

As important as the developmental timing of economic strategies for Asian labor movements is the historical timing of such strategies. It was noted that labor-intensive EOI under post-Fordist production regimes differs from earlier standard-production EOI in shifting the locus of labor control from the state to enterprise and in fragmenting and dispersing the workforce to a greater extent than in the earlier period. Similarly, the global-temporal context, within which there is industrial deepening into more capital and technology-intensive production, has shifted appreciably. Despite unfavorable developmental sequencing, earlier Fordist industrial deepening gave somewhat greater encouragement and scope to emergent labor movements, as seen in South Korea and Taiwan during the 1980s. By contrast, incipient deepening in high value-added industrial production in Thailand and Malaysia has encouraged preemptive enterprise participative structures that often displace and undercut unions. In Thailand, resourceful and market-dominant firms such as Toyota, Siam Cement, and Yamaha have instituted skill-based job ladders, suggestion systems, enterprise unions, carefully circumscribed quality circles, dualistic internal labor markets, and other measures that at once mobilize worker ideas and involvement (Siengthai, 1988) while discouraging independent or oppositional collective action. In Malaysia, state encouragement for Japanese-style enterprise unionism contributes further to such an effect (Rajasekaran, 1993). More advanced technology deepening in Singapore, Taiwan, and South Korea has been associated with even greater official sponsorship and encouragement of labor management councils, sponsored enterprise unions, and other preemptive participatory forums that displace unions by ostensibly assuming many of their functions (Deyo, 1989; Kuruvilla, 1994).

CONCLUSION

In response to new imperatives of changing technology, more volatile and fragmented markets, and global economic liberalization, firms in the successfully industrializing countries of East Asia have instituted greater adaptability and flexibility in all phases of production. From the standpoint of human resources, such flexibility has taken both static and autocratic-dynamic forms. Static flexibility has entailed increased reliance on temporary and contract workers and on outsourcing to low-cost suppliers, and dynamic-autocratic flexibility has been based on increased internal "functional" flexibility, higher skill levels, circumscribed worker participation in production, and more adequate wages and worker benefits. In contrast to patterns of dynamic flexibility adopted in industrially more advanced countries, these two types of flexibility have at once reflected and reinforced labor's subordinate position at the enterprise level.

Characteristics of economic governance and of the export niches occupied by firms in most countries and industrial sectors of developing East Asia would seem to structurally impede an early shift from static and autocratic to more participative forms of flexibility, thus reducing the likelihood that continued industrial development will empower workers and unions in future years. Such nonconvergence on industrial organizational patterns that are being instituted in industrially more advanced countries will entail variable economic costs. Industries adopting static forms of flexibility will experience difficulty in moving into higher value-added product niches that require continuing process and product innovation. This transitional difficulty will prove particularly problematic in Thailand, Malaysia, and other countries now attempting to shift from cost-based to higher value-added niches in world markets. Industries adopting dynamic-autocratic forms of flexibility will struggle to move into more innovative and technology-intensive market niches requiring more deeply penetrating human resource systems and correspondingly greater employee participation and involvement in shopfloor change. This second transitional difficulty will most affect South Korea, Taiwan, and Singapore, where continued industrial advance is increasingly impeded by the negative legacies of state and enterprise autocracy.

Although the political implications of industrial restructuring are far more uncertain, a few speculative comments may be offered. To the extent that both the nature and timing of East Asian economic strategies have generally undercut the capacity of organized labor to participate in shaping industrial restructuring at enterprise or national levels, national governments may enjoy somewhat greater scope in responding positively to growing domestic and international demands for political liberalization and labor market deregulation without precipitating increased labor militancy and thus threatening processes of capital accumulation. Such a pattern also provides a solution to the problem posed by the internal instability of authoritarian regimes under sustained economic development, in part, by enhancing the prospects for democracy by reducing the likelihood that labor can exploit new political opportunities offered by parliamentary reforms. Alternatively stated, the structurally rooted exclusion of labor from democratic politics may enhance both the usefulness to business of parliamentary institutions and business support for further democratic reforms.

NOTE

1. This finding is based on conversations with a Thai Labor Department factory inspector during factory site visits in 1993.

REFERENCES

Amsden, A. (1989). *Asia's next giant: South Korea and late industrialization*. New York: Oxford University Press.

Arudsothy, P., & Littler, C. R. (1993). State regulation and union fragmentation in Malaysia. In S. Frenkel (Ed.), *Organized labor in the Asia-Pacific region* (pp. 107-130). Ithaca, NY: ILR Press.

Begin, J. P. (1995). Singapore's industrial relations system: Is it congruent with its second phase of industrialization? In S. Frenkel & J. Harrod (Eds.), *Industrialization and labor relations* (pp. 64-87). Ithaca, NY: ILR Press.

Brown, A., & Frenkel, S. (1993). Union unevenness and insecurity in Thailand. In S. Frenkel (Ed.), *Organized labor in the Asia-Pacific region* (pp. 82-106). Ithaca, NY: ILR Press.

Charoenloet, V. (1993). Export-oriented industry in Thailand: Implications for employment and labour. In A. Wehmhorner (Ed.), *NIC's in Asia: A challenge to trade unions.* Singapore: Friedrich-Ebert-Stiftung.

Chiu, S., & Levin, D. A. (1993). The world economy, state, and sectors in industrial change: Labor relations in Hong Kong's textile and garment-making industries. In S. Frenkel (Ed.), *Organized labor in the Asia-Pacific region.* Ithaca, NY: ILR Press.

Chiu, S., & Levin, D. A. (1995, May-June). *Prosperity without citizenship: Industrial relations and industrial democracy in Hong Kong.* Paper presented at the 10th World Congress of the International Industrial Relations Association, Washington, DC.

Chiu, S., & Lui, T. (1994). *Horizontal expansion and spatial relocation: Production and employment restructuring of the electronics industry in Hong Kong.* Unpublished manuscript, Chinese University of Hong Kong, Department of Sociology.

Colclough, G., & Tolbert, C. M., II. (1992). *Work in the fast lane: Flexibility, divisions of labor, and inequality in high-tech industries.* Albany: State University of New York Press.

Cole, R. E. (1989). *Strategies for learning: Small-group activities in American, Japanese, and Swedish industry.* Berkeley: University of California Press.

Deyo, F. (1989). *Beneath the miracle: Labor subordination in the new Asian industrialism.* Berkeley: University of California Press.

Deyo, F. (1992). The political economy of social policy formation: East Asia's newly industrialized countries. In R. Appelbaum & J. Henderson (Eds.), *States and development in the Asian Pacific Rim* (pp. 289-306). Newbury Park, CA: Sage.

Deyo, F. (1995). Human resource strategies and industrial restructuring in Thailand. In S. Frenkel & J. Harrod (Eds.), *Industrialization and labor relations* (pp. 23-36). Ithaca, NY: ILR Press.

Doner, R. (1991). *Driving a bargain: Automobile industrialization and Japanese firms in Southeast Asia.* Berkeley: University of California Press.

The Europa world yearbook. (1995). London: Europa Publications Ltd.

Frenkel, S. (1993). Variations in patterns of trade unionism: A synthesis. In S. Frenkel (Ed.), *Organized labor in the Asia-Pacific region* (pp. 309-346). Ithaca, NY: ILR Press.

Frenkel, S., Hong, H.-C., & Lee, B.-L. (1993). The resurgence and fragility of trade unions in Taiwan. In S. Frenkel (Ed.), *Organized labor in the Asia-Pacific region.* Ithaca, NY: ILR Press.

Friedman, D. (1988). *The misunderstood miracle: Industrial development and political change in Japan.* Ithaca, NY: Cornell University Press.

Gereffi, G. (1990). Paths of industrialization: An overview. In G. Gereffi & D. Wyman (Eds.), *Manufacturing miracles* (pp. 3-31). Princeton, NJ: Princeton University Press.

Herzenberg, S. (1996). Regulatory frameworks and development in the North American auto industry. In F. Deyo (Ed.), *Social reconstructions of the world automobile industry* (pp. 261-294). London: Macmillan/New York: St. Martin's.

Hollingsworth, J. R., & Streeck, W. (1994). Countries and sectors: Concluding remarks on performance, convergence, and competitiveness. In J. R. Hollingsworth, P. C. Schmitter, & W. Streeck (Eds.), *Governing capitalist economies.* New York: Oxford University Press.

International Labour Organization (ILO). (1995a). *World employment 1995.* Geneva, Switzerland: Author.

International Labour Organization (ILO). (1995b). *World labor report 1995.* Geneva, Switzerland: Author.

Kenney, M., & Florida, R. (1993). *Beyond mass production: The Japanese system and its transfer to the U.S.* New York: Oxford University Press.

Kim, H.-J. (1993). The Korean union movement in transition. In S. Frenkel (Ed.), *Organized labor in the Asia-Pacific region.* Ithaca, NY: ILR Press.

Kim, T. (1995). Human resource management for production workers in large Korean manufacturing enterprises. In S. Frenkel & J. Harrod (Eds.), *Industrialization and labor relations* (pp. 216-235). Ithaca, NY: ILR Press.

Kuruvilla, S. (1994, January). *Industrialization strategy and IR policy in Malaysia and the Philippines: Implications for comparative industrial relations.* Paper presented at the 46th Annual Meeting of the Industrial Relations Research Association, Boston.

Kuruvilla, S. (1995). Industrialization strategy and industrial relations policy in Malaysia. In S. Frenkel & J. Harrod (Eds.), *Industrialization and labor relations* (pp. 37-63). Ithaca, NY: ILR Press.

Lee, J., & Park, Y.-B. (1995). Employment, labour standards and economic development in Taiwan and Korea. *Labour: Review of Labour Economics and Industrial Relations,* S223-S242.

Levin, D., & Chiu, S. (1993). Dependent capitalism, a colonial state, and marginal unions: The case of Hong Kong. In S. Frenkel (Ed.), *Organized labor in the Asia-Pacific region* (pp. 187-222). Ithaca, NY: ILR Press.

Ofreneo, R. E. (1994). The labour market, protective labour institutions and economic growth in the Philippines. In G. Rodgers (Ed.), *Workers, institutions and economic growth in Asia* (pp. 255-301). Geneva, Switzerland: International Institute for Labour Studies.

Ofreneo, R. E. (1995). *The changing terrains for trade union organizing.* Unpublished manuscript, University of the Philippines, School of Labor and Industrial Relations.

Rajasekaran, G. (1993). Look East policy: Successful in which way? In A. Wehmhorner (Ed.), *Trade unions in NICs* (pp. 24-28). Singapore: Friedrich-Ebert-Stiftung.

Rasiah, R. (1994). Flexible production systems and local machine tool subcontracting: Case of electronics components transnationals in Malaysia. *Cambridge Journal of Economics, 18.*

Rodgers, R. A., & Yit-Yeng, J. W. (1995). *Transferring Japanese manufacturing methods to Singapore* (Working Papers Series No. 95-10). Singapore: National University of Singapore, Faculty of Business Administration.

Sabel, C. (1989). Flexible specialization and regional development. In P. Hirst & J. Zeitlin (Eds.), *Reversing industrial decline.* London: Berg.

Sabel, C. (1995, Winter). Bootstrapping reform: Rebuilding firms, the welfare state, and unions. *Politics and Society.*

Scott, A. J. (1992). The Roepke lecture in economic geography: The collective order of flexible production agglomerations: Lessons for local economic development policy and strategic choice. *Economic Geography, 68*(3), 219-233.

Siengthai, S. (1988). Thai-Hino Industry Co., Ltd. In International Labour Office (Ed.), *Case studies in labour-management cooperation for productivity improvement* (pp. 265-308). Bangkok: ILO.

Song, H. K. (1993). After the struggle: Labor unions in the politics of liberalization in South Korea. In A. Wehmhorner (Ed.), *Trade unions in NICs* (pp. 60-73). Singapore: Friedrich-Ebert-Stiftung.

Standing, G. (1989). *The growth of external labour flexibility in a nascent NIC: Malaysian Labor Flexibility Survey (MLFS)* (World Employment Programme Research Working Paper No. 35). Geneva, Switzerland: ILO.

Streeck, W. (1990). *The social foundations for diversified quality production* [Mimeo]. Madison: University of Wisconsin, Department of Sociology.

Womack, J. P., Jones, D. T., & Roos, D. (1990). *The machine that changed the world.* New York: Rawson.

World almanac. (1994). Mahwah, NJ: Funk & Wagnalls.

World Bank. (1995). *World development report.* New York: Oxford University Press.

Conclusion

What are the research implications of workplace restructuring? As a transformation of workplace social structure, restructuring raises for researchers in the sociology of work questions about fundamental shifts in the distribution of authority in the firm, the depth of mutual commitment between employer and employee, and in the actors that bargain over the terms of employment. Restructuring also compels researchers to examine the consequences of these fundamental shifts for worker livelihoods and life chances.

The two chapters in this concluding section offer complementary research agendas. Both argue that workplace restructuring challenges the standard image in the sociology of work of the "organization man's and woman's" long-term careers in the pyramidal, bureaucratic internal labor market of a single firm. Indeed, labor union decline, downsizing, displacement, decentralization and casualization invoke other images of career mobility processes. Hirsch and Naquin's research agenda calls for a broadening of the typology of careers that are treated by theories of careers; Kalleberg's agenda embraces the full variety of new, flexible firms and the research implications of flexibility.

Hirsch and Naquin are not convinced by the "hype" over the prevalence of workplace restructuring. They argue in Chapter 23 that restructuring constitutes a departure from the bureaucratic internal labor market, a departure that compels researchers to develop new theories of careers. Nonetheless, their analysis of patterns and trends in worker tenure and displacement and temporary employment leads them to conclude that the pace and diffusion of restructuring are modest, signaling the continuing significance of the bounded organizational career. Consequently, researchers need to develop new theories of careers that incorporate both enduring and emerging models of careers.

In Chapter 24, Kalleberg extracts a research agenda from a threefold typology of firm flexibility: functional flexibility, numerical flexibility, and network organizations. He argues that functional flexibility, or adjustments by the firm in the assignment of employees to different jobs, calls for research on the nature and direction of worker participation in decision making. Numerical flexibility, or adjustments by management in the size of its workforce, raises research questions about the emergence of a dualism in job security and life chances between core and periphery workers within the restructured firm. The advent of network organizations—that is, organizations that are embedded in market-mediated cooperative relations—challenges researchers to analyze the depth of trust between organizations and the durability of interorganizational relations.

Together these two chapters encapsulate the themes of *Working in Restructured Workplaces* and point sociologists of work to central questions about the prevalence, nature, and consequences of restructuring.

The Changing Sociology of Work and the Reshaping of Careers

PAUL M. HIRSCH
CHARLES E. NAQUIN

Developments during the past quarter-century have given rise to the sense that we have entered into a new economic order (Ashkenas, Ulrich, Jick, & Kerr, 1995; Carnevale, 1991; Drucker, 1992; Huey, 1994; Mirvis, 1993). In this new business environment, it is claimed that the "traditional" ways of doing business are no longer adequate to maintain high performance (Nadler, Gerstein, & Shaw, 1992). The prevalent view is that organizations must be as streamlined and flexible as possible in order to survive in an increasingly competitive and ever changing economic environment (Dunlap, 1996; Hammer & Champy, 1994; Volberda, 1996). Wasteful work routines and large overhead staffs are a luxury of the bygone mass production era and must be eliminated in order to maintain shareholder value. Such objectives are typically achieved by way of such practices as (a) "strategic" layoffs (also called "rightsizing" or "delayering") and (b) the use of easily added and eliminated temporary workers. Evidence suggests that these strategies are indeed popular as traditional leaders and continuing role models of industry such as IBM, General Motors, Boeing, Sears, and AT&T have all downsized their workforce. In 1996, three out of four households claimed to have had a close encounter with layoffs, and 450,000 workers actually lost their jobs due to downsizing (Cascio, 1997). In step with this downsizing, temporary service agencies have today become one of the fastest growing industries (Carey & Hazelbaker, 1986; Plunkert & Hayghe, 1995), and the temporary employee service agency, Manpower, Inc., is often cited as the largest employer in the United States (Smith, 1998). These changes in how work is accomplished are also argued to be far reaching, extending beyond that of blue-collar workers—who have traditionally shouldered the burden of economic turbulence—to that of white-collar workers. The sign of the times seems to be that organizations must find a way to deliver outstanding performance with less human capital: Stock prices rise when employment goes down! A harsh perspective, but it constitutes the generally agreed-upon road to organizational survival. However, whether such "contemporary" strategies truly lead to enhanced organizational performance in this new economic era is unclear (Hilmer & Donaldson, 1996). But what is clear is that a diversity of organizational practices have been created as the structure of work is being reinvented (Smith, 1997).

Changes in how work is structured are often linked to changes in the nature of careers (Allred, Snow, & Miles, 1996; Miles & Snow, 1996; Stewart, 1995). As such, amid the sensationalized "strategic" layoffs and rapid temporary workforce growth, numerous and popular claims have been made that the traditional view of a career (as a relatively safe and upward movement through an organization) is now considered an artifact of a bygone era (Arthur & Rousseau, 1996; Bird, 1994; Delfillippi & Arthur, 1994; Dolan, 1996; Glassner, 1994; Kanter, 1989a, 1989b; Nicholson, 1996; Pfeffer & Baron, 1988). Instead, it is widely argued that career stability is on the decline as successful contemporary careers are often marked by continual mobility (Brown, 1995; Hirsch, 1987).

This chapter focuses on two of the more popular claims—indeed, hallmark characteristics—of the contemporary career literature. More specifically, we examine empirical evidence that explores the claims of (1) a decline in organizational tenure, and (2) the phenomenal growth in the temporary workforce. As will be evident, the nature of careers may very well be changing, but the empirical evidence suggests that strong claims about how far these changes have already diffused remain exaggerated.

TABLE 23.1 Job Retention Rates

Current Tenure Group	*1983-1987*	*1987-1991*
0 to <2	.335	.346
2 to <9	.568	.522
9 to <15	.806	.805
15+	.671	.712
All	.537	.527

NOTE: Calculated by Diebold, Newmark, and Polsky (1997).

CHANGES IN ORGANIZATIONAL TENURE

The traditional career literature has two prominent characteristics. The first is that careers are typically viewed as a succession of jobs with vertical mobility (Barley, 1989). Many common terms that we use to explain careers reflect this perspective—for example, "fast tracker," "topped out," "upward mobility," "downward mobility," "entry level," "promotions," "demotions," "glass ceilings," and "sticky floors." Alongside this hierarchical ascension is the second characteristic, that of white-collar workers as above the fray of economic cycles, unlike blue-collar workers who have traditionally shouldered the majority of burden in times of economic turbulence.

This stands in contrast to claims made in the contemporary career literature. The hallmark characteristic of contemporary careers is that they are marked by continuous mobility for *both* blue- and white-collar workers (e.g., Arthur, 1994; Arthur & Rousseau, 1996; Bird, 1994; Brousseau, Driver, Eneroth, & Larsson, 1996; Delfillippi & Arthur, 1994; Dolan, 1996; Glassner, 1994; Hall, 1996; Kiechel, 1993; Newman, 1988; Nicholson, 1996; Pfeffer & Baron, 1988; Schein, 1996). In addition, the psychological contract binding workers to the company and vice versa are shattered (Rousseau & Wade-Benzoni, 1995), job security is dead, and in its place is job insecurity. Thus, those who wish to survive and prosper in this new economic era should reshape their personal bag of skills such that they have the ability to make career-advancing moves that are horizontal in direction. To do so, the recommendation is to (a) develop the appropriate mind-set in which "corporate loyalty is dead" (O'Reilly, 1994), that you must "take care of yourself" (Bridges, 1994) and (b) develop the appropriate skill base—broad skills, not firm specific, are key (Henkoff, 1995). This has resulted in a growing body of rhetoric around the new notion that careers are marked by the continual mobility across multiple employers—consider, for example, "job shopping," "marketable or transferable skills," "temp work," "job mobility," and, of course, "boundaryless."

A number of researchers have attempted to empirically document this claim of increased job mobility (e.g., Diebold, Neumark, & Polsky, 1997; Rose, 1995; Swinnerton & Wial, 1995). For example, as displayed in Table 23.1, Diebold et al. (1997) calculated aggregate retention rates for U.S. workers from the census. Their findings indicated that of those who worked for a particular employer in 1983, 54% were still employed by the same firm 4 years later. Similarly, the

TABLE 23.2 Job Retention Rates, by Occupation

	Current Tenure Group (years)				
Occupation	*0 to <2*	*2 to <9*	*9 to <15*	*15+*	*Total*
Blue-collar					
1983-1987	.340	.603	.870	.675	.571
1987-1991	.332	.491	.798	.640	.507
Change	–.008	–.112	–.072	–.035	–.064
White-collar					
1983-1987	.228	.505	.877	.830	.469
1987-1991	.212	.487	.880	.899	.473
Change	–.016	–.018	.003	.069	–.007

NOTE: Calculated by Diebold, Neumark, and Polsky (1997).

retention rate was 53% between 1987 and 1991. While these findings need to be updated, in this chapter we posit that there is little evidence to suggest that the aggregate stability exhibited through 1991 dropped appreciably later in the 1990s. Indeed, there were dramatic instances of job losses and downsizings during the years covered by their study, the mid-1980s and early 1990s. However, we argue that the extent to which this instability impacted broader labor markets has been exaggerated. If there had been a significant increase in job switching (as much contemporary literature suggests as its basis for extolling "boundaryless careers"), one would expect to see a decline in the retention rates. However, Diebold et al.'s (1997) findings support the counterhypothesis that job retention rates have remained surprisingly stable.

These overall findings are consistent with more recent data on median years of tenure (for ages 28-31), as derived from both the Current Population Survey and the National Longitudinal Survey of Youth (Nardone, Veum, & Yates, 1997). In 1988, the CPS and NLSY average total tenure rate was 2.5 and 2.52, respectively, and 2.87 and 3.0 in 1993—relatively small shifts in tenure (and both are upward).

Data on the retention rates of blue- and white-collar workers are displayed in Table 23.2. Here, it appears that blue-collar workers have been more affected by a reduction in retention rates than white-collar workers (as has traditionally been true). Whereas 57% of blue-collar workers remained with the same employer between 1983 and 1987, the number fell to 51% between the years 1987 and 1991. However, during that same time period, the white-collar retention rates were relatively constant, at 46.9% and 47.3%, respectively.

In a similar study, Rose (1995) examined changes in retention rates over a longer period, using Panel Study of Income Dynamics (PSID) data (see Table 23.3). He reported a decline from the overall job stability during the 1970s to that of the 1980s, across all job categories. Rose also found that both white- and blue-collar workers witnessed relatively equal declines in employment stability.

Examining this same issue from the angle of job loss rate, Kletzer (1998), using data from 1984 to 1996 Displaced Worker Surveys (DWS), reported a pattern consistent with Rose's (1995) discovery of increasing job insecurity. As illustrated in Figure 23.1, although job displacement rates fell steadily from the 1981-1983 rate, they rose again in the 1989-1995 time period. It should be noted that these numbers are consistent with the economy's cycles, given the eco-

TABLE 23.3 Job Stability (percentage), by Occupation

	Occupation		
	Managers	*Professionals*	*Blue-Collar*
1970s			
0 to 1 changes	79	78	70
2 to 3 changes	18	14	20
4+ changes	1	7	8
1980s			
0 to 1 changes	67	68	60
2 to 3 changes	23	20	24
4+ changes	9	11	14
Difference			
0 to 1 changes	–12	–10	–10
2 to 3 changes	5	6	4
4+ changes	8	4	6

NOTE: Calculated by Rose (1995).

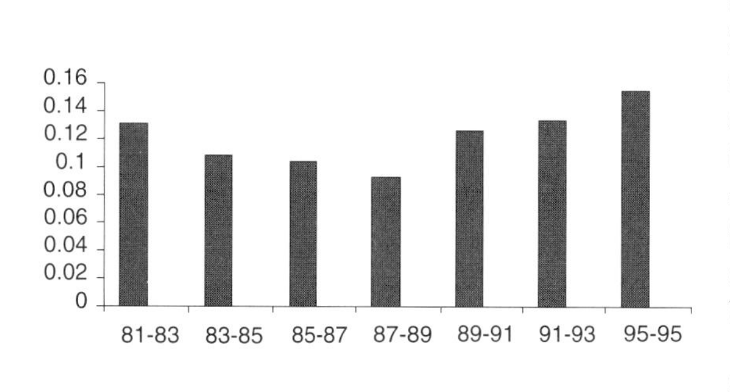

Figure 23.1. Fraction of Workers With Job Loss
SOURCE: Kletzer (1998).

nomic expansion from 1983 to 1989 and the economic weakening from 1989 to 1991. However, the economic cycles do not explain the "high" displacement rates found in the 1993 to 1995 time frame when there was relatively steady growth in the economy. Still, the overall difference in reported job loss rates remains fairly small.[1]

When broken down by occupation, blue-collar workers still bore the brunt of job loss over the past 15 years. As illustrated in Table 23.4, job loss rates for blue-collar workers (craftspeople, operatives, and laborers) remain considerably higher than those of other occupations. However, it must be noted that the difference between rates for occupational categories is narrowing—that the job-loss rates for other occupations have grown over the past 15 years but have been falling for blue-collar labor.

And so what is one to make of all these findings? Taking these studies together suggests that *a change in job stability may very well be under way in this new economic era, but caution is warranted before making strong claims as to the extent of this change.* The empirical evidence is mixed and even raises the question whether a shift in job stability has actually occurred at all. And, if it has, it may be the case that blue-collar workers are still absorbing the brunt of this turbulence as they have traditionally in the past.

One of the well-publicized factors contributing to the rhetoric of increased job mobility is the notion of temporary work, so we now turn our attention to the phenomenal rise of the temporary workforce.

TABLE 23.4 Percentage of Workers With Job Loss, by Occupation, in 3-Year Period

Occupation	*1981-1983*	*1983-1985*	*1985-1987*	*1987-1989*	*1989-1991*	*1991-1993*	*1993-1995*
Managers, Executives	8.2	7.0	7.4	6.4	9.3	9.7	7.8
Professional, Technical	5.1	5.3	4.3	3.5	5.4	5.5	5.9
Sales, Admininstrative Support	8.5	6.7	7.5	6.9	9.2	9.1	9.3
Service	5.9	5.7	5.6	4.8	6.8	6.5	7.3
Crafts, Operatives, Laborers	21.2	16.8	12.8	11.1	17.3	13.7	13.5

SOURCE: Kletzer (1998).

TEMPING

Growth in the temporary workforce over the past two decades has indeed been dramatic. When examining the growth in temporary employee service agencies—which supply temporary workers to organizations on an "as needed" basis—Segal and Sullivan (1997) found an annual growth rate of approximately 11% between 1972 and 1995 (calculations were derived from data gathered by the National Association of Temporary Staff and Services). Workers in temporary service agencies grew from 165,000 in 1972 (less than 0.5% of the workforce) to over 2 million in 1995 (less than 2% of total U.S. employment). Along a similar line, the February 1995 CPS also determined that the number of contingent workers (defined as those who expect their current jobs to last less than a year) is less than 5% (U.S. Department of Labor, 1995). No doubt, the growth in the temporary workforce has been dramatic, and it currently makes up a notable percentage of the U.S. working population.

However, although the growth in size of the temporary workforce is remarkable, three qualifying points must also be noted. First, the initial base upon which this number is based is quite small (165,000 workers, less than 0.5% of the U.S. workforce). Thus a relatively small change in the number of temporary workers will yield a significant growth rate while the absolute size of the temporary workforce may remain relatively small compared to the total population.

Second, the proportion of workers who hold contingent jobs, according to the CPS (as reported by Devens, 1998) has actually declined slightly between 1995 and 1997—from 4.9% to 4.4%. This potentially indicates that a plateau has been reached or may even be the initial indicator of a reversal in the upward trend.

Finally, the absolute size of the temporary workforce isn't nearly as large as might appear from the great attention (albeit praise or alarm) it has received from both scholars and journalists. Two popular claims often cited are that (a) 25% of the workforce are now temporary workers (Morrow, 1993) and (b) Manpower Inc., a temporary service agency, is the nation's largest employer (Smith, 1998). The first claim is misleading because it includes both part-time workers (17.5% of the workforce) and the self-employed (11.8% of the workforce) along with temporary workers (less than 3%) (calculations by Segal & Sullivan, 1997). Granted, combined they make up a respectable portion of the labor force, but one must also note that part-timers and the self-employed make up a significantly larger portion of the workforce than do the temporary and that neither of these two larger categories has seen the dramatic growth rate as has the temporary workforce (Segal, 1996).

Another frequently cited statistic is that the temporary workforce has grown so large that the temporary service agency, Manpower, Inc. is now the largest employer in the United States. While it is true that Manpower issues more W-2 forms than any other organizations, when Segal and Sullivan (1997) take their remarkably high turnover rates into account, Manpower's equivalent employment level is less than 25% of that of General Motors.

Finally, when examining this growth from a blue- versus white-collar work perspective, we find that a large portion of this growth has resulted from blue-collar work. The fraction of temporaries working in blue-collar and pink-collar (administrative support) occupations grew from 64% in 1983 to 75% in 1993 (derived from data presented in Segal & Sullivan, 1997), with blue-collar work accounting for the vast majority of this growth, from 18% to 36% over the respective time frame. In 1995, it is estimated that 39% of those in temporary service agencies actually did their work in manufacturing (i.e., blue-collar) settings (Polivka, 1996). As traditionally has been the case in the past, the temporary industry is largely dominated by blue- (and pink-) versus white-collar workers.

FINDING THE BALANCE

In a paradox reminiscent of the mythical Chinese curse "May you live in interesting times," the rapidly changing economic environment of the late 20th century created simultaneously a confusing time for workers and practitioners and an exciting opportunity for career researchers and theorists. Recent changes brought on by the new economic era have blurred traditional workplace assumptions upon which prior career theory had been based (e.g., an organization's commitment to internal promotions).

As a result, new theories and predictions flourished. A downside to the rich intellectual chaos that ensued is that it is not clear which theories best explain the current nature of careers both in and about the workplace. Hilmer and Donaldson (1996) critically suggest this has contributed to a willingness by both scholars and practitioners to follow the latest fashion or fad. The satirical practice (see Adams, 1996) is one where everyone desires to stay abreast of the latest developments and not fall behind, but has resulted in a misplaced emphasis upon such trends and fashions of the time as downsizing, reengineering, empowerment, decentralization, and more recently, boundaryless careers. Such concerns over faddish career-related claims have grown over the past 15 years, resulting in the commonly given prescriptive advice that the greatest opportunities are for those who no longer align themselves with a particular job or company (Bridges, 1994) and who succeed best in smart networking (Baker, 1994). Yet as we have seen, the jury is still out regarding the conclusion to be reached on the empirical evidence for this contemporary career perspective (Hirsch & Shanley, 1996; Swinnerton & Wial, 1995). It is contradictory in some cases (as with changes in organizational tenure) or suggests a much more modest change than what has been claimed (as with the size of the temporary workforce). What is crystal clear is that employment relationships can no longer be considered a strictly bounded or boundaryless quid pro quo of wages in exchange for labor; they are certainly much more diverse and complex.

The basic theme of this chapter was to more closely examine some of the popular claims in contemporary career literature. We have reviewed the empirical evidence, but it would be incomplete if we did not also take a step back to examine the broader picture. In doing so, we note two interesting situations. First, in addition to the "financial fanatic" perspective of protecting shareholder value at all costs, there is another perspective that may not receive as much attention in contemporary career texts but is prevalent within organizations nonetheless. We refer to this alternative perspective as the *relationship builder.*

Relationship builders generally view the downsizing as destructive to the organization, shedding critical resources that are essential for generating high performance (Katzenbach et al., 1995). Remaining in the rubble of downsized organizations may be workers too shell-shocked to deliver the necessary organizational results for success. Thus, downsizing, according to the relationship builder, leads to a competitive disadvantage. Relationship builders instead view the interaction among employees as a source of competitive advantage (Bluestone & Bluestone, 1992; Gordon, 1996; Hallowell, 1996; Harrison, 1994; Heskett, Sasser, & Hart, 1990; Osterman, 1996; Webber, 1993). From this perspective, the development of highly participative internal relationships may be a critical key to achieving the innovation and flexibility necessary for high performance. As a result, and at its best, the focus can move to the use of teams as a basic building block of organizational structure (Donnellon, 1996; Jacob, 1995; Katzenbach et al., 1995; Nadler et al., 1992). Effective teamwork is seen as better able to deliver high performance results due to its ability to integrate the variety of skills of its members in producing a collective product no single person could have generated (Katzenbach & Smith, 1993). In addition, relationship builders also believe that satisfied employees constitute an asset that can be converted into shareholder value. For example, Southwest Airlines attributes a large part of its financial success to the happiness and commitment of its workforce (Hallowell, 1996). Overall, this alternative perspective views the worker within the organization as a competitive advantage to be developed.

Also when taking a step back and examining the broader picture, we find that some basic ideas about work and careers have survived the sweeping changes. Which brings us to our second observation, that this new economic era is still dominated by the traditional multitier hierarchical bureaucracy. Granted, some individuals have lost opportunities in this new economic era, but it must also be pointed out that many new opportunities have been created, and that there are still workers within organizations to take advantage of these numerous opportunities that abound.

Our overall point is simple: Although the nature of work is changing, how these changes affect the nature of careers is yet to be seen. If anything, the recent social and economic developments have led to the realization that viewing careers as taking place solely within the firm is no longer sufficient to encompass the increasing range of work experiences that people encounter. However, the full extent of the current transformation under way has yet to play itself out to completion, and it is unclear as to where it will eventually lead. Under such conditions of large-scale change, it is only natural that both practitioners and scholars bring into question their "old" beliefs and assumptions in order to determine if they are still applicable in explaining the altered state of events. Those assumptions and theories that are found lacking in some manner are appropriately adjusted. We argue that it is premature for contemporary career theorists to draw the rigid conclusion that the bounded organizational career is dead. Rather, if anything has changed at all, it has become one of a variety of career forms in an increasingly diverse organizational environment. Thus, we suggest taking a pluralistic approach to careers that integrates the diverse possibilities and balance the mix as appropriate. On the whole, this would create something that is totally new and generate a number of productive benefits.

NOTE

1. In periods of economic growth, job tenure is generally expected to fall given the increased number of job opportunities offered by new employers.

REFERENCES

Adams, S. (1996). *The Dilbert principle.* New York: HarperCollins.

Allred, B. B., Snow, C. C., & Miles, R. E. (1996). Characteristics of managerial careers in the 21st century. *The Academy of Management Executive, 10,* 17-27.

Arthur, M. B. (1994). The boundaryless career: A new perspective for organizational inquiry. *Journal of Organizational Behavior, 15,* 295-306.

Arthur, M. B., & Rousseau, D. M. (Eds.). (1996). *The boundaryless career: A new employment principle of a new organizational era.* New York: Oxford University Press.

Ashkenas, R., Ulrich, D., Jick, T., & Kerr, S. (1995). *The boundaryless organization: Breaking the chains of organizational structure.* San Francisco: Jossey-Bass.

Baker, W. E. (1994). *Networking smart: How to build relationships for personal and organizational success.* New York: McGraw-Hill.

Barley, S. R. (1989). Careers, identities, and institutions: The legacy of the Chicago School of Sociology. In M. B. Arthur, D. T. Hall, & B. S. Lawrence (Eds.), *Handbook of career theory* (pp. 41-65). New York: Cambridge University Press.

Bird, A. (1994). Careers as repositories of knowledge: A new perspective on boundaryless careers. *Journal of Organizational Behavior, 15,* 325-344.

Bluestone, B., & Bluestone, I. (1992). *Negotiating the future: A labor perspective on American business.* New York: Basic Books.

Bridges, W. (1994). *Jobshift: How to prosper in a workplace without jobs.* Reading, MA: Addison-Wesley.

Brown, P. (1995). Cultural capital and social exclusion: Some observations on recent trends in education, employment and the labour market. *Work, Employment & Society, 9,* 29-51.

Brousseau, K. R., Driver, M. J., Eneroth, K., & Larsson, R. (1996). Career pandemonium: Realigning organizations and individuals. *The Academy of Management Executive, 10,* 52-66.

Carey, M., & Hazelbaker, K. (1986, April). Employment growth in the temporary help industry. *Monthly Labor Review,* pp. 37-44.

Carnevale, A. P. (1991). *America and the new economy: How new competitive standards are radically changing American workplaces.* San Francisco: Jossey-Bass.

Cascio, W. (1997, August). *Consequences of downsizing and some alternatives.* Paper presented to the Academy of Management, Boston.

Delfillippi, R. J., & Arthur, M. B. (1994). The boundaryless career: A competency based perspective. *Journal of Organizational Behavior, 15,* 307-324.

Devens, R. M. (1998, March). Gains in job security. *Monthly Labor Review,* pp. 74-75.

Diebold, F. X., Neumark, D., & Polsky, D. (1997). Job stability in the United States. *Journal of Labor Economics, 15,* 206-233.

Dolan, K. A. (1996, November 18). When money isn't enough. *Forbes,* pp. 164-170.

Donnellon, A. (1996). *Team talk: The power in language in team dynamics.* Boston: Harvard Business School Press.

Drucker, P. F. (1992, September-October). The new society of organizations. *Harvard Business Review,* pp. 95-104.

Dunlap, A. J. (1996). *Mean business: How I save bad companies and make good companies great.* New York: Times Books.

Glassner B. (1994). *Career crash: America's new crisis and who survives.* New York: Simon & Schuster.

Gordon, D. M. (1996). *Fat and mean: The corporate squeeze of working americans and the myth of managerial downsizing.* New York: Martin Kessler Books/Free Press.

Hall, D. T. (1996). Protean careers of the 21st century. *The Academy of Management Executive, 10,* 8-15.

Hallowell, R. (1996). Southwest Airlines: A case study linking employee needs satisfaction and organizational capabilities to competitive advantage. *Human Resource Management, 35,* 513-534.

Hammer, M., & Champy, J. (1994). *Reengineering the corporation: A manifesto for business revolution.* New York: HarperCollins.

Harrison, B. (1994). *Lean and mean: The changing landscape of corporate power in the age of flexibility.* New York: Basic Books.

Henkoff, R. (1995, July 12). Winning the new career game. *Fortune,* pp. 46-49.

Heskett, J. L., Sasser, W. E., & Hart, C. W. L. (1990). *Breakthrough service.* New York: Free Press.

Hilmer F., & Donaldson, L. (1996). *Management redeemed: Debunking the fads that undermine our corporations.* New York: Free Press.

Hirsch, P. (1987). Pack your own parachute: How to survive mergers, takeovers, and other corporate disasters. Reading, MA: Addison-Wesley.

Hirsch, P. M., & Shanley, M. (1996). The rhetoric of boundaryless—or, how the newly empowered managerial class bought into its own marginalization. In M. Author & D. Rousseau (Eds.), *The boundaryless career: A new employment principle of a new organizational era* (pp. 218-233). New York: Oxford University Press.

Huey, J. (1994, June 27). Waking up to the new economy. *Fortune,* pp. 36-46.

Jacob, R. (1995, April 3). The struggle to create an organization for the 21st century. *Fortune,* pp. 90-99.

Kanter, R. M. (1989a). *When giants learn to dance: Mastering the challenge of strategy, management, and careers in the 1990's.* New York: Simon & Schuster.

Kanter, R. M. (1989b). Careers and the wealth of nations: A macro perspective on the structure and implications of career forms. In M. Arthur, D. Hall, & B. Lawrence (Eds.), *Handbook of career theory* (pp. 506-522). New York: Cambridge University Press.

Katzenbach, J. R., Beckett, F., Dichter, S., Feigen, M., Gagnon, C., Hope, Q., & Ling, T. (1995). *Real change leaders: How you can create growth and high performance at your company.* New York: Times Books.

Katzenbach, J. R., & Smith, D. K. (1993). *The wisdom of teams: Creating the high-performance organization.* Boston: Harvard Business School Press.

Kiechel, W. (1993, May 17). How we will work in the year 2000. *Fortune,* pp. 38-52.

Kletzer, L. G. (1988). Job displacement. *Journal of Economic Perspectives, 12,* 115-136.

Miles, R. E., & Snow, C. C. (1996). Twenty-first-century careers. In M. Author & D. Rousseau (Eds.), *The boundaryless career: A new employment principle of a new organizational era* (pp. 97-115). New York: Oxford University Press.

Mirvis, P. H. (1993). *Building the competitive workforce: Investing in human capital for corporate success.* New York: John Wiley.

Morrow, L. (1993, March 29). The temping of America. *Time*, pp. 40-41.

Nadler, D. A., Gerstein, M. S., & Shaw, R. B. (1992). *Organizational architecture: Designs for changing organizations.* San Francisco: Jossey-Bass.

Nardone, T., Veum, J., & Yates, J. (1997, June). Measuring job security. *Monthly Labor Review*, pp. 26-33.

Newman, K. S. (1988). *Falling from grace: The experience of downward mobility in American middle class.* New York: Random House.

Nicholson, N. (1996). Career systems in crisis: Change and opportunity in the information age. *The Academy of Management Executive, 10*, 40-51.

O'Rielly, B. (1994, June 13). The new deal: What companies and employees owe one another. *Fortune*, pp. 44-48.

Osterman, P. (1996). *Broken ladders: Managerial careers in the new economy.* New York: Oxford University Press.

Pfeffer, J., & Baron, J. (1988). Taking the workers back out: Recent trends in the structuring of employment. In B. Staw (Ed.), *Research in organizational behavior* (Vol. 10, pp. 257-303). Westport, CT: JAI.

Plunkert, L., & Hayghe, H. (1995, February). Strong employment gains continue in 1994. *Monthly Labor Review*, pp. 3-17.

Polivka, A. (1996). *Are temporary help agency workers substitutes for direct hire temps? Searching for an alternative explanation of growth in the temporary help industry.* Washington, DC: Bureau of Labor Statistics.

Rose, S. (1995). *Declining job security and the professionalization of opportunity* (NCEP Research Report No. 95-04). Washington, DC: National Commission on Employment Policy.

Rousseau, D. M., & Wade-Benzoni, K. A. (1995). Changing individual-organizational attachments: A two-way street. In A. Howard (Ed.), *The changing nature of work* (pp. 290-322). San Francisco: Jossey-Bass.

Schein, E. H. (1996). Career anchors revisited: Implications for career development in the 21st century. *The Academy of Management Executive, 10*, 80-88.

Segal, L. (1996). Flexible employment: Composition and trends. *Journal of Labor Research, 17*, 527-542.

Segal, L. M., & Sullivan, D. G. (1997). The growth of temporary services work. *Journal of Economic Perspectives, 11*, 117-136.

Smith, V. (1997). New forms of work organization. *Annual Review of Sociology, 23*, 315-410.

Smith, V. (1998). The fractured world of the temporary worker: Power, participation, and fragmentation in the contemporary workplace. *Social Problems, 45*, 411-430.

Stewart, T. A. (1995, March 20). Planning a career in a world without managers. *Fortune*, pp. 72-80.

Swinnerton, K., & Wial, H. (1995). Is job stability declining in the U.S. economy? *Industrial and Labor Relations Review, 48*, 293-304.

U.S. Department of Labor. (1995, February). *Current population survey.* Washington, DC: Government Printing Office.

Volberda, H. W. (1996). Toward the flexible form: How to remain vital in hypercompetitive environments. *Organization Science, 7*, 359-374.

Webber, A. M. (1993, January-February). What's so new about the new economy? *Harvard Business Review*, pp. 24-42.

The Advent of the Flexible Workplace

Implications for Theory and Research

ARNE L. KALLEBERG

Flexibility has become an increasingly central theme in scholarly as well as popular writings on work and workplaces. *Flexibility* refers to the "capacity to adapt to change" (Meulders & Wilkin, 1987), and individuals, organizations, and nations in the past two decades have all had to adapt to a variety of technological, economic, social, political, and demographic changes. These changes include the growth of international competition and trade, increased rapidity of technological innovation (especially in information technologies and communications), and increasing diversity in labor force composition (such as the continued increase in women and non-White workers). Flexibility is widely seen as the way in which organizations and societies can adapt to these changes, and so flexibility has become both the corporate watchword for the 1990s (Cappelli et al., 1997; Christensen, 1989) and the proposed solution to societywide problems of recession and uncertainty (Pollert, 1988).

Flexibility has been an elusive concept, and its many meanings have often produced confusion (Meulders & Wilkin, 1987; Piore, 1986; Sengenberger, 1990; Smith, 1993, 1997; Streeck, 1987; Vallas, 1999). For example, flexibility has been conceptualized at multiple levels of analysis. At the macroscopic level, employment and wage flexibility are strategies that nations have used to seek to overcome unemployment and labor market rigidities that have impeded efficiency in periods of reduced economic growth and lowered productivity rates (Organization for Economic Cooperation and Development, 1990). In this context, flexibility is part of the "regimes of accumulation" and "modes of regulation" that constitute the historically contingent political and economic conditions affecting work (Boyer, 1987, 1988). At the mezzoscopic level of the workplace, flexibility is an organizational strategy designed to redeploy labor among tasks or to adjust the size of the labor force to adapt to changes in product and labor markets. At the individual level, flexibility is a goal of workers seeking to balance work with family and other nonwork activities. At each of these levels of analysis, flexibility impacts on work and workplaces: Macroscopic employment policies affect the likelihood that people are able to find good jobs; workplace flexibility influences the attachment of individuals to their organizations and their ability to perform various kinds of tasks; and individuals' needs for flexible schedules have helped shift production to the home, encouraged the spread of job sharing and part-time work, and so on.

This chapter focuses on flexibility in the workplace, where most work is carried out in industrial societies. Workplaces have adapted in two main ways to their needs for flexibility (see Smith, 1997, for a review). Some organizations have emphasized "functional" flexibility and sought to increase the participation of employees in decision making and to provide them with multiple skills so that they can be redeployed from one task to another. Other organizations have adopted strategies based on "numerical" flexibility, removing their dependence on "permanent" employees who are fixed costs and replacing them by nonstandard workers such as temporary and contract workers. These two types of flexibility are alternative ways that employers can obtain flexibility: changing the people who work in the organization (in the case of numerical flexibility) or changing what the employees do (in the case of functional flexibility).

Both of these types of flexibility represent a challenge to much theory and research in the sociology of work, which has been dominated by a relatively static, bureaucratic model of organizations.[1] The advent of the flexible firm implies a need to redirect the sociology of work toward studying dynamic workplaces and peoples' responses—individually and collectively—to the changing organization of work. As a consequence of the greater importance placed on flexible firms, some kinds of research questions have increased in importance, especially those related to workplace dynamism and corporate restructuring and to individual and collective agency. Unfortunately, the literature on work and occupations has not always kept pace with these changes, and researchers often continue to study problems and issues that were much more relevant in the 1970s than they are likely to be in the 2000s.

I first discuss briefly some of the challenges to our thinking about work and workplaces posed by the advent of the flexible firm. I then outline three main models or conceptions of the flexible firm that have dominated recent literature. Next, I briefly describe some of the research questions that are raised by these conceptions of the flexible firm and also some research strategies that will become increasingly important in studying work and workplaces. My goal in this chapter is to synthesize recent writings on the flexible firm and to indicate some of the implications of the advent of the flexible firm for research and theory in the sociology of work and occupations.

FLEXIBLE WORKPLACES: CHALLENGING OUR THINKING ABOUT WORK

Sociologists studying work have often ignored the organizational contexts within which work is embedded, just as organizational researchers have rarely studied work. To the extent that research and theory in the sociology of work during the post-World War II period have taken into account organizations, they have been heavily influenced by a bureaucratic view of work and workplaces (e.g., Baron & Bielby, 1980; Bendix, 1956; Doeringer & Piore, 1971; Kanter, 1977). Writers in this period tended to view work as organized hierarchically in relatively large, stable workplaces. Manufacturing organizations—the subjects of most studies of work—were assumed to be characterized by a "Fordist" model of work organization and mechanization that used assembly-line techniques to mass-produce and mass-market complex products cheaply (Wood, 1989). The Fordist model was reinforced by Taylorist principles of job design, which separated managers' conception of work from both blue- and white-collar workers' execution of deskilled tasks (Braverman, 1974). The tasks of motivating and training workers were accomplished mainly by the construction of job ladders or firm internal labor markets, which were central aspects of the bureaucratic control systems that emerged in many large corporations after World War II (Edwards, 1979).

Fordism, Taylorism, and bureaucratic control flourished in a larger social and economic context characterized by high growth rates, the expansion of markets for mass-produced goods, and high product market concentration fueled (in the United States) by the relative lack of foreign competition. Relations between labor and management in the United States from the end of World War II to the late 1970s were generally characterized by a social contract that fostered harmony between these groups, as both benefitted from the growing pie made possible by the postwar expansion in mass-product markets (Rubin, 1995). Social consensus also characterized, for the most part, western European nations (interrupted briefly by the massive student unrest and strike waves of May 1968 and the Italian Hot Autumn), which saw much progress in social and distributional policies during this period (Standing, 1997).

Accompanying this social contract in the United States was a psychological contract between the employer and the employee in which job security was exchanged for loyalty. These social and psychological contracts formed the basis for what may be described as a "standard" employment relation. There is little consensus on what constitutes a standard employer-employee relationship, although in the United States during the post-World War II period it typically involved the exchange of labor by an employee for monetary compensation by an employer, with the work performed on a preset schedule at the employer's place of business, under the employer's control, and often with the shared expectation of continued employment, assuming satisfactory performance by the employee (Kalleberg, Reskin, & Hudson, 2000).

During this period, sociologists typically studied work-related phenomena within relatively large workplaces. Labor process theorists debated the veracity of Braverman's (1974) claims about deskilling in mass-production firms and the role of collective agency in resisting Taylorist practices (e.g., Wood, 1982). Stratification researchers analyzed the rate and patterns of mobility of individuals along job ladders within large corporations (e.g., Rosenbaum, 1979), and organizational researchers examined how workplace size was related to bureaucratic structures such as differentiation, centralization, and formalization (Blau & Schoenherr, 1971).

Beginning in the late 1970s, changes in political, social, technological, and economic environments made the bureaucratic model of work less viable in most sectors of the economies of the United States and other industrial nations. Declines in economic growth rates in the 1980s—after substantial and steady increases in the postwar period—threatened companies' profits as well as governments' budgets (Harrison, 1994; Harvey, 1989; Rubin, 1995). Piore and Sabel (1984) saw these changes as representing fundamental challenges to the effectiveness of mass production technologies and announced the arrival of a "second industrial divide" whereby craft-based, smaller-scale, flexible workplaces would displace bureaucratic organizations employing Fordist mass-production processes. They argued that this new industrial order—based on flexible specialization—was made possible by computer-based technologies and was necessary to enable organizations to adapt quickly to changing market opportunities.

The need for flexibility posed by these changes was described differently in different countries. In Great Britain, Atkinson (1984) sparked a "flexibility debate" in the 1980s by outlining a core-periphery model that provided a framework for identifying the main practices on which managers and government policymakers should focus to achieve functional as well as numerical flexibility (see also Pollert, 1988). In Japan, the *genryō-keiei* (the "slimming management" debate) in the mid-1970s emphasized ways of achieving numerical flexibility, as obtaining internal, functional flexibility was less problematic for Japanese firms (Wood, 1989). In Germany, restrictive union contracts severely constrained employers' ability to attain numerical flexibility, and so debate centered on the "new production concepts" that facilitated functional flexibility (e.g., Kern & Schumann, 1987).

This focus on flexibility in the 1980s and 1990s underscores the conditional nature of work organization and the employment relation: These are shaped by historically specific circumstances and are not universal manifestations of an inherent logic of capitalist production (Tilly & Tilly, 1998). It is not surprising that bureaucratic organizations do not do well in turbulent environments; this outcome is predictable on the basis of the structural contingency theory of organizations that grew up in the 1960s, which maintained that the efficiency of organizational structures depends on the characteristics of the environments in which they operate (Lawrence & Lorsch, 1967; Thompson, 1967). The tightly integrated, hierarchical company that bases its work organization on principles of scientific management and Fordism was not a necessary feature of capitalist production. Rather, it was an efficient response to stable and predictable environments in the post-World War II period in which some corporations controlled their markets and both GNP (gross national product) and productivity were on the rise (Hyman, 1988; Piore, 1986). By contrast, making firms more flexible is a rational response to conditions of rapid change: During such circumstances, organizations will seek to externalize or redeploy workers in order to try to deal with the uncertainty (Pfeffer & Baron, 1988).

Although an image of firms as flexible rather than static is more realistic in the present period of rapid change, we should note that the bureaucratic model of firms was misleading in important ways even when it served as the basis for much of our thinking about work. Most organizations were (and continue to be) small (Granovetter, 1984) and not bureaucratically organized (Kalleberg, Knoke, Marsden, & Spaeth, 1996). Indeed, the centrality of large workplaces to the study of work in the postwar period has always exceeded their prevalence; rather, they were the public face of American business that symbolized postwar prosperity and represented to many workers the ideal employer (Rudolph, 1998). Moreover, the majority of the labor force (especially women and non-Whites) never enjoyed the relational contracts with their employers that were implied by the model of bureaucratic control. For example, the idea of job security—which was often associated with employment in "core" bureaucratically controlled firms—is a phenomenon that was uncommon in most of the 20th century. As Jacoby (1985) points out, there was not much job security in U.S. work organizations in the early part of the 20th century and job security was purported to be especially high only during the postwar period (1945-1973, around the time of the first OPEC oil shock) (see also Farber, 1997). Similarly, Hirsch (1993) argues that the firm internal labor market model is of fairly recent origin: It was in place in the United States only during the period 1950 to1985.

It is likely, then, that the flexible workplace may be the "normal" state of affairs and that the post-World War II period in the United States simply represented a deviation from the norm of flexibility. In any event, the changes discussed above have made bureaucratic images of work—such as organizing jobs in highly structured internal labor markets—less useful as models for understanding the organization of work as well as for capturing contemporary corporate career realities. Numerical and functional flexibility challenge our thinking about work. Findings about functional flexibility (that employees work in teams and work groups which blur formal organizational structures) and numerical flexibility (such as the permeability of organizational boundaries, the downsizing of managers, and the scarcity of relational employment contracts) both suggest the need for more dynamic and multilevel views of organizations. The next section discusses various ways that flexible firms have been conceptualized.

THREE MODELS OF FLEXIBLE FIRMS

Numerical and functional flexibility form the basis—in varying degrees—of three main models of flexible firms:

1. The functionally flexible, high-performance work organization that seeks to overcome rigid and detailed divisions of labor by multiskilling, broadbanding, and eliciting greater participation in decision making by employees
2. The numerically flexible organization, which externalizes some of its work and relies less on a psychological contract by

which job security is exchanged for loyalty and commitment

3. The network organization, which is characterized by a logic of embeddedness and is governed by relatively durable trust-based relations among workplaces

Flexible organizations may be characterized as using primarily one or another of these approaches, although combinations of these models may be used in different parts of the organization. Similarly, entire societies have typically sought to achieve a balance between types of flexibility in their economies (OECD, 1990). I briefly consider each of these models of the flexible firm.

Functionally Flexible High-Performance Work Organizations

Functional flexibility refers to an organization's ability to deploy its employees and other resources among a variety of tasks and skills and thereby to adjust its division of labor to changes in demand, technology, production methods, labor markets, and other conditions (Wood, 1989). Some functionally flexible organizations are able to modify their production systems as needed and to produce a variety of products via "flexible specialization" (Piore & Sabel, 1984) in response to changing demand for their goods and services.

Studies of functional flexibility typically focus on workers in manufacturing who are employed in regular, full-time work arrangements (Smith, 1993; Vallas, 1999). Functional flexibility represents a departure from Fordist principles of manufacturing and from Taylorist methods of job simplification. Unlike the Taylorist detailed division of labor associated with rigid, hierarchical production organizations, functionally flexible workers have general skills and can therefore adapt to changing technologies and ways of organizing work. Functionally flexible work synthesizes mental and manual skills, providing workers with "responsible autonomy" (Friedman, 1977) or a high degree of employee involvement in decision making; such work has been alternatively described as representing "new production concepts" (Kern & Schumann, 1987) and as characteristic of the "posthierarchical workplace" (Zuboff, 1988).

The idea of functional flexibility overlaps with the concept of "high performance" work organizations, the subject of a rapidly growing literature in the United States (for reviews, see Appelbaum & Batt, 1994; Smith, 1997). High-performing organizations (also called "transformed" systems, "salaried" systems, or "high commitment" organizations—see Osterman, 1994) represent a departure from hierarchical, top-down management and are characterized by high degrees of employee involvement in decision making, employee discretion, and skills.

The notion of "high performing" organizations has been used to refer to workplaces adopting a wide variety of practices, including just-in-time inventory practices, job expansion and rotation, technologically sophisticated work such as the use of computers, and the utilization of team production such as quality circles and self-directed work teams (Appelbaum & Batt, 1994; Smith, 1997). Some of these practices are designed to foster employee involvement in production and thereby elicit greater employee discretion in the workplace (Bailey, 1992). Others (e.g., just-in-time inventory practices) are intended to increase efficiency in production by removing barriers to the smooth functioning of the production process—also a goal in Japanese lean production methods—or to increase product quality by diagnosing and solving production problems. Still others (e.g., group incentives) are human resource practices that support the "high performance" structures by motivating employees to "do whatever it takes" to help the organization succeed (Osterman, 1994). Appelbaum and Batt (1994) identify two models of high-performing systems in the United States: one characterized by high employee involvement in decision making and a heavy reliance on team production; the other an American version of Japanese lean production that maintains a hierarchical structure but adopts various practices designed to enhance quality.

An emergent theme in the literature on high-performing work organizations is that organizations adopting systems or "bundles" of work organization, technology, and human resource practices achieve greater complementarities among them and thus attain higher performance and other benefits of functional flexibility (Pil & MacDuffie, 1996). Thus, involved and secure workers are more likely to be motivated to undergo training, to be willing to be redeployed to new job assignments, and to put forth the discretionary effort that is often needed when companies are in the midst of rapid and uncertain change (Bailey, 1992). MacDuffie's (1995) study of automotive assembly plants provides support for this view: He found that flexible production plants with team-based work systems, low inventory and repair buffers, and "high commitment" human resource practices such as contingent compensation and extensive training performed better than mass-production plants but that plants which combined these practices performed even better (see also Arthur, 1992; Kochan, Cutcher-Gershenfeld, & MacDuffie, 1991; Levine & Tyson, 1990).

The extent to which workers as well as managers benefit from functionally flexible, "high performing" work systems is debatable. On one hand, some writers (e.g., Piore & Sabel, 1984; Womack, Jones, & Roos, 1990) argue that these work systems provide workers with greater control over their work and promote harmonious collaboration between managers and workers. On the other hand, critics maintain that the Japanese lean production model in particular is a coercive system that uses peer pressure to obtain worker compliance without providing workers with any real voice in decision making (e.g., Berggren, 1992; Dohse, Jurgens, & Malsch, 1985; Graham, 1995; see also the discussion of concertive control by Barker, 1993, and Grenier's, 1988, analysis of the tyranny of teams).

Regardless of whom benefits from functional flexibility, the number of organizations using one or more practices designed to enhance it appears to be growing rapidly. A study of the adoption of employee involvement programs conducted in the late 1980s (Lawler, Ledford, & Mohrman, 1989) found that 80% of large *Fortune* 1000 companies had implemented some type of involvement program within the past 5 years; these programs were typically survey feedback systems or employee participation groups such as quality circles. However, only 10% of these companies had at least three types of these systems with more than 40% of employees covered by each. When these companies were surveyed again in 1990, the authors found substantial increases in the number of firms using self-managed work teams or job enrichment practices (Lawler, Mohrman, & Ledford, 1992; see also Cappelli, 1995; Commission on the Skills of the American Workforce, 1989). Osterman's (1994) survey—of a sample of private sector establishments in the United States with more than 50 employees—defined "transformed" organizations as those in which more than half of the employees in the core occupation (an occupation considered to be central to the organization's main product or service) were involved in at least two of four practices designed to enhance employee participation (self-directed teams, problem-solving groups, and Total Quality Management principles) and deployment (job rotation). He concluded that 37% of all establishments (43% of nonmanufacturing, 36% of manufacturing) represented the "new breed" of transformed, functionally flexible establishments. This estimate is probably on the high side, due to his focus on a core occupation, his sampling of relatively large organizations, and his broad definition of functional flexibility.

The rise of functionally flexible workplaces represents an adaptation by organizations to the growing uncertainty, increased competition, and rapid changes in technology that we have discussed above. Managers have had to cope with such conditions before, and their adaptations to uncertainty in the past similarly sought to elicit their employees' discretionary efforts (Bailey, 1992). For example, the human relations movement in the 1930s—like the high-performance work systems of the 1990s—emphasized teams and work groups as vehicles for enhancing the motivation of employees and harnessing their energies to further organizational goals (Bailey, 1992; Guillén, 1994). The need to elicit employees' participation in decision making is perhaps more pressing now due to the reductions in numbers of managers and supervisors that have accompanied recent waves of downsizing,[2] for eliminating layers of management has forced firms to rely more on decisions made by employees at all levels of the organization. In any event, the current focus on functional flexibility may well represent only the latest oscillation of managerial control between rational (e.g., Taylorist) and normative (e.g., human relations, high-performance organization) control systems (Barley & Kunda, 1992). Key questions are whether the pace of change and competition will abate in the future and whether this will diminish the need for functionally flexible firms.

Numerically Flexible, Core-Periphery, Dualistic Models

Numerical or external flexibility refers to an organization's ability to adjust the size of its labor force so as to cope with changes in demand for products and labor, to reduce labor costs (especially the cost of fringe benefits), or to avoid legal requirements associated with the status of the employer (Gonos, 1997, p. 86; Houseman, 2001). Organizations are typically unable to freely hire and fire their employees. This is due to constraints imposed by the existence of relational contracts such as psychological contracts (in which employers have an obligation to provide job security in return for their employees' loyal efforts—see Rousseau, 1995), employment laws, union contracts, and shortages of trained workers. The nature of these constraints—particularly employment laws and union contracts—differs among countries, although numerical flexibility is problematic in all industrial nations, even in the United States, which is characterized by relatively low union power and, at least theoretically, the doctrine of employment at will (Piore, 1986). The importance for employers of obtaining numerical flexibility also depends on labor market conditions; as demands for labor increase, organizations more often attempt to hire "standard" employees and to internalize them so as to prevent raiding by competitors.

Organizations seek to achieve numerical flexibility through the use of "nonstandard" staffing arrangements. Nonstandard work arrangements—by contrast to the "standard" work arrangements we discussed earlier—are characterized by the absence of a single employer (as with independent contractors) or by persons working at an organization that is not their employer (e.g., temps are employees of temporary help agencies, not the client organizations at which they work—see Gonos, 1997). Nonstandard workers include those hired through employment intermediaries (e.g., temporary help agencies, contract companies, and subcontracting networks) as well as workers hired directly by the organization (e.g., fixed-term employees and on-call workers who may be maintained by in-house temp pools). Nonstandard arrangements provide organizations with flexible staffing options; by contrast, organizations typically use flexible scheduling (e.g., flextime, part-time work, job sharing, and home-based work) to accommodate the schedules of valued "permanent" employees (Christensen, 1989). In 1995, about 30% of the U.S. labor force worked in nonstandard work arrangements, with about 34% of female workers and about 25% of males working in nonstandard jobs (see Kalleberg et al., 1997).

There is mounting evidence that organizations are increasingly using temporary, part-time, and subcontracted work arrangements (e.g., Abraham, 1990; Christensen, 1989; Hakim, 1990). This growth is most marked among temporary help agencies, in which employment has increased by about 11% per year since 1972 (Gonos, 1997; Segal & Sullivan, 1997). Part-time employment grew from 16.4% of the labor force in 1970 to 18% in 1990, almost entirely because of the expansion of involuntary part-time employment (Tilly, 1996). There was also an increase in the proportion of persons reporting income only as self-employed or independent contractors, which is suggestive of the increase in independent contracting (Callaghan & Hartmann, 1991).

Organizations rarely rely solely on nonstandard employment relations, and so there are not likely to be "numerically flexible" organizations in the same sense as there are "functionally flexible" organizations. An extreme, and probably rare, example of an organization characterized by high levels of numerical flexibility is the "virtual organization" (such as the computer sales company that "builds" computers to customers' orders by contracting out manufacturing), which may be largely made up of nonstandard workers. More typically, organizations use a numerically flexible, nonstandard, "peripheral" workforce to buffer or protect their regular, "core" labor force from fluctuations in demand and other variations in the need for workers. Indeed, the achievement of internal, functional flexibility may only be possible if there is a demand buffer provided by external flexibility.

The coexistence within the same organization of numerical and functional flexibility is the hallmark of the core-periphery model of the flexible firm, a conception that gained popularity in the mid-1980s through the work of John Atkinson (1984, 1987) in Great Britain. This model was quickly adopted by writers on both sides of the Atlantic and has become the subject of a lively debate (e.g., Abraham, 1990; Cappelli, 1995; Davis-Blake & Uzzi, 1993; Hakim, 1990; Hunter, McGregor, MacInnes, & Sproull, 1993; Mangum, Mayall, & Nelson, 1985; Pfeffer & Baron, 1988; Pollert, 1988; Procter, Rowlinson, McArdle, Hassard, & Forrester, 1994). The core-periphery model revived the concept of economic dualism in describing work and the workplace, a theoretical idea that has declined in popularity in American sociology since the late 1970s. It is ironic that theory and research on dualism largely vanished from the academic scene at precisely the moment—in the late 1980s and 1990s—when polarizing and dualizing tendencies increased most rapidly. The multidimensional view of flexibility suggested by the core-periphery model is also a potentially useful correction to one-dimensional representations of flexible work structures that emphasize *either* functional *or* numerical flexibility.

The appeal of the core-periphery model is due largely to its combining established management thinking (such as Thompson's, 1967, idea that organizations should buffer or protect their central capabilities and resources) with a variety of management fads such as Japanese management and the need for the organization to define strategically its core competence (Pollert, 1988). The core-periphery model also applies the concept of economic dualism to the organization, rather than using it to describe differences among jobs within the society as a whole, as the dual labor market theorists did in the 1970s (see Kalleberg & Sørensen, 1979, for a review). Moreover, this model suggests that firms' needs for flexibility result in increased segmentation and polarization between advantaged and disadvantaged labor force members (Hyman, 1988).

The idea that employers seek to combine functional and numerical flexibility is not new. For example, immigrants, by providing a "reserve army" of potential employees, disciplined and buffered the organization's permanent workforce in much the same way as temporary help agencies and business service firms now do (Pfeffer & Baron, 1988, p. 276; see also Sabel & Zeitlin, 1985). Moreover, contract work arrangements are not new phenomena; Buttrick (1952), for example, describes the inside-contracting system common in the late 1800s. Nonstandard work arrangements never disappeared from the economy and have been used fairly consistently as a buffer to protect the jobs of "permanent" employees (Harrison, 1994; Morse, 1969).

Some writers have criticized the core-periphery model, on both theoretical and empirical grounds. Theoretically, Pollert (1988) argued that the model is ambiguous and circular, and that it confuses description, prediction, and prescription. Empirically, there is little quantitative evidence that the increased use of these nonstandard work arrangements is driven by management's desire to buffer their core employees. For example, Hakim's (1990) analysis of several national British surveys found that only 5% of workplaces pursued what might be called a "core-periphery" strategy (or, for that matter, had a human resource strategy at all!). Similarly, Cappelli's (1995) review concluded there is little evidence that managers in the United States have adopted such a strategy. Yet over half of the respondents in a recent survey of more than 1,000 establishments in the United States (see Kalleberg, Knoke, & Marsden, 1995) "agreed" or "strongly agreed" with the statement "Your human resource management strategy divides the workforce into permanent and nonpermanent employees."

Network Organizations: Numerical and Functional Flexibility Via Embeddedness

The increase in recent years of market-mediated work arrangements such as contract companies, subcontracting, and temporary help agencies (Abraham & Taylor, 1996) underscores the importance of network relations among organizations and the pervasiveness of the embeddedness of social and economic life (Granovetter 1985). During the past decade, a growing literature has sought to combine organization theory and social network theory via the notion of network organizations. These are forms of cooperative endeavor characterized by reciprocal patterns of communication and exchange ("embeddedness") and governed by trust between parties rather than by the market logic of price or hierarchical power and decision making (Powell, 1990; Uzzi, 1996, 1997). Even though network forms of organization are not new, in some cases predating markets or hierarchies (Powell, 1990, p. 299), many writers claim that network forms of organization are more common now due to a fertile environment for networking produced by global and segmented markets and by cheap information technology (Grandori & Soda, 1995; Miles & Snow, 1986).

As with the core-periphery model, the idea of network organizations suggests ways in which organizations can achieve both numerical and functional flexibility. Numerical flexibility may be obtained by outsourcing functions such as production, maintenance, repair, clerical, and other activities that were previously done within the organization (Harrison & Kelley, 1993). Functional flexibility can be achieved by collaborative relations among specialized suppliers and producers, as illustrated in the Emilia-Romagna industrial district of Italy (Piore & Sabel, 1984), and by the network of computer-oriented firms centered around Route 28 in Massachusetts and clustered around Silicon Valley in California. The close, trust-based relations among organizations in these networks enable producers to reconfigure their relationships with suppliers and to develop interorganizational competencies, thus achieving flexible specialization by being able to redeploy their resources as needed so as to adapt to changes in the environment (Harrison & Kelley, 1993).

The creation of network relations among organizations is in part an attempt by employers to reduce resource dependencies and otherwise respond to the changes in competition, technology, and other environmental conditions that we have discussed. In turbulent environments, organizations will try to become more interconnected with other organizations, in order to cope with the uncertainty (Pfeffer & Baron, 1988, p. 277). Powell, Koput, and Smith-Doerr (1996) use data from the biotechnology industry to illustrate that the locus of innovation will be in organizational networks—rather than individual firms—when an industry's knowledge base is complex and growing and when sources of expertise are widely dispersed. Organizational networks may also form when large, vertically integrated firms search for greater flexibility by spinning off and decoupling parts of the organization ("dedifferentiation"; Clegg, 1990) and establishing collaborations with other organizations (DiTomaso, 2001; Miles & Snow, 1986). Joint ventures between multinational firms and alliances between producers and suppliers are two examples of network arrangements based on close collaborations between organizations. Powell (1996) sees these as illustrative of a broader phenomenon: the emergence of network or alliance capitalism in which projects replace jobs and organizational boundaries become porous and replaced by interorganizational relations.

Organizational networks are most interesting when they are durable and when they have ties based on trust rather than price (as in the market model) or authority (as in the hierarchical model) (Powell, 1990). Examples of such networks are home-building contractors (Eccles, 1981) and movie production companies (Faulkner & Anderson, 1987), which exhibit trust, reliance on implicit knowledge, and strong economic incentives for efficiently creating and disbanding projects. Such craft or project networks based on trust are likely to persist when turnover in skills and knowledge is slow enough to enable holders of implicit knowledge to maintain their edge. In general, network organizations are likely to be most durable when continuing rapid change in the state-of-the-art of knowledge and technology creates situations where it is very difficult for any firm to be certain that it will be able to purchase what it needs through markets or hierarchies (Baker & Kalleberg, 1998). When such conditions no longer exist, organizations in networks may eventually adopt either market or hierarchical forms of governance, and it is unclear whether their interorganizational relations are then best described as "network organizations" (see, e.g., the discussion in Harrison, 1994).

SOME RESEARCH QUESTIONS RAISED BY THE RISE OF THE FLEXIBLE FIRM

The advent of the flexible workplace raises important questions for research. For example, we need to understand better the determinants and correlates of organizational restructuring and the individual and collective responses to workplace changes. The three models of flexible firms we have described suggest a variety of issues that need to be addressed: functional flexibility directs our attention toward the changing organization of production; numerical flexibility focuses our concern on questions related to the changing nature of employment relations; and the idea of network organizations leads to the study of interorganizational relations and how organizations are embedded in institutional contexts. Our discussion of these three models has identified a number of unresolved issues related to the growth of flexibility in the workplace, such as whether functional flexibility really results in greater worker control, the extent to which dualism exists in workplaces, and the durability of network organizational forms. The next section illustrates some additional research questions raised by the advent of the flexible firm.

Changing Organization of Work

Theories that predict a decline in rigidly structured jobs and a rise in "high performance" work organizations designed to promote functional flexibility suggest various hypotheses about changes in skills, worker participation in decision making, and the structure of work. For example, it is assumed that the Taylorist distinction between conception and execution will be eliminated and replaced by higher skill levels and greater worker participation in decisions.

Evidence on these changes is mixed (see the reviews by Appelbaum & Batt, 1994; Vallas, 1999). I discussed earlier some studies that support the hypothesis that the growth of flexible specialization increases workers' participation in decision making. Additional support for this view is provided by a recent investigation of work organization and workers in the steel, apparel, and medical electronic instruments and imaging industries. The investigators found that workers in high-performance work systems had more opportunities to participate in decisions and experienced higher intrinsic rewards (challenging work) (Appelbaum, Bailey, Berg, & Kalleberg, 1999).

Vallas and Beck (1996), however, found only partial support for post-Fordist theory in their study of four pulp-and-paper manufacturing plants. Even though the skills required of manual workers have risen, as predicted by post-Fordist theory, they found that Fordist principles of work organization remained prevalent; there was little evidence of the expansion of craft discretion or of the synthesis of mental and manual labor. Moreover, Taplin's (1995) analysis of apparel manufacturing suggests that firms achieve manufacturing flexibility—and improvements in productivity and quality—by using new technology to deskill high-skilled functional tasks and preserve distinctions between managers and workers. This restructuring appeared to represent a modification of Fordist principles rather than a new, post-Fordist paradigm. In addition, Hodson's (1988) interviews with workers and managers in high-tech firms revealed that segmentation between mental and manual labor persisted and that participation was limited to professional employees. Furthermore, his analysis of workplace ethnographies (Hodson, 1996) yielded results at least partly consistent with a pessimistic view of participative management: Even though workers had more positive experiences under modern participative forms of management, these experiences were not as positive as those characteristic of the craft organization of work.

Hyman (1988) offers an explanation of why workforce flexibility does not necessarily accompany the use of flexible specialization in product strategies, arguing that flexibility will not result in industrial democracy unless flexibility is "liberated from the dominance of capital" (p. 59). This observation points to the importance of continued research on the relationship between firms' productive strategies and organization of production. It also emphasizes the need for cross-national studies that examine how work is organized under differing "regimes of accumulation."

Changing Employment Relations

The growth of nonstandard work arrangements has led to changes both in the social contract between labor and management in the broader society and in the psychological contract between individual employers and employees (especially White males). Even the most successful and enlightened U.S. companies no longer guarantee career security. These changes provide an opportunity to study the conditional nature of linkages between employers and employees. Rousseau's (e.g., 1995) research on the mutual obligations, promises, and expectations that are involved in the creation of psychological contracts illustrates a promising area of research on this topic.

Studies of nonstandard work arrangements have also suggested that flexibility may have a "dark side" that has costs for workers at the same time as they benefit their employers. Evidence from Europe, for example, indicates that increased labor market flexibility may be associated with increased job insecurity (Standing, 1997). Moreover, studies in the United States demonstrate that nonstandard jobs are more likely to be "bad" than are regular full-time jobs: Nonstandard jobs are more likely to be contingent, to pay low wages, and to lack fringe benefits such as health insurance and pension benefits (Kalleberg et al., 2000). The debate about the consequences of nonstandard work arrangements is only beginning (e.g., see Blank, 1998), and research is needed on questions such as what is the relationship between nonstandard work arrangements and job quality, and what groups of workers (defined by demographic categories such as gender, race, and age) are helped or hurt by working in nonstandard work arrangements?

Changing Nature of Internal Labor Markets and Careers

The changes we have discussed—downsizing, the redefinition of the psychological contract, and an increased emphasis on numerical flexibility—suggest that workers have less reason to be attached to a particular organization and that it is more rational for them instead to be committed to an occupation or to their careers. More research is needed on how changes in the organization of work is likely to affect careers, as many aspects of these dynamics are poorly understood (see Hirsch, 1993).

We need to understand better, for example, which workers have been most affected by recent changes associated with the advent of the flexible firm. Although the evidence showed an erosion of job security between the 1980s and 1990s for white-collar Americans, it remains unclear whether overall job security has decreased: Statistics from the Department of Labor's Displaced Workers Surveys show that white-collar layoff rates rose from 2.6% in 1981 to 1982 to 3.6% in 1991 to 1992 before falling to 3.2% in 1993 to 1994 (Rudolph, 1998). This suggests that what is new about downsizing may not be its overall incidence but the fact that it has affected the formerly privileged white-collar sector: Job security in white-collar jobs had been a hallmark of U.S. workplaces since World War II.

The demise of internal labor markets may be overstated. This is especially true if one conceives of the firm internal labor market broadly as encompassing a company's overall human resource strategy, that is, as including wage systems, job classifications, and rules regarding the deployment of labor and employment security, in addition to job ladders (Osterman, 1993). Viewed in this sense, firm internal labor markets may still be important, although they may be "fraying" around the edges. For example, Osterman (1993) argues that long-term employment relationships are growing in importance for women and are still important for men, even though there was a drop in job tenure for middle-aged men in the 1980s. Moreover, he suggests that contingent employment does not necessarily decrease long-term relationships as people could have long-term employment with a company that acts as a contractor to other companies. These findings are consistent with other analyses (e.g., by Groshen & Levine, 1998) that find no evidence of a decline in the importance of internal labor markets in large firms (as measured by deviations of company wage policies from market averages).

The concept of the occupational internal labor market may be especially relevant for explaining the changing nature of careers (Althauser & Kalleberg, 1981). The decline of organizational careers (and "lifetime" jobs), for example, may be compensated by the growth of occupational careers, "stochastic careers," job hopping, and an emphasis on employability. Occupational careers are characterized by greater portability of skills and more importance placed on general rather than specific training and skills (Arthur & Rousseau, 1996). People are expected increasingly to manage their own careers, as the career of the 21st century will be "protean," needing to be reinvented by the person from time to time as the individual and the environment change (Hall, 1996). Heckscher (1995) describes this as the growth of a new professional loyalty, in which people are loyal to the task or occupation rather than the company. The rise of networks among organizations, such as joint ventures and alliances, provide opportunities for people to move from one organization to another.

The use of contingent workers may also affect the mobility of noncontingent workers, in the sense that their careers may be interdependent. Thus, Barnett and Miner (1992) found in the clerical workforce of a large, formalized organization that hiring temporaries reduced the mobility chances of permanent workers in lower level jobs, but increased permanent workers' promotion chances in higher level jobs.

Some Research Strategies Implied by the Rise of the Flexible Firm

The advent of the flexible firm, and the growing importance of the research questions discussed above, suggest the increasing utility of several kinds of research strategies.

Studying organizational networks. Studying work within a single organization may not be as useful in the future, as organizations are embedded in networks and the boundaries of what constitutes the "organization" have become blurred (Hirsch, 1993). Moreover, fewer workers will spend the bulk of their work careers in single organizations. The linkages between organizations provide the skeletal structure for careers in the 21st century in much the same way as the linkages among jobs in internal labor markets within bureaucratic structures served this purpose in the latter half of the 20th century.

Longitudinal studies. Panel and longitudinal studies, rather than cross-sectional investigations, are needed to examine changes in the nature of work, as workplaces are increasingly dynamic. Questions such as whether layers of management are being eliminated through downsizing require the analysis of data over time. Further, microdata linking organizations and individuals are needed to study the changing employment relations between individuals and organizations.

Comparative research. Cross-national and historical research is needed to examine how macro level factors impact on work and workplaces (e.g., Gallie, 1978; Lincoln & Kalleberg, 1990). Cross-national research has been invaluable as a source of insights about flexible firms: Many of the debates about flexibility originated in Europe (Hartmann, Nicholas, Sorge, & Warner, 1983; Lane, 1988), and Japan has long been held up as the ideal type of the core-periphery model of the flexible firm. Moreover, historical research is needed to help contextualize debates about correlates and consequences of flexibility. As Standing (1997, p. 7) observes, systems of work relations evolve through phases of flexibility and inflexibility or rigidity. Comparative research may hold the clues to answering the key question of whether the forms of flexibility that we are now observing represent transitional forms or fundamental changes in the organization of work.

Diversity. Studies of flexible work and workplaces need to take into account the fact that the changes described here may affect both organizations and people differently. Thus, there is a need to study service organizations as well as manufacturing firms and to consider the role of gender and race in organizing work and employment contracting. For example, Smith (1993) shows that women do not benefit as much as men from correlates of flexible specialization such as employee participation or worker self-management practices; women in professional occupations who seek more flexible work may be assigned to the "periphery" while men remain in the "core." Moreover, women more often desire and need to work in flexible staffing arrangements, particularly part-time work.

Combining qualitative ethnographies and quantitative surveys of organizations. Quantitative studies such as those based on surveys are useful for testing theories, whereas ethnographic and qualitative studies are particularly well suited for generating hypotheses. Studies that combine these two approaches (e.g., Uzzi, 1996) are likely to be particularly fruitful for advancing our understanding of the correlates and consequences of flexibility.

CONCLUSIONS

The advent of the flexible firm has important implications for research and theory in the study of work, organizations, and occupations. It requires new theories of work organization and employment relations that address the dynamic and changing nature of work and workplaces. The development of such theories faces the challenge posed by the high complexity associated with the notion of "flexibility," which is often used synonymously with change and dynamism. This chapter discussed two types of flexibility: numerical and functional. These two types underlie three different models of the flexible workplace. We also indicated some of the theoretical issues raised by these models. A comprehensive theory of flexible organizations should synthesize these three models and explain why organizations use one or the other, or combinations of them. Research focusing on questions related to work organization, employment relations, and network relations is likely to be especially important for enhancing our understanding of the changes in the nature of work.

Some questions that have preoccupied students of work, organizations, and occupations are likely to decline in importance in the face of the growth in dynamic workplaces. For example, studying patterns of career mobility within organizational labor markets is likely to be less useful in the future as careers increasingly span organizations. Also, focusing on organizational units such as establishments or even firms may have less utility as organizational boundaries become more permeable.

Other, older issues may still be important but may take on new twists. Thus, firm internal labor markets are still useful to study, especially if they are conceived broadly as the rules governing deployment of labor. Moreover, studies of organizational commitment could usefully be expanded to include commitments to other work structures, such as occupations, professions, and unions, as well as to work itself.

Despite concerns raised in the early 1990s that flexibility had run its course as a framework for research on work, organizations and occupations (e.g., Pollert, 1991), the topic of workplace flexibility continues to raise many important theoretical and empirical questions as we enter the 21st century. It is likely that the flexible firm is here to stay.

NOTES

1. These two types do not exhaust the possible forms of flexibility. Some writers have emphasized wage flexibility, for example, which is the ability of organizations or societies to adjust wage levels to changing market conditions (e.g., Boyer, 1987). This type of flexibility is hard to implement, however, as wages are made sticky in all nations by institutional and cultural factors, and so is not likely to play a major role in work organization. Reilly (1998) also identifies temporal and locational flexibility.

2. Not everyone, however, agrees that downsizing has decreased the number of managers and supervisors in U.S. firms (see, e.g., Gordon, 1996).

REFERENCES

Abraham, K. G. (1990). Restructuring the employment relationship: The growth of market-mediated work arrangements. In K. G. Abraham & R. B. McKersie (Eds.), *New developments in the labor market: Toward a new institutional paradigm* (pp. 85-120). Cambridge: MIT Press.

Abraham, K. G., & Taylor, S. K. (1996). Firms' use of outside contractors: Theory and evidence. *Journal of Labor Economics, 14,* 394-424.

Althauser, R. P., & Kalleberg, A. L. (1981). Firms, occupations, and the structure of labor markets: A conceptual analysis. In I. Berg (Ed.), *Sociological perspectives on labor markets* (pp. 119-149). New York: Academic Press.

Appelbaum, E., Bailey, T., Berg, P., & Kalleberg, A. L. (2000). *Manufacturing Advantage: Why High-Performance Work Systems Pay Off.* Ithaca, NY: Cornell University Press.

Appelbaum, E., & Batt, R. (1994). *The new American workplace: Transforming work systems in the United States.* Ithaca, NY: ILR Press.

Arthur, J. B. (1992). The link between business strategy and industrial relations systems in American steel minimills. *Industrial and Labor Relations Review, 45,* 488-506.

Arthur, M. B., & Rousseau, D. M. (Eds.). (1996). *Boundaryless careers: Employment in the new organizational era.* New York: Oxford University Press.

Atkinson, J. (1984). Manpower strategies for flexible organizations. *Personnel Management, 16*(8), 28-31.

Atkinson, J. (1987). Flexibility or fragmentation? The United Kingdom labour market in the eighties. *Labour and Society, 12,* 88-105.

Bailey, T. (1992). *Discretionary effort and the organization of work: Employee participation and work reform since Hawthorne.* Unpublished manuscript, Teachers College, Columbia University, New York.

Baker, T., & Kalleberg, A. L. (1998). *Trust-centered organizational networks: Emerging durable forms?* Unpublished manuscript, Department of Sociology, University of North Carolina at Chapel Hill.

Barker, J. R. (1993). Tightening the iron cage: Concertive control in self-managing teams. *Administrative Science Quarterly, 38,* 408-437.

Barley, S. R., & Kunda, G. (1992). Design and devotion: Surges of rational and normative ideologies of control in managerial discourse. *Administrative Science Quarterly, 33,* 24-60.

Barnett, W. P., & Miner, A. S. (1992). Standing on the shoulders of others: Career interdependence in job mobility. *Administrative Science Quarterly, 37,* 262-281.

Baron, J. N., & Bielby, W. T. (1980). Bringing the firms back in: Stratification, segmentation, and the organization of work. *American Sociological Review, 45,* 737-765.

Bendix, R. (1956). *Work and authority in industry: Ideologies of management in the course of industrialization.* New York: John Wiley.

Berggren, C. (1992). *Alternative to lean production: Work organization in the Swedish auto industry.* Ithaca, NY: ILR Press.

Blank, R. M. (1998). Contingent work in a changing labor market. In R. B. Freeman & P. Gottschalk (Eds.), *Generating jobs: How to increase demand for less-skilled workers* (pp. 258-294). New York: Russell Sage.

Blau, P. M., & Schoenherr, R. A. (1971). *The structure of organizations.* New York: Basic Books.

Boyer, R. (1987). Labour flexibilities: Many forms, uncertain effects. *Labour and Society, 12,* 107-129.

Boyer, R. (1988). Defensive or offensive flexibility? In R. Boyer (Ed.), *The search for labour market flexibility: The European economies in transition* (pp. 274-290). Oxford, UK: Clarendon.

Braverman, H. (1974). *Labor and monopoly capital: The degradation of work in the twentieth century.* New York: Monthly Review Press.

Buttrick, J. (1952). The inside contracting system. *Journal of Economic History, 12,* 205-221.

Callaghan, P., & Hartmann, H. (1991). *Contingent work: A chart book on part-time and temporary employment.* Washington, DC: Economic Policy Institute.

Cappelli, P. (1995). Rethinking employment. *British Journal of Industrial Relations, 33,* 563-602.

Cappelli, P., Bassi, L., Katz, H., Knoke, D., Osterman, P., & Useem, M. (1997). *Change at work.* New York: Oxford University Press.

Christensen, K. (1989). *Flexible staffing and scheduling in U.S. corporations* (Research Bulletin No. 240). New York: The Conference Board.

Clegg, S. R. (1990). *Modern organizations: Organization studies in the postmodern world.* London: Sage.

Commission on the Skills of the American Workforce. (1989). *America's choice: High skills or low wages?* Rochester, NY: National Center on Education and the Economy.

Davis-Blake, A., & Uzzi, B. (1993). Determinants of employment externalization: A study of temporary workers and independent contractors. *Administrative Science Quarterly, 38,* 195-223.

DiTomaso, N. (2001). The loose coupling of jobs: The subcontracting of everyone? In I. Berg & A. L. Kalleberg (Eds.), *Sourcebook of labor markets: Evolving structures and processes.* New York: Kluwer Academic/Plenum Publishers.

Doeringer, P. B., & Piore, M. J. (1971). *Internal labor markets and manpower analysis.* Lexington, MA: D. C. Heath.

Dohse, K., Jurgens, U., & Malsch, T. (1985). From "Fordism" to "Toyotism"? The social organization of the labor process in the Japanese automobile industry. *Politics and Society, 14,* 115-146.

Eccles, R. G. (1981). The quasifirm in the construction industry. *Journal of Economic Behavior and Organization, 2,* 335-357.

Edwards, R. (1979). *Contested terrain: The transformation of the workplace in the twentieth century.* New York: Basic Books.

Farber, H. S. (1997, January). *Job creation in the United States: Good jobs or bad?* Paper presented at conference on Labor Market Inequality, Madison, WI.

Faulkner, R. R., & Anderson, A. B. (1987). Short-term projects and emergent careers: Evidence from Hollywood. *American Journal of Sociology, 92,* 879-909.

Friedman, A. L. (1977). *Industry and labour: Class struggle at work and monopoly capitalism.* London: Macmillan.

Gallie, D. (1978). *In search of the new working class: Automation and social integration within the capitalist enterprise.* New York: Cambridge University Press.

Gonos, G. (1997). The contest of "employer" status in the postwar United States: The case of temporary help firms. *Law and Society Review, 31,* 81-110.

Gordon, D. M. (1996). *Fat and mean: The corporate squeeze of working Americans and the myth of managerial downsizing.* New York: Free Press.

Graham, L. (1995). *On the line at Subaru-Isuzu: The Japanese model and the American worker.* Ithaca, NY: ILR Press.

Grandori, A., & Soda, G. (1995). Inter-firm networks: Antecedents, mechanisms, and forms. *Organization Studies, 16,* 183-214.

Granovetter, M. (1984). Small is bountiful: Labor markets and establishment size. *American Sociological Review, 49,* 323-334.

Granovetter, M. (1985). Economic action and social structure: The problem of embeddedness. *American Journal of Sociology, 91,* 481-510.

Grenier, G. (1988). *Inhuman relations: Quality circles and anti-unionism in American industry.* Philadelphia: Temple University Press.

Groshen, E. L., & Levine, D. I. (1998). *The rise and decline (?) of U.S. internal labor markets.* Unpublished manuscript, Federal Reserve Bank of New York.

Guillén, M. F. (1994). *Models of management: Work, authority, and organization in a comparative perspective.* Chicago: University of Chicago Press.

Hakim, C. (1990). Core and periphery in employers' workforce strategies: Evidence from the 1987 E.L.U.S. Survey. *Work, Employment and Society, 4,* 157-188.

Hall, D. T. (1996). Protean careers of the 21st century. *Academy of Management Executive, 10,* 8-16.

Harrison, B. (1994). *Lean and mean: The changing landscape of corporate power in the age of flexibility.* New York: Basic Books.

Harrison, B., & Kelley, M. E. (1993). Outsourcing and the search for "flexibility." *Work, Employment and Society, 7,* 213-235.

Hartmann, G. I., Nicholas, I., Sorge, A., & Warner, M. (1983). Computerized machine tools, manpower consequences, and skill utilization: A study of British and West German manufacturing firms. *British Journal of Industrial Relations, 21,* 221-231.

Harvey, D. (1989). *The condition of postmodernity: An enquiry into the origins of cultural change.* Oxford, UK: Basil Blackwell.

Heckscher, C. C. (1995). *White-collar blues: Management loyalties in an age of corporate restructuring.* New York: Basic Books.

Hirsch, P. M. (1993). Undoing the managerial revolution? Needed research on the decline of middle management and internal labor markets. In R. Swedberg (Ed.), *Explorations in economic sociology* (pp. 145-157). New York: Russell Sage.

Hodson, R. (1988). Good jobs and bad management: How new problems evoke old solutions in high tech settings. In G. Farkas & P. England (Eds.), *Industries, firms, and jobs: Sociological and economic approaches* (pp. 247-279). New York: Plenum.

Hodson, R. (1996). Dignity in the workplace under participative management: Alienation and freedom revisited. *American Sociological Review, 61,* 719-738.

Houseman, S. (in press). Why employees use flexible staffing arrangements: Evidence from an establishment survey. *Industrial and Labor Relations Review.*

Hunter, L., McGregor, A., MacInnes, J., & Sproull, A. (1993). The "flexible firm": Strategy and segmentation. *British Journal of Industrial Relations, 31,* 383-407.

Hyman, R. (1988). Flexible specialization: Miracle or myth? In R. Hyman & W. Streeck (Eds.), *New technology and industrial relations* (pp. 48-60). Oxford, UK: Basil Blackwell.

Jacoby, S. M. (1985). *Employing bureaucracy: Managers, unions, and the transformation of work in American industry, 1900-1945.* New York: Columbia University Press.

Kalleberg, A. L., Knoke, D., & Marsden, P. V. (1995). Interorganizational networks and the changing employment contract. *Connections, 18,* 32-49.

Kalleberg, A. L., Knoke, D., Marsden, P. V., & Spaeth, J. L. (1996). *Organizations in America: Analyzing their structures and human resource practices.* Thousand Oaks, CA: Sage.

Kalleberg, A. L., Rasell, E., Cassirer, N., Reskin, B. F., Hudson, K., Webster, D., Appelbaum, E., & Spalter-Roth, R. M. (1997). *Nonstandard work, substandard jobs: Flexible work arrangements in the U.S.* Washington, DC: Economic Policy Institute.

Kalleberg, A. L., Reskin, B. F., & Hudson, K. (2000). Bad jobs in America: Standard and nonstandard employment relations and job quality in the United States. *American Sociological Review, 65,* 256-278.

Kalleberg, A. L., & Sørensen, A. B. (1979). The sociology of labor markets. *Annual Review of Sociology, 5,* 351-379.

Kanter, R. M. (1977). *Men and women of the corporation.* New York: Basic Books.

Kern, H., & Schumann, M. (1987). Limits of the division of labour: New production and employment concepts in West German industry. *Economic and Industrial Democracy, 8,* 151-170.

Kochan, T. A., Cutcher-Gernshenfeld, J., & MacDuffie, J. P. (1991). Employee participation, work redesign, and new technology: Implications for manufacturing and engineering practice. In G. Salvendy (Ed.), *Handbook of industrial engineering* (2nd ed., pp. 798-814). New York: John Wiley.

Lane, C. (1988). Industrial change in Europe: The pursuit of flexible specialization in Britain and W. Germany. *Work, Employment, and Society, 2,* 141-168.

Lawler, E. E., III, Ledford, G. E., Jr., & Mohrman, S. A. (1989). *Employee involvement in America: A study of contemporary practices.* Houston, TX: American Productivity and Quality Center.

Lawler, E. E., III, Mohrman, S. A., & Ledford, G. E., Jr. (1992). *Employee involvement and total quality management.* San Francisco: Jossey-Bass.

Lawrence, P. R., & Lorsch, J. W. (1967). *Organization and environment: Managing differentiation and integration.* Homewood, IL: Irwin.

Levine, D., & Tyson, L. D. (1990). Participation, productivity, and the firm's environment. In A. Blinder (Ed.), *Paying for productivity* (pp. 183-243). Washington, DC: Brookings Institution.

Lincoln, J. R., & Kalleberg, A. L. (1990). *Culture, control and commitment: A study of work organization and work attitudes in the United States and Japan.* Cambridge, UK: Cambridge University Press.

MacDuffie, J. P. (1995). Human resource bundles and manufacturing performance: Organizational logic and flexible production systems in the world auto industry. *Industrial and Labor Relations Review, 48,* 197-221.

Mangum, G., Mayall, D., & Nelson, K. (1985). The temporary help industry: A response to the dual internal labor market. *Industrial and Labor Relations Review, 38,* 599-611.

Meulders, D., & Wilkin, L. (1987). Labour market flexibility: Critical introduction to the analysis of a concept. *Labour and Society, 12,* 3-17.

Miles, R. E., & Snow, C. C. (1986). Organizations: New concepts for new forms. *California Management Review, 28,* 62-73.

Morse, D. (1969). *The peripheral worker.* New York: Columbia University Press.

Organization for Economic Cooperation and Development. (1990). *Labour market policies for the 1990s.* Paris: OECD.

Osterman, P. (1993). Internal labor markets in a changing environment: Models and evidence. In D. Lewin, O. Mitchell, & P. Sherer (Eds.), *Research frontiers in industrial relations and human resources* (pp. 273-308). Madison, WI: Industrial Relations Research Association.

Osterman, P. (1994). How common is workplace transformation and who adopts it? *Industrial and Labor Relations Review, 47,* 173-188.

Pfeffer, J., & Baron, J. N. (1988). Taking the workers back out: Recent trends in the structuring of employment. *Research in Organizational Behavior, 10,* 257-303.

Pil, F. K., & MacDuffie, J. P. (1996). The adoption of high-involvement work practices. *Industrial Relations, 35,* 423-455.

Piore, M. (1986). Perspectives on labor market flexibility. *Industrial Relations, 25,* 146-166.

Piore, M., & Sabel, C. F. (1984). *The second industrial divide: Possibilities for prosperity.* New York: Basic Books.

Pollert, A. (1988). The "flexible firm": Fixation or fact? *Work, Employment, and Society, 2,* 281-316.

Pollert, A. (Ed.). (1991). *Farewell to flexibility?* Oxford, UK: Basil Blackwell.

Powell, W. W. (1990). Neither market nor hierarchy: Network forms of organization. *Research in Organizational Behavior, 12,* 295-336.

Powell, W. W. (1996, August). *The capitalist firm in the 21st century: Emerging patterns.* Paper presented at the annual meeting of the American Sociological Association, New York City.

Powell, W. W., Koput, K. W., & Smith-Doerr, L. (1996). Interorganizational collaboration and the locus of innovation: Networks of learning in biotechnology. *Administrative Science Quarterly, 41,* 116-145.

Procter, S. J., Rowlinson, M., McArdle, L., Hassard, J., & Forrester, P. (1994). Flexibiltity, politics and strategy: In defense of the model of the flexible firm. *Work, Employment, and Society, 8,* 221-242.

Reilly, P. A. (1998). Balancing flexibility—Meeting the interests of employer and employee. *European Journal of Work and Organizational Psychology, 7,* 7-22.

Rosenbaum, J. E. (1979). Tournament mobility: Career patterns in a corporation. *Administrative Science Quarterly, 24,* 220-241.

Rousseau, D. M. (1995). *Psychological contracts in organizations.* Thousand Oaks, CA: Sage.

Rubin, B. (1995). Flexible accumulation: The decline of contract and social transformation. *Research in Social Stratification and Mobility, 14,* 297-323.

Rudolph, B. (1998). *Disconnected.* New York: Free Press.

Sabel, C., & Zeitlin, J. (1985). Historical alternatives to mass production: Politics, markets and technology in 19th century industrialization. *Past and Present, 108,* 133-176.

Segal, L. M., & Sullivan, D. G. (1997). The growth of temporary services work. *Journal of Economic Perspectives, 11,* 117-136.

Sengenberger, W. (1990). Flexibility in the labor market: Internal versus external adjustment. In E. Appelbaum & R. Schettkat (Eds.), *Labor market adjustments to structural change and technological progress* (pp. 144-162). New York: Praeger.

Smith, V. (1993). Flexibility in work and employment: The impact on women. *Research in the Sociology of Organizations, 11,* 195-216.

Smith, V. (1997). New forms of work organization. *Annual Review of Sociology, 23,* 315-339.

Standing, G. (1997). Globalization, labour flexibility and insecurity: The era of market regulation. *European Journal of Industrial Relations, 3,* 7-37.

Streeck, W. (1987). The uncertainties of management in the management of uncertainty: Employers, labor relations and industrial adjustment in the 1980s. *Work, Employment, and Society, 1,* 281-308.

Taplin, I. (1995). Flexible production, rigid jobs: Lessons from the clothing industry. *Work and Occupations, 22,* 412-438.

Thompson, J. D. (1967). *Organizations in action.* New York: McGraw-Hill.

Tilly, C. (1996). *Half a job: Bad and good part-time jobs in a changing labor market.* Philadelphia: Temple University Press.

Tilly, C., & Tilly, C. (1998). *Work under capitalism.* Boulder, CO: Westview.

Uzzi, B. (1996). Embeddedness and the economic performance of organizations: The network effect. *American Sociological Review, 61,* 674-698.

Uzzi, B. (1997). Social structure and competition in interfirm networks: The paradox of embeddedness. *Administrative Science Quarterly, 42,* 35-67.

Vallas, S. P. (1999). Rethinking post-Fordism: The meaning of workplace flexibility. *Sociological Theory 17,* 68-101.

Vallas, S. P., & Beck, J. P. (1996). The transformation of work revisited: The limits of flexibility in American manufacturing. *Social Problems, 43,* 339-361.

Womack, J., Jones, D., & Roos, D. (1990). *The machine that changed the world.* New York: Rawson Associates.

Wood, S. (Ed.). (1982). *The degradation of work?* London: Hutchinson.

Wood, S. (1989). The transformation of work? In S. Wood (Ed.), *The transformation of work? Skill, flexibility and the labour process* (pp. 1-43). London: Unwin Hyman.

Zuboff, S. (1988). *In the age of the smart machine.* New York: Basic Books.

Index

About the Contributors

Roy J. Adams is Professor Emeritus of Industrial Relations at McMaster University in Hamilton, Canada. He has written extensively on international and comparative employment issues. Currently, his research is focused on the emergence of an international consensus regarding human rights in employment and its implications for labor policy and practice.

Linda H. Aiken is Claire M. Fagin Professor of Nursing and Sociology and Director of the Center for Health Outcomes and Policy Research at the University of Pennsylvania. Her primary research interests concern the effects of the organization of health care on the outcomes of patients and health professionals.

Marietta L. Baba is Professor of Anthropology and Department Chair and founding director of the Business and Industrial Anthropology Graduate Sequence at Wayne State University. Her research interests lie at the intersection of organizational culture and technological innovation.

Terry Boswell is Professor of Sociology and Department Chair at Emory University. Recent publications include (with Chris Chase-Dunn) *The Spiral of Capitalism and Socialism: Toward Global Democracy* (2000) and (with Cliff Brown) "The Scope of General Theory" in *Sociological Methods and Research* (1999). His current research focuses on revolutions, inequality and growth, and international union organizing.

Elizabeth K. Briody is a cultural anthropologist employed by General Motors Research and Development Center. Her title is Staff Research Scientist. Her field research has focused on employees, including product development personnel, material handlers, and expatriates. Her current work examines strategic alliances and global product programs.

Mauricio Bustos received his master's degree in regional development from El Colegio de la Frontera Norte in Tijuana, Mexico. He is currently working in the Baja California State Government at the Ministry of Economic Development.

Karen E. Campbell is Associate Professor and Director of Graduate Studies in Sociology at Vanderbilt University. She (with Holly McCammon) is studying state woman suffrage movements and is also interested in gender differences in social networks, attitudes toward gender inequality, and the state regulation of nurse practitioners.

Deborah Carr is Assistant Professor of Sociology and Assistant Research Scientist in the Institute for Social Research at the University of Michigan. Her research focuses on the psychological consequences of work and family roles over the life course. She is currently using quantitative and qualitative data to examine career transitions at midlife. She also studies widowhood among older adults.

Mariah Mantsun Cheng is Research Associate in the Carolina Population Center at the University of North Carolina, Chapel Hill. Her research interests are in demography, social mobility, applied statistics, and quantitative methodology. Besides her work in labor market studies, her recent research is on health-risk behaviors of disabled adolescents.

Oscar Contreras is Director of the Industrial Relations Program at El Colegio de Sonora and editor of the Mexican academic journal *Región y Sociedad*. He is author of *Global Companies, Local Actors* and presently is completing a book on the reorganization of the TV industry in North America and conducting a project on the impact of the Internet in regional development in Mexico.

Lindsay Cooper is a Lecturer in Anthropology and Women's Studies at Oakland University in Rochester, Michigan. Her current research interests include organizational anthropology and sex differences in various aspects of social work.

Daniel B. Cornfield is Professor of Sociology and Department Chair at Vanderbilt University and editor of *Work and Occupations.* His research addresses labor movement revitalization, workplace restructuring, employment relations, and cross-national patterns in the intellectual history of the sociology of work. His most recent book is (with Toby Parcel) *Work and Family: Research Informing Policy* (Sage, 2000).

Frederic C. Deyo is Professor of Sociology at the State University of New York at Brockport and Honorary Professor/Research Fellow at the University of Auckland, New Zealand. His current research interests include economic development, labor movements, industrial organization, and industrial subcontracting. His most recent book is *Economic Governance and the Challenge of Flexibility in East Asia* (2000).

Deborah M. Figart is Professor of Economics at Richard Stockton College in Pomona, New Jersey. She is a founding member of the International Association for Feminist Economics. Her current research is on working time, living wages, pay equity, and other labor market policies in the United States.

W. Richard Goe is Associate Professor of Sociology at Kansas State University. His research focuses on the implications of the growth of the service sector and the development of computers and information technology for labor processes, corporate and industry structure, and communities.

Paul M. Hirsch is James Allen Distinguished Professor of Strategy and Organization Behavior in the Kellogg Graduate School of Management at Northwestern University. He has written extensively about careers and organizational change. He is a "Distinguished Scholar" of the Organization and Management Theory Division of the American Academy of Management and former chair of the American Sociological Association's Section on Occupations, Organizations and Work.

Randy Hodson is Professor of Sociology at Ohio State University. He is author of *Working With Dignity* (2001), coauthor (with Teresa A. Sullivan) of *The Social Organization of Work* (3rd edition, 2001), and editor of the JAI Press annual series *Research in the Sociology of Work.* His research interests include both coworker and worker-management relations.

Timothy J. Hoff is Assistant Professor in the School of Public Health at the State University of New York at Albany. His research examines the changing work lives and roles of physicians under managed care. This work has appeared in a variety of sociological and health care journals. Currently, he is planning a project on medical errors within the physician training culture and looking at collective representation within medicine.

Richard Hyman is Professor of Industrial Relations at the London School of Economics, founding editor of the *European Journal of Industrial Relations,* and president of the Research Committee on Labor Movements of the International Sociological Association. His research interests include labor movements, political economy, European integration, and industrial relations. His most recent book is *Understanding European Trade Unionism* (Sage, 2001).

Nancy C. Jurik is Professor of Justice Studies at Arizona State University. Her publications focus on gender and work organization. With Susan Ehrlich Martin, she published *Doing Justice, Doing Gender: Women in Law and Criminal Justice Occupations* (Sage, 1996) and presently is writing a book on U.S. microenterprise development.

Arne L. Kalleberg is Kenan Professor of Sociology at the University of North Carolina, Chapel Hill. His current research focuses on: U.S. organizations' use of flexible staffing arrangements; cross-national differences in the job rewards and work attitudes of nonstandard (especially part-time and temporary) workers versus regular full-time workers; and what companies can do to promote work-life balance.

Martin Kenney is Professor of Human and Community Development at the University of California, Davis and Senior Project Director at the Berkeley Roundtable on the International Economy. His research includes the transfer of industrial relations systems overseas, the development of high-technology regions, and the venture capital industry. *Understanding Silicon Valley* is his most recent book.

June Lapidus is Associate Professor of Economics in the School of Policy Studies at Roosevelt University. Her current research interests include welfare reform and the economics of education. She to works with the Center for Popular Economics in an attempt to keep alive an alternative to market mania.

James R. Lincoln is Spieker Professor in the Haas School of Business and Director of the Institute of Industrial Relations at the University of California, Berkeley. He is author (with Arne Kalleberg) of *Culture, Control, and Commitment: A Study of Work Organizations and Work Attitudes in the U.S. and Japan* (1990) and numerous articles on Japanese economy and society.

Anthony C. Masi is Vice Principal (Information Systems and Technology) and a member of the Department of Sociology, McGill University. He is also a Research Fellow at the Italian National Statistics Institute (ISTAT). Utilizing labor force and general social surveys, he is conducting research on flexibility in the Italian labor market.

David P. McCaffrey is Professor of Public Administration and Policy at the State University of New York at Albany. He studies organizational processes in financial markets and other sectors and is author (with David Hart) of *Wall Street Polices Itself* (1998) and other related books and articles.

Holly J. McCammon is Associate Professor of Sociology at Vanderbilt University. She has studied the U.S. labor movement, particularly the ways in which labor law has influenced the movement and in turn been utilized by labor, and currently is studying the U.S. women's suffrage movement. Work on these topics is forthcoming in the journals *Work and Occupations, American Sociological Review,* and *Gender & Society.*

Yoshifumi Nakata is Professor of Industrial Relations at Doshisha University in Kyoto, Japan. He has published extensively on Japanese labor topics and is a frequent consultant to national labor unions and government agencies.

Charles E. Naquin is Assistant Professor of Management in the Mendoza College of Business at the University of Notre Dame. His current research interests include negotiation, teams, and the role of technology in organizational behavior.

Jackie Krasas Rogers is Assistant Professor of Labor Studies and Industrial Relations, Sociology, and Women's Studies at Pennsylvania State University. Her research focuses on nonstandard employment and gender and racial inequalities at work. She is author of *Temps: The Many Faces of the Changing Workplace* (2000).

Jairo Romero is currently a consultant on labor relations issues in Davis, California. His research has focused on labor-management relations in maquiladoras.

Catherine E. Ross is Professor of Sociology at Ohio State University. She studies the effects of socioeconomic status, work, family and community on men's and women's physical and mental health and their sense of control versus powerlessness. She is currently working on the second edition of her book with John Mirowsky, *Social Causes of Psychological Distress.*

Beth A. Rubin is Associate Professor of Sociology and Adjunct Associate Professor in the A.B. Freeman School of Business at Tulane University. In addition to her research on employment and reemployment in the new economy, she is examining organizational change and its relationship to the 24/7 economy.

Kathryn Schellenberg is Assistant Professor of Sociology at the University of Michigan, Flint. Her areas of scholarly research include workplace instability, impacts of information technologies on policing, and organizational justice. She has also served as editor of *Annual Editions: Computers in Society.*

Douglas M. Sloane is Adjunct Associate Professor in the Center for Health Outcomes and Policy Research at University of Pennsylvania School of Nursing, Associate Professor of Sociology at the Life Cycle Institute at Catholic University of America, and Social Science Analyst at the U.S. General Accounting Office in Washington, D.C.

Brian T. Smith is a contingent sociologist finishing up his second year as Visiting Assistant Professor in the Department of Sociology at Loyola University in New Orleans. While to date his research interests have centered on employment relationships, he currently is examining the social implications of the increasingly large familial caretaker population associated with victims of Alzheimer's disease.

Michael R. Smith is Professor of Sociology at McGill University. His recent publications have dealt with trends in employment security and the effects of employment security. His current research examines the effects of technology and globalization on employment and on earnings inequality.

Vicki Smith is Professor of Sociology at the University of California, Davis. Her book *Crossing the Great Divide: Worker Risk and Opportunity in the New Economy* (2001) analyzes and compares new forms of work and employment relations in diverse occupational settings.

Joseph Smucker is Adjunct Professor of Sociology at Concordia University in Montreal. His publications include works on the history of industrialization in Canada, philosophies of management, labor unions, and labor markets. He is currently a member of a research team studying business practices of firms in foreign countries.

Dimitris Stevis is Associate Professor of Political Science at Colorado State University. His research focuses on international environmental and labor politics and policy. His recent work has appeared in *Journal of World-System Research, Strategies, and Environmental Politics.* He coedited *The International Political Economy of the Environment: Critical Perspectives,* Volume 12 of the *IPE Yearbook* (2001).

Ian M. Taplin is Professor of Sociology and International Studies at Wake Forest University and Visiting Professor of Management at ESC in Toulouse, France. Current research interests include strategies of work restructuring and technological innovation in the clothing industries of high-wage economies, the changing contours of employment relations, and comparative management systems.

Axel van den Berg is Professor of Sociology at McGill University. His recent research has focused on the sociology of labor markets, the debates about rational choice theory in the social sciences, contemporary sociological theory, and a cross-cultural comparison of aesthetic criteria of visual art.

Marylyn P. Wright works as a market researcher for Fitch Inc., a design consultancy firm in Columbus, Ohio.

James R. Zetka, Jr. is Associate Professor of Sociology at the State University of New York at Albany. He is author of *Militancy, Market Dynamics, and Workplace Authority* (1995) and is currently writing a book that examines the impact of competition within the medical division of labor on the development of video surgery.